SPIDER-GIRL

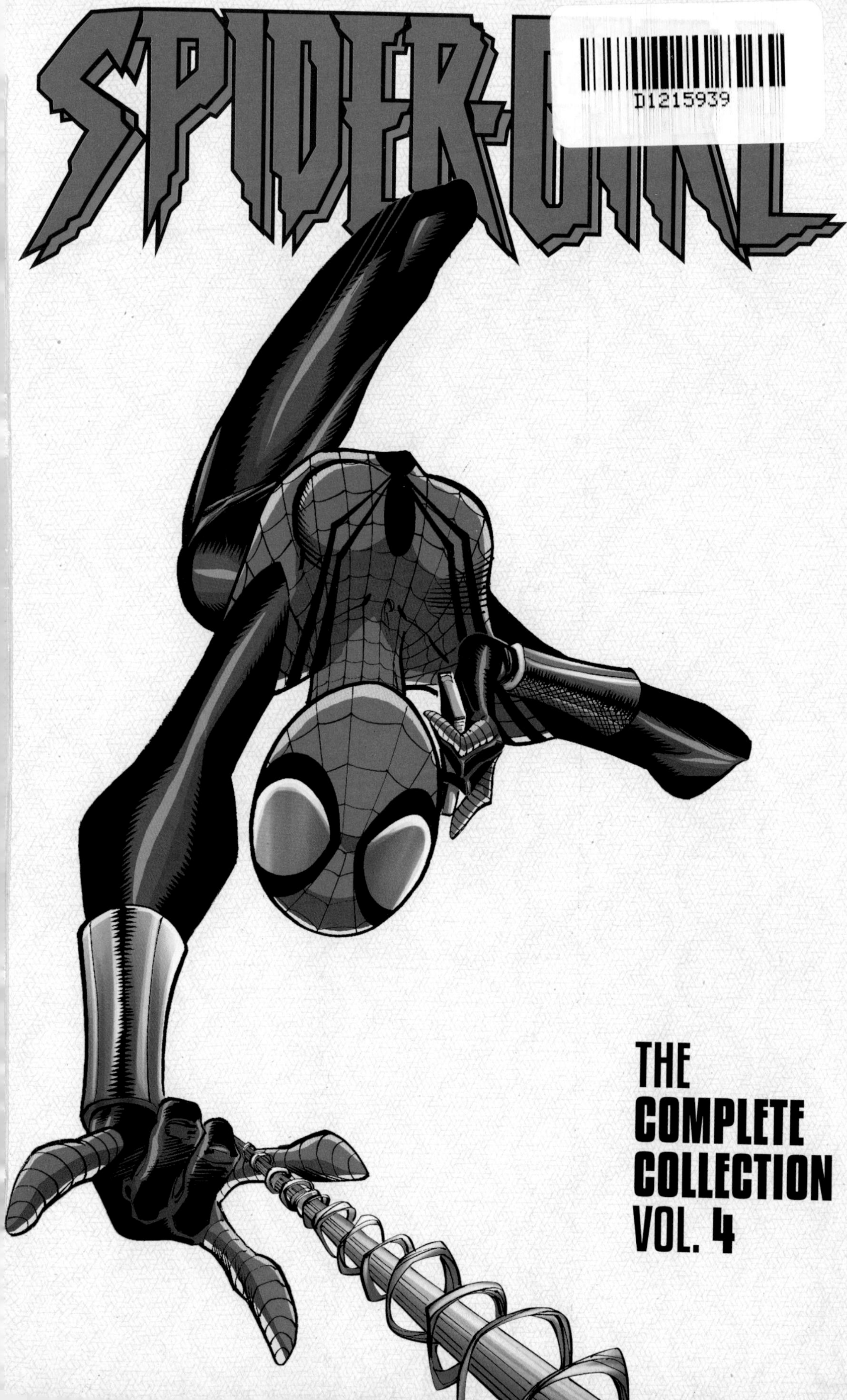

THE COMPLETE COLLECTION VOL. 4

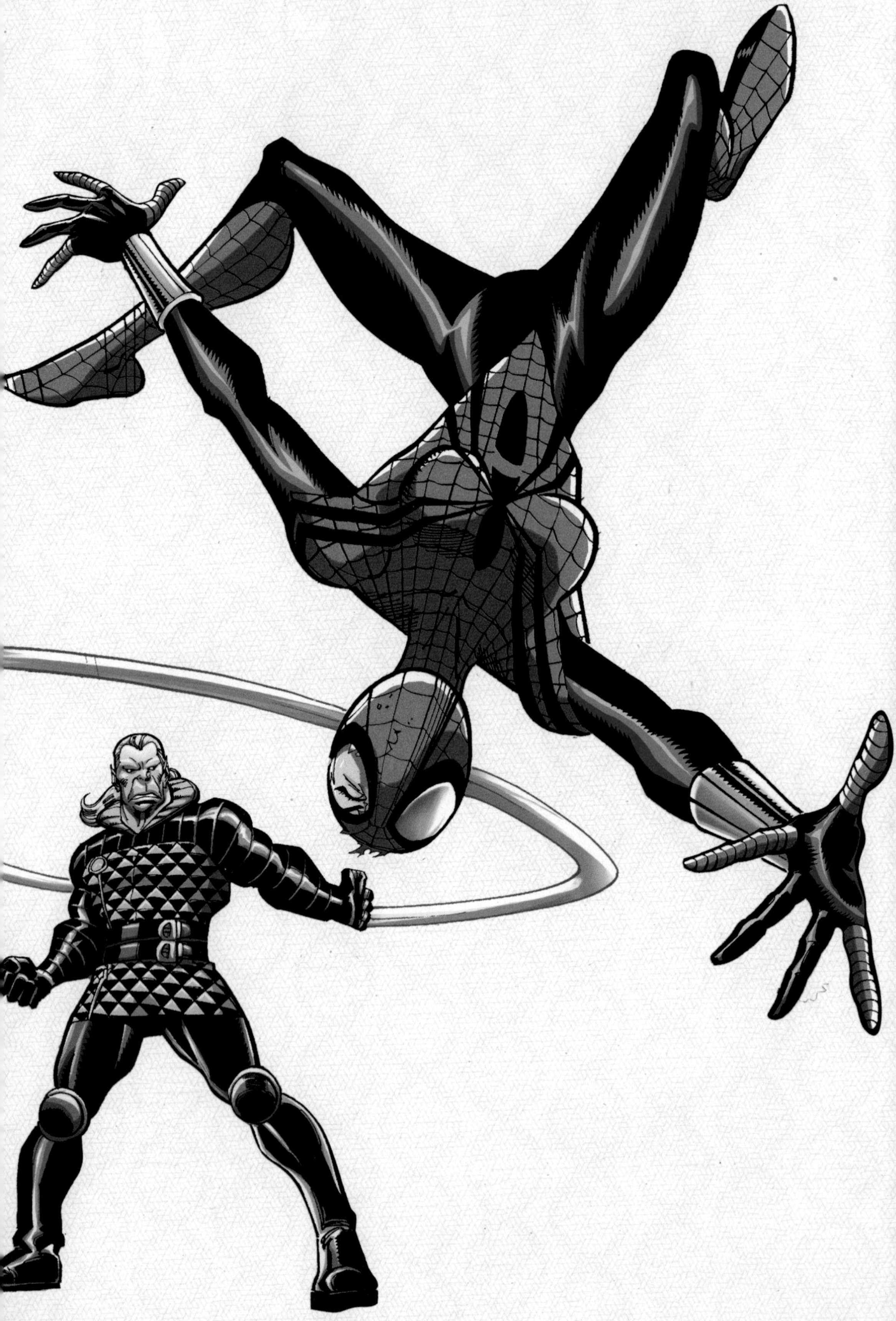

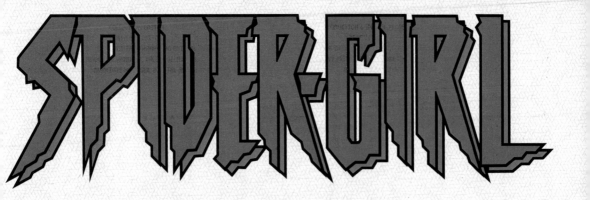

SPIDER-GIRL

THE COMPLETE COLLECTION VOL. 4

SPIDER-GIRL #51

WRITER **Sean McKeever**
ARTIST **Casey Jones**

SPIDER-GIRL #53-54 & #56

WRITER **Tom DeFalco**
PENCILER **Pat Olliffe**
INKER **Al Williamson**

SPIDER-GIRL #55

WRITER **Tom DeFalco**
BREAKDOWNS **Pat Olliffe**
FINISHER **Sal Buscema**

SPIDER-GIRL #52, #57-58 & #60

WRITER **Tom DeFalco**
CO-PLOTTER & PENCILER **Ron Frenz**
INKERS **Al Williamson** with **Rodney Ramos** (#58)

SPIDER-GIRL #59 & #61-67

WRITER **Tom DeFalco**
CO-PLOTTER & BREAKDOWNS **Ron Frenz**
FINISHER **Sal Buscema**

COLORIST **UDON Studios**
LETTERERS **VC's Randy Gentile** (#51-63), **Rus Wooton** (#64-65), **Cory Petit** (#66) & **Dave Sharpe** (#67)

Casey Jones & **UDON's Jamie Noguchi** (#51); **Ron Frenz**, **Al Williamson** & **UDON's Jamie Noguchi** (#52 & #54-56); **Pat Olliffe**, **Al Williamson** & **UDON Studios** (#53); **Pat Olliffe** & **Chris Sotomayor** (#57); **Pat Olliffe**, **Al Williamson** & **UDON's Angelo Tsang** (#58-59); **Ron Frenz**, **Al Williamson** & **UDON's Angelo Tsang** (#60); **Howard Porter** & **UDON's Angelo Tsang** (#61); **Barry Kitson** & **UDON Studios** (#62); **Gurihiru** (#63); **Ron Frenz**, **Klaus Janson** & **UDON Studios** (#64-65); **Ron Frenz**, **Sal Buscema** & **UDON's Angelo Tsang** (#66); and **Ron Frenz**, **Sal Buscema** & **UDON Studios** (#67)
COVER ART

Marc Sumerak & **Andy Schmidt**
ASSISTANT EDITORS

Tom Brevoort & **Andy Schmidt**
EDITORS

Tom Brevoort
SUPERVISING EDITOR

COLLECTION EDITOR: **Jennifer Grünwald**
ASSISTANT EDITOR: **Daniel Kirchhoffer**
ASSISTANT MANAGING EDITOR: **Maia Loy**
ASSOCIATE MANAGER, TALENT RELATIONS: **Lisa Montalbano**
ASSOCIATE MANAGER, DIGITAL ASSETS: **Joe Hochstein**
VP PRODUCTION & SPECIAL PROJECTS: **Jeff Youngquist**
PRODUCTION: **Joe Frontirre**
BOOK DESIGNER: **Stacie Zucker** with **Adam Del Re**
SVP PRINT, SALES & MARKETING: **David Gabriel**
EDITOR IN CHIEF: **C.B. Cebulski**

SPIDER-GIRL: THE COMPLETE COLLECTION VOL. 4. Contains material originally published in magazine form as SPIDER-GIRL (1998) #51-67. First printing 2022. ISBN 978-1-302-93479-8. Published by MARVEL WORLDWIDE, INC., a subsidiary of MARVEL ENTERTAINMENT, LLC. OFFICE OF PUBLICATION: 1290 Avenue of the Americas, New York, NY 10104. **Printed in Canada.** KEVIN FEIGE, Chief Creative Officer; DAN BUCKLEY, President, Marvel Entertainment; JOE QUESADA, EVP & Creative Director; DAVID BOGART, Associate Publisher & SVP of Talent Affairs; TOM BREVOORT, VP, Executive Editor; NICK LOWE, Executive Editor, VP of Content, Digital Publishing; DAVID GABRIEL, VP of Print & Digital Publishing; MARK ANNUNZIATO, VP of Planning & Forecasting; JEFF YOUNGQUIST, VP of Production & Special Projects; ALEX MORALES, Director of Publishing Operations; DAN EDINGTON, Director of Editorial Operations; RICKEY PURDIN, Director of Talent Relations; JENNIFER GRÜNWALD, Director of Production & Special Projects; SUSAN CRESPI, Production Manager; STAN LEE, Chairman Emeritus. For information regarding advertising in Marvel Comics or on Marvel.com, please contact Vit DeBellis, Custom Solutions & Integrated Advertising Manager, at vdebellis@marvel.com. For Marvel subscription inquiries, please call 888-511-5480. **Manufactured between 1/28/2022 and 3/1/2022 by SOLISCO PRINTERS, SCOTT, QC, CANADA.**

10 9 8 7 6 5 4 3 2 1

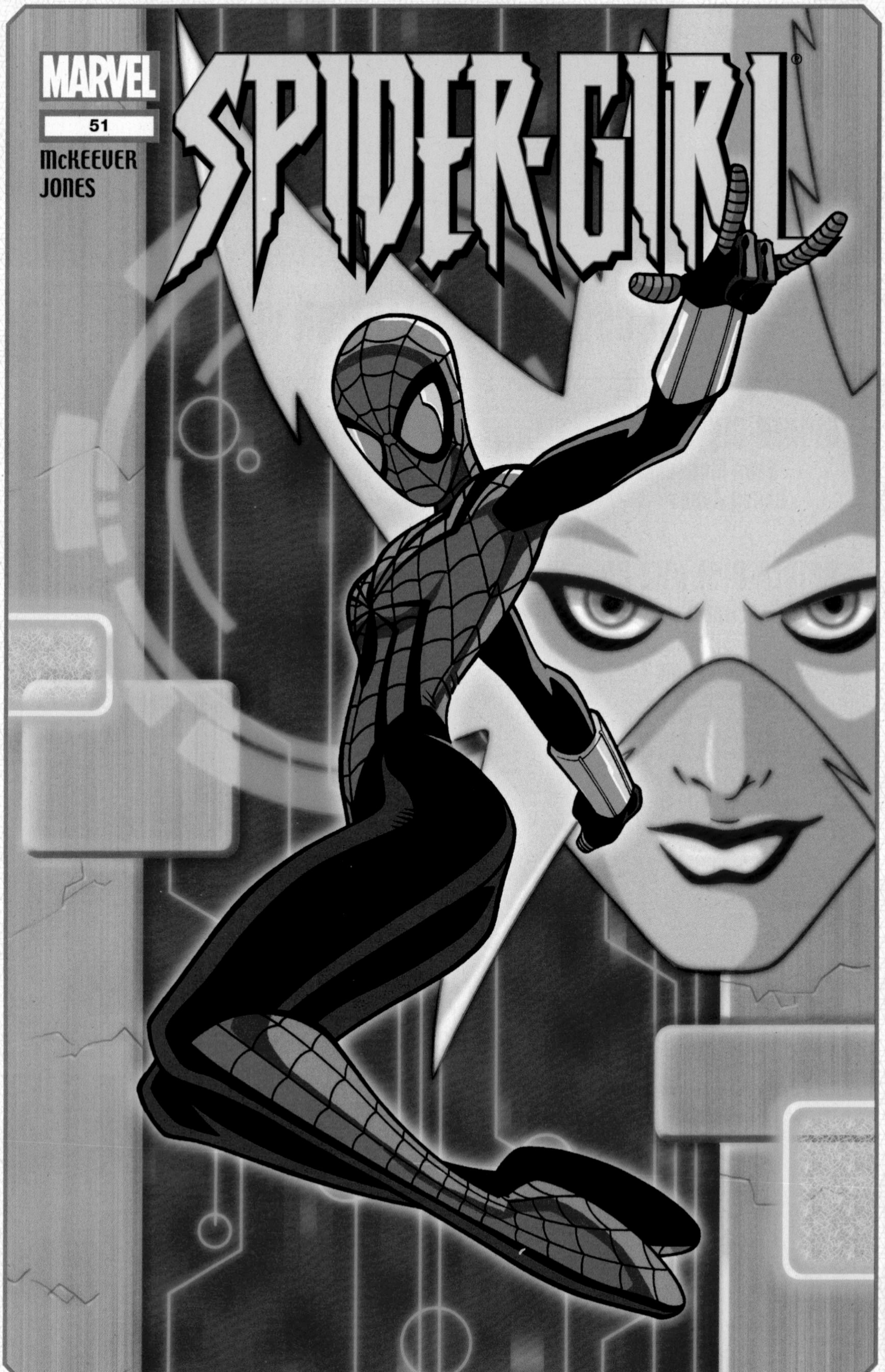
MARVEL
51
McKEEVER
JONES
SPIDER-GIRL

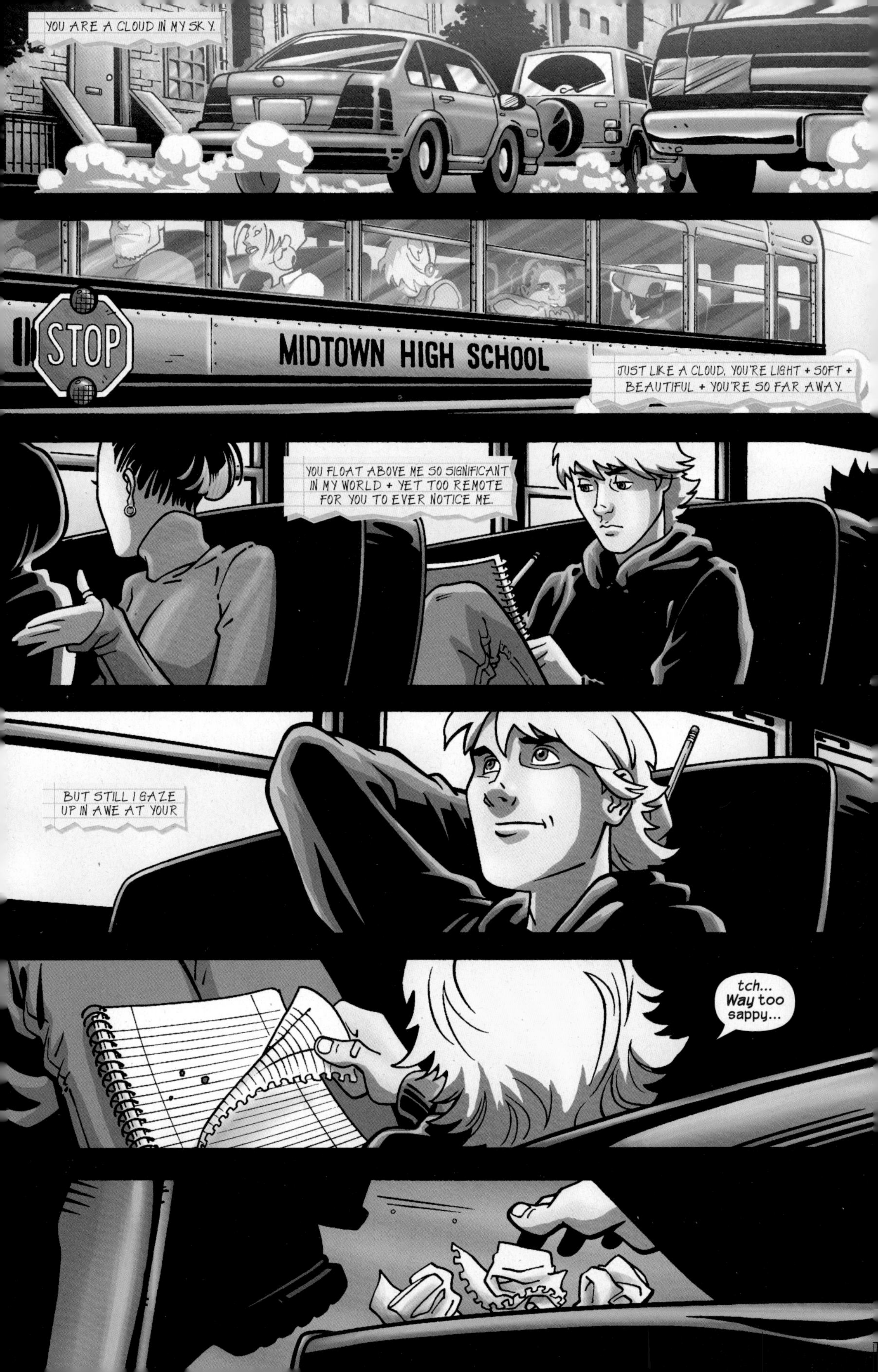
YOU ARE A CLOUD IN MY SKY.
MIDTOWN HIGH SCHOOL
STOP
JUST LIKE A CLOUD, YOU'RE LIGHT + SOFT + BEAUTIFUL + YOU'RE SO FAR AWAY.
YOU FLOAT ABOVE ME SO SIGNIFICANT IN MY WORLD + YET TOO REMOTE FOR YOU TO EVER NOTICE ME.
BUT STILL I GAZE UP IN AWE AT YOUR
tch... Way too sappy...

The daughter of the original Spider-Man, May "Mayday" Parker has inherited her father's amazing powers. Possessing the proportionate strength, speed, and agility of a spider, as well as the ability to cling to walls, she now follows in his web-lines! Stan Lee presents... **SPIDER-GIRL!**

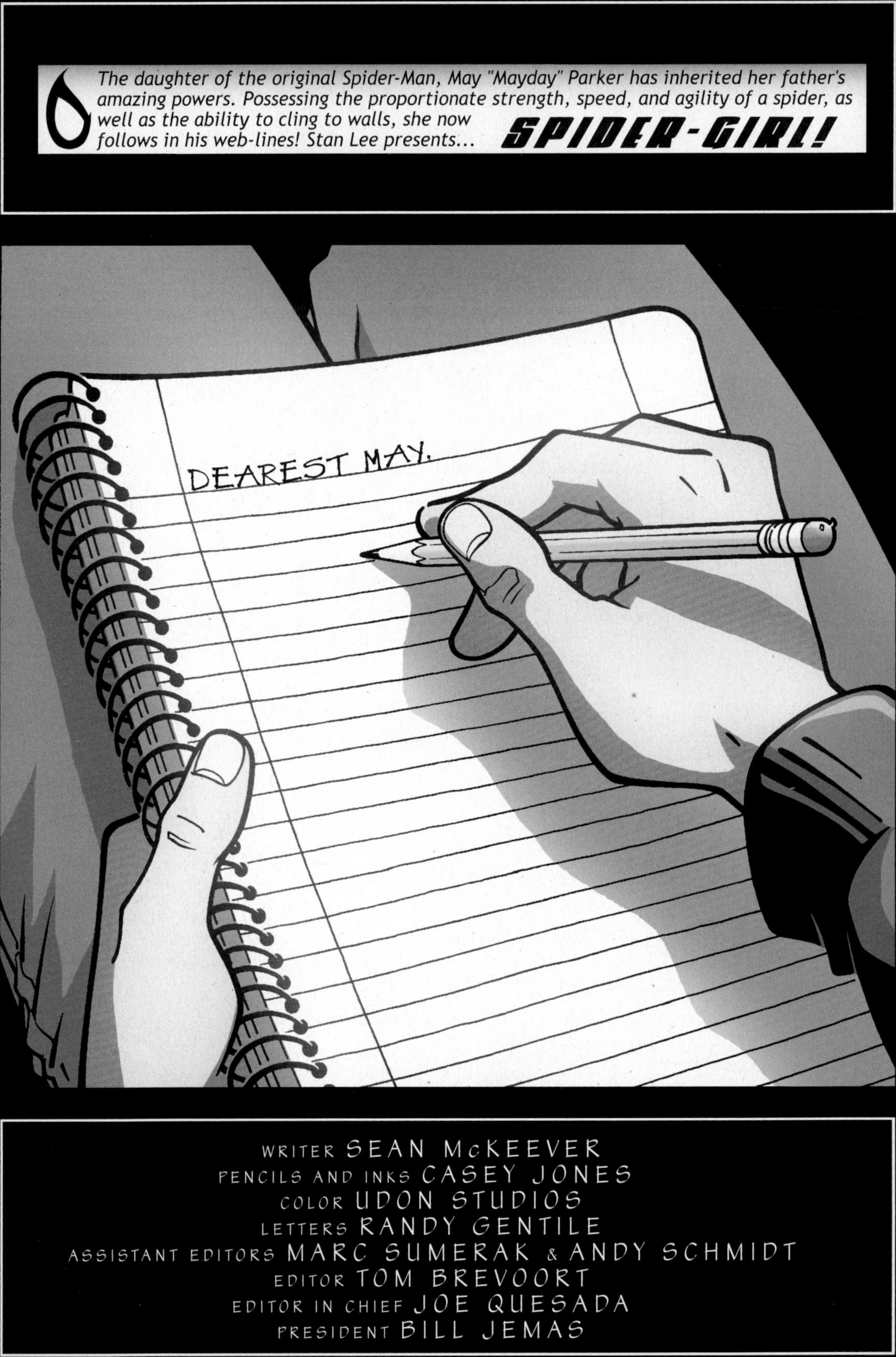
DEAREST MAY,

WRITER SEAN McKEEVER
PENCILS AND INKS CASEY JONES
COLOR UDON STUDIOS
LETTERS RANDY GENTILE
ASSISTANT EDITORS MARC SUMERAK & ANDY SCHMIDT
EDITOR TOM BREVOORT
EDITOR IN CHIEF JOE QUESADA
PRESIDENT BILL JEMAS

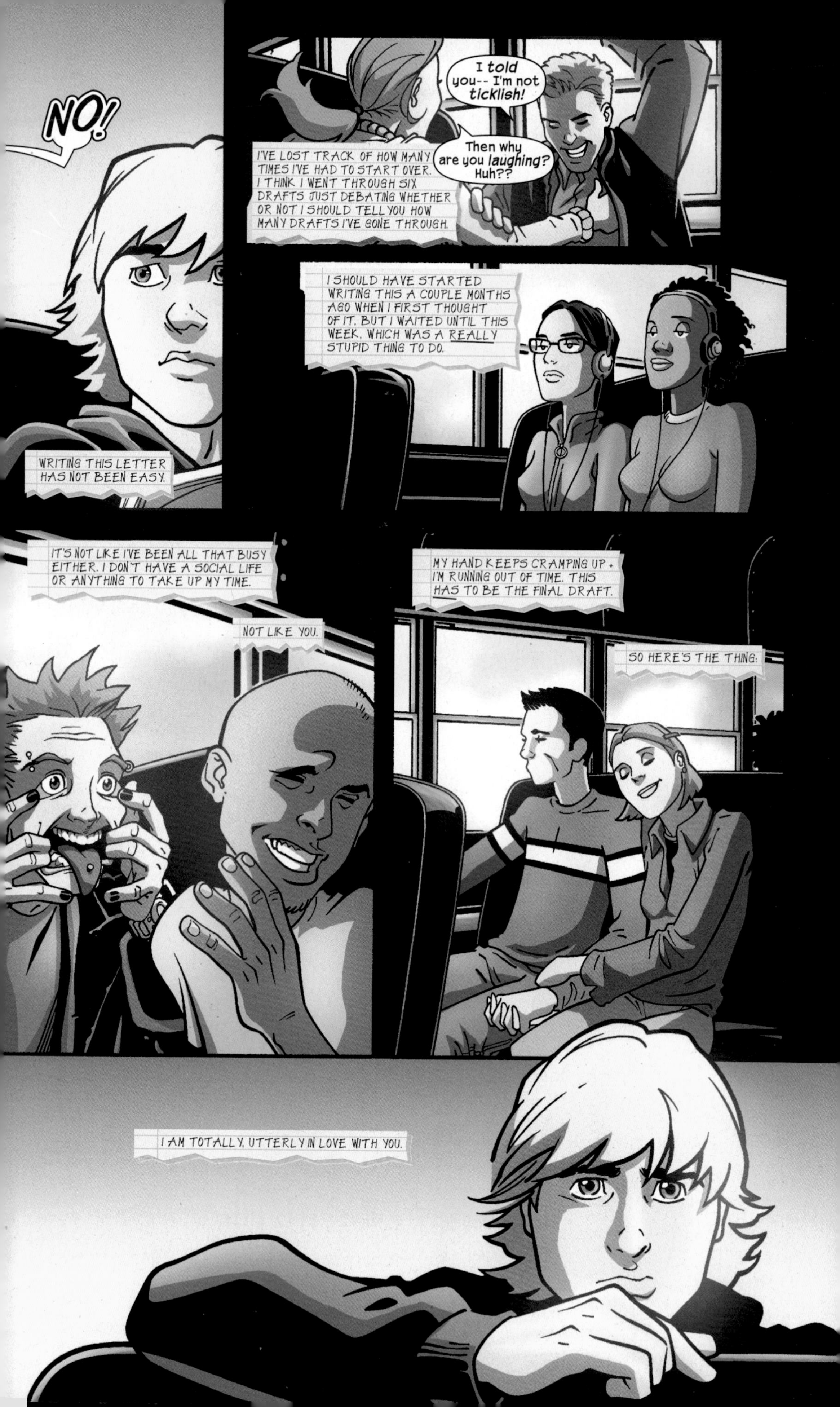
NO!
WRITING THIS LETTER HAS NOT BEEN EASY.
I'VE LOST TRACK OF HOW MANY TIMES I'VE HAD TO START OVER. I THINK I WENT THROUGH SIX DRAFTS JUST DEBATING WHETHER OR NOT I SHOULD TELL YOU HOW MANY DRAFTS I'VE GONE THROUGH.
I told you-- I'm not ticklish!
Then why are you laughing? Huh??
I SHOULD HAVE STARTED WRITING THIS A COUPLE MONTHS AGO WHEN I FIRST THOUGHT OF IT, BUT I WAITED UNTIL THIS WEEK, WHICH WAS A REALLY STUPID THING TO DO.
IT'S NOT LIKE I'VE BEEN ALL THAT BUSY EITHER. I DON'T HAVE A SOCIAL LIFE OR ANYTHING TO TAKE UP MY TIME.
NOT LIKE YOU.
MY HAND KEEPS CRAMPING UP + I'M RUNNING OUT OF TIME. THIS HAS TO BE THE FINAL DRAFT.
SO HERE'S THE THING:
I AM TOTALLY, UTTERLY IN LOVE WITH YOU.

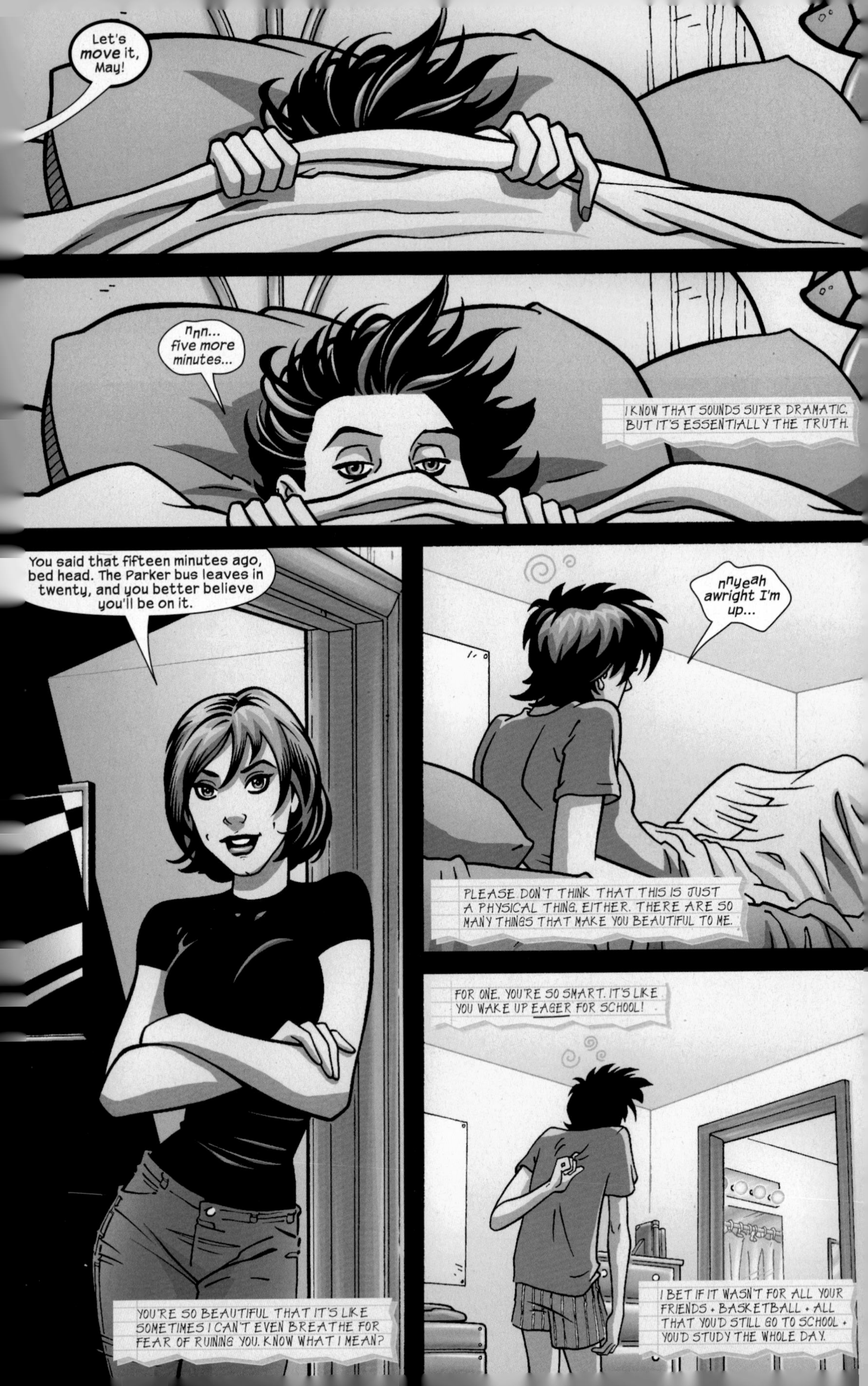
Let's move it, May!
nnn... five more minutes...
I KNOW THAT SOUNDS SUPER DRAMATIC, BUT IT'S ESSENTIALLY THE TRUTH.
You said that fifteen minutes ago, bed head. The Parker bus leaves in twenty, and you better believe you'll be on it.
YOU'RE SO BEAUTIFUL THAT IT'S LIKE SOMETIMES I CAN'T EVEN BREATHE FOR FEAR OF RUINING YOU. KNOW WHAT I MEAN?
nnyeah awright I'm up...
PLEASE DON'T THINK THAT THIS IS JUST A PHYSICAL THING, EITHER. THERE ARE SO MANY THINGS THAT MAKE YOU BEAUTIFUL TO ME.
FOR ONE, YOU'RE SO SMART. IT'S LIKE YOU WAKE UP EAGER FOR SCHOOL!
I BET IF IT WASN'T FOR ALL YOUR FRIENDS + BASKETBALL + ALL THAT YOU'D STILL GO TO SCHOOL + YOU'D STUDY THE WHOLE DAY.

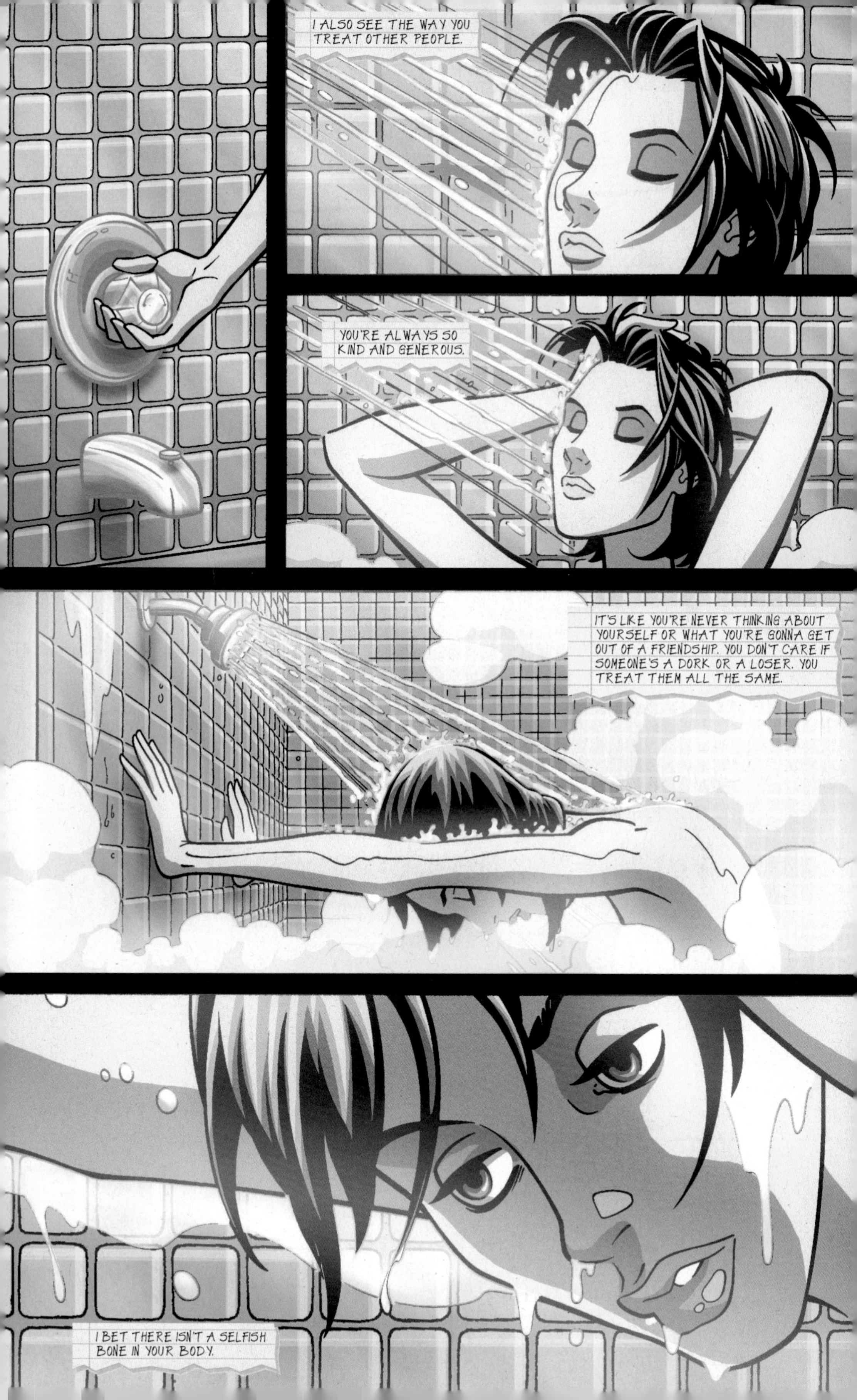
I ALSO SEE THE WAY YOU TREAT OTHER PEOPLE.
YOU'RE ALWAYS SO KIND AND GENEROUS.
IT'S LIKE YOU'RE NEVER THINKING ABOUT YOURSELF OR WHAT YOU'RE GONNA GET OUT OF A FRIENDSHIP. YOU DON'T CARE IF SOMEONE'S A DORK OR A LOSER. YOU TREAT THEM ALL THE SAME.
I BET THERE ISN'T A SELFISH BONE IN YOUR BODY.

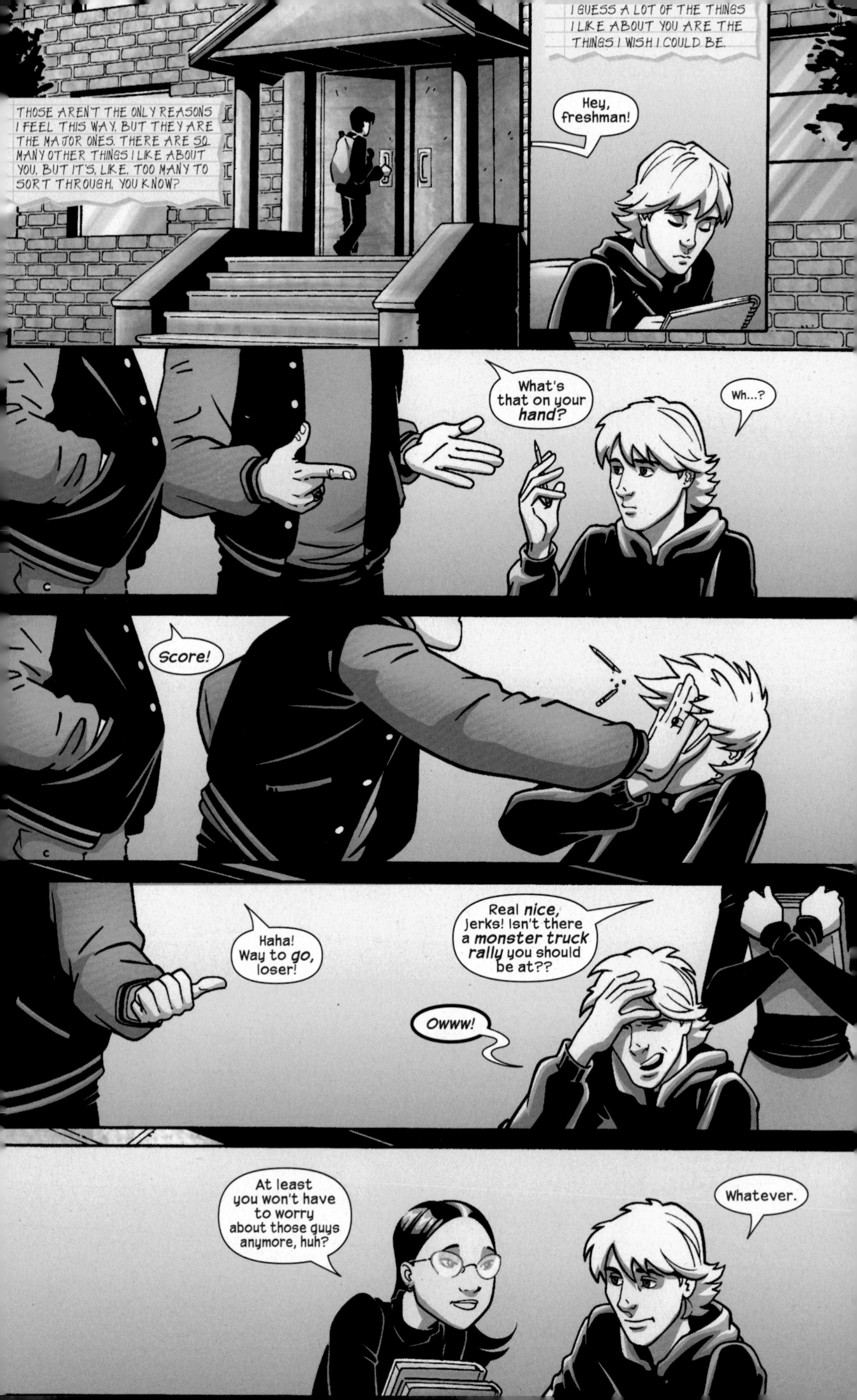
THOSE AREN'T THE ONLY REASONS I FEEL THIS WAY. BUT THEY ARE THE MAJOR ONES. THERE ARE SO MANY OTHER THINGS I LIKE ABOUT YOU, BUT IT'S, LIKE, TOO MANY TO SORT THROUGH, YOU KNOW?
I GUESS A LOT OF THE THINGS I LIKE ABOUT YOU ARE THE THINGS I WISH I COULD BE.
Hey, freshman!
What's that on your *hand?*
Wh...?
Score!
Haha! Way to *go*, loser!
Real *nice*, jerks! Isn't there a *monster truck rally* you should be at??
Owww!
At least you won't have to worry about those guys anymore, huh?
Whatever.

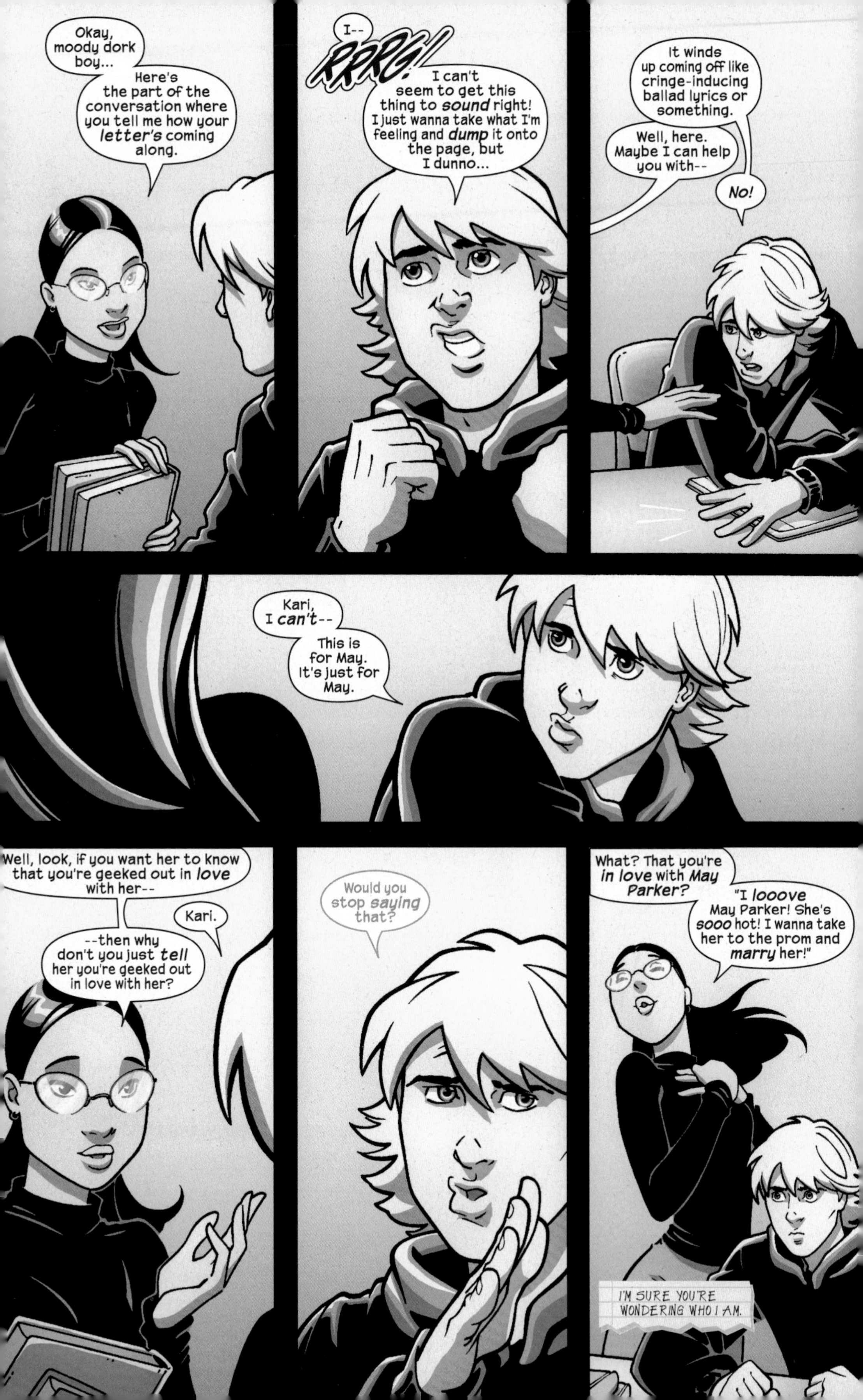
Okay, moody dork boy...
Here's the part of the conversation where you tell me how your *letter's* coming along.
I--
RRRG!
I can't seem to get this thing to *sound* right! I just wanna take what I'm feeling and *dump* it onto the page, but I dunno...
It winds up coming off like cringe-inducing ballad lyrics or something.
Well, here. Maybe I can help you with--
No!
Kari, I *can't*--
This is for May. It's just for May.
Well, look, if you want her to know that you're geeked out in *love* with her--
Kari.
--then why don't you just *tell* her you're geeked out in love with her?
Would you stop *saying* that?
What? That you're *in love* with *May Parker?*
"I *looove* May Parker! She's *sooo* hot! I wanna take her to the prom and *marry* her!"
I'M SURE YOU'RE WONDERING WHO I AM.

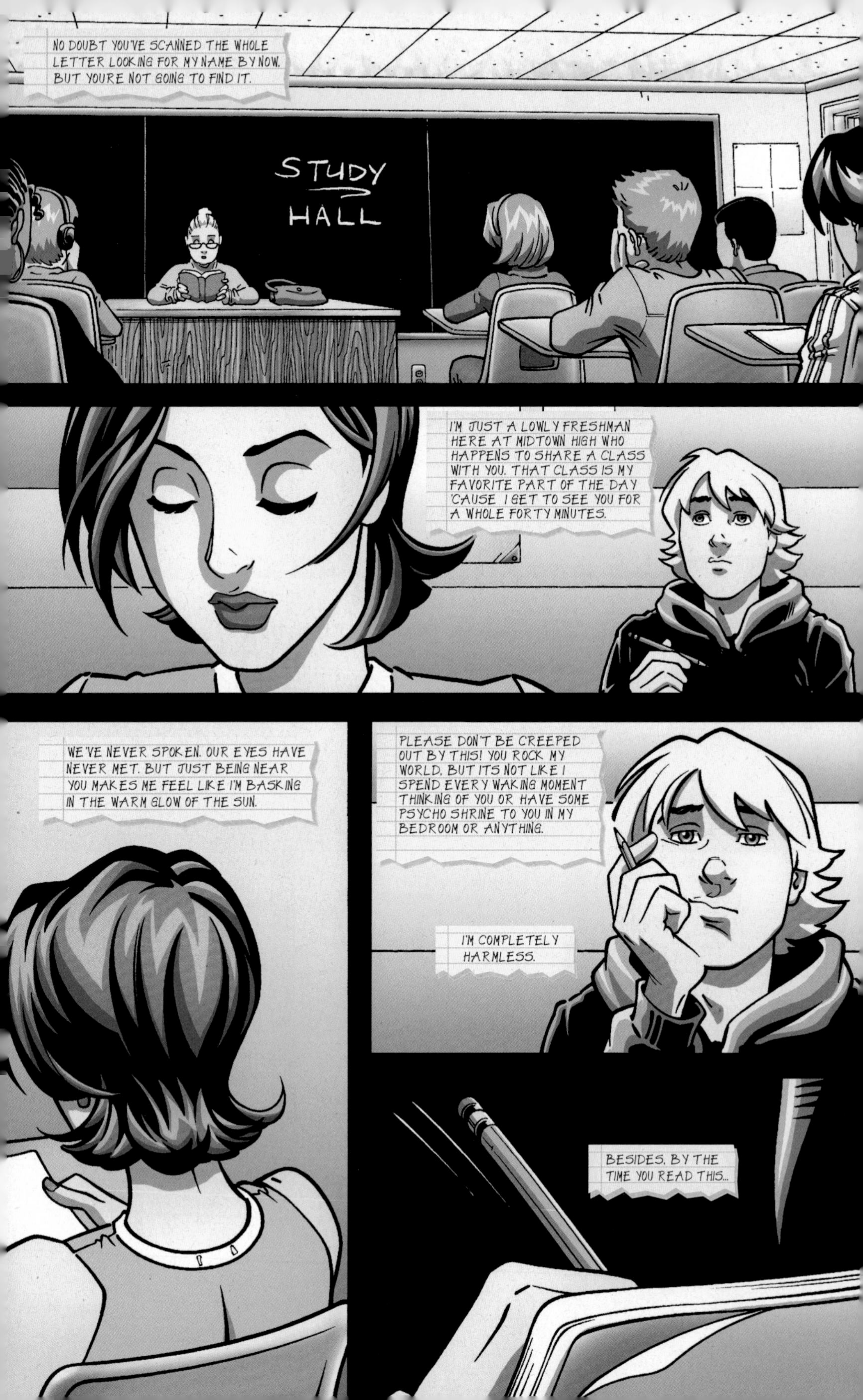

NO DOUBT YOU'VE SCANNED THE WHOLE LETTER LOOKING FOR MY NAME BY NOW. BUT YOU'RE NOT GOING TO FIND IT.
STUDY HALL
I'M JUST A LOWLY FRESHMAN HERE AT MIDTOWN HIGH WHO HAPPENS TO SHARE A CLASS WITH YOU. THAT CLASS IS MY FAVORITE PART OF THE DAY 'CAUSE I GET TO SEE YOU FOR A WHOLE FORTY MINUTES.
WE'VE NEVER SPOKEN. OUR EYES HAVE NEVER MET. BUT JUST BEING NEAR YOU MAKES ME FEEL LIKE I'M BASKING IN THE WARM GLOW OF THE SUN.
PLEASE DON'T BE CREEPED OUT BY THIS! YOU ROCK MY WORLD. BUT ITS NOT LIKE I SPEND EVERY WAKING MOMENT THINKING OF YOU OR HAVE SOME PSYCHO SHRINE TO YOU IN MY BEDROOM OR ANYTHING.
I'M COMPLETELY HARMLESS.
BESIDES, BY THE TIME YOU READ THIS...

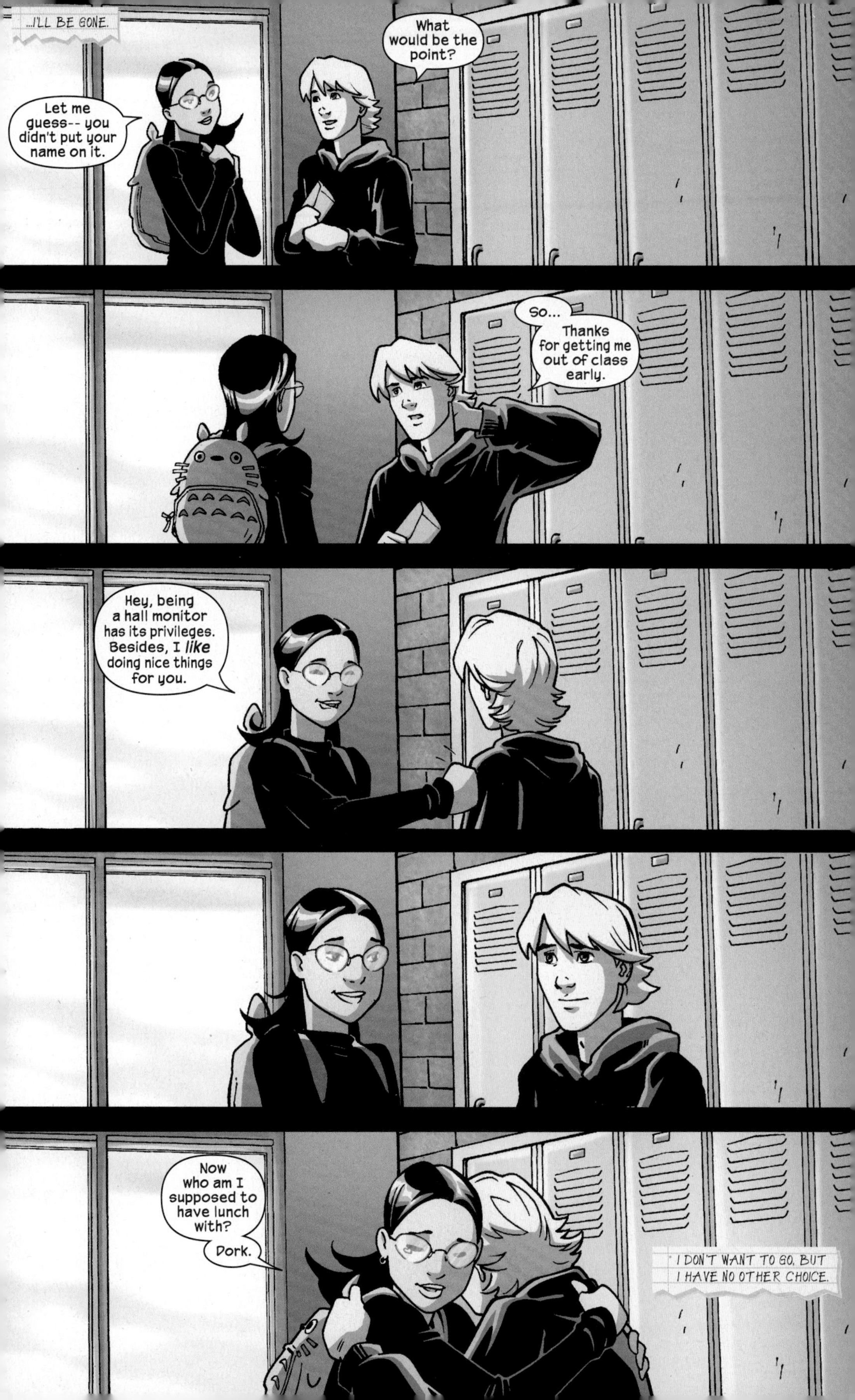
...I'LL BE GONE.
What would be the point?
Let me guess-- you didn't put your name on it.
So...
Thanks for getting me out of class early.
Hey, being a hall monitor has its privileges. Besides, I *like* doing nice things for you.
Now who am I supposed to have lunch with?
Dork.
I DON'T WANT TO GO, BUT I HAVE NO OTHER CHOICE.

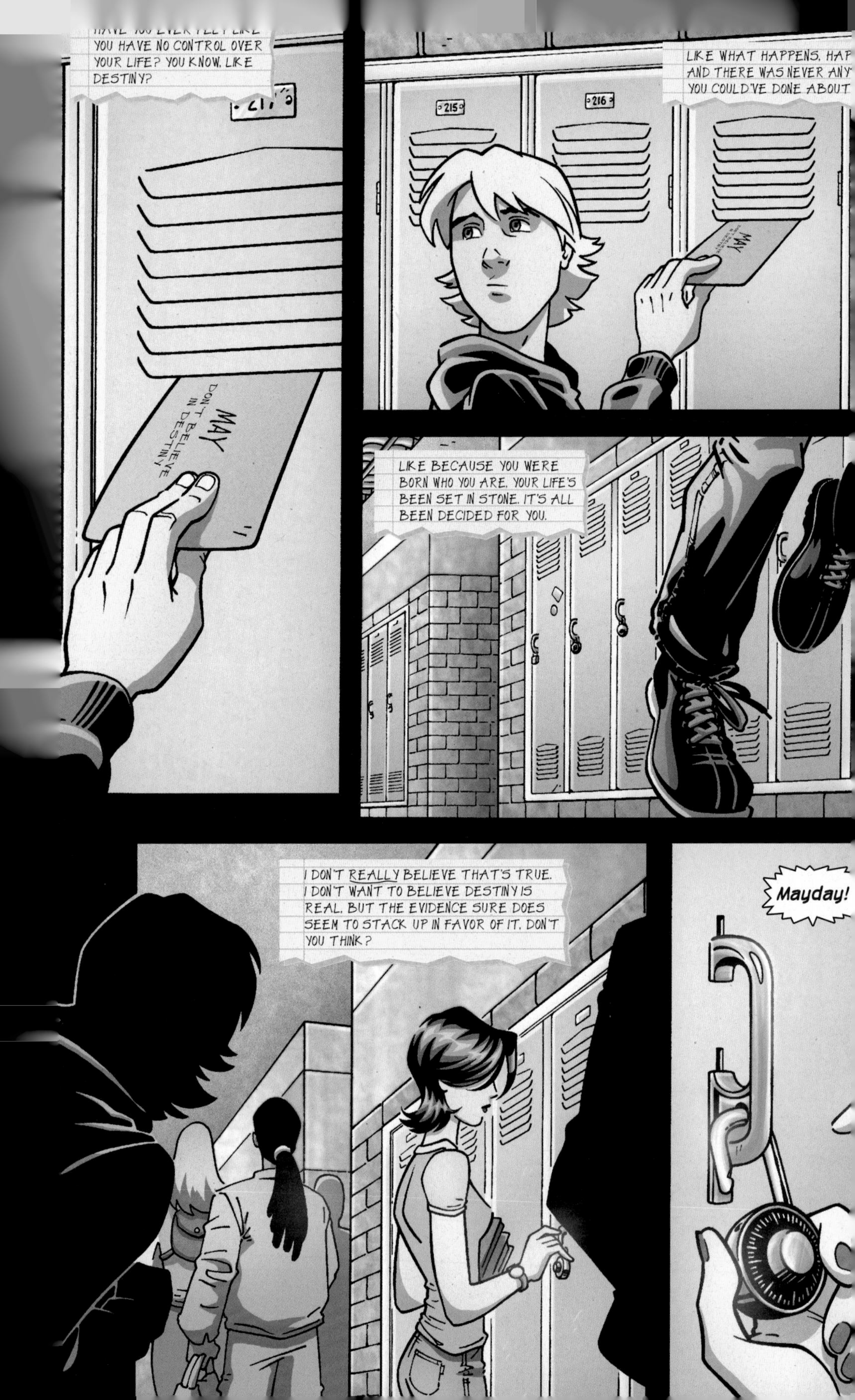
YOU HAVE NO CONTROL OVER YOUR LIFE? YOU KNOW, LIKE DESTINY?
MAY
DON'T BELIEVE IN DESTINY
215
216
LIKE WHAT HAPPENS, HAP
AND THERE WAS NEVER ANY
YOU COULD'VE DONE ABOUT
LIKE BECAUSE YOU WERE BORN WHO YOU ARE, YOUR LIFE'S BEEN SET IN STONE. IT'S ALL BEEN DECIDED FOR YOU.
I DON'T REALLY BELIEVE THAT'S TRUE. I DON'T WANT TO BELIEVE DESTINY IS REAL. BUT THE EVIDENCE SURE DOES SEEM TO STACK UP IN FAVOR OF IT, DON'T YOU THINK?
Mayday!

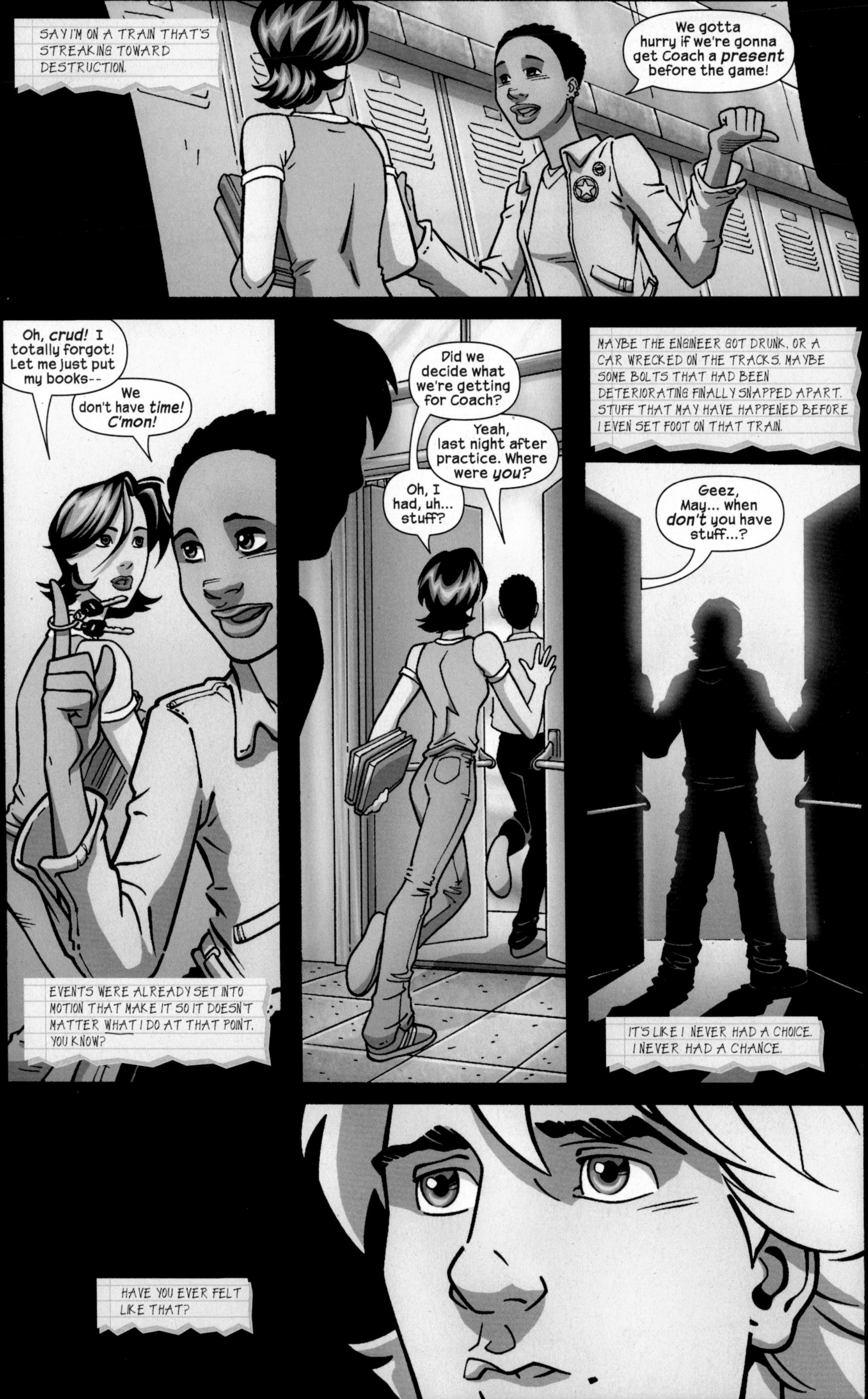
SAY I'M ON A TRAIN THAT'S STREAKING TOWARD DESTRUCTION.
We gotta hurry if we're gonna get Coach a *present* before the game!
Oh, *crud!* I totally forgot! Let me just put my books--
We don't have *time! C'mon!*
EVENTS WERE ALREADY SET INTO MOTION THAT MAKE IT SO IT DOESN'T MATTER WHAT I DO AT THAT POINT. YOU KNOW?
Did we decide what we're getting for Coach?
Yeah, last night after practice. Where were *you?*
Oh, I had, uh... stuff?
MAYBE THE ENGINEER GOT DRUNK. OR A CAR WRECKED ON THE TRACKS. MAYBE SOME BOLTS THAT HAD BEEN DETERIORATING FINALLY SNAPPED APART. STUFF THAT MAY HAVE HAPPENED BEFORE I EVEN SET FOOT ON THAT TRAIN.
Geez, May... when *don't* you have stuff...?
IT'S LIKE I NEVER HAD A CHOICE. I NEVER HAD A CHANCE.
HAVE YOU EVER FELT LIKE THAT?

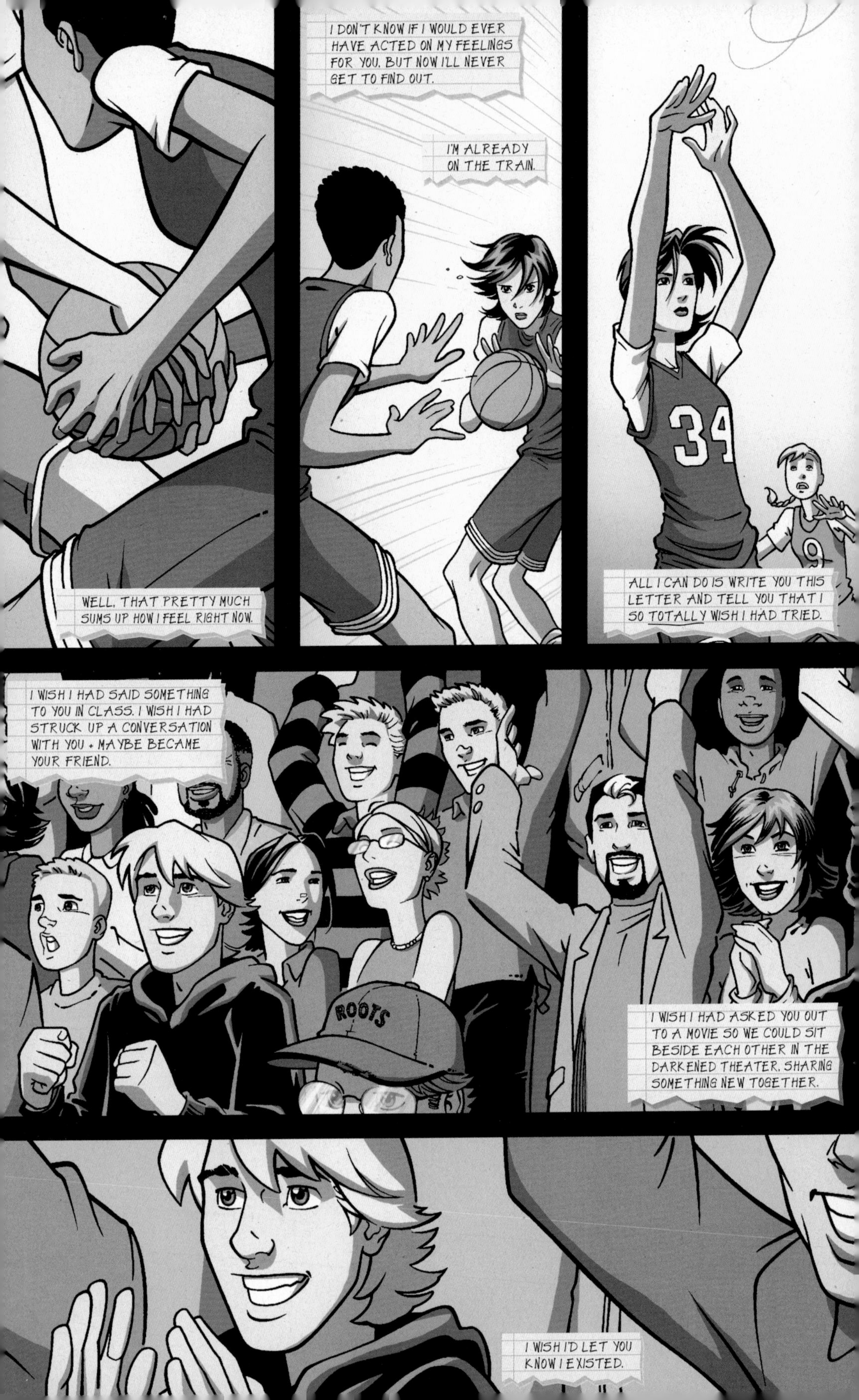
WELL, THAT PRETTY MUCH SUMS UP HOW I FEEL RIGHT NOW.
I DON'T KNOW IF I WOULD EVER HAVE ACTED ON MY FEELINGS FOR YOU, BUT NOW I'LL NEVER GET TO FIND OUT.
I'M ALREADY ON THE TRAIN.
34
9
ALL I CAN DO IS WRITE YOU THIS LETTER AND TELL YOU THAT I SO TOTALLY WISH I HAD TRIED.
I WISH I HAD SAID SOMETHING TO YOU IN CLASS. I WISH I HAD STRUCK UP A CONVERSATION WITH YOU + MAYBE BECAME YOUR FRIEND.
ROOTS
I WISH I HAD ASKED YOU OUT TO A MOVIE SO WE COULD SIT BESIDE EACH OTHER IN THE DARKENED THEATER, SHARING SOMETHING NEW TOGETHER.
I WISH I'D LET YOU KNOW I EXISTED.

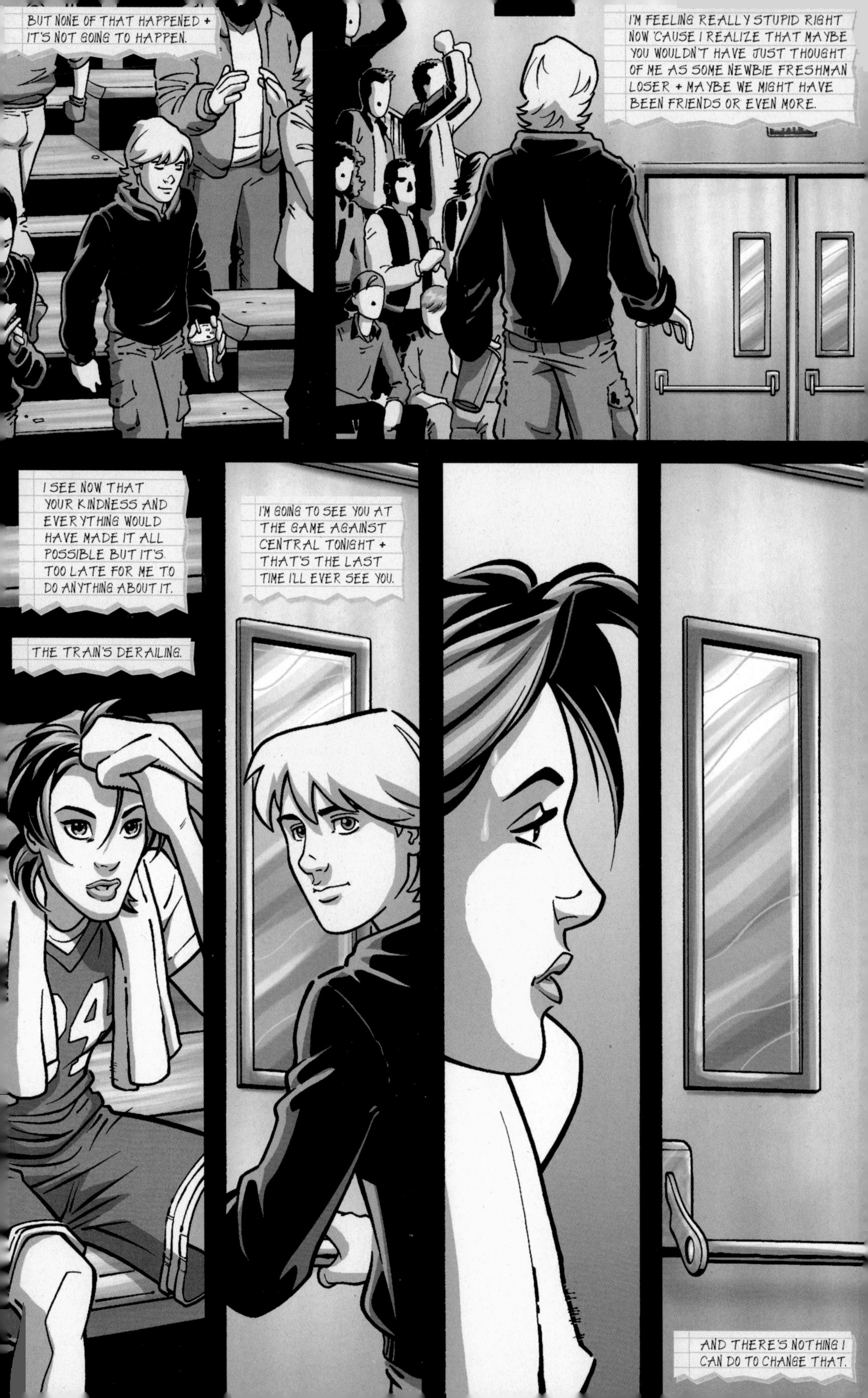
BUT NONE OF THAT HAPPENED + IT'S NOT GOING TO HAPPEN.
I'M FEELING REALLY STUPID RIGHT NOW 'CAUSE I REALIZE THAT MAYBE YOU WOULDN'T HAVE JUST THOUGHT OF ME AS SOME NEWBIE FRESHMAN LOSER + MAYBE WE MIGHT HAVE BEEN FRIENDS OR EVEN MORE.
I SEE NOW THAT YOUR KINDNESS AND EVERYTHING WOULD HAVE MADE IT ALL POSSIBLE BUT IT'S TOO LATE FOR ME TO DO ANYTHING ABOUT IT.
THE TRAIN'S DERAILING.
I'M GOING TO SEE YOU AT THE GAME AGAINST CENTRAL TONIGHT + THAT'S THE LAST TIME I'LL EVER SEE YOU.
AND THERE'S NOTHING I CAN DO TO CHANGE THAT.

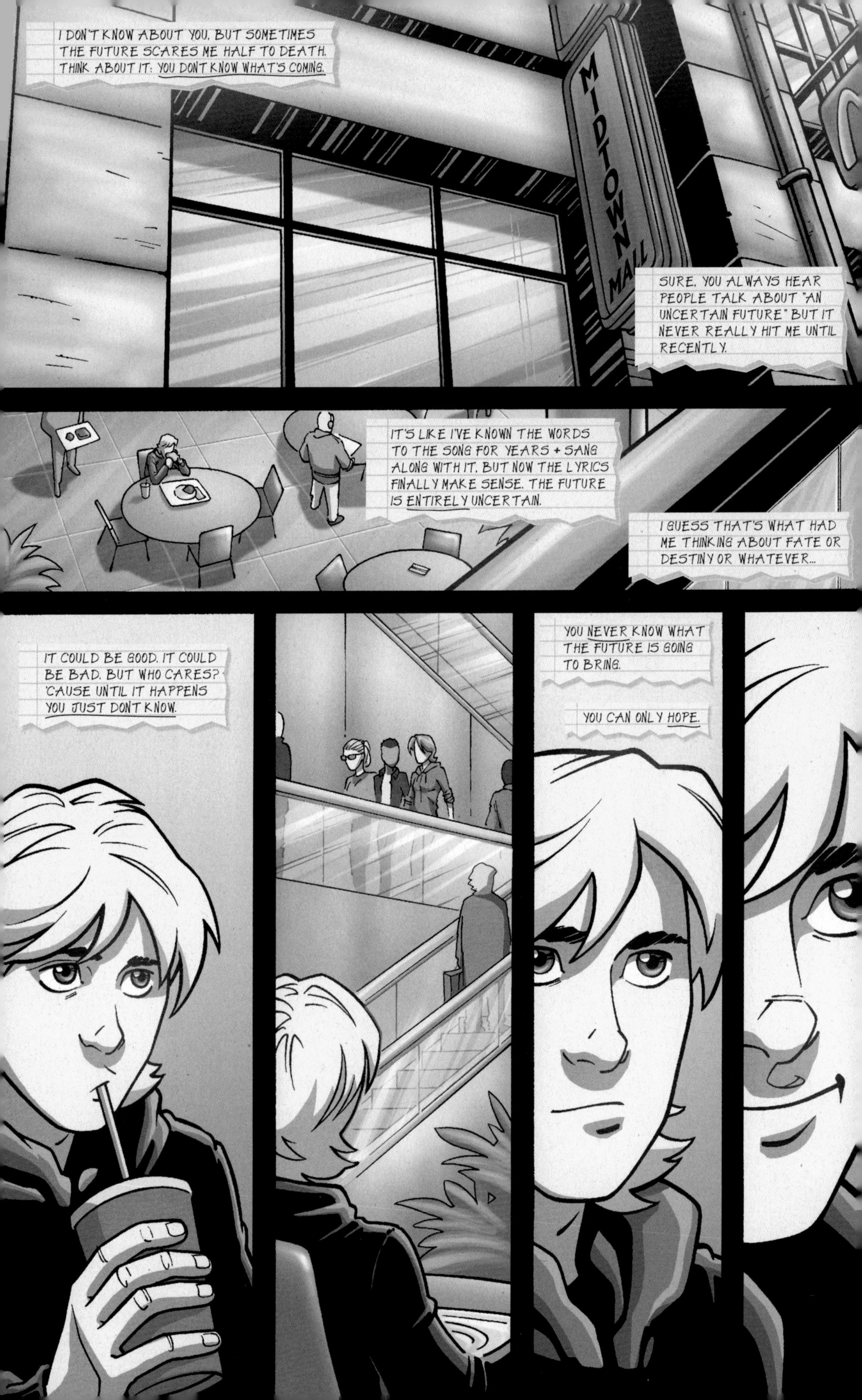
I DON'T KNOW ABOUT YOU, BUT SOMETIMES THE FUTURE SCARES ME HALF TO DEATH. THINK ABOUT IT: YOU DON'T KNOW WHAT'S COMING.
MIDTOWN MALL
SURE, YOU ALWAYS HEAR PEOPLE TALK ABOUT "AN UNCERTAIN FUTURE" BUT IT NEVER REALLY HIT ME UNTIL RECENTLY.
IT'S LIKE I'VE KNOWN THE WORDS TO THE SONG FOR YEARS + SANG ALONG WITH IT, BUT NOW THE LYRICS FINALLY MAKE SENSE. THE FUTURE IS ENTIRELY UNCERTAIN.
I GUESS THAT'S WHAT HAD ME THINKING ABOUT FATE OR DESTINY OR WHATEVER...
IT COULD BE GOOD. IT COULD BE BAD. BUT WHO CARES? 'CAUSE UNTIL IT HAPPENS YOU JUST DON'T KNOW.
YOU NEVER KNOW WHAT THE FUTURE IS GOING TO BRING.
YOU CAN ONLY HOPE.

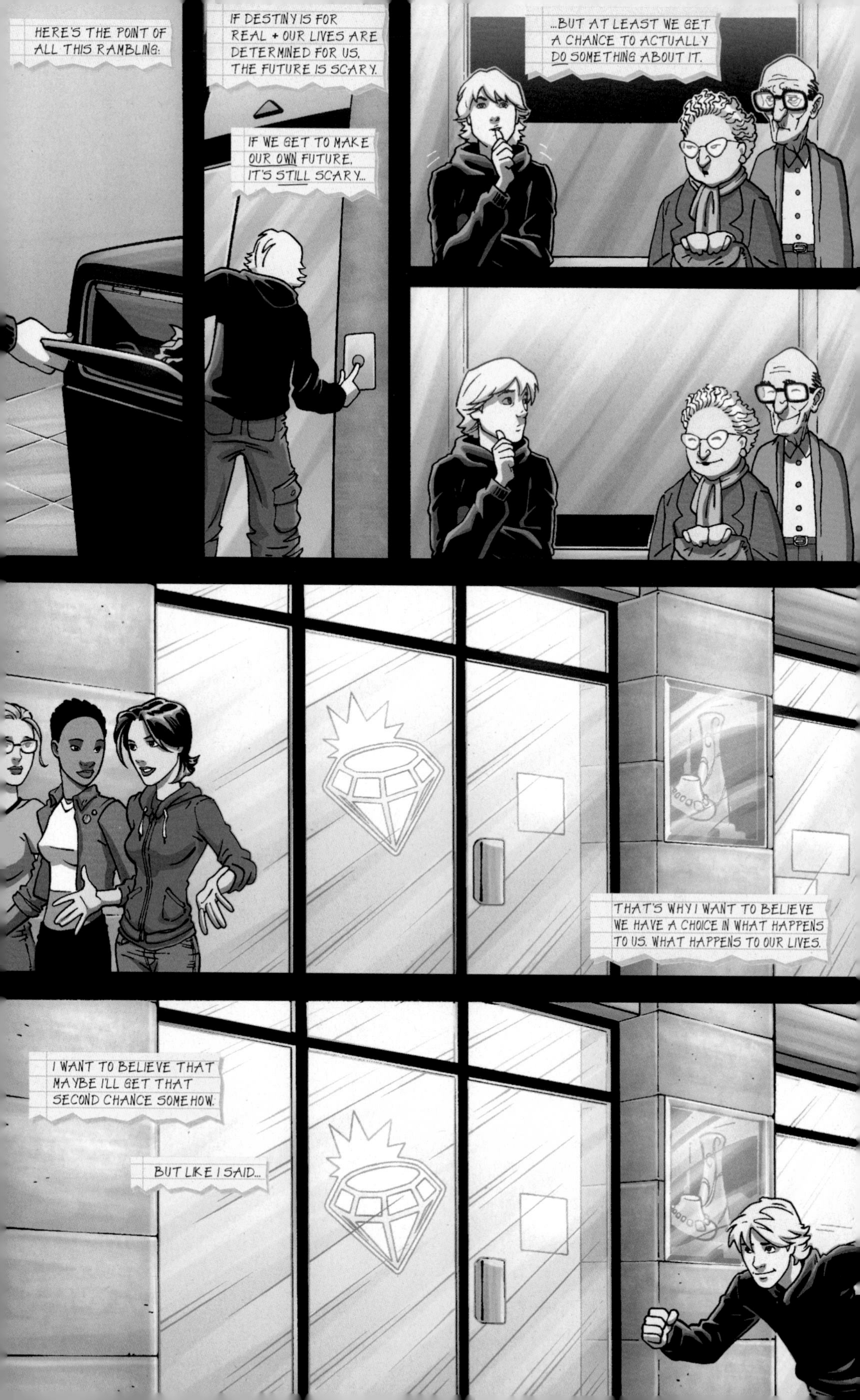
HERE'S THE POINT OF ALL THIS RAMBLING:
IF DESTINY IS FOR REAL + OUR LIVES ARE DETERMINED FOR US, THE FUTURE IS SCARY.
IF WE GET TO MAKE OUR OWN FUTURE, IT'S STILL SCARY...
...BUT AT LEAST WE GET A CHANCE TO ACTUALLY DO SOMETHING ABOUT IT.
THAT'S WHY I WANT TO BELIEVE WE HAVE A CHOICE IN WHAT HAPPENS TO US. WHAT HAPPENS TO OUR LIVES.
I WANT TO BELIEVE THAT MAYBE I'LL GET THAT SECOND CHANCE SOMEHOW.
BUT LIKE I SAID...

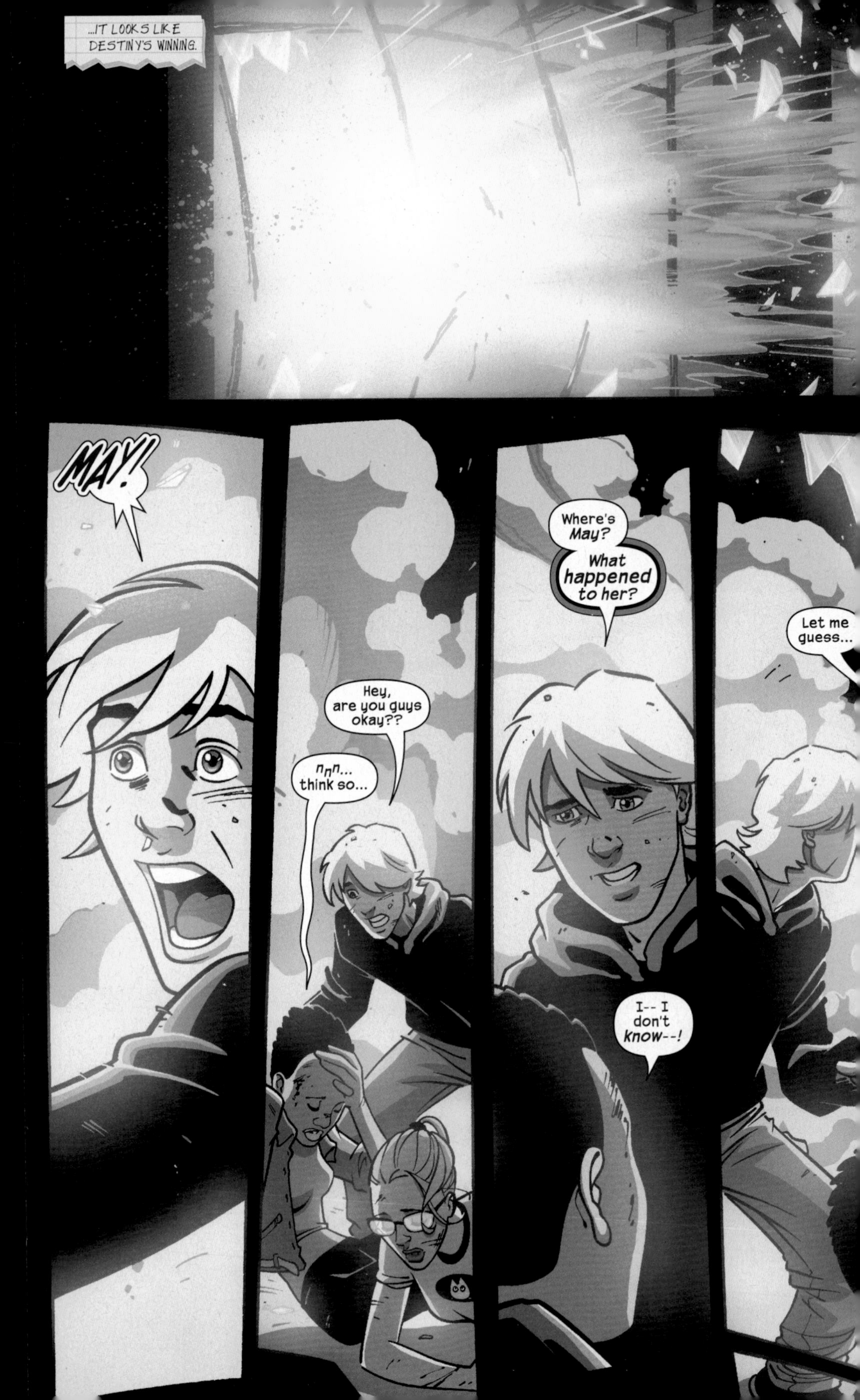
...IT LOOKS LIKE DESTINY'S WINNING.
MAY!
Hey, are you guys okay??
nnn... think so...
Where's May?
What happened to her?
I-- I don't know--!
Let me guess...

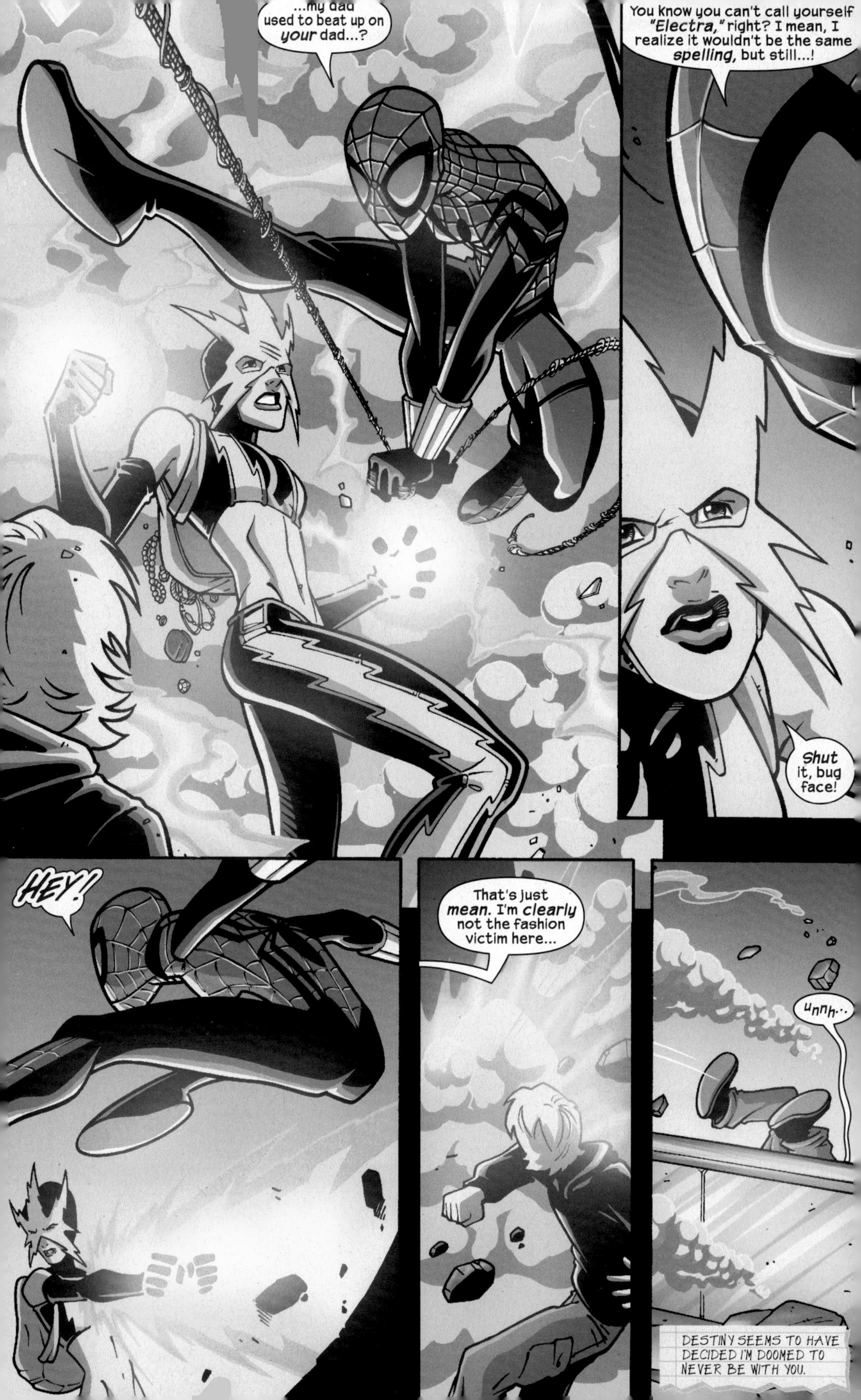
...my dad
used to beat up on
your dad...?
You know you can't call yourself "*Electra*," right? I mean, I realize it wouldn't be the same *spelling*, but still...!
Shut it, bug face!
HEY!
That's just *mean*. I'm *clearly* not the fashion victim here...
unnh...
DESTINY SEEMS TO HAVE DECIDED I'M DOOMED TO NEVER BE WITH YOU.

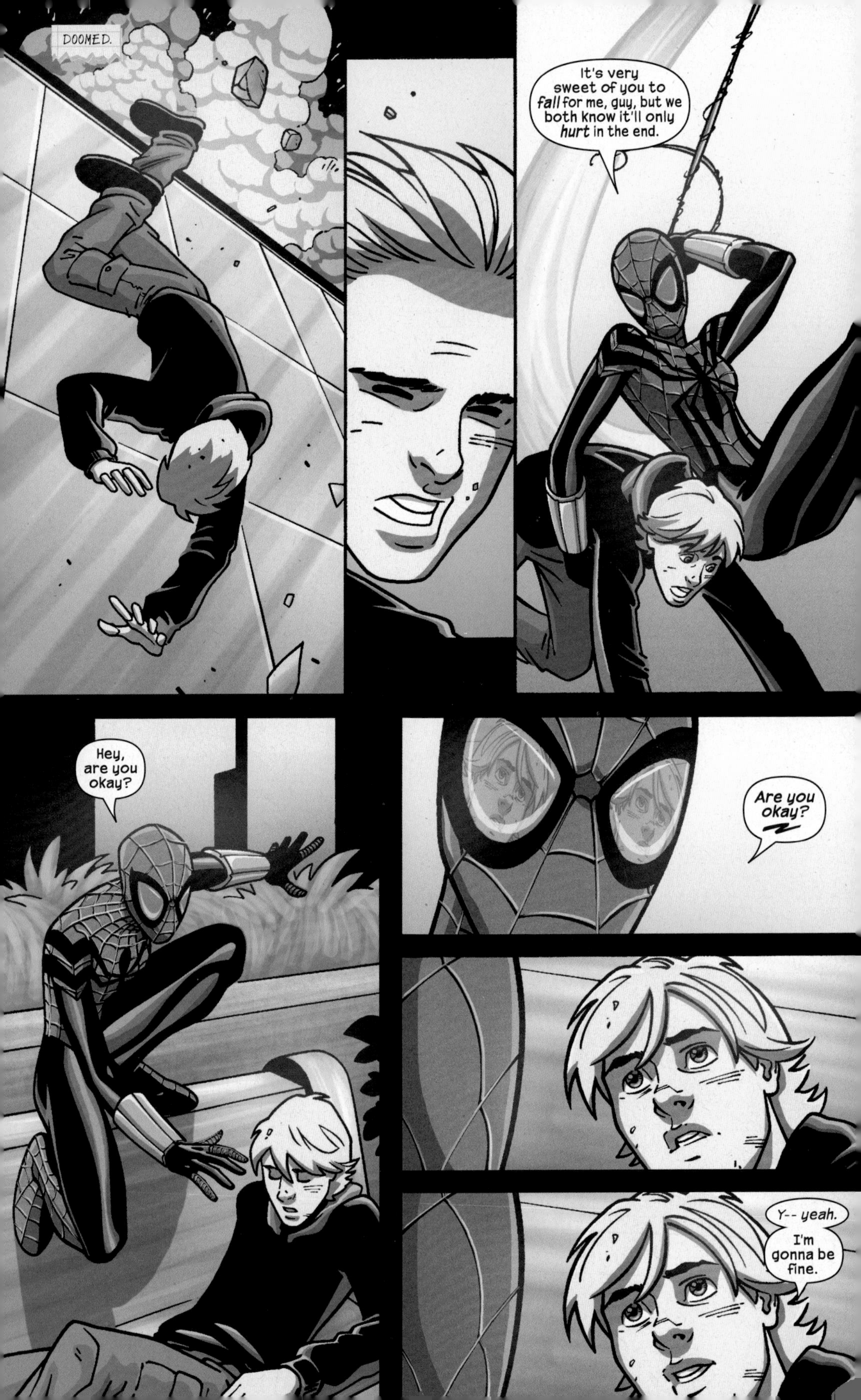
DOOMED.
It's very sweet of you to fall for me, guy, but we both know it'll only hurt in the end.
Hey, are you okay?
Are you okay?
Y-- yeah.
I'm gonna be fine.

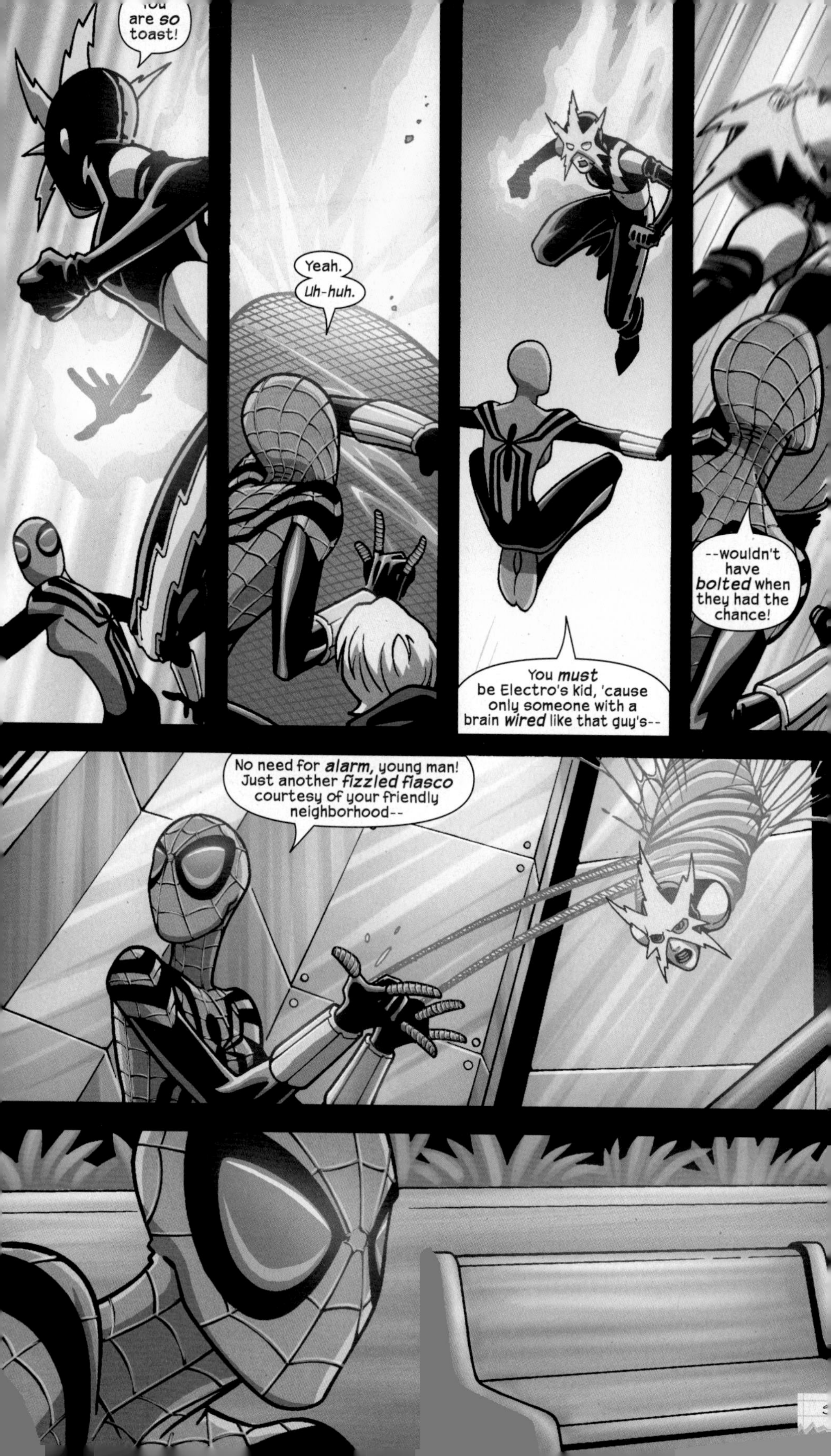

are so toast!
Yeah.
Uh-huh.
You must be Electro's kid, 'cause only someone with a brain wired like that guy's--
--wouldn't have bolted when they had the chance!
No need for alarm, young man! Just another fizzled fiasco courtesy of your friendly neighborhood--

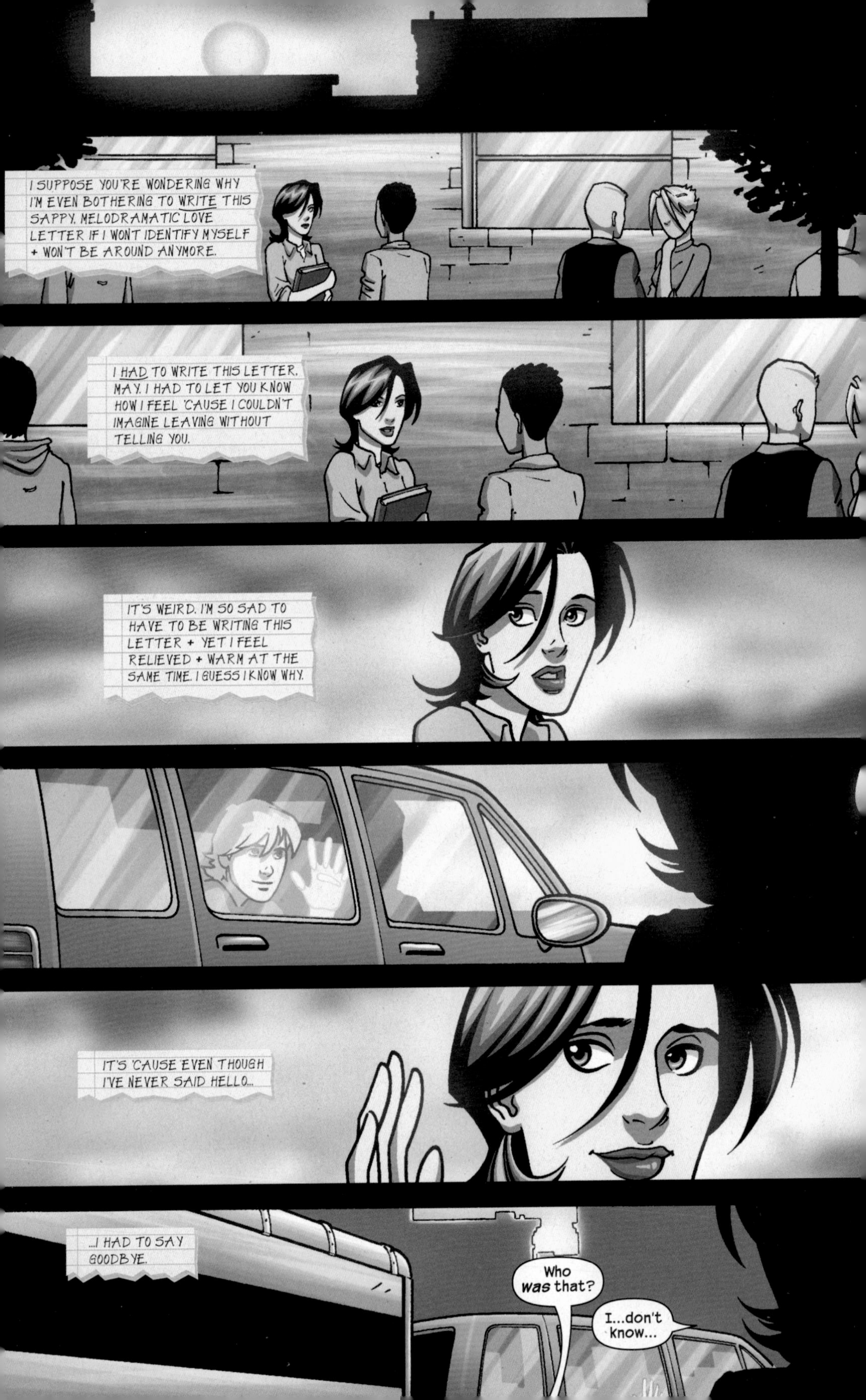
I SUPPOSE YOU'RE WONDERING WHY I'M EVEN BOTHERING TO WRITE THIS SAPPY, MELODRAMATIC LOVE LETTER IF I WON'T IDENTIFY MYSELF + WON'T BE AROUND ANYMORE.
I HAD TO WRITE THIS LETTER, MAY. I HAD TO LET YOU KNOW HOW I FEEL 'CAUSE I COULDN'T IMAGINE LEAVING WITHOUT TELLING YOU.
IT'S WEIRD. I'M SO SAD TO HAVE TO BE WRITING THIS LETTER + YET I FEEL RELIEVED + WARM AT THE SAME TIME. I GUESS I KNOW WHY.
IT'S 'CAUSE EVEN THOUGH I'VE NEVER SAID HELLO...
...I HAD TO SAY GOODBYE.
Who *was* that?
I...don't know...

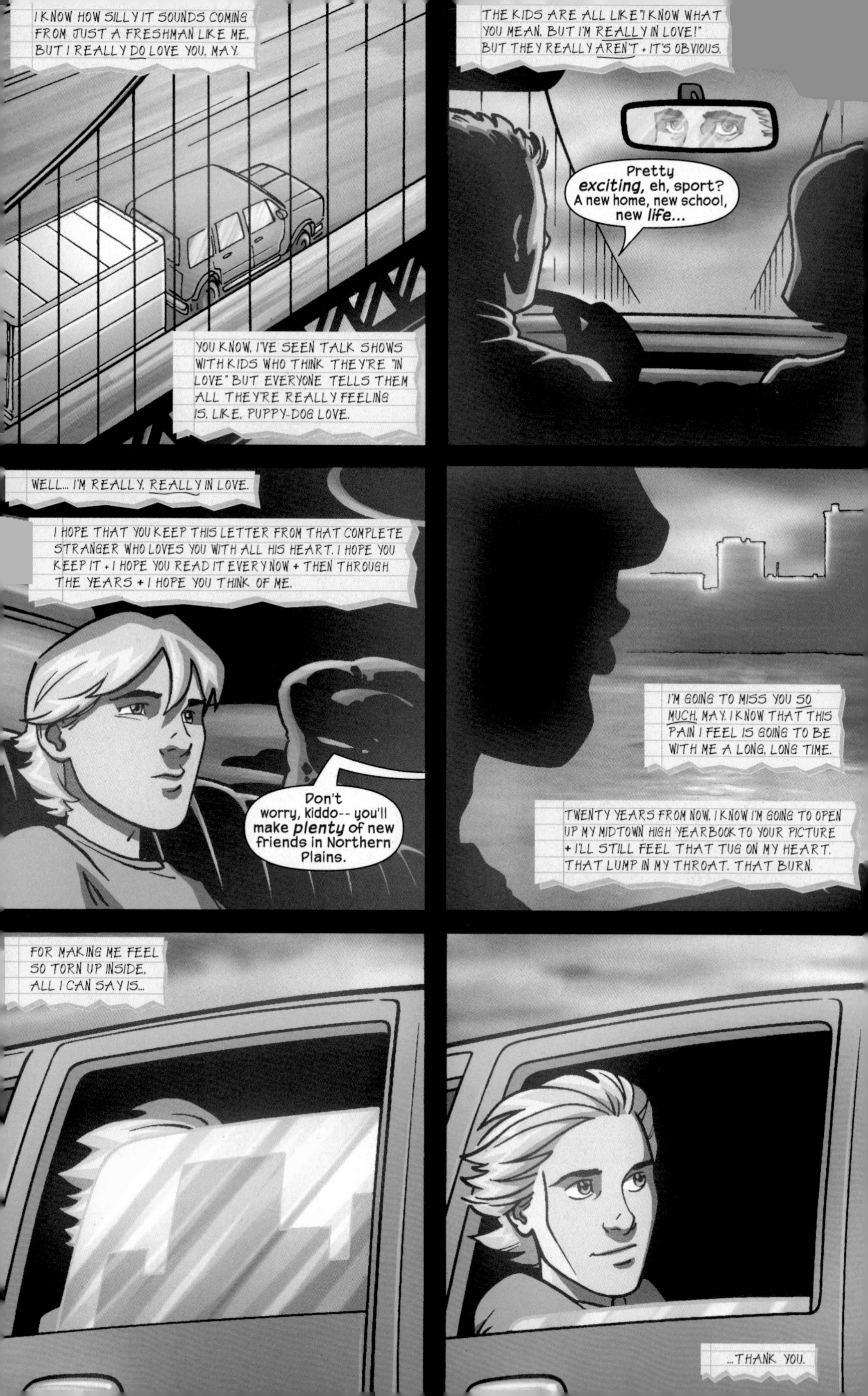
I KNOW HOW SILLY IT SOUNDS COMING FROM JUST A FRESHMAN LIKE ME. BUT I REALLY DO LOVE YOU, MAY.
YOU KNOW, I'VE SEEN TALK SHOWS WITH KIDS WHO THINK THEY'RE "IN LOVE" BUT EVERYONE TELLS THEM ALL THEY'RE REALLY FEELING IS, LIKE, PUPPY-DOG LOVE.
THE KIDS ARE ALL LIKE "I KNOW WHAT YOU MEAN, BUT I'M REALLY IN LOVE!" BUT THEY REALLY AREN'T + IT'S OBVIOUS.
Pretty exciting, eh, sport? A new home, new school, new life...
WELL... I'M REALLY, REALLY IN LOVE.
I HOPE THAT YOU KEEP THIS LETTER FROM THAT COMPLETE STRANGER WHO LOVES YOU WITH ALL HIS HEART. I HOPE YOU KEEP IT + I HOPE YOU READ IT EVERY NOW + THEN THROUGH THE YEARS + I HOPE YOU THINK OF ME.
Don't worry, kiddo-- you'll make plenty of new friends in Northern Plains.
I'M GOING TO MISS YOU SO MUCH, MAY. I KNOW THAT THIS PAIN I FEEL IS GOING TO BE WITH ME A LONG, LONG TIME.
TWENTY YEARS FROM NOW, I KNOW I'M GOING TO OPEN UP MY MIDTOWN HIGH YEARBOOK TO YOUR PICTURE + I'LL STILL FEEL THAT TUG ON MY HEART. THAT LUMP IN MY THROAT. THAT BURN.
FOR MAKING ME FEEL SO TORN UP INSIDE, ALL I CAN SAY IS...
...THANK YOU.

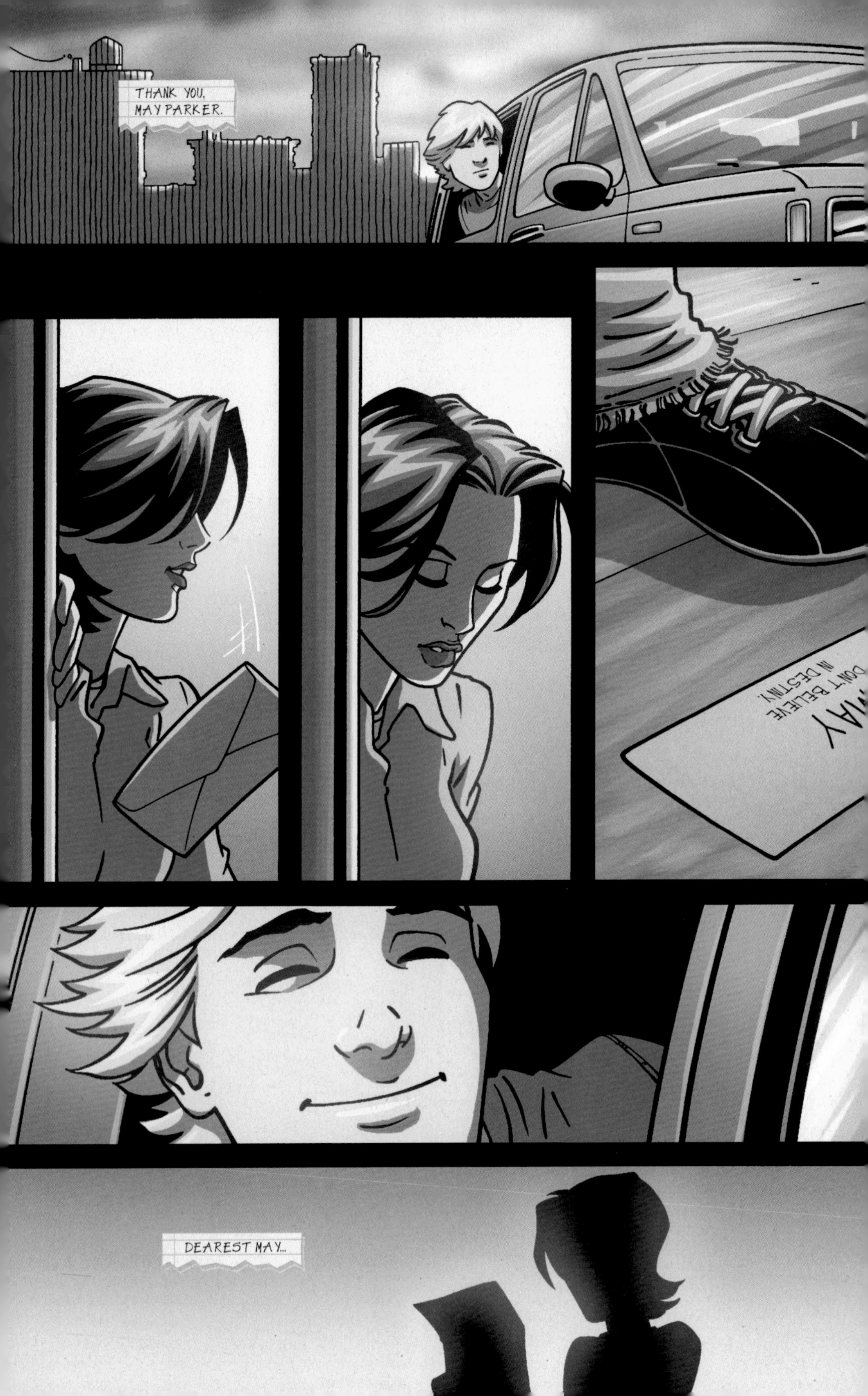
THANK YOU, MAY PARKER.
DON'T BELIEVE IN DESTINY.
DEAREST MAY...

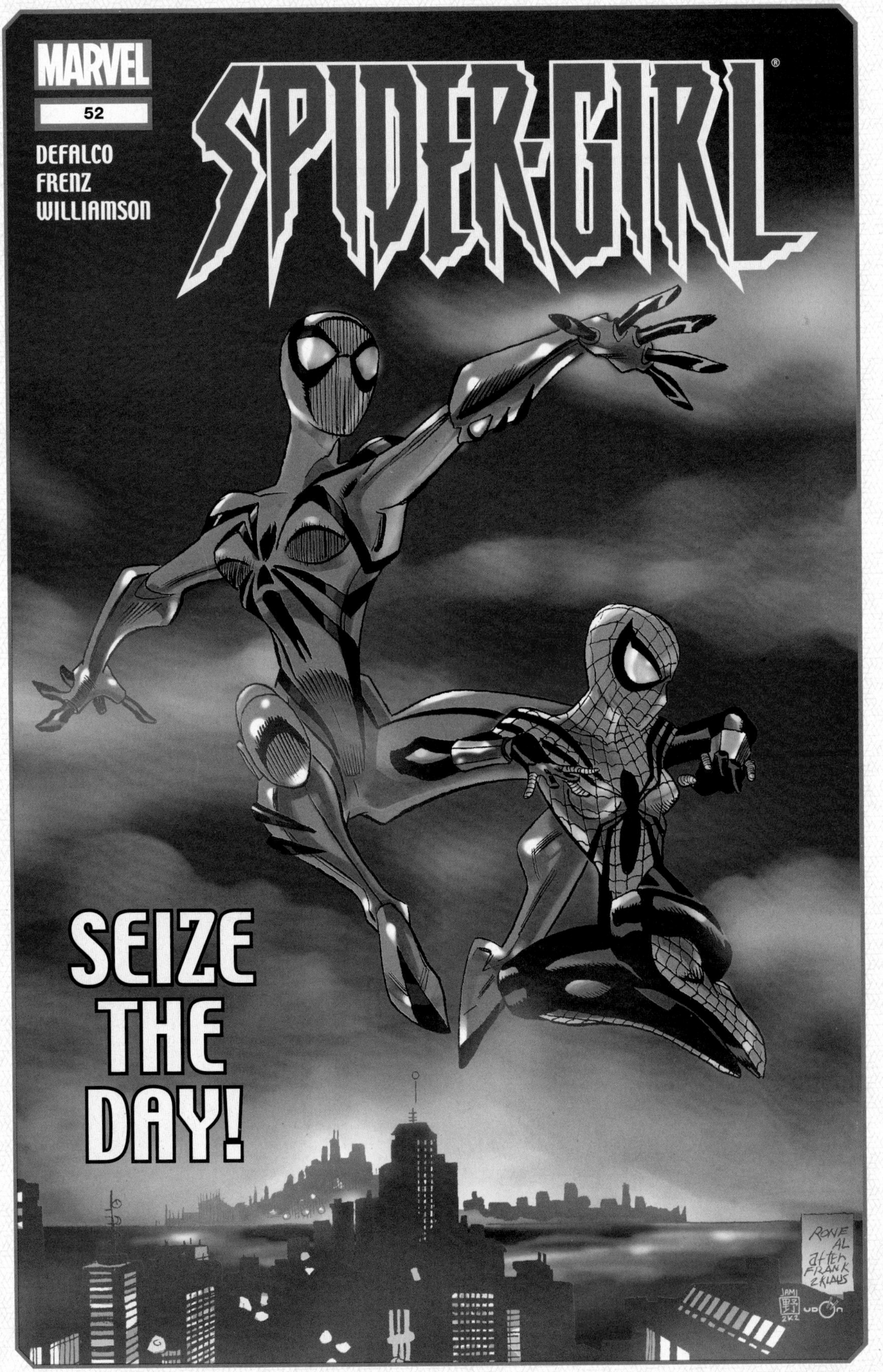
MARVEL
52
DEFALCO
FRENZ
WILLIAMSON
SPIDER-GIRL
SEIZE THE DAY!

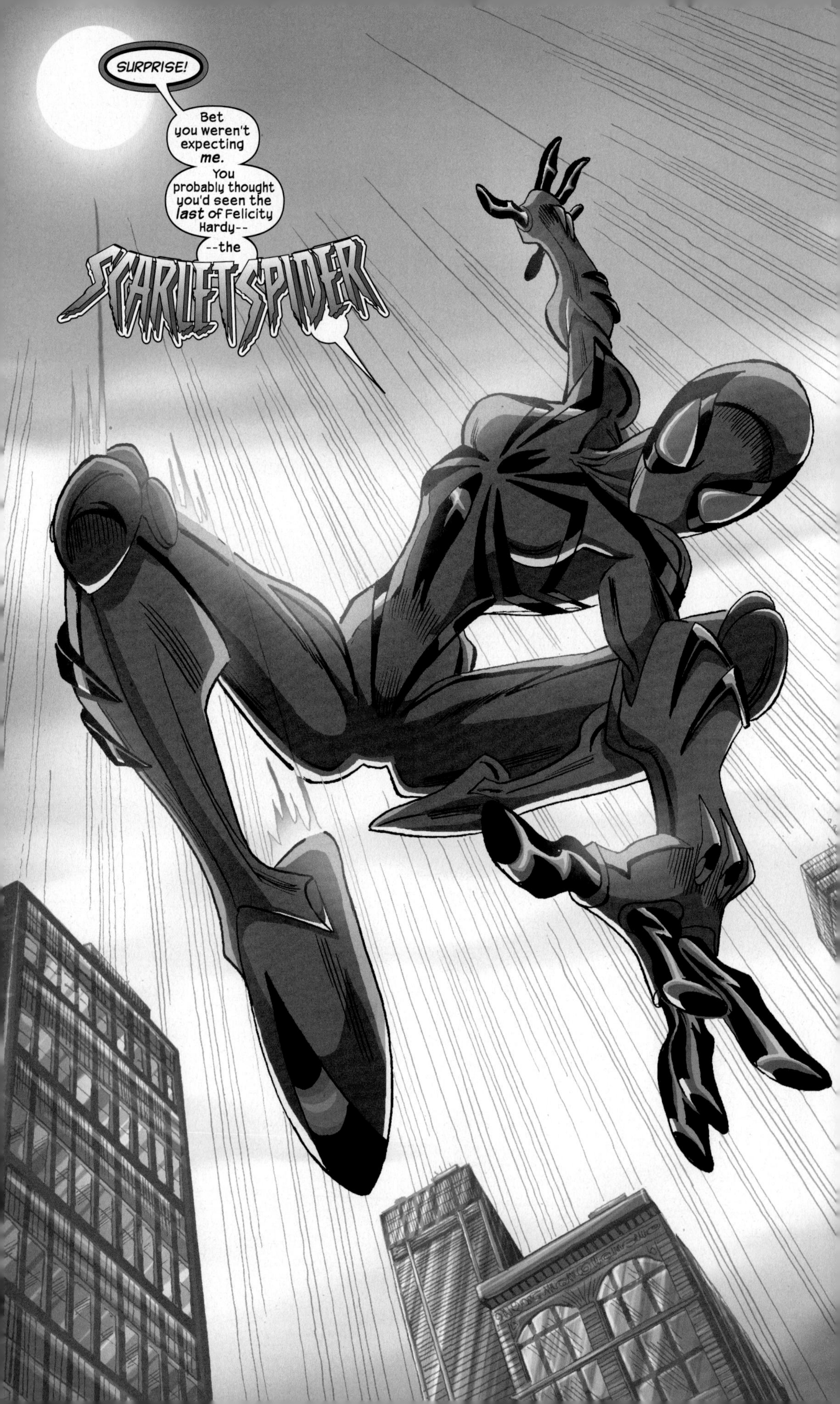

SURPRISE!
Bet you weren't expecting *me*.
You probably thought you'd seen the *last* of Felicity Hardy--
--the
SCARLET SPIDER

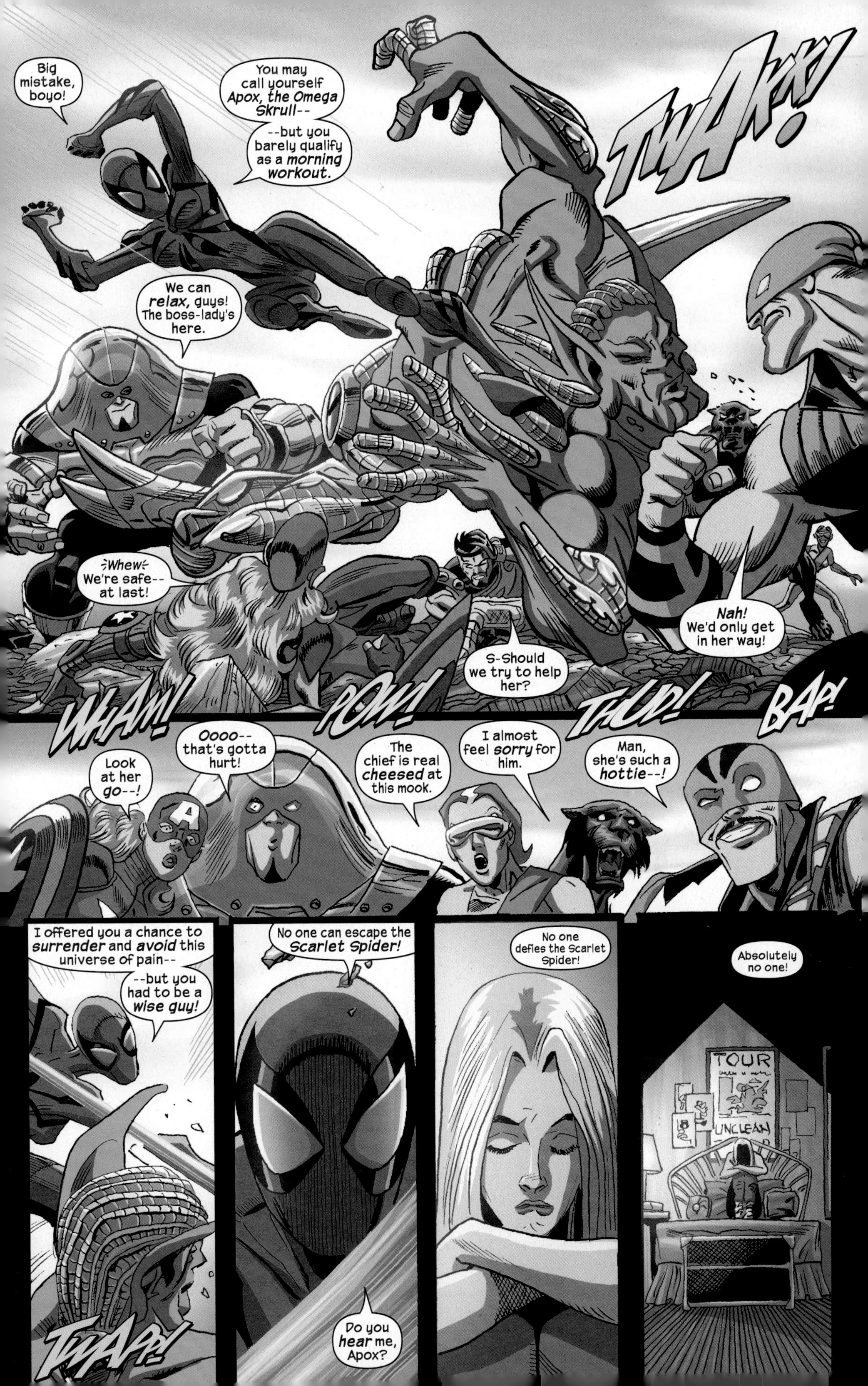
Big mistake, boyo!
You may call yourself Apox, the Omega Skrull--
--but you barely qualify as a morning workout.
THWAKK!
We can relax, guys! The boss-lady's here.
Whew We're safe-- at last!
S-Should we try to help her?
Nah! We'd only get in her way!
WHAM!
POW!
THUD!
BAP!
Look at her go--!
Oooo-- that's gotta hurt!
The chief is real cheesed at this mook.
I almost feel sorry for him.
Man, she's such a hottie--!
I offered you a chance to surrender and avoid this universe of pain--
--but you had to be a wise guy!
THWAPP!
No one can escape the Scarlet Spider!
Do you hear me, Apox?
No one defies the Scarlet Spider!
Absolutely no one!
TOUR
UNCLEAN

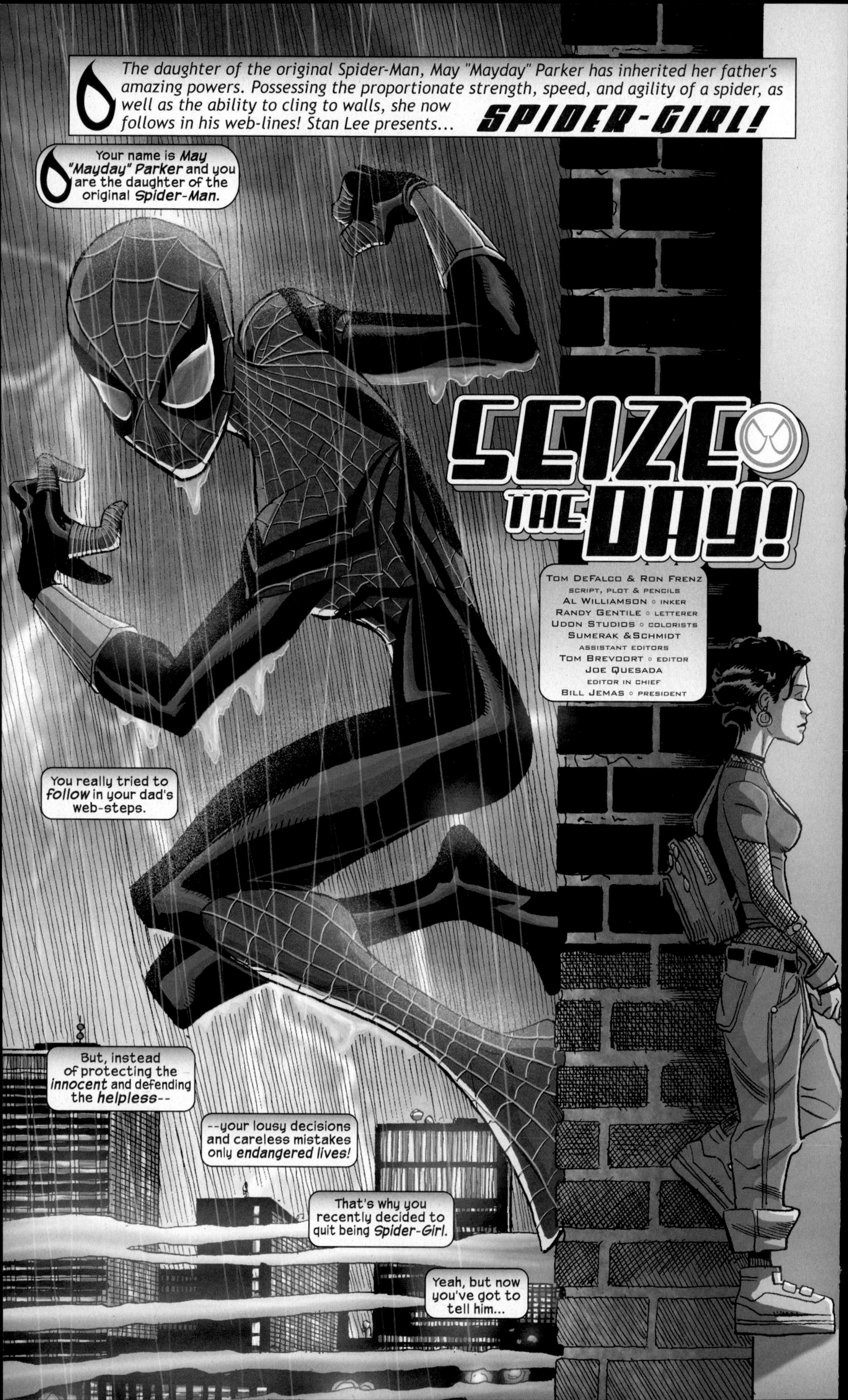
The daughter of the original Spider-Man, May "Mayday" Parker has inherited her father's amazing powers. Possessing the proportionate strength, speed, and agility of a spider, as well as the ability to cling to walls, she now follows in his web-lines! Stan Lee presents... SPIDER-GIRL!
Your name is May "Mayday" Parker and you are the daughter of the original Spider-Man.
SEIZE THE DAY!
Tom DeFalco & Ron Frenz script, plot & pencils
Al Williamson ○ inker
Randy Gentile ○ letterer
Udon Studios ○ colorists
Sumerak &Schmidt assistant editors
Tom Brevoort ○ editor
Joe Quesada editor in chief
Bill Jemas ○ president
You really tried to follow in your dad's web-steps.
But, instead of protecting the innocent and defending the helpless--
--your lousy decisions and careless mistakes only endangered lives!
That's why you recently decided to quit being Spider-Girl.
Yeah, but now you've got to tell him...

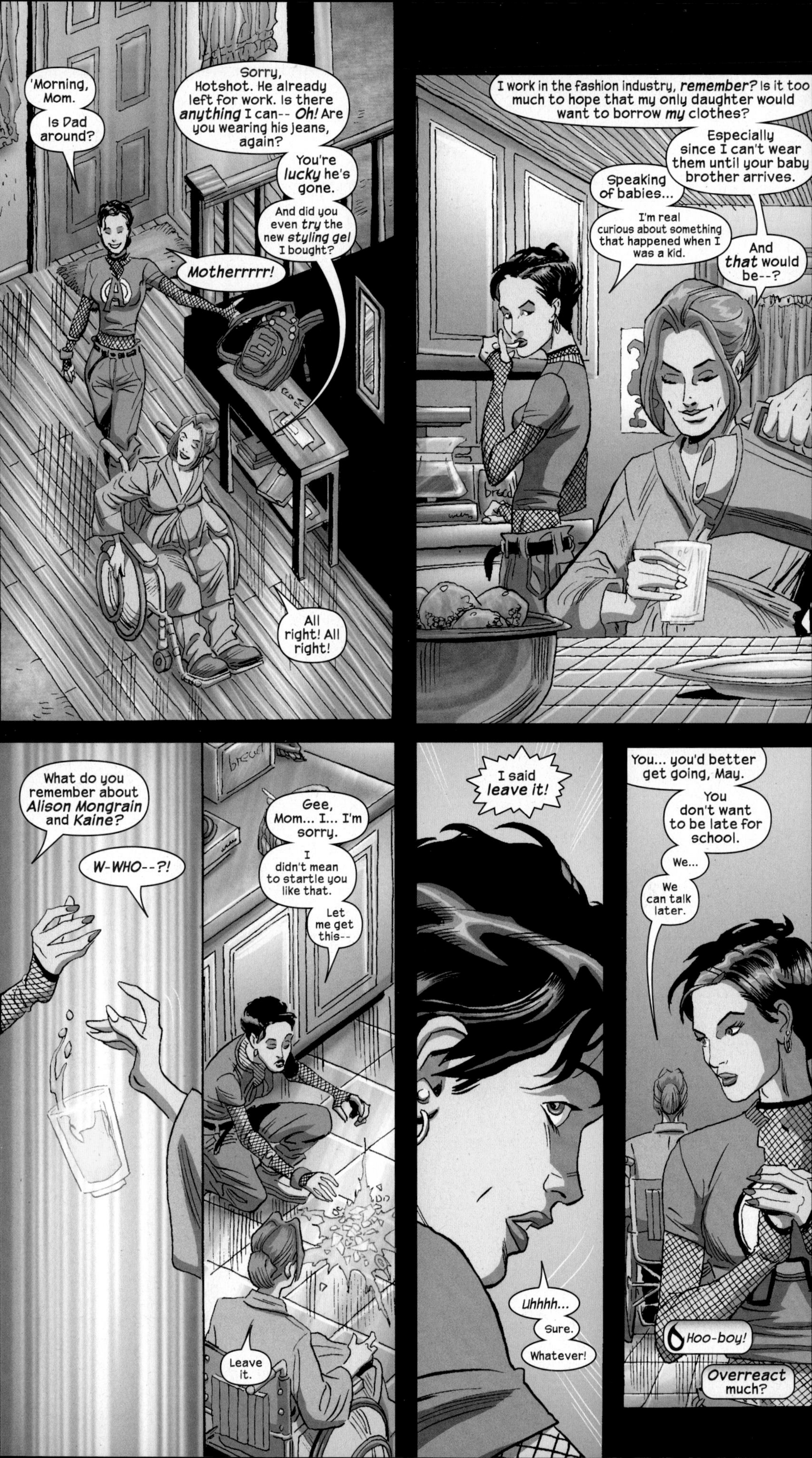
'Morning, Mom.
Is Dad around?
Sorry, Hotshot. He already left for work. Is there *anything* I can-- *Oh!* Are you wearing his jeans, again?
You're *lucky* he's gone.
And did you even *try* the new *styling gel* I bought?
Motherrrrr!
All right! All right!
I work in the fashion industry, *remember?* Is it too much to hope that my only daughter would want to borrow *my* clothes?
Especially since I can't wear them until your baby brother arrives.
Speaking of babies...
I'm real curious about something that happened when I was a kid.
And *that* would be--?
What do you remember about *Alison Mongrain* and *Kaine?*
W-WHO--?!
Gee, Mom... I... I'm sorry.
I didn't mean to startle you like that.
Let me get this--
Leave it.
I said *leave it!*
Uhhhh...
Sure.
Whatever!
You... you'd better get going, May.
You don't want to be late for school.
We...
We can talk later.
Hoo-boy!
Overreact much?

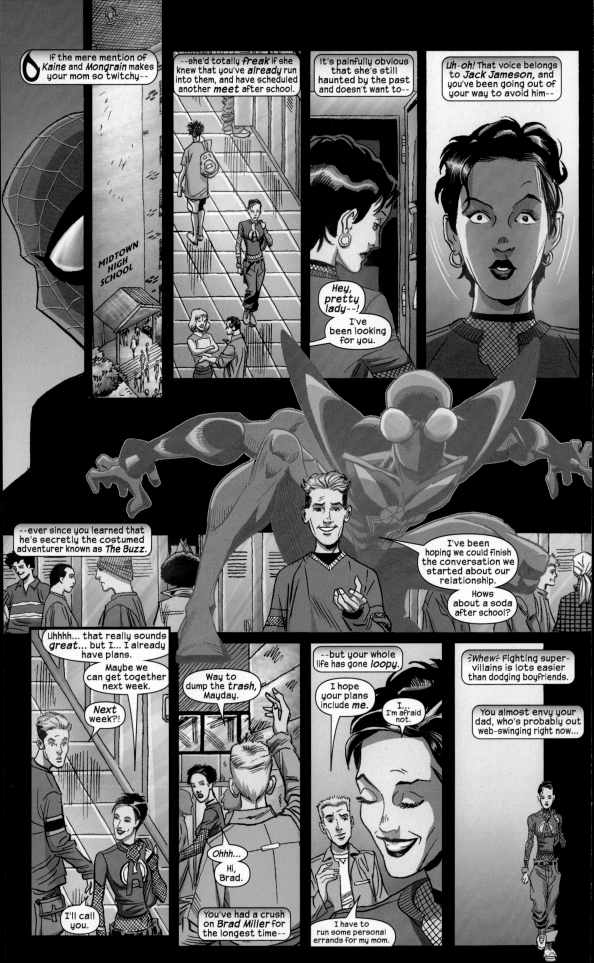

If the mere mention of *Kaine* and *Mongrain* makes your mom so twitchy--

--she'd totally *freak* if she knew that you've *already* run into them, and have scheduled another *meet* after school.

It's painfully obvious that she's still haunted by the past and doesn't want to--

Uh-oh! That voice belongs to *Jack Jameson,* and you've been going out of your way to avoid him--

MIDTOWN HIGH SCHOOL

Hey, pretty lady--! I've been looking for you.

--ever since you learned that he's secretly the costumed adventurer known as *The Buzz.*

I've been hoping we could finish the conversation we started about our relationship.

Hows about a soda after school?

Uhhhh... that really sounds *great*... but I... I already have plans.

Maybe we can get together next week.

Next week?!

I'll call you.

Way to dump the *trash,* Mayday.

Ohhh... Hi, Brad.

You've had a crush on *Brad Miller* for the longest time--

--but your whole life has gone *loopy.*

I hope your plans include *me.*

I... I'm afraid not.

I have to run some personal errands for my mom.

Whew-- Fighting super-villains is lots easier than dodging boyfriends.

You almost envy your dad, who's probably out web-swinging right now...

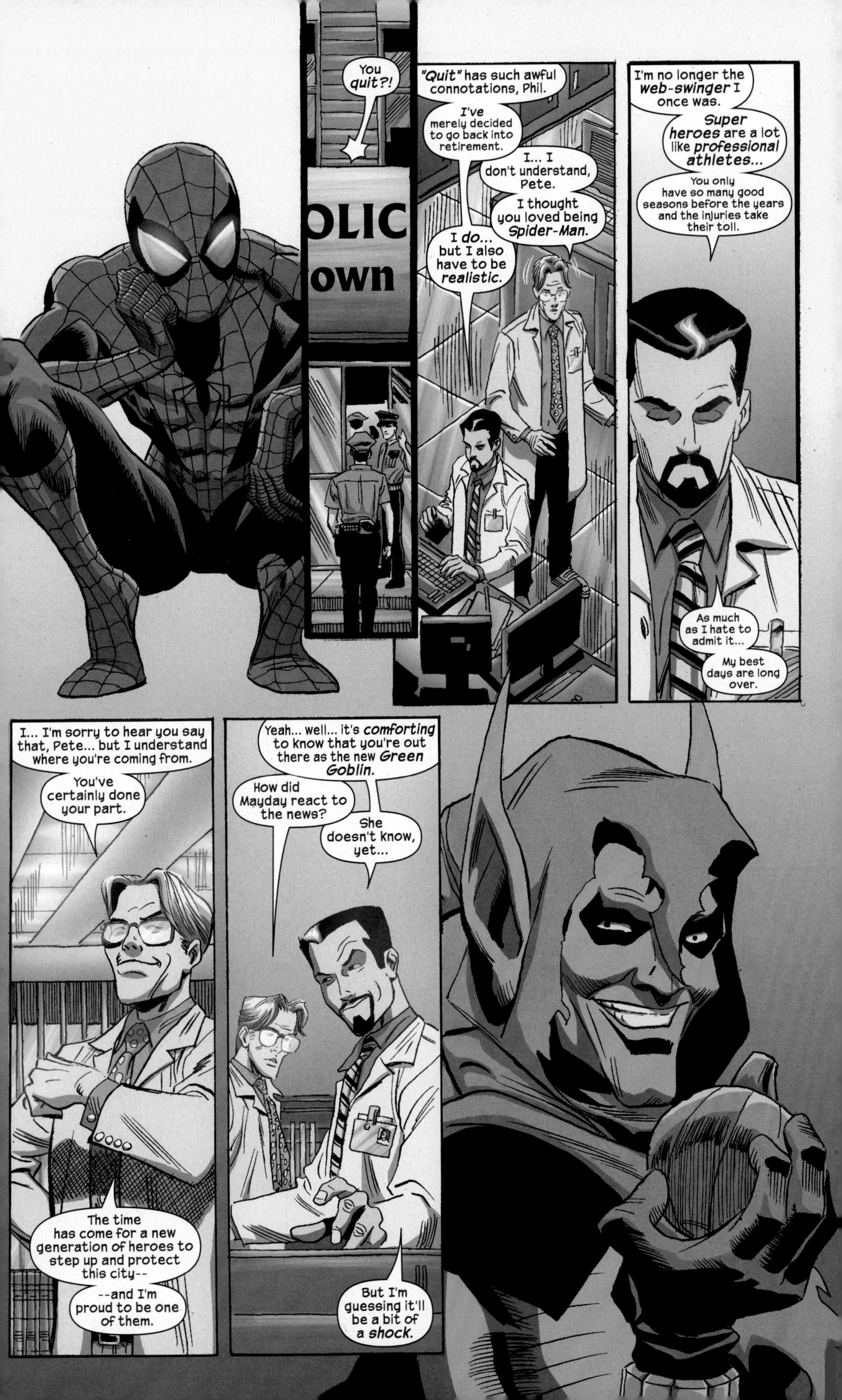

You quit?!
OLIC
own
"Quit" has such awful connotations, Phil.
I've merely decided to go back into retirement.
I... I don't understand, Pete.
I thought you loved being Spider-Man.
I do... but I also have to be realistic.
I'm no longer the web-swinger I once was.
Super heroes are a lot like professional athletes...
You only have so many good seasons before the years and the injuries take their toll.
As much as I hate to admit it...
My best days are long over.
I... I'm sorry to hear you say that, Pete... but I understand where you're coming from.
You've certainly done your part.
The time has come for a new generation of heroes to step up and protect this city--
--and I'm proud to be one of them.
Yeah... well... it's comforting to know that you're out there as the new Green Goblin.
How did Mayday react to the news?
She doesn't know, yet...
But I'm guessing it'll be a bit of a shock.

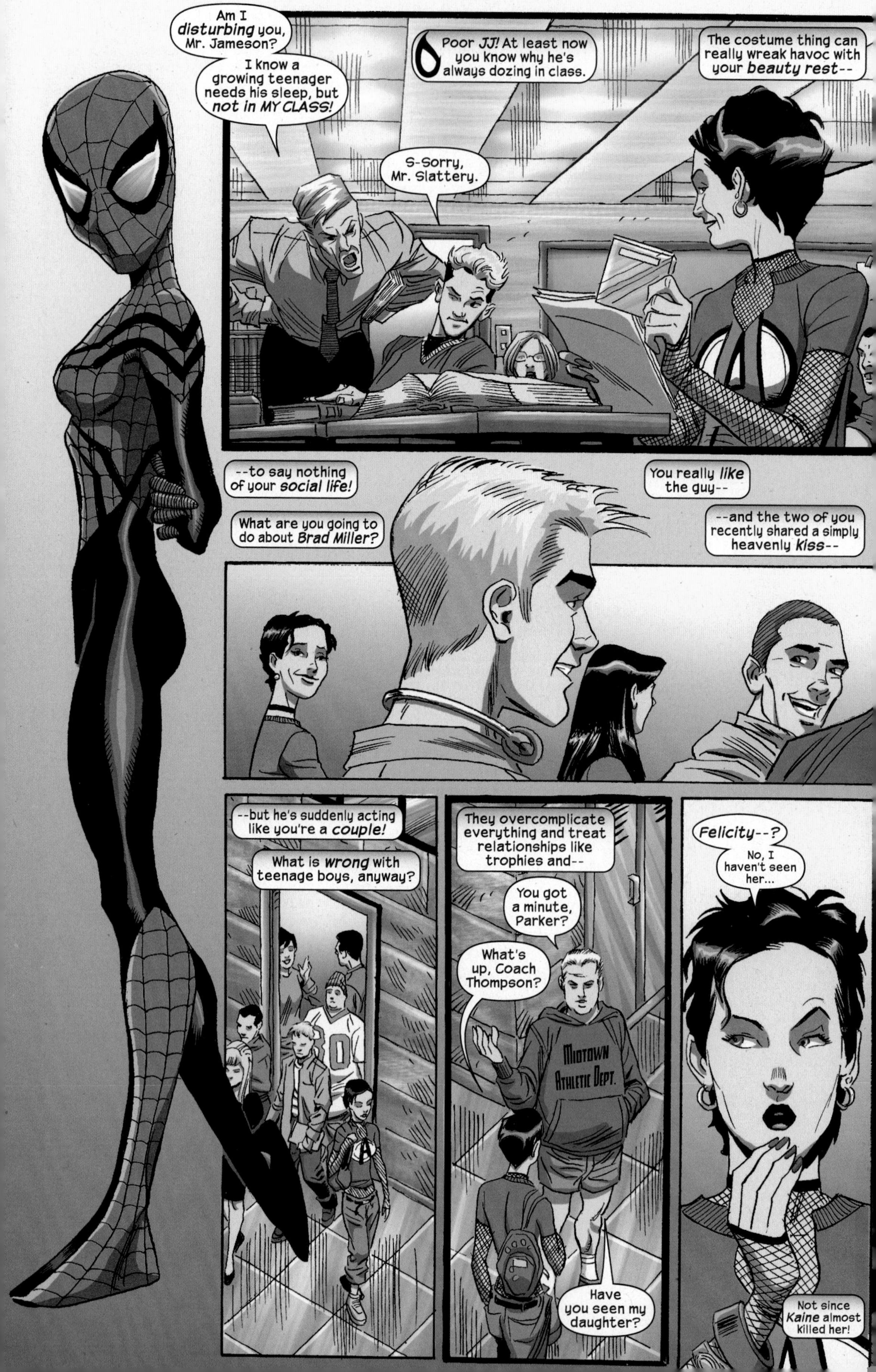

Am I disturbing you, Mr. Jameson?
I know a growing teenager needs his sleep, but not in MY CLASS!
Poor JJ! At least now you know why he's always dozing in class.
The costume thing can really wreak havoc with your beauty rest--
S-Sorry, Mr. Slattery.
--to say nothing of your social life!
What are you going to do about Brad Miller?
You really like the guy--
--and the two of you recently shared a simply heavenly kiss--
--but he's suddenly acting like you're a couple!
What is wrong with teenage boys, anyway?
They overcomplicate everything and treat relationships like trophies and--
You got a minute, Parker?
What's up, Coach Thompson?
MIDTOWN ATHLETIC DEPT.
Have you seen my daughter?
Felicity--?
No, I haven't seen her...
Not since Kaine almost killed her!

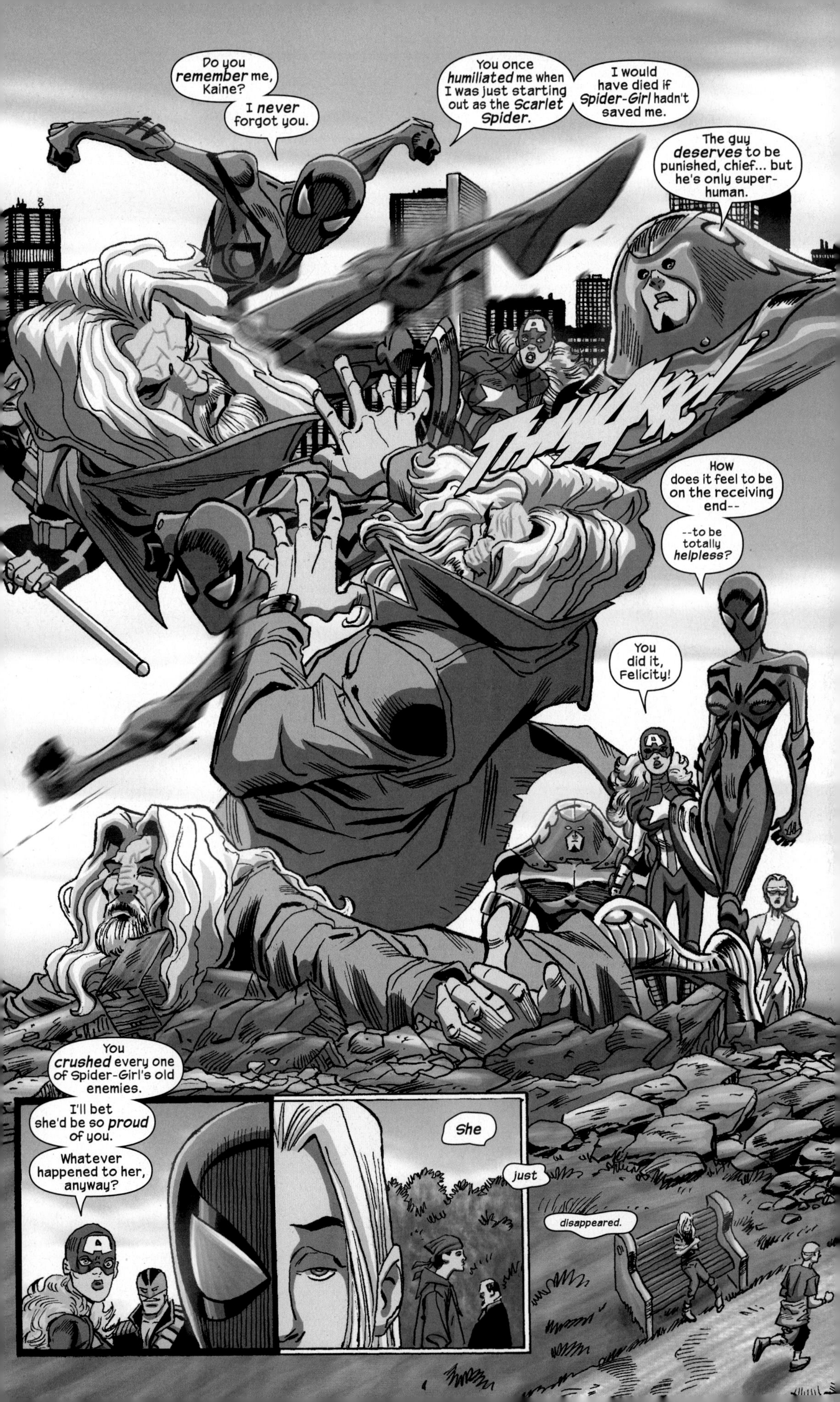

Do you remember me, Kaine?
I never forgot you.
You once humiliated me when I was just starting out as the Scarlet Spider.
I would have died if Spider-Girl hadn't saved me.
The guy deserves to be punished, chief... but he's only super-human.
THWAKK!
How does it feel to be on the receiving end--
--to be totally helpless?
You did it, Felicity!
You crushed every one of Spider-Girl's old enemies.
I'll bet she'd be so proud of you.
Whatever happened to her, anyway?
She
just
disappeared.

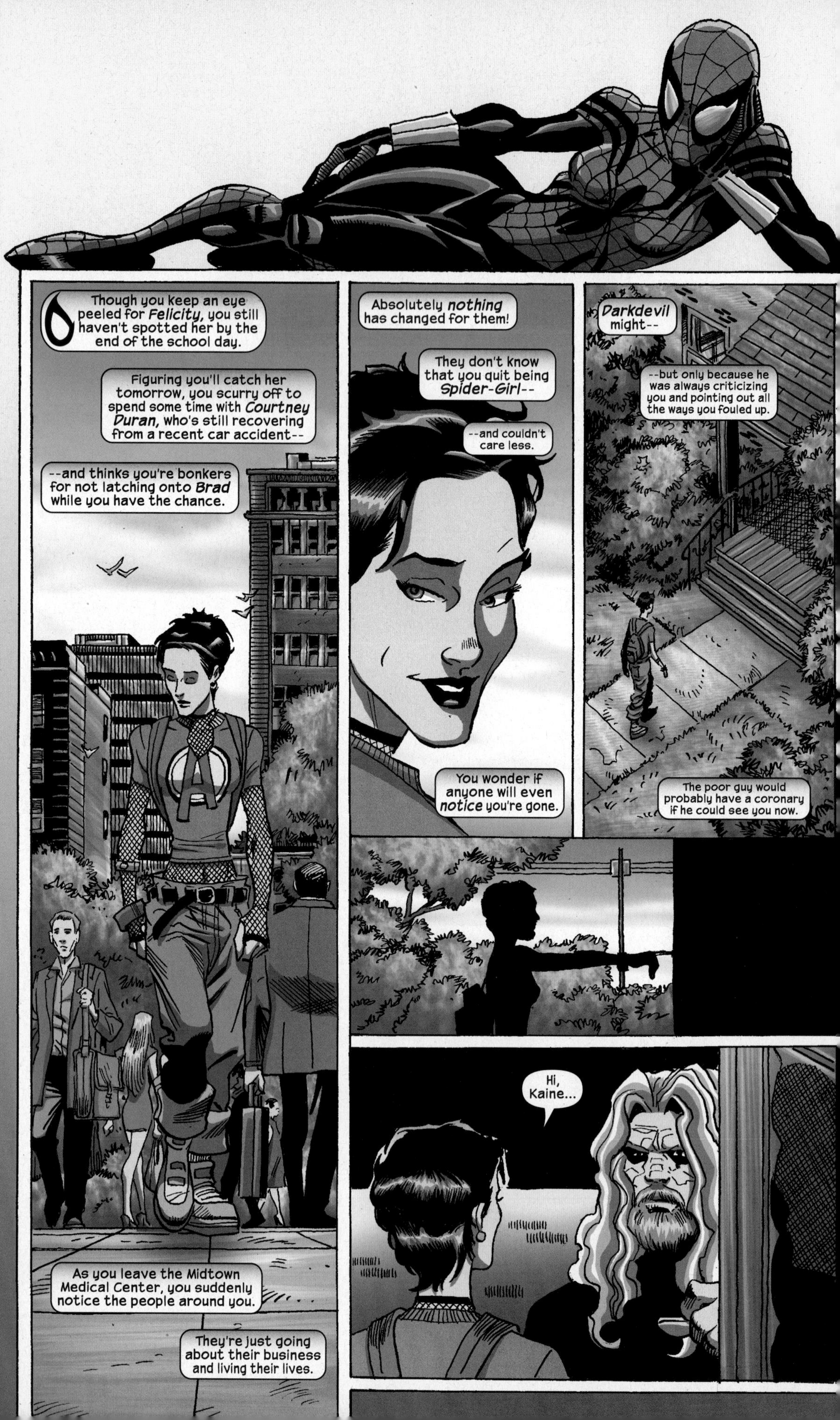
Though you keep an eye peeled for Felicity, you still haven't spotted her by the end of the school day.
Figuring you'll catch her tomorrow, you scurry off to spend some time with Courtney Duran, who's still recovering from a recent car accident--
--and thinks you're bonkers for not latching onto Brad while you have the chance.
As you leave the Midtown Medical Center, you suddenly notice the people around you.
They're just going about their business and living their lives.
Absolutely nothing has changed for them!
They don't know that you quit being Spider-Girl--
--and couldn't care less.
You wonder if anyone will even notice you're gone.
Darkdevil might--
--but only because he was always criticizing you and pointing out all the ways you fouled up.
The poor guy would probably have a coronary if he could see you now.
Hi, Kaine...

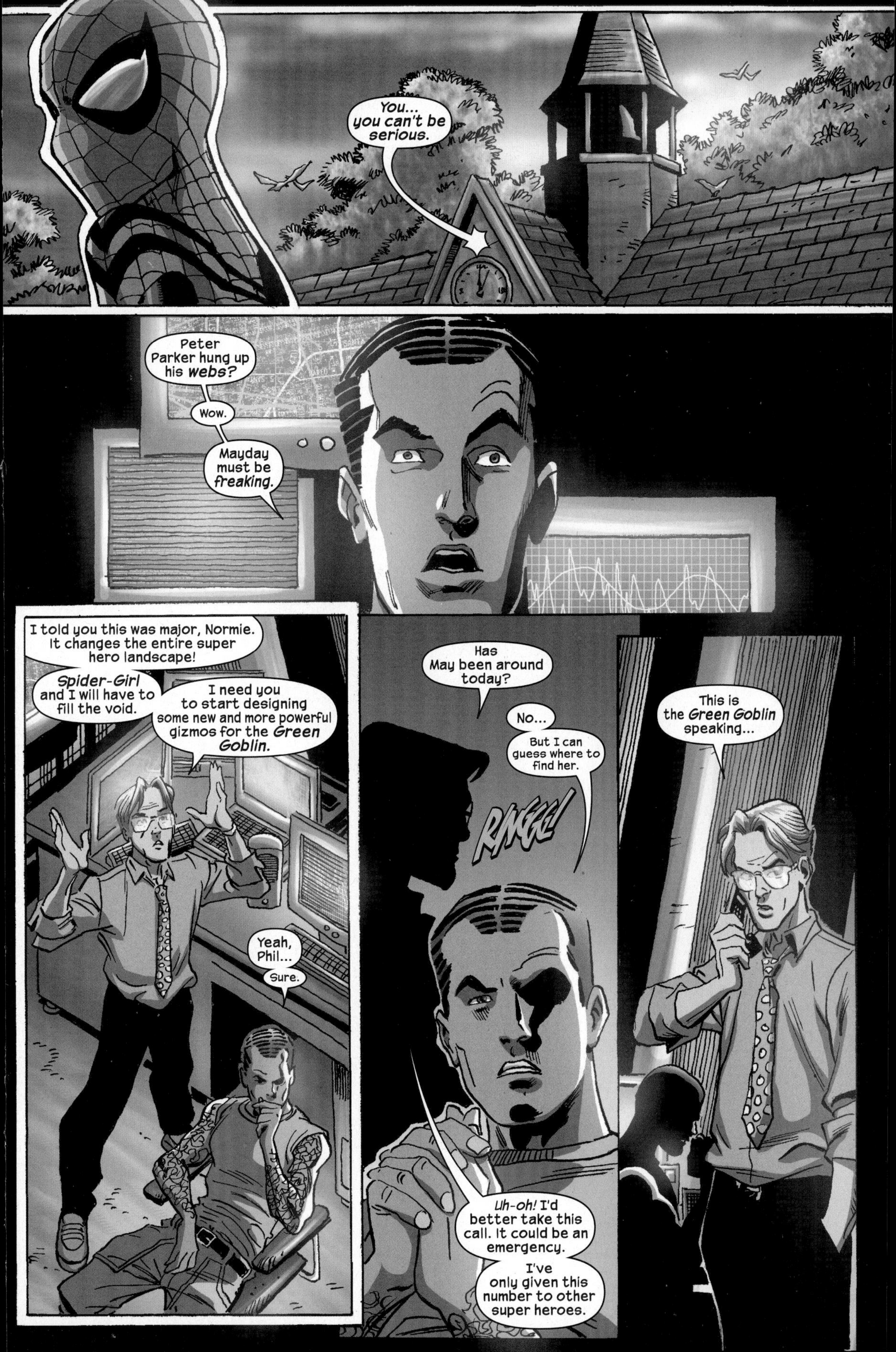
You... you can't be serious.
Peter Parker hung up his *webs*?
Wow.
Mayday must be *freaking*.
I told you this was major, Normie. It changes the entire super hero landscape!
Spider-Girl and I will have to fill the void.
I need you to start designing some new and more powerful gizmos for the *Green Goblin*.
Yeah, Phil...
Sure.
Has May been around today?
No...
But I can guess where to find her.
RINGG!
Uh-oh! I'd better take this call. It could be an emergency.
I've only given this number to other super heroes.
This is the *Green Goblin* speaking...

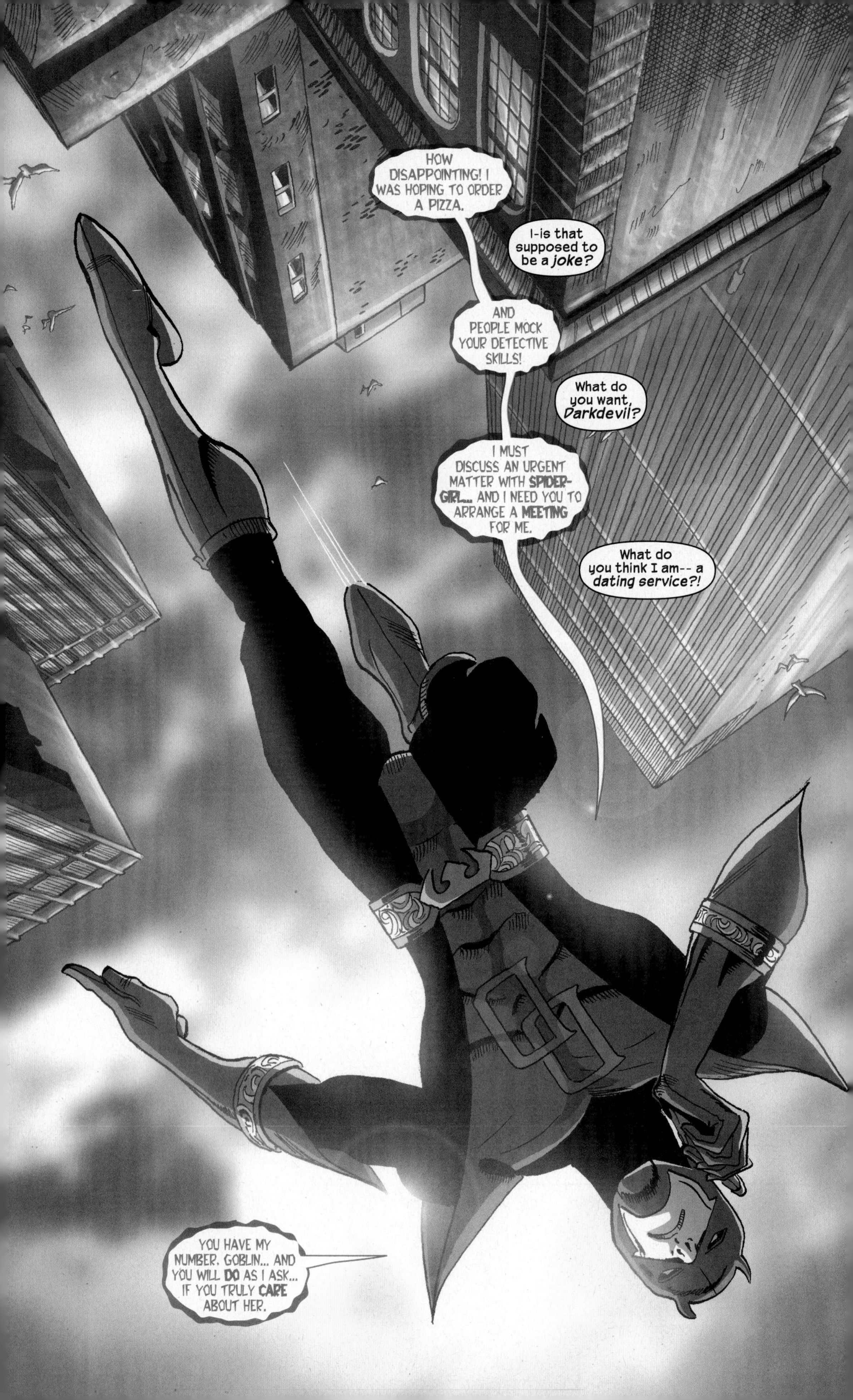
HOW DISAPPOINTING! I WAS HOPING TO ORDER A PIZZA.
I-is that supposed to be a *joke?*
AND PEOPLE MOCK YOUR DETECTIVE SKILLS!
What do you want, *Darkdevil?*
I MUST DISCUSS AN URGENT MATTER WITH **SPIDER-GIRL...** AND I NEED YOU TO ARRANGE A **MEETING** FOR ME.
What do you think I am-- a *dating service?!*
YOU HAVE MY NUMBER, GOBLIN... AND YOU WILL **DO** AS I ASK... IF YOU TRULY **CARE** ABOUT HER.

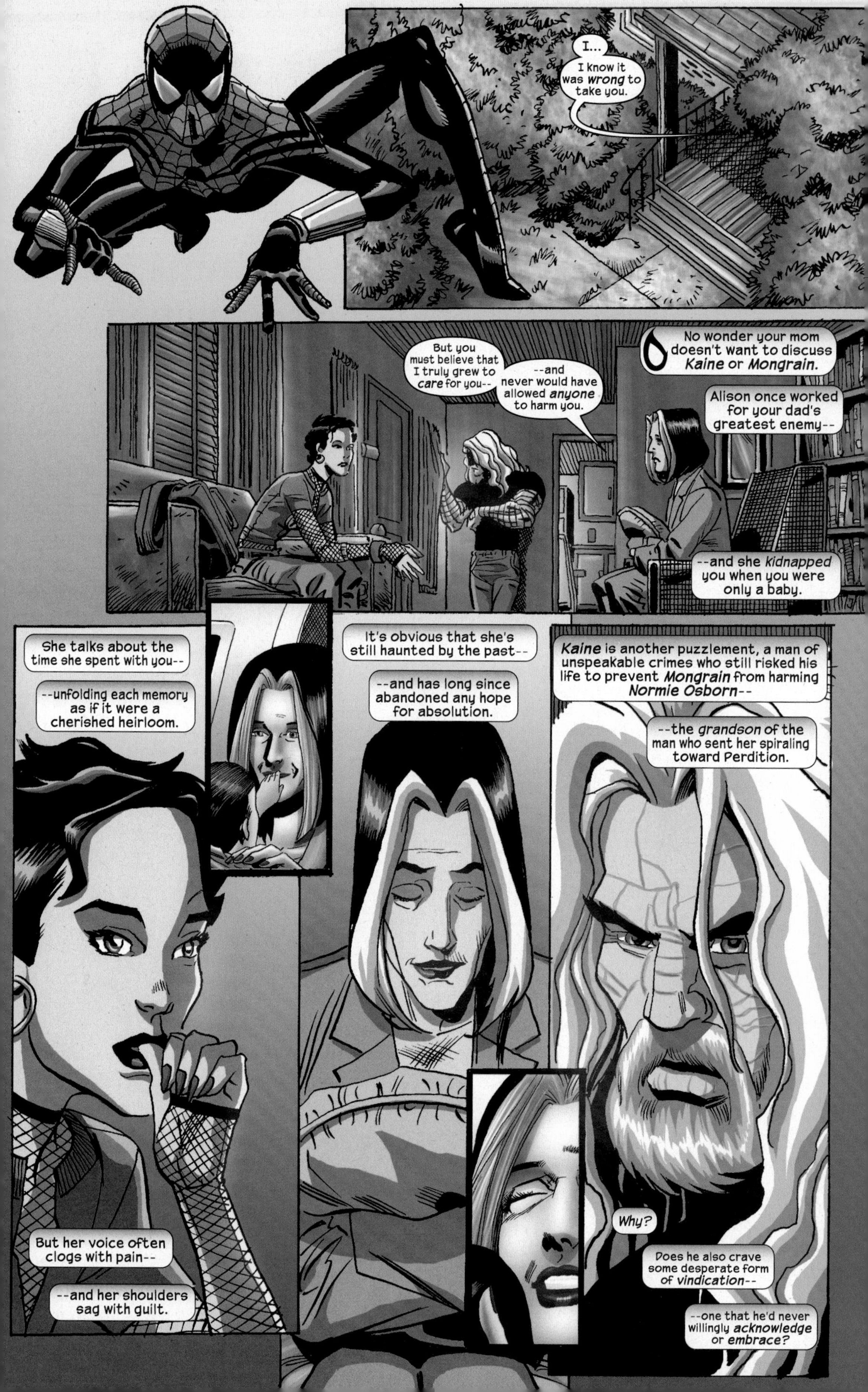

I...
I know it was *wrong* to take you.
But you must believe that I truly grew to *care* for you--
--and never would have allowed *anyone* to harm you.
No wonder your mom doesn't want to discuss *Kaine* or *Mongrain.*
Alison once worked for your dad's greatest enemy--
--and she *kidnapped* you when you were only a baby.
She talks about the time she spent with you--
--unfolding each memory as if it were a cherished heirloom.
But her voice often clogs with pain--
--and her shoulders sag with guilt.
It's obvious that she's still haunted by the past--
--and has long since abandoned any hope for absolution.
Kaine is another puzzlement, a man of unspeakable crimes who still risked his life to prevent *Mongrain* from harming *Normie Osborn*--
--the *grandson* of the man who sent her spiraling toward Perdition.
Why?
Does he also crave some desperate form of *vindication*--
--one that he'd never willingly *acknowledge* or *embrace?*

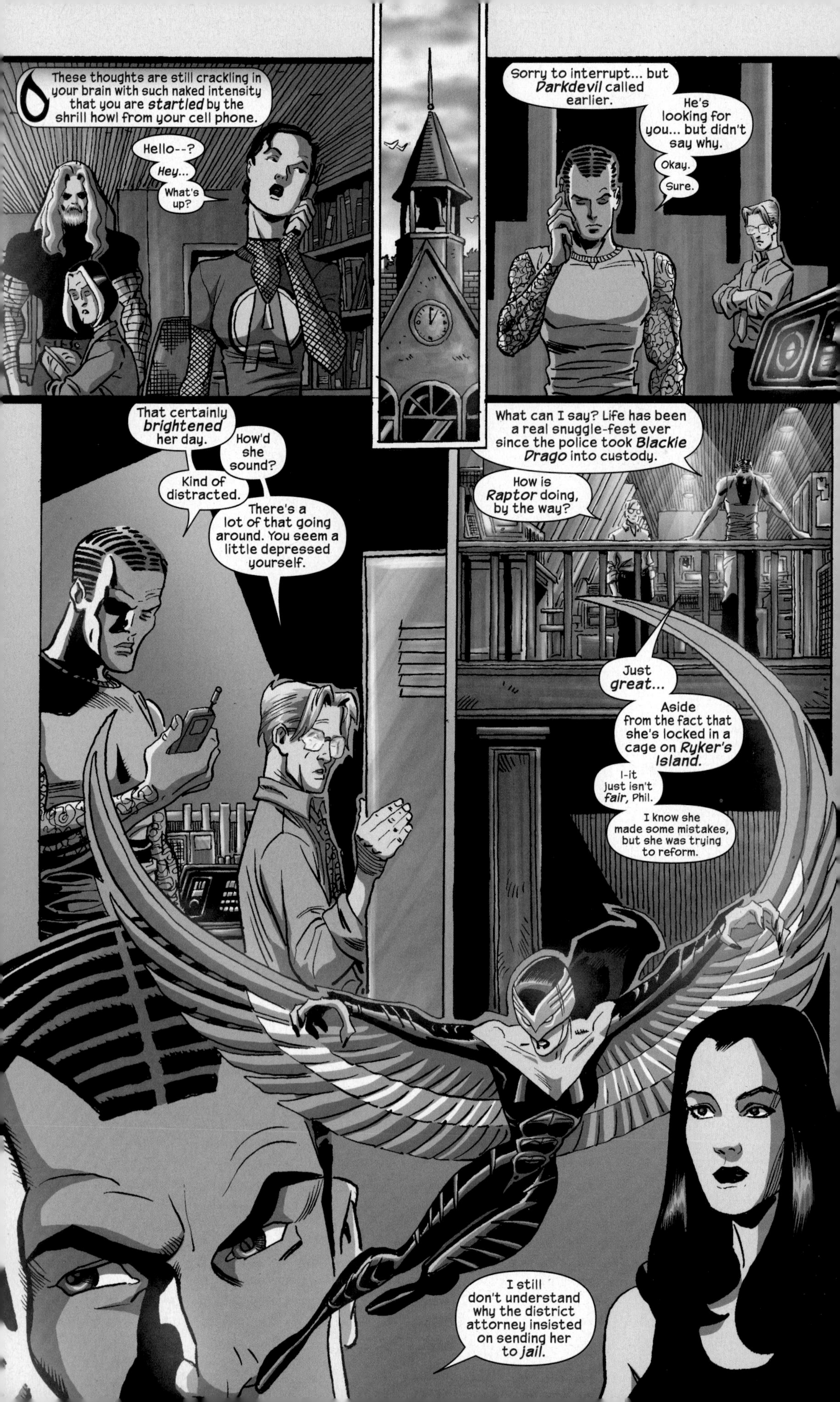
These thoughts are still crackling in your brain with such naked intensity that you are *startled* by the shrill howl from your cell phone.
Hello--?
Hey...
What's up?
Sorry to interrupt... but *Darkdevil* called earlier.
He's looking for you... but didn't say why.
Okay.
Sure.
That certainly *brightened* her day.
How'd she sound?
Kind of distracted.
There's a lot of that going around. You seem a little depressed yourself.
What can I say? Life has been a real snuggle-fest ever since the police took *Blackie Drago* into custody.
How is *Raptor* doing, by the way?
Just *great...*
Aside from the fact that she's locked in a cage on *Ryker's Island.*
I-it just isn't *fair,* Phil.
I know she made some mistakes, but she was trying to reform.
I still don't understand why the district attorney insisted on sending her to *jail.*

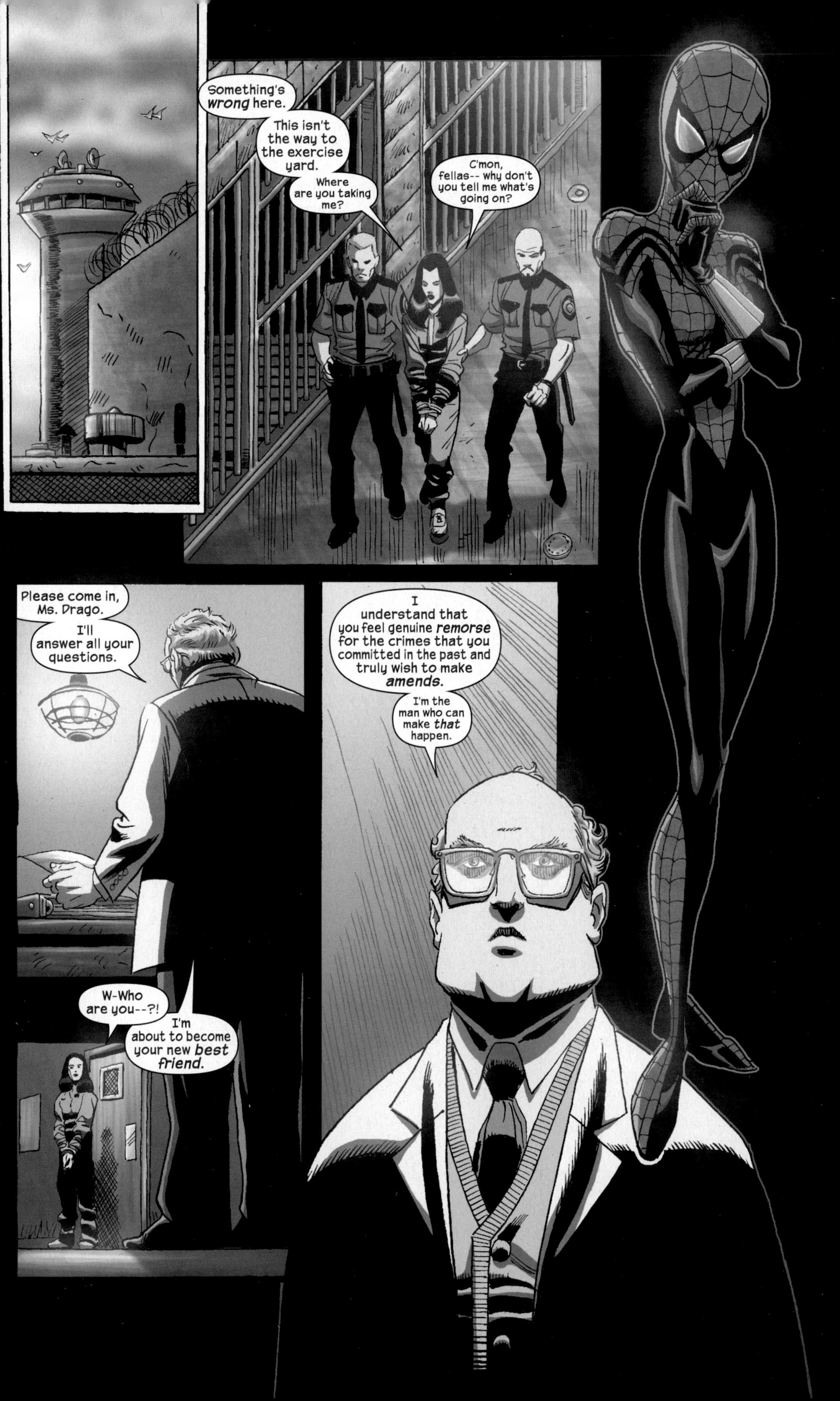
Something's *wrong* here.
This isn't the way to the exercise yard.
Where are you taking me?
C'mon, fellas-- why don't you tell me what's going on?
Please come in, Ms. Drago.
I'll answer all your questions.
W-Who are you--?!
I'm about to become your new *best friend*.
I understand that you feel genuine *remorse* for the crimes that you committed in the past and truly wish to make *amends*.
I'm the man who can make *that* happen.

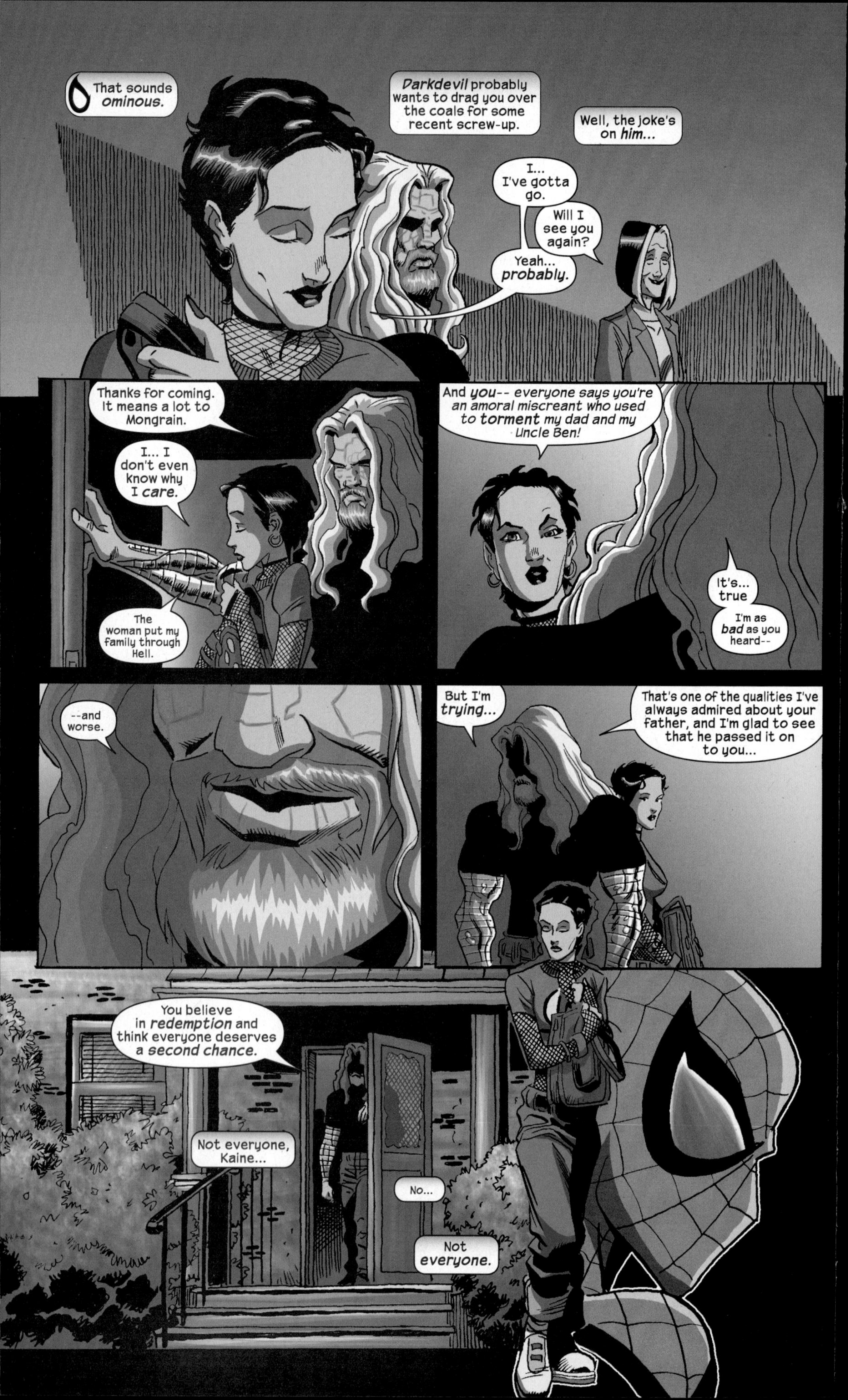
That sounds ominous.
Darkdevil probably wants to drag you over the coals for some recent screw-up.
Well, the joke's on him...
I... I've gotta go.
Will I see you again?
Yeah... probably.
Thanks for coming. It means a lot to Mongrain.
I... I don't even know why I care.
The woman put my family through Hell.
And you-- everyone says you're an amoral miscreant who used to torment my dad and my Uncle Ben!
It's... true
I'm as bad as you heard--
--and worse.
But I'm trying...
That's one of the qualities I've always admired about your father, and I'm glad to see that he passed it on to you...
You believe in redemption and think everyone deserves a second chance.
Not everyone, Kaine...
No...
Not everyone.

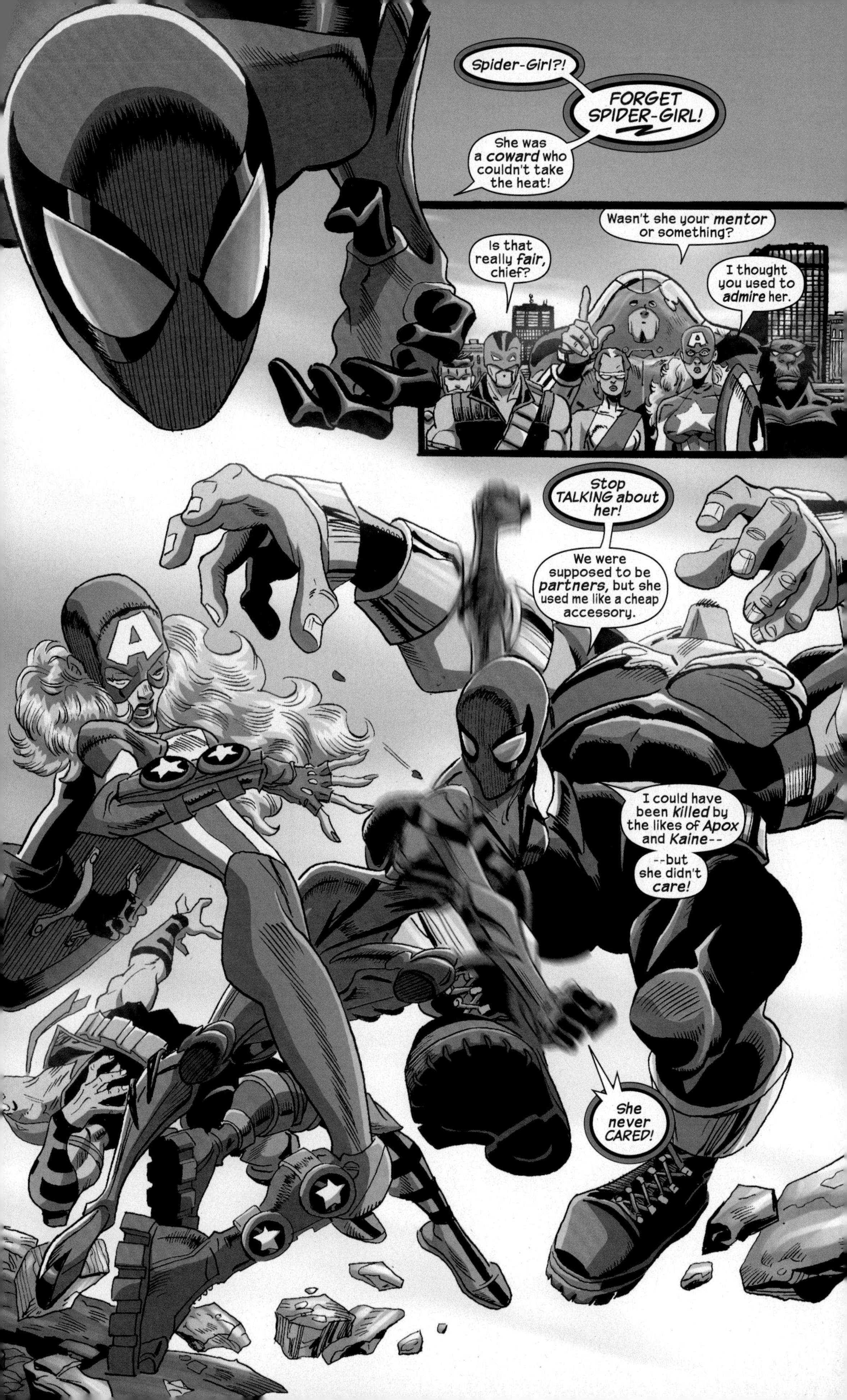
Spider-Girl?!
FORGET SPIDER-GIRL!
She was a coward who couldn't take the heat!
Wasn't she your mentor or something?
Is that really fair, chief?
I thought you used to admire her.
Stop TALKING about her!
We were supposed to be partners, but she used me like a cheap accessory.
I could have been killed by the likes of Apox and Kaine--
--but she didn't care!
She never CARED!

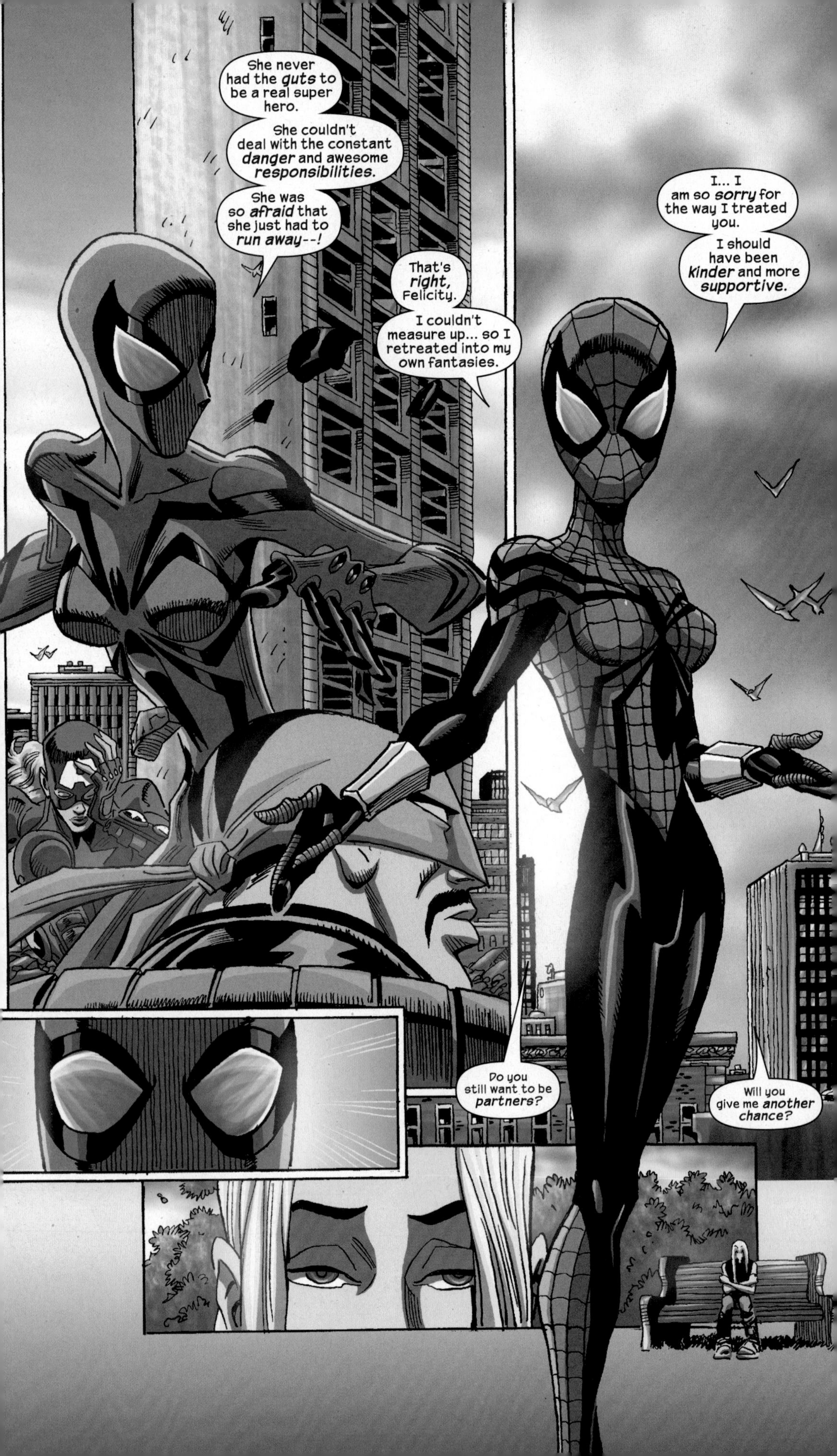

She never had the *guts* to be a real super hero.
She couldn't deal with the constant *danger* and awesome *responsibilities.*
She was so *afraid* that she just had to *run away*--!
That's *right,* Felicity.
I couldn't measure up... so I retreated into my own fantasies.
I... I am so *sorry* for the way I treated you.
I should have been *kinder* and more *supportive.*
Do you still want to be *partners?*
Will you give me *another chance?*

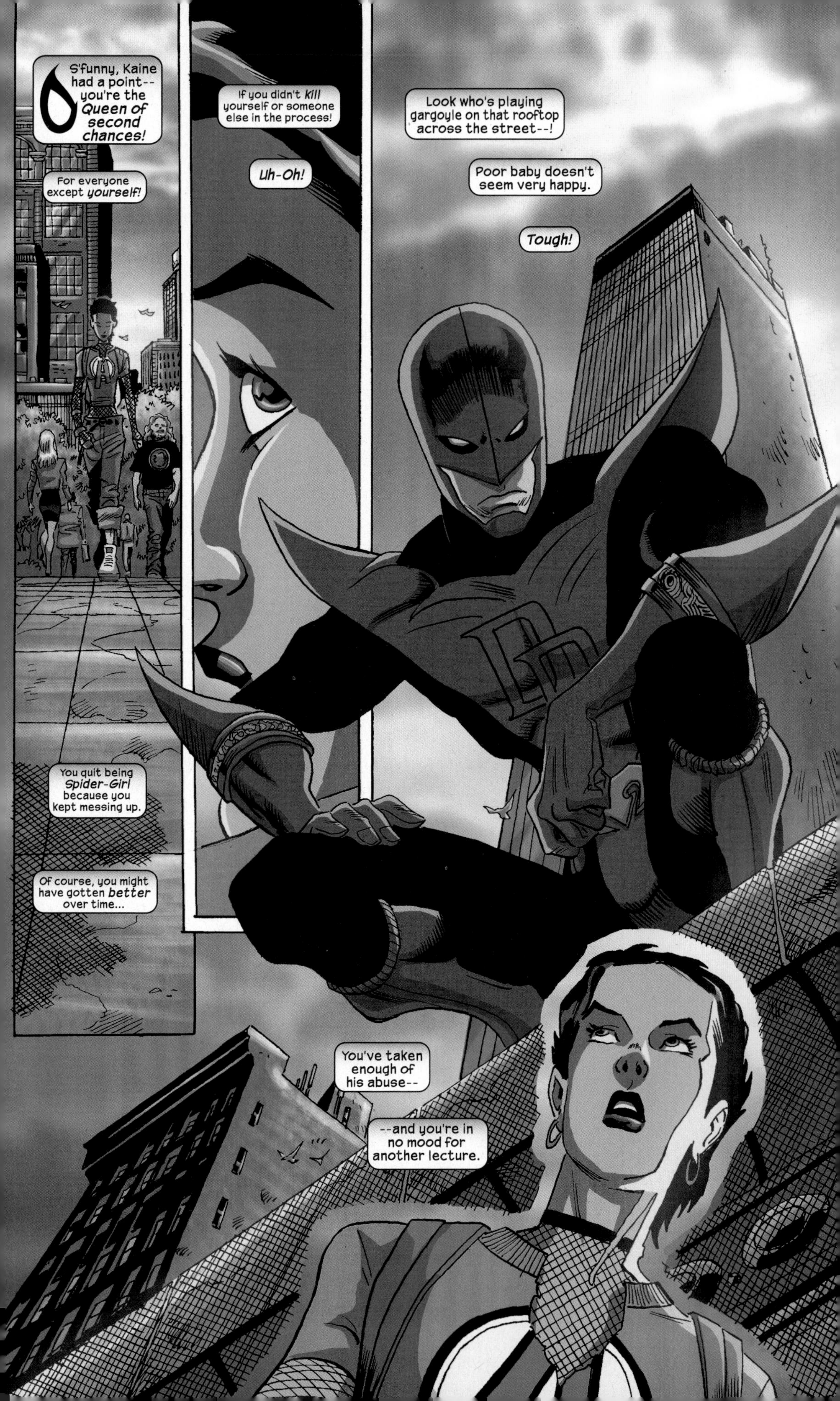
S'funny, Kaine had a point--you're the Queen of second chances!
For everyone except yourself!
If you didn't kill yourself or someone else in the process!
Uh-Oh!
Look who's playing gargoyle on that rooftop across the street--!
Poor baby doesn't seem very happy.
Tough!
You quit being Spider-Girl because you kept messing up.
Of course, you might have gotten better over time...
You've taken enough of his abuse--
--and you're in no mood for another lecture.

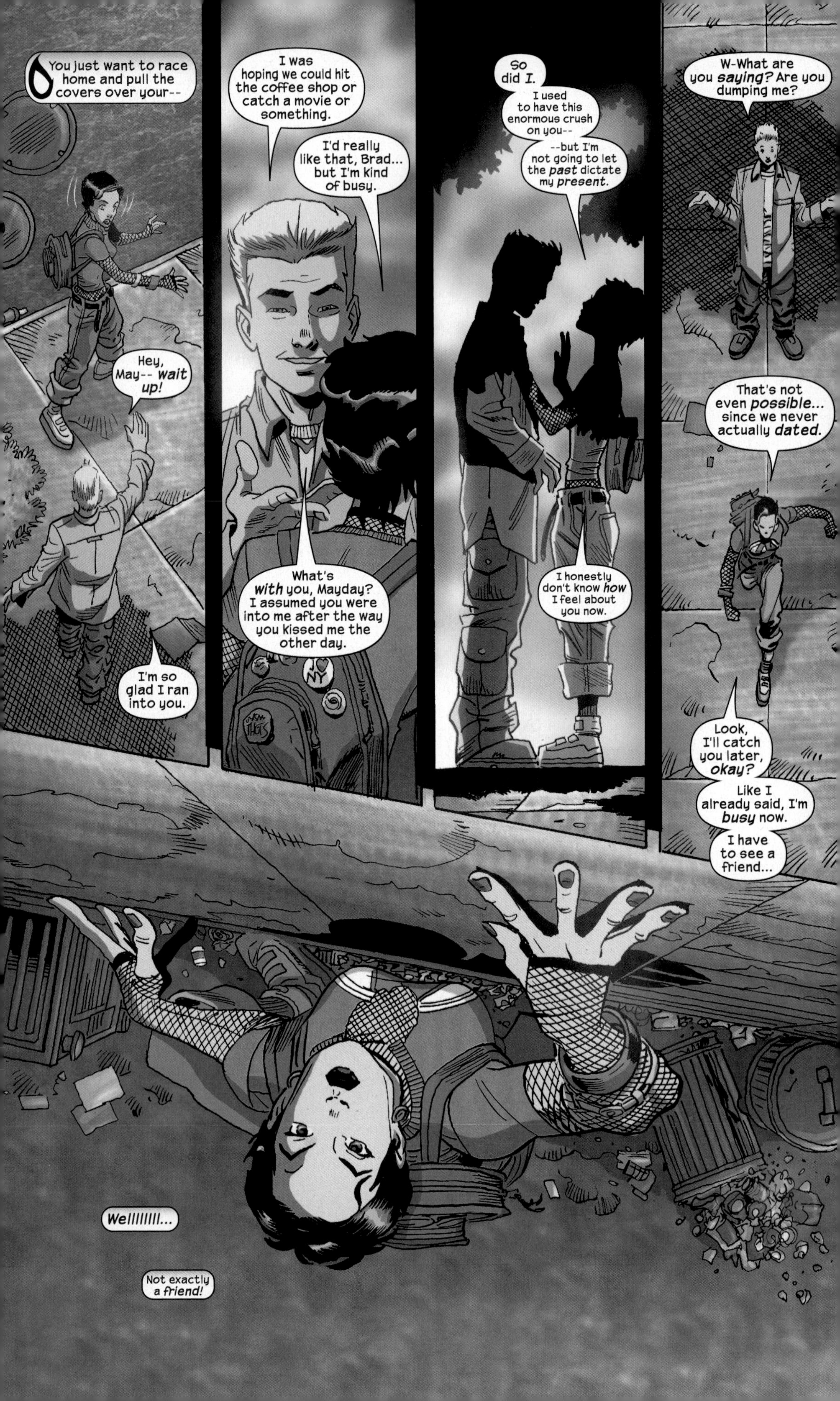

You just want to race home and pull the covers over your--
Hey, May-- *wait up!*
I'm so glad I ran into you.
I was hoping we could hit the coffee shop or catch a movie or something.
I'd really like that, Brad... but I'm kind of busy.
What's *with* you, Mayday? I assumed you were into me after the way you kissed me the other day.
So did *I*.
I used to have this enormous crush on you--
--but I'm not going to let the *past* dictate my *present*.
I honestly don't know *how* I feel about you now.
W-What are you *saying*? Are you dumping me?
That's not even *possible*... since we never actually *dated*.
Look, I'll catch you later, *okay?*
Like I already said, I'm *busy* now.
I have to see a friend...
Wellllllll...
Not exactly a *friend!*

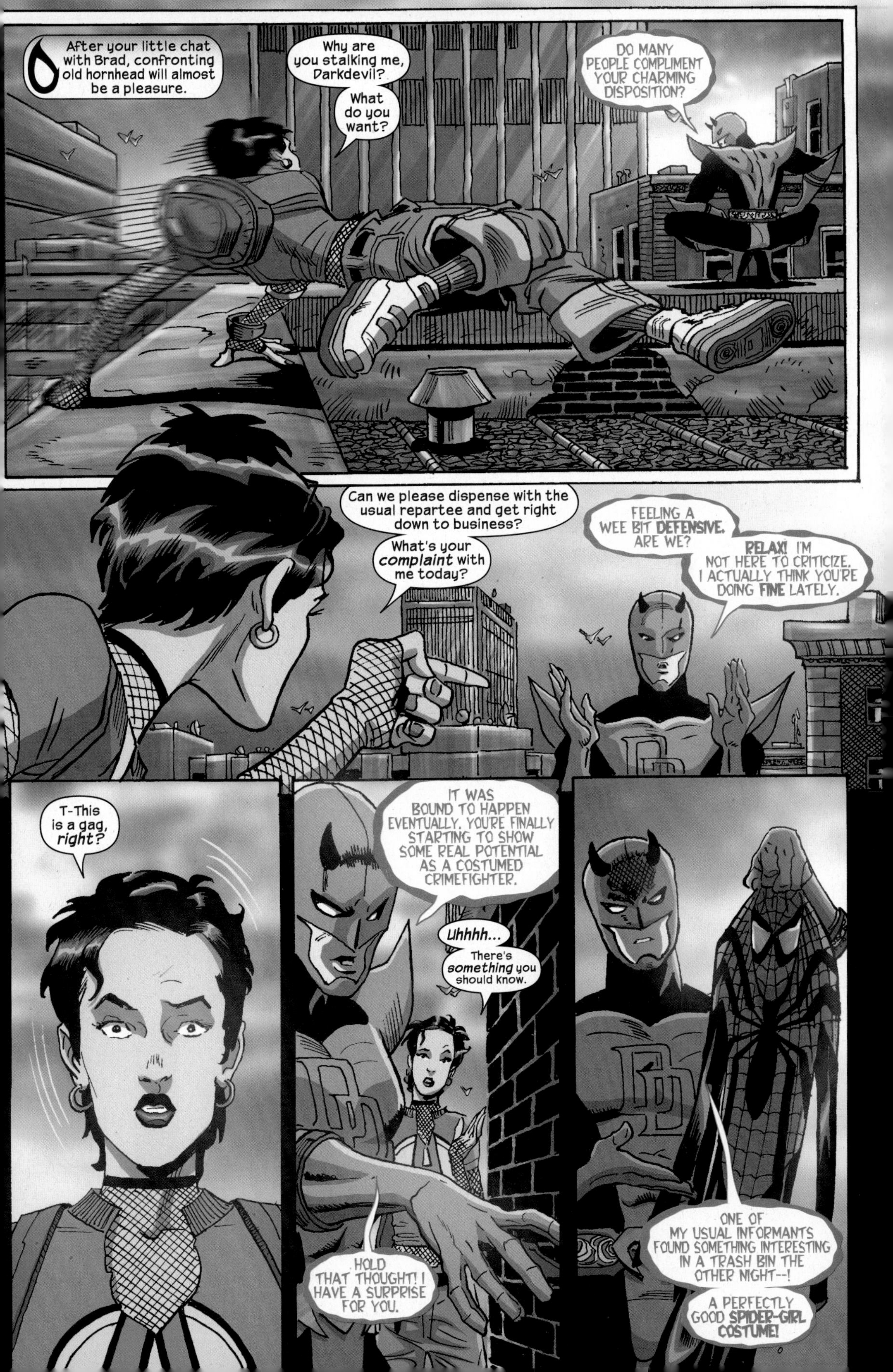
After your little chat with Brad, confronting old hornhead will almost be a pleasure.
Why are you stalking me, Darkdevil?
What do you want?
DO MANY PEOPLE COMPLIMENT YOUR CHARMING DISPOSITION?
Can we please dispense with the usual repartee and get right down to business?
What's your *complaint* with me today?
FEELING A WEE BIT **DEFENSIVE**, ARE WE?
RELAX! I'M NOT HERE TO CRITICIZE. I ACTUALLY THINK YOU'RE DOING **FINE** LATELY.
T-This is a gag, *right*?
IT WAS BOUND TO HAPPEN EVENTUALLY. YOU'RE FINALLY STARTING TO SHOW SOME REAL POTENTIAL AS A COSTUMED CRIMEFIGHTER.
Uhhhh...
There's *something* you should know.
HOLD THAT THOUGHT! I HAVE A SURPRISE FOR YOU.
ONE OF MY USUAL INFORMANTS FOUND SOMETHING INTERESTING IN A TRASH BIN THE OTHER NIGHT--!
A PERFECTLY GOOD **SPIDER-GIRL COSTUME!**

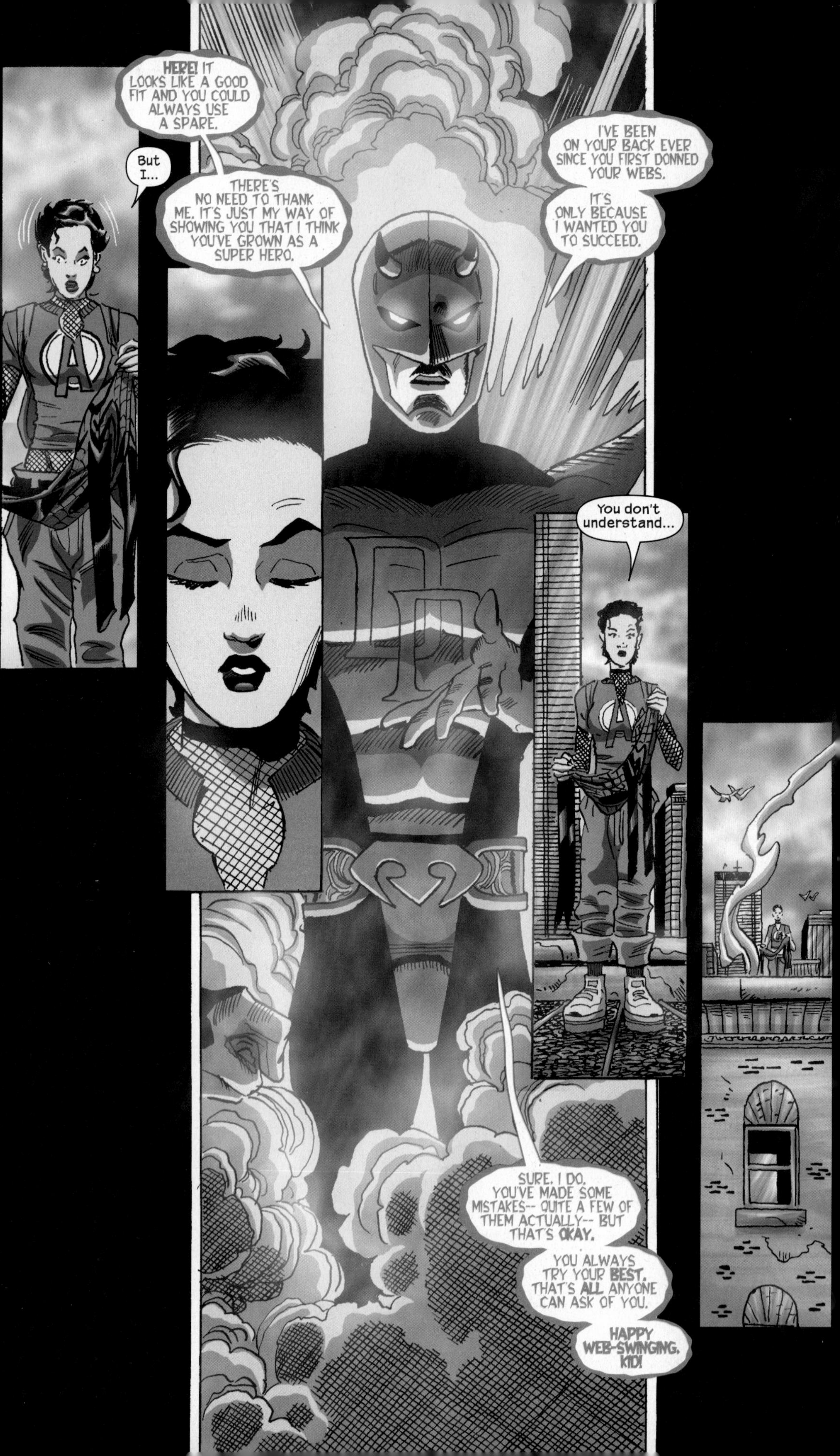
HERE! IT LOOKS LIKE A GOOD FIT AND YOU COULD ALWAYS USE A SPARE.
But I...
THERE'S NO NEED TO THANK ME. IT'S JUST MY WAY OF SHOWING YOU THAT I THINK YOU'VE GROWN AS A SUPER HERO.
I'VE BEEN ON YOUR BACK EVER SINCE YOU FIRST DONNED YOUR WEBS.
IT'S ONLY BECAUSE I WANTED YOU TO SUCCEED.
You don't understand...
SURE, I DO. YOU'VE MADE SOME MISTAKES-- QUITE A FEW OF THEM ACTUALLY-- BUT THAT'S OKAY.
YOU ALWAYS TRY YOUR BEST. THAT'S ALL ANYONE CAN ASK OF YOU.
HAPPY WEB-SWINGING, KID!

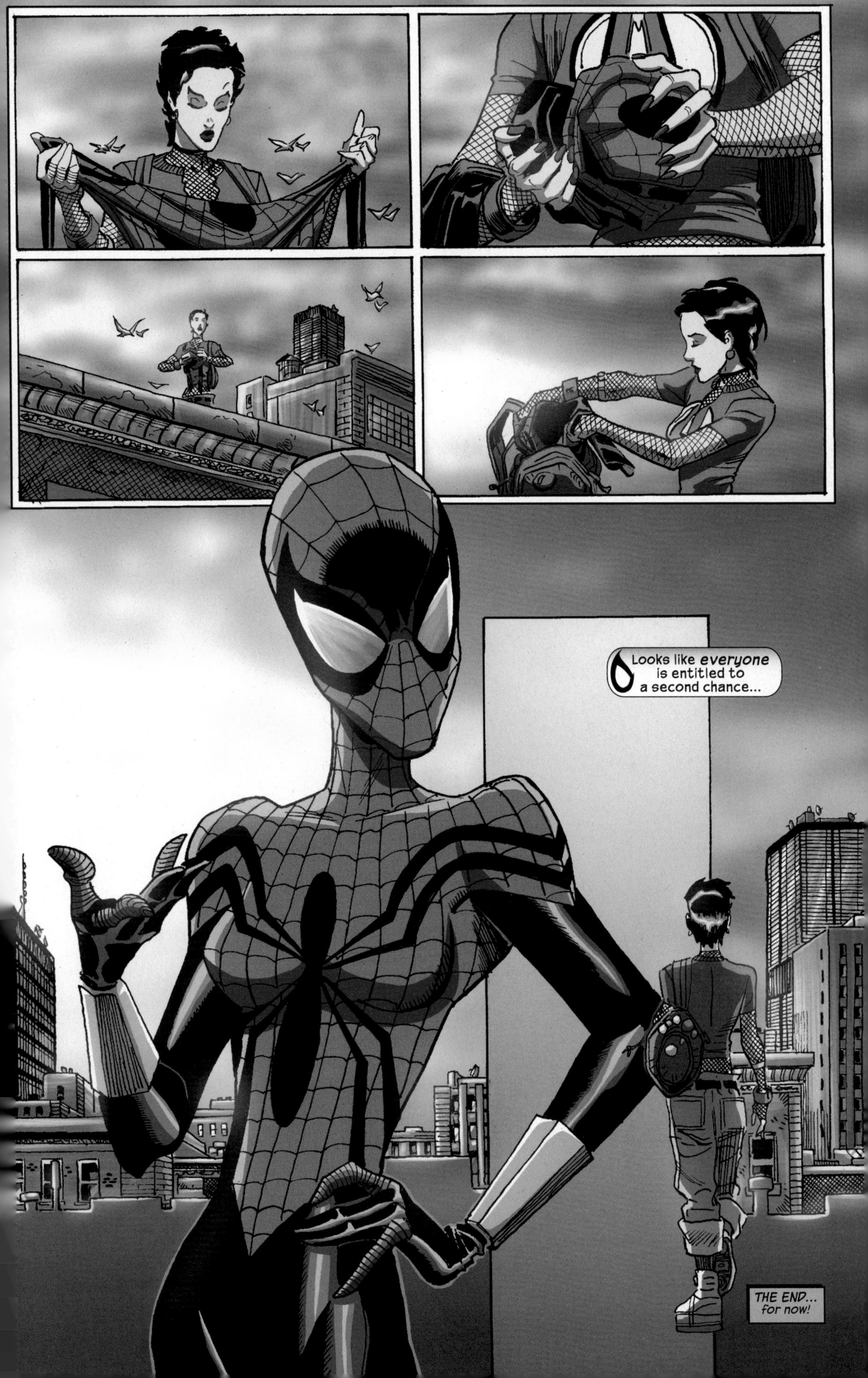
Looks like everyone is entitled to a second chance...
THE END... for now!

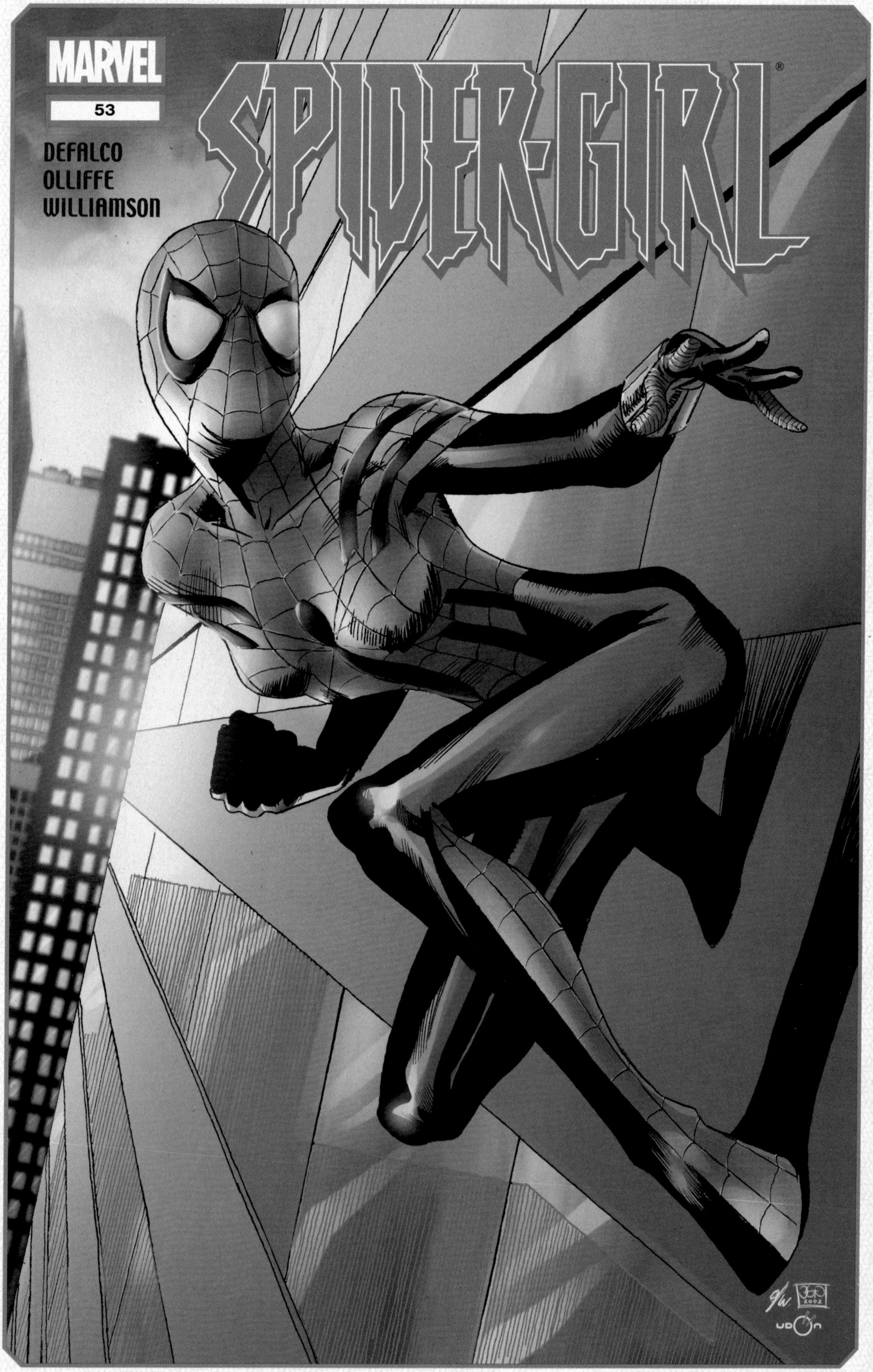
MARVEL
53
SPIDER-GIRL
DEFALCO
OLLIFFE
WILLIAMSON

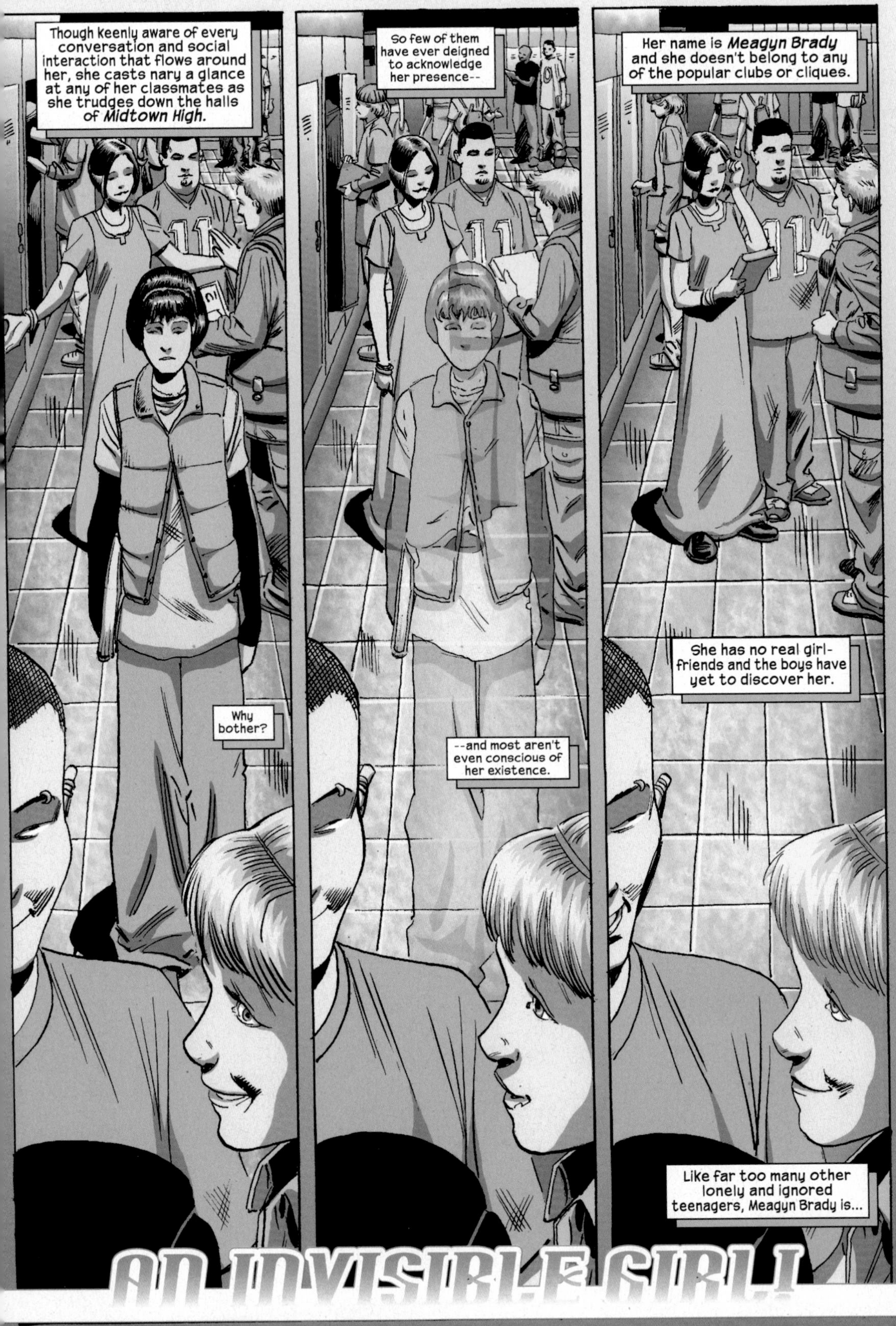
Though keenly aware of every conversation and social interaction that flows around her, she casts nary a glance at any of her classmates as she trudges down the halls of Midtown High.
Why bother?
So few of them have ever deigned to acknowledge her presence--
--and most aren't even conscious of her existence.
Her name is Meagyn Brady and she doesn't belong to any of the popular clubs or cliques.
She has no real girl-friends and the boys have yet to discover her.
Like far too many other lonely and ignored teenagers, Meagyn Brady is...
AN INVISIBLE GIRL!

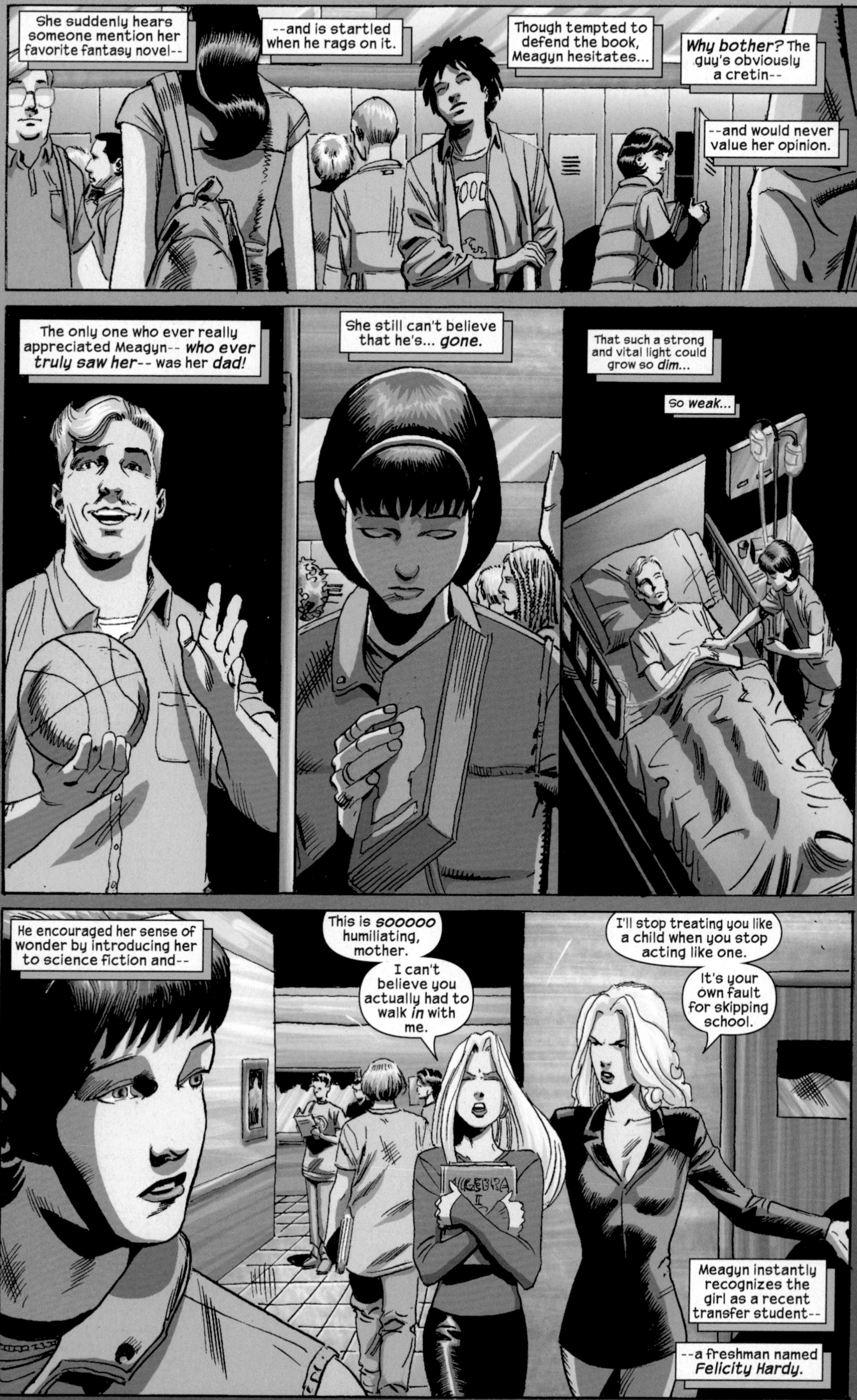
She suddenly hears someone mention her favorite fantasy novel--
--and is startled when he rags on it.
Though tempted to defend the book, Meagyn hesitates...
Why bother? The guy's obviously a cretin--
--and would never value her opinion.
The only one who ever really appreciated Meagyn-- who ever truly saw her-- was her dad!
She still can't believe that he's... gone.
That such a strong and vital light could grow so dim...
So weak...
He encouraged her sense of wonder by introducing her to science fiction and--
This is sooooo humiliating, mother.
I can't believe you actually had to walk in with me.
I'll stop treating you like a child when you stop acting like one.
It's your own fault for skipping school.
Meagyn instantly recognizes the girl as a recent transfer student--
--a freshman named Felicity Hardy.

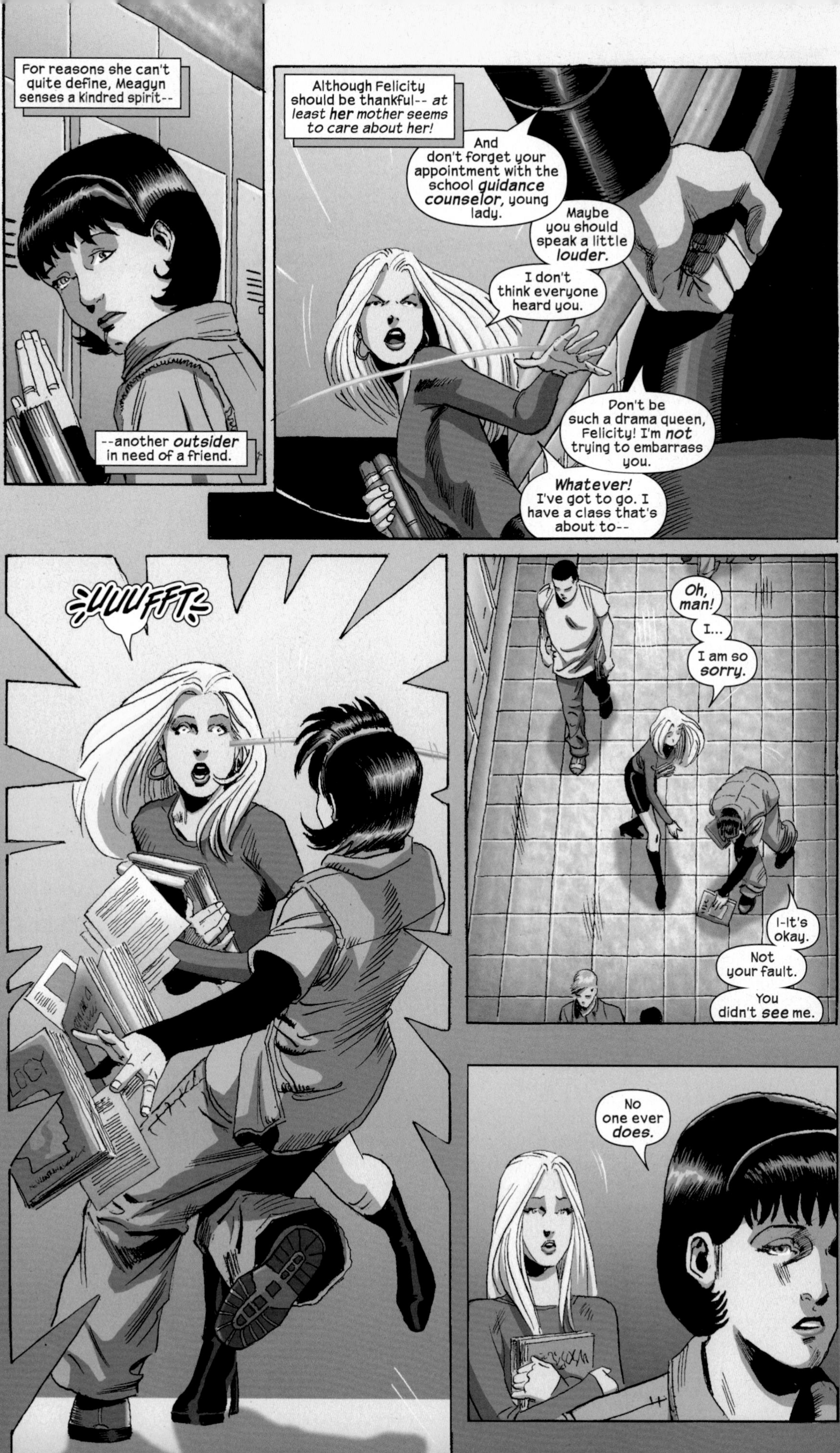
For reasons she can't quite define, Meagyn senses a kindred spirit--
--another *outsider* in need of a friend.
Although Felicity should be thankful-- *at least **her** mother seems to care about her!*
And don't forget your appointment with the school *guidance counselor,* young lady.
Maybe you should speak a little *louder.*
I don't think everyone heard you.
Don't be such a drama queen, Felicity! I'm *not* trying to embarrass you.
Whatever! I've got to go. I have a class that's about to--
UUUFFT
Oh, man!
I...
I am so *sorry.*
I-It's okay.
Not your fault.
You didn't *see* me.
No one ever *does.*

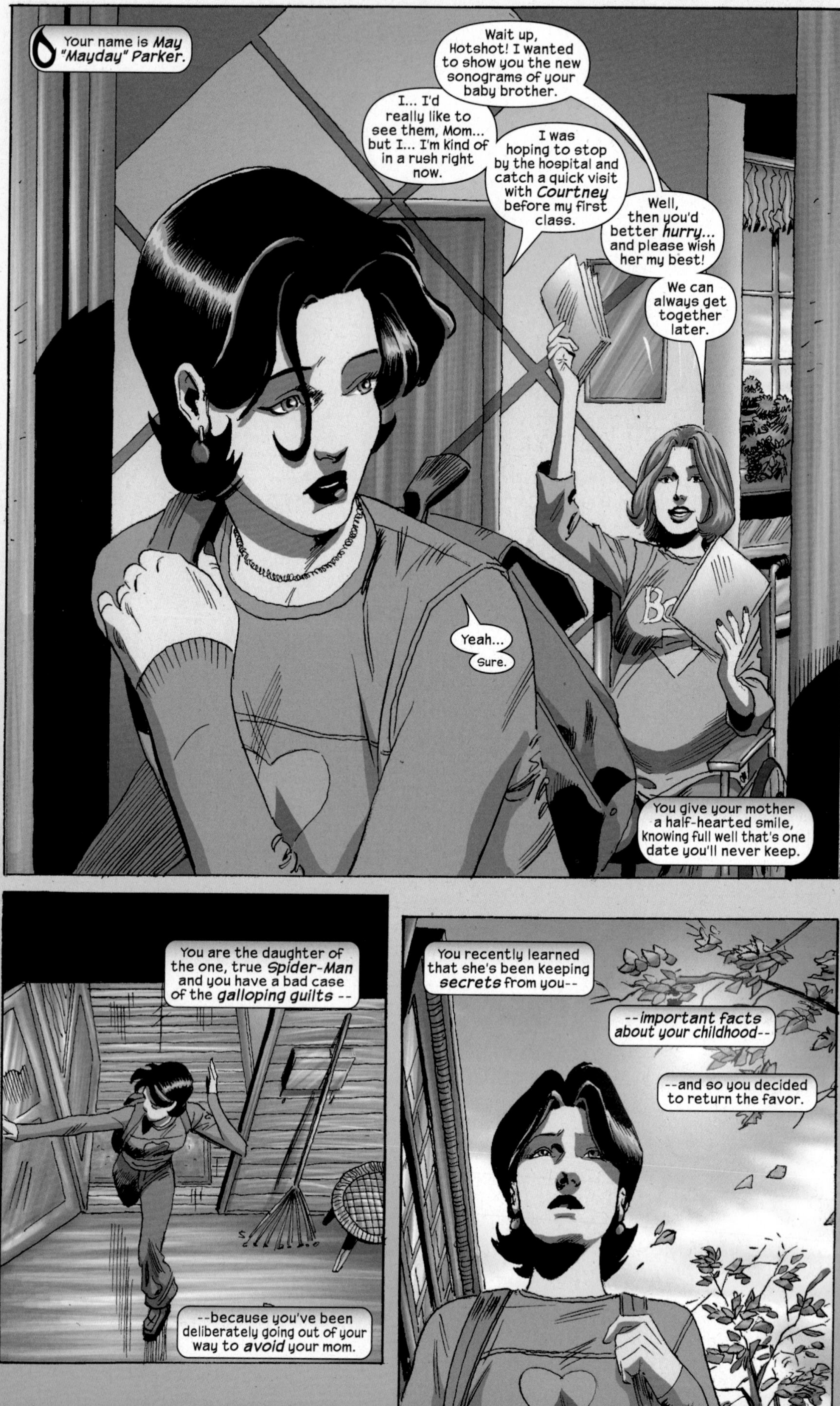
Your name is May "Mayday" Parker.
Wait up, Hotshot! I wanted to show you the new sonograms of your baby brother.
I... I'd really like to see them, Mom... but I... I'm kind of in a rush right now.
I was hoping to stop by the hospital and catch a quick visit with Courtney before my first class.
Well, then you'd better hurry... and please wish her my best!
We can always get together later.
Yeah...
Sure.
You give your mother a half-hearted smile, knowing full well that's one date you'll never keep.
You are the daughter of the one, true Spider-Man and you have a bad case of the galloping guilts --
--because you've been deliberately going out of your way to avoid your mom.
You recently learned that she's been keeping secrets from you--
--important facts about your childhood--
--and so you decided to return the favor.

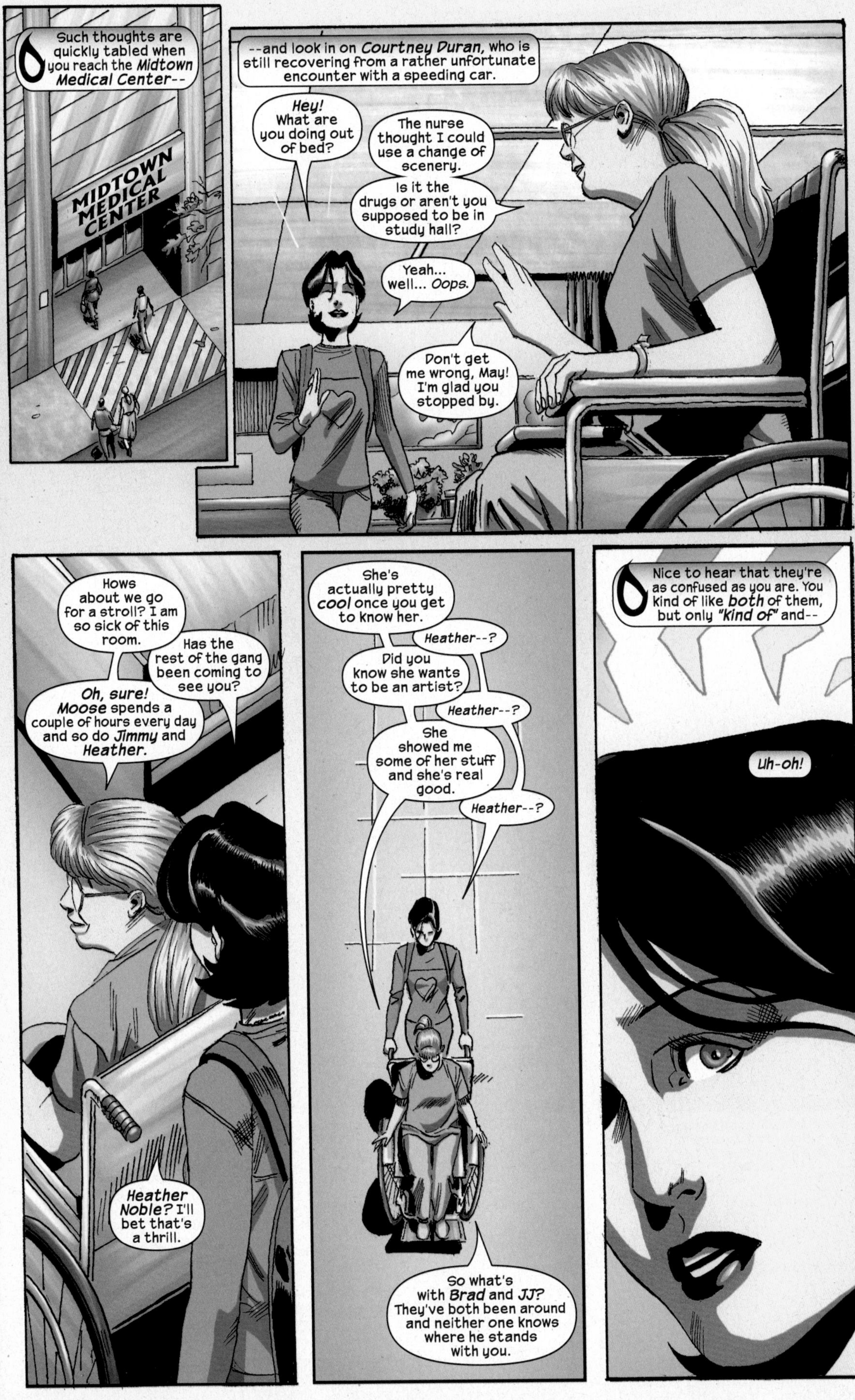
Such thoughts are quickly tabled when you reach the Midtown Medical Center--
MIDTOWN MEDICAL CENTER
--and look in on Courtney Duran, who is still recovering from a rather unfortunate encounter with a speeding car.
Hey! What are you doing out of bed?
The nurse thought I could use a change of scenery.
Is it the drugs or aren't you supposed to be in study hall?
Yeah... well... Oops.
Don't get me wrong, May! I'm glad you stopped by.
Hows about we go for a stroll? I am so sick of this room.
Has the rest of the gang been coming to see you?
Oh, sure! Moose spends a couple of hours every day and so do Jimmy and Heather.
Heather Noble? I'll bet that's a thrill.
She's actually pretty cool once you get to know her.
Heather--?
Did you know she wants to be an artist?
Heather--?
She showed me some of her stuff and she's real good.
Heather--?
So what's with Brad and JJ? They've both been around and neither one knows where he stands with you.
Nice to hear that they're as confused as you are. You kind of like both of them, but only "kind of" and--
Uh-oh!

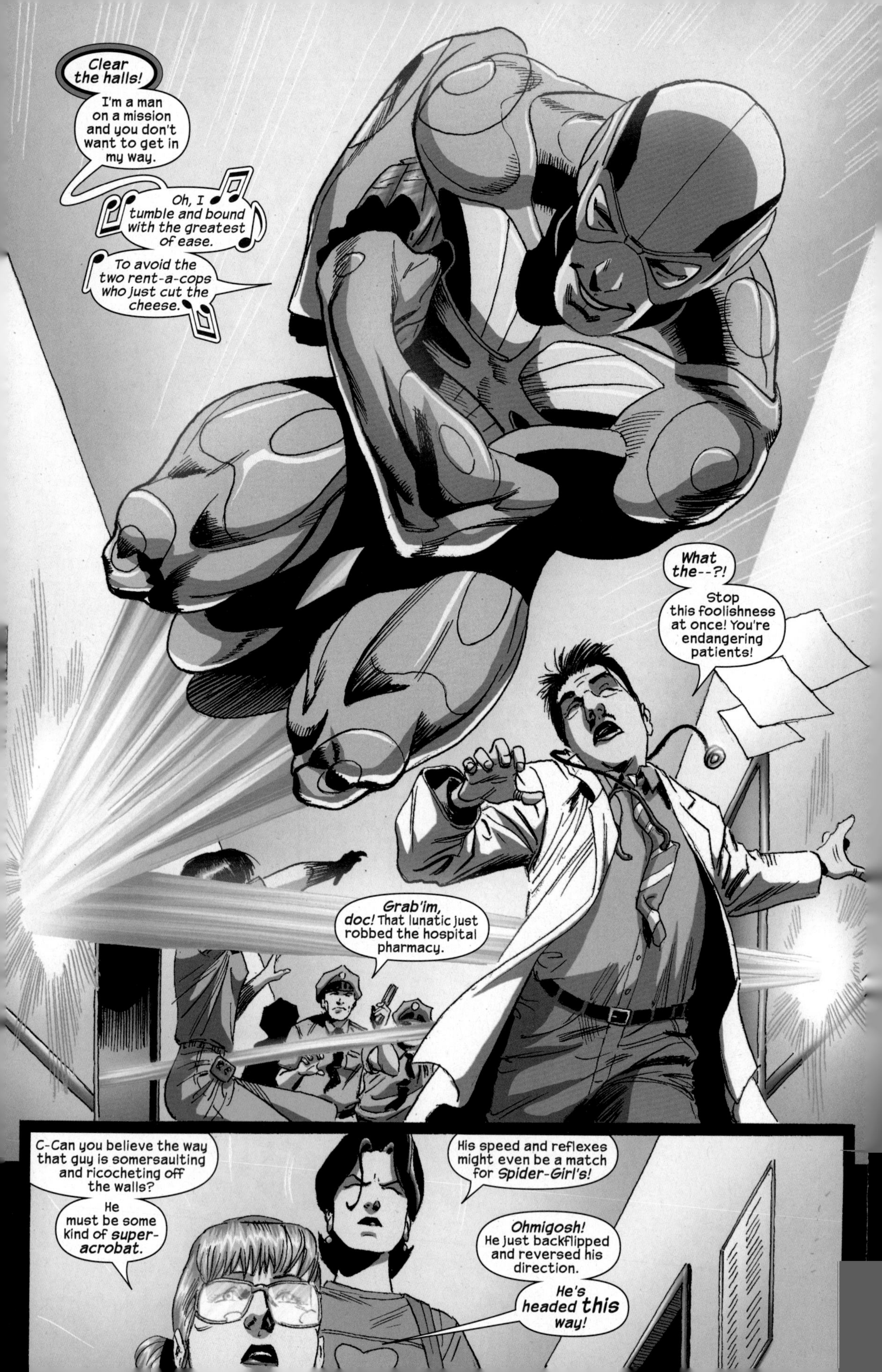
Clear the halls!
I'm a man on a mission and you don't want to get in my way.
Oh, I tumble and bound with the greatest of ease.
To avoid the two rent-a-cops who just cut the cheese.
What the--?!
Stop this foolishness at once! You're endangering patients!
Grab'im, doc! That lunatic just robbed the hospital pharmacy.
C-Can you believe the way that guy is somersaulting and ricocheting off the walls?
He must be some kind of super-acrobat.
His speed and reflexes might even be a match for Spider-Girl's!
Ohmigosh! He just backflipped and reversed his direction.
He's headed this way!

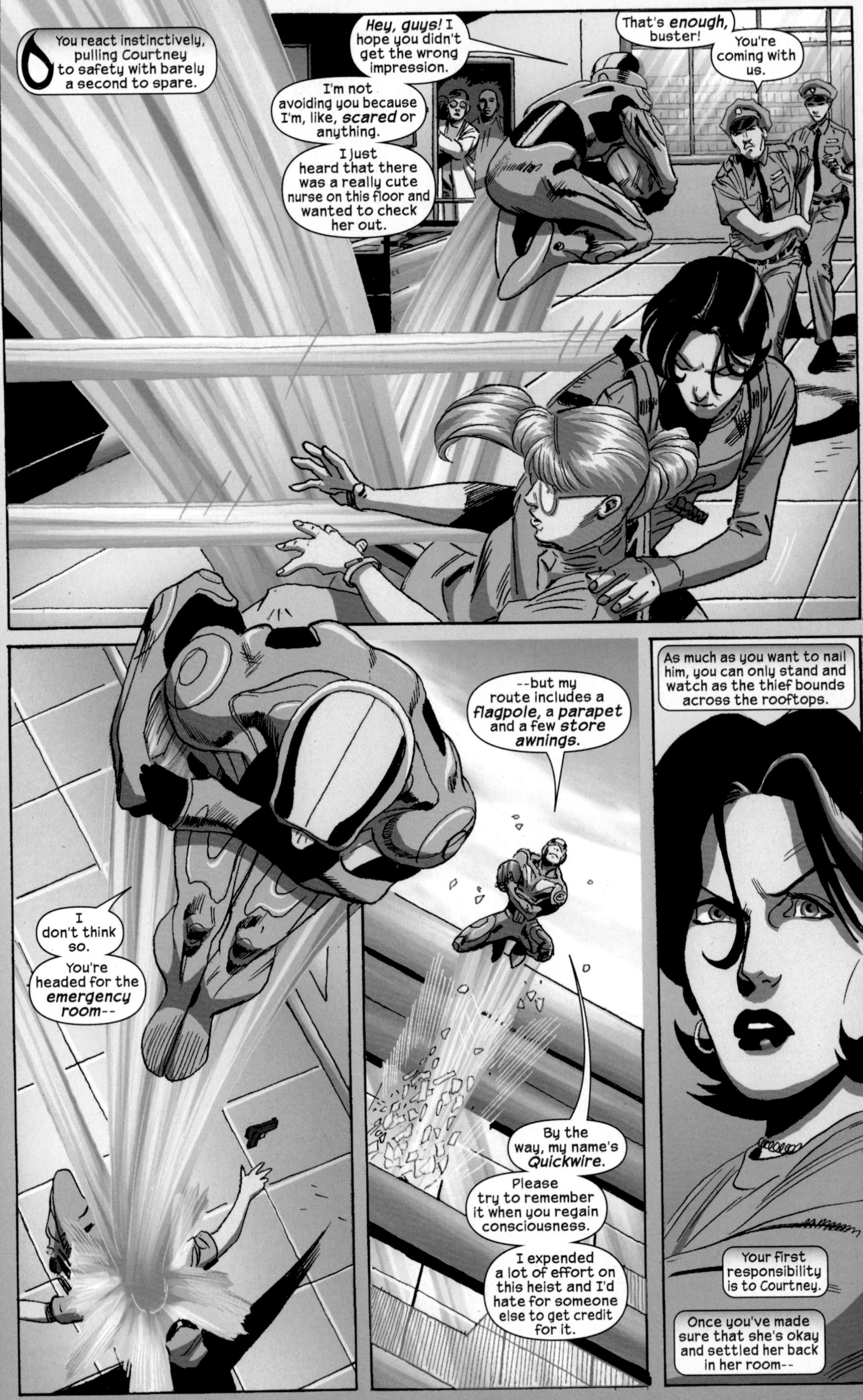

You react instinctively, pulling Courtney to safety with barely a second to spare.
Hey, guys! I hope you didn't get the wrong impression.
I'm not avoiding you because I'm, like, scared or anything.
I just heard that there was a really cute nurse on this floor and wanted to check her out.
That's enough, buster!
You're coming with us.
I don't think so.
You're headed for the emergency room--
--but my route includes a flagpole, a parapet and a few store awnings.
By the way, my name's Quickwire.
Please try to remember it when you regain consciousness.
I expended a lot of effort on this heist and I'd hate for someone else to get credit for it.
As much as you want to nail him, you can only stand and watch as the thief bounds across the rooftops.
Your first responsibility is to Courtney.
Once you've made sure that she's okay and settled her back in her room--

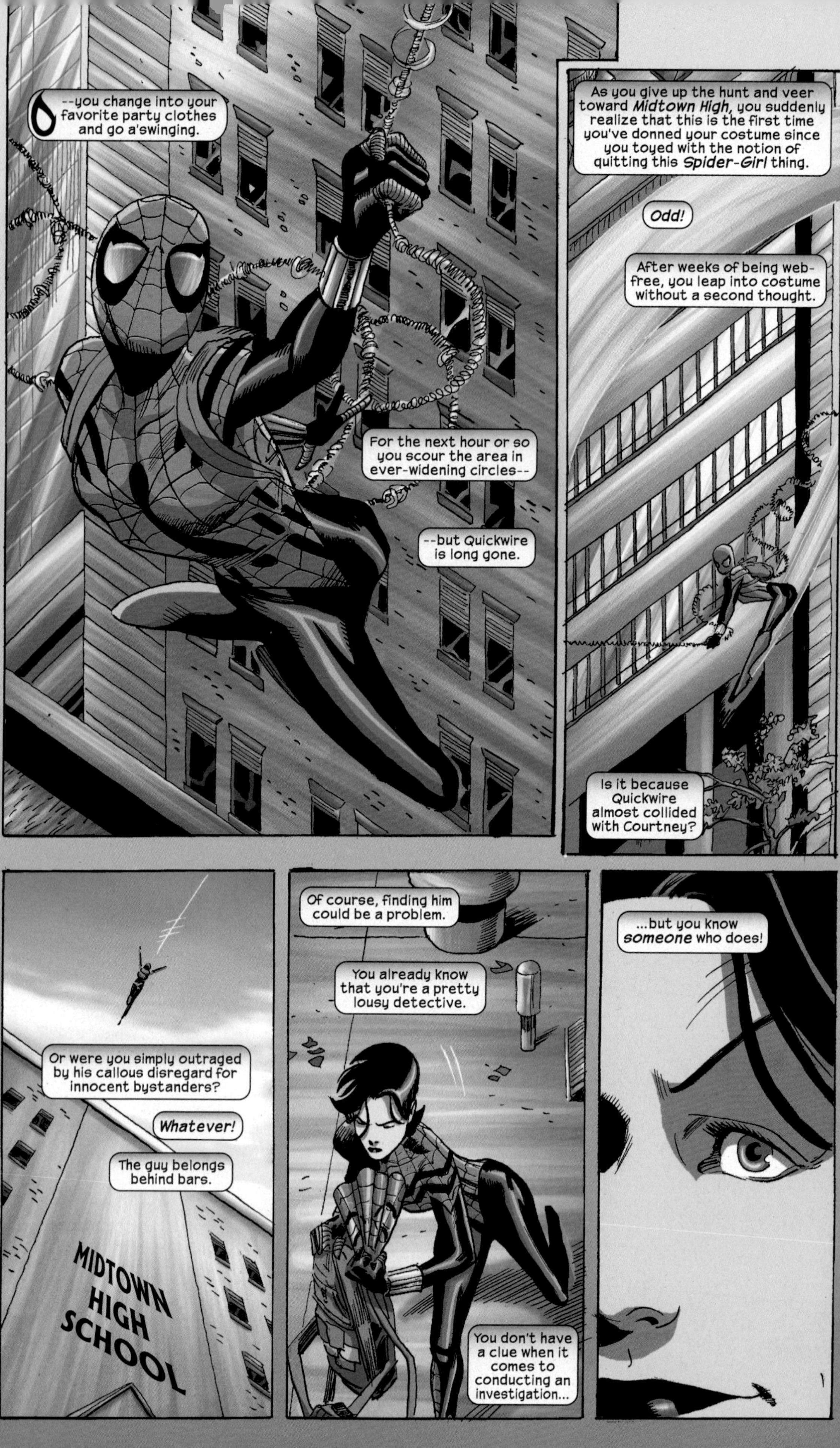

--you change into your favorite party clothes and go a'swinging.
For the next hour or so you scour the area in ever-widening circles--
--but Quickwire is long gone.
As you give up the hunt and veer toward *Midtown High*, you suddenly realize that this is the first time you've donned your costume since you toyed with the notion of quitting this *Spider-Girl* thing.
Odd!
After weeks of being web-free, you leap into costume without a second thought.
Is it because Quickwire almost collided with Courtney?
Or were you simply outraged by his callous disregard for innocent bystanders?
Whatever!
The guy belongs behind bars.
MIDTOWN HIGH SCHOOL
Of course, finding him could be a problem.
You already know that you're a pretty lousy detective.
You don't have a clue when it comes to conducting an investigation...
...but you know *someone* who does!

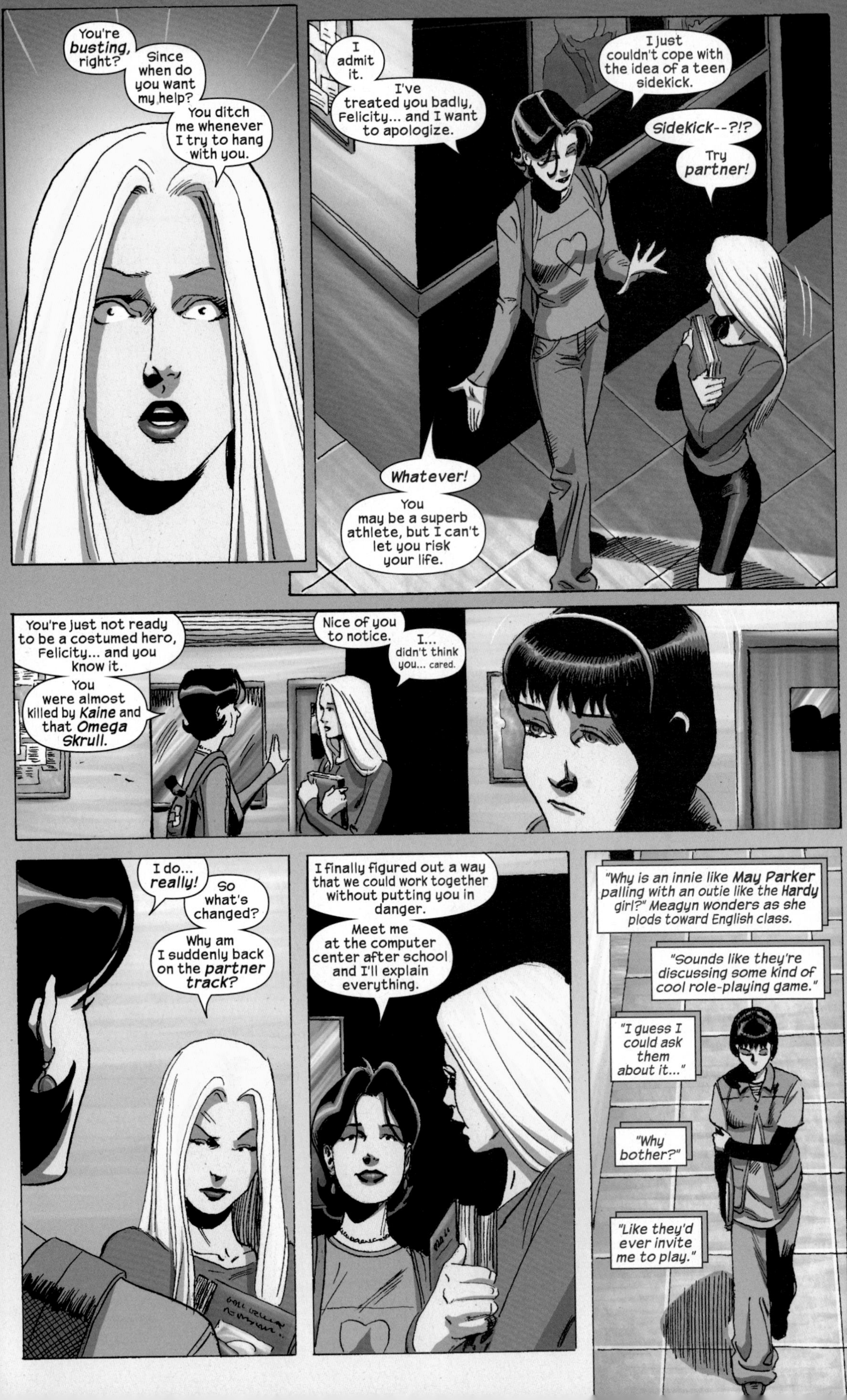
You're busting, right?
Since when do you want my help?
You ditch me whenever I try to hang with you.
I admit it.
I've treated you badly, Felicity... and I want to apologize.
I just couldn't cope with the idea of a teen sidekick.
Sidekick--?!?
Try partner!
Whatever!
You may be a superb athlete, but I can't let you risk your life.
You're just not ready to be a costumed hero, Felicity... and you know it.
You were almost killed by Kaine and that Omega Skrull.
Nice of you to notice.
I... didn't think you... cared.
I do... really!
So what's changed?
Why am I suddenly back on the partner track?
I finally figured out a way that we could work together without putting you in danger.
Meet me at the computer center after school and I'll explain everything.
"Why is an innie like May Parker palling with an outie like the Hardy girl?" Meagyn wonders as she plods toward English class.
"Sounds like they're discussing some kind of cool role-playing game."
"I guess I could ask them about it..."
"Why bother?"
"Like they'd ever invite me to play."

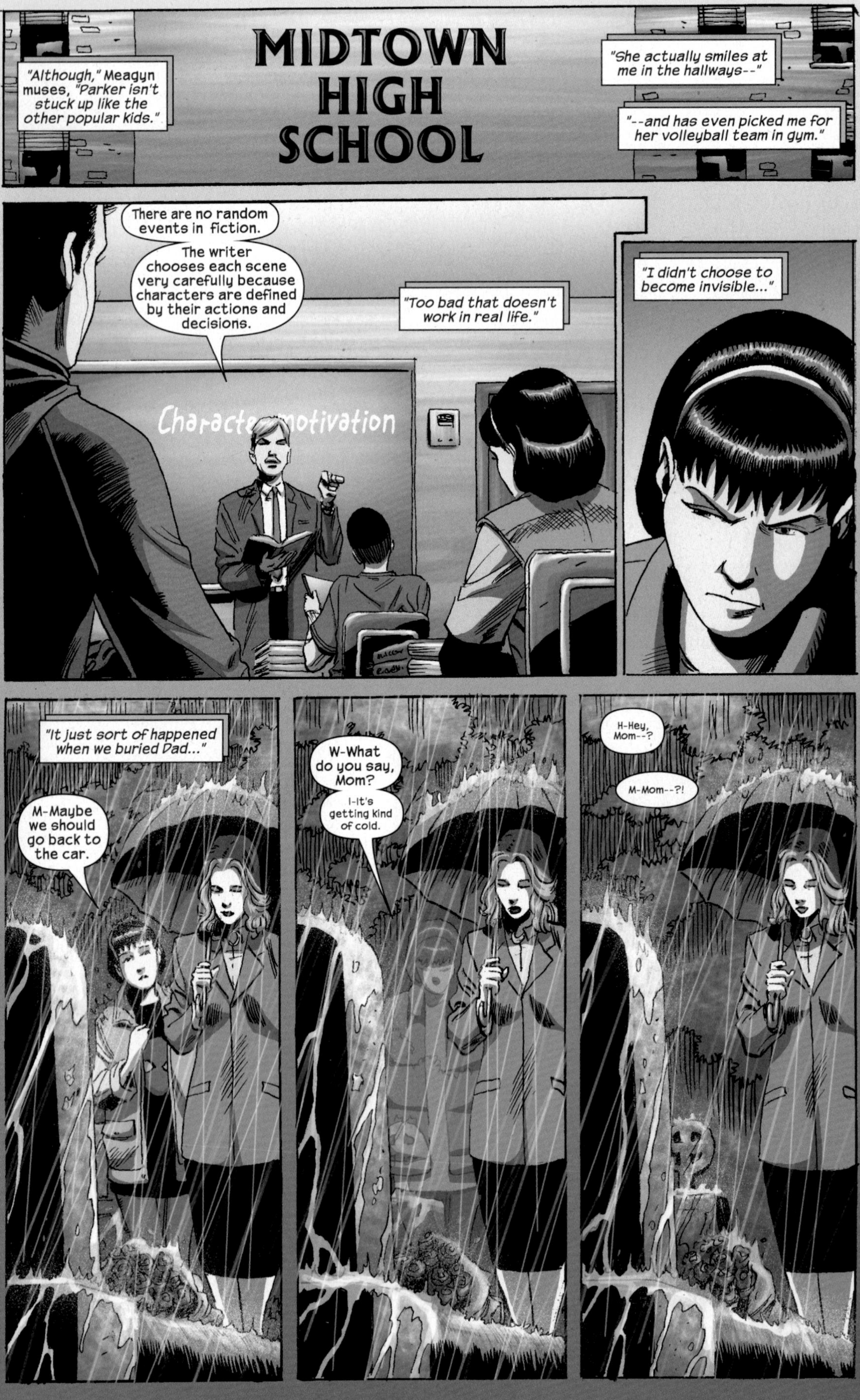
MIDTOWN HIGH SCHOOL
"Although," Meagyn muses, "Parker isn't stuck up like the other popular kids."
"She actually smiles at me in the hallways--"
"--and has even picked me for her volleyball team in gym."
There are no random events in fiction.
The writer chooses each scene very carefully because characters are defined by their actions and decisions.
"Too bad that doesn't work in real life."
"I didn't choose to become invisible..."
"It just sort of happened when we buried Dad..."
M-Maybe we should go back to the car.
W-What do you say, Mom?
I-It's getting kind of cold.
H-Hey, Mom--?
M-Mom--?!

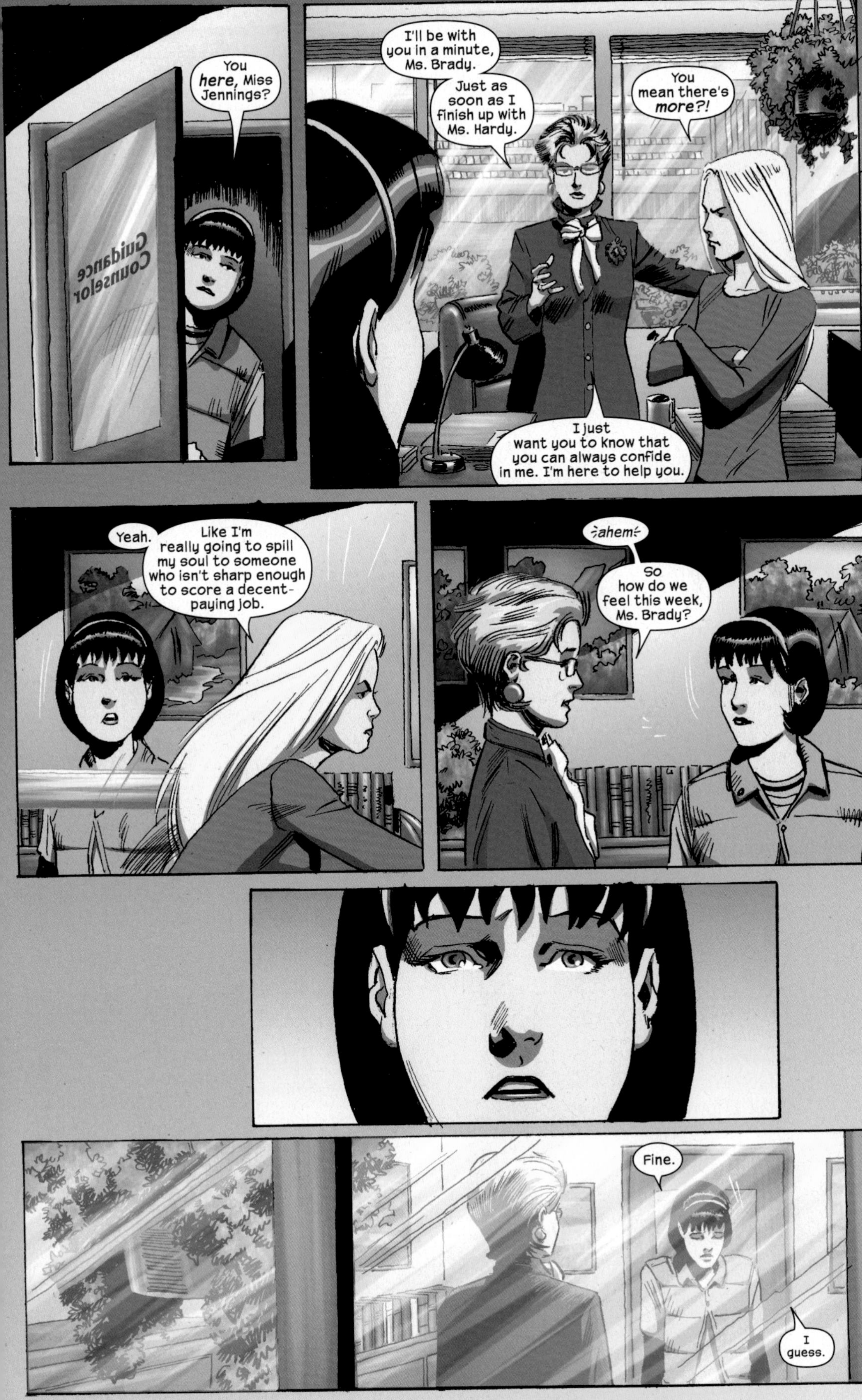

Guidance Counselor
You here, Miss Jennings?
I'll be with you in a minute, Ms. Brady.
Just as soon as I finish up with Ms. Hardy.
You mean there's more?!
I just want you to know that you can always confide in me. I'm here to help you.
Yeah.
Like I'm really going to spill my soul to someone who isn't sharp enough to score a decent-paying job.
ahem
So how do we feel this week, Ms. Brady?
Fine.
I guess.

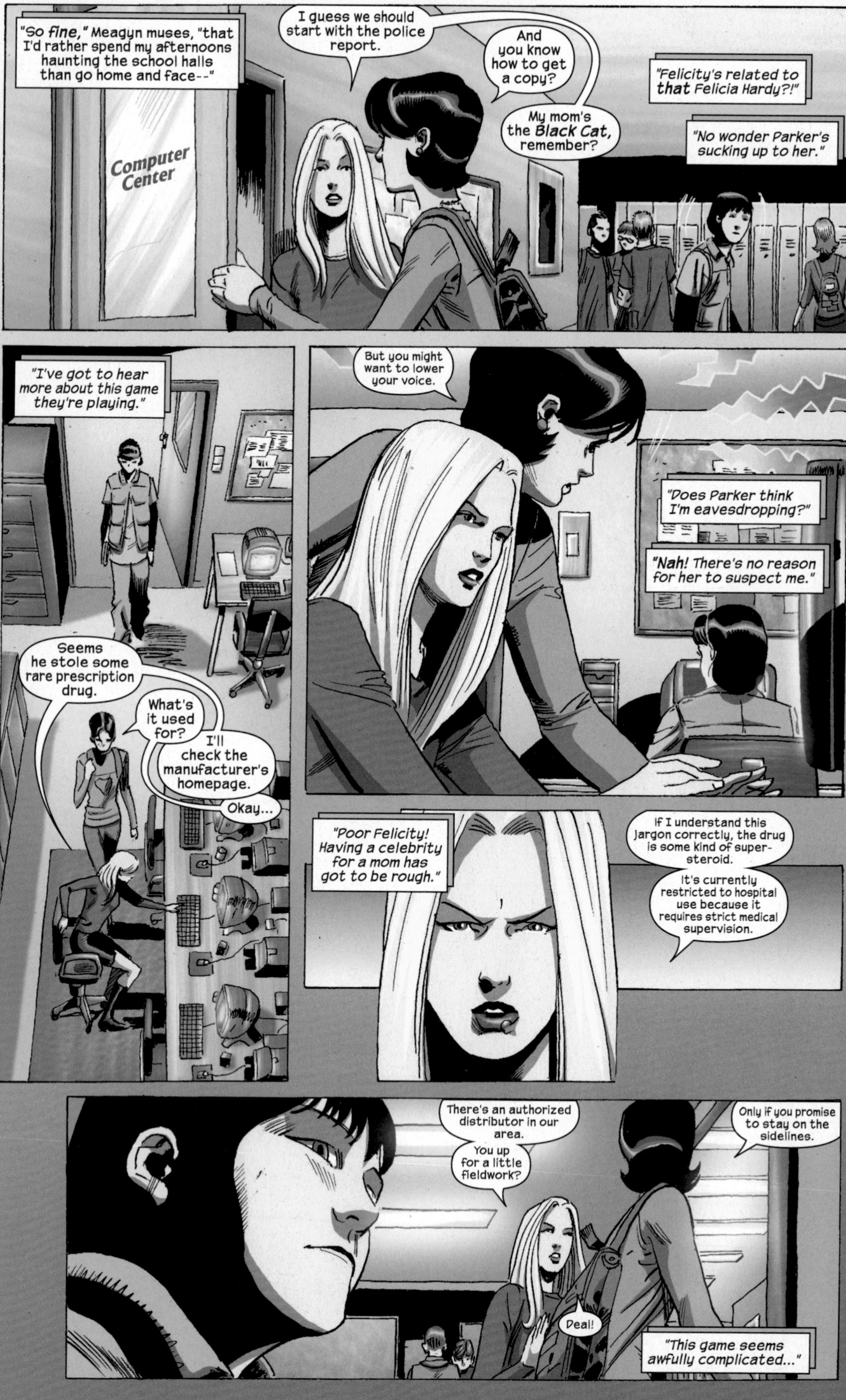
"So *fine*," Meagyn muses, "that I'd rather spend my afternoons haunting the school halls than go home and face--"
Computer Center
I guess we should start with the police report.
And you know how to get a copy?
My mom's the *Black Cat*, remember?
"Felicity's related to **that** Felicia Hardy?!"
"No wonder Parker's sucking up to her."
"I've got to hear more about this game they're playing."
Seems he stole some rare prescription drug.
What's it used for?
I'll check the manufacturer's homepage.
Okay...
But you might want to lower your voice.
"Does Parker think I'm eavesdropping?"
"**Nah!** There's no reason for her to suspect me."
"Poor Felicity! Having a celebrity for a mom has got to be rough."
If I understand this jargon correctly, the drug is some kind of super-steroid.
It's currently restricted to hospital use because it requires strict medical supervision.
There's an authorized distributor in our area.
You up for a little fieldwork?
Only if you promise to stay on the sidelines.
Deal!
"This game seems awfully complicated..."

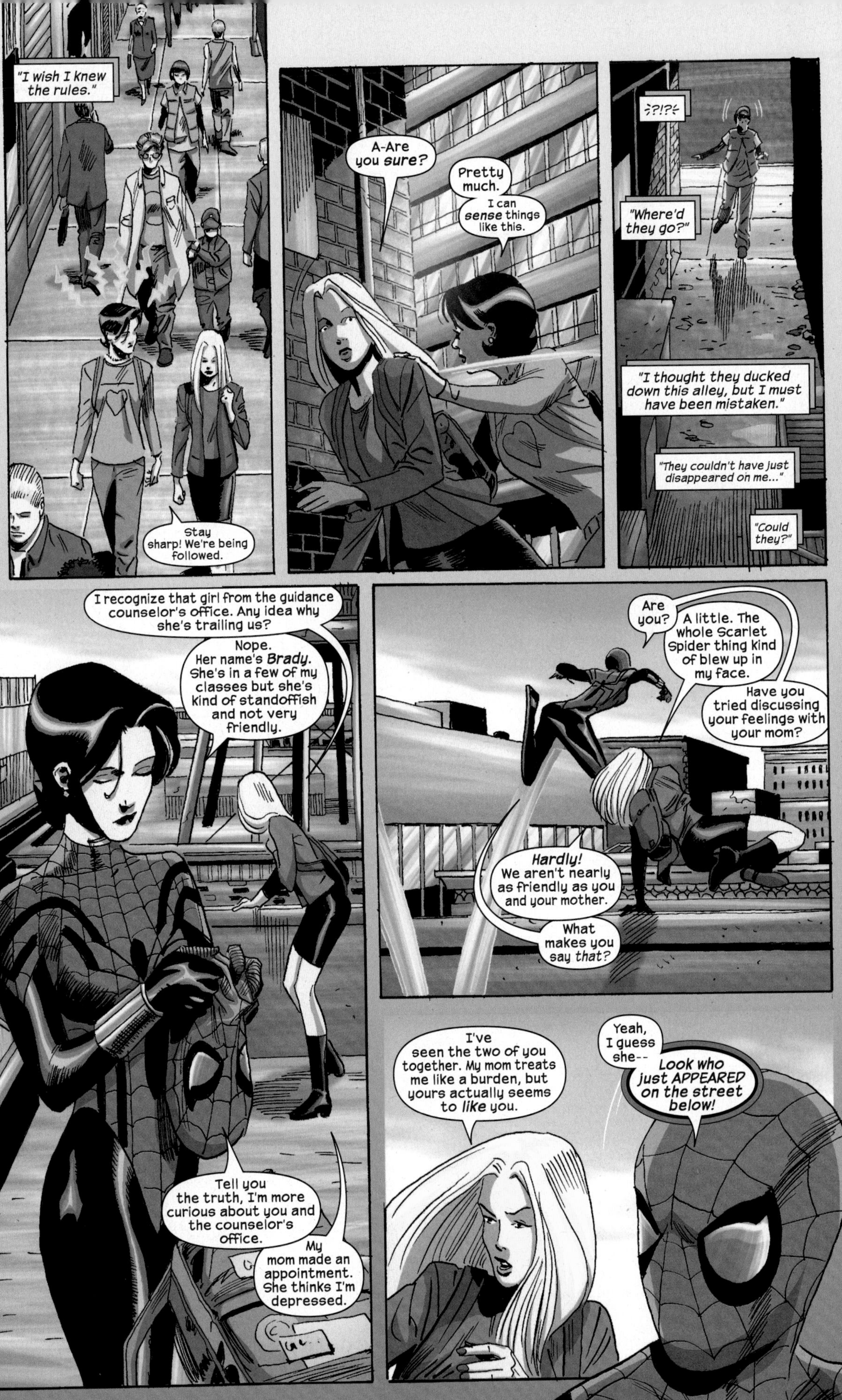
"I wish I knew the rules."
Stay sharp! We're being followed.
A-Are you *sure*?
Pretty much.
I can *sense* things like this.
?!?!?
"Where'd they go?"
"I thought they ducked down this alley, but I must have been mistaken."
"They couldn't have just disappeared on me..."
"Could they?"
I recognize that girl from the guidance counselor's office. Any idea why she's trailing us?
Nope. Her name's *Brady*. She's in a few of my classes but she's kind of standoffish and not very friendly.
Tell you the truth, I'm more curious about you and the counselor's office.
My mom made an appointment. She thinks I'm depressed.
Are you?
A little. The whole Scarlet Spider thing kind of blew up in my face.
Have you tried discussing your feelings with your mom?
Hardly! We aren't nearly as friendly as you and your mother.
What makes you say *that*?
I've seen the two of you together. My mom treats me like a burden, but yours actually seems to *like* you.
Yeah, I guess she--
Look who just APPEARED on the street below!

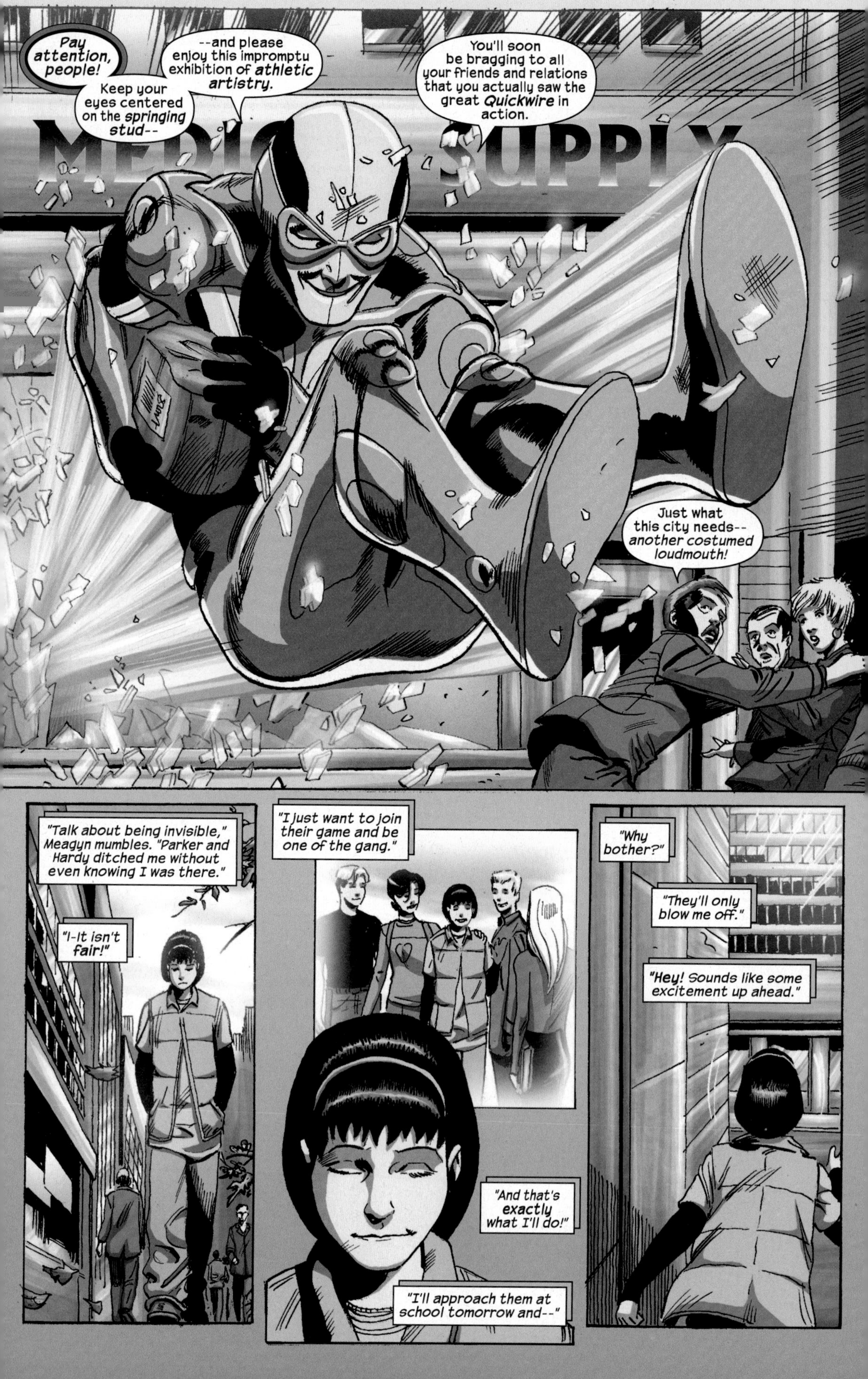
Pay attention, people!
Keep your eyes centered on the springing stud--
--and please enjoy this impromptu exhibition of athletic artistry.
You'll soon be bragging to all your friends and relations that you actually saw the great Quickwire in action.
Just what this city needs-- another costumed loudmouth!
"Talk about being invisible," Meagyn mumbles. "Parker and Hardy ditched me without even knowing I was there."
"I-It isn't fair!"
"I just want to join their game and be one of the gang."
"And that's exactly what I'll do!"
"I'll approach them at school tomorrow and--"
"Why bother?"
"They'll only blow me off."
"Hey! Sounds like some excitement up ahead."

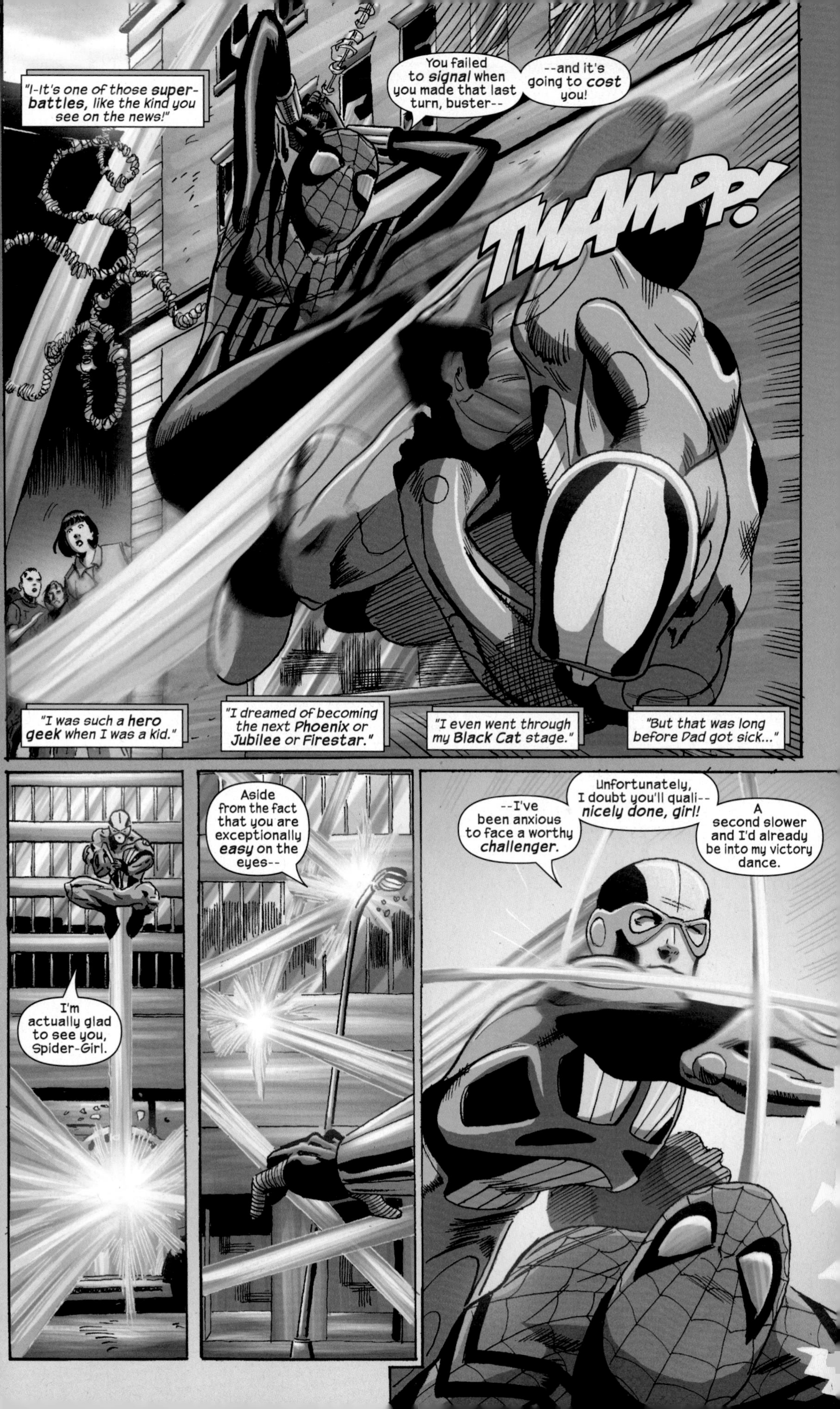
"I-It's one of those super-battles, like the kind you see on the news!"
You failed to signal when you made that last turn, buster--
--and it's going to cost you!
THWAMPP!
"I was such a hero geek when I was a kid."
"I dreamed of becoming the next Phoenix or Jubilee or Firestar."
"I even went through my Black Cat stage."
"But that was long before Dad got sick..."
I'm actually glad to see you, Spider-Girl.
Aside from the fact that you are exceptionally easy on the eyes--
--I've been anxious to face a worthy challenger.
Unfortunately, I doubt you'll quali-- nicely done, girl!
A second slower and I'd already be into my victory dance.

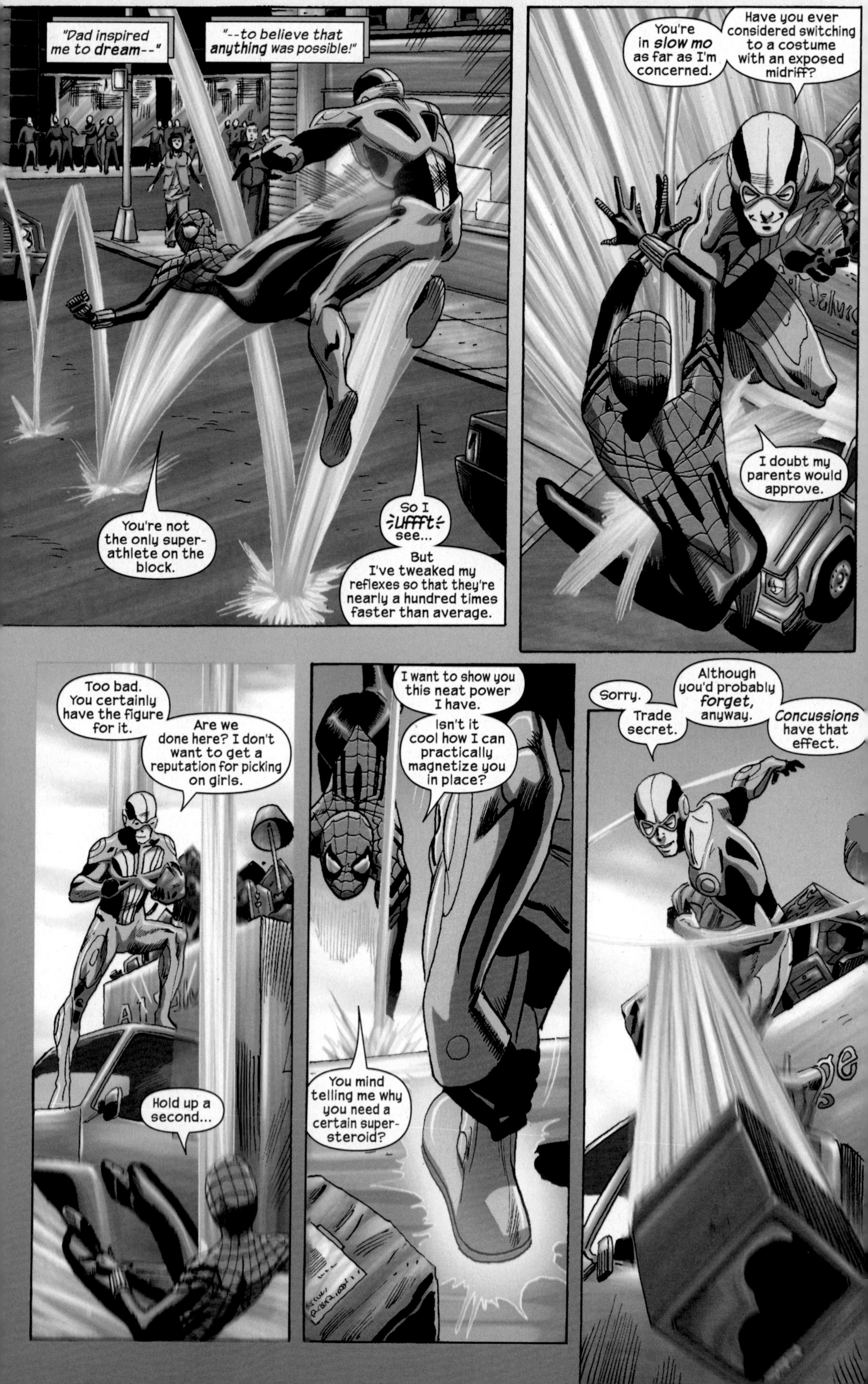
"Dad inspired me to *dream*--"
"--to believe that *anything* was possible!"
You're not the only super-athlete on the block.
So I
UFFFt
see...
But I've tweaked my reflexes so that they're nearly a hundred times faster than average.
You're in *slow mo* as far as I'm concerned.
Have you ever considered switching to a costume with an exposed midriff?
I doubt my parents would approve.
Too bad. You certainly have the figure for it.
Are we done here? I don't want to get a reputation for picking on girls.
Hold up a second...
I want to show you this neat power I have.
Isn't it cool how I can practically magnetize you in place?
You mind telling me why you need a certain super-steroid?
Sorry.
Trade secret.
Although you'd probably *forget,* anyway.
Concussions have that effect.

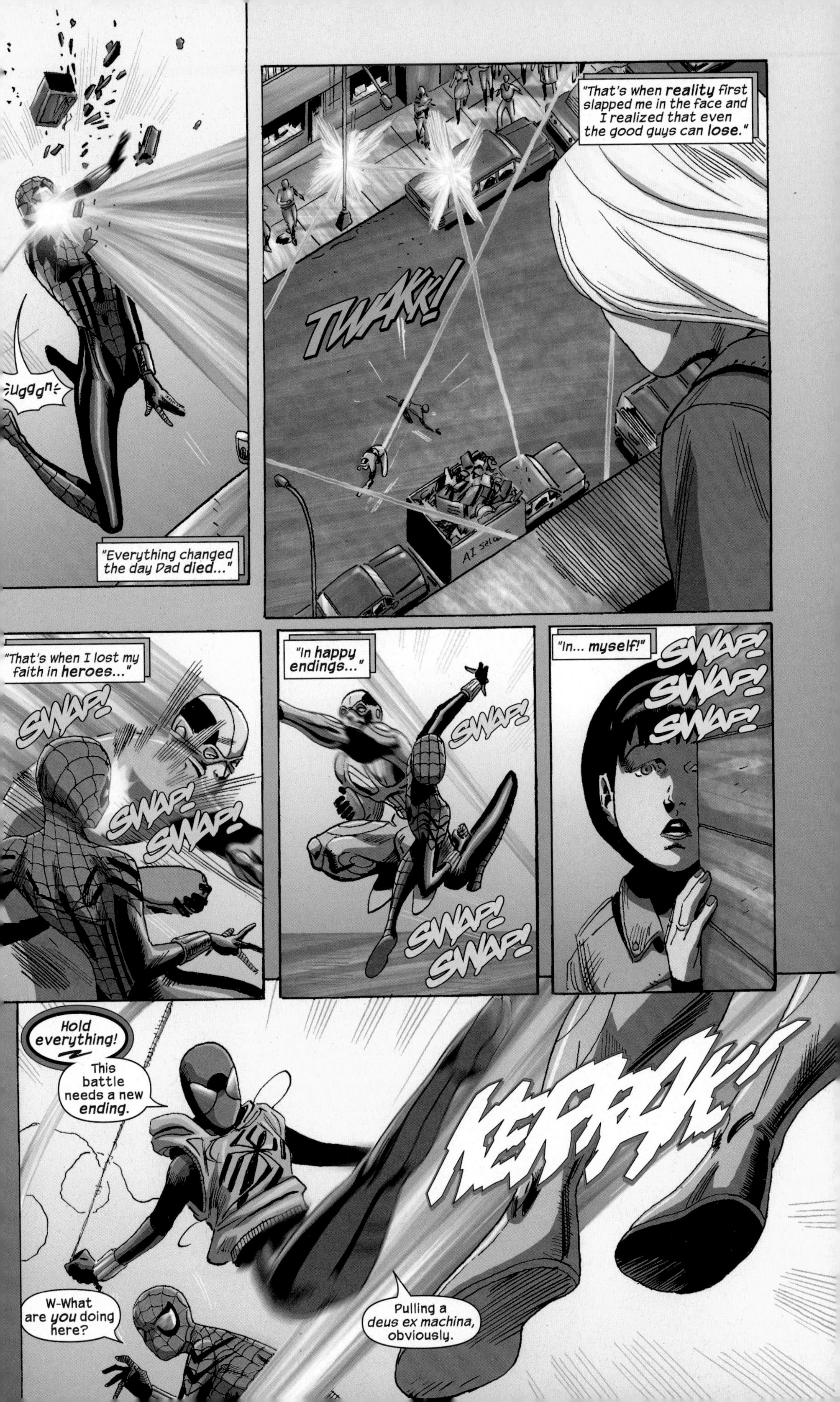

Uggghn
"Everything changed the day Dad died..."
"That's when reality first slapped me in the face and I realized that even the good guys can lose."
TWAKK!
"That's when I lost my faith in heroes..."
SWAP!
SWAP!
SWAP!
"In happy endings..."
SWAP!
SWAP!
SWAP!
"In... myself!"
SWAP!
SWAP!
SWAP!
Hold everything!
This battle needs a new ending.
KERRAK!
W-What are you doing here?
Pulling a deus ex machina, obviously.

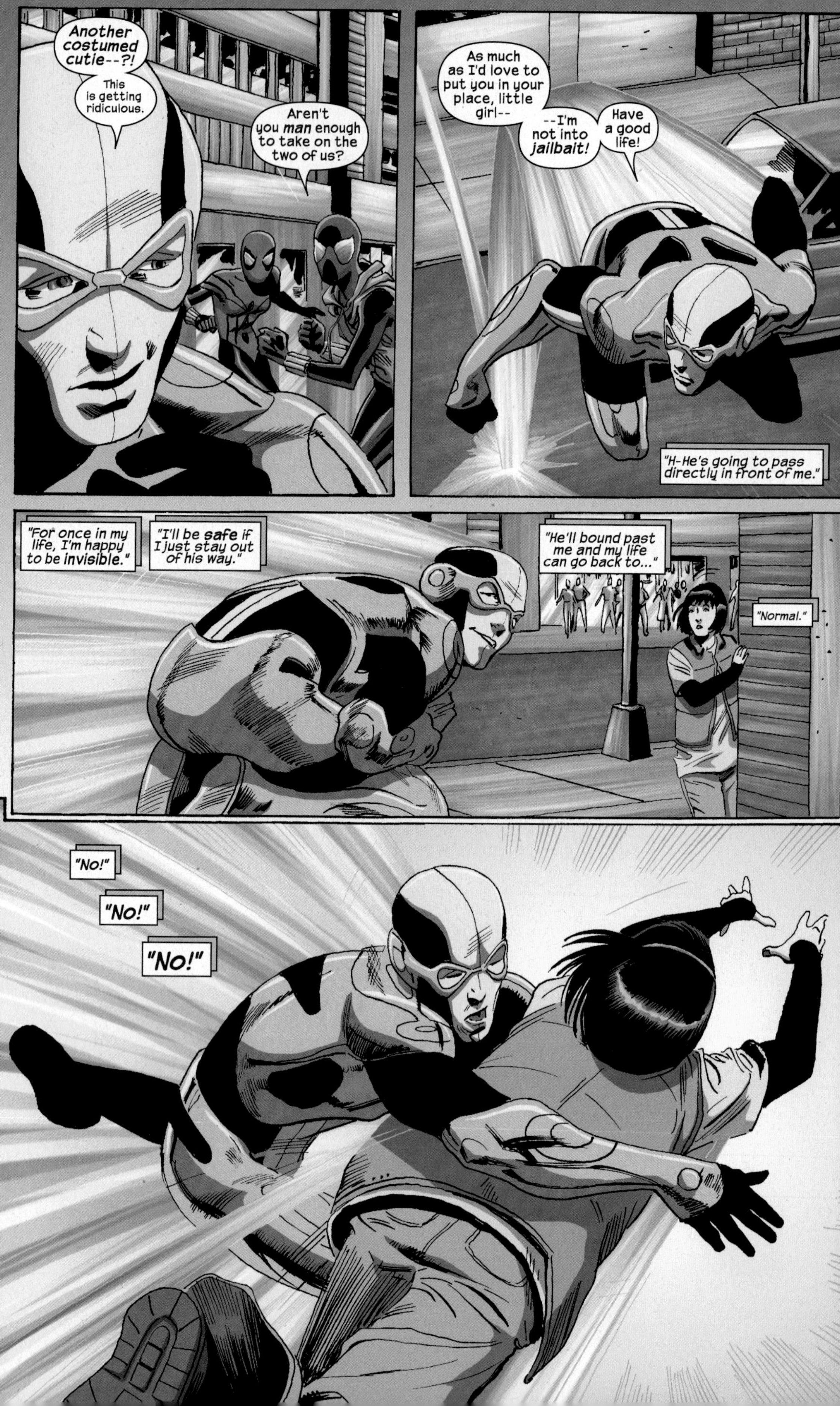
Another costumed cutie--?!
This is getting ridiculous.
Aren't you man enough to take on the two of us?
As much as I'd love to put you in your place, little girl--
--I'm not into jailbait!
Have a good life!
"H-He's going to pass directly in front of me."
"For once in my life, I'm happy to be invisible."
"I'll be safe if I just stay out of his way."
"He'll bound past me and my life can go back to..."
"Normal."
"No!"
"No!"
"No!"

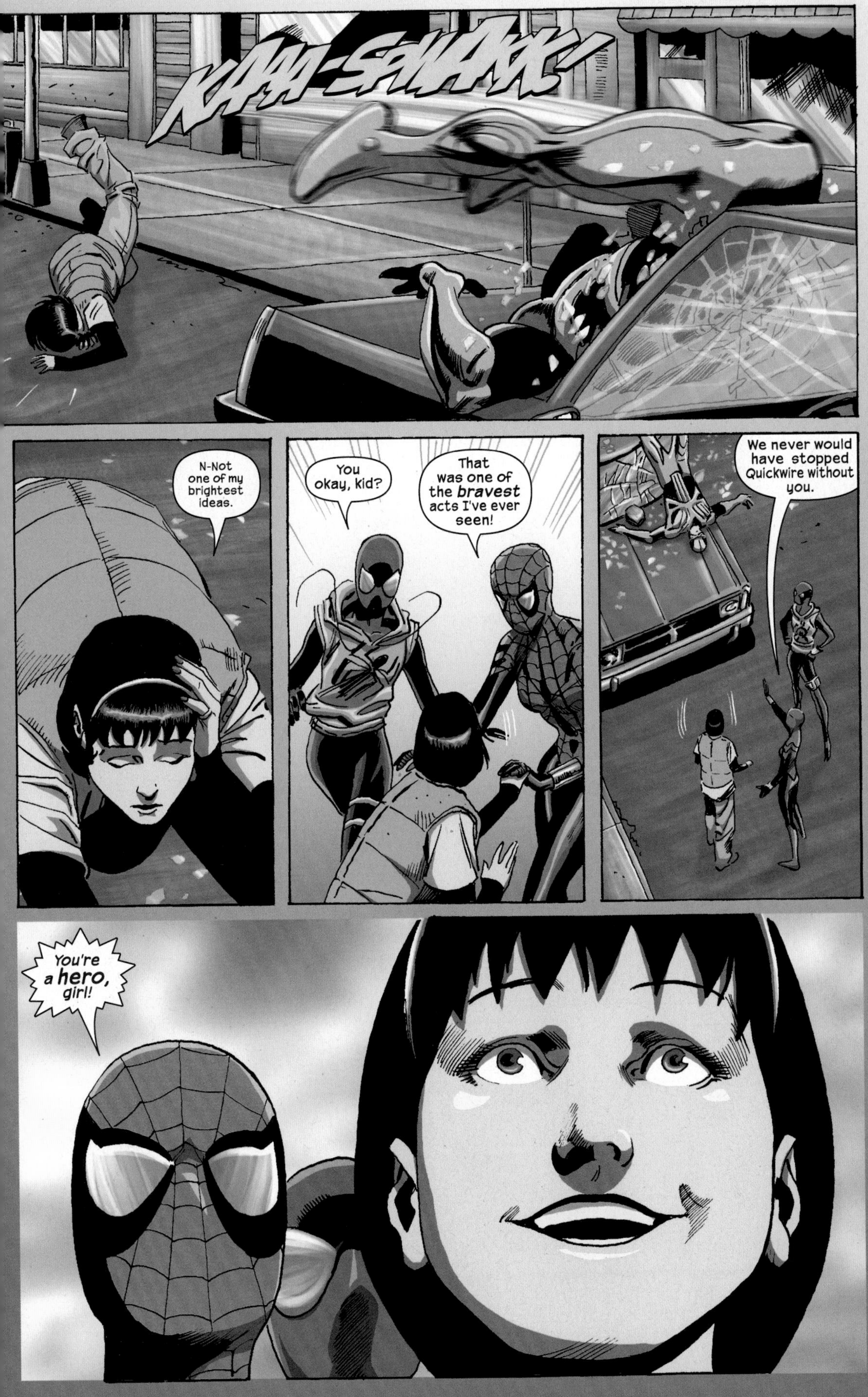
KAAA-SPWAKK!
N-Not one of my brightest ideas.
You okay, kid?
That was one of the *bravest* acts I've ever seen!
We never would have stopped Quickwire without you.
You're a **hero**, girl!

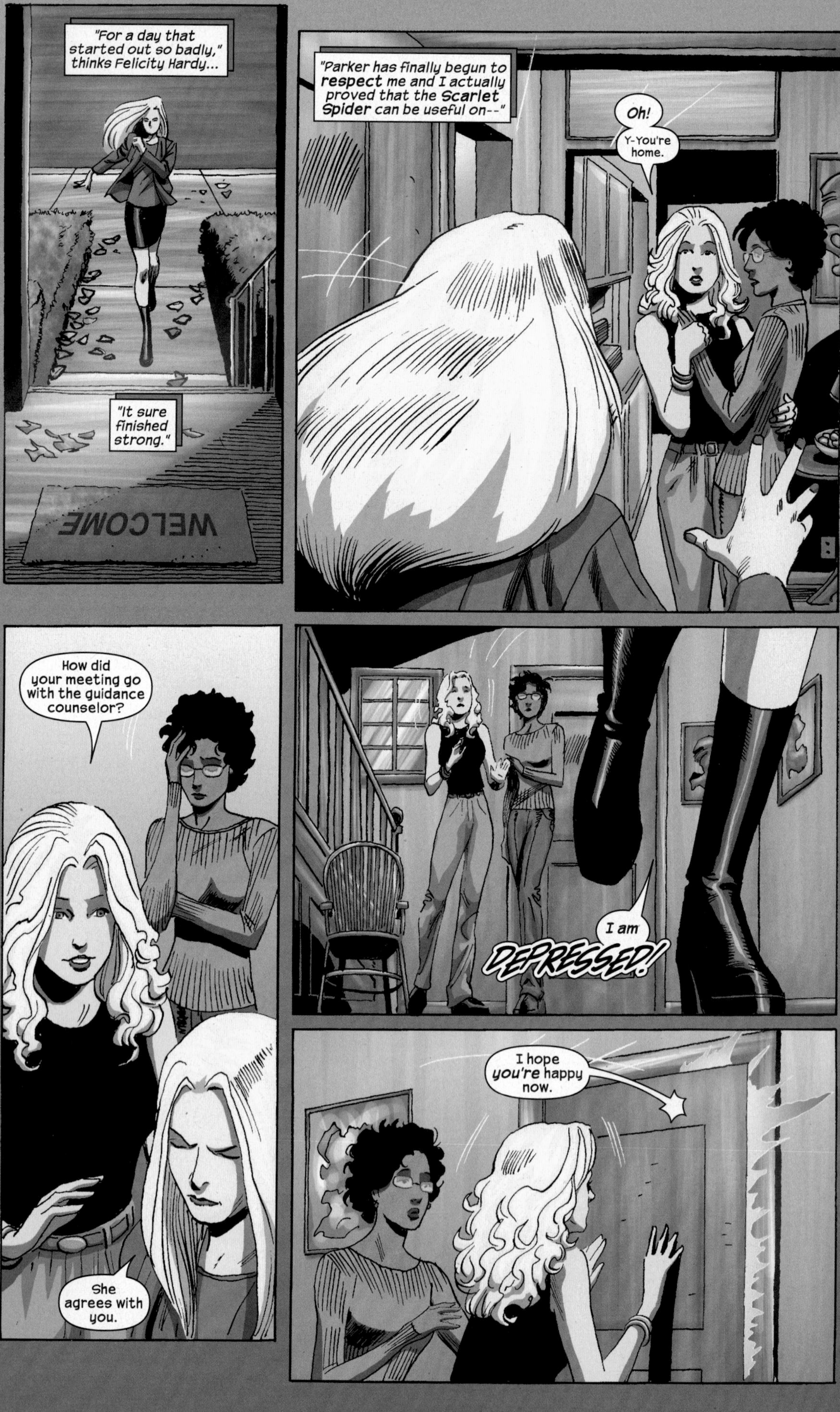
"For a day that started out so badly," thinks Felicity Hardy...
"It sure finished strong."
WELCOME
"Parker has finally begun to respect me and I actually proved that the Scarlet Spider can be useful on--"
Oh!
Y-You're home.
How did your meeting go with the guidance counselor?
She agrees with you.
I am DEPRESSED!
I hope you're happy now.

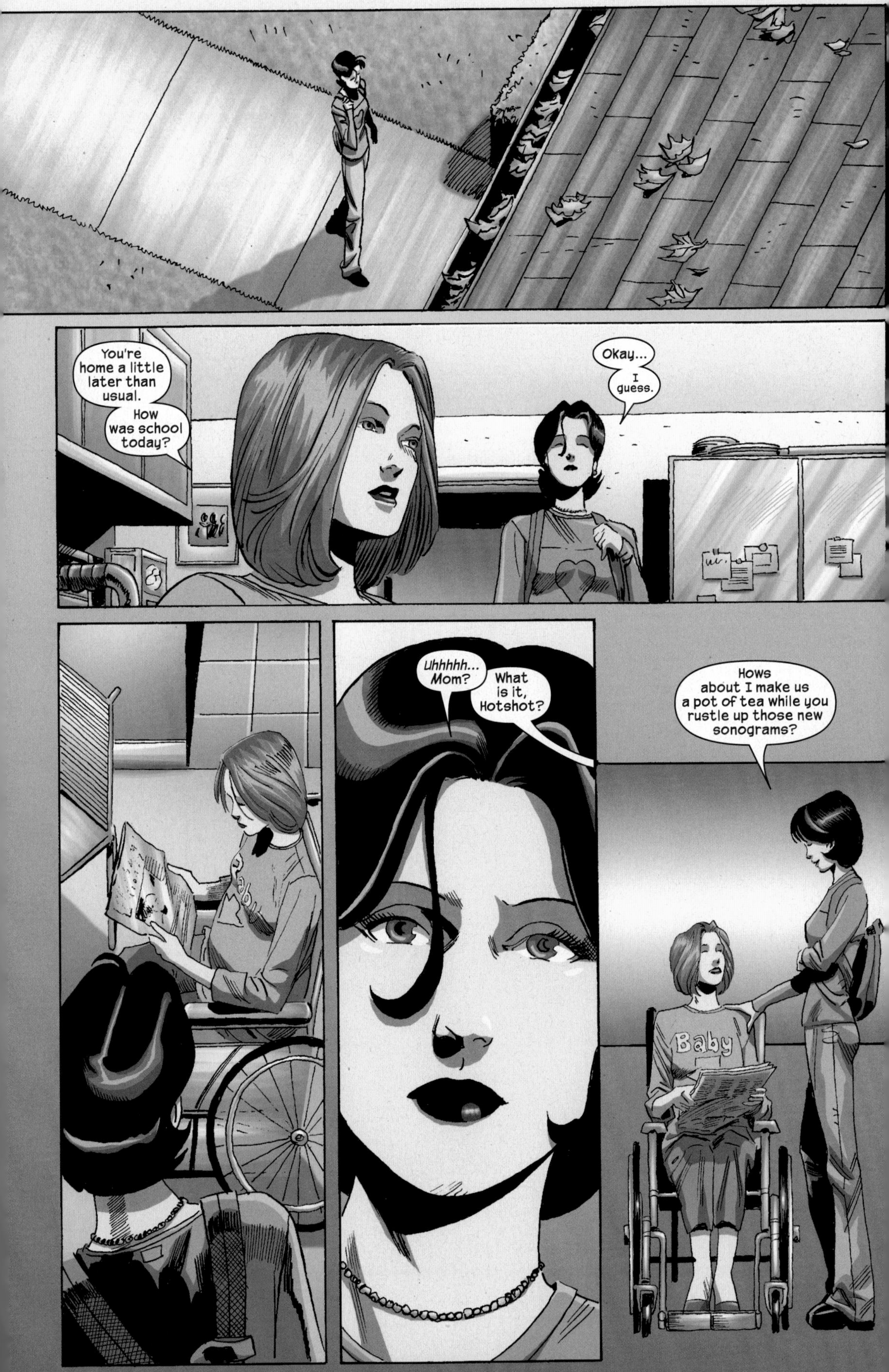

You're home a little later than usual.
How was school today?
Okay...
I guess.
Uhhhhh... Mom?
What is it, Hotshot?
Hows about I make us a pot of tea while you rustle up those new sonograms?

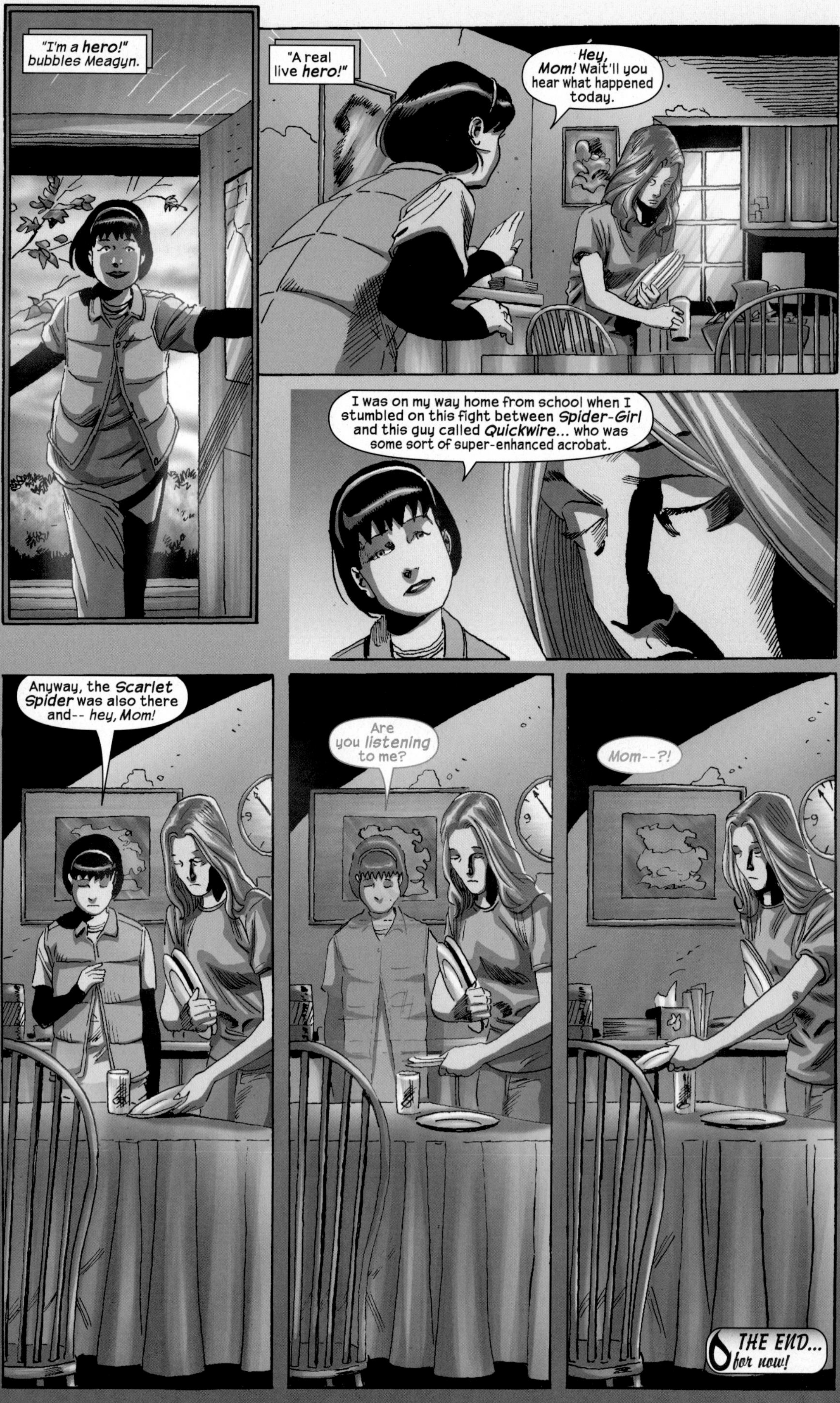
"I'm a hero!" bubbles Meagyn.
"A real live hero!"
Hey, Mom! Wait'll you hear what happened today.
I was on my way home from school when I stumbled on this fight between Spider-Girl and this guy called Quickwire... who was some sort of super-enhanced acrobat.
Anyway, the Scarlet Spider was also there and-- hey, Mom!
Are you listening to me?
Mom--?!
THE END... for now!

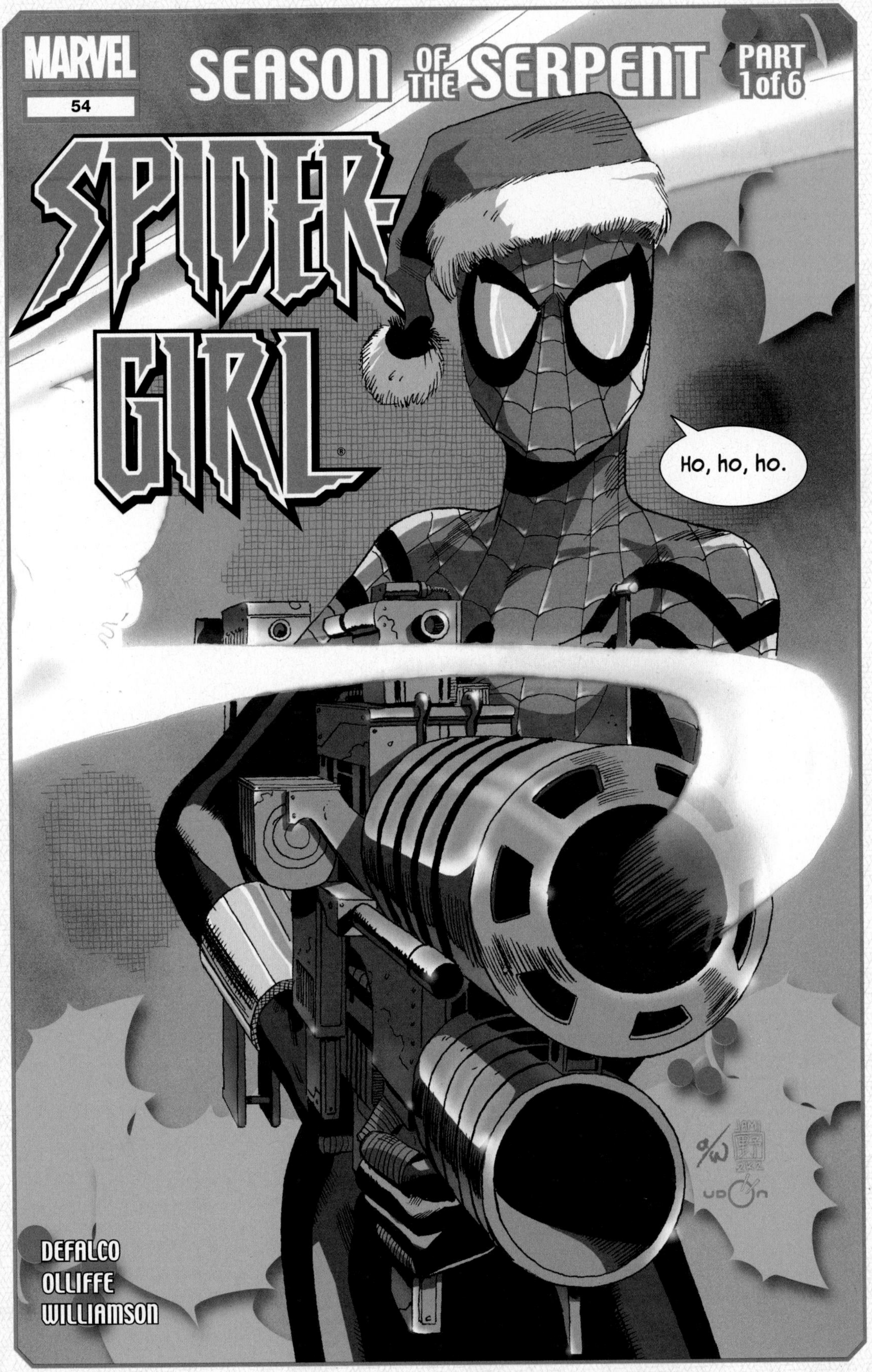
MARVEL
54
SEASON OF THE SERPENT
PART 1 of 6
SPIDER-GIRL
Ho, ho, ho.
DEFALCO
OLLIFFE
WILLIAMSON

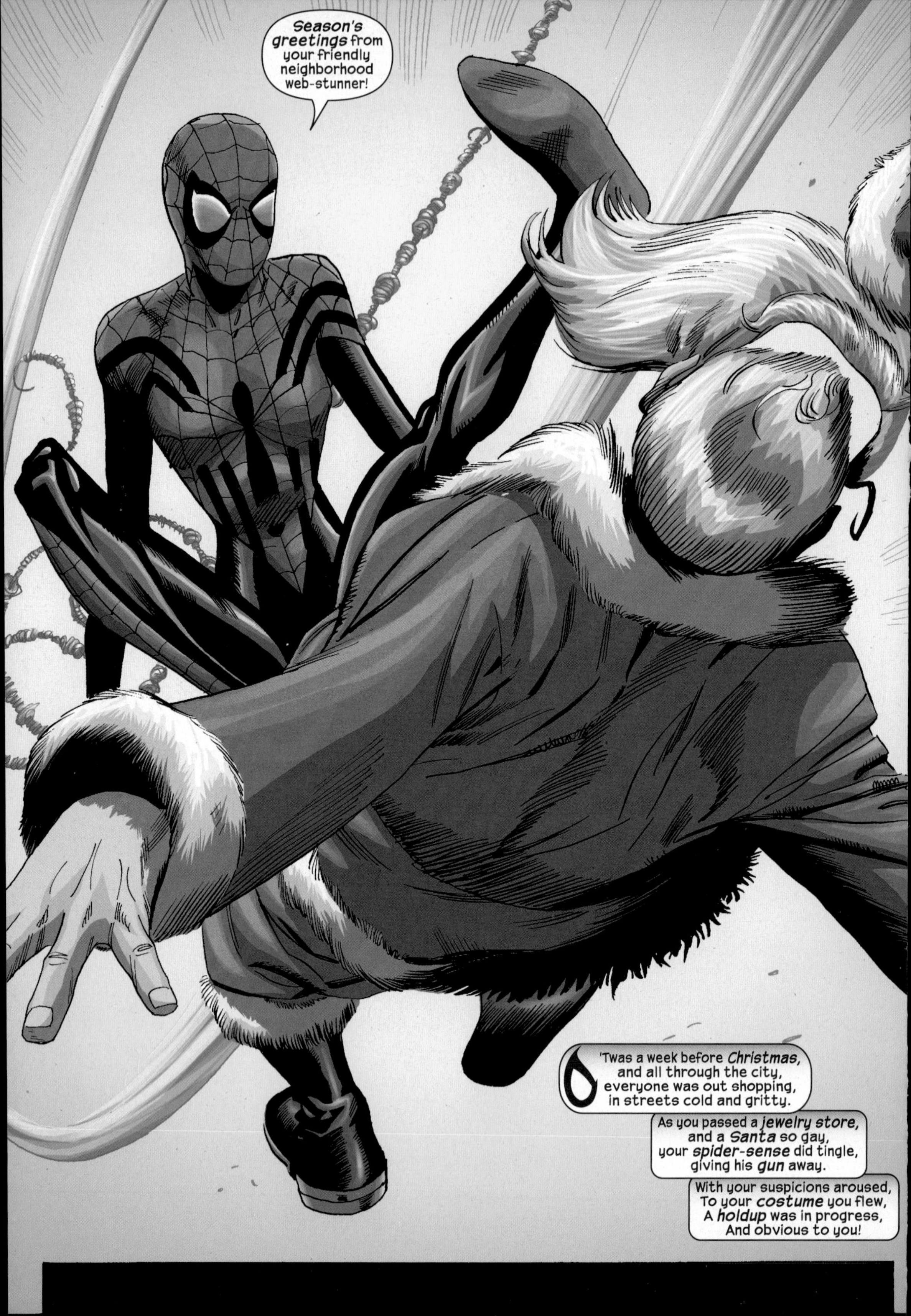
Season's greetings from your friendly neighborhood web-stunner!
'Twas a week before Christmas, and all through the city, everyone was out shopping, in streets cold and gritty.
As you passed a jewelry store, and a Santa so gay, your spider-sense did tingle, giving his gun away.
With your suspicions aroused, To your costume you flew, A holdup was in progress, And obvious to you!

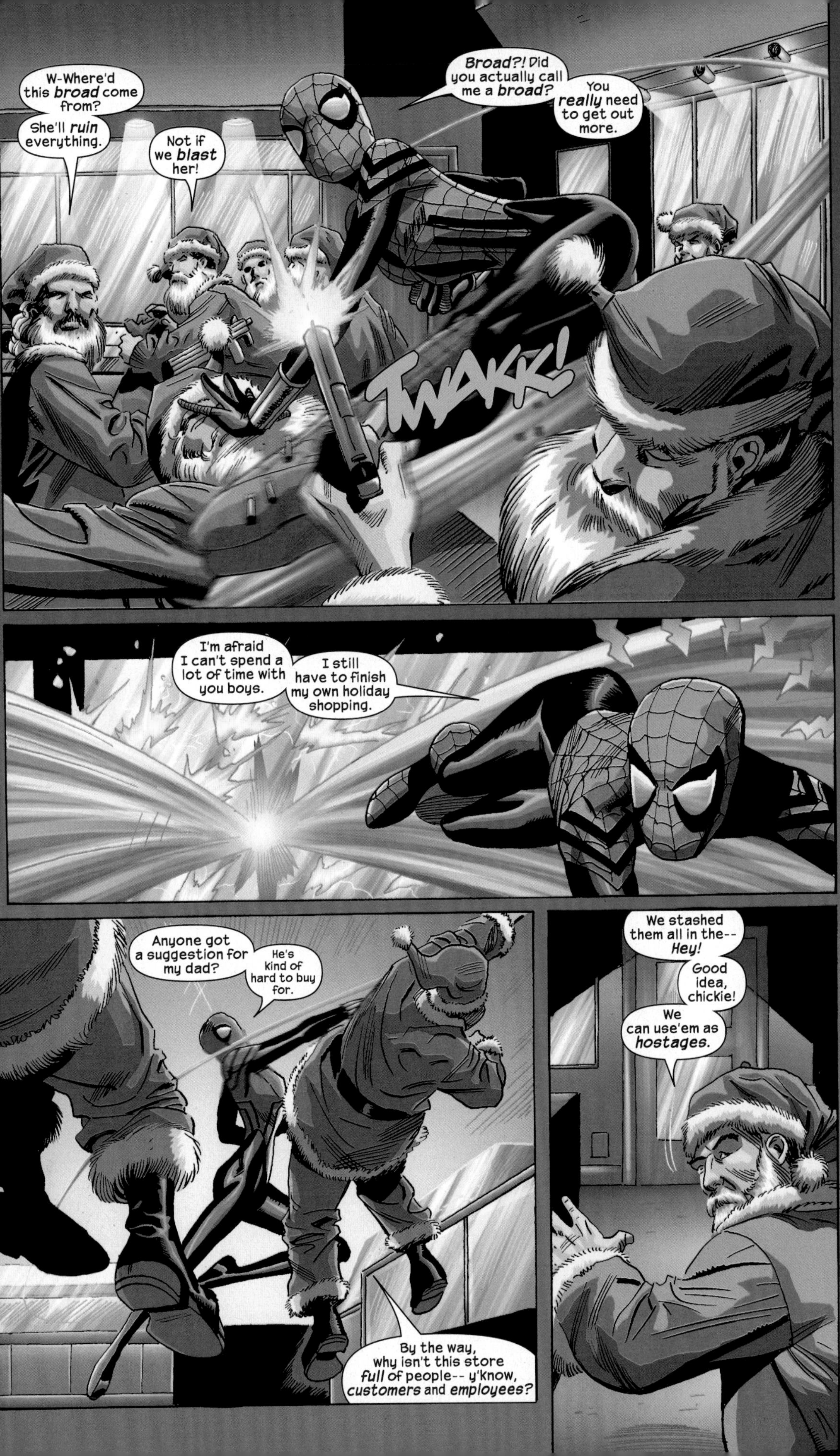
W-Where'd this broad come from?
She'll ruin everything.
Not if we blast her!
Broad?! Did you actually call me a broad?
You really need to get out more.
TWAKK!
I'm afraid I can't spend a lot of time with you boys.
I still have to finish my own holiday shopping.
Anyone got a suggestion for my dad?
He's kind of hard to buy for.
By the way, why isn't this store full of people-- y'know, customers and employees?
We stashed them all in the-- Hey!
Good idea, chickie!
We can use'em as hostages.

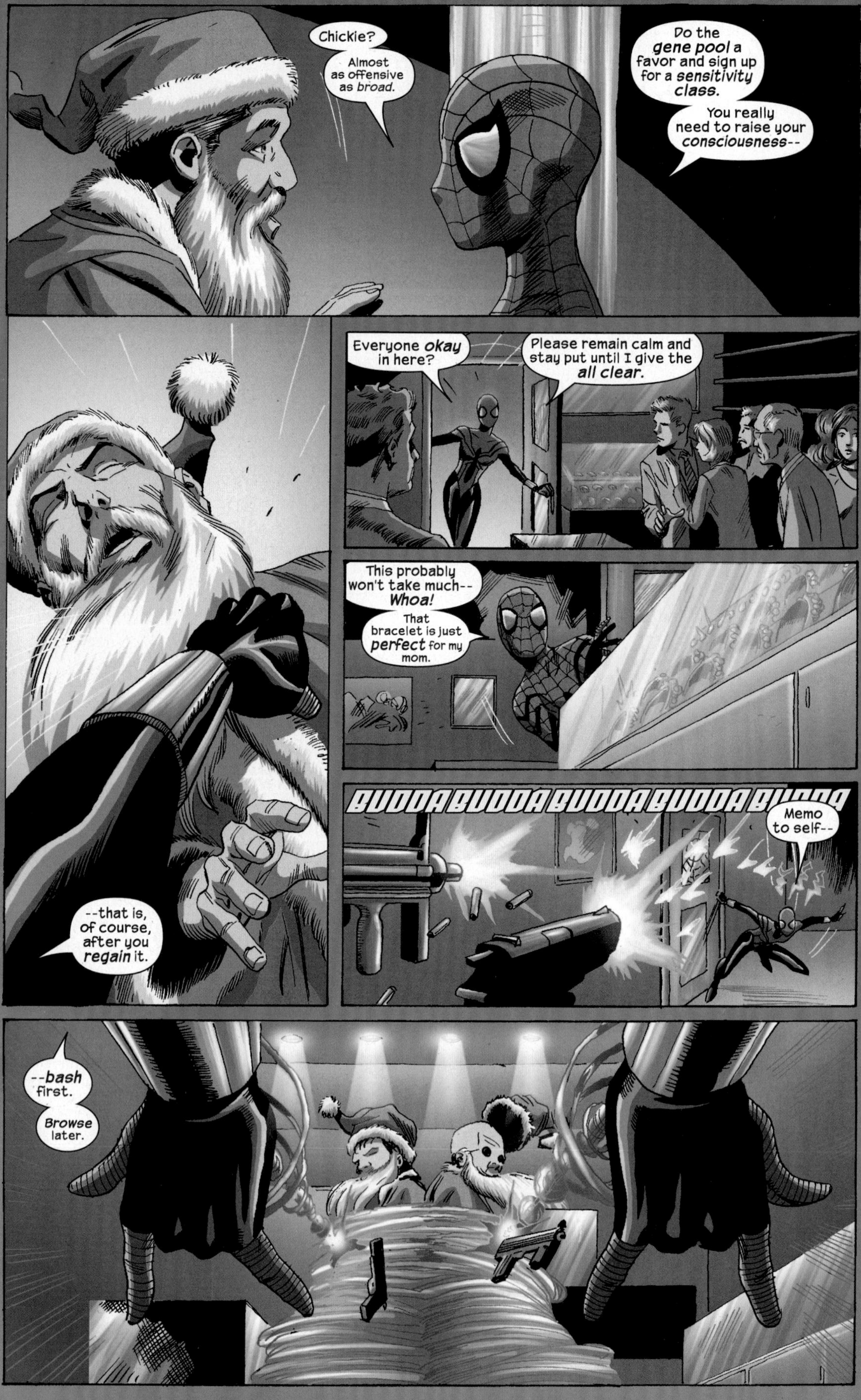
Chickie?
Almost as offensive as broad.
Do the gene pool a favor and sign up for a sensitivity class.
You really need to raise your consciousness--
--that is, of course, after you regain it.
Everyone okay in here?
Please remain calm and stay put until I give the all clear.
This probably won't take much-- Whoa!
That bracelet is just perfect for my mom.
BUDDA BUDDA BUDDA BUDDA BUDDA
Memo to self--
--bash first.
Browse later.

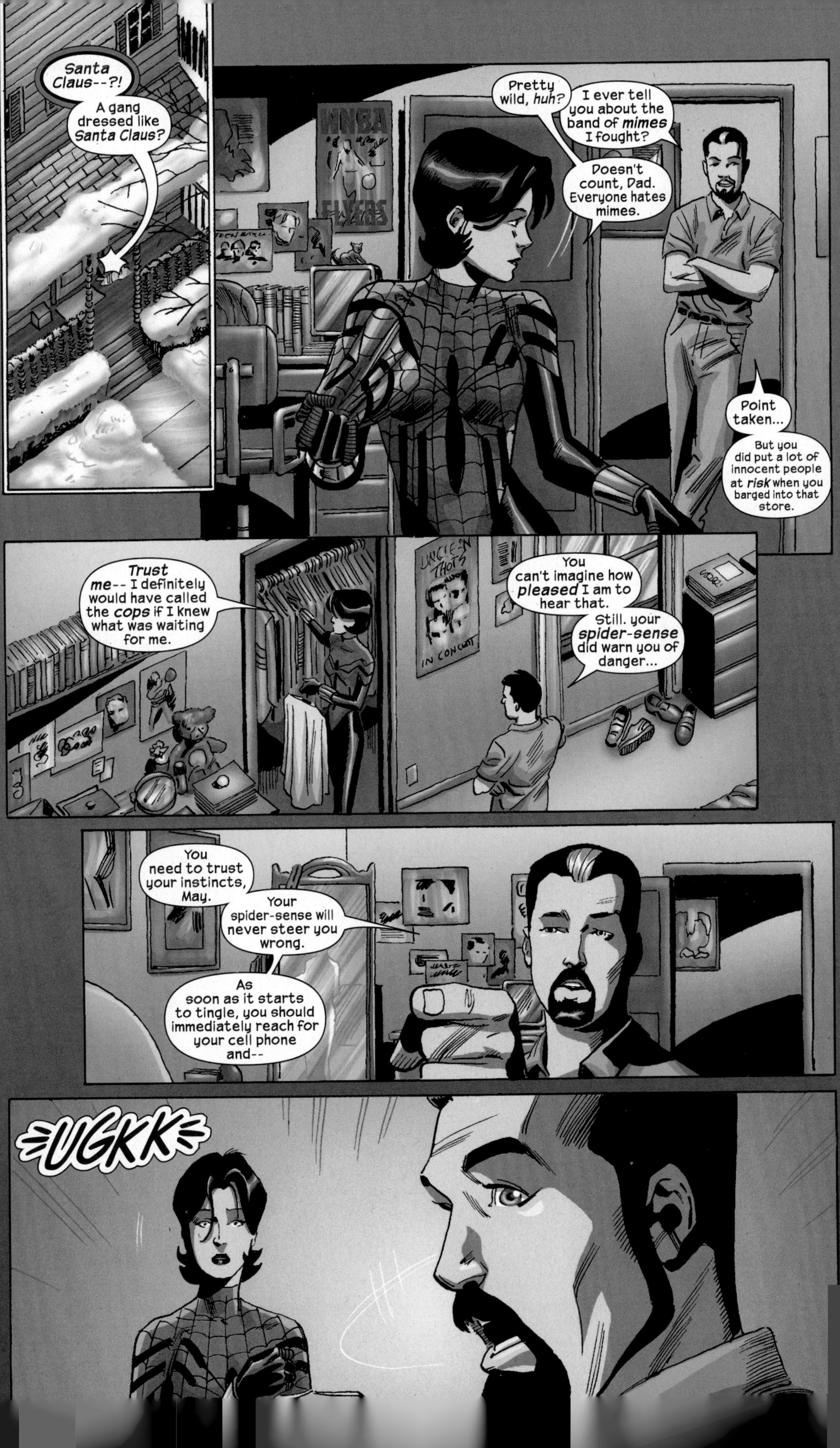
Santa Claus--?!
A gang dressed like Santa Claus?
Pretty wild, huh?
I ever tell you about the band of mimes I fought?
Doesn't count, Dad. Everyone hates mimes.
Point taken...
But you did put a lot of innocent people at risk when you barged into that store.
Trust me-- I definitely would have called the cops if I knew what was waiting for me.
You can't imagine how pleased I am to hear that.
Still, your spider-sense did warn you of danger...
You need to trust your instincts, May.
Your spider-sense will never steer you wrong.
As soon as it starts to tingle, you should immediately reach for your cell phone and--
UGKK

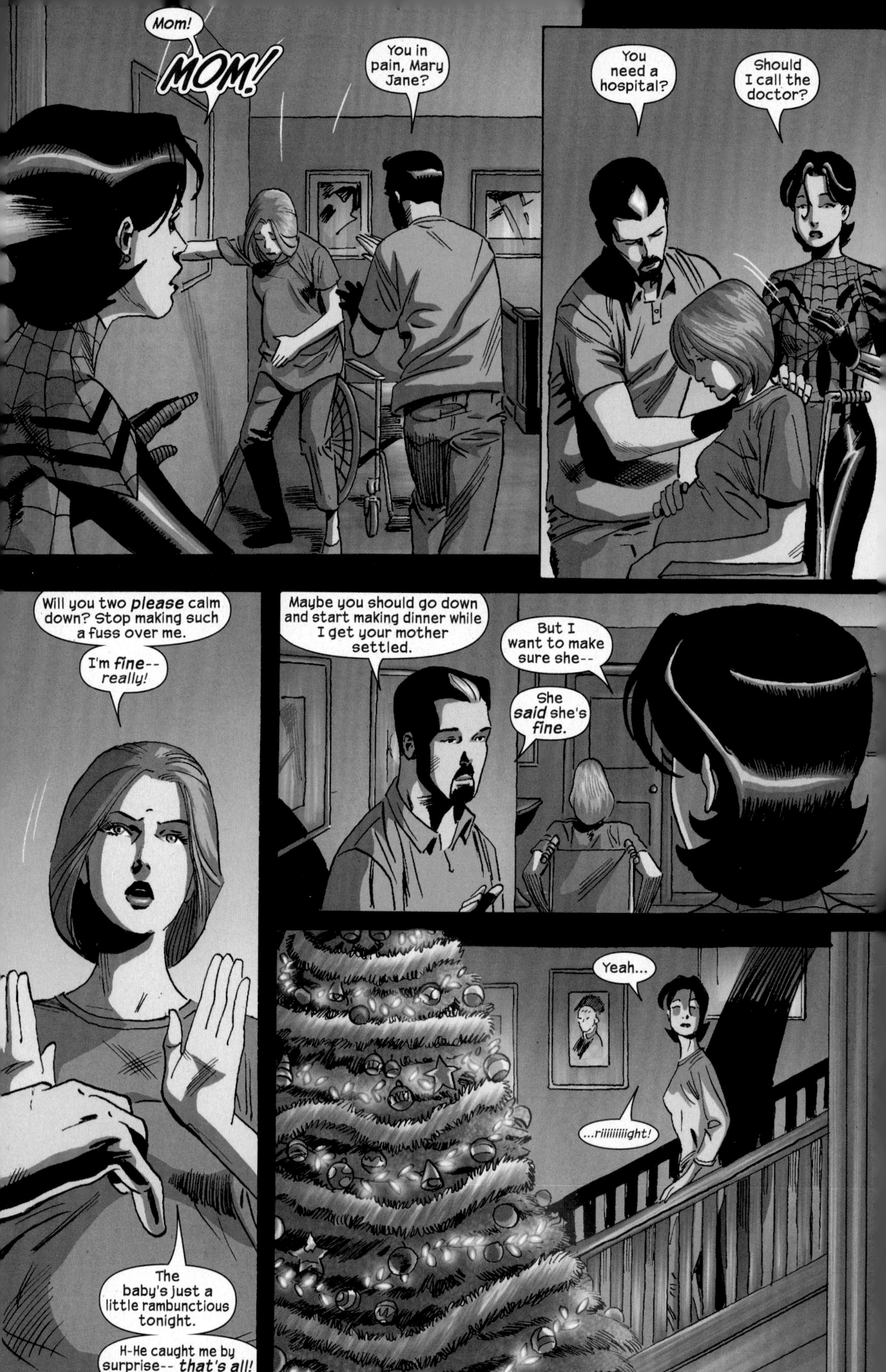
Mom!
MOM!
You in pain, Mary Jane?
You need a hospital?
Should I call the doctor?
Will you two please calm down? Stop making such a fuss over me.
I'm fine-- really!
The baby's just a little rambunctious tonight.
H-He caught me by surprise-- that's all!
Maybe you should go down and start making dinner while I get your mother settled.
But I want to make sure she--
She said she's fine.
Yeah...
...riiiiiiiight!

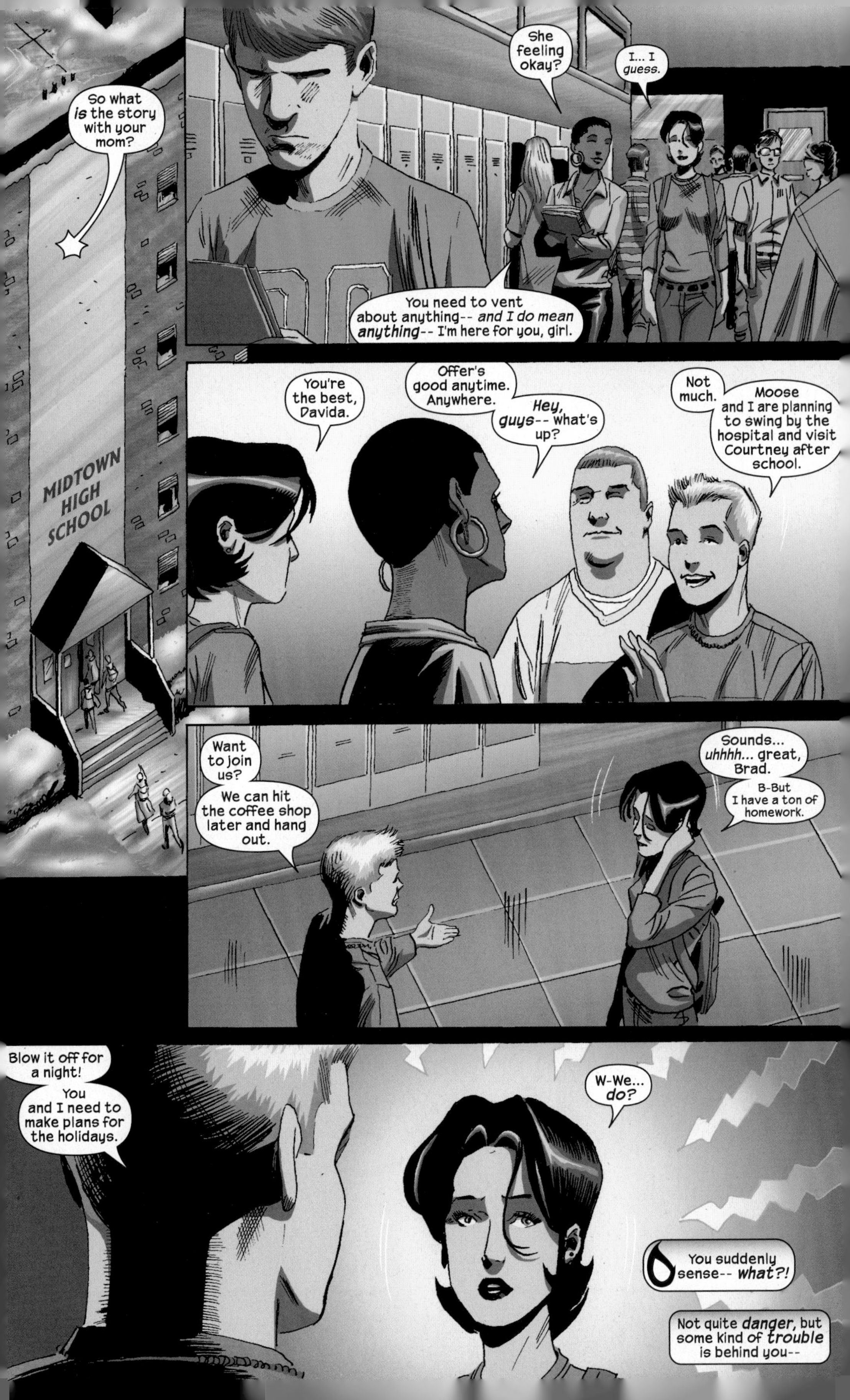

So what *is* the story with your mom?
She feeling okay?
I... I guess.
You need to vent about anything-- *and I do mean anything*-- I'm here for you, girl.
MIDTOWN HIGH SCHOOL
You're the best, Davida.
Offer's good anytime. Anywhere.
Hey, guys-- what's up?
Not much.
Moose and I are planning to swing by the hospital and visit Courtney after school.
Want to join us?
We can hit the coffee shop later and hang out.
Sounds... *uhhhh*... great, Brad.
B-But I have a ton of homework.
Blow it off for a night!
You and I need to make plans for the holidays.
W-We... *do?*
You suddenly sense-- *what?!*
Not quite *danger*, but some kind of *trouble* is behind you--

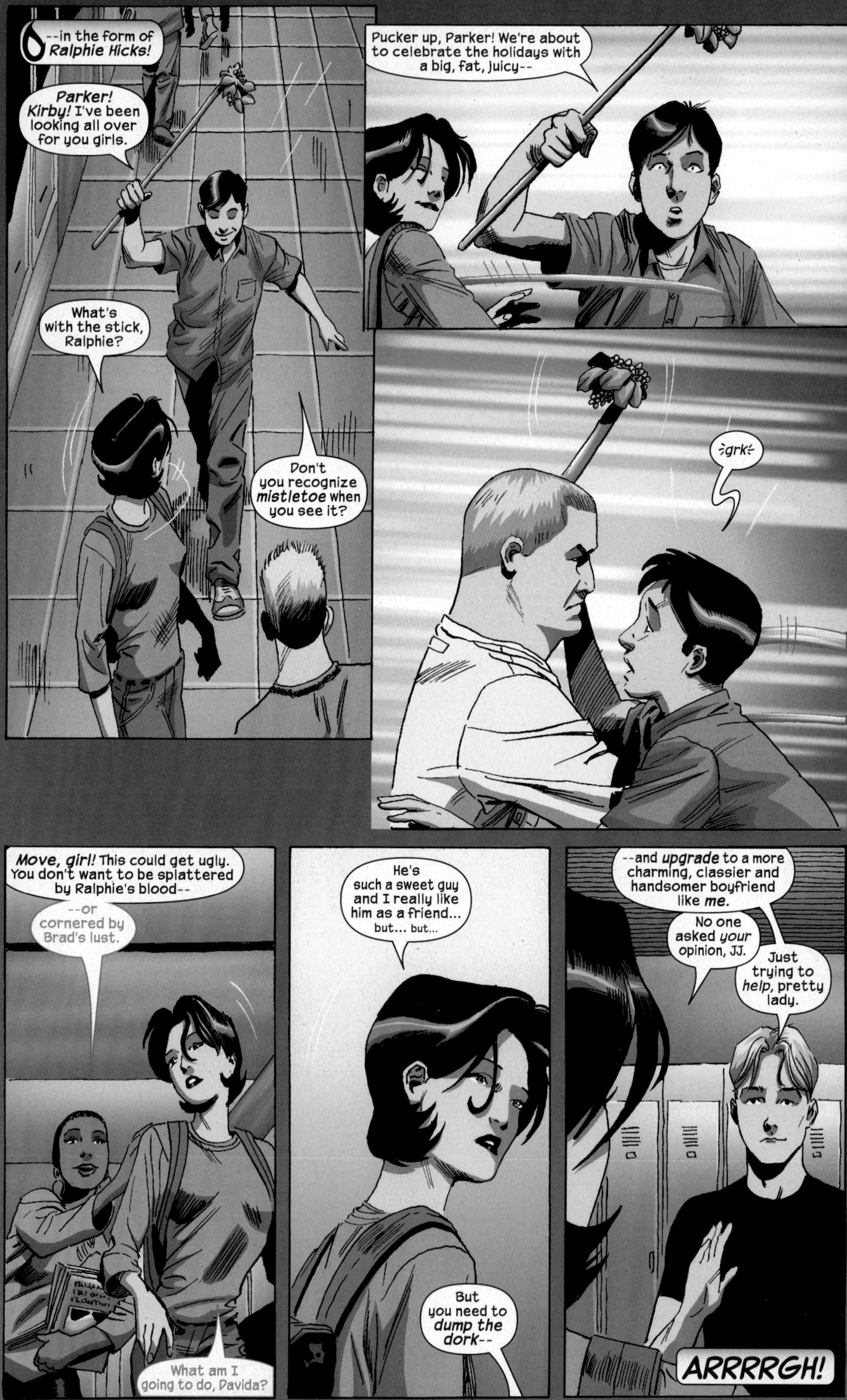
--in the form of Ralphie Hicks!
Parker! Kirby! I've been looking all over for you girls.
What's with the stick, Ralphie?
Don't you recognize mistletoe when you see it?
Pucker up, Parker! We're about to celebrate the holidays with a big, fat, juicy--
grk
Move, girl! This could get ugly. You don't want to be splattered by Ralphie's blood--
--or cornered by Brad's lust.
What am I going to do, Davida?
He's such a sweet guy and I really like him as a friend... but... but...
But you need to dump the dork--
--and upgrade to a more charming, classier and handsomer boyfriend like me.
No one asked your opinion, JJ.
Just trying to help, pretty lady.
ARRRRGH!

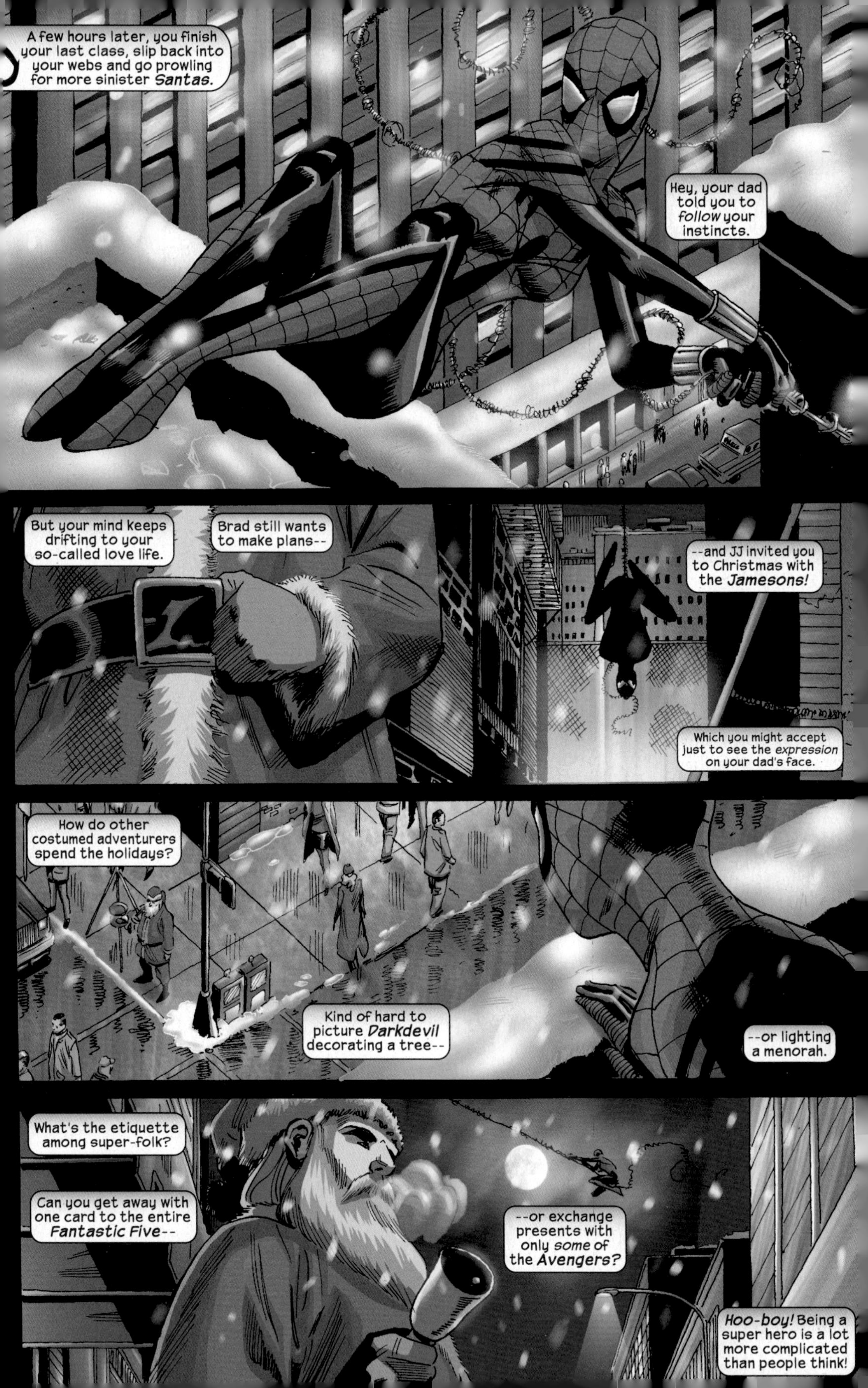

A few hours later, you finish your last class, slip back into your webs and go prowling for more sinister *Santas*.
Hey, your dad told you to *follow* your instincts.
But your mind keeps drifting to your so-called love life.
Brad still wants to make plans--
--and JJ invited you to Christmas with the *Jamesons!*
Which you might accept just to see the *expression* on your dad's face.
How do other costumed adventurers spend the holidays?
Kind of hard to picture *Darkdevil* decorating a tree--
--or lighting a menorah.
What's the etiquette among super-folk?
Can you get away with one card to the entire *Fantastic Five*--
--or exchange presents with only *some* of the *Avengers?*
Hoo-boy! Being a super hero is a lot more complicated than people think!

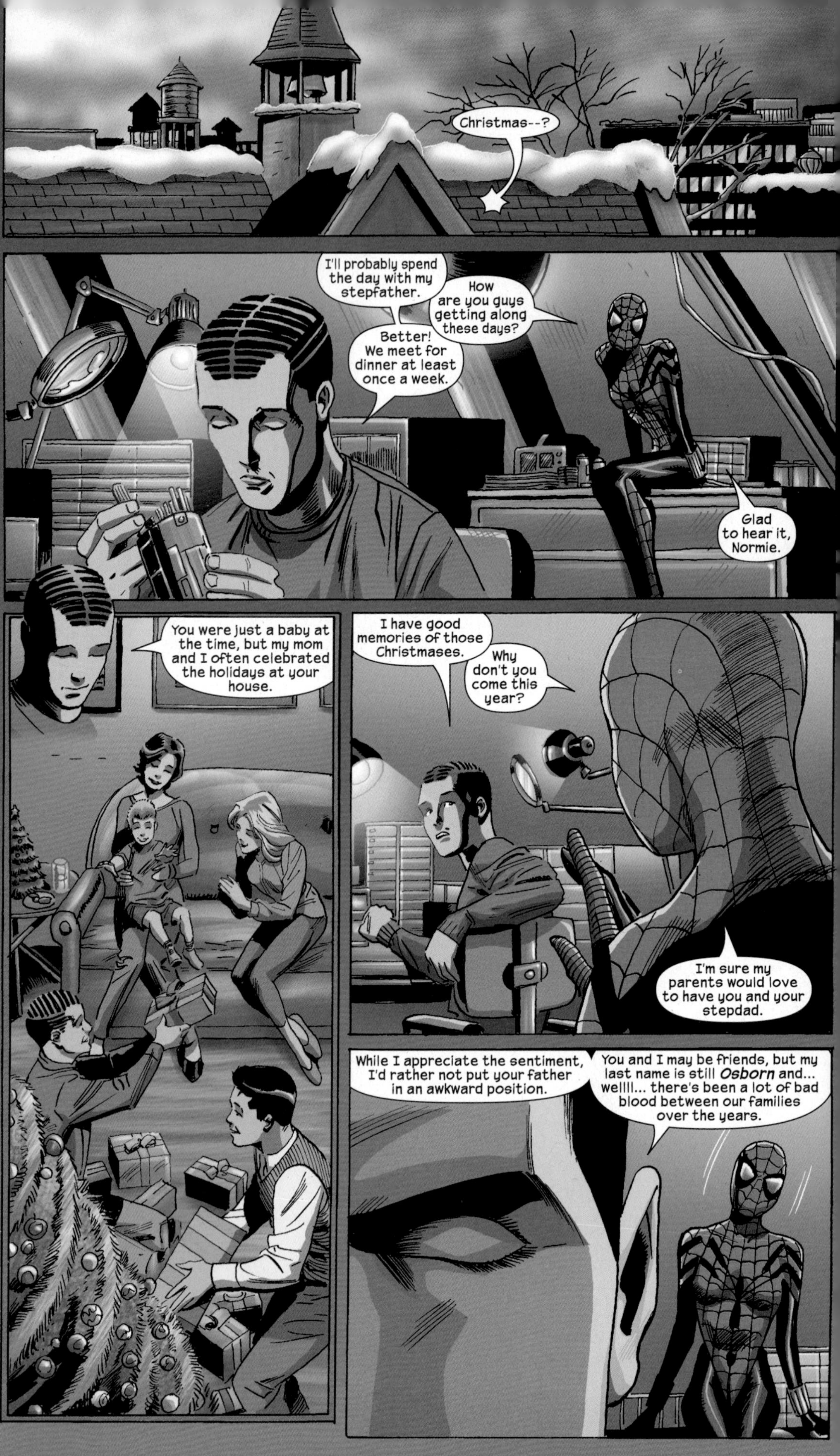
Christmas--?
I'll probably spend the day with my stepfather.
How are you guys getting along these days?
Better! We meet for dinner at least once a week.
Glad to hear it, Normie.
You were just a baby at the time, but my mom and I often celebrated the holidays at your house.
I have good memories of those Christmases.
Why don't you come this year?
I'm sure my parents would love to have you and your stepdad.
While I appreciate the sentiment, I'd rather not put your father in an awkward position.
You and I may be friends, but my last name is still *Osborn* and... wellll... there's been a lot of bad blood between our families over the years.

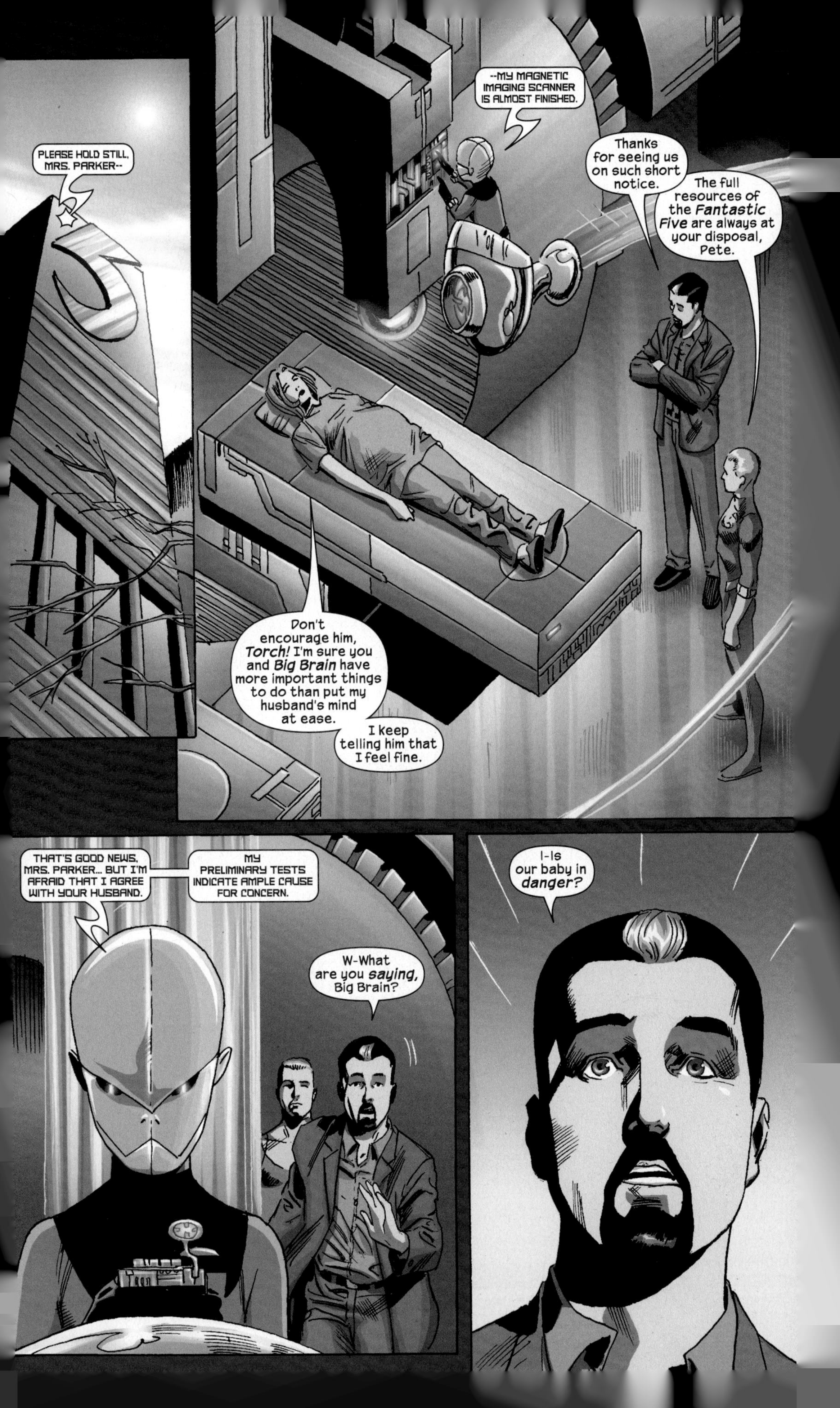
PLEASE HOLD STILL, MRS. PARKER--
--MY MAGNETIC IMAGING SCANNER IS ALMOST FINISHED.
Thanks for seeing us on such short notice.
The full resources of the Fantastic Five are always at your disposal, Pete.
Don't encourage him, Torch! I'm sure you and Big Brain have more important things to do than put my husband's mind at ease.
I keep telling him that I feel fine.
THAT'S GOOD NEWS, MRS. PARKER... BUT I'M AFRAID THAT I AGREE WITH YOUR HUSBAND.
MY PRELIMINARY TESTS INDICATE AMPLE CAUSE FOR CONCERN.
W-What are you saying, Big Brain?
I-Is our baby in danger?

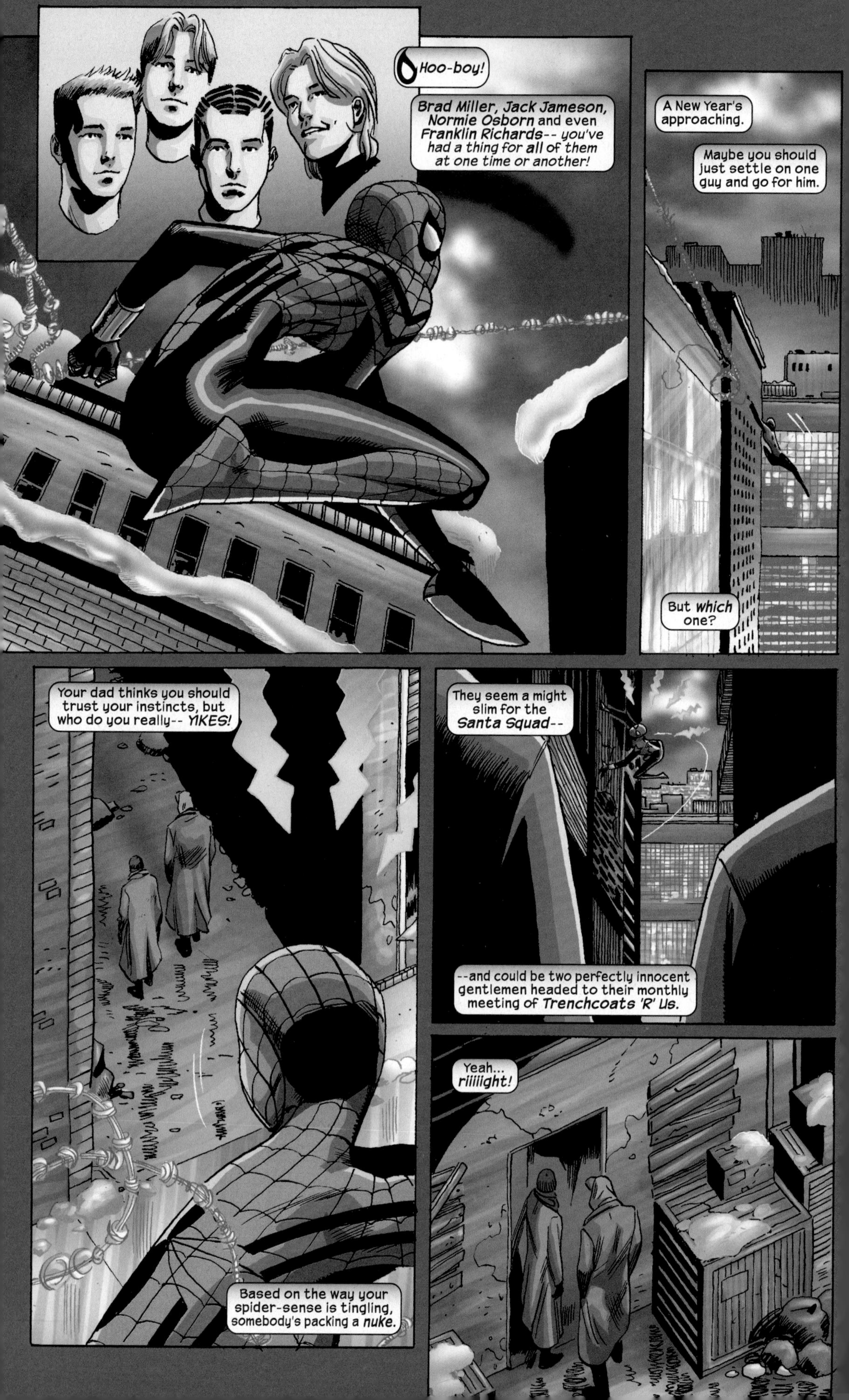

Hoo-boy!
Brad Miller, Jack Jameson, Normie Osborn and even Franklin Richards-- you've had a thing for all of them at one time or another!
A New Year's approaching.
Maybe you should just settle on one guy and go for him.
But which one?
Your dad thinks you should trust your instincts, but who do you really-- YIKES!
Based on the way your spider-sense is tingling, somebody's packing a nuke.
They seem a might slim for the Santa Squad--
--and could be two perfectly innocent gentlemen headed to their monthly meeting of Trenchcoats 'R' Us.
Yeah... riiiiight!

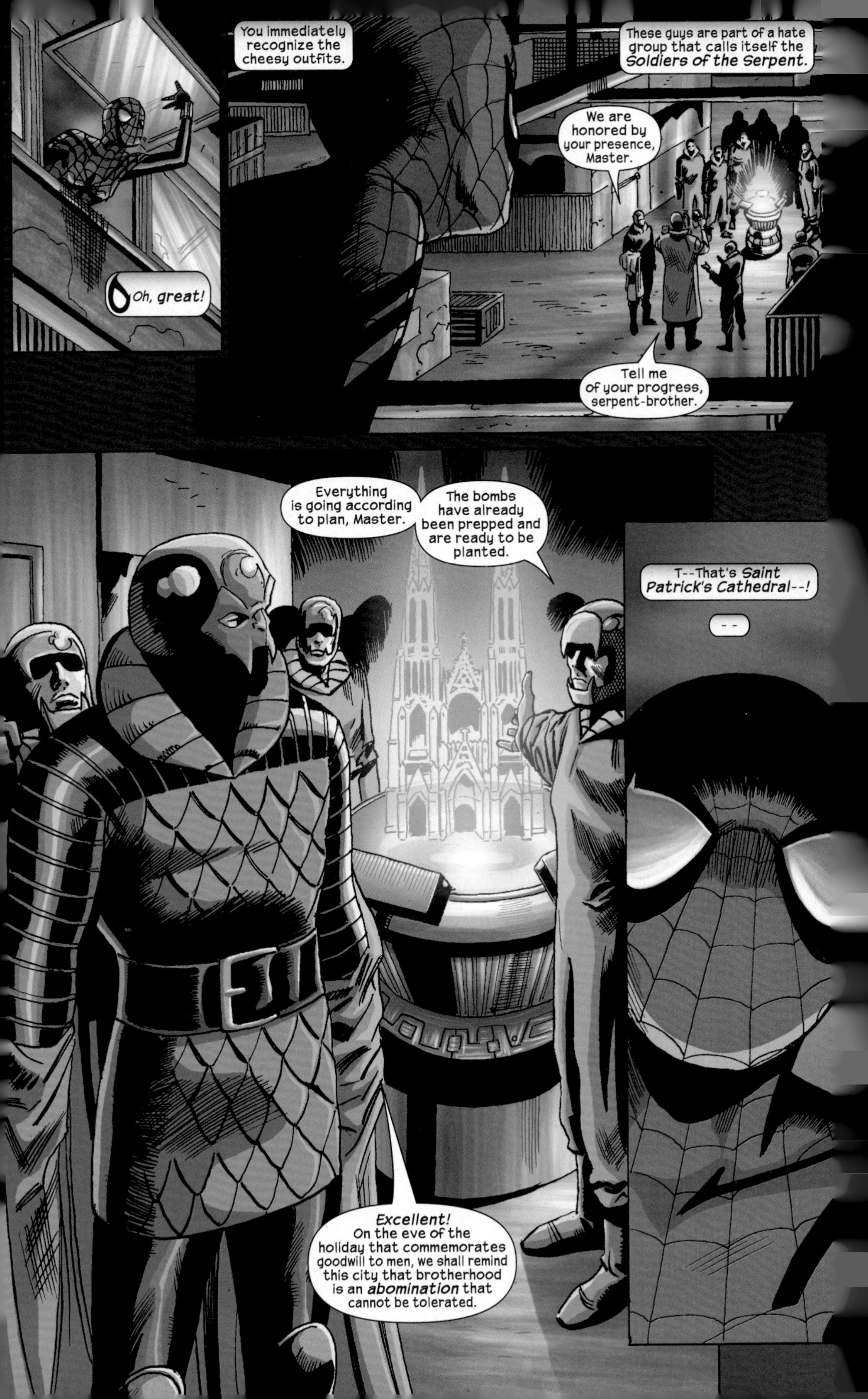
Oh, great!
You immediately recognize the cheesy outfits.
These guys are part of a hate group that calls itself the *Soldiers of the Serpent.*
We are honored by your presence, Master.
Tell me of your progress, serpent-brother.
Everything is going according to plan, Master.
The bombs have already been prepped and are ready to be planted.
T--That's *Saint Patrick's Cathedral*--!
--
Excellent! On the eve of the holiday that commemorates goodwill to men, we shall remind this city that brotherhood is an *abomination* that cannot be tolerated.

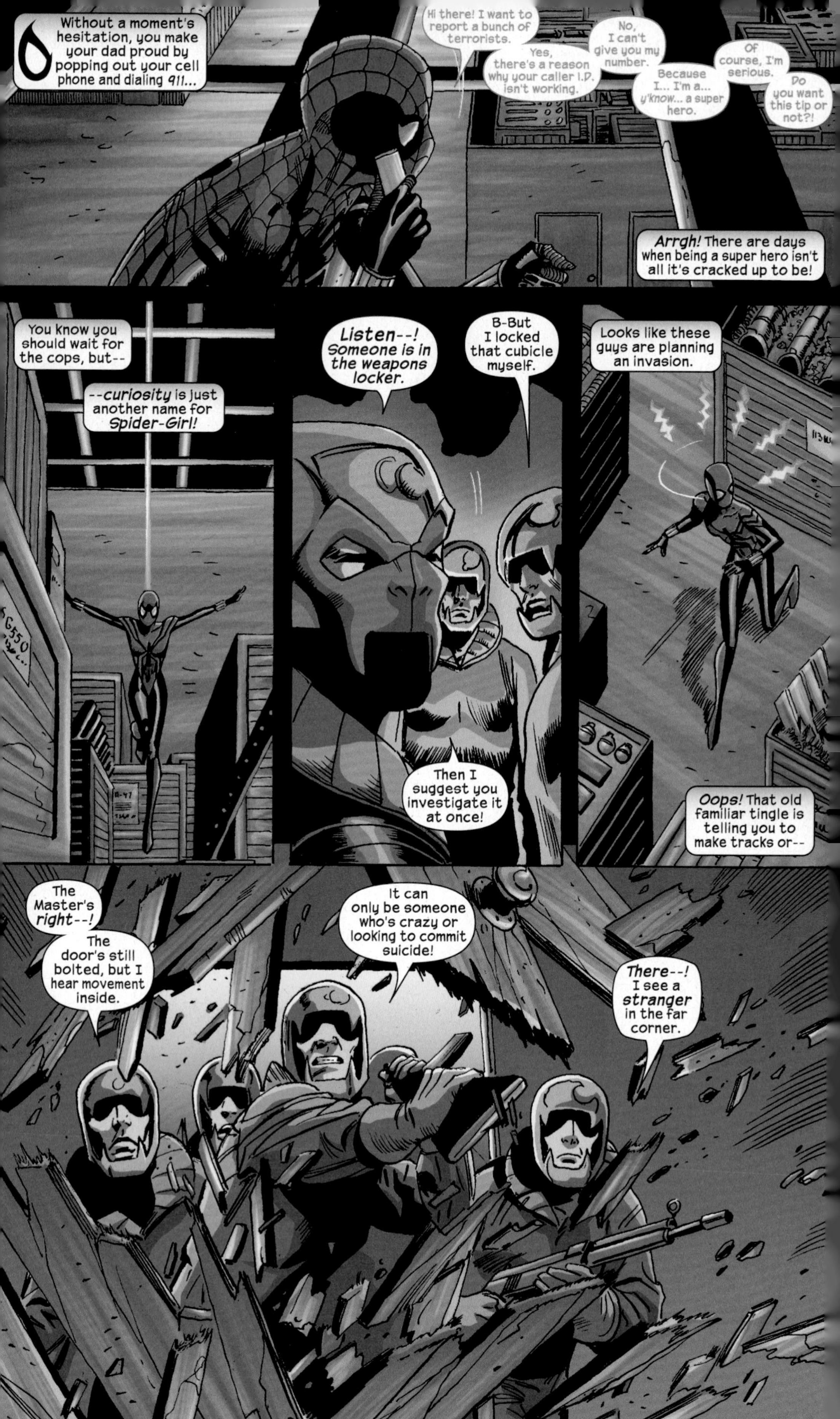

Without a moment's hesitation, you make your dad proud by popping out your cell phone and dialing 911...
Hi there! I want to report a bunch of terrorists.
Yes, there's a reason why your caller I.D. isn't working.
No, I can't give you my number.
Because I... I'm a... y'know... a super hero.
Of course, I'm serious.
Do you want this tip or not?!
Arrgh! There are days when being a super hero isn't all it's cracked up to be!
You know you should wait for the cops, but--
--curiosity is just another name for Spider-Girl!
Listen--! Someone is in the weapons locker.
B-But I locked that cubicle myself.
Then I suggest you investigate it at once!
Looks like these guys are planning an invasion.
Oops! That old familiar tingle is telling you to make tracks or--
The Master's right--!
The door's still bolted, but I hear movement inside.
It can only be someone who's crazy or looking to commit suicide!
There--! I see a stranger in the far corner.

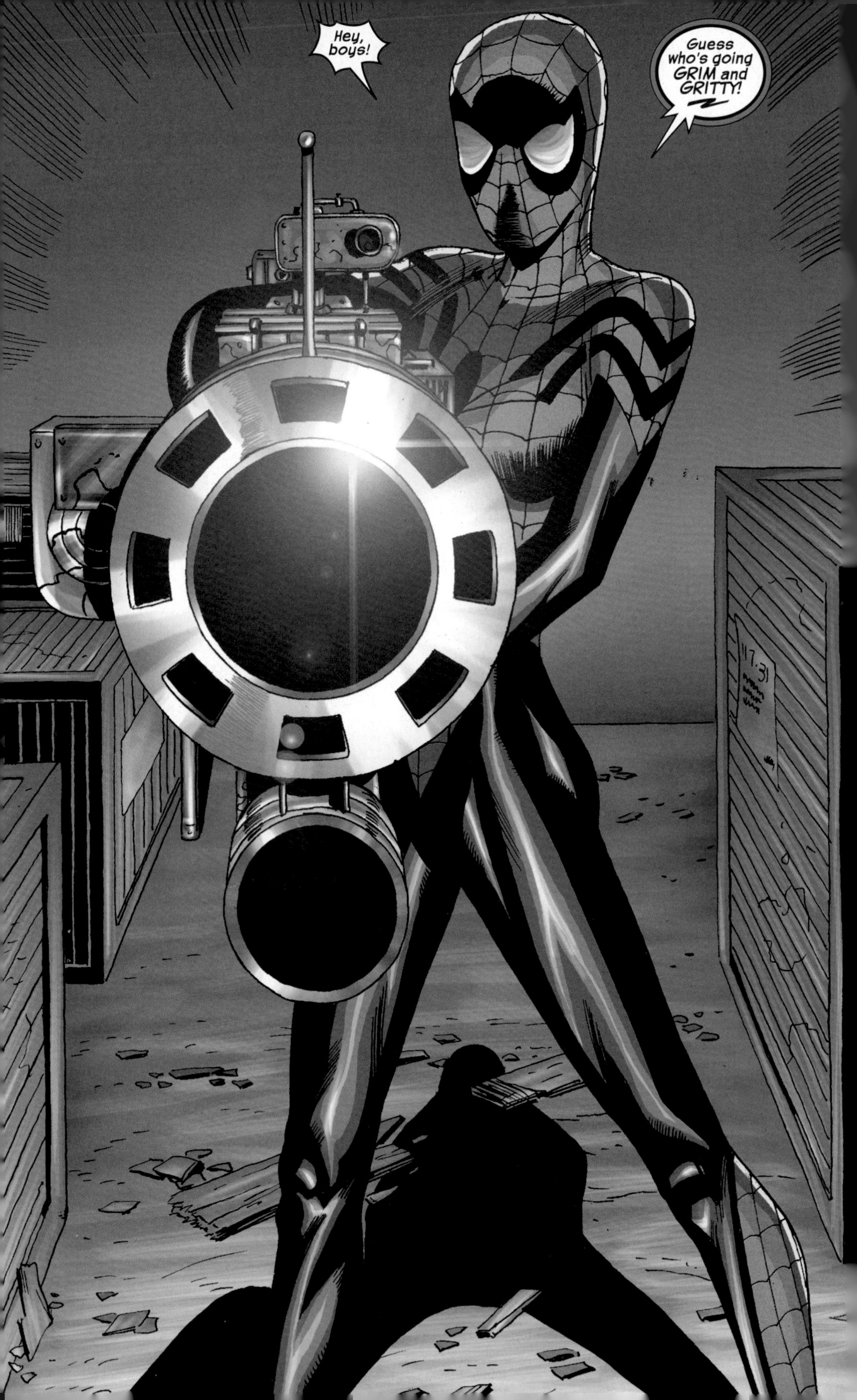
Hey, boys!
Guess who's going GRIM and GRITTY!

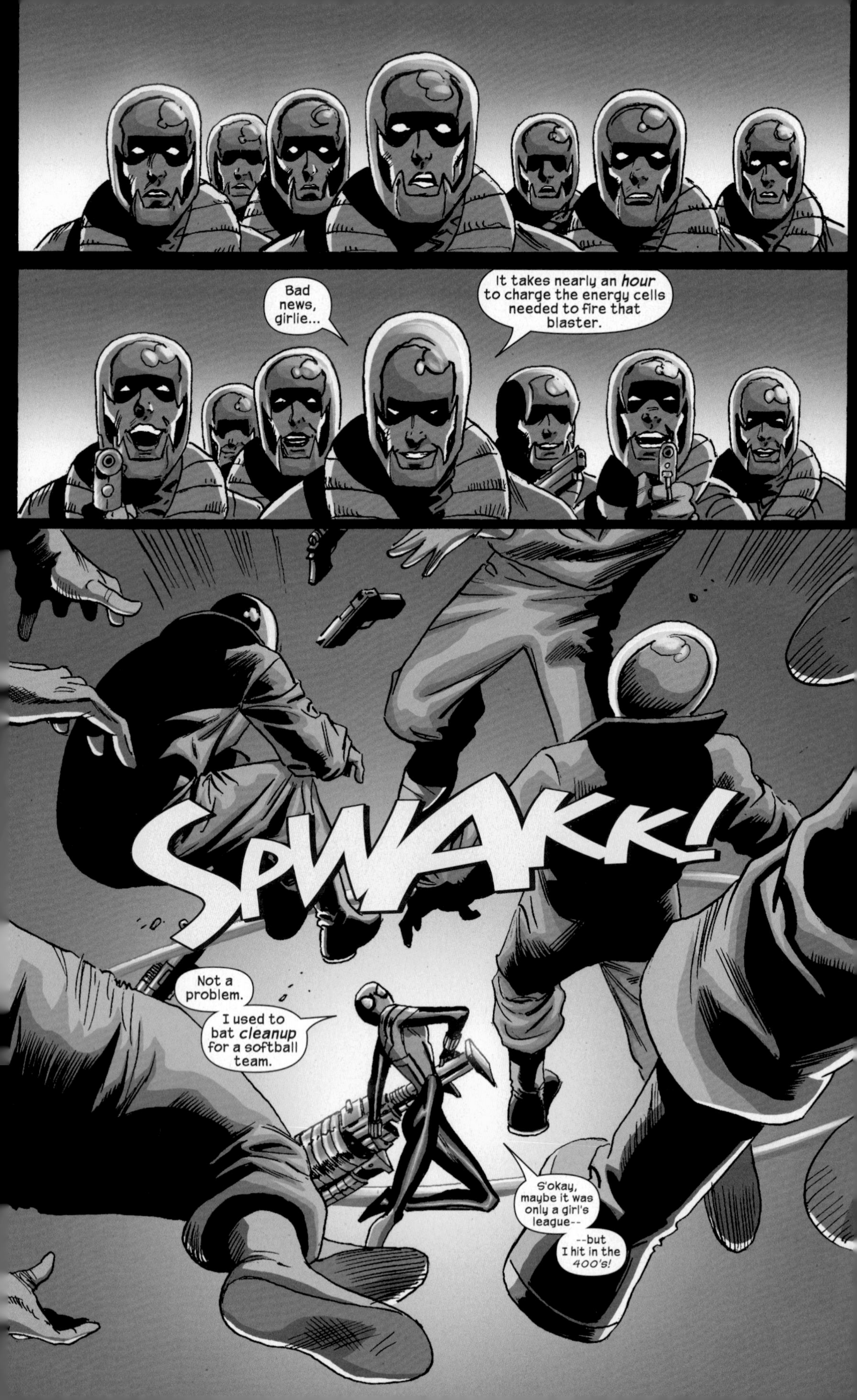
Bad news, girlie...
It takes nearly an *hour* to charge the energy cells needed to fire that blaster.
SPWAKK!
Not a problem.
I used to bat *cleanup* for a softball team.
S'okay, maybe it was only a girl's league--
--but I hit in the *400's*!

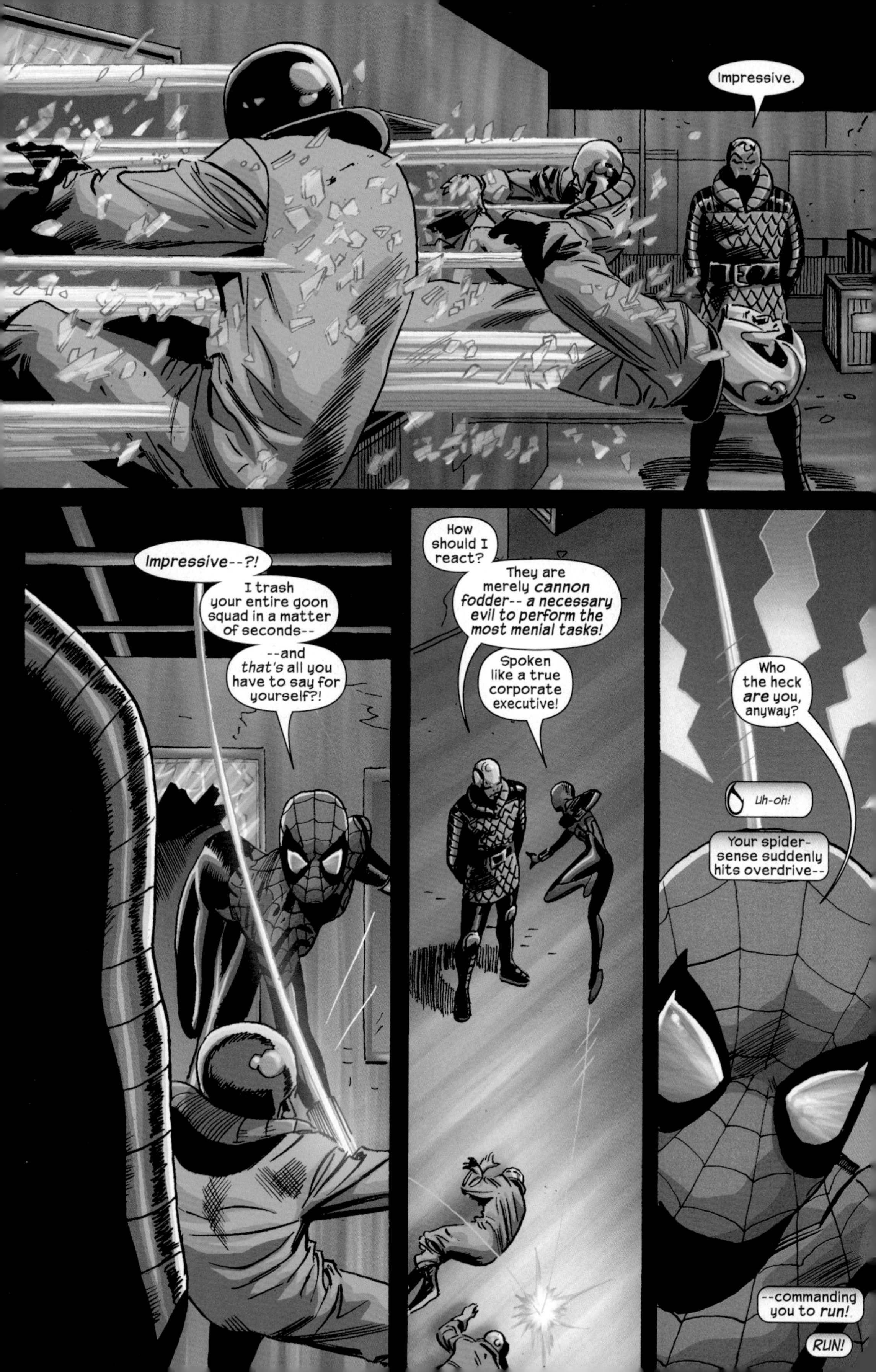
Impressive.
Impressive--?!
I trash your entire goon squad in a matter of seconds--
--and that's all you have to say for yourself?!
How should I react?
They are merely cannon fodder-- a necessary evil to perform the most menial tasks!
Spoken like a true corporate executive!
Who the heck are you, anyway?
Uh-oh!
Your spider-sense suddenly hits overdrive--
--commanding you to run!
RUN!

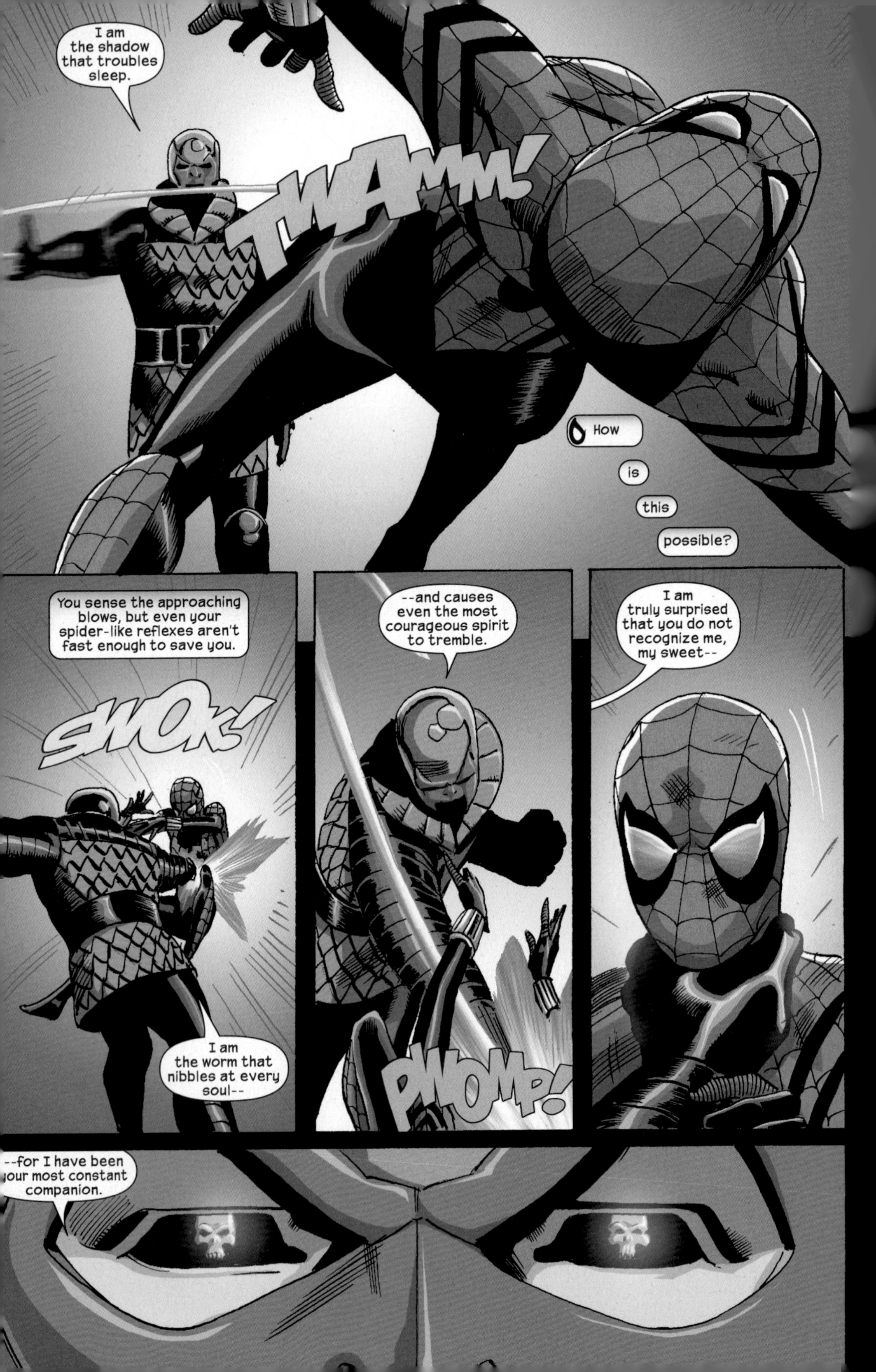

I am the shadow that troubles sleep.
THWAMM!
How
is
this
possible?
You sense the approaching blows, but even your spider-like reflexes aren't fast enough to save you.
SWOK!
I am the worm that nibbles at every soul--
--and causes even the most courageous spirit to tremble.
PHOMP!
I am truly surprised that you do not recognize me, my sweet--
--for I have been your most constant companion.

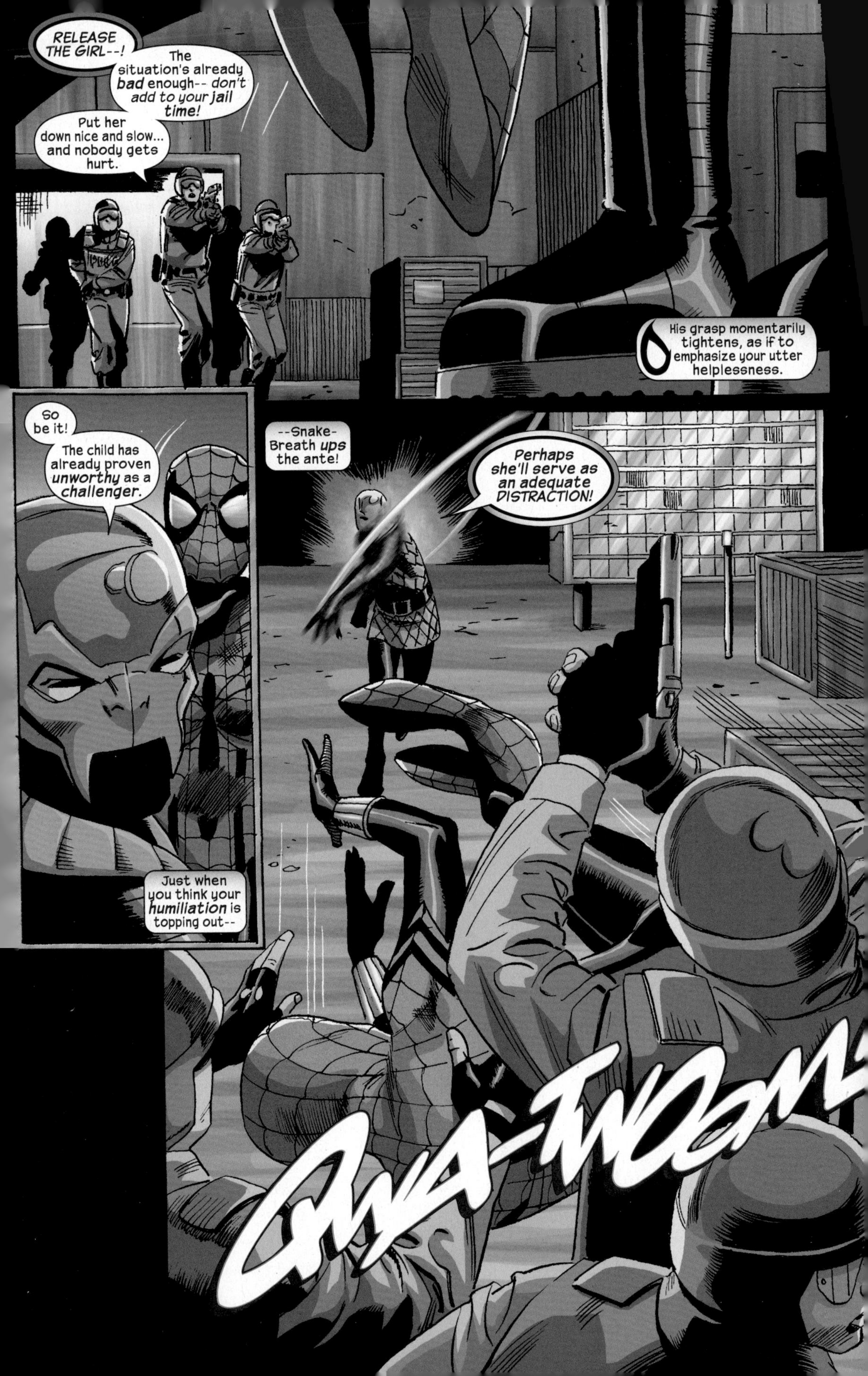
RELEASE THE GIRL--!
The situation's already bad enough-- don't add to your jail time!
Put her down nice and slow... and nobody gets hurt.
His grasp momentarily tightens, as if to emphasize your utter helplessness.
So be it!
The child has already proven unworthy as a challenger.
Just when you think your humiliation is topping out--
--Snake-Breath ups the ante!
Perhaps she'll serve as an adequate DISTRACTION!

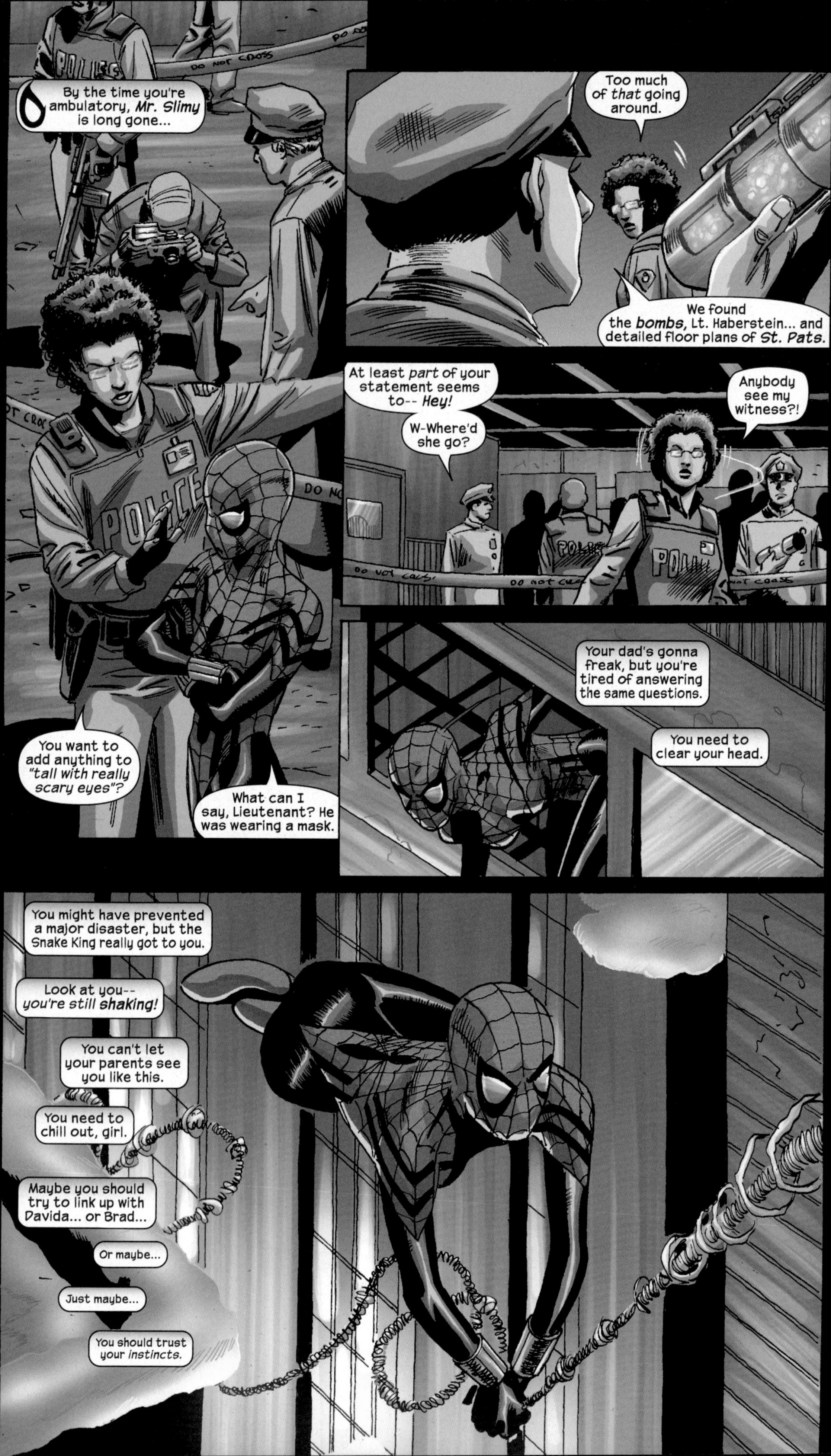

By the time you're ambulatory, Mr. Slimy is long gone...
POLICE
DO NOT CROSS
Too much of that going around.
We found the bombs, Lt. Haberstein... and detailed floor plans of St. Pats.
POLICE
You want to add anything to "tall with really scary eyes"?
What can I say, Lieutenant? He was wearing a mask.
At least part of your statement seems to-- Hey!
W-Where'd she go?
Anybody see my witness?!
POLICE
DO NOT CROSS
Your dad's gonna freak, but you're tired of answering the same questions.
You need to clear your head.
You might have prevented a major disaster, but the Snake King really got to you.
Look at you-- you're still shaking!
You can't let your parents see you like this.
You need to chill out, girl.
Maybe you should try to link up with Davida... or Brad...
Or maybe...
Just maybe...
You should trust your instincts.

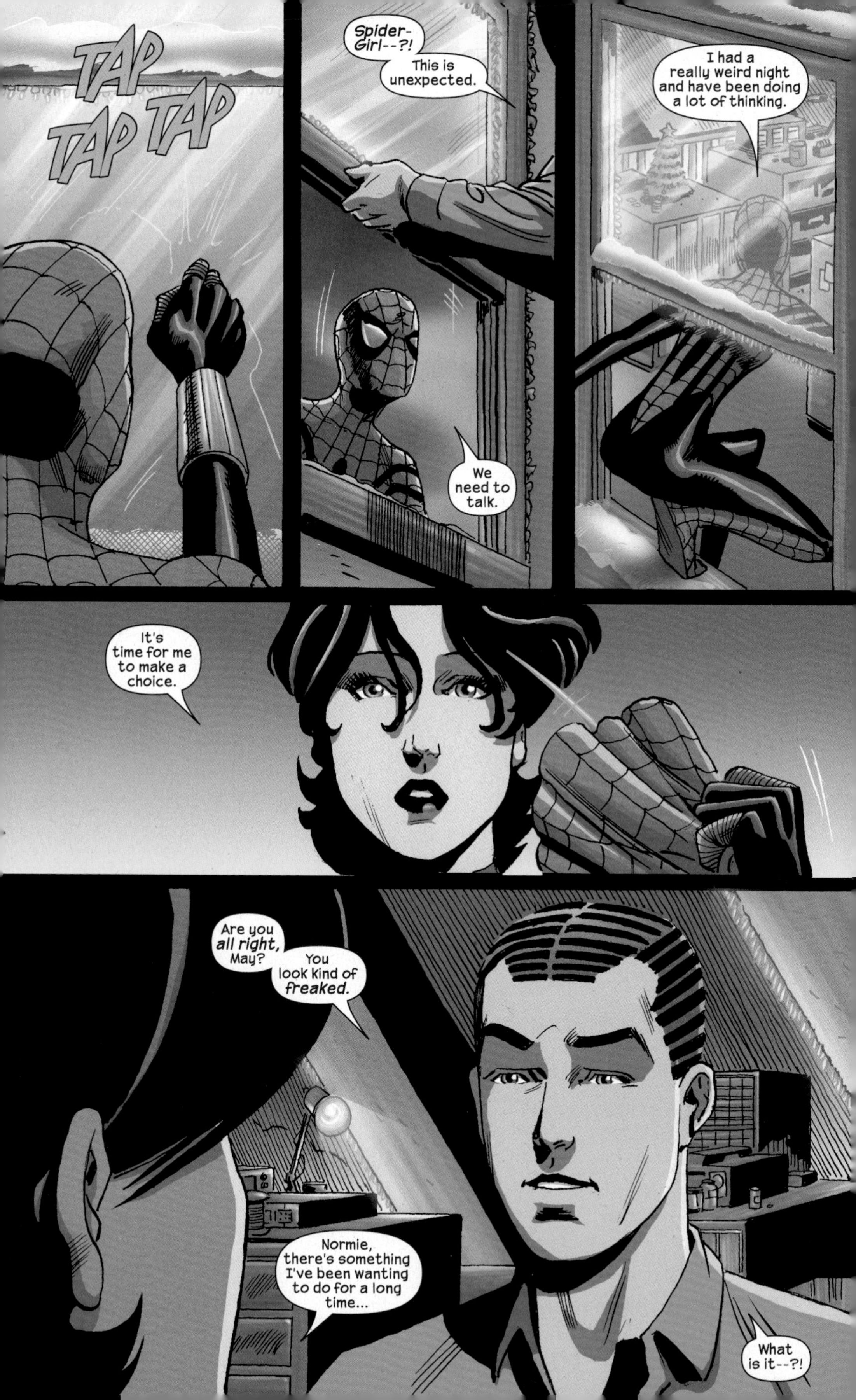
TAP TAP TAP
Spider-Girl--?!
This is unexpected.
We need to talk.
I had a really weird night and have been doing a lot of thinking.
It's time for me to make a choice.
Are you all right, May?
You look kind of freaked.
Normie, there's something I've been wanting to do for a long time...
What is it--?!

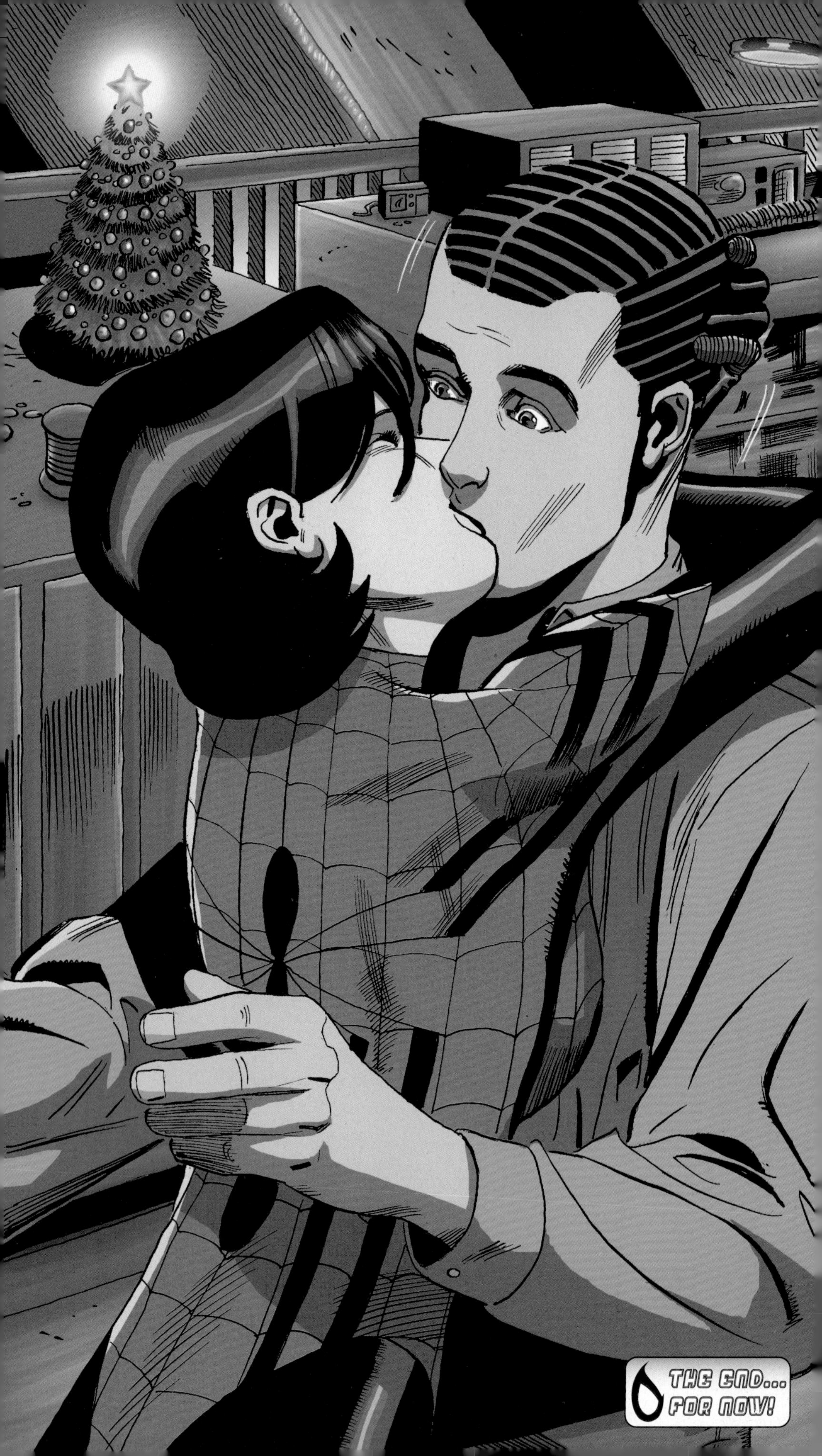
THE END... FOR NOW!

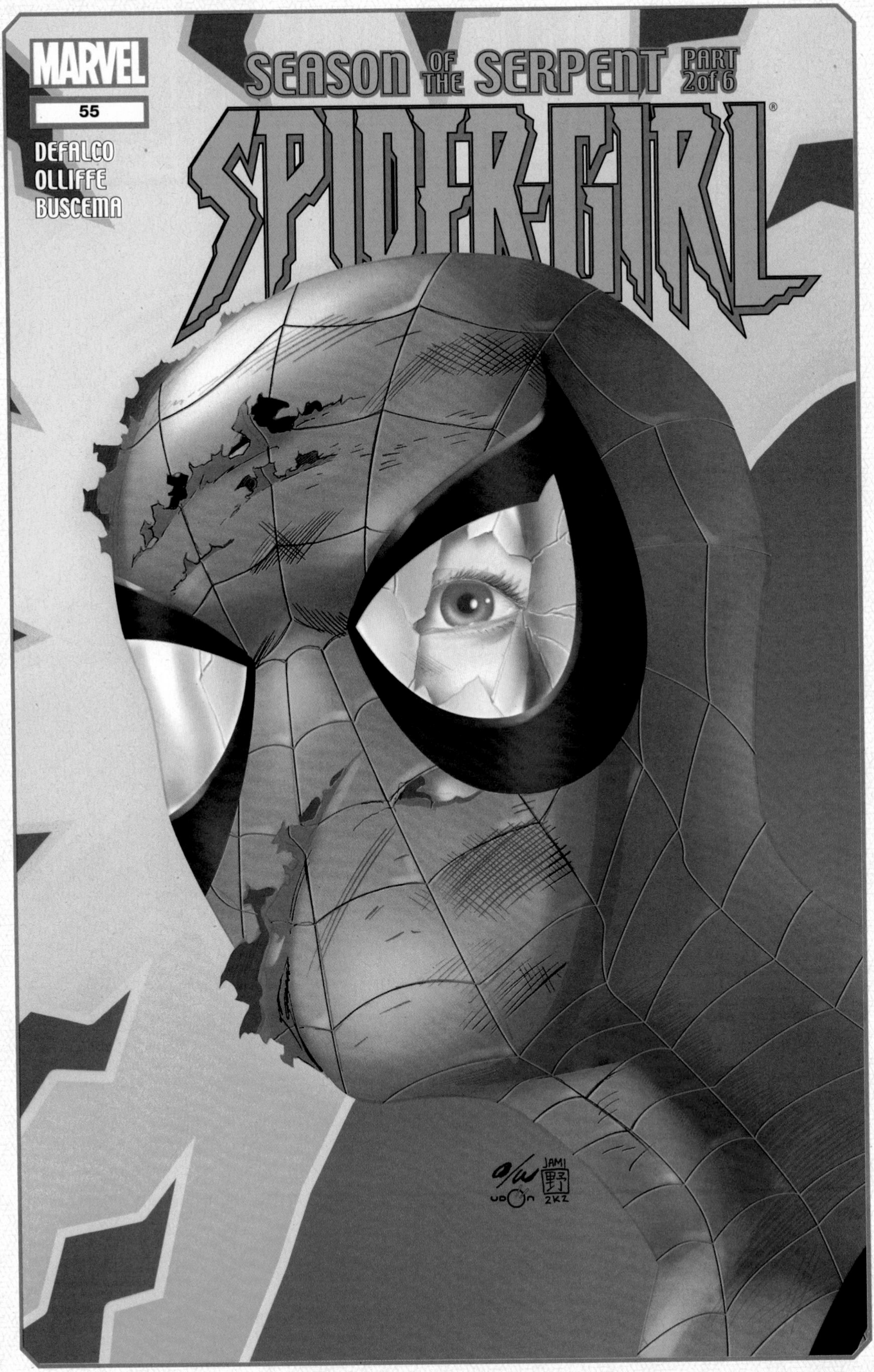

MARVEL
55
DEFALCO
OLLIFFE
BUSCEMA
SEASON OF THE SERPENT PART 2 of 6
SPIDER-GIRL®

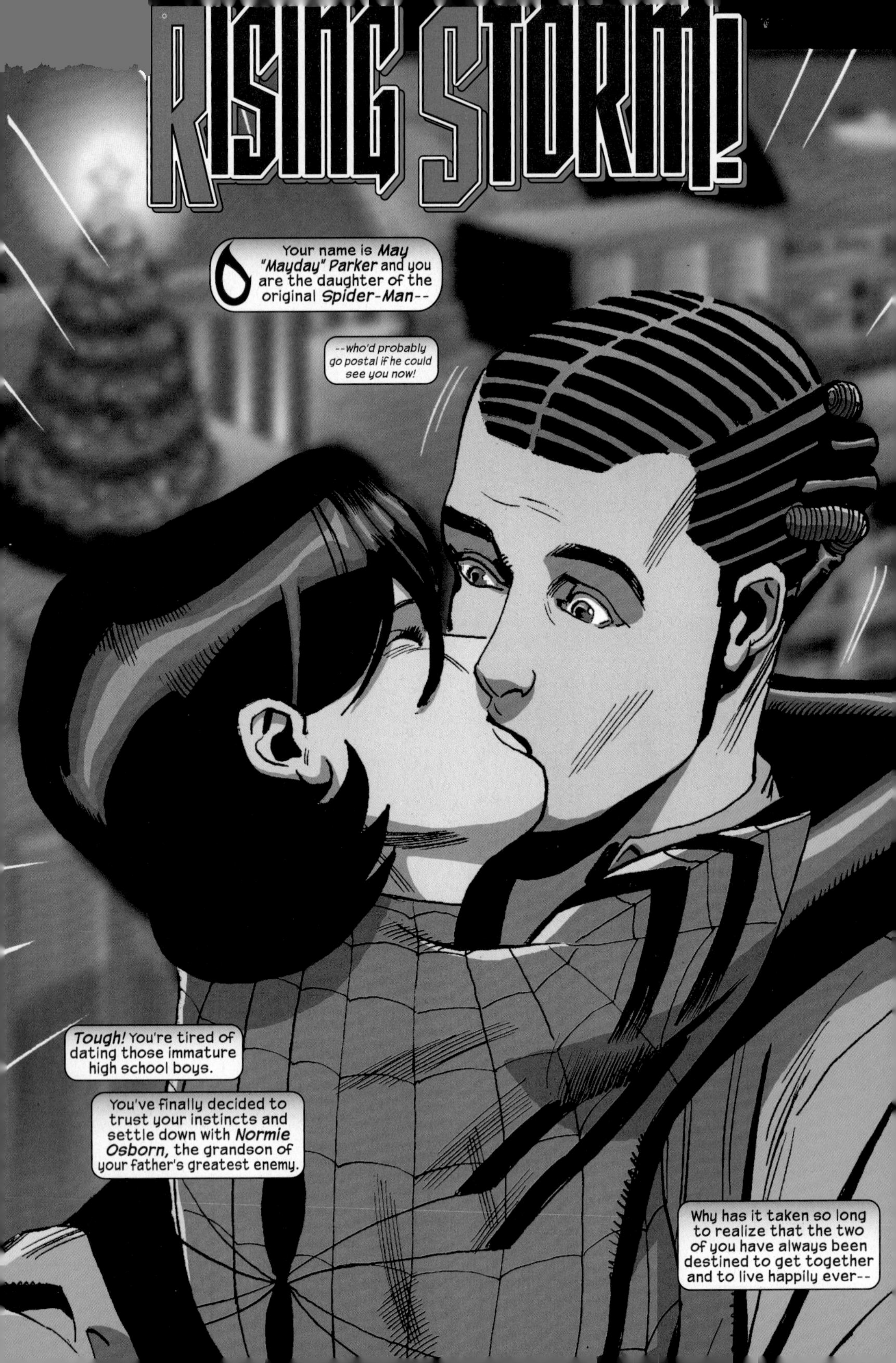
RISING STORM!
Your name is May "Mayday" Parker and you are the daughter of the original Spider-Man--
--who'd probably go postal if he could see you now!
Tough! You're tired of dating those immature high school boys.
You've finally decided to trust your instincts and settle down with Normie Osborn, the grandson of your father's greatest enemy.
Why has it taken so long to realize that the two of you have always been destined to get together and to live happily ever--

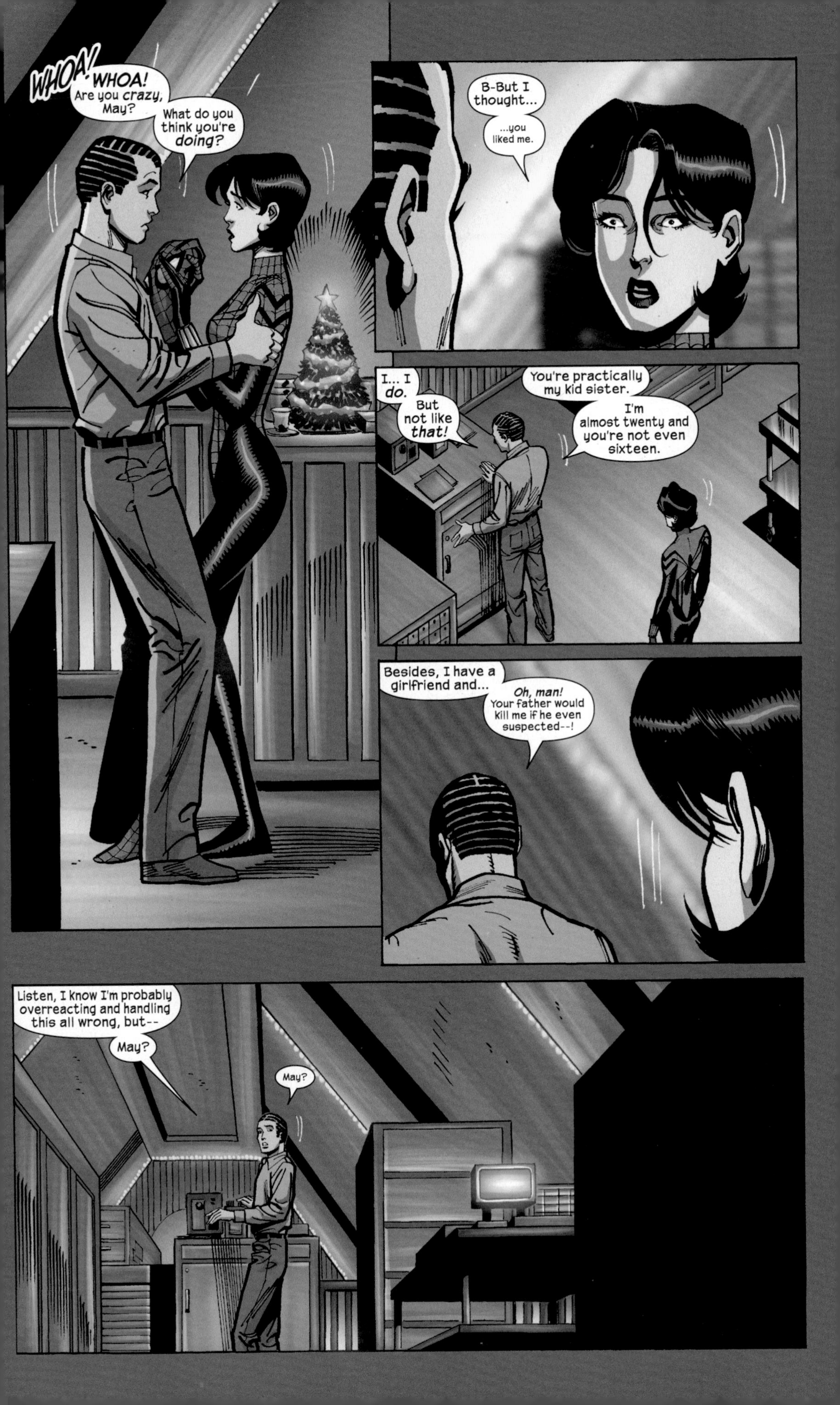
WHOA!
WHOA! Are you crazy, May?
What do you think you're doing?
B-But I thought...
...you liked me.
I... I do.
But not like that!
You're practically my kid sister.
I'm almost twenty and you're not even sixteen.
Besides, I have a girlfriend and...
Oh, man! Your father would kill me if he even suspected--!
Listen, I know I'm probably overreacting and handling this all wrong, but--
May?
May?

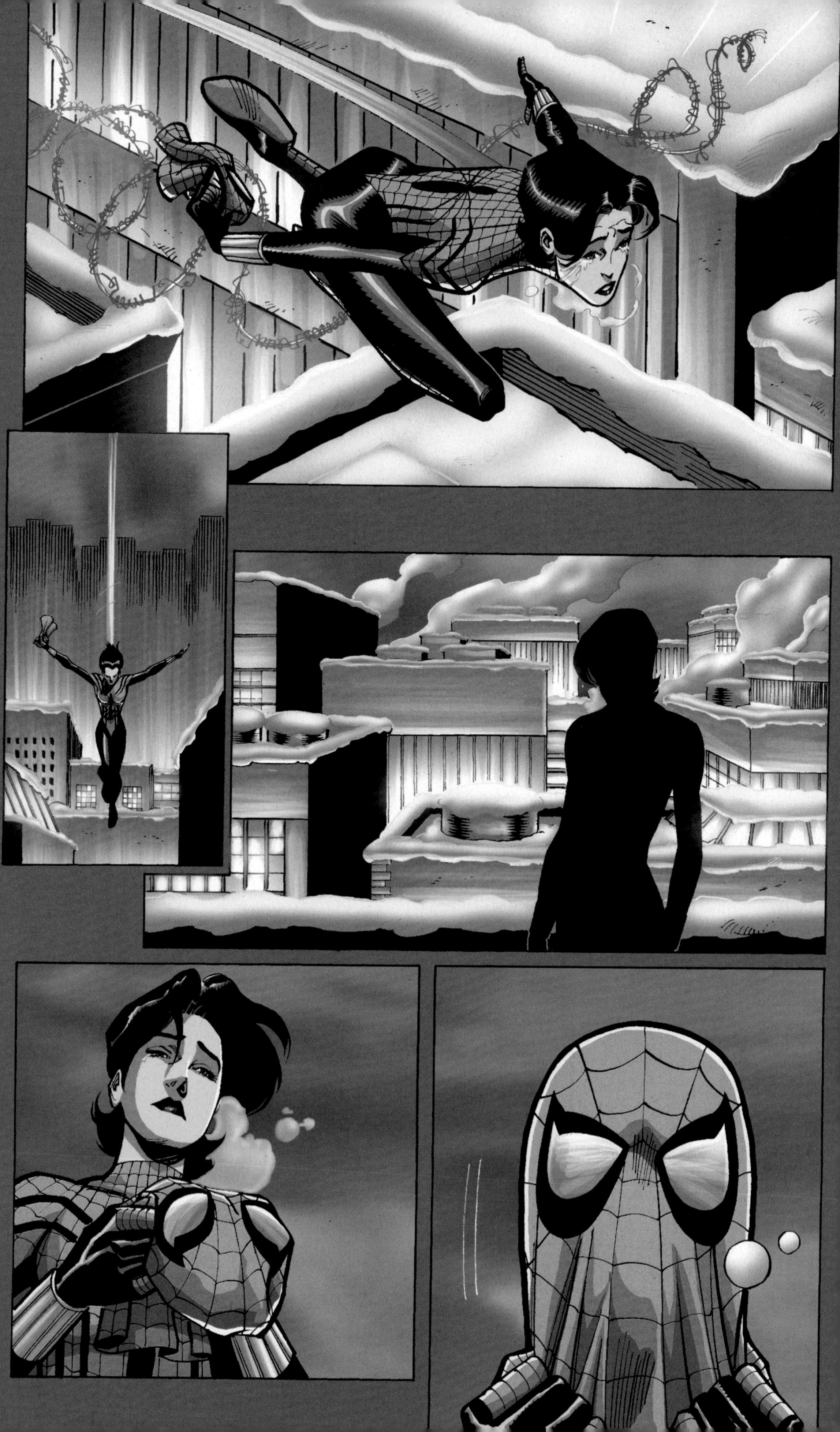

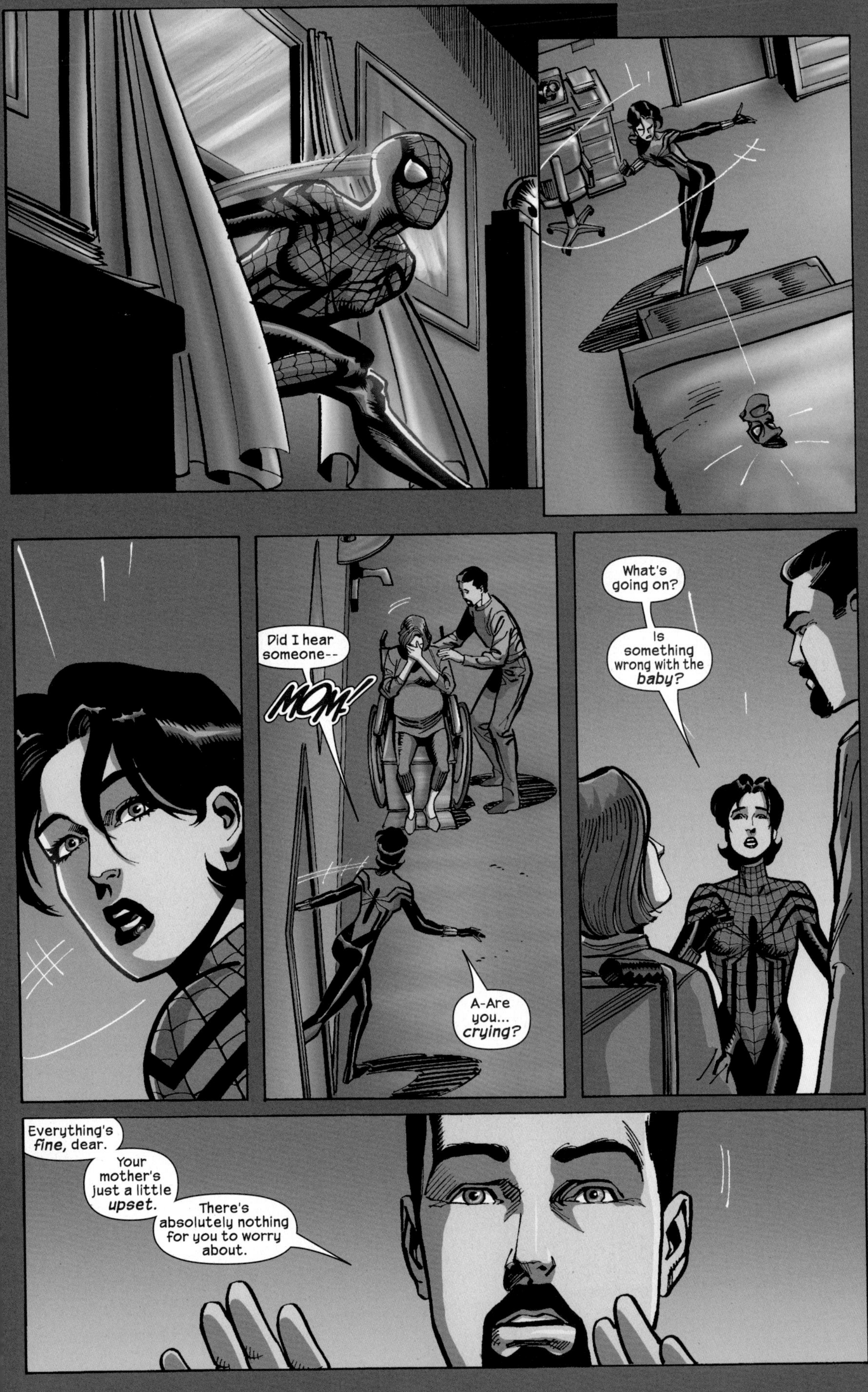
Did I hear someone--
MOM!
A-Are you... *crying?*
What's going on?
Is something wrong with the *baby?*
Everything's *fine,* dear.
Your mother's just a little *upset.*
There's absolutely nothing for you to worry about.

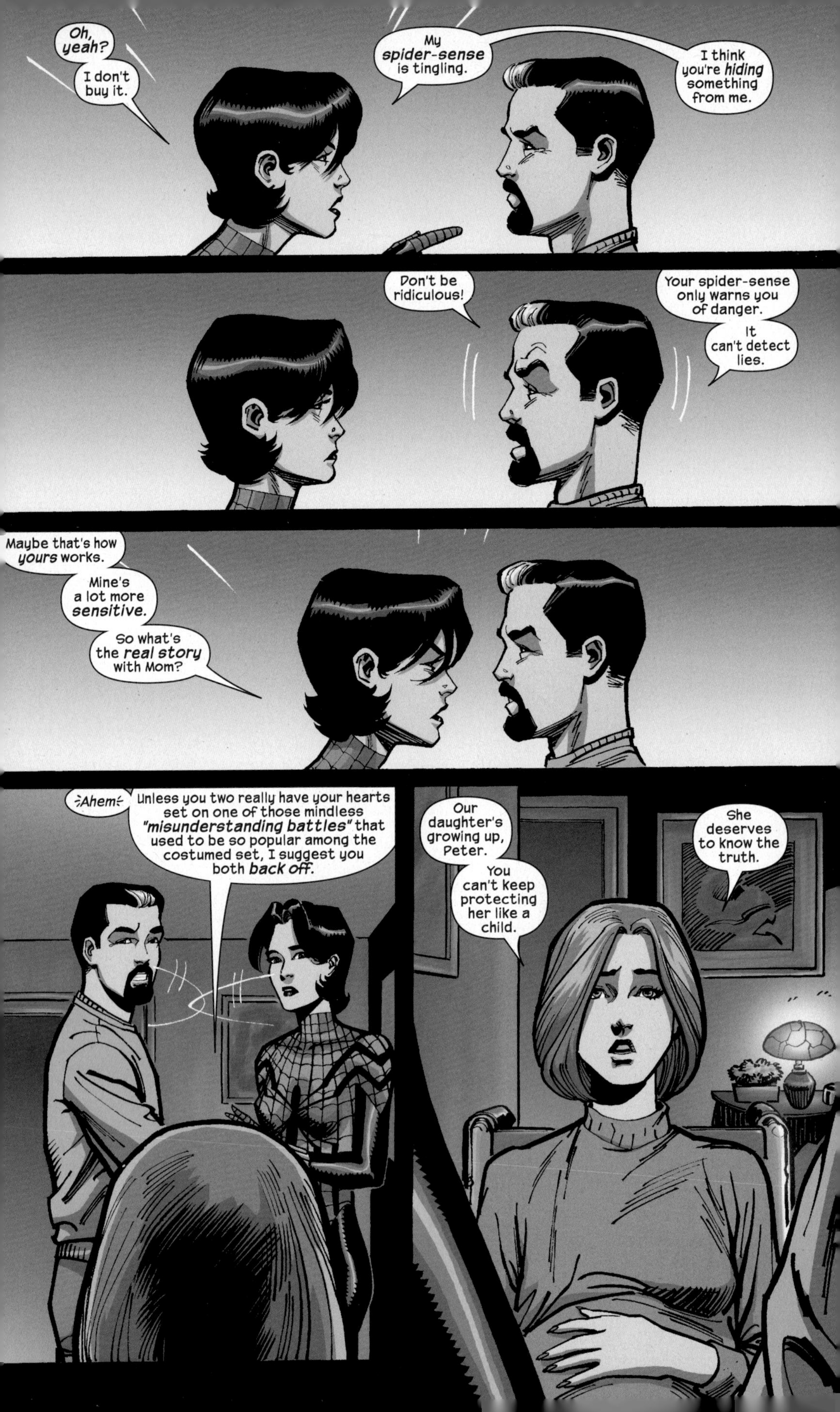

Oh, yeah?
I don't buy it.
My spider-sense is tingling.
I think you're hiding something from me.
Don't be ridiculous!
Your spider-sense only warns you of danger.
It can't detect lies.
Maybe that's how yours works.
Mine's a lot more sensitive.
So what's the real story with Mom?
Ahem
Unless you two really have your hearts set on one of those mindless "misunderstanding battles" that used to be so popular among the costumed set, I suggest you both back off.
Our daughter's growing up, Peter.
You can't keep protecting her like a child.
She deserves to know the truth.

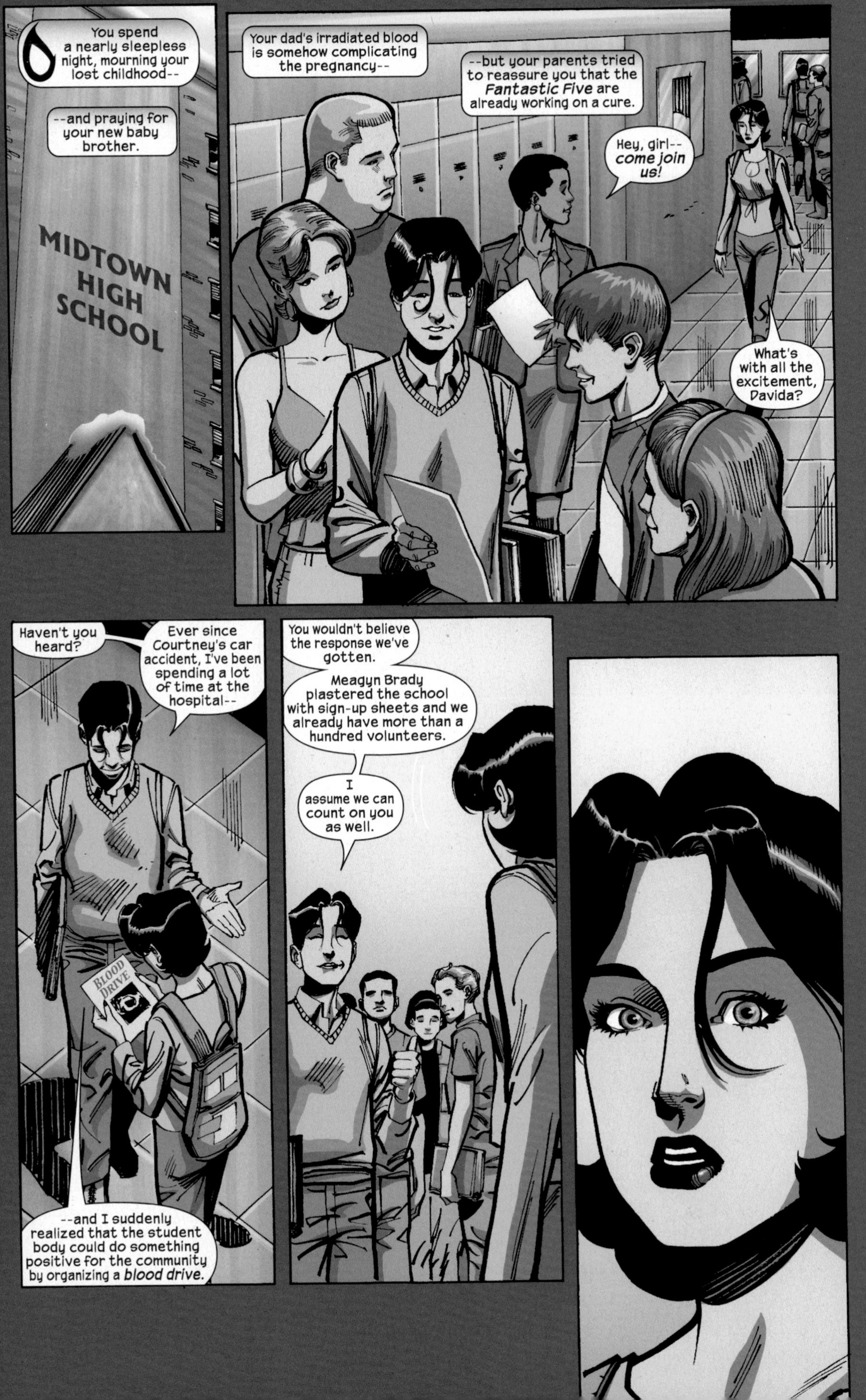
You spend a nearly sleepless night, mourning your lost childhood--
--and praying for your new baby brother.
MIDTOWN HIGH SCHOOL
Your dad's irradiated blood is somehow complicating the pregnancy--
--but your parents tried to reassure you that the *Fantastic Five* are already working on a cure.
Hey, girl-- *come join us!*
What's with all the excitement, Davida?
Haven't you heard?
Ever since Courtney's car accident, I've been spending a lot of time at the hospital--
BLOOD DRIVE
--and I suddenly realized that the student body could do something positive for the community by organizing a *blood drive.*
You wouldn't believe the response we've gotten.
Meagyn Brady plastered the school with sign-up sheets and we already have more than a hundred volunteers.
I assume we can count on you as well.

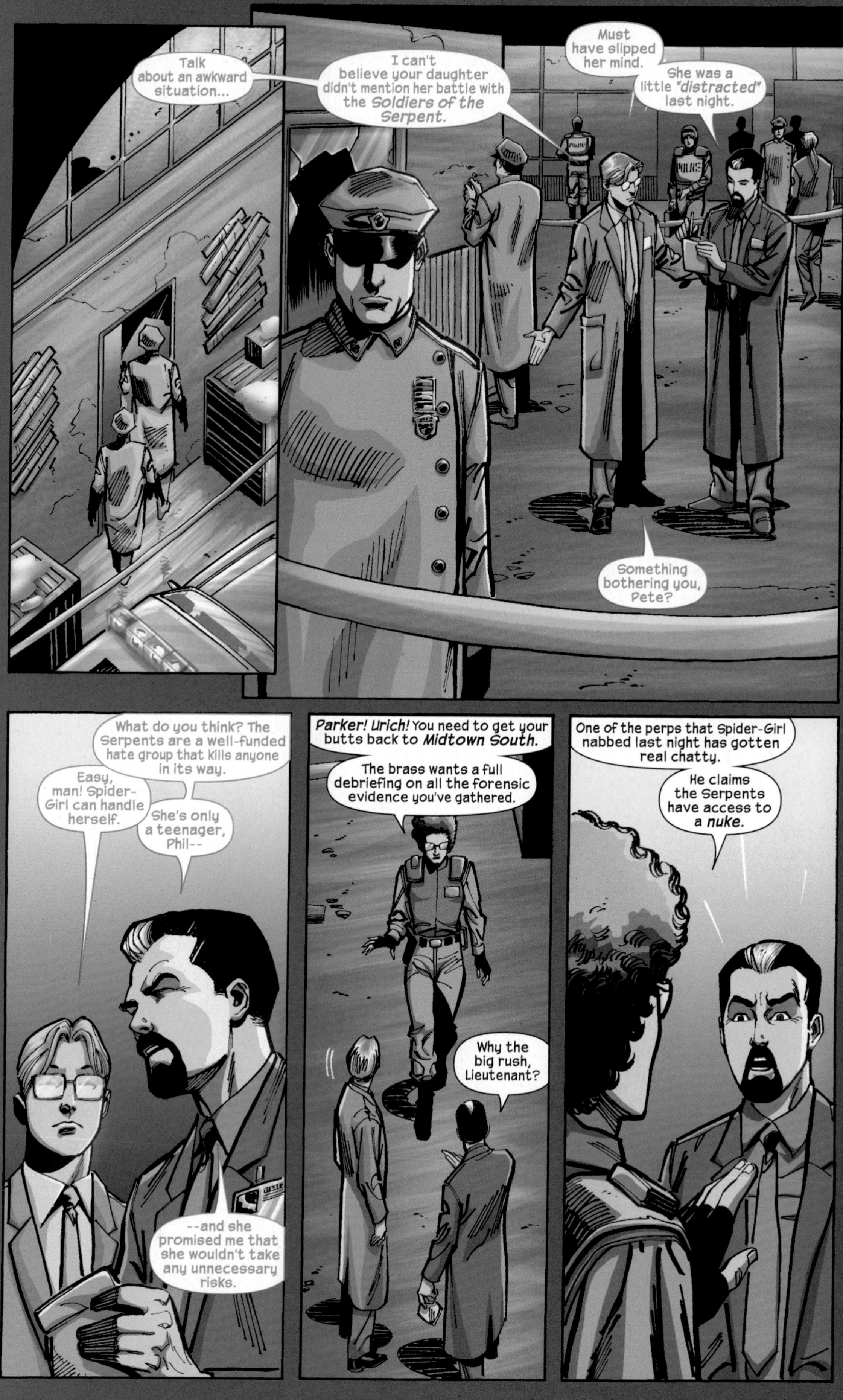
Talk about an awkward situation...
I can't believe your daughter didn't mention her battle with the Soldiers of the Serpent.
Must have slipped her mind.
She was a little "distracted" last night.
Something bothering you, Pete?
What do you think? The Serpents are a well-funded hate group that kills anyone in its way.
Easy, man! Spider-Girl can handle herself.
She's only a teenager, Phil--
--and she promised me that she wouldn't take any unnecessary risks.
Parker! Urich! You need to get your butts back to Midtown South.
The brass wants a full debriefing on all the forensic evidence you've gathered.
Why the big rush, Lieutenant?
One of the perps that Spider-Girl nabbed last night has gotten real chatty.
He claims the Serpents have access to a nuke.

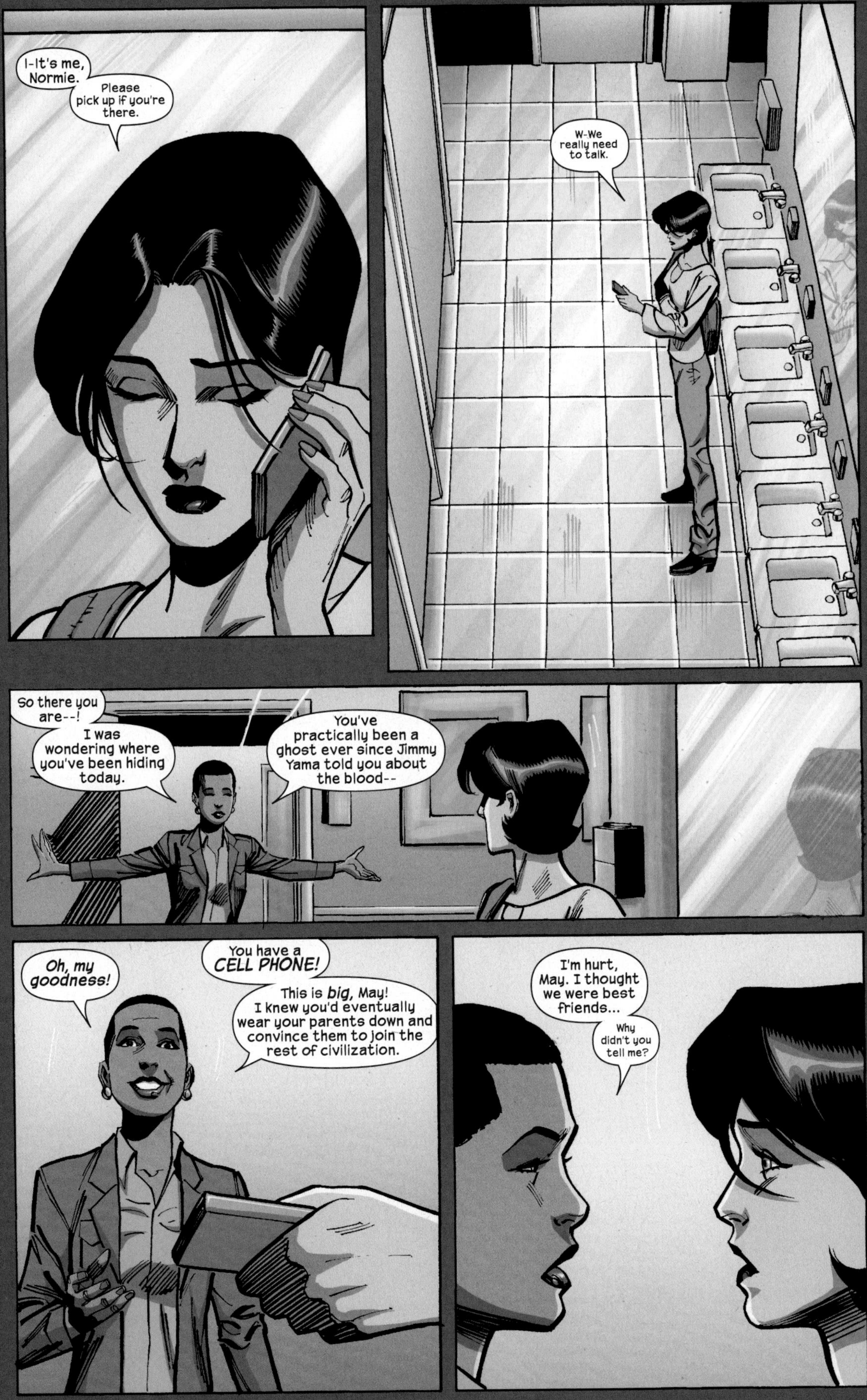

I-It's me, Normie.
Please pick up if you're there.
W-We really need to talk.
So there you are--!
I was wondering where you've been hiding today.
You've practically been a ghost ever since Jimmy Yama told you about the blood--
Oh, my goodness!
You have a CELL PHONE!
This is big, May! I knew you'd eventually wear your parents down and convince them to join the rest of civilization.
I'm hurt, May. I thought we were best friends...
Why didn't you tell me?

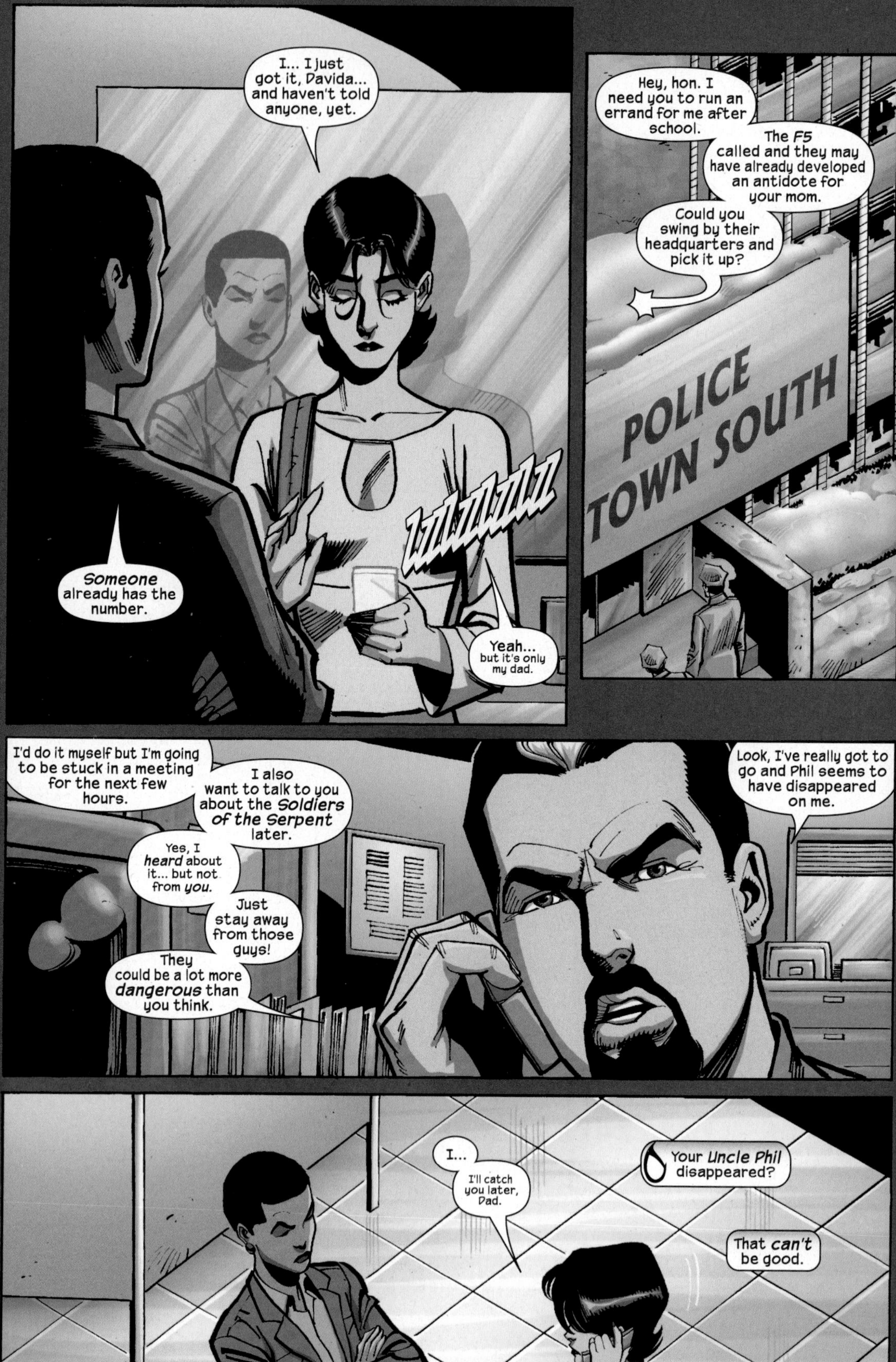
I... I just got it, Davida... and haven't told anyone, yet.
Someone already has the number.
ZZZZZZZ
Yeah... but it's only my dad.
Hey, hon. I need you to run an errand for me after school.
The F5 called and they may have already developed an antidote for your mom.
Could you swing by their headquarters and pick it up?
POLICE TOWN SOUTH
I'd do it myself but I'm going to be stuck in a meeting for the next few hours.
I also want to talk to you about the Soldiers of the Serpent later.
Yes, I heard about it... but not from you.
Just stay away from those guys!
They could be a lot more dangerous than you think.
Look, I've really got to go and Phil seems to have disappeared on me.
I...
I'll catch you later, Dad.
Your Uncle Phil disappeared?
That can't be good.

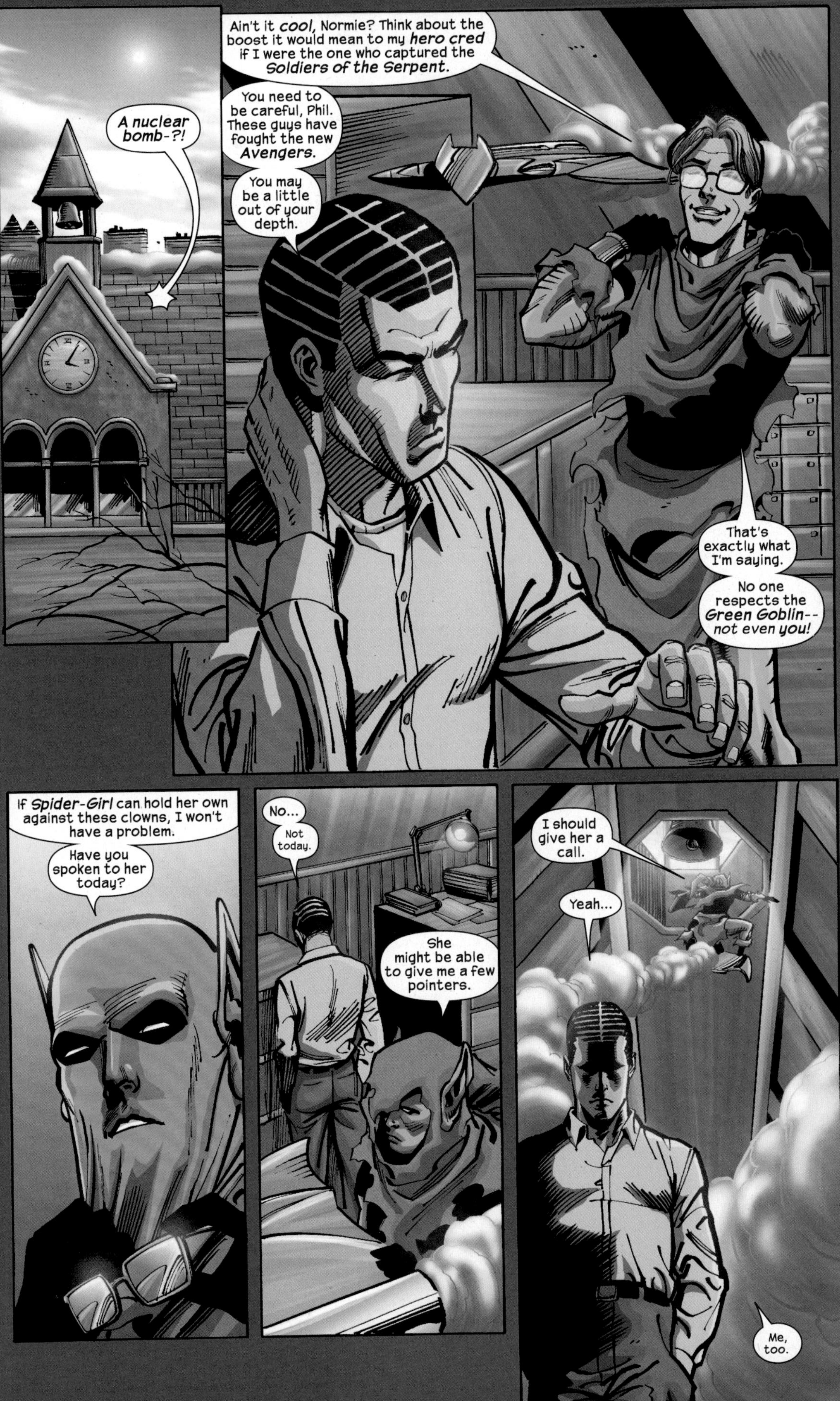
A nuclear bomb-?!
Ain't it cool, Normie? Think about the boost it would mean to my hero cred if I were the one who captured the Soldiers of the Serpent.
You need to be careful, Phil. These guys have fought the new Avengers.
You may be a little out of your depth.
That's exactly what I'm saying.
No one respects the Green Goblin-- not even you!
If Spider-Girl can hold her own against these clowns, I won't have a problem.
Have you spoken to her today?
No...
Not today.
She might be able to give me a few pointers.
I should give her a call.
Yeah...
Me, too.

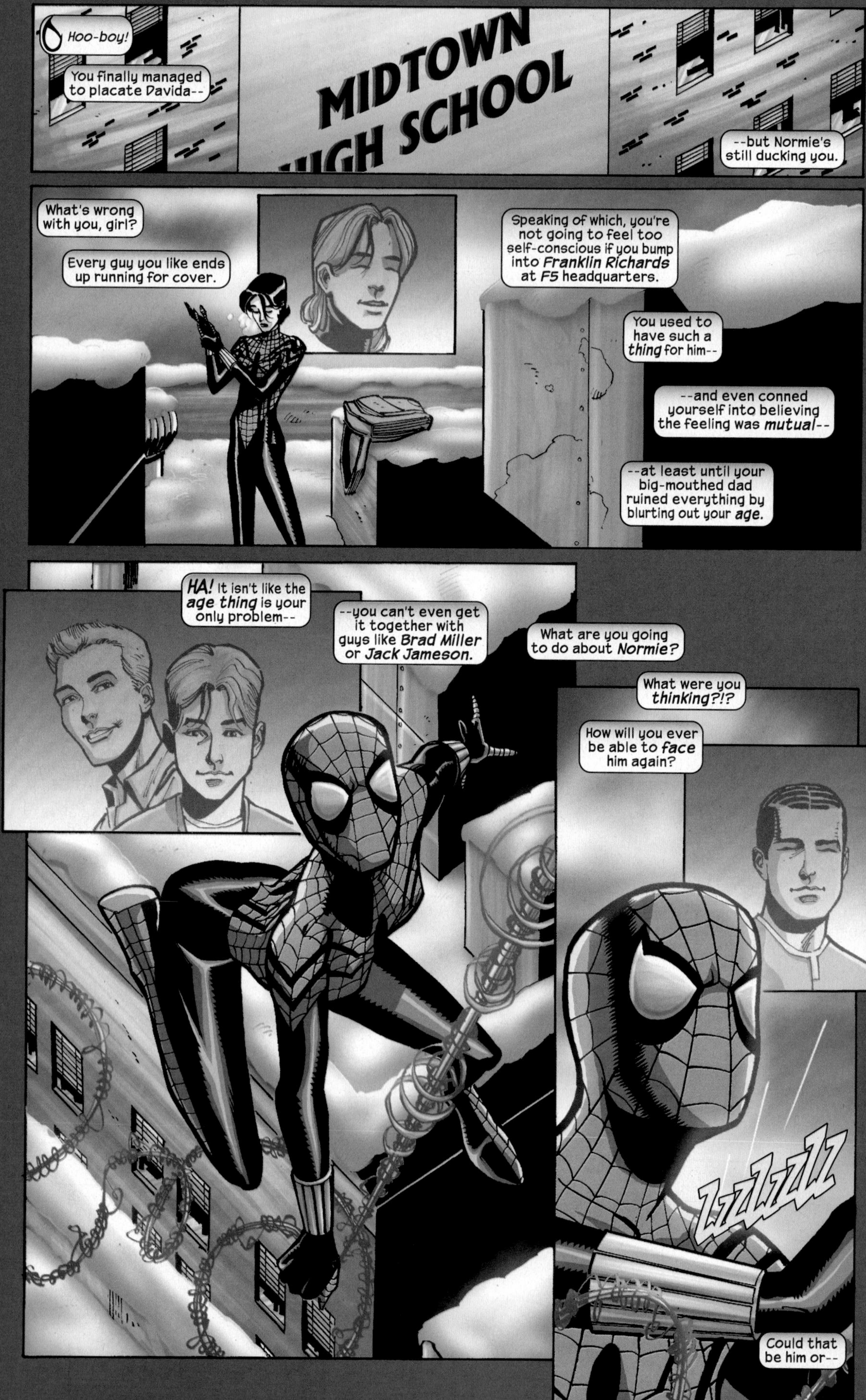
Hoo-boy!
You finally managed to placate Davida--
MIDTOWN HIGH SCHOOL
--but Normie's still ducking you.
What's wrong with you, girl?
Every guy you like ends up running for cover.
Speaking of which, you're not going to feel too self-conscious if you bump into Franklin Richards at F5 headquarters.
You used to have such a thing for him--
--and even conned yourself into believing the feeling was mutual--
--at least until your big-mouthed dad ruined everything by blurting out your age.
HA! It isn't like the age thing is your only problem--
--you can't even get it together with guys like Brad Miller or Jack Jameson.
What are you going to do about Normie?
What were you thinking?!?
How will you ever be able to face him again?
ZZZZZZZZ
Could that be him or--

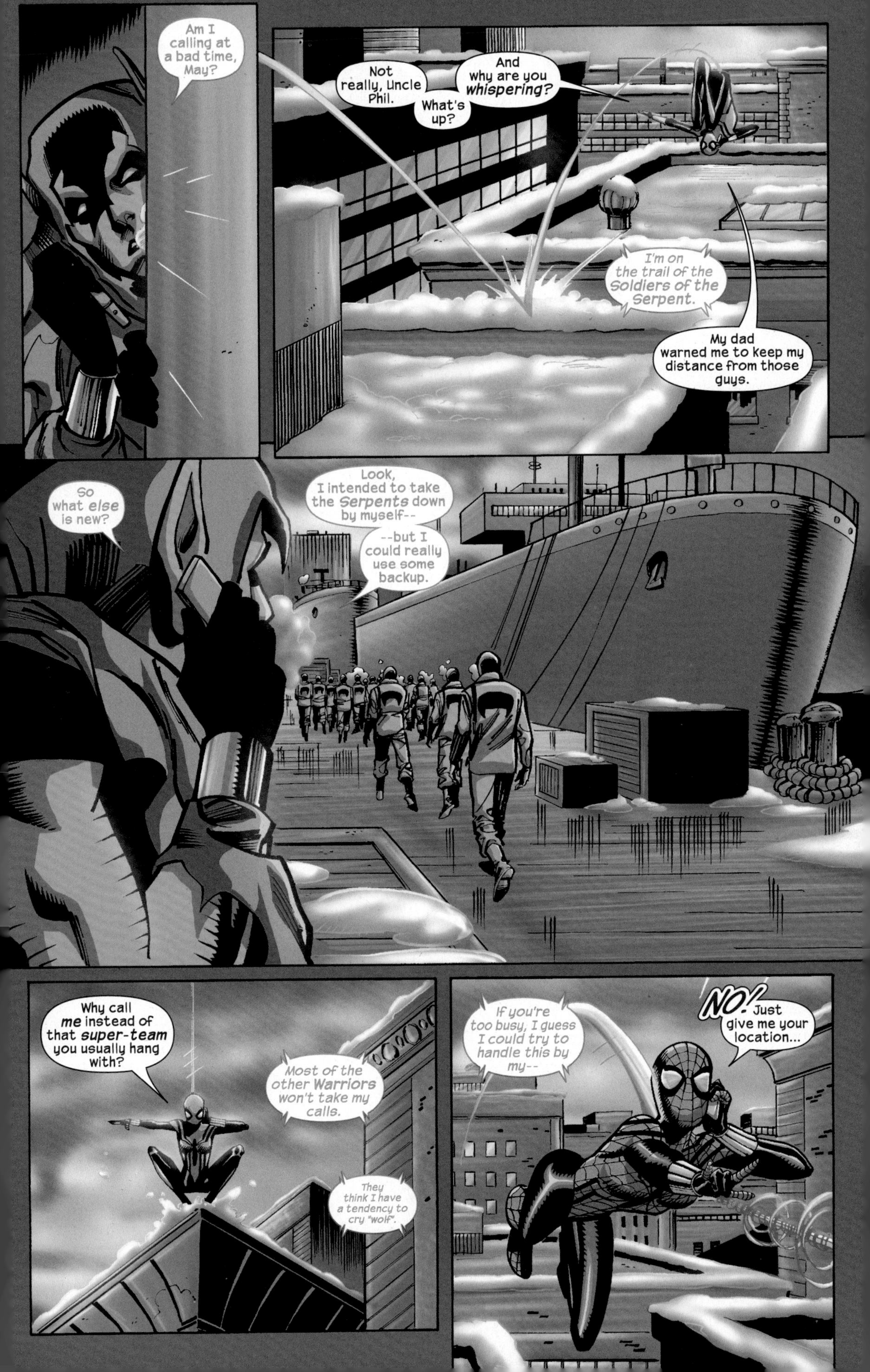
Am I calling at a bad time, May?
Not really, Uncle Phil.
What's up?
And why are you whispering?
I'm on the trail of the Soldiers of the Serpent.
My dad warned me to keep my distance from those guys.
So what else is new?
Look, I intended to take the Serpents down by myself--
--but I could really use some backup.
Why call me instead of that super-team you usually hang with?
Most of the other Warriors won't take my calls.
They think I have a tendency to cry "wolf".
If you're too busy, I guess I could try to handle this by my--
NO! Just give me your location...

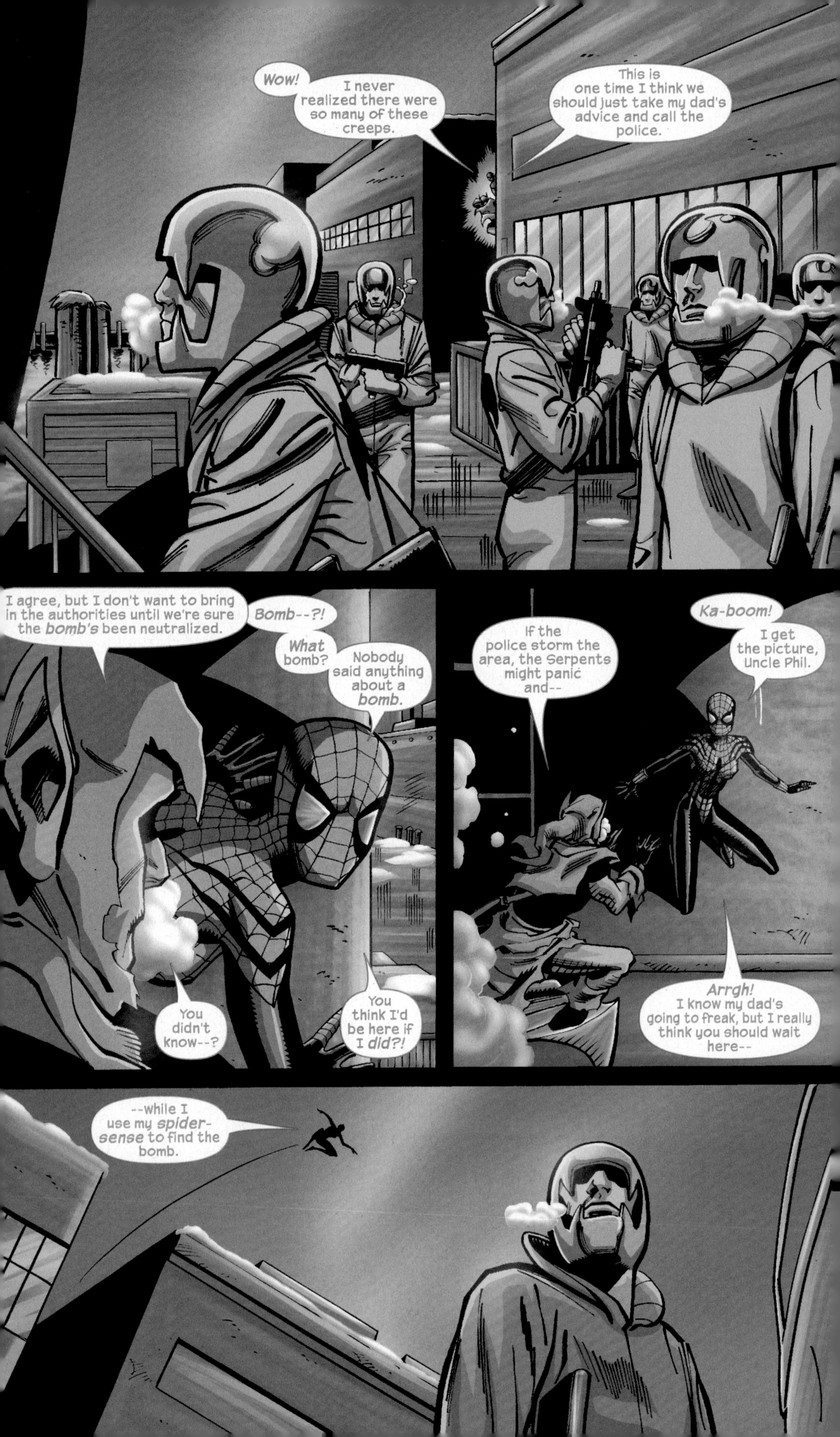
Wow!
I never realized there were so many of these creeps.
This is one time I think we should just take my dad's advice and call the police.
I agree, but I don't want to bring in the authorities until we're sure the bomb's been neutralized.
Bomb--?!
What bomb?
Nobody said anything about a bomb.
You didn't know--?
You think I'd be here if I did?!
If the police storm the area, the Serpents might panic and--
Ka-boom!
I get the picture, Uncle Phil.
Arrgh!
I know my dad's going to freak, but I really think you should wait here--
--while I use my spider-sense to find the bomb.

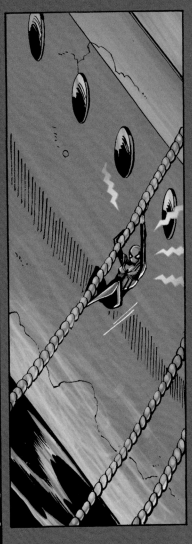

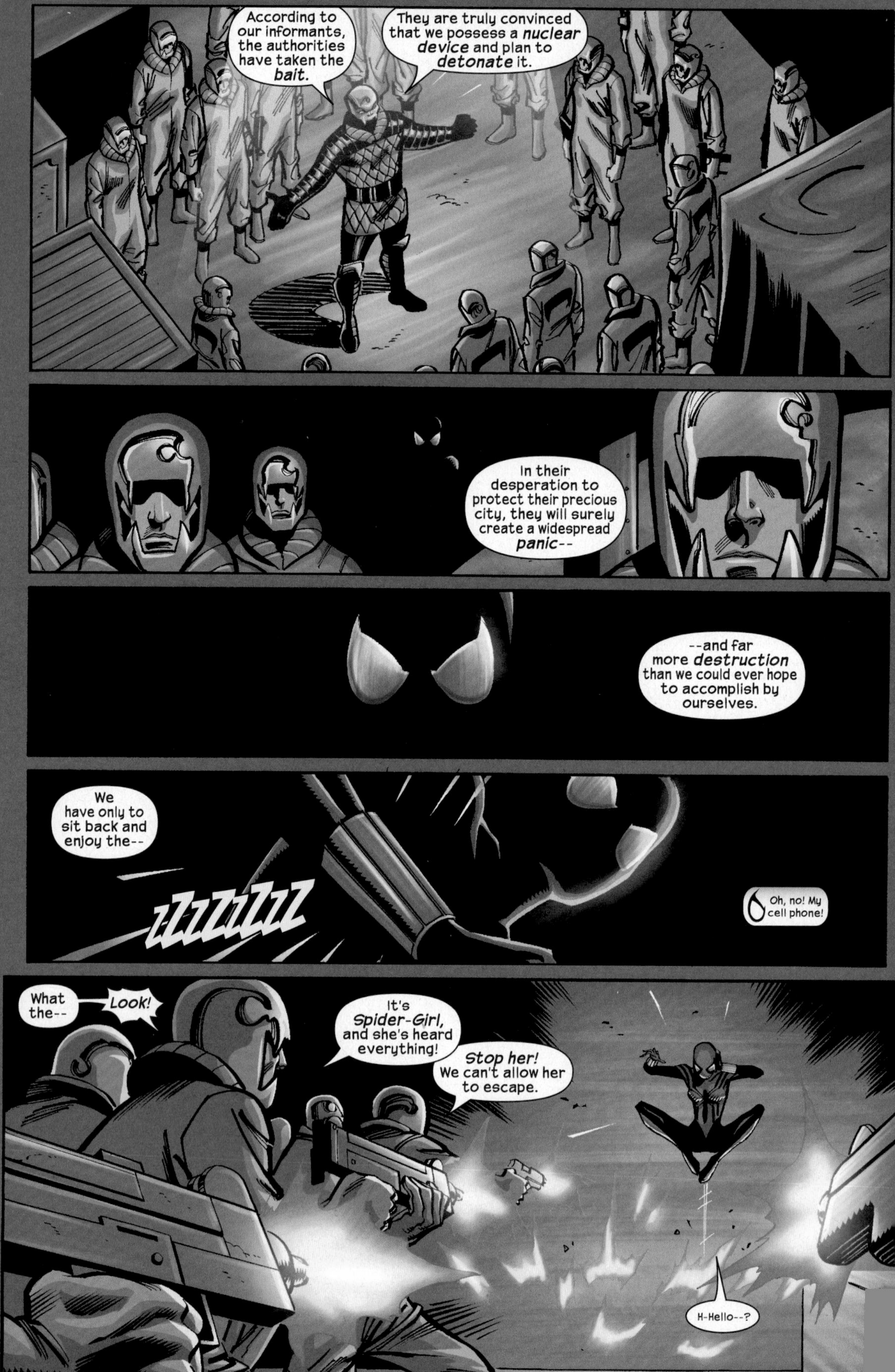
According to our informants, the authorities have taken the bait.
They are truly convinced that we possess a nuclear device and plan to detonate it.
In their desperation to protect their precious city, they will surely create a widespread panic--
--and far more destruction than we could ever hope to accomplish by ourselves.
We have only to sit back and enjoy the--
ZZZZZZZZ
Oh, no! My cell phone!
What the--
Look!
It's Spider-Girl, and she's heard everything!
Stop her! We can't allow her to escape.
H-Hello--?

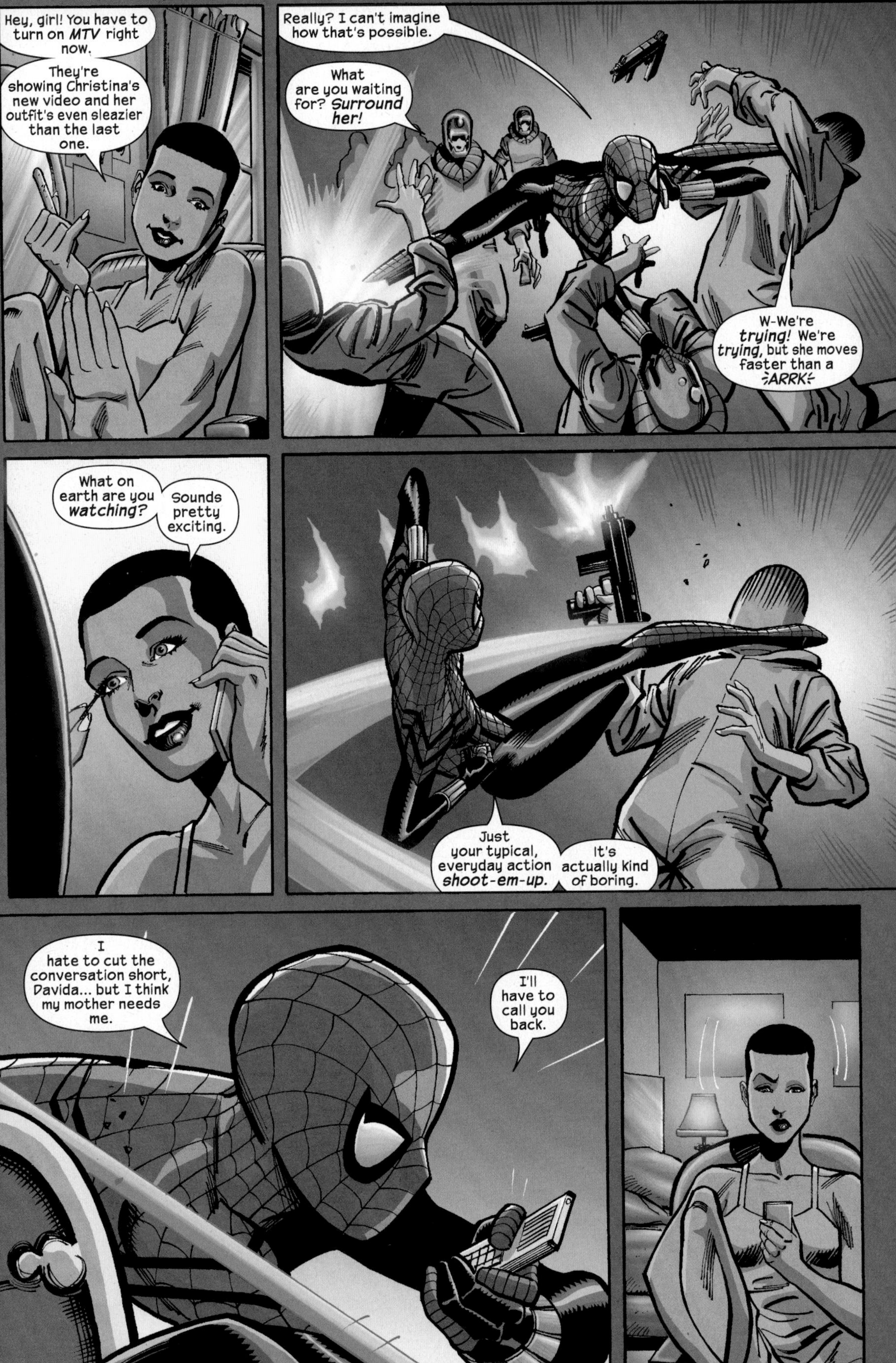

Hey, girl! You have to turn on MTV right now.
They're showing Christina's new video and her outfit's even sleazier than the last one.
Really? I can't imagine how that's possible.
What are you waiting for? Surround her!
W-We're trying! We're trying, but she moves faster than a
ARRK
What on earth are you watching?
Sounds pretty exciting.
Just your typical, everyday action shoot-em-up.
It's actually kind of boring.
I hate to cut the conversation short, Davida... but I think my mother needs me.
I'll have to call you back.

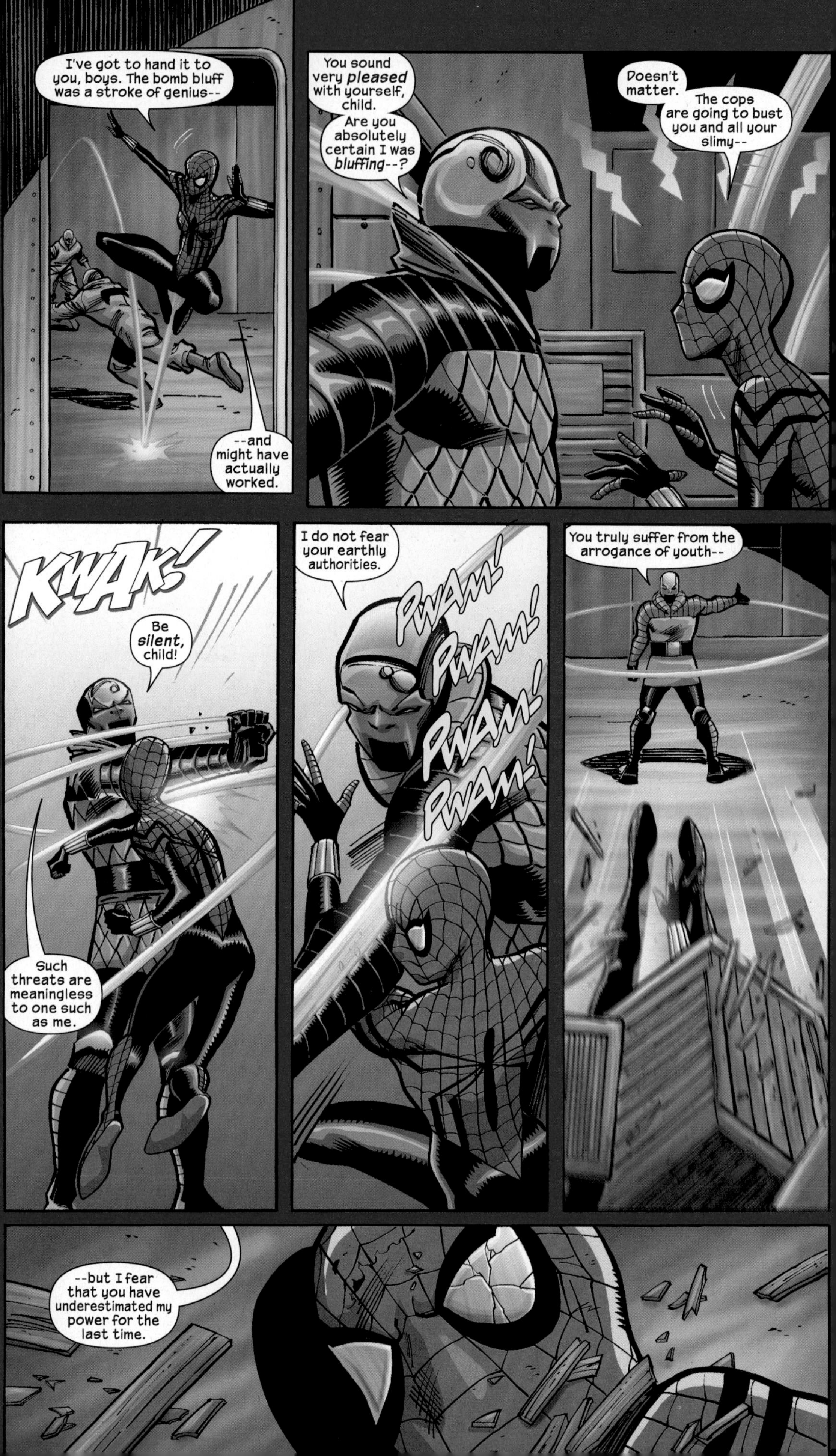

I've got to hand it to you, boys. The bomb bluff was a stroke of genius--
--and might have actually worked.
You sound very *pleased* with yourself, child.
Are you absolutely certain I was *bluffing*--?
Doesn't matter.
The cops are going to bust you and all your slimy--
KWAK!
Be *silent*, child!
Such threats are meaningless to one such as me.
I do not fear your earthly authorities.
PWAM! PWAM! PWAM! PWAM!
You truly suffer from the arrogance of youth--
--but I fear that you have underestimated my power for the last time.

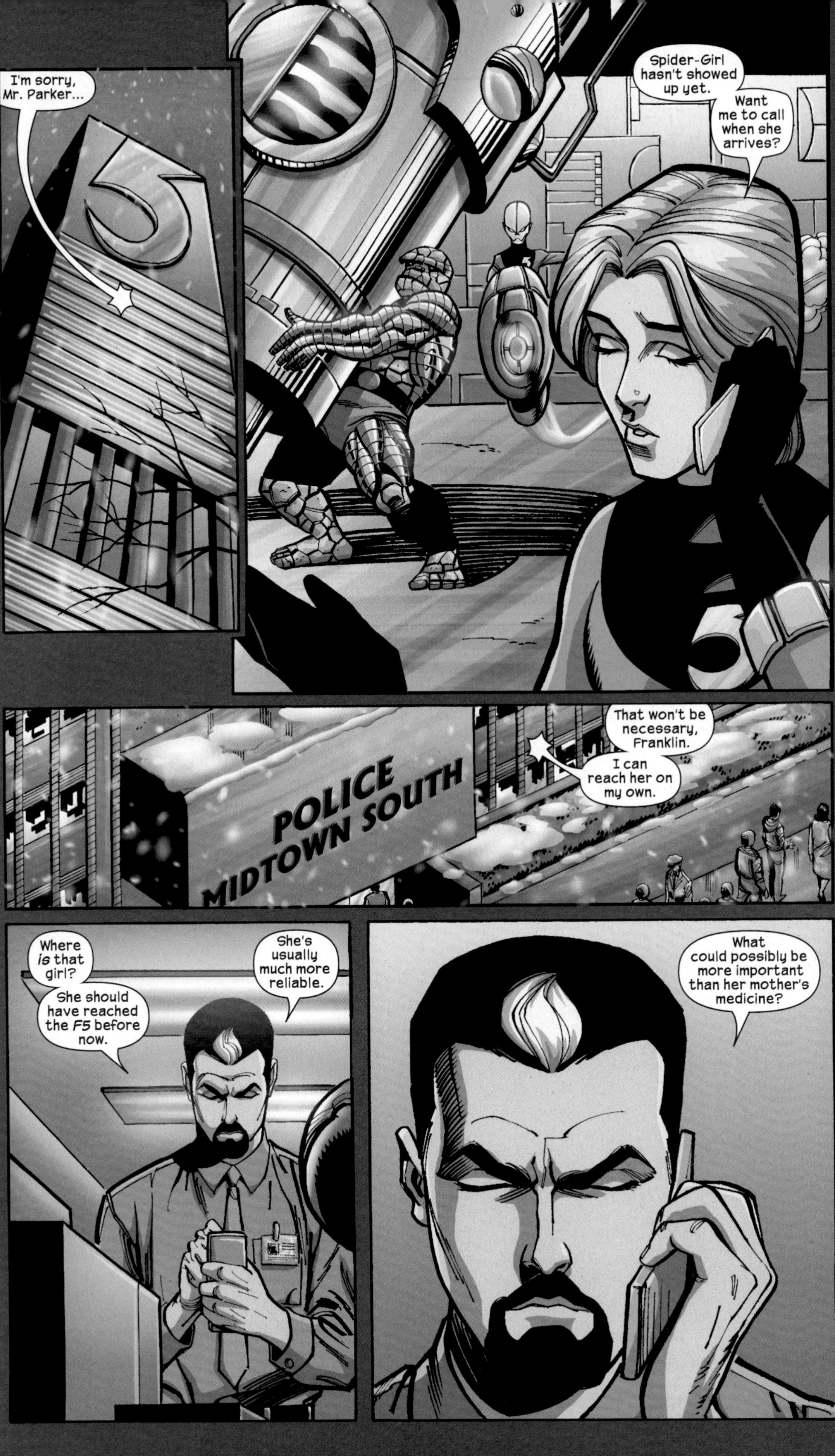

I'm sorry, Mr. Parker...
Spider-Girl hasn't showed up yet.
Want me to call when she arrives?
POLICE MIDTOWN SOUTH
That won't be necessary, Franklin.
I can reach her on my own.
Where *is* that girl?
She should have reached the *F5* before now.
She's usually much more reliable.
What could possibly be more important than her mother's medicine?

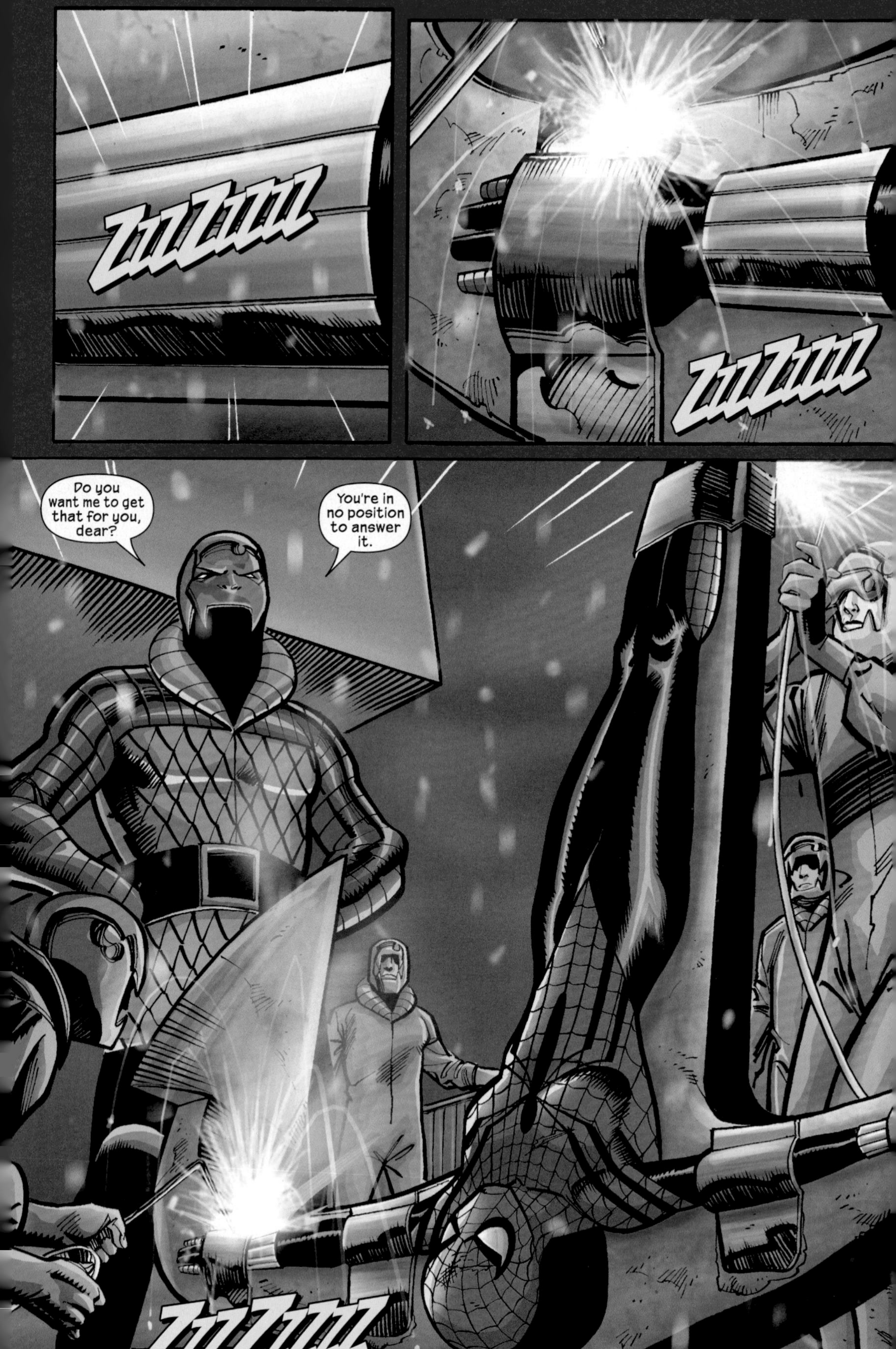
ZZZZZZZ
ZZZZZZZ
Do you want me to get that for you, dear?
You're in no position to answer it.
ZZZZZZZ

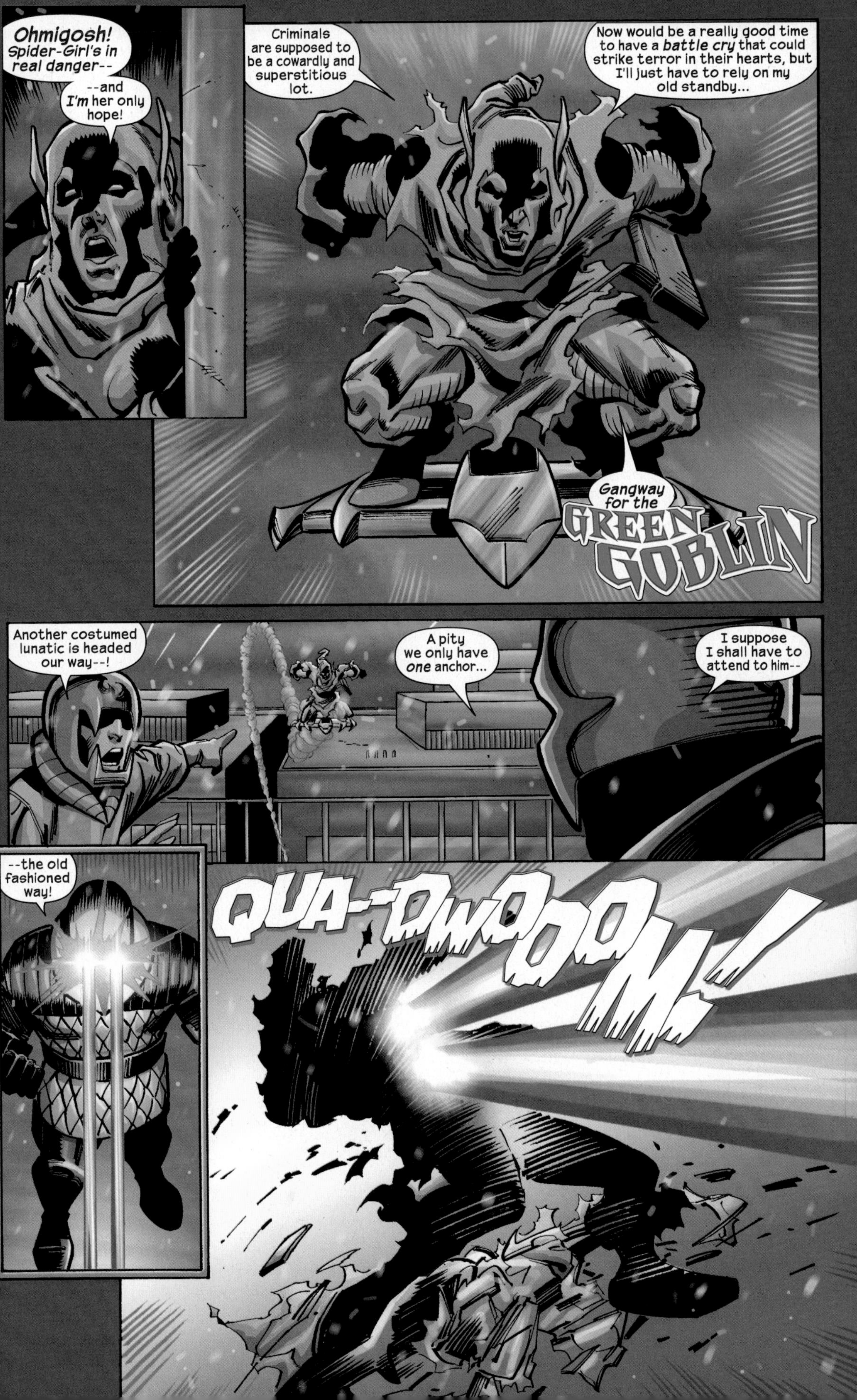

Ohmigosh! Spider-Girl's in real danger--
--and I'm her only hope!
Criminals are supposed to be a cowardly and superstitious lot.
Now would be a really good time to have a battle cry that could strike terror in their hearts, but I'll just have to rely on my old standby...
Gangway for the
GREEN GOBLIN
Another costumed lunatic is headed our way--!
A pity we only have one anchor...
I suppose I shall have to attend to him--
--the old fashioned way!
QUA--DWOOOOM!

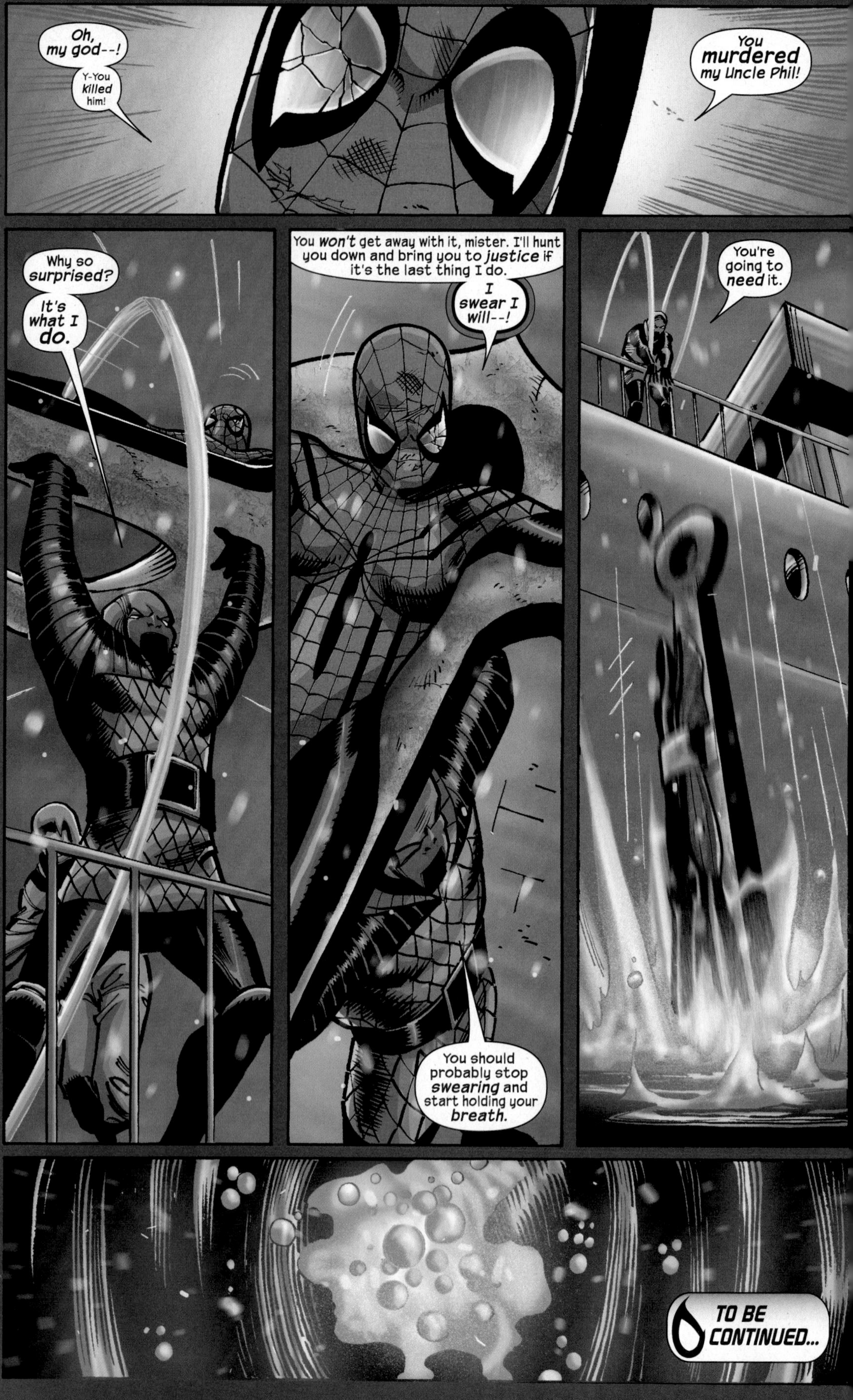
Oh, my god--!
Y-You killed him!
You murdered my Uncle Phil!
Why so surprised?
It's what I do.
You won't get away with it, mister. I'll hunt you down and bring you to justice if it's the last thing I do.
I swear I will--!
You should probably stop swearing and start holding your breath.
You're going to need it.
TO BE CONTINUED...

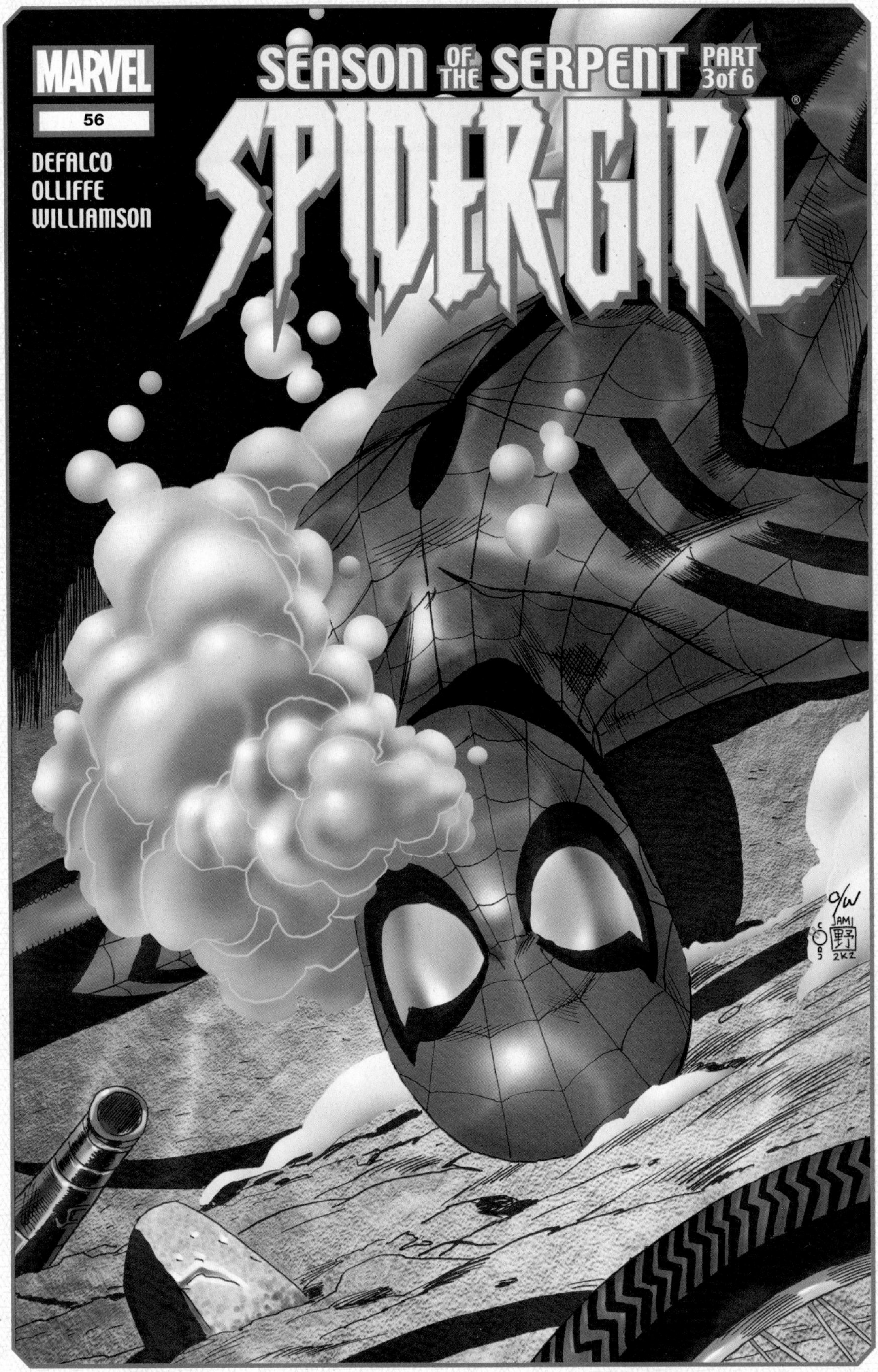
MARVEL
56
SEASON OF THE SERPENT PART 3 of 6
SPIDER-GIRL
DEFALCO
OLLIFFE
WILLIAMSON

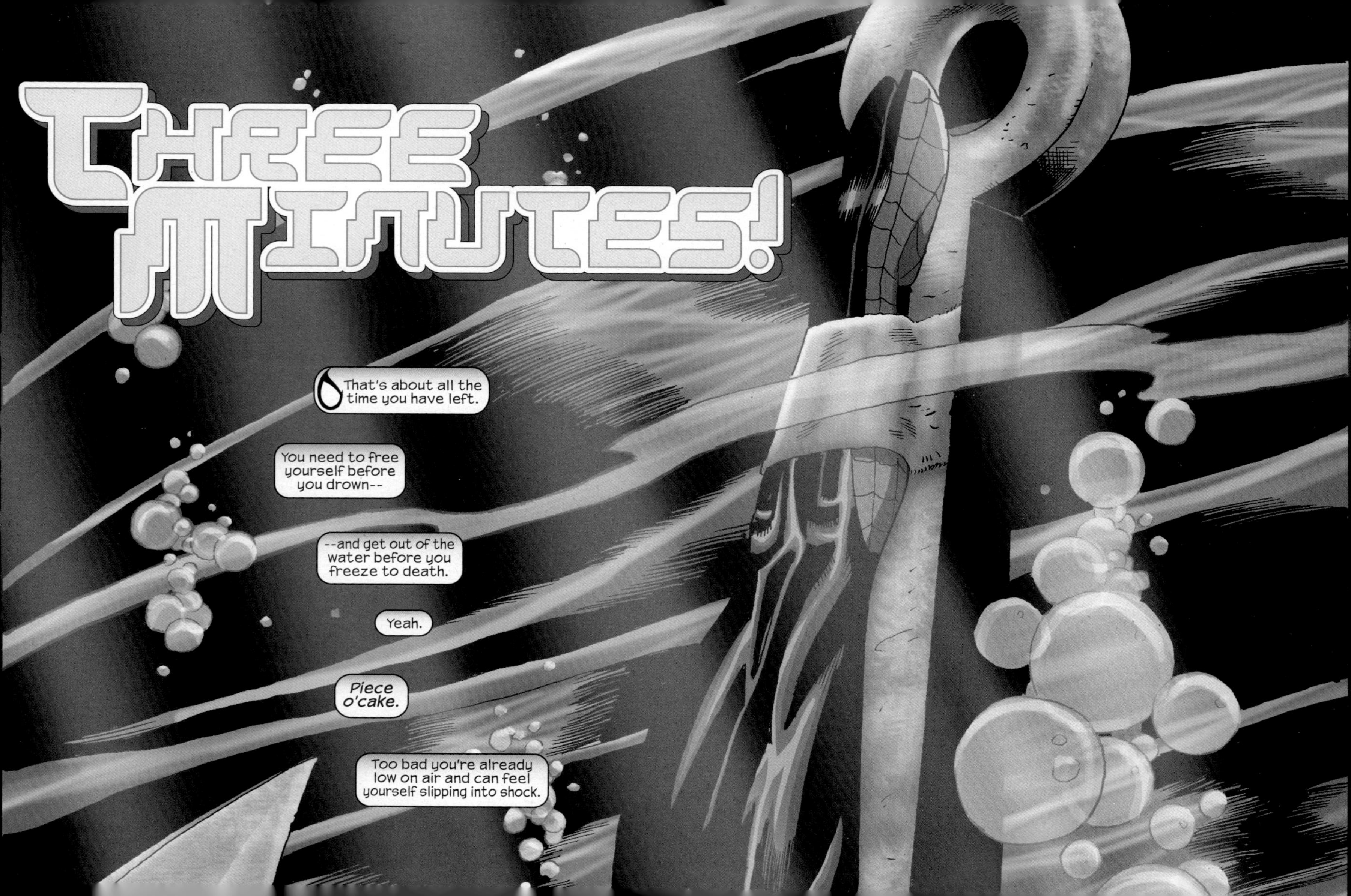
THREE MINUTES!
That's about all the time you have left.
You need to free yourself before you drown--
--and get out of the water before you freeze to death.
Yeah.
Piece o'cake.
Too bad you're already low on air and can feel yourself slipping into shock.

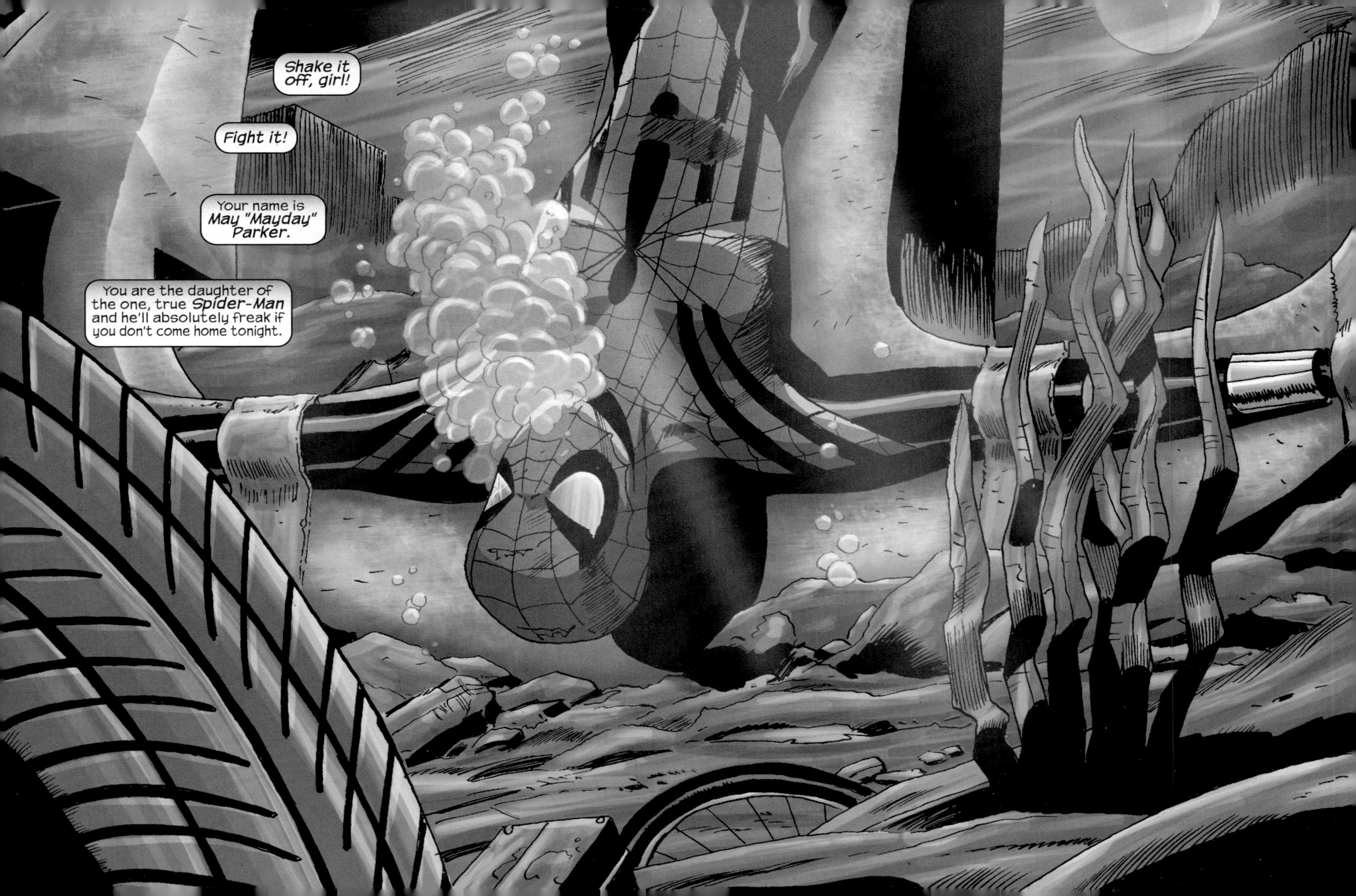
Shake it off, girl!
Fight it!
Your name is May "Mayday" Parker.
You are the daughter of the one, true Spider-Man and he'll absolutely freak if you don't come home tonight.

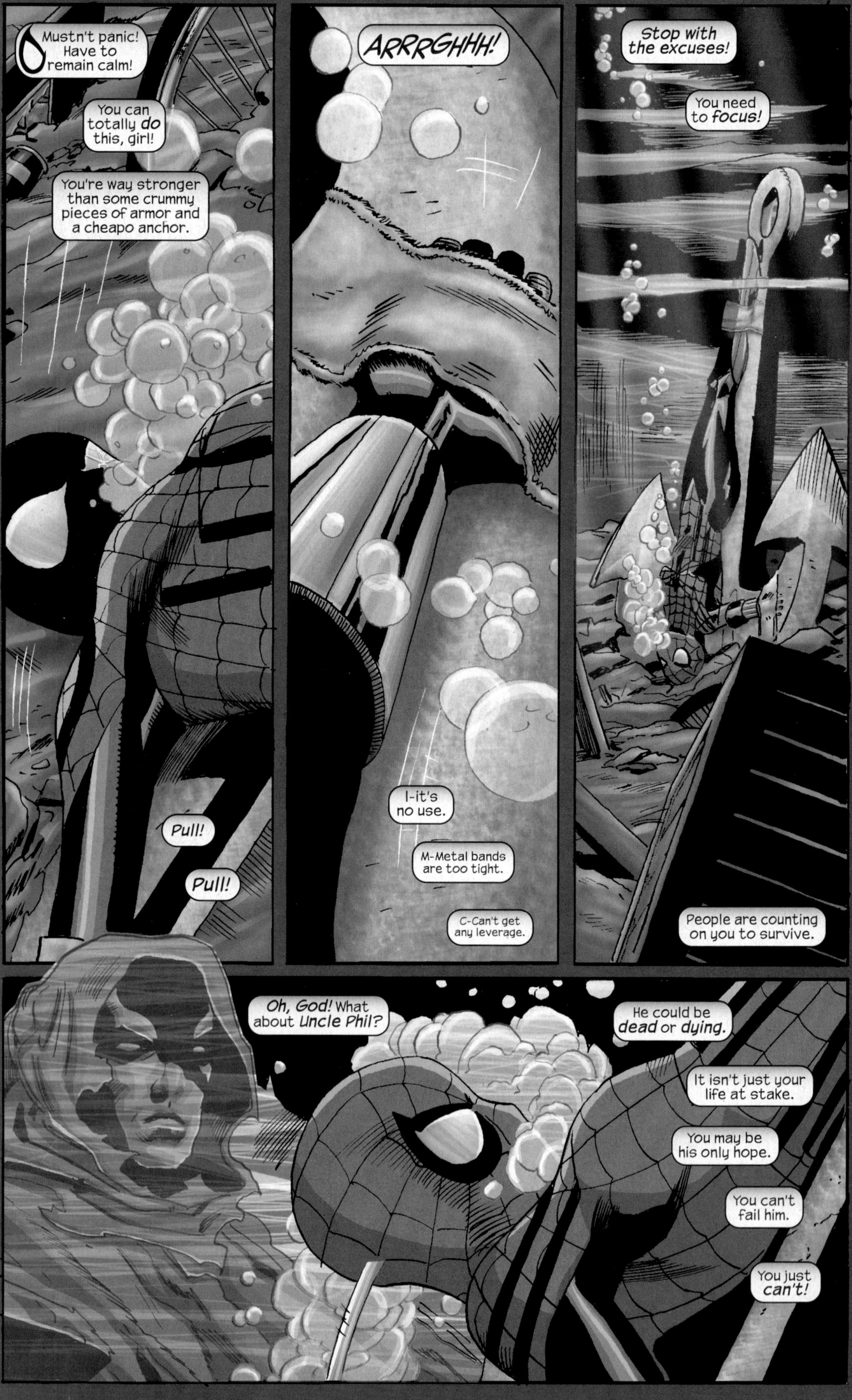

Mustn't panic! Have to remain calm!
You can totally do this, girl!
You're way stronger than some crummy pieces of armor and a cheapo anchor.
Pull!
Pull!
ARRRGHHH!
I-it's no use.
M-Metal bands are too tight.
C-Can't get any leverage.
Stop with the excuses!
You need to focus!
People are counting on you to survive.
Oh, God! What about Uncle Phil?
He could be dead or dying.
It isn't just your life at stake.
You may be his only hope.
You can't fail him.
You just can't!

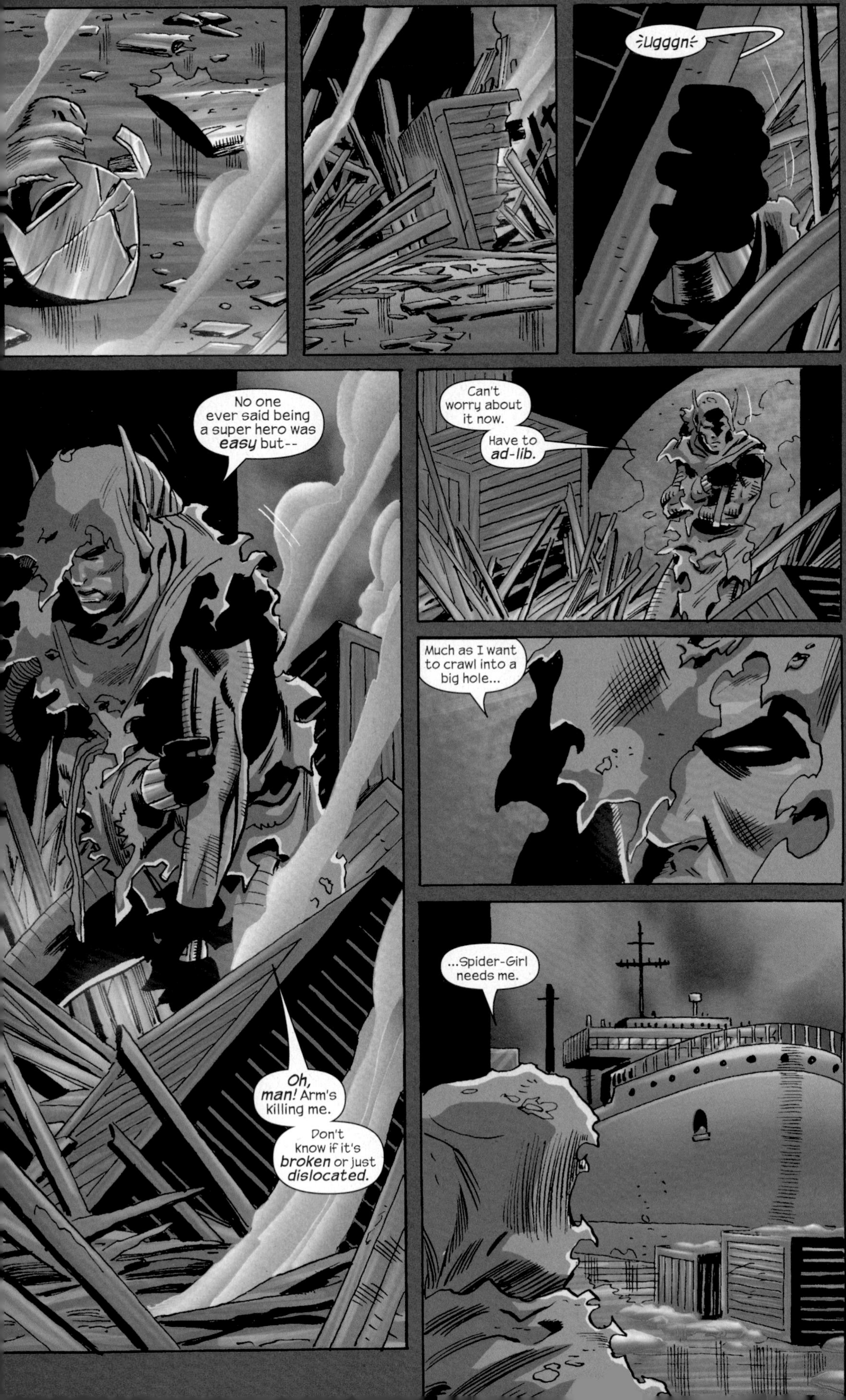
Ugggn
No one ever said being a super hero was easy but--
Oh, man! Arm's killing me.
Don't know if it's broken or just dislocated.
Can't worry about it now.
Have to ad-lib.
Much as I want to crawl into a big hole...
...Spider-Girl needs me.

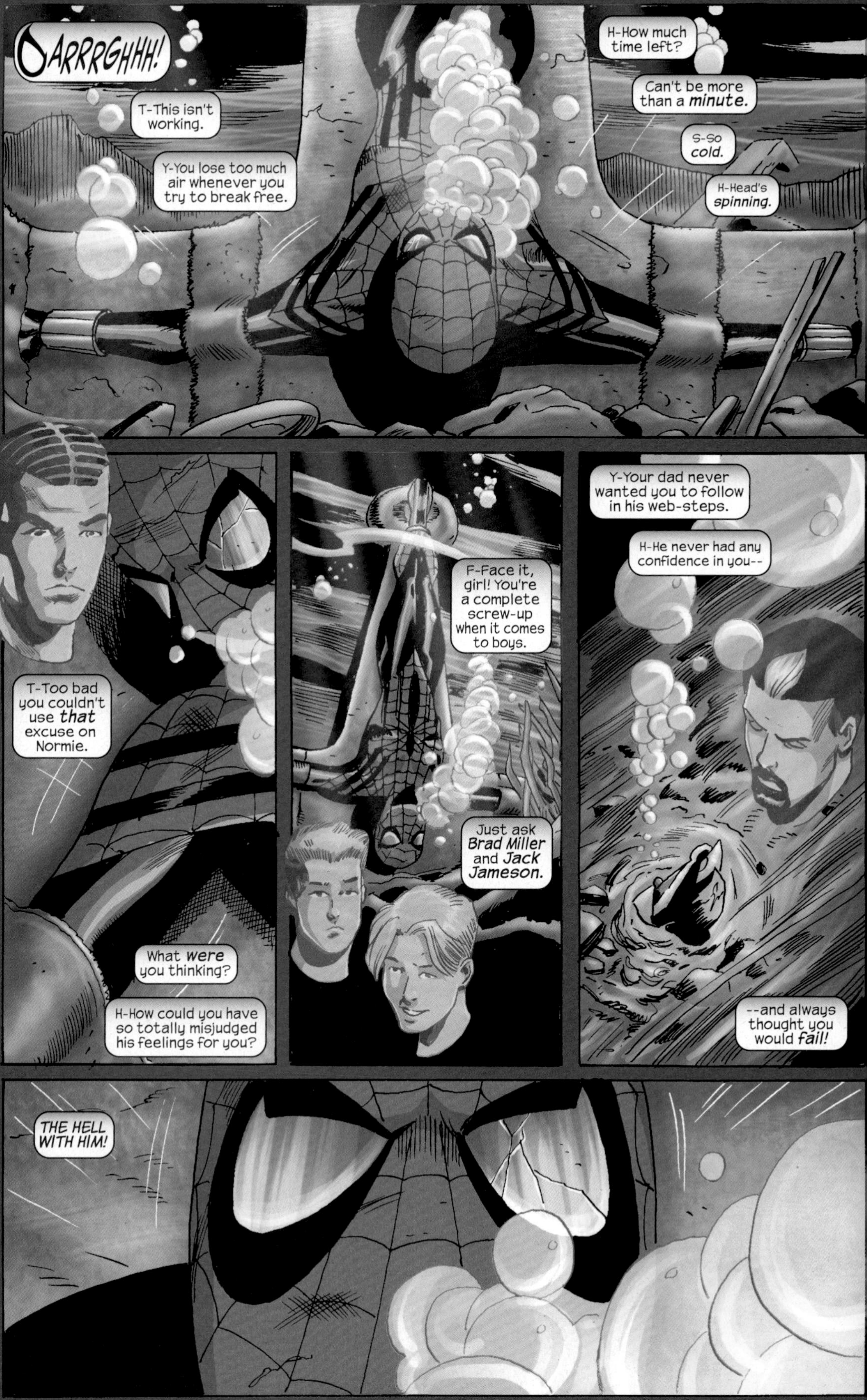
GARRRGHHH!
T-This isn't working.
Y-You lose too much air whenever you try to break free.
H-How much time left?
Can't be more than a *minute.*
S-So *cold.*
H-Head's *spinning.*
T-Too bad you couldn't use *that* excuse on Normie.
What *were* you thinking?
H-How could you have so totally misjudged his feelings for you?
F-Face it, girl! You're a complete screw-up when it comes to boys.
Just ask *Brad Miller* and *Jack Jameson.*
Y-Your dad never wanted you to follow in his web-steps.
H-He never had any confidence in you--
--and always thought you would *fail!*
THE HELL WITH HIM!

Y-Your mother needs her medicine--

--and she'd be *crushed* if anything ever happened to you.

S-So would your *dad*--

--but you've got something more to prove to *him*.

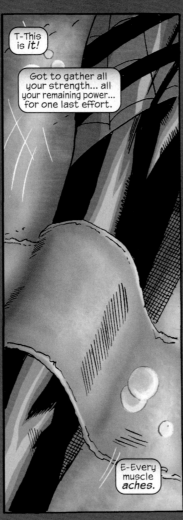

T-This is *it!*

Got to gather all your strength... all your remaining power... for one last effort.

E-Every muscle *aches.*

S-Strain's *unbearable.*

W-Water feels like it's growing *colder.*

C-Can't stop!

M-Must keep fighting!

Or you'll never get to meet your new baby brother.

S-Someone's got to show him the ropes--

--and keep dad off his back.

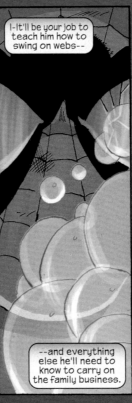

I-It'll be your job to teach him how to swing on webs--

--and everything else he'll need to know to carry on the family business.

Yeah.

YEAH!

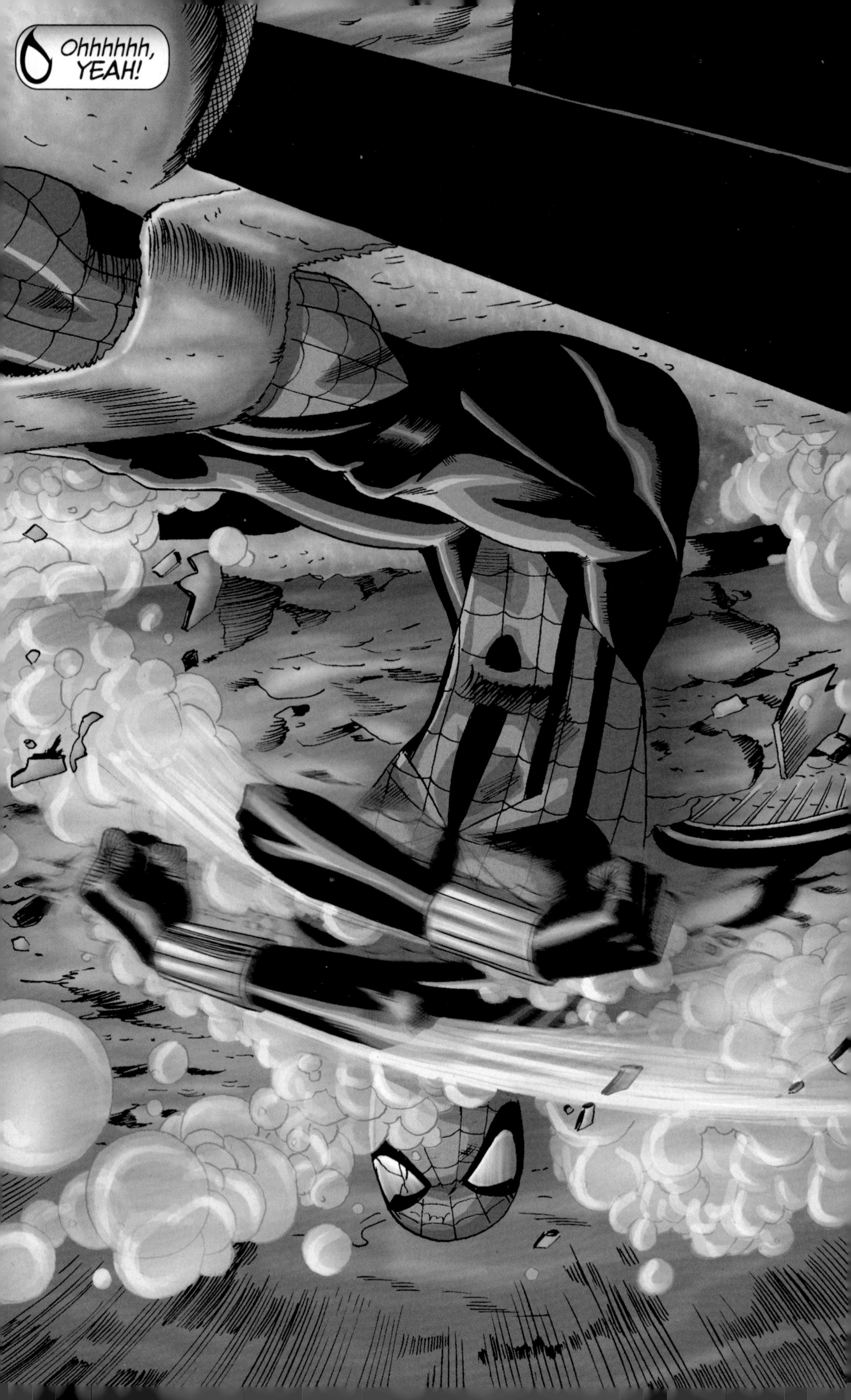
Ohhhhhh, YEAH!

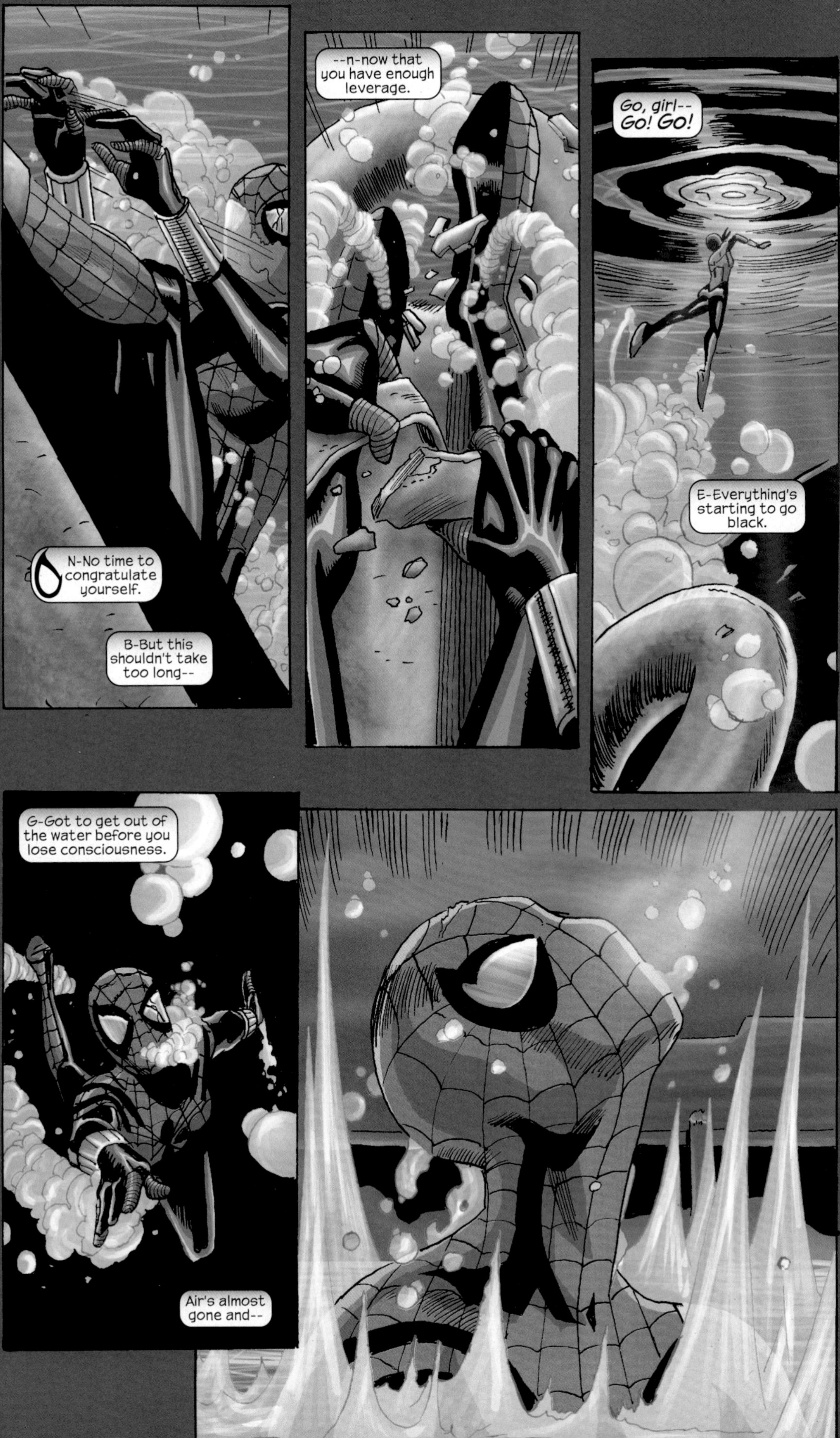
N-No time to congratulate yourself.
B-But this shouldn't take too long--
--n-now that you have enough leverage.
Go, girl-- Go! Go!
E-Everything's starting to go black.
G-Got to get out of the water before you lose consciousness.
Air's almost gone and--

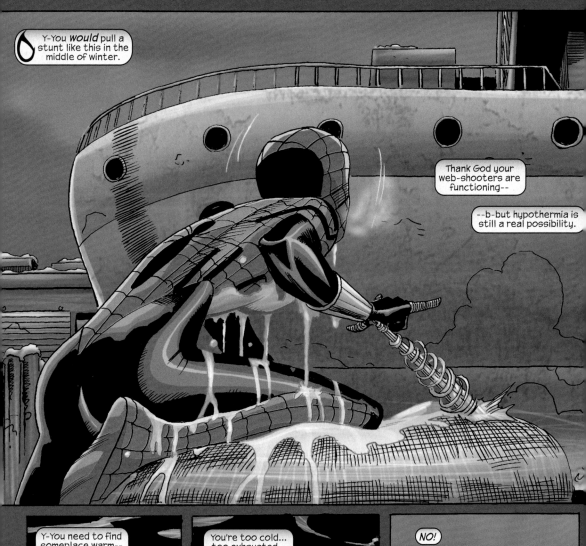

Y-You *would* pull a stunt like this in the middle of winter.

Thank *God* your web-shooters are functioning--

--b-but hypothermia is still a real possibility.

Y-You need to find someplace *warm*--

--where you can raise your body temperature.

Y-You've had *enough*, girl.

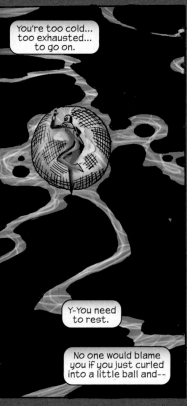

You're too *cold*... too exhausted... to go on.

Y-You need to rest.

No one would blame you if you just curled into a little ball and--

NO!

Not yet.

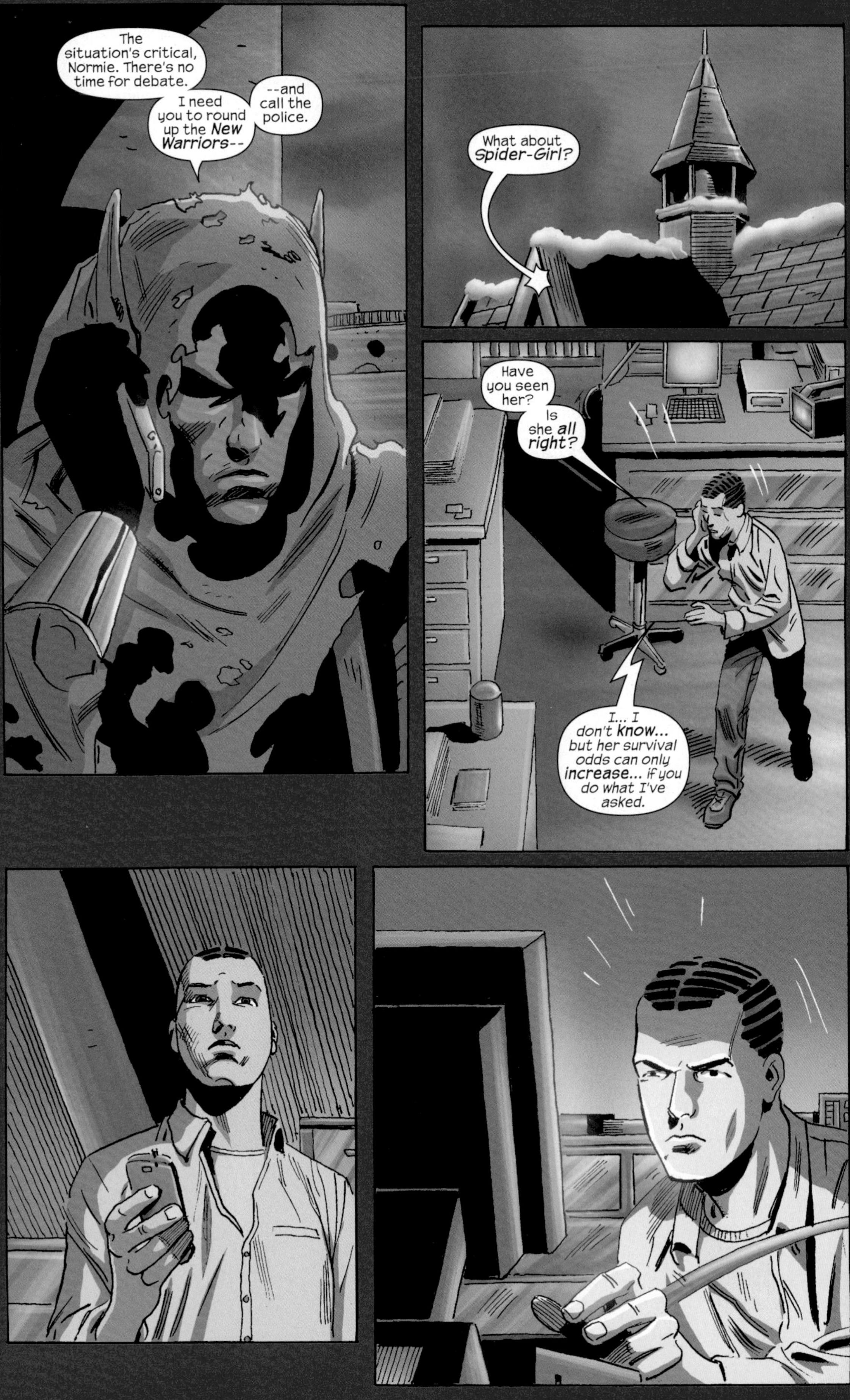
The situation's critical, Normie. There's no time for debate.
I need you to round up the New Warriors--
--and call the police.
What about Spider-Girl?
Have you seen her?
Is she all right?
I... I don't know... but her survival odds can only increase... if you do what I've asked.

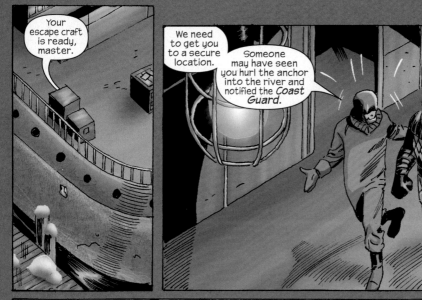

Your escape craft is ready, master.

We need to get you to a secure location.

Someone may have seen you hurl the anchor into the river and notified the *Coast Guard.*

You are overly cautious, Serpent-brother.

I do not fear the local authorities.

My master plan is too close to completion.

No power on Earth can possibly stop it now.

Wanna *bet?*

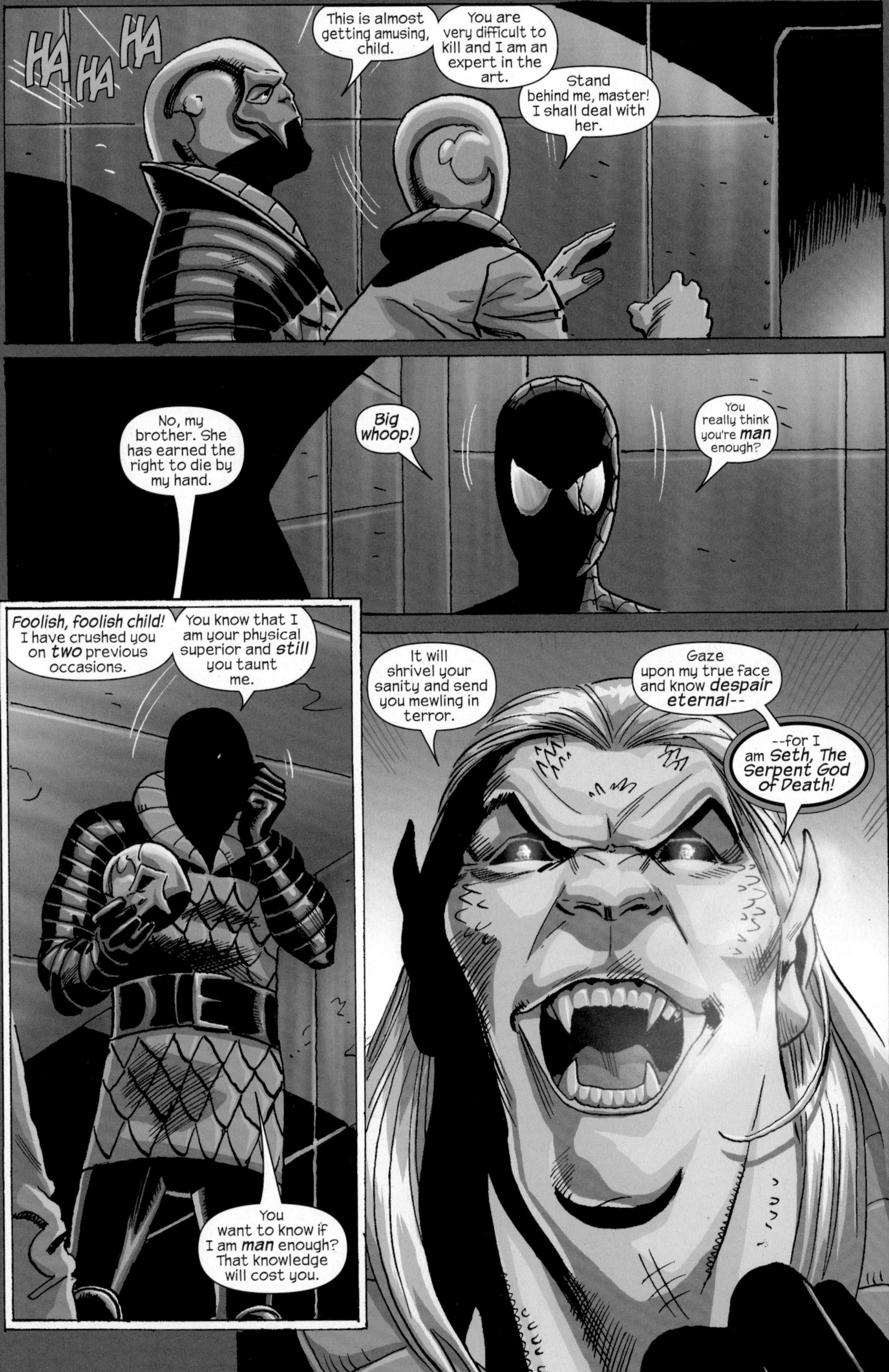
HA HA HA
This is almost getting amusing, child.
You are very difficult to kill and I am an expert in the art.
Stand behind me, master! I shall deal with her.
No, my brother. She has earned the right to die by my hand.
Big whoop!
You really think you're *man* enough?
Foolish, foolish child! I have crushed you on **two** previous occasions.
You know that I am your physical superior and **still** you taunt me.
You want to know if I am **man** enough? That knowledge will cost you.
It will shrivel your sanity and send you mewling in terror.
Gaze upon my true face and know **despair eternal**--
--for I am **Seth, The Serpent God of Death!**

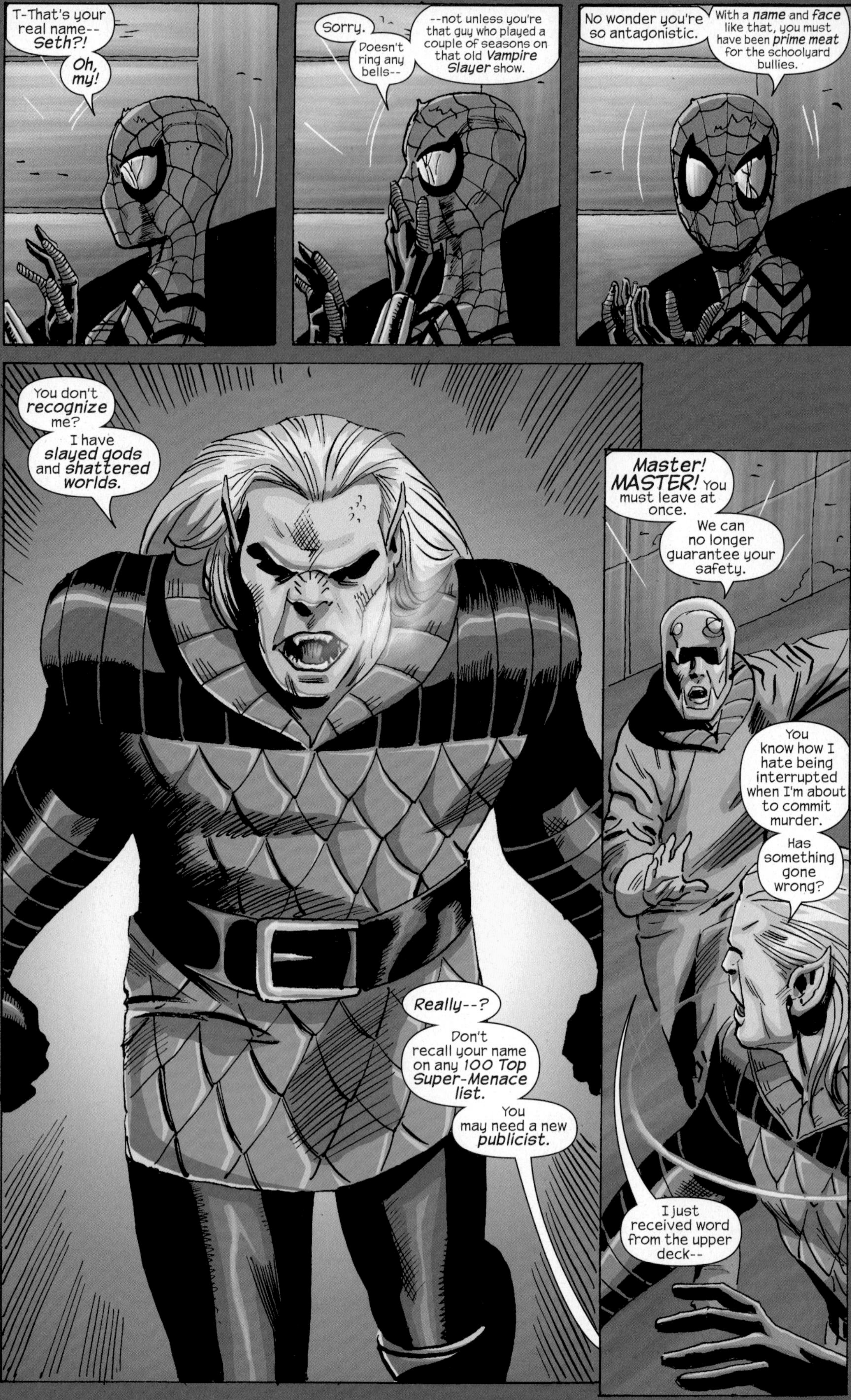

T-That's your real name-- Seth?!
Oh, my!
Sorry.
Doesn't ring any bells--
--not unless you're that guy who played a couple of seasons on that old Vampire Slayer show.
No wonder you're so antagonistic.
With a name and face like that, you must have been prime meat for the schoolyard bullies.
You don't recognize me?
I have slayed gods and shattered worlds.
Master! MASTER! You must leave at once.
We can no longer guarantee your safety.
You know how I hate being interrupted when I'm about to commit murder.
Has something gone wrong?
Really--?
Don't recall your name on any 100 Top Super-Menace list.
You may need a new publicist.
I just received word from the upper deck--

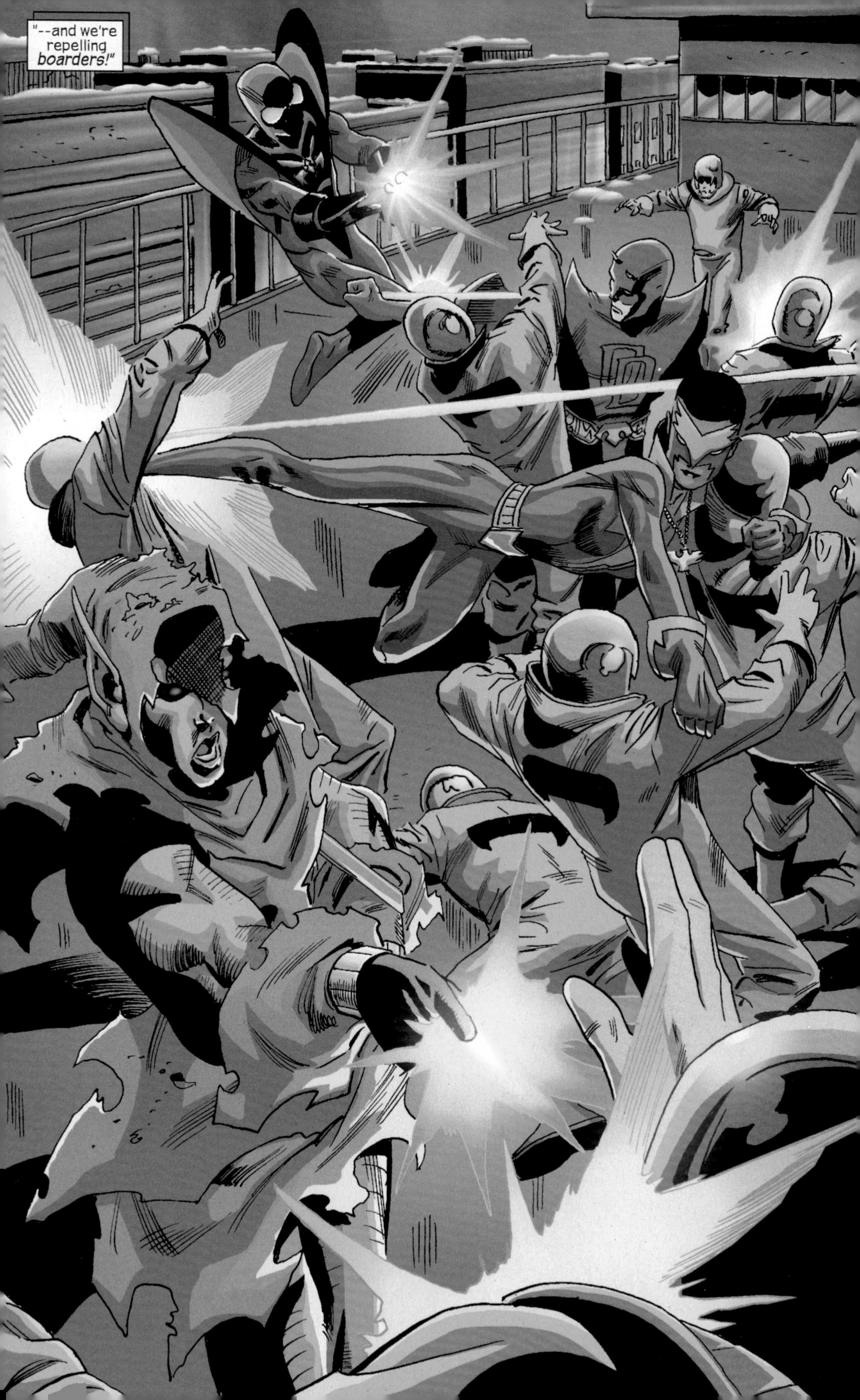
"--and we're repelling *boarders!*"

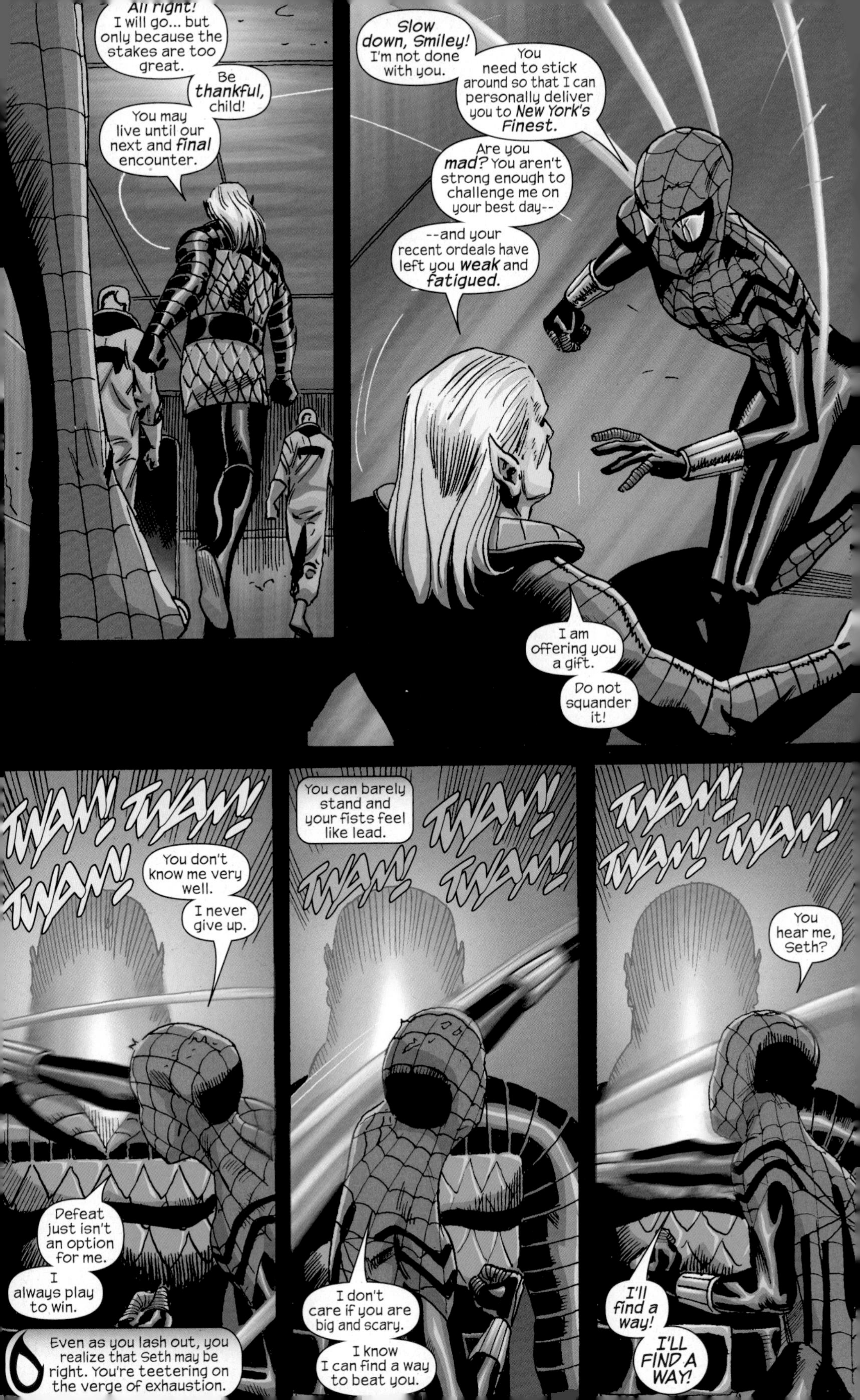
All right! I will go... but only because the stakes are too great.
Be thankful, child!
You may live until our next and final encounter.
Slow down, Smiley! I'm not done with you.
You need to stick around so that I can personally deliver you to New York's Finest.
Are you mad? You aren't strong enough to challenge me on your best day--
--and your recent ordeals have left you weak and fatigued.
I am offering you a gift.
Do not squander it!
TWAN! TWAN! TWAN!
You don't know me very well.
I never give up.
Defeat just isn't an option for me.
I always play to win.
Even as you lash out, you realize that Seth may be right. You're teetering on the verge of exhaustion.
You can barely stand and your fists feel like lead.
TWAN! TWAN! TWAN!
I don't care if you are big and scary.
I know I can find a way to beat you.
TWAN! TWAN! TWAN!
You hear me, Seth?
I'll find a way!
I'LL FIND A WAY!

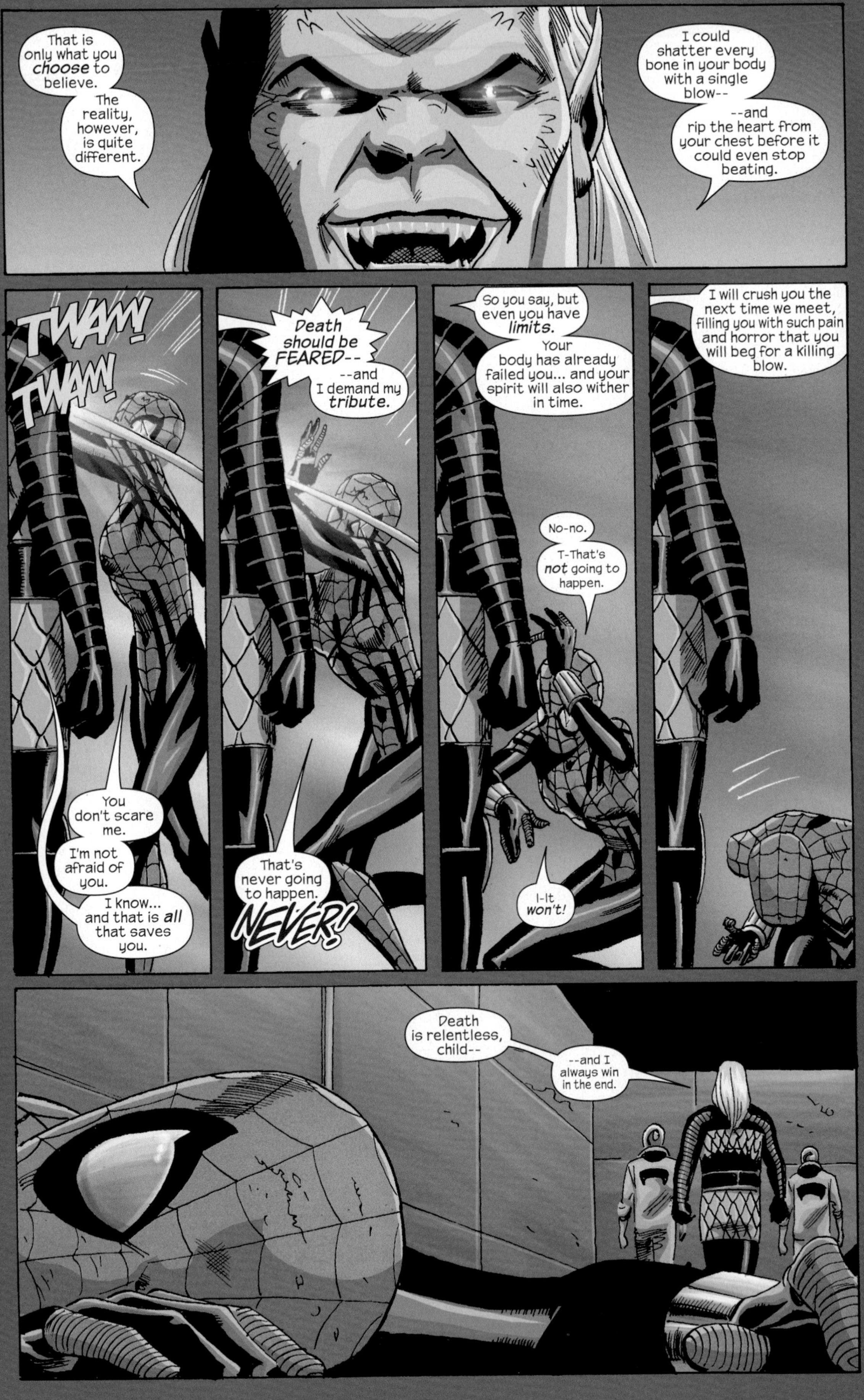

That is only what you *choose* to believe.
The reality, however, is quite different.
I could shatter every bone in your body with a single blow--
--and rip the heart from your chest before it could even stop beating.
TWAM!
TWAM!
You don't scare me.
I'm not afraid of you.
I know... and that is *all* that saves you.
Death should be FEARED--
--and I demand my *tribute.*
That's never going to happen.
NEVER!
So you say, but even you have *limits.*
Your body has already failed you... and your spirit will also wither in time.
No-no.
T-That's *not* going to happen.
I-It *won't!*
I will crush you the next time we meet, filling you with such pain and horror that you will beg for a killing blow.
Death is relentless, child--
--and I always win in the end.

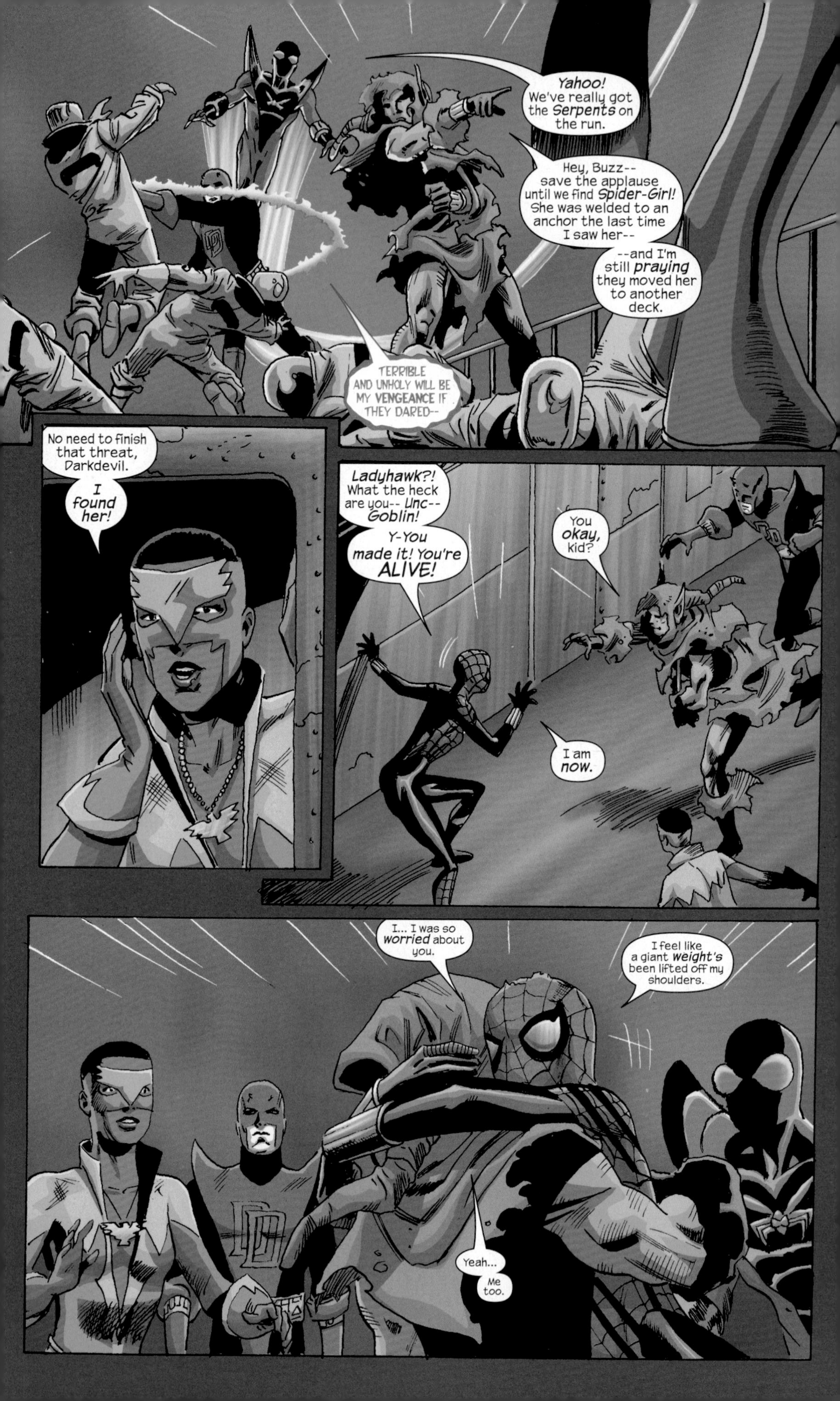
Yahoo! We've really got the Serpents on the run.
Hey, Buzz-- save the applause until we find Spider-Girl! She was welded to an anchor the last time I saw her--
--and I'm still praying they moved her to another deck.
TERRIBLE AND UNHOLY WILL BE MY VENGEANCE IF THEY DARED--
No need to finish that threat, Darkdevil.
I found her!
Ladyhawk?! What the heck are you-- Unc-- Goblin!
Y-You made it! You're ALIVE!
You okay, kid?
I am now.
I... I was so worried about you.
I feel like a giant weight's been lifted off my shoulders.
Yeah...
Me too.

WHAT ABOUT THE SERPENT LEADER?

DID YOU SEE HIM?

Yes... but I'm afraid he's long *gone.*

I... I *tried* to stop him, but I...

I *failed.*

What a loser! We took out a few *dozen* of these clowns and you couldn't even stop *one.*

What kind of *hero* are you, anyway?

You sure you're in the right biz?

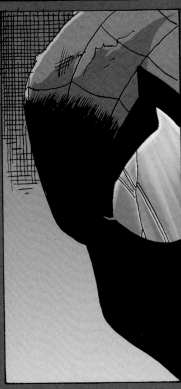

Look, I hate to break up the party, but I really gotta go.

I need to be elsewhere.

I'll catch you *whenever.*

Hold up, girl! No need to get so huffy. I was just messing with you and--

HEY, BUZZ...

SHUT UP!

B-But I... Okay. Sure.

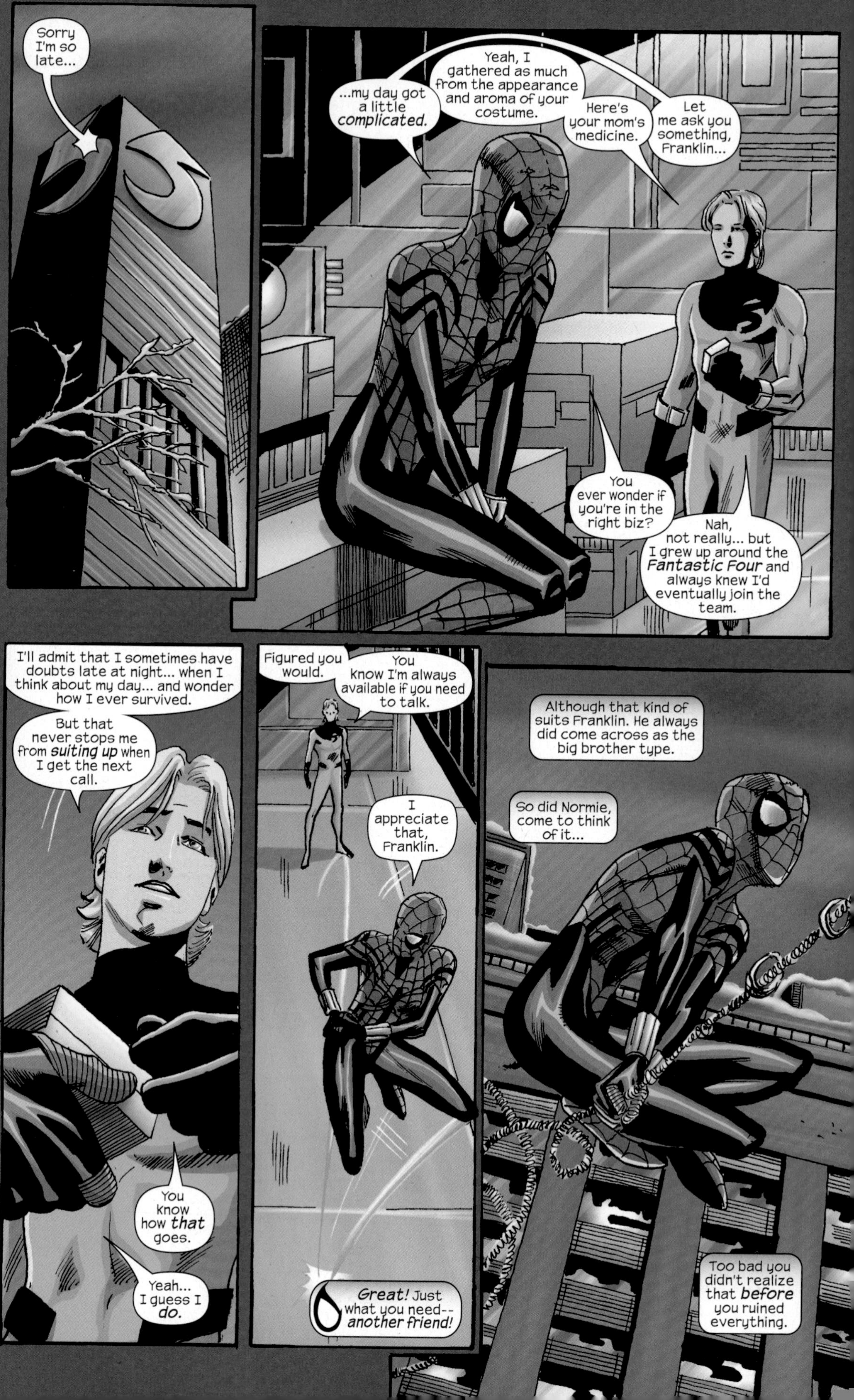

Sorry I'm so late...
...my day got a little complicated.
Yeah, I gathered as much from the appearance and aroma of your costume.
Here's your mom's medicine.
Let me ask you something, Franklin...
You ever wonder if you're in the right biz?
Nah, not really... but I grew up around the Fantastic Four and always knew I'd eventually join the team.
I'll admit that I sometimes have doubts late at night... when I think about my day... and wonder how I ever survived.
But that never stops me from suiting up when I get the next call.
You know how that goes.
Yeah... I guess I do.
Figured you would.
You know I'm always available if you need to talk.
I appreciate that, Franklin.
Great! Just what you need-- another friend!
Although that kind of suits Franklin. He always did come across as the big brother type.
So did Normie, come to think of it...
Too bad you didn't realize that before you ruined everything.

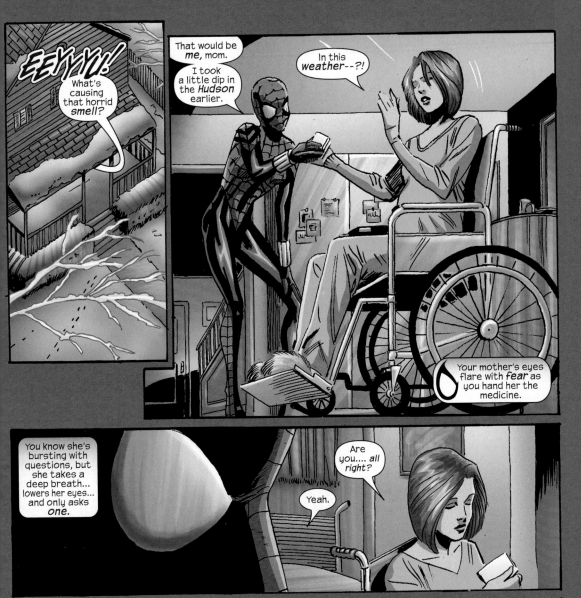

EEYYY!! What's causing that horrid *smell?*

That would be *me,* mom. I took a little dip in the *Hudson* earlier.

In this *weather--?!*

Your mother's eyes flare with *fear* as you hand her the medicine.

You know she's bursting with questions, but she takes a deep breath... lowers her eyes... and only asks *one.*

Are you.... *all right?*

Yeah.

You... you'd better lose that costume before your father gets home. You know how he worries.

S'funny, you know what it costs you to suit up and can imagine what it cost your dad.

But you suddenly realize that your mom may be paying the highest price of all.

And May... Take a *shower!*

Trust me, I can't wait to renew my acquaintance with *Mr. Bubbles.*

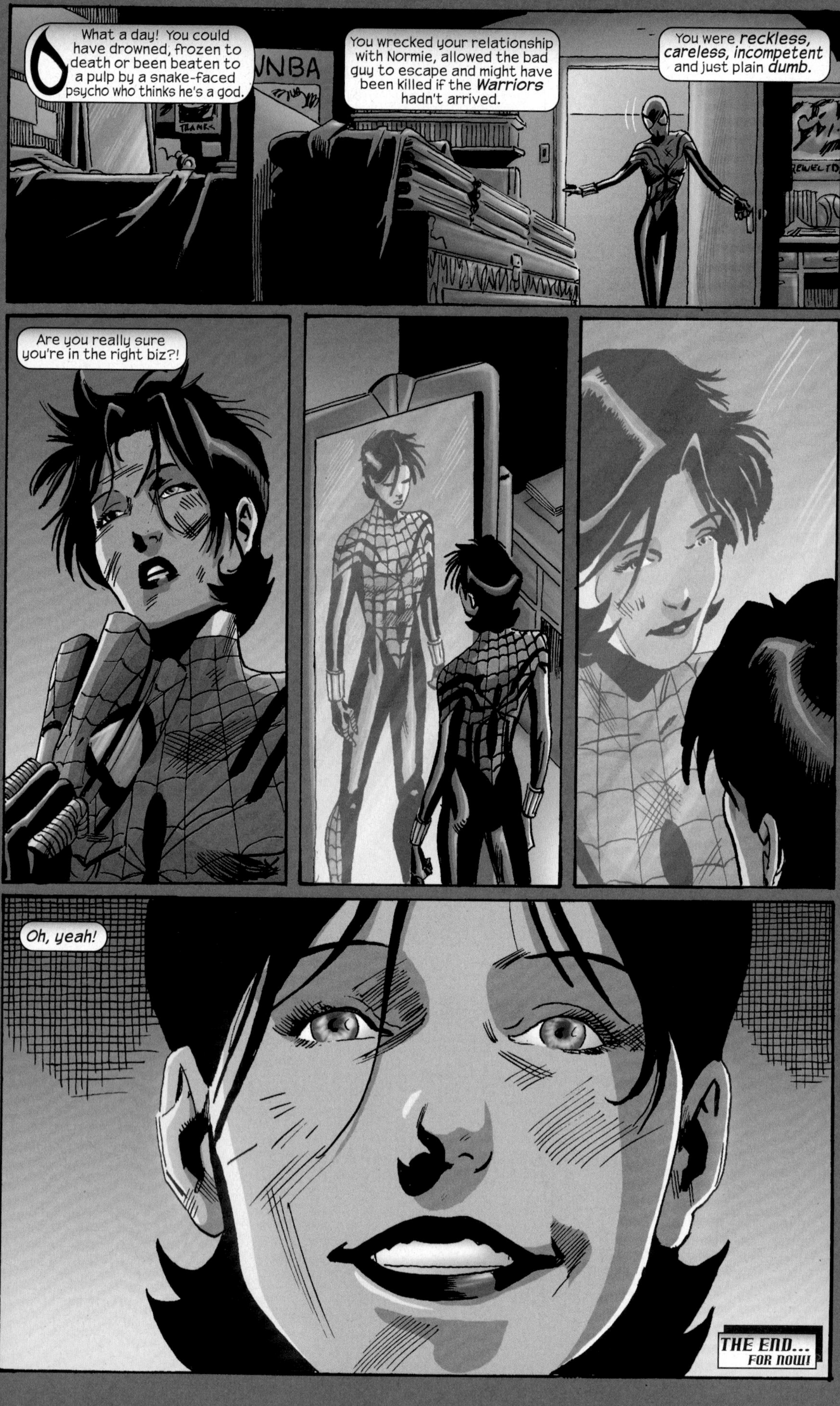
What a day! You could have drowned, frozen to death or been beaten to a pulp by a snake-faced psycho who thinks he's a god.
WNBA
THANKS
You wrecked your relationship with Normie, allowed the bad guy to escape and might have been killed if the *Warriors* hadn't arrived.
You were ***reckless, careless, incompetent*** and just plain ***dumb.***
Are you really sure you're in the right biz?!
Oh, yeah!
THE END... FOR NOW!

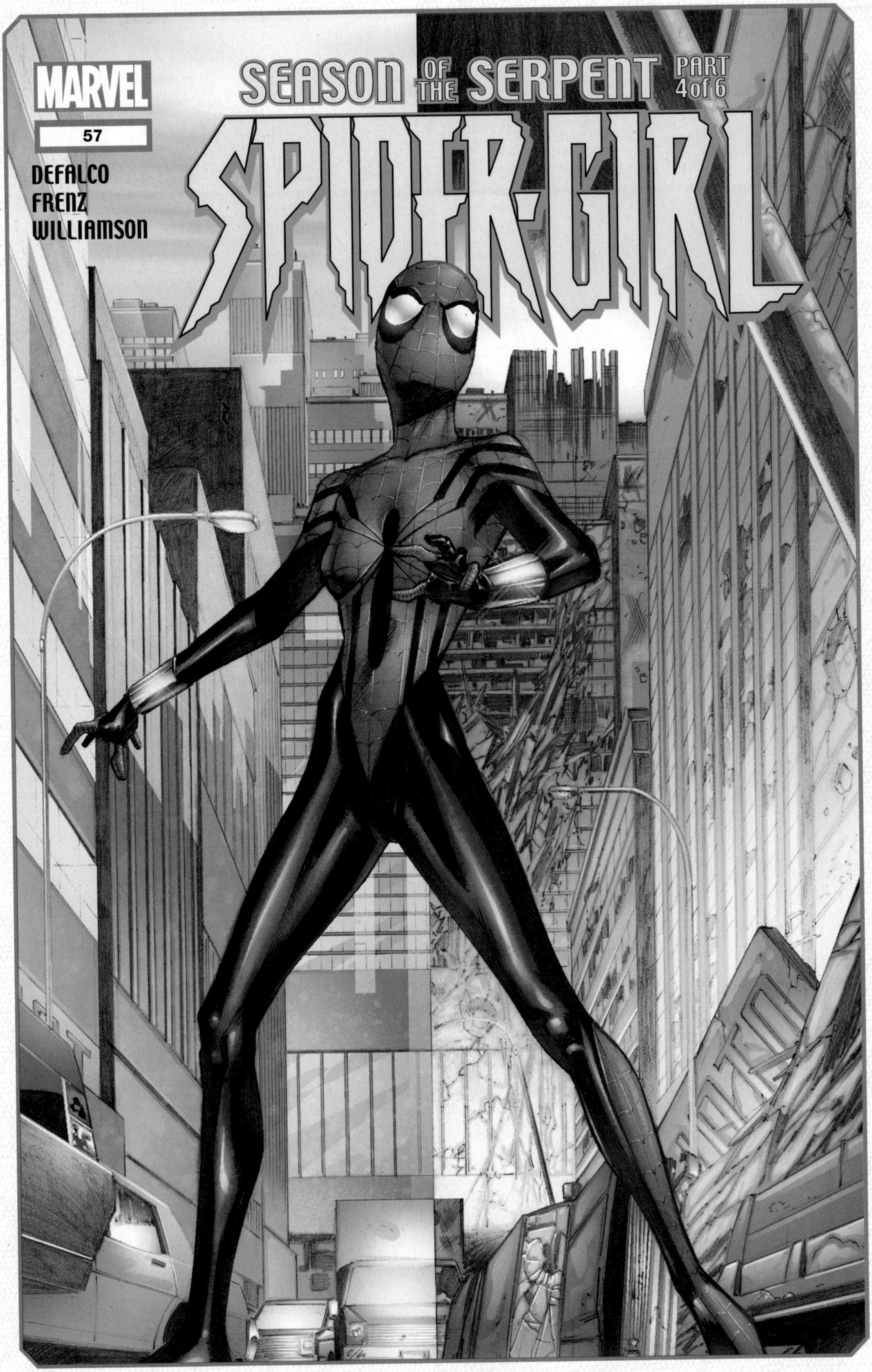
SEASON OF THE SERPENT PART 4 of 6
MARVEL
57
DEFALCO
FRENZ
WILLIAMSON
SPIDER-GIRL

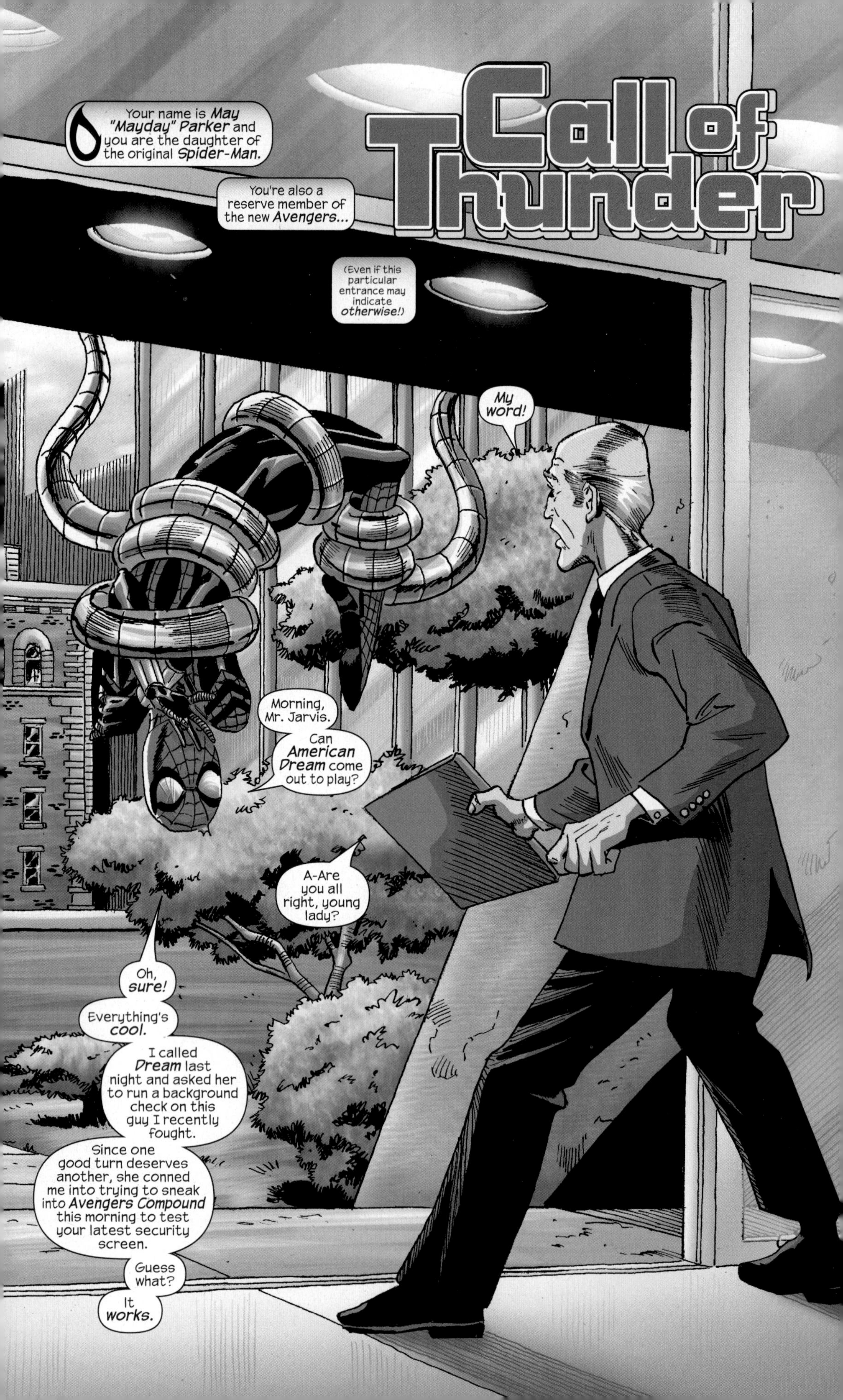

Call of Thunder
Your name is May "Mayday" Parker and you are the daughter of the original Spider-Man.
You're also a reserve member of the new Avengers...
(Even if this particular entrance may indicate otherwise!)
My word!
Morning, Mr. Jarvis.
Can American Dream come out to play?
A-Are you all right, young lady?
Oh, sure!
Everything's cool.
I called Dream last night and asked her to run a background check on this guy I recently fought.
Since one good turn deserves another, she conned me into trying to sneak into Avengers Compound this morning to test your latest security screen.
Guess what?
It works.

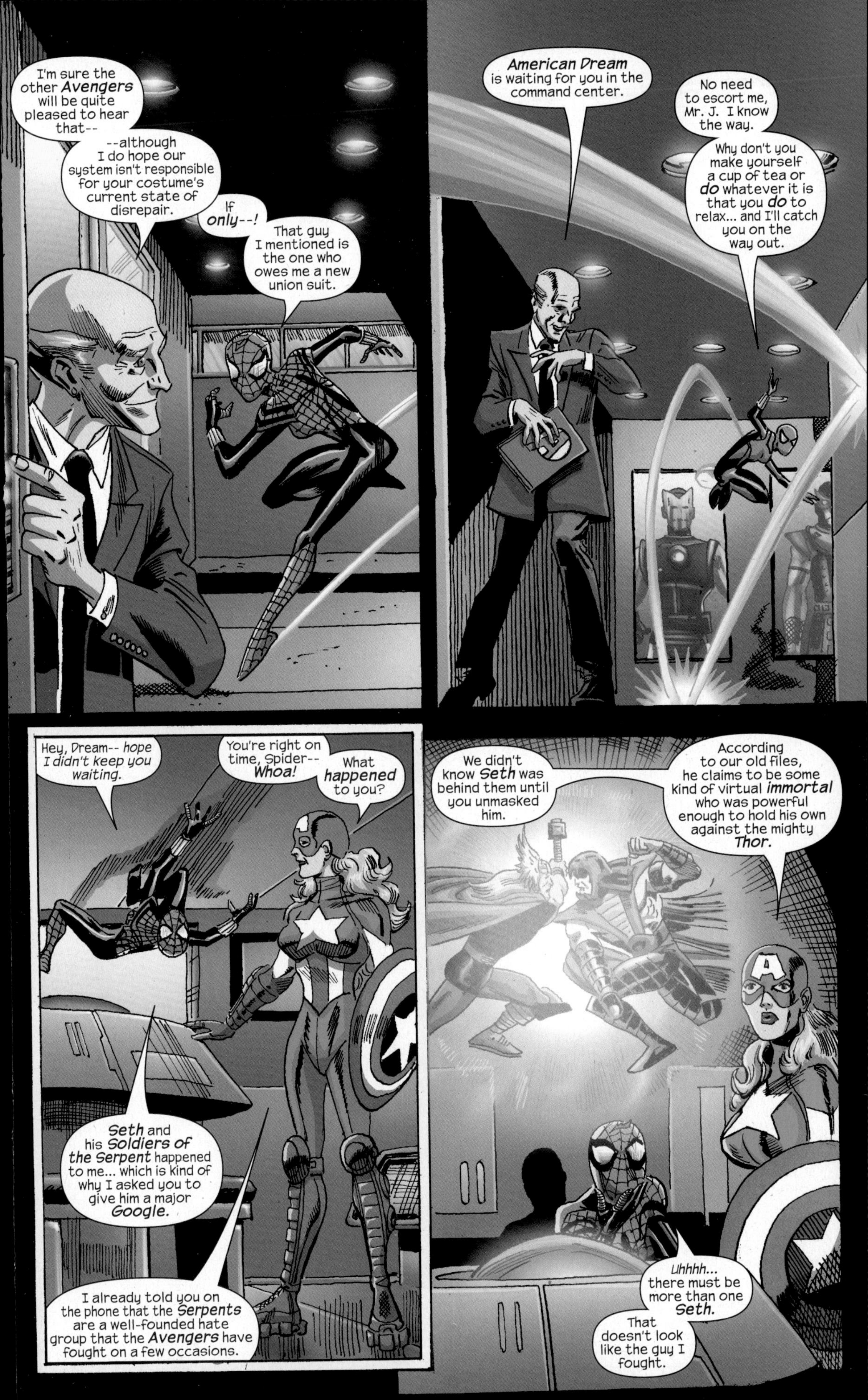
I'm sure the other Avengers will be quite pleased to hear that--
--although I do hope our system isn't responsible for your costume's current state of disrepair.
If only--!
That guy I mentioned is the one who owes me a new union suit.
American Dream is waiting for you in the command center.
No need to escort me, Mr. J. I know the way.
Why don't you make yourself a cup of tea or do whatever it is that you do to relax... and I'll catch you on the way out.
Hey, Dream-- hope I didn't keep you waiting.
You're right on time, Spider-- Whoa!
What happened to you?
Seth and his Soldiers of the Serpent happened to me... which is kind of why I asked you to give him a major Google.
I already told you on the phone that the Serpents are a well-founded hate group that the Avengers have fought on a few occasions.
We didn't know Seth was behind them until you unmasked him.
According to our old files, he claims to be some kind of virtual immortal who was powerful enough to hold his own against the mighty Thor.
Uhhhh... there must be more than one Seth.
That doesn't look like the guy I fought.

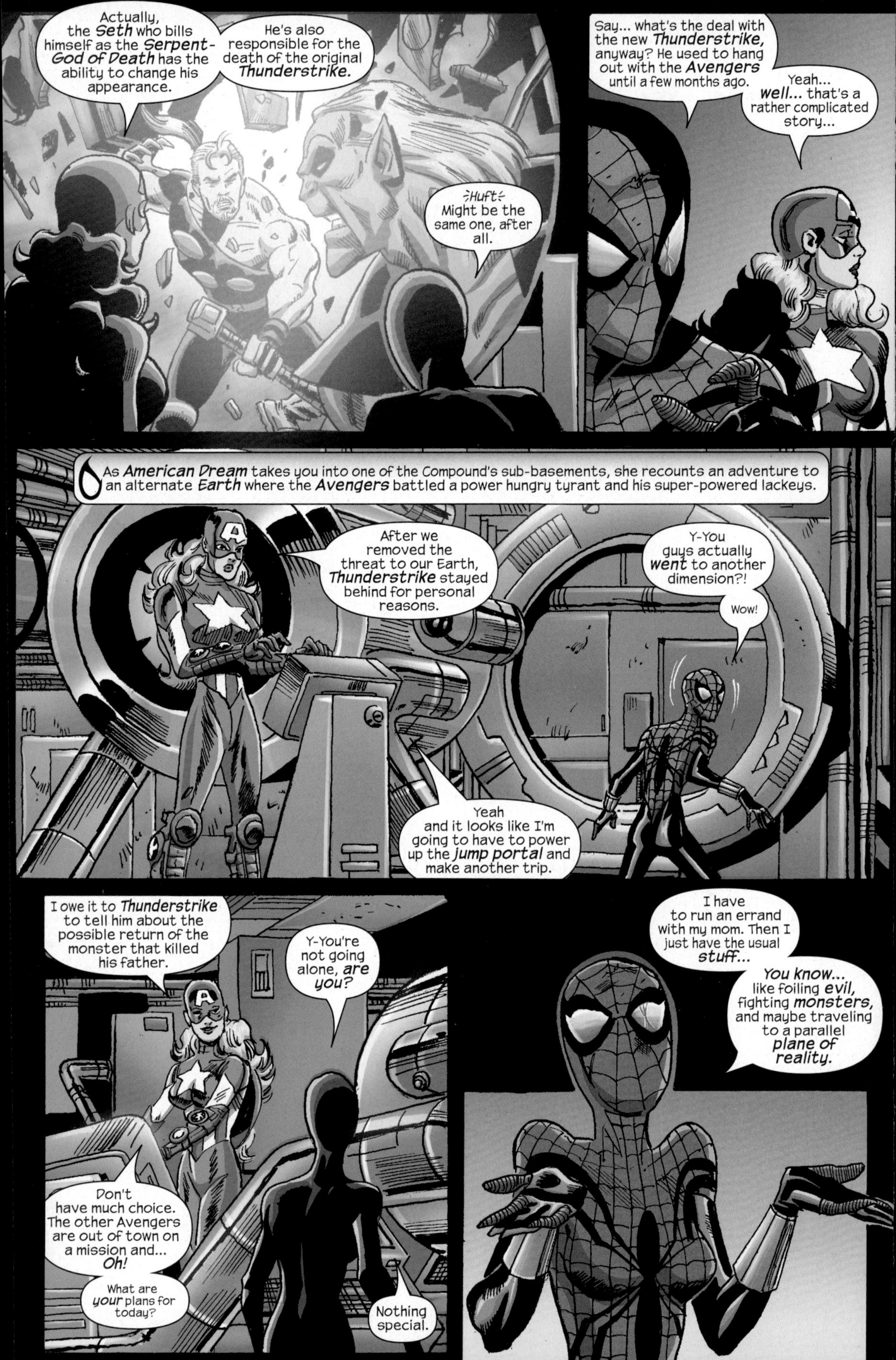

Actually, the Seth who bills himself as the Serpent-God of Death has the ability to change his appearance.
He's also responsible for the death of the original Thunderstrike.
Huft
Might be the same one, after all.
Say... what's the deal with the new Thunderstrike, anyway? He used to hang out with the Avengers until a few months ago.
Yeah... well... that's a rather complicated story...
As American Dream takes you into one of the Compound's sub-basements, she recounts an adventure to an alternate Earth where the Avengers battled a power hungry tyrant and his super-powered lackeys.
After we removed the threat to our Earth, Thunderstrike stayed behind for personal reasons.
Y-You guys actually went to another dimension?!
Wow!
Yeah and it looks like I'm going to have to power up the jump portal and make another trip.
I owe it to Thunderstrike to tell him about the possible return of the monster that killed his father.
Y-You're not going alone, are you?
Don't have much choice. The other Avengers are out of town on a mission and... Oh!
What are your plans for today?
Nothing special.
I have to run an errand with my mom. Then I just have the usual stuff...
You know... like foiling evil, fighting monsters, and maybe traveling to a parallel plane of reality.

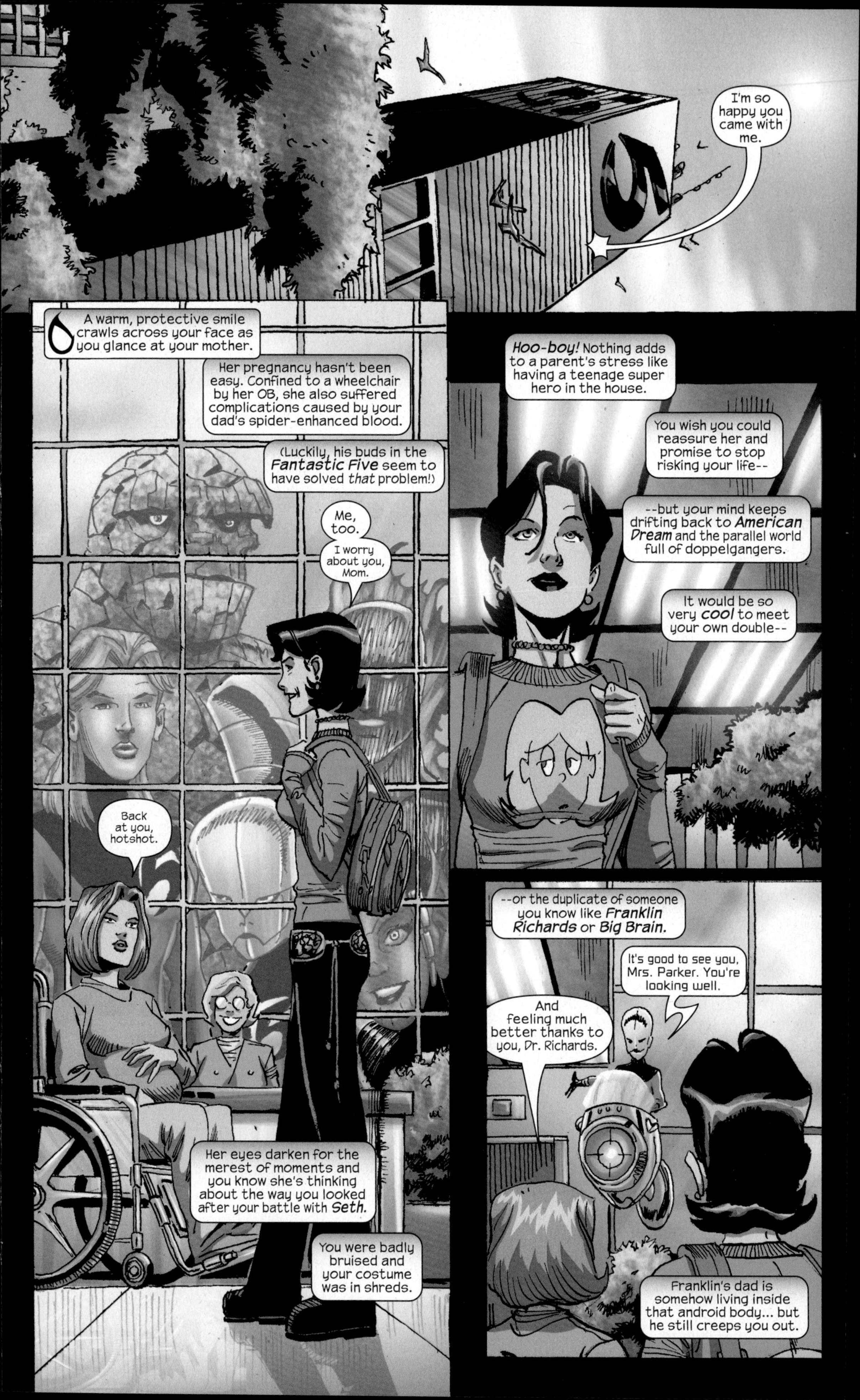
I'm so happy you came with me.
A warm, protective smile crawls across your face as you glance at your mother.
Her pregnancy hasn't been easy. Confined to a wheelchair by her OB, she also suffered complications caused by your dad's spider-enhanced blood.
(Luckily, his buds in the *Fantastic Five* seem to have solved *that* problem!)
Me, too.
I worry about you, Mom.
Back at you, hotshot.
Her eyes darken for the merest of moments and you know she's thinking about the way you looked after your battle with *Seth*.
You were badly bruised and your costume was in shreds.
Hoo-boy! Nothing adds to a parent's stress like having a teenage super hero in the house.
You wish you could reassure her and promise to stop risking your life--
--but your mind keeps drifting back to *American Dream* and the parallel world full of doppelgangers.
It would be so very *cool* to meet your own double--
--or the duplicate of someone you know like *Franklin Richards* or *Big Brain.*
It's good to see you, Mrs. Parker. You're looking well.
And feeling much better thanks to you, Dr. Richards.
Franklin's dad is somehow living inside that android body... but he still creeps you out.

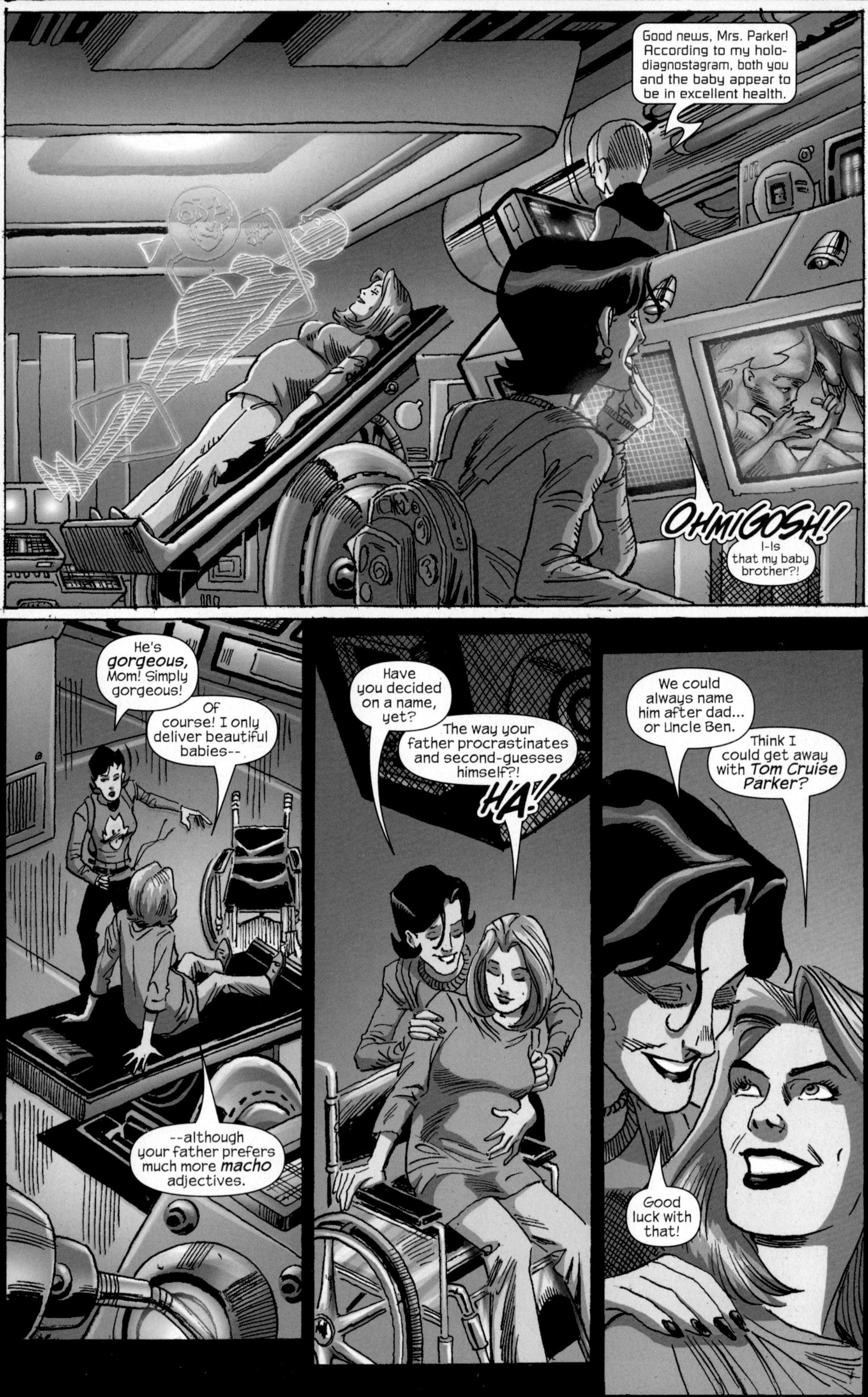
Good news, Mrs. Parker! According to my holo-diagnostagram, both you and the baby appear to be in excellent health.
OHMIGOSH!
I-Is that my baby brother?!
He's **gorgeous,** Mom! Simply gorgeous!
Of course! I only deliver beautiful babies--
--although your father prefers much more ***macho*** adjectives.
Have you decided on a name, yet?
The way your father procrastinates and second-guesses himself?!
HA!
We could always name him after dad... or Uncle Ben.
Think I could get away with ***Tom Cruise Parker?***
Good luck with that!

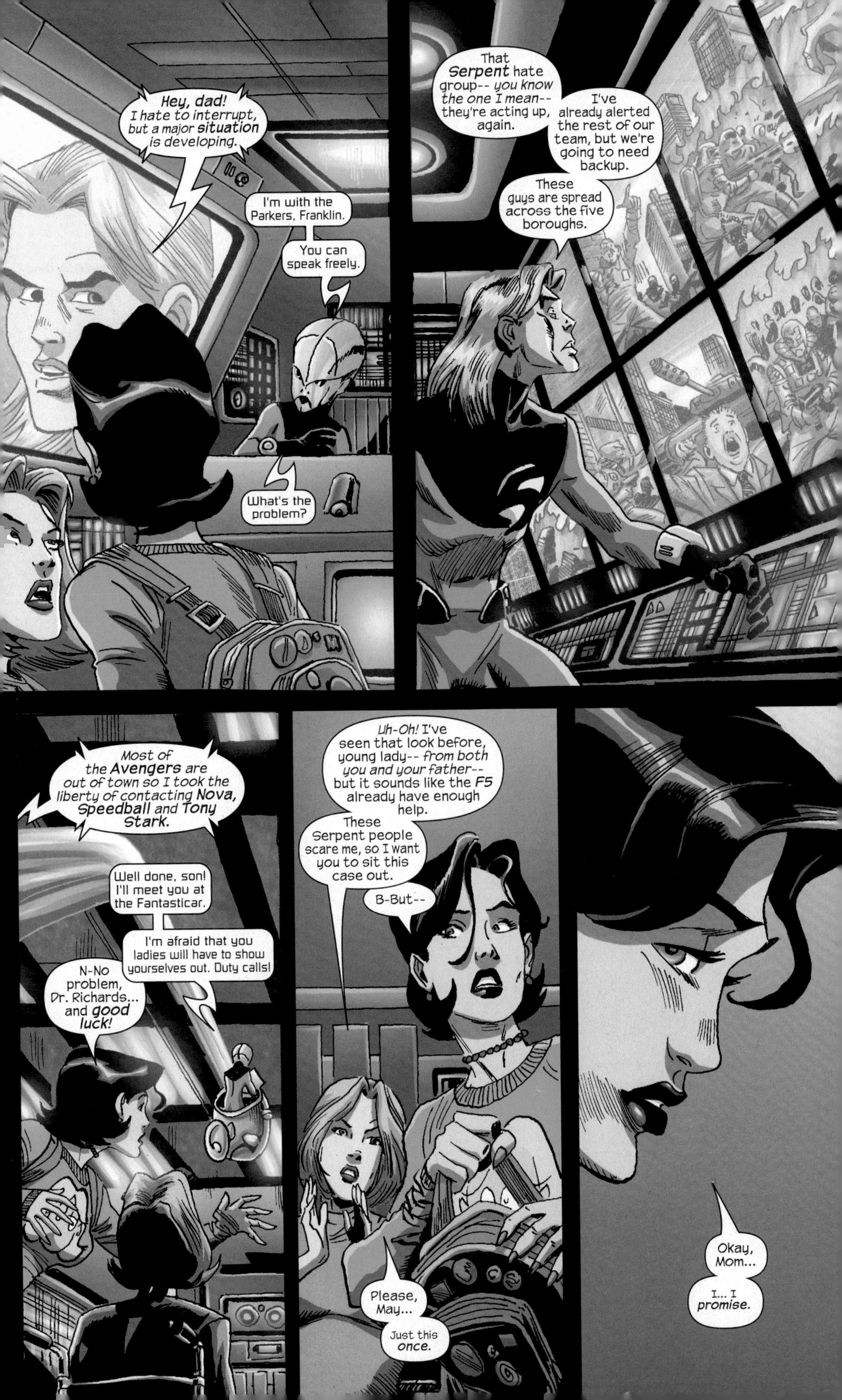
Hey, dad! I hate to interrupt, but a major situation is developing.
I'm with the Parkers, Franklin.
You can speak freely.
What's the problem?
That Serpent hate group-- you know the one I mean-- they're acting up, again.
I've already alerted the rest of our team, but we're going to need backup.
These guys are spread across the five boroughs.
Most of the Avengers are out of town so I took the liberty of contacting Nova, Speedball and Tony Stark.
Well done, son! I'll meet you at the Fantasticar.
I'm afraid that you ladies will have to show yourselves out. Duty calls!
N-No problem, Dr. Richards... and good luck!
Uh-Oh! I've seen that look before, young lady-- from both you and your father-- but it sounds like the F5 already have enough help.
These Serpent people scare me, so I want you to sit this case out.
B-But--
Please, May...
Just this once.
Okay, Mom...
I... I promise.

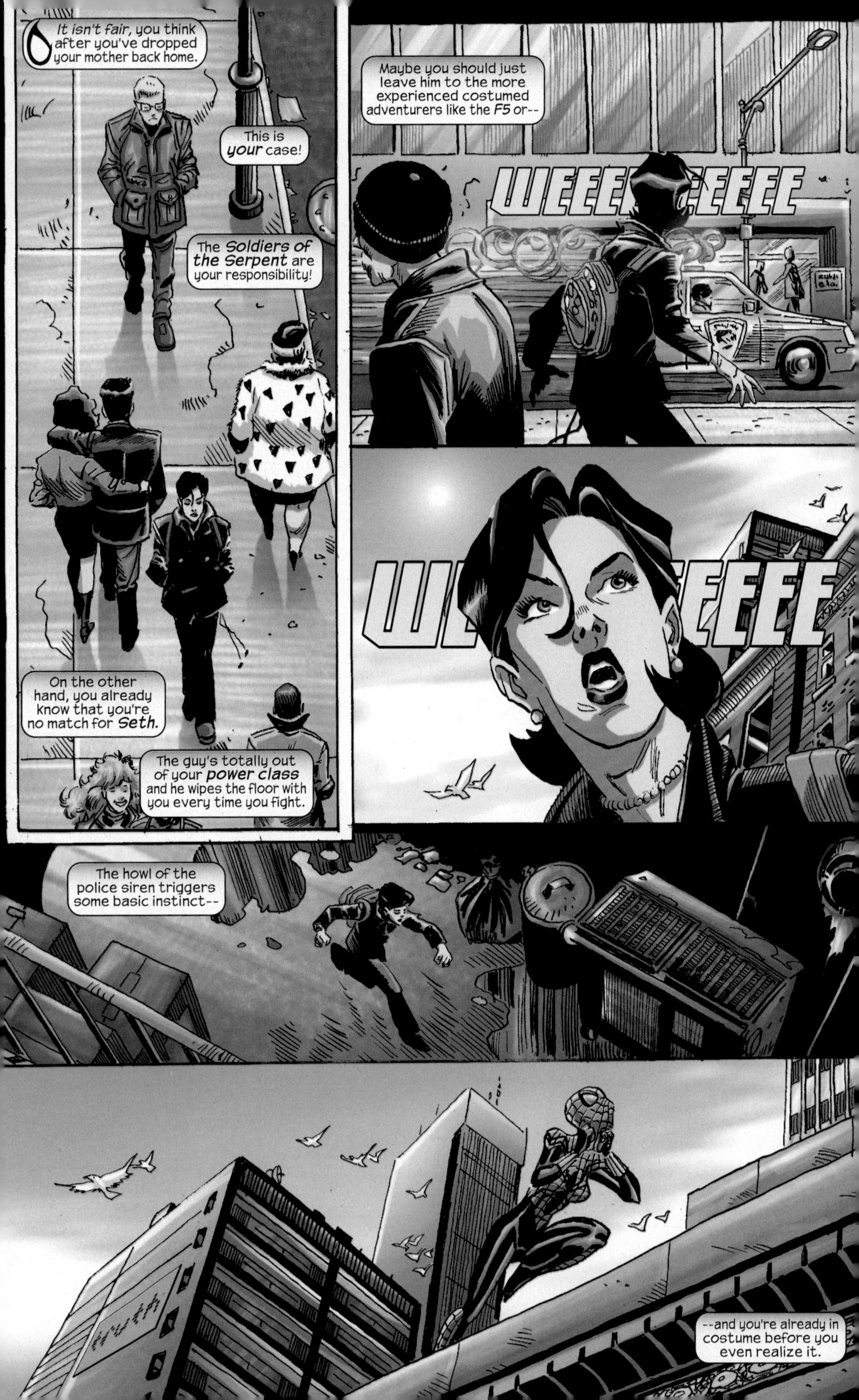

It isn't fair, you think after you've dropped your mother back home.
This is your case!
The Soldiers of the Serpent are your responsibility!
On the other hand, you already know that you're no match for Seth.
The guy's totally out of your power class and he wipes the floor with you every time you fight.
Maybe you should just leave him to the more experienced costumed adventurers like the F5 or--
WEEEEEEEEE
WEEEEEEEE
The howl of the police siren triggers some basic instinct--
--and you're already in costume before you even realize it.

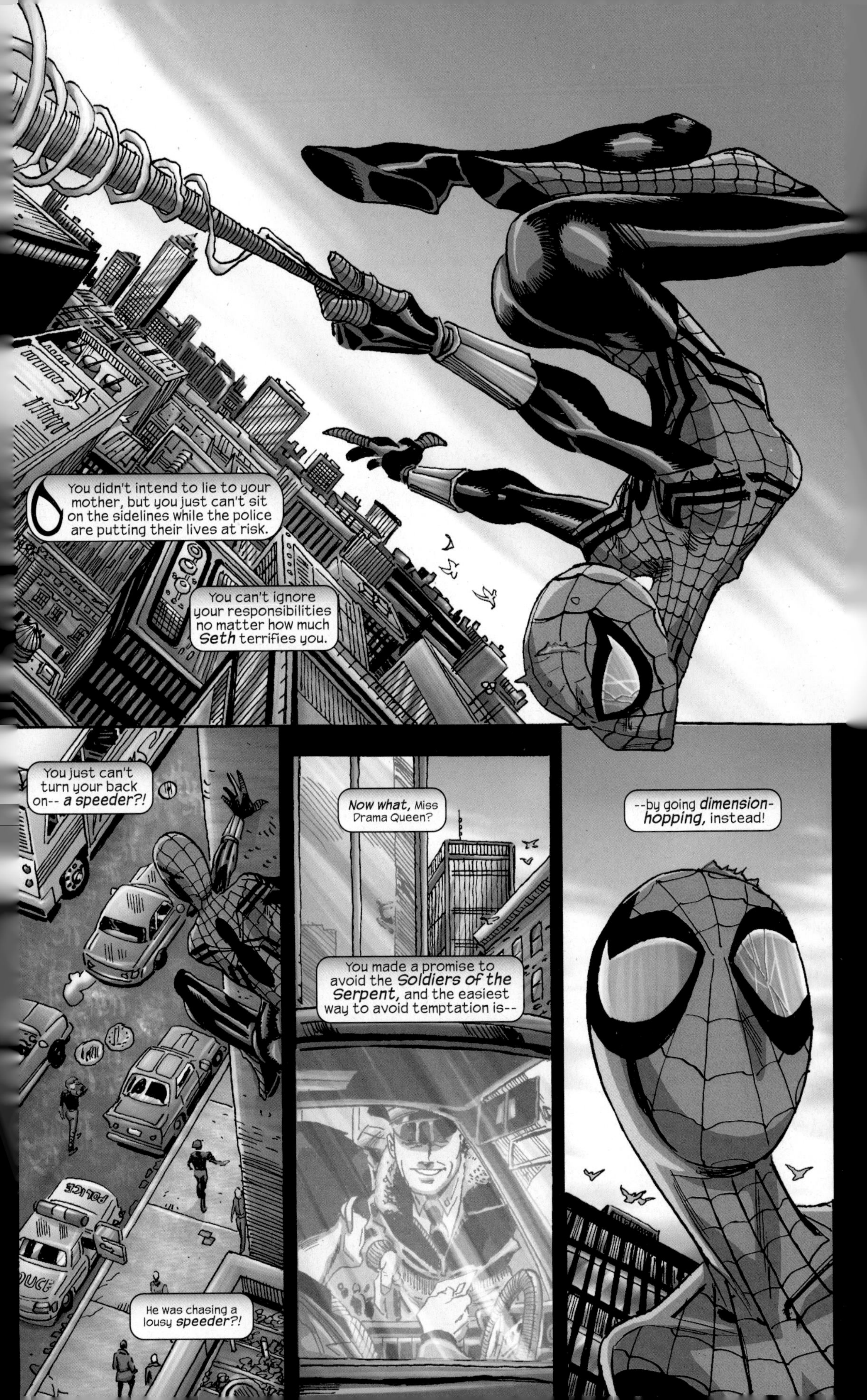

You didn't intend to lie to your mother, but you just can't sit on the sidelines while the police are putting their lives at risk.
You can't ignore your responsibilities no matter how much *Seth* terrifies you.
You just can't turn your back on-- *a speeder?!*
He was chasing a lousy *speeder?!*
Now what, Miss Drama Queen?
You made a promise to avoid the *Soldiers of the Serpent,* and the easiest way to avoid temptation is--
--by going *dimension-hopping,* instead!

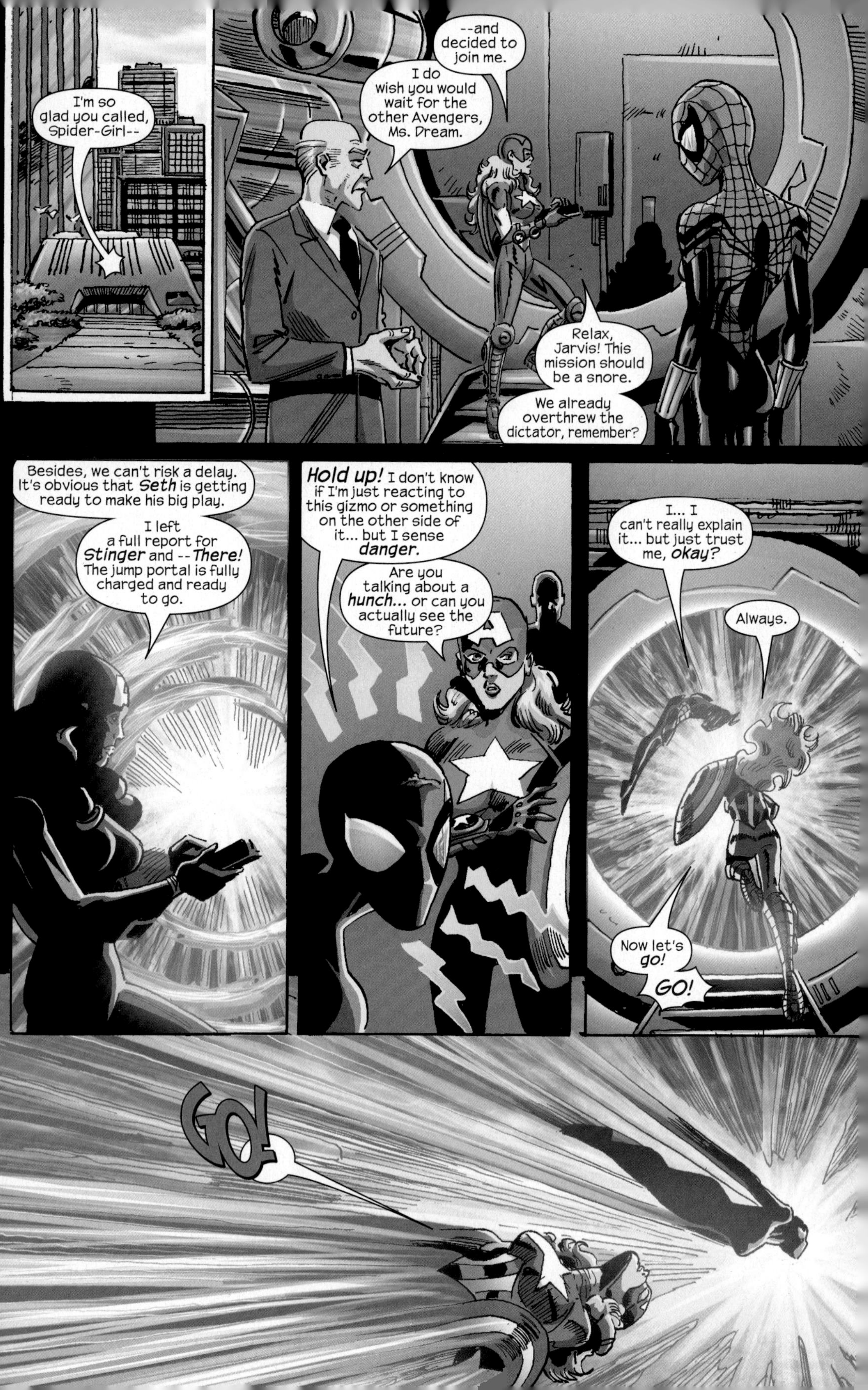
I'm so glad you called, Spider-Girl--
--and decided to join me.
I do wish you would wait for the other Avengers, Ms. Dream.
Relax, Jarvis! This mission should be a snore.
We already overthrew the dictator, remember?
Besides, we can't risk a delay. It's obvious that Seth is getting ready to make his big play.
I left a full report for Stinger and --There! The jump portal is fully charged and ready to go.
Hold up! I don't know if I'm just reacting to this gizmo or something on the other side of it... but I sense danger.
Are you talking about a hunch... or can you actually see the future?
I... I can't really explain it... but just trust me, okay?
Always.
Now let's go!
GO!
GO!

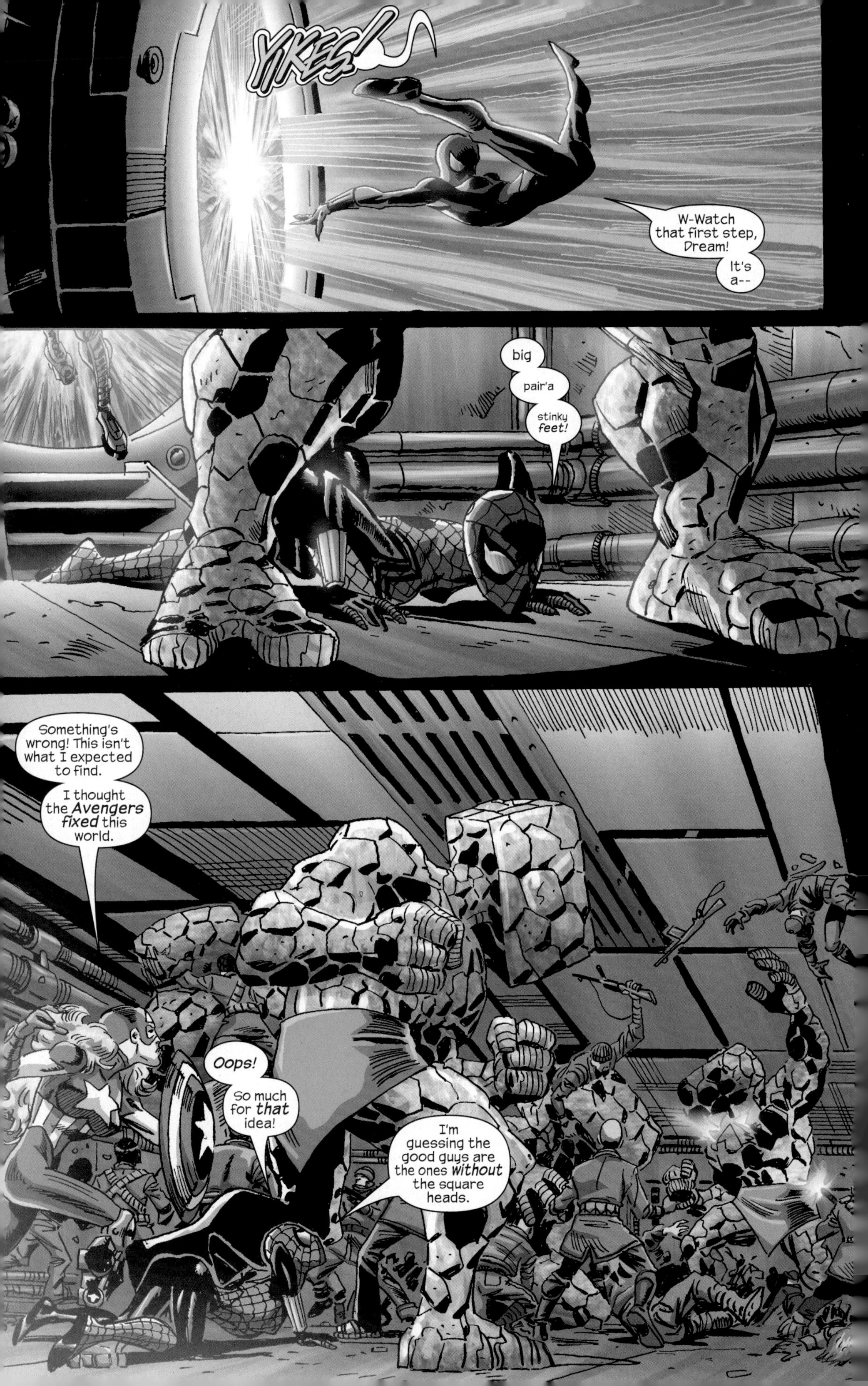
YIKES!
W-Watch that first step, Dream!
It's a--
big
pair'a
stinky *feet!*
Something's wrong! This isn't what I expected to find.
I thought the *Avengers fixed* this world.
Oops!
So much for *that* idea!
I'm guessing the good guys are the ones *without* the square heads.

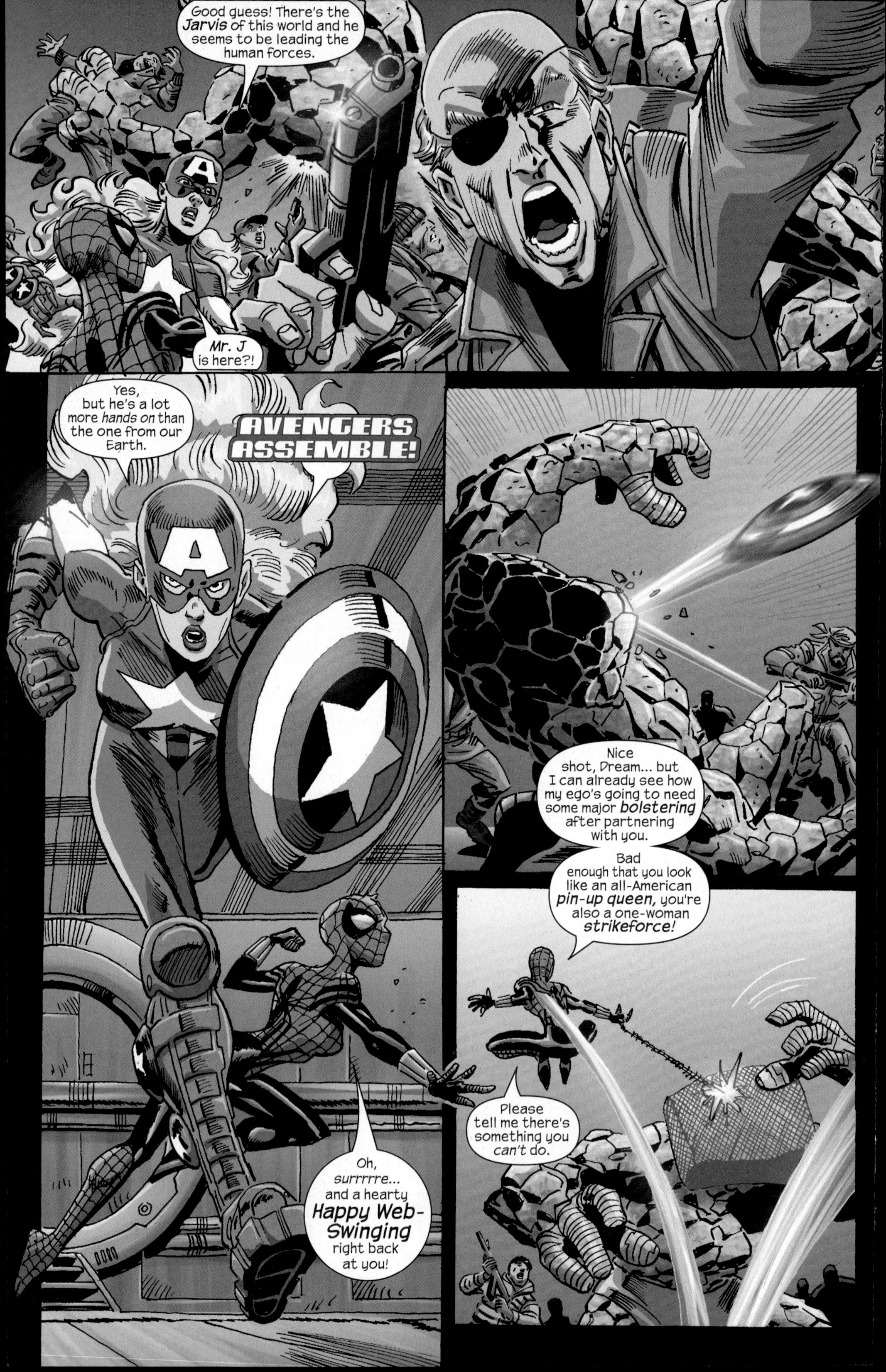
Good guess! There's the Jarvis of this world and he seems to be leading the human forces.
Mr. J is here?!
Yes, but he's a lot more hands on than the one from our Earth.
AVENGERS ASSEMBLE!
Nice shot, Dream... but I can already see how my ego's going to need some major bolstering after partnering with you.
Bad enough that you look like an all-American pin-up queen, you're also a one-woman strikeforce!
Please tell me there's something you can't do.
Oh, surrrrre... and a hearty Happy Web-Swinging right back at you!

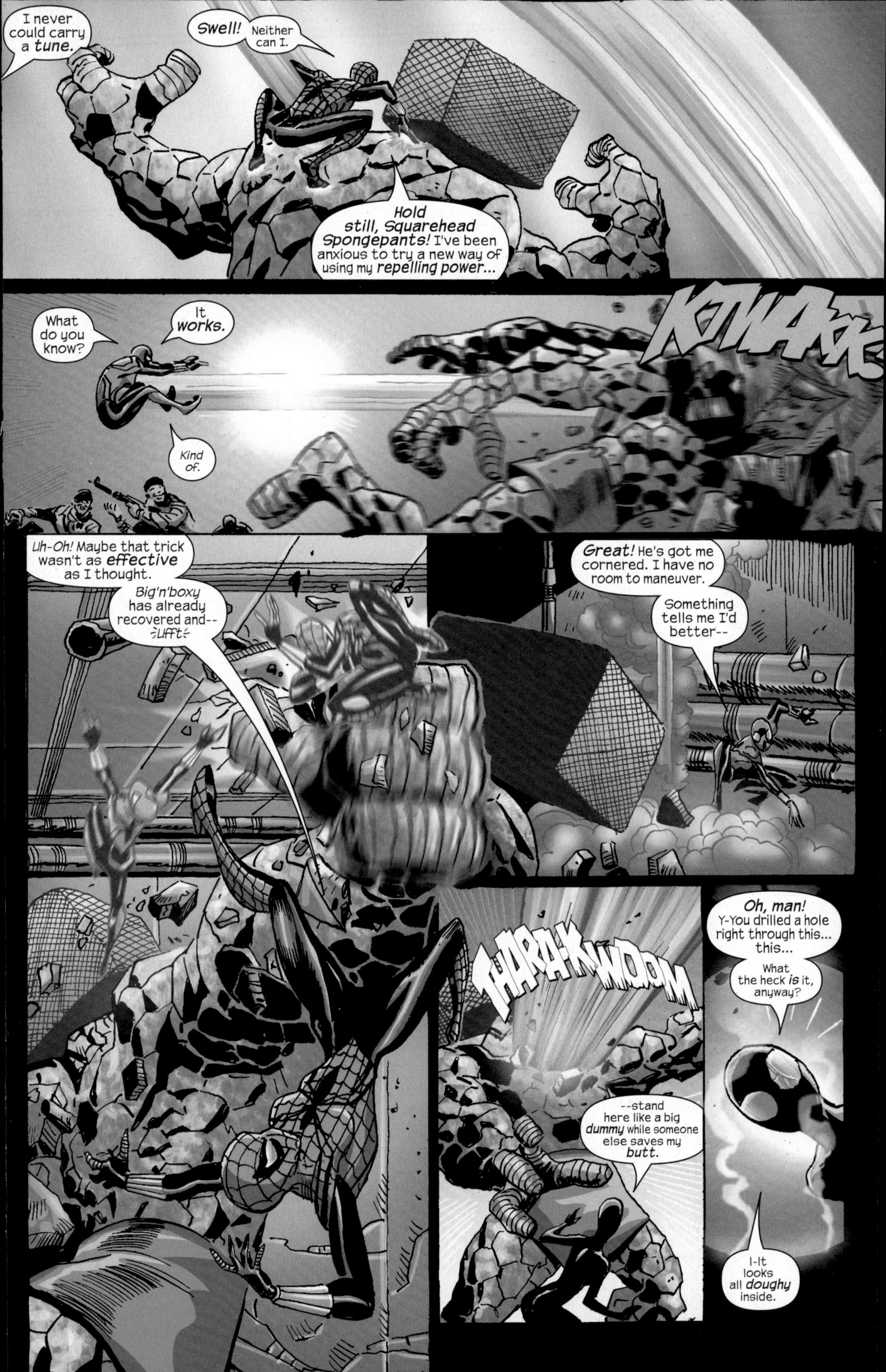

I never could carry a tune.
Swell! Neither can I.
Hold still, Squarehead Spongepants! I've been anxious to try a new way of using my repelling power...
What do you know?
It works.
Kind of.
KTWAKK
Uh-Oh! Maybe that trick wasn't as effective as I thought.
Big'n'boxy has already recovered and-- UFFT
Great! He's got me cornered. I have no room to maneuver.
Something tells me I'd better--
THRA-KWOOM
--stand here like a big dummy while someone else saves my butt.
Oh, man! Y-You drilled a hole right through this... this...
What the heck is it, anyway?
I-It looks all doughy inside.

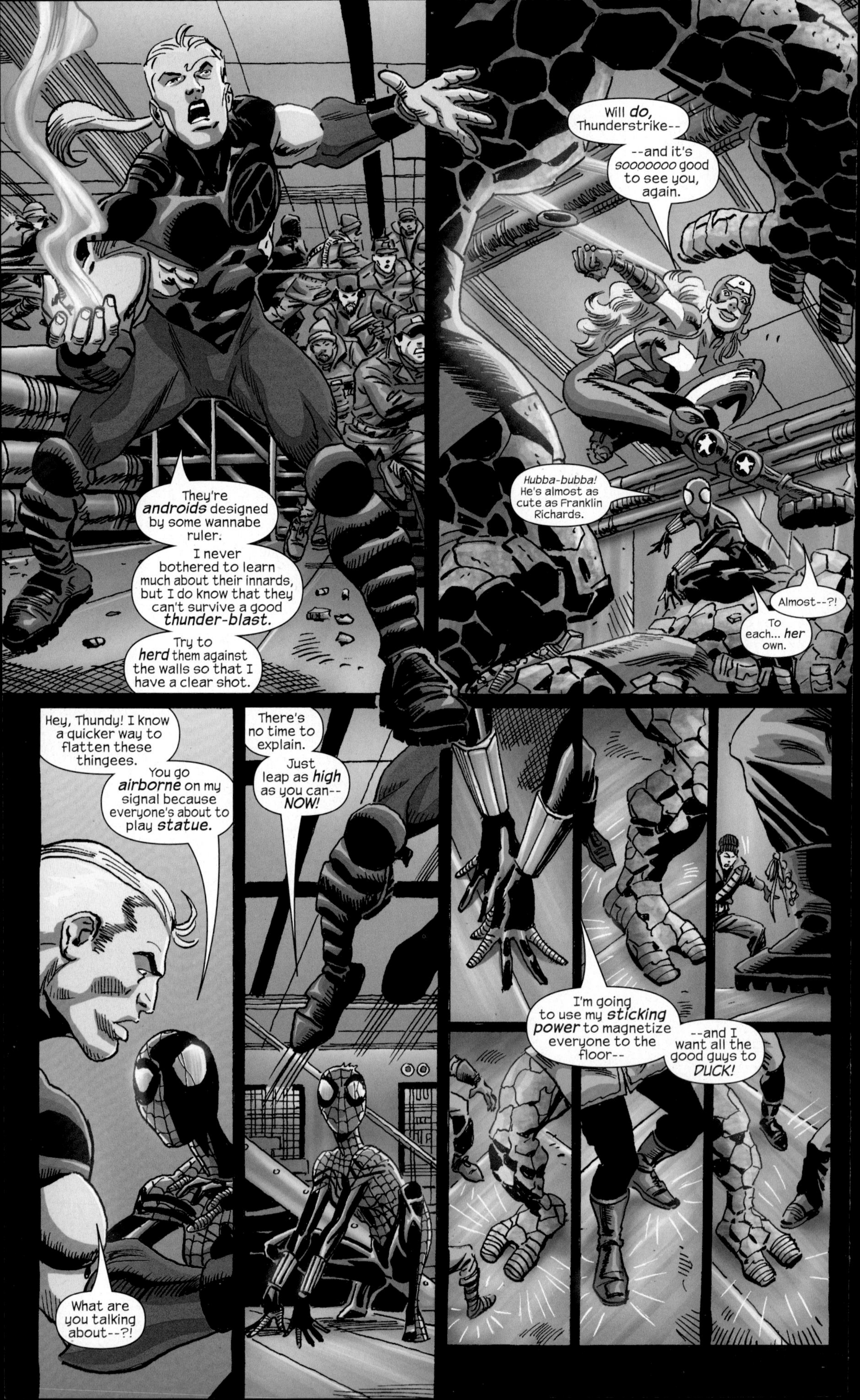
They're *androids* designed by some wannabe ruler.
I never bothered to learn much about their innards, but I do know that they can't survive a good *thunder-blast.*
Try to *herd* them against the walls so that I have a clear shot.
Will *do,* Thunderstrike--
--and it's *sooooooo* good to see you, again.
Hubba-bubba! He's almost as cute as Franklin Richards.
Almost--?!
To each... *her* own.
Hey, Thundy! I know a quicker way to flatten these thingees.
You go *airborne* on my signal because everyone's about to play *statue.*
What are you talking about--?!
There's no time to explain.
Just leap as *high* as you can-- *NOW!*
I'm going to use my *sticking power* to magnetize everyone to the floor--
--and I want all the good guys to *DUCK!*

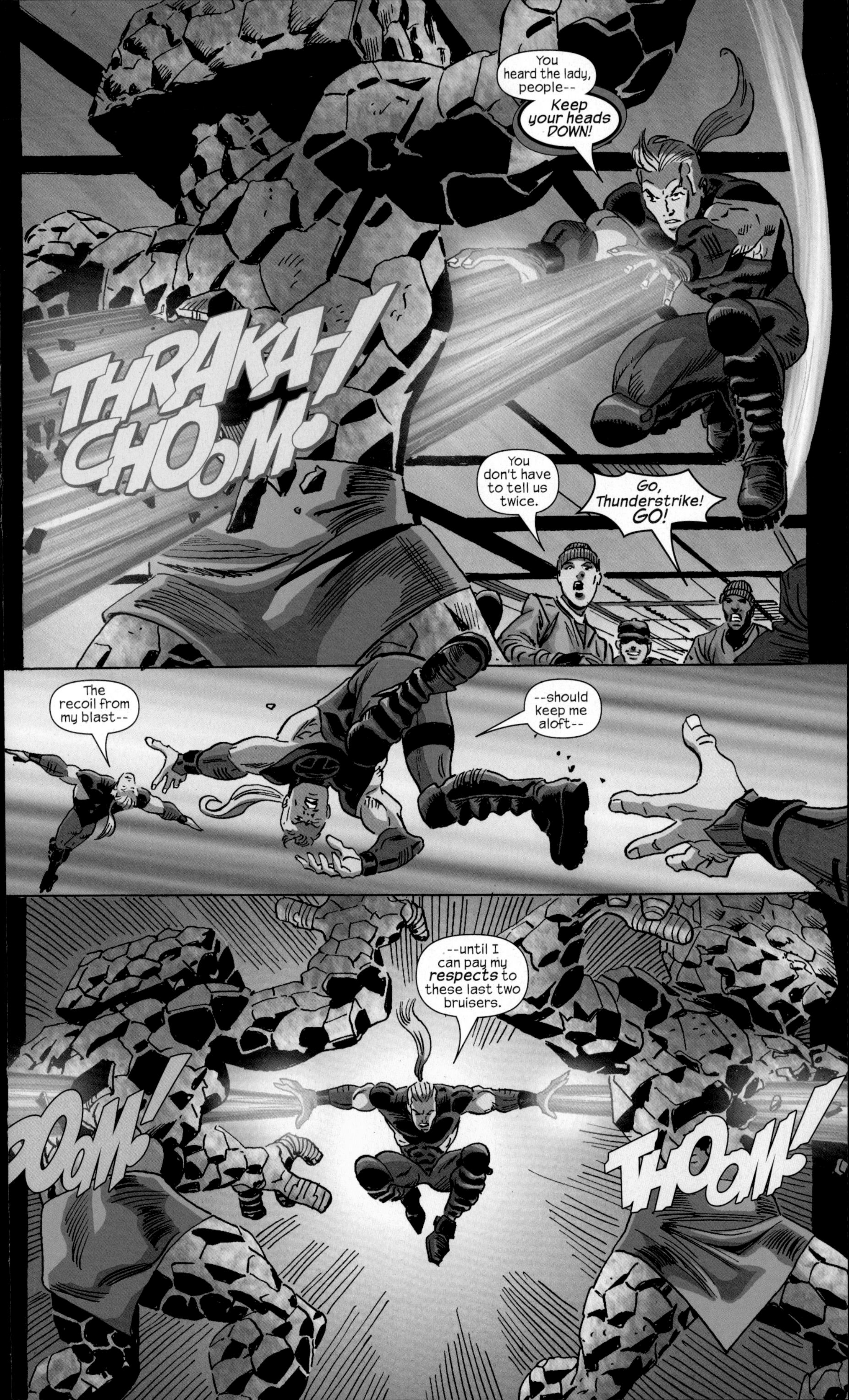

You heard the lady, people-- Keep your heads DOWN!
THRAKA-! CHOOM!
You don't have to tell us twice.
Go, Thunderstrike! GO!
The recoil from my blast--
--should keep me aloft--
--until I can pay my respects to these last two bruisers.
OOM!
THOOM!

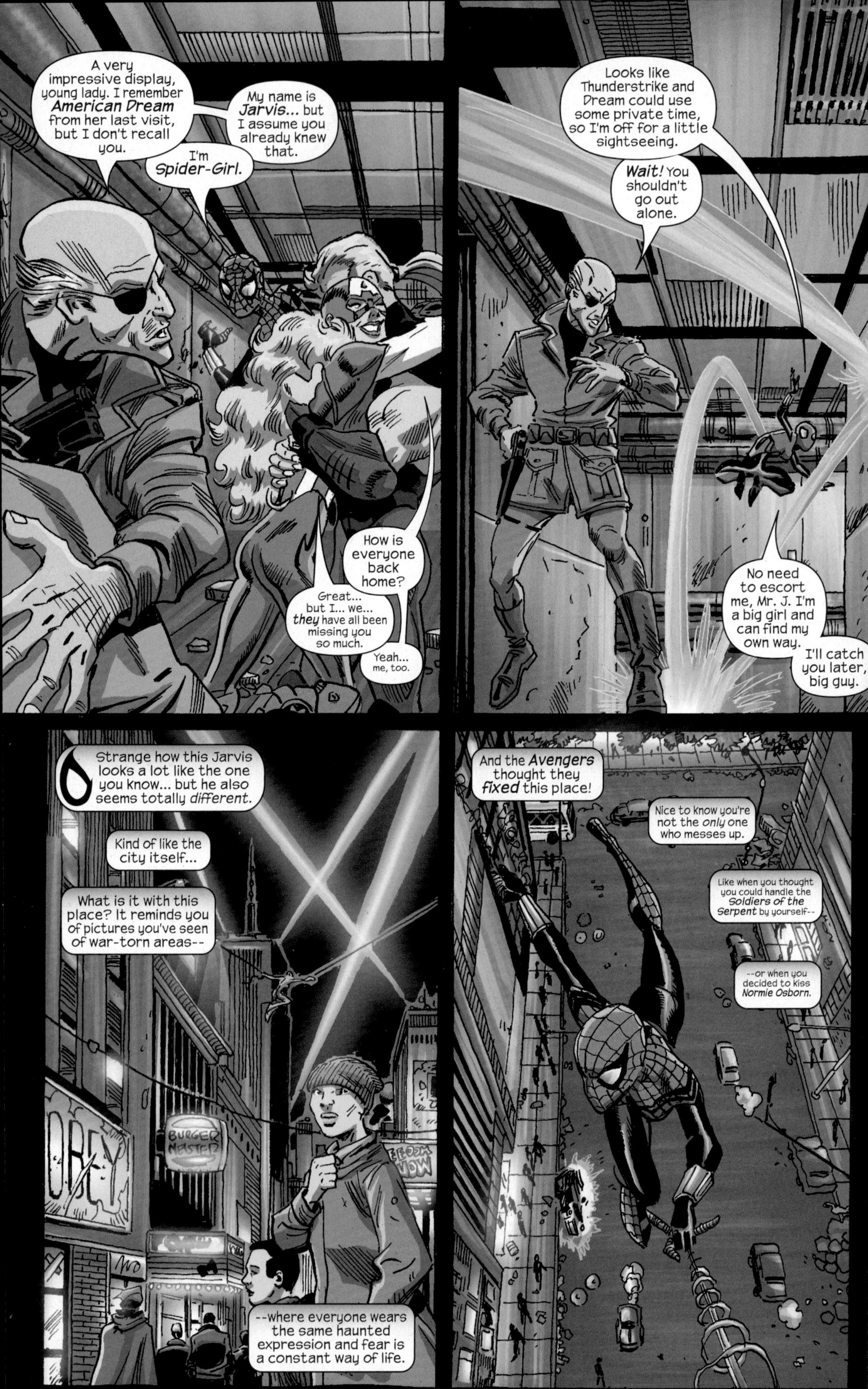

A very impressive display, young lady. I remember American Dream from her last visit, but I don't recall you.
My name is Jarvis... but I assume you already knew that.
I'm Spider-Girl.
How is everyone back home?
Great... but I... we... they have all been missing you so much.
Yeah... me, too.
Looks like Thunderstrike and Dream could use some private time, so I'm off for a little sightseeing.
Wait! You shouldn't go out alone.
No need to escort me, Mr. J. I'm a big girl and can find my own way.
I'll catch you later, big guy.
Strange how this Jarvis looks a lot like the one you know... but he also seems totally different.
Kind of like the city itself...
What is it with this place? It reminds you of pictures you've seen of war-torn areas--
--where everyone wears the same haunted expression and fear is a constant way of life.
BURGER MASTER
And the Avengers thought they fixed this place!
Nice to know you're not the only one who messes up.
Like when you thought you could handle the Soldiers of the Serpent by yourself--
--or when you decided to kiss Normie Osborn.

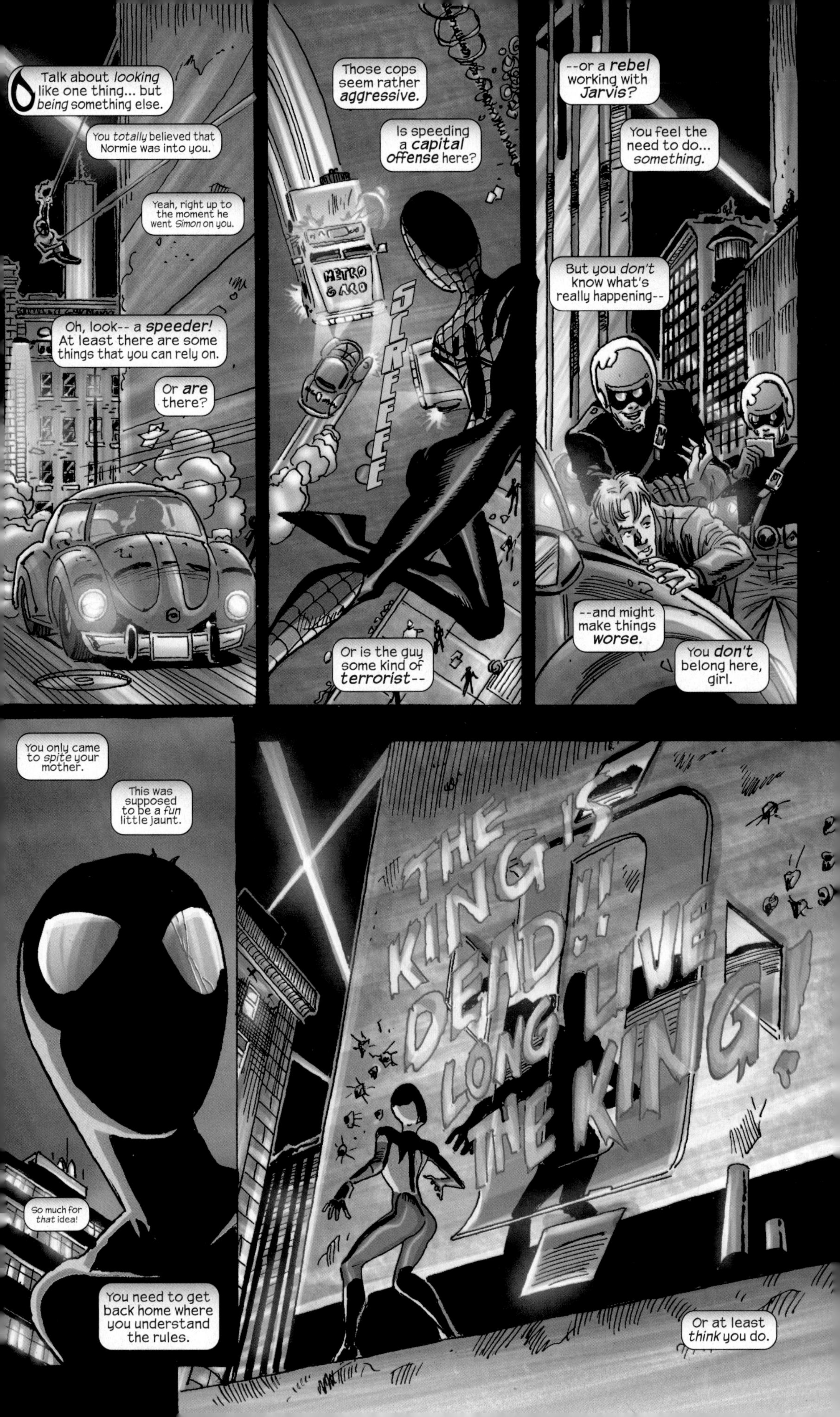
Talk about *looking* like one thing... but *being* something else.
You *totally* believed that Normie was into you.
Yeah, right up to the moment he went *Simon* on you.
Oh, look-- a ***speeder!*** At least there are some things that you can rely on.
Or ***are*** there?
Those cops seem rather ***aggressive.***
Is speeding a ***capital offense*** here?
METRO GARD
SCREEEE
Or is the guy some kind of ***terrorist--***
--or a ***rebel*** working with ***Jarvis?***
You feel the need to do... *something.*
But you *don't* know what's really happening--
--and might make things ***worse.***
You ***don't*** belong here, girl.
You only came to *spite* your mother.
This was supposed to be a *fun* little jaunt.
So much for *that* idea!
You need to get back home where you understand the rules.
THE KING IS DEAD!! LONG LIVE THE KING!
Or at least *think* you do.

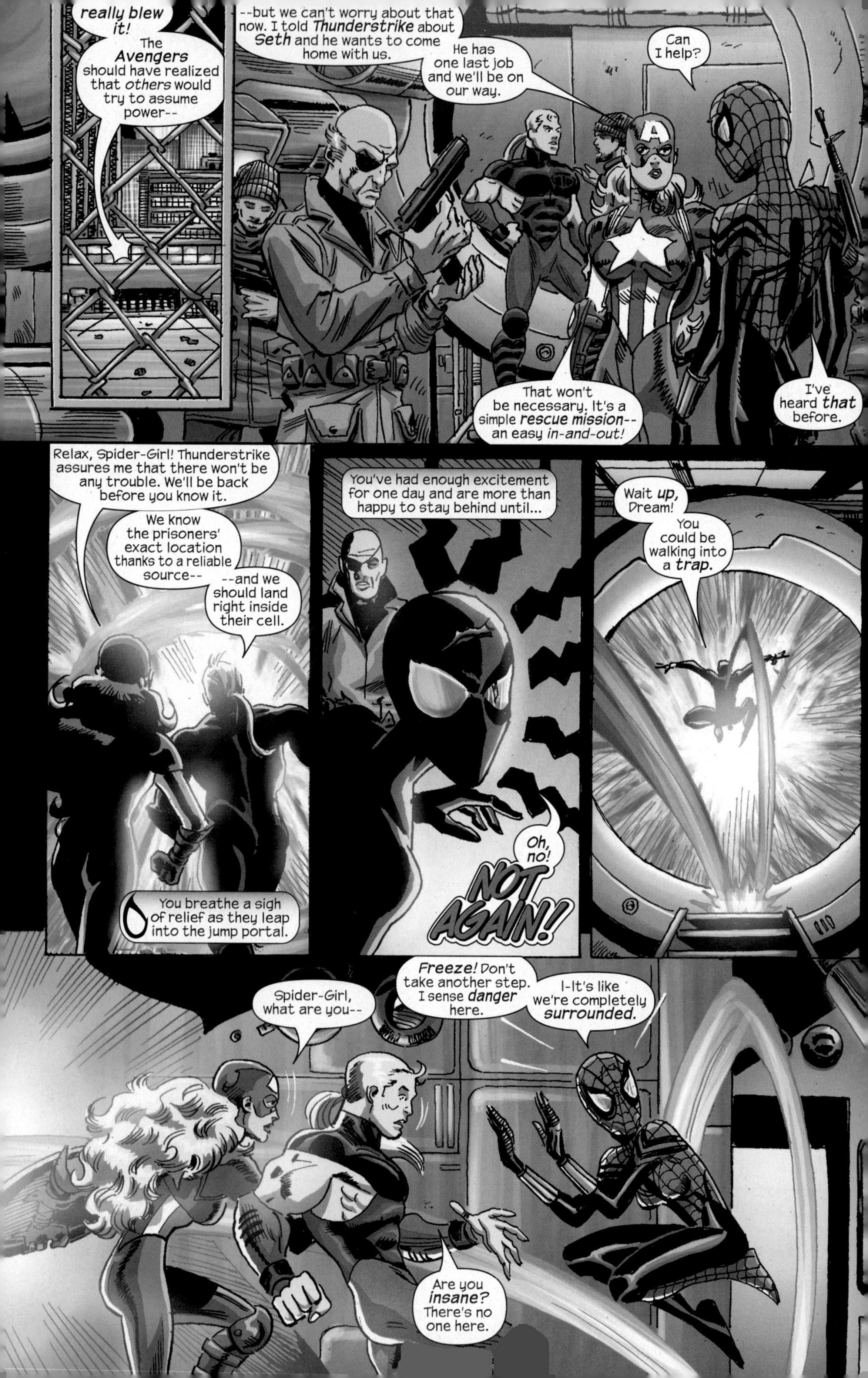

really blew it!
The Avengers should have realized that others would try to assume power--
--but we can't worry about that now. I told Thunderstrike about Seth and he wants to come home with us.
He has one last job and we'll be on our way.
Can I help?
That won't be necessary. It's a simple rescue mission-- an easy in-and-out!
I've heard that before.
Relax, Spider-Girl! Thunderstrike assures me that there won't be any trouble. We'll be back before you know it.
We know the prisoners' exact location thanks to a reliable source--
--and we should land right inside their cell.
You breathe a sigh of relief as they leap into the jump portal.
You've had enough excitement for one day and are more than happy to stay behind until...
Oh, no!
NOT AGAIN!
Wait up, Dream!
You could be walking into a trap.
Spider-Girl, what are you--
Freeze! Don't take another step. I sense danger here.
I-It's like we're completely surrounded.
Are you insane? There's no one here.

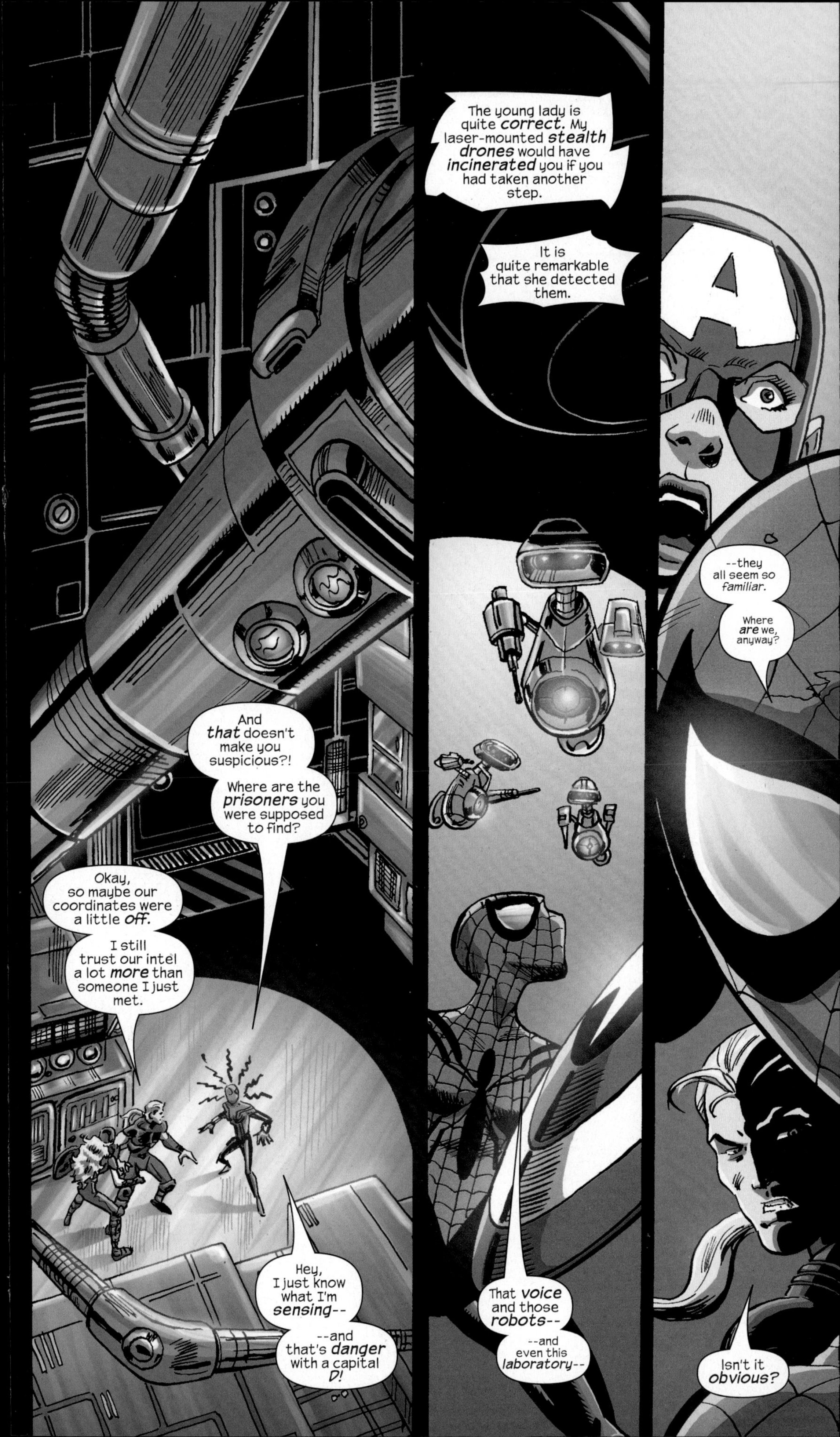

And that doesn't make you suspicious?!
Where are the prisoners you were supposed to find?
Okay, so maybe our coordinates were a little off.
I still trust our intel a lot more than someone I just met.
Hey, I just know what I'm sensing--
--and that's danger with a capital D!
The young lady is quite correct. My laser-mounted stealth drones would have incinerated you if you had taken another step.
It is quite remarkable that she detected them.
That voice and those robots--
--and even this laboratory--
--they all seem so familiar.
Where are we, anyway?
Isn't it obvious?

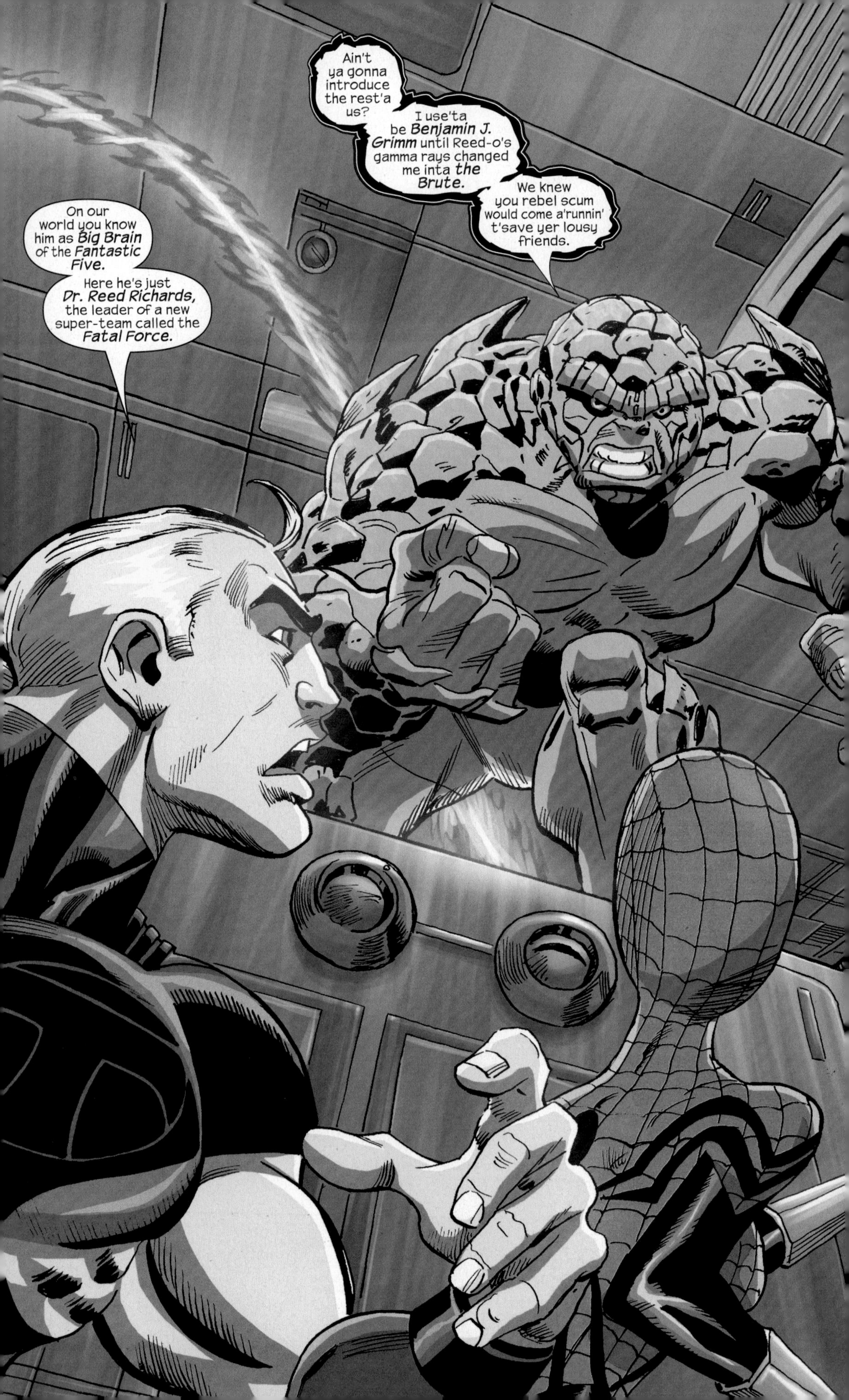
On our world you know him as Big Brain of the Fantastic Five.
Here he's just Dr. Reed Richards, the leader of a new super-team called the Fatal Force.
Ain't ya gonna introduce the rest'a us?
I use'ta be Benjamin J. Grimm until Reed-o's gamma rays changed me inta the Brute.
We knew you rebel scum would come a'runnin' t'save yer lousy friends.

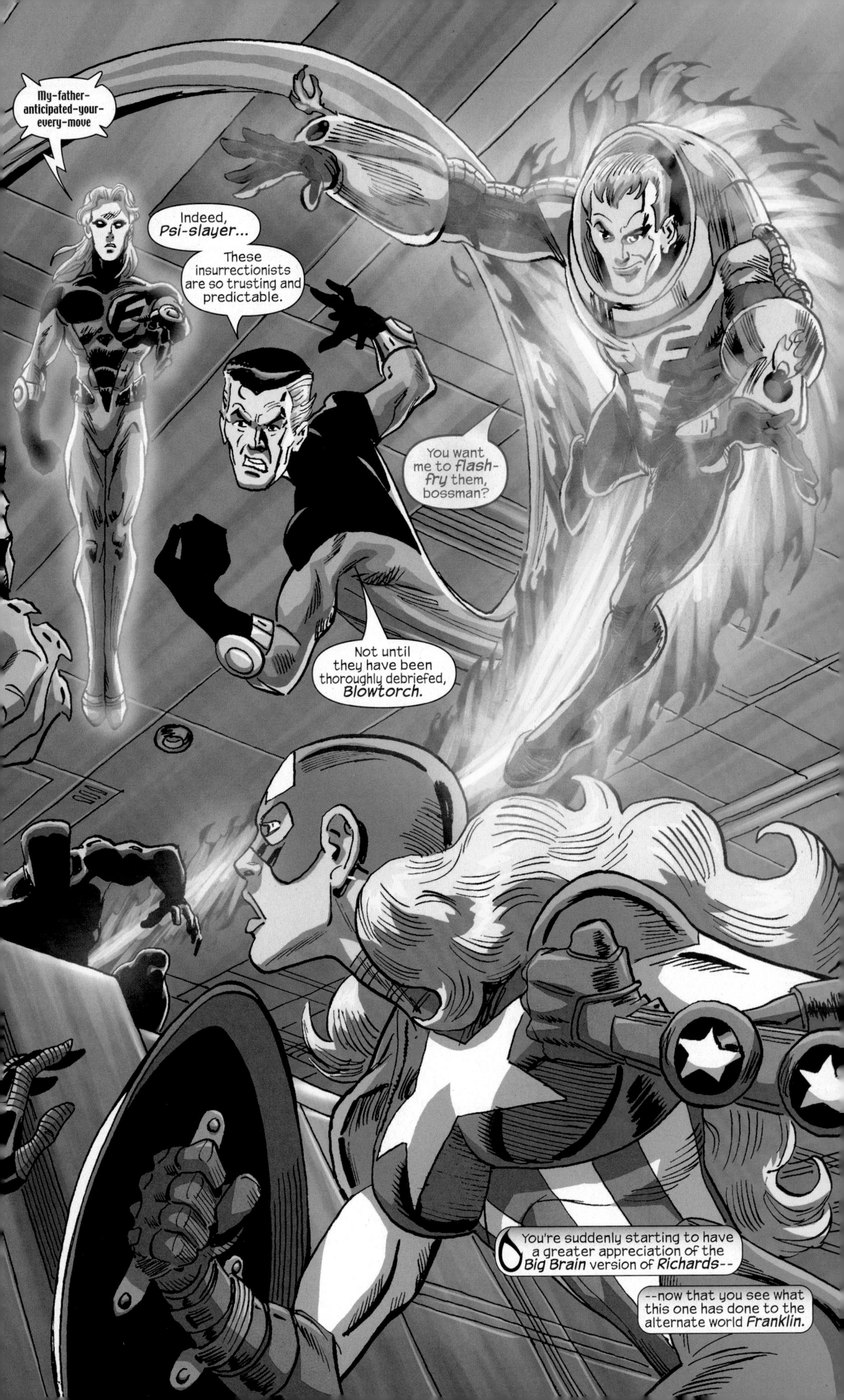
My-father-anticipated-your-every-move
Indeed, Psi-slayer...
These insurrectionists are so trusting and predictable.
You want me to flash-fry them, bossman?
Not until they have been thoroughly debriefed, Blowtorch.
You're suddenly starting to have a greater appreciation of the Big Brain version of Richards--
--now that you see what this one has done to the alternate world Franklin.

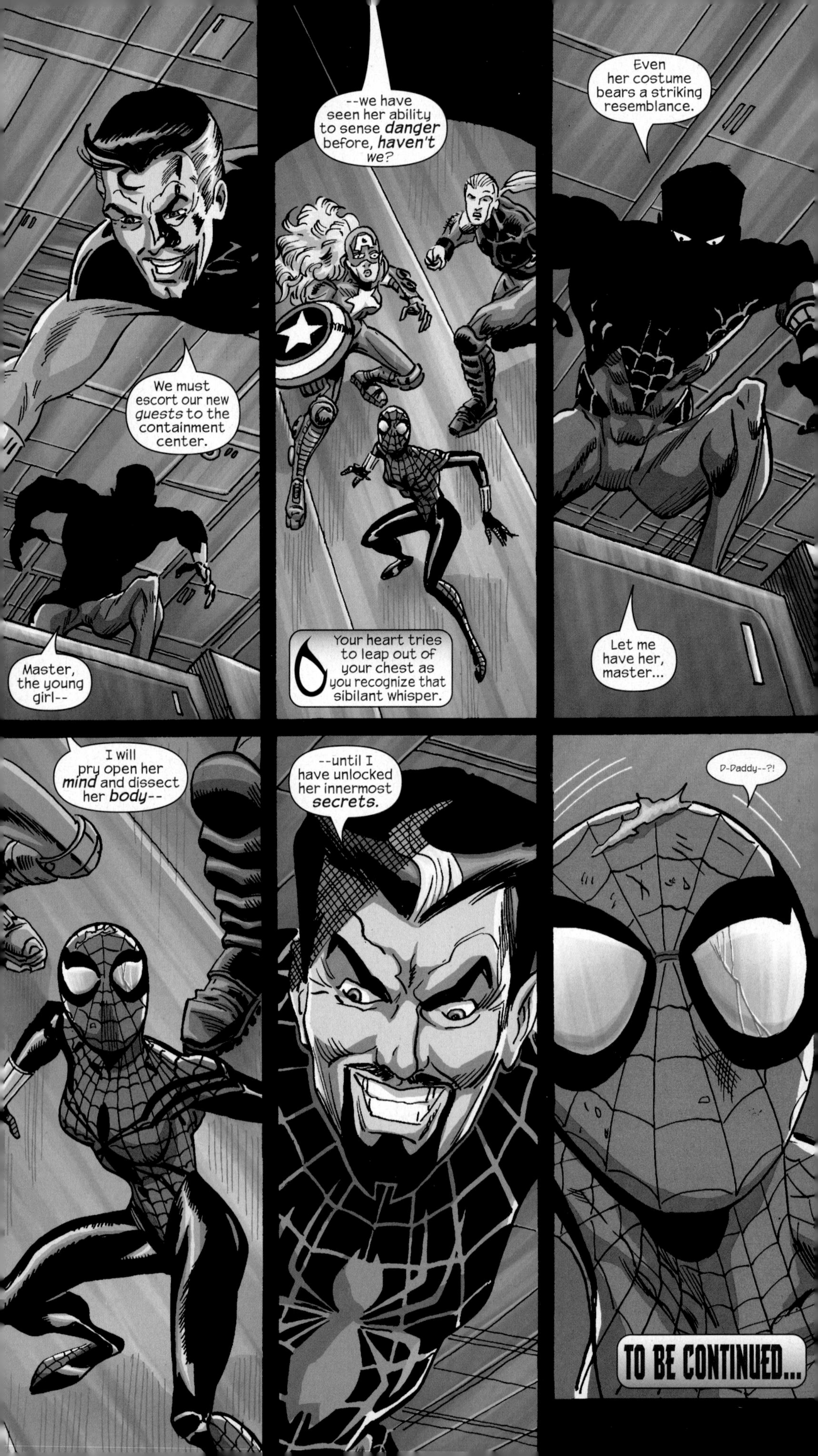

We must escort our new *guests* to the containment center.
Master, the young girl--
--we have seen her ability to sense *danger* before, *haven't* we?
Your heart tries to leap out of your chest as you recognize that sibilant whisper.
Even her costume bears a striking resemblance.
Let me have her, master...
I will pry open her *mind* and dissect her *body*--
--until I have unlocked her innermost *secrets.*
D-Daddy--?!
TO BE CONTINUED...

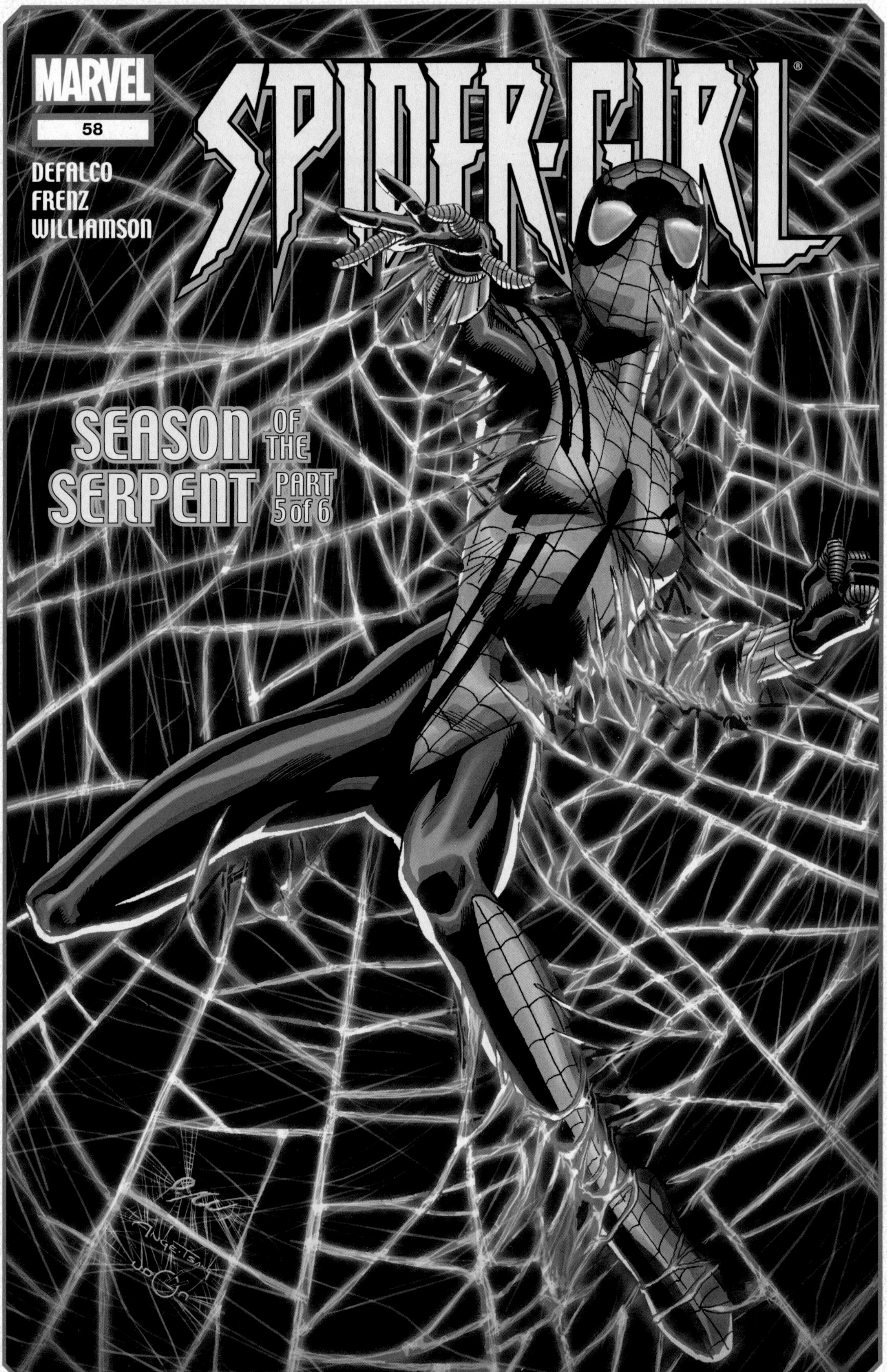
MARVEL
58
SPIDER-GIRL®
DEFALCO
FRENZ
WILLIAMSON
SEASON OF THE SERPENT PART 5 of 6

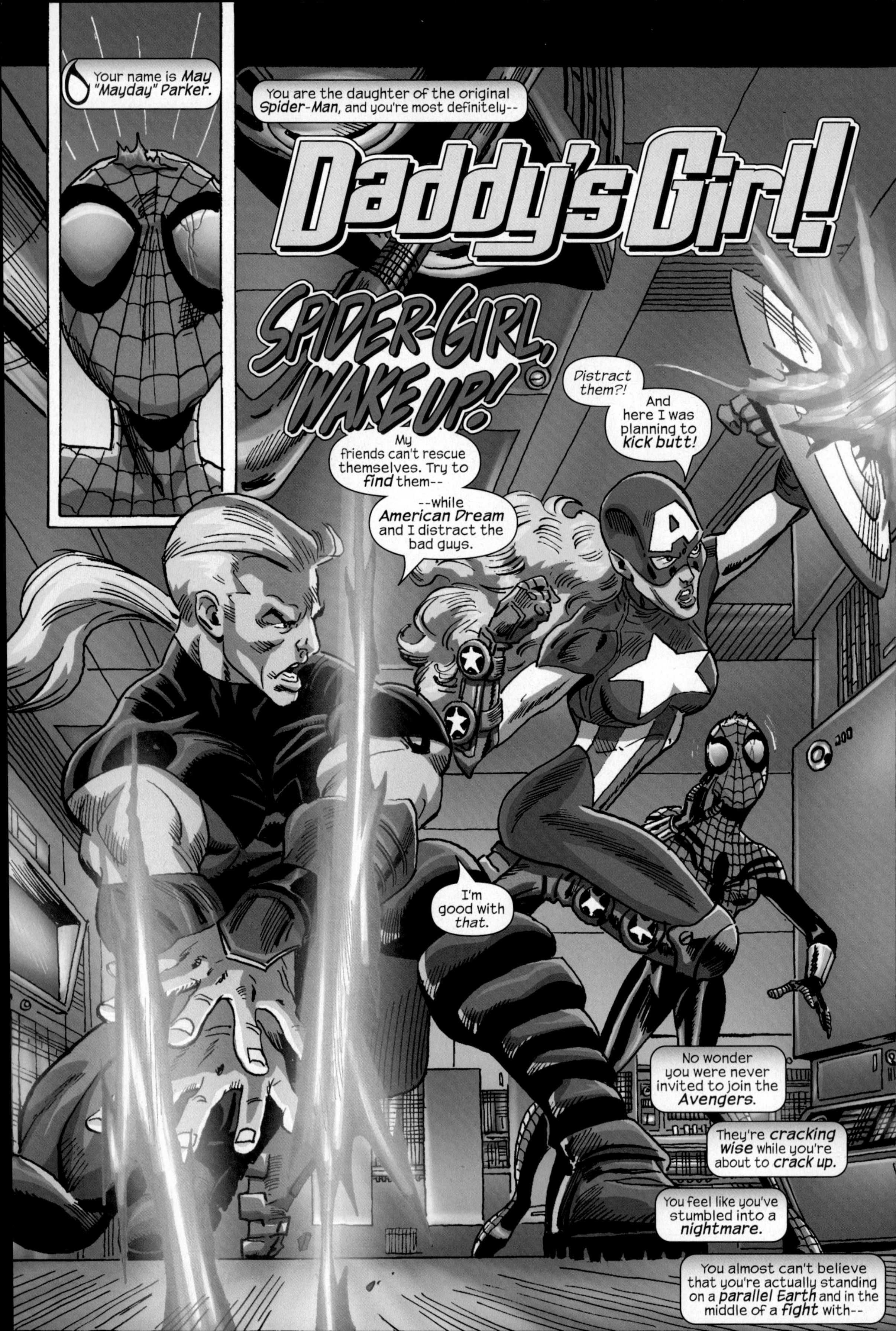
Your name is May "Mayday" Parker.
You are the daughter of the original Spider-Man, and you're most definitely--
Daddy's Girl!
SPIDER-GIRL, WAKE UP!
My friends can't rescue themselves. Try to find them--
--while American Dream and I distract the bad guys.
Distract them?!
And here I was planning to kick butt!
I'm good with that.
No wonder you were never invited to join the Avengers.
They're cracking wise while you're about to crack up.
You feel like you've stumbled into a nightmare.
You almost can't believe that you're actually standing on a parallel Earth and in the middle of a fight with--

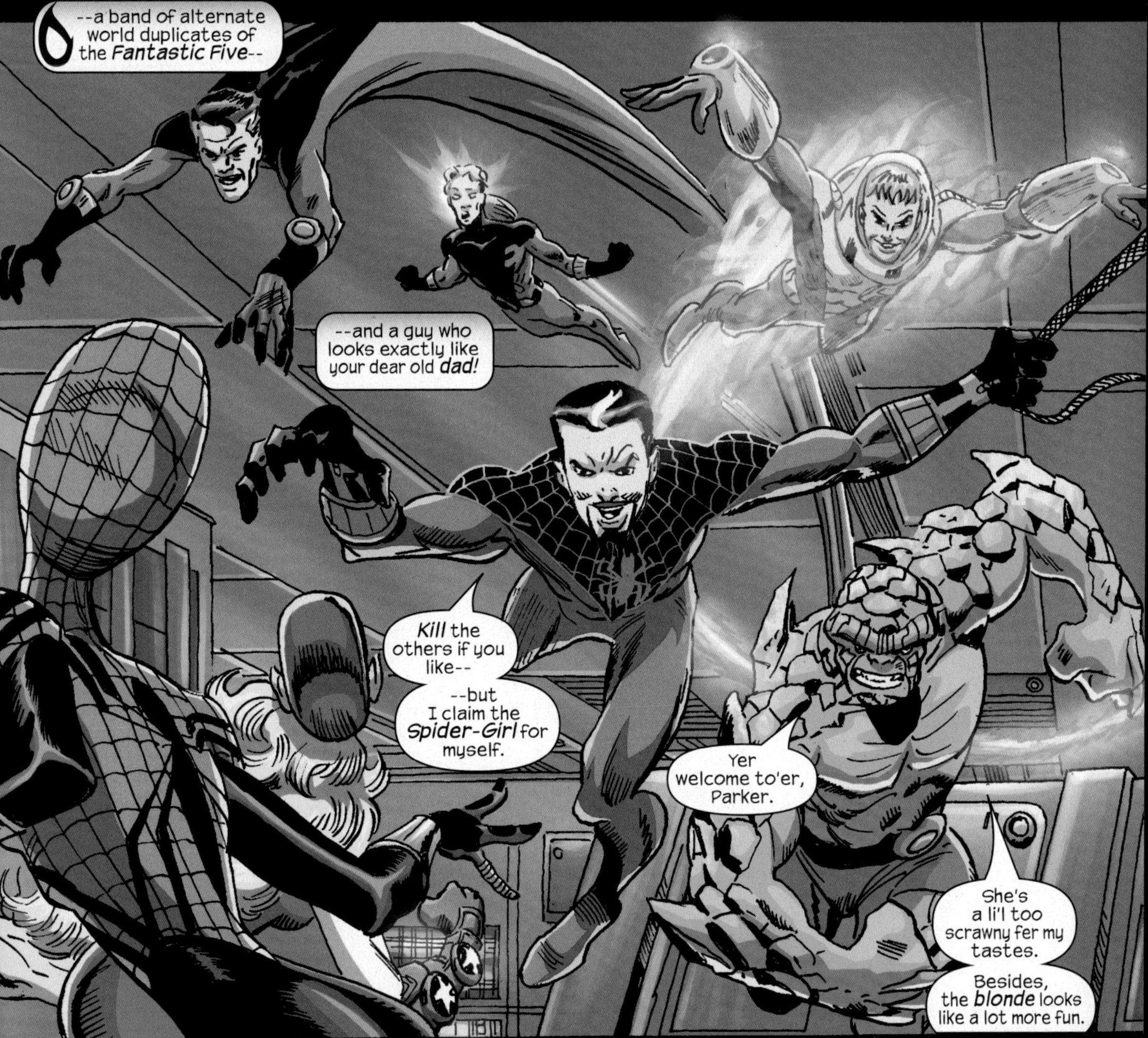
--a band of alternate world duplicates of the *Fantastic Five*--
--and a guy who looks exactly like your dear old *dad!*
Kill the others if you like--
--but I claim the *Spider-Girl* for myself.
Yer welcome to'er, Parker.
She's a li'l too scrawny fer my tastes.
Besides, the *blonde* looks like a lot more fun.

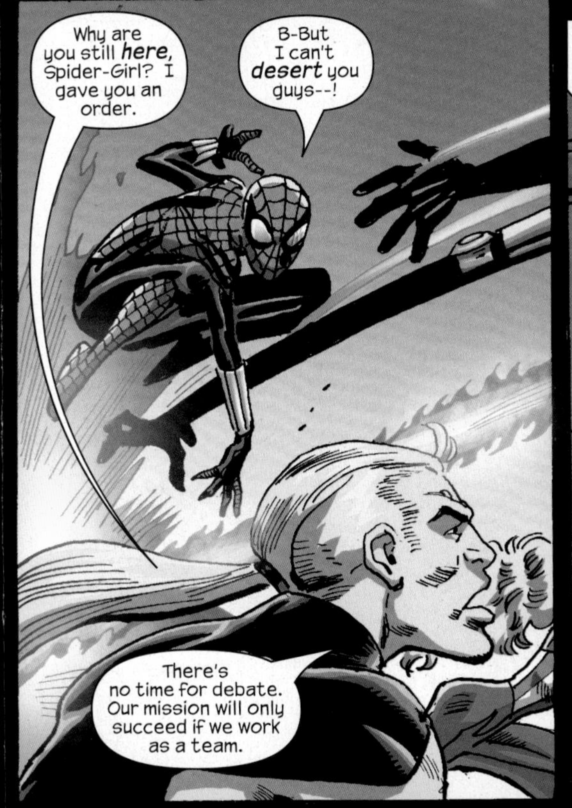
Why are you still *here*, Spider-Girl? I gave you an order.
B-But I can't *desert* you guys--!
There's no time for debate. Our mission will only succeed if we work as a team.

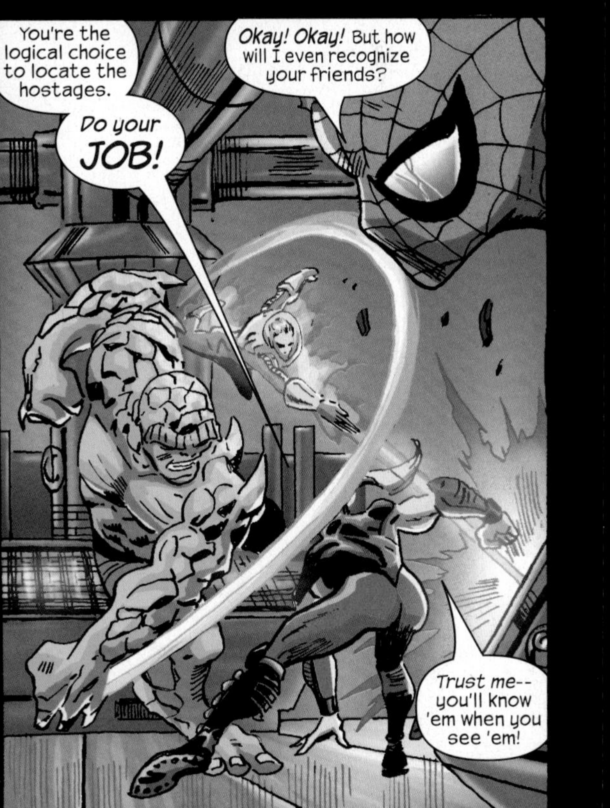
You're the logical choice to locate the hostages.
Do your **JOB!**
Okay! Okay! But how will I even recognize your friends?
Trust me-- you'll know 'em when you see 'em!

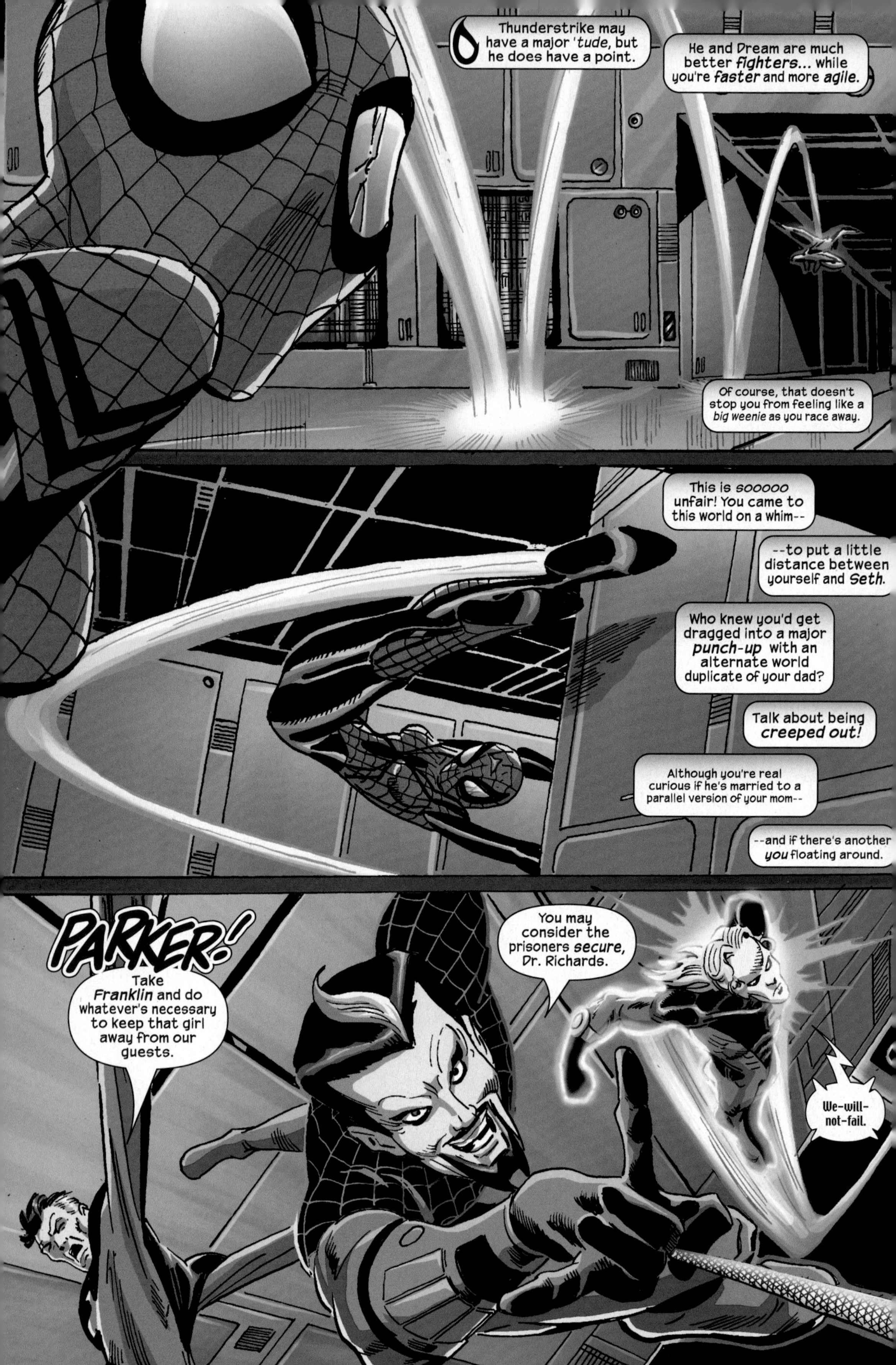
Thunderstrike may have a major 'tude, but he does have a point.
He and Dream are much better fighters... while you're faster and more agile.
Of course, that doesn't stop you from feeling like a big weenie as you race away.
This is sooooo unfair! You came to this world on a whim--
--to put a little distance between yourself and Seth.
Who knew you'd get dragged into a major punch-up with an alternate world duplicate of your dad?
Talk about being creeped out!
Although you're real curious if he's married to a parallel version of your mom--
--and if there's another you floating around.
PARKER!
Take Franklin and do whatever's necessary to keep that girl away from our guests.
You may consider the prisoners secure, Dr. Richards.
We-will-not-fail.

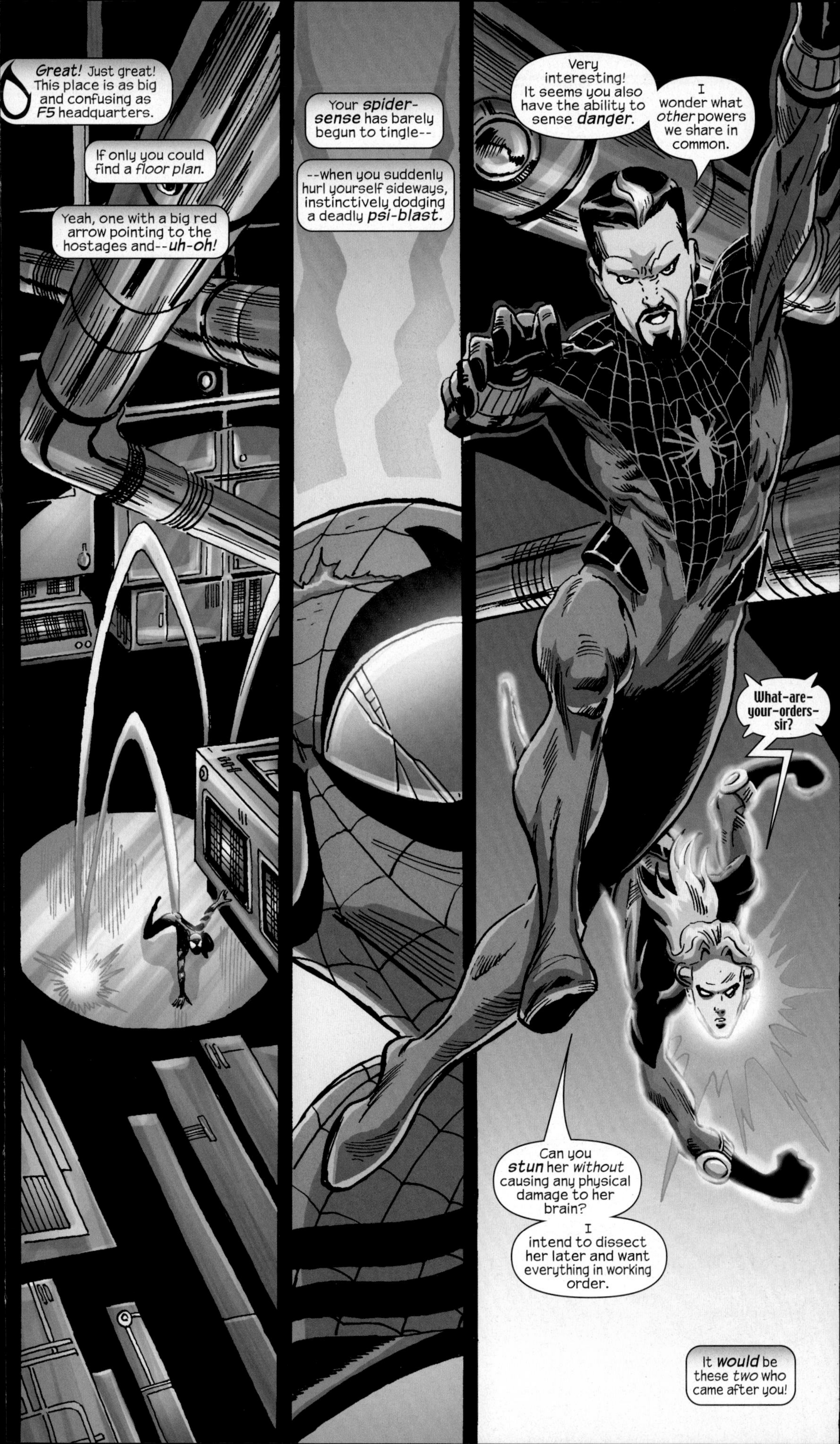
Great! Just great! This place is as big and confusing as F5 headquarters.
If only you could find a floor plan.
Yeah, one with a big red arrow pointing to the hostages and--uh-oh!
Your spider-sense has barely begun to tingle--
--when you suddenly hurl yourself sideways, instinctively dodging a deadly psi-blast.
Very interesting! It seems you also have the ability to sense danger.
I wonder what other powers we share in common.
What-are-your-orders-sir?
Can you stun her without causing any physical damage to her brain?
I intend to dissect her later and want everything in working order.
It would be these two who came after you!

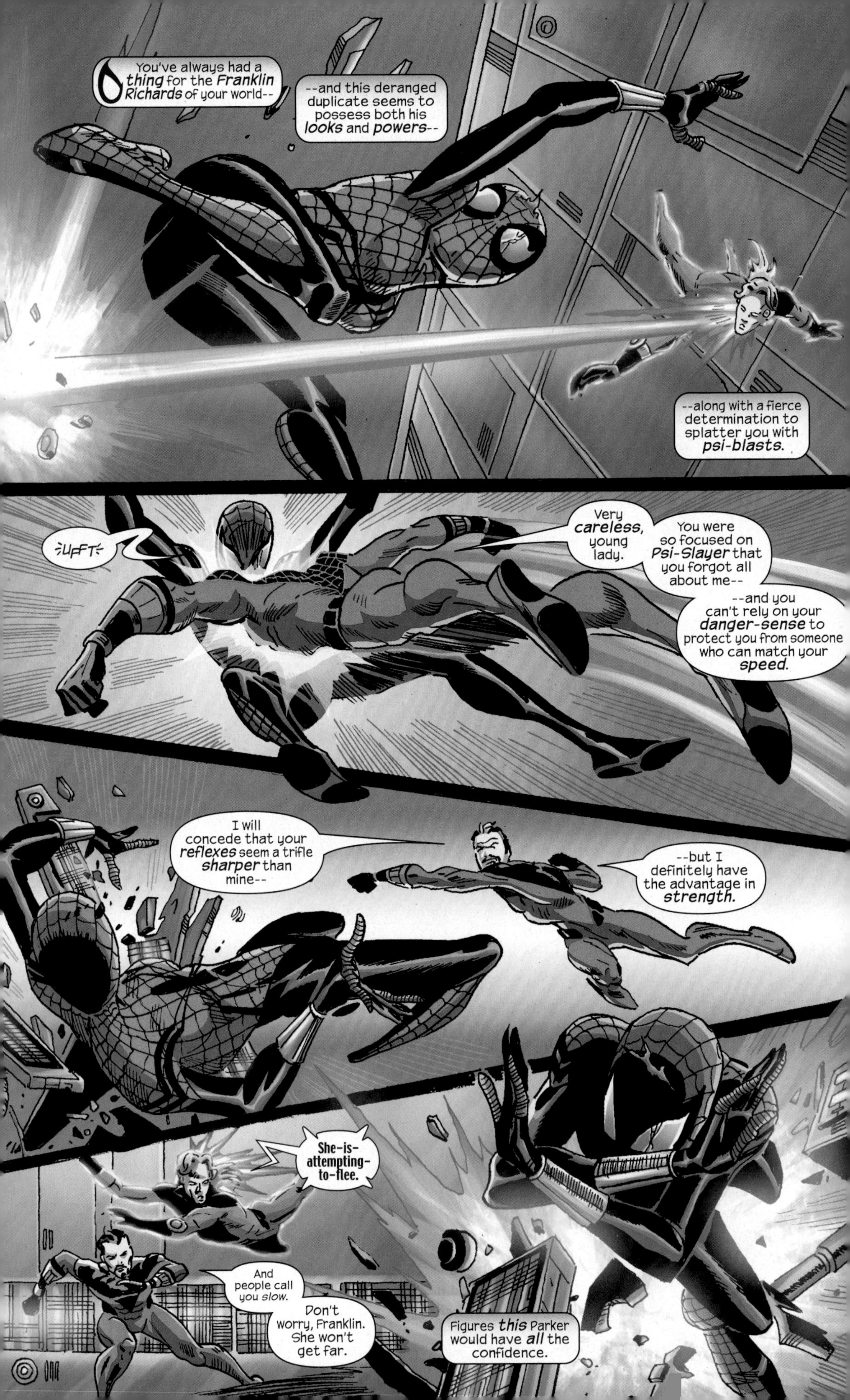
You've always had a thing for the Franklin Richards of your world--
--and this deranged duplicate seems to possess both his looks and powers--
--along with a fierce determination to splatter you with psi-blasts.
UFFT
Very careless, young lady.
You were so focused on Psi-Slayer that you forgot all about me--
--and you can't rely on your danger-sense to protect you from someone who can match your speed.
I will concede that your reflexes seem a trifle sharper than mine--
--but I definitely have the advantage in strength.
She-is-attempting-to-flee.
And people call you slow.
Don't worry, Franklin. She won't get far.
Figures this Parker would have all the confidence.

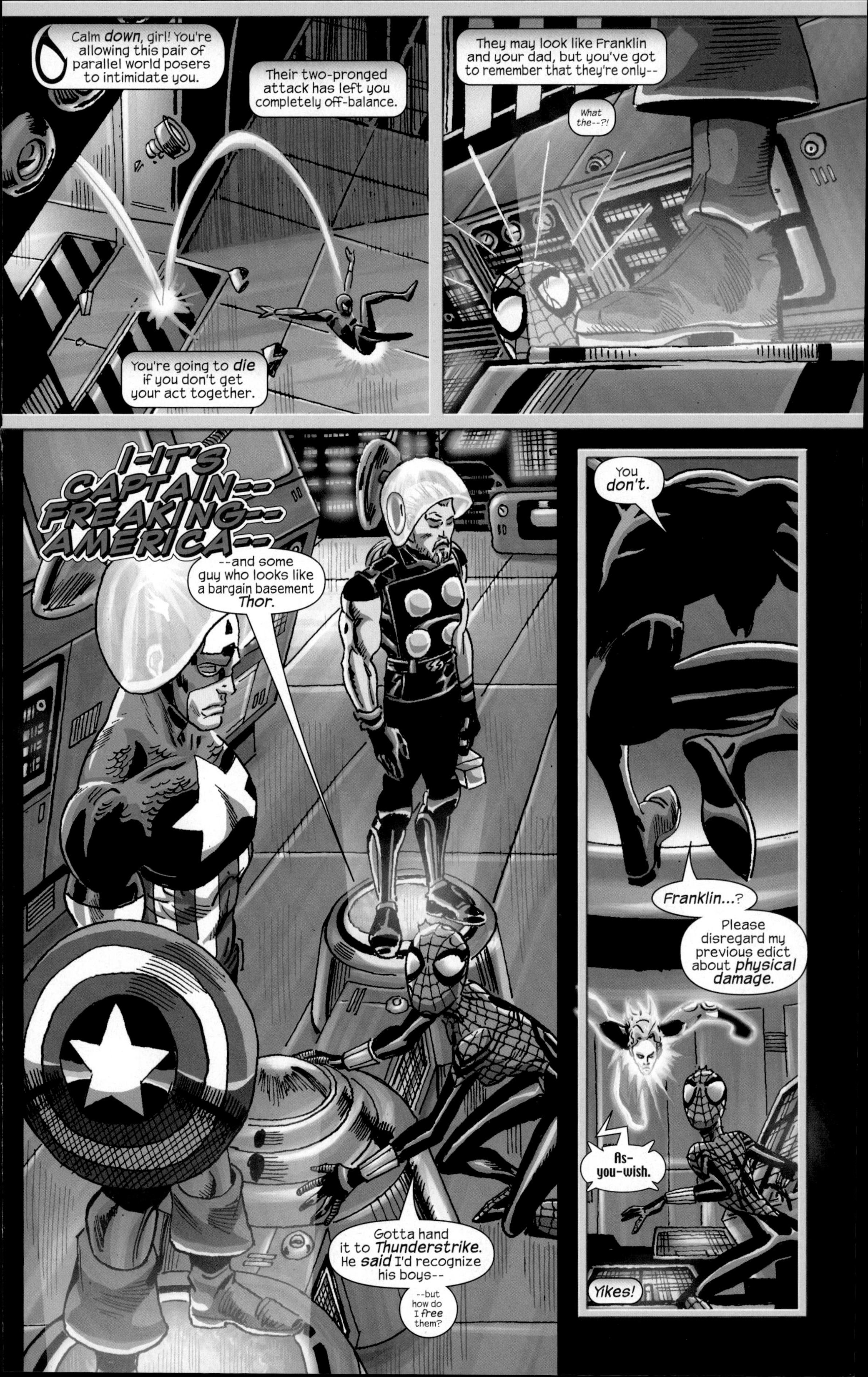
Calm down, girl! You're allowing this pair of parallel world posers to intimidate you.
Their two-pronged attack has left you completely off-balance.
You're going to die if you don't get your act together.
They may look like Franklin and your dad, but you've got to remember that they're only--
What the--?!
I-IT'S CAPTAIN-- FREAKING-- AMERICA--
--and some guy who looks like a bargain basement Thor.
Gotta hand it to Thunderstrike. He said I'd recognize his boys--
--but how do I free them?
You don't.
Franklin...?
Please disregard my previous edict about physical damage.
As-you-wish.
Yikes!

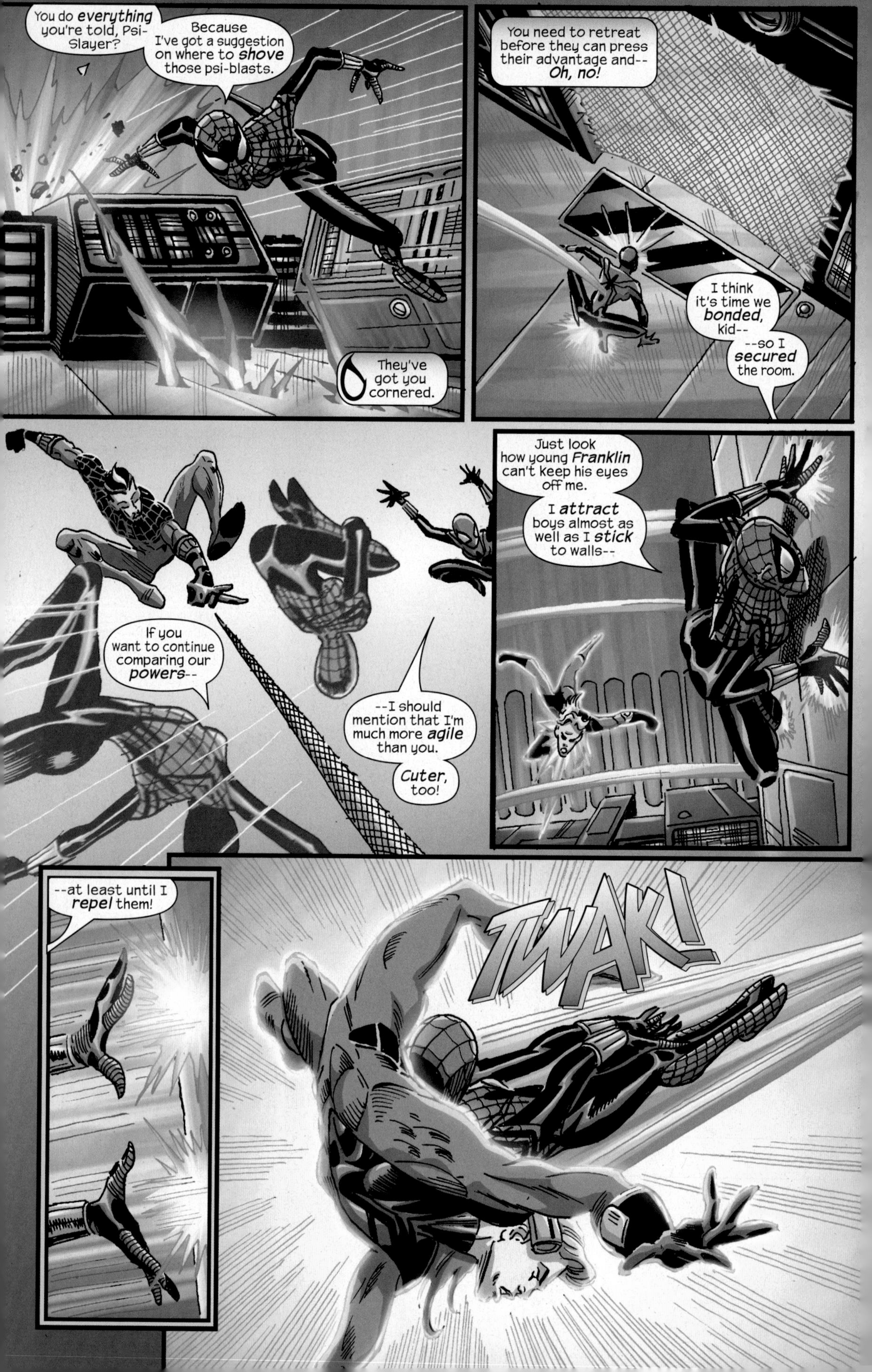

You do everything you're told, Psi-Slayer?
Because I've got a suggestion on where to shove those psi-blasts.
They've got you cornered.
You need to retreat before they can press their advantage and-- Oh, no!
I think it's time we bonded, kid--
--so I secured the room.
If you want to continue comparing our powers--
--I should mention that I'm much more agile than you.
Cuter, too!
Just look how young Franklin can't keep his eyes off me.
I attract boys almost as well as I stick to walls--
--at least until I repel them!
TWAK!

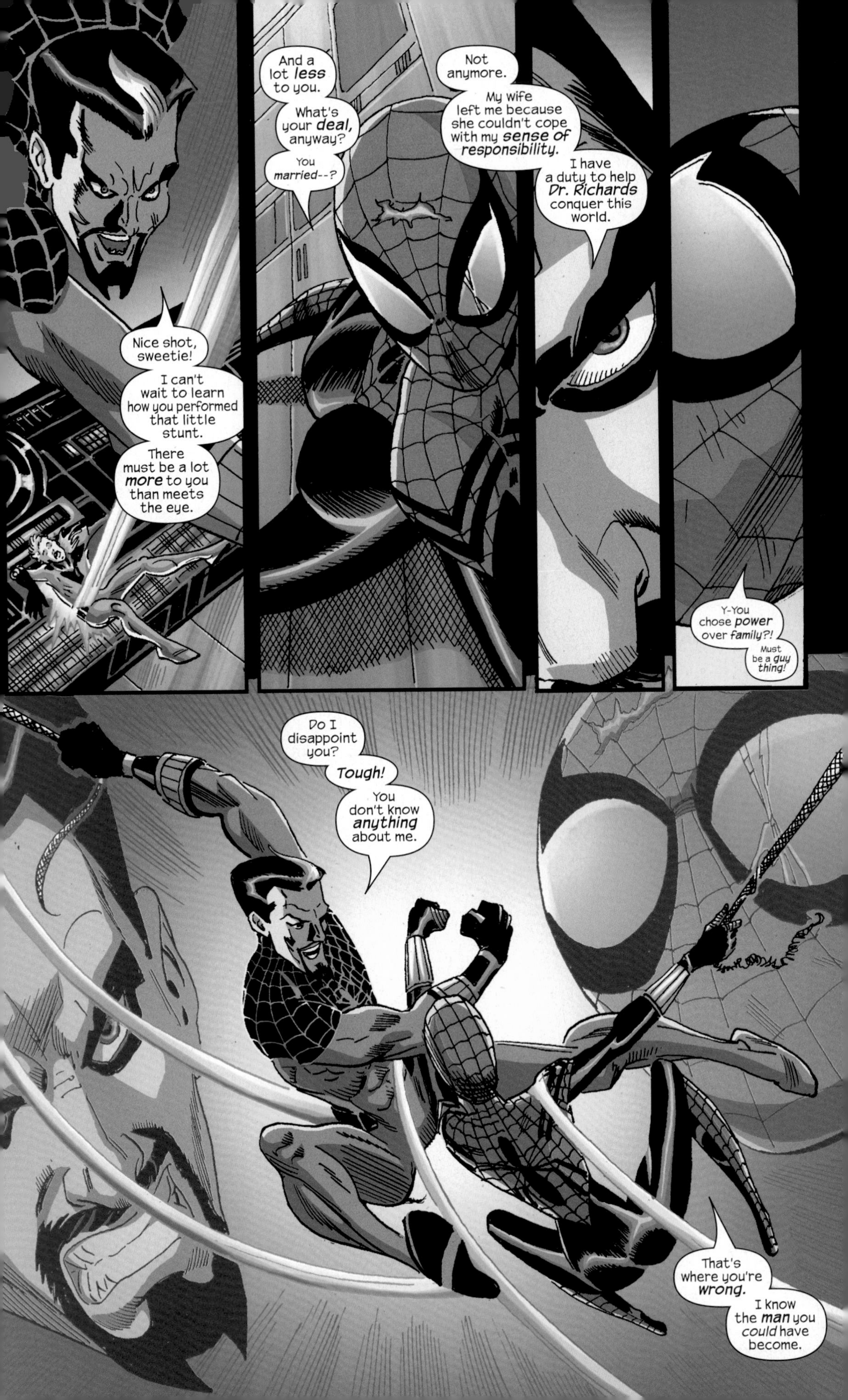
Nice shot, sweetie!
I can't wait to learn how you performed that little stunt.
There must be a lot more to you than meets the eye.
And a lot less to you.
What's your deal, anyway?
You married--?
Not anymore.
My wife left me because she couldn't cope with my sense of responsibility.
I have a duty to help Dr. Richards conquer this world.
Y-You chose power over family?!
Must be a guy thing!
Do I disappoint you?
Tough!
You don't know anything about me.
That's where you're wrong.
I know the man you could have become.

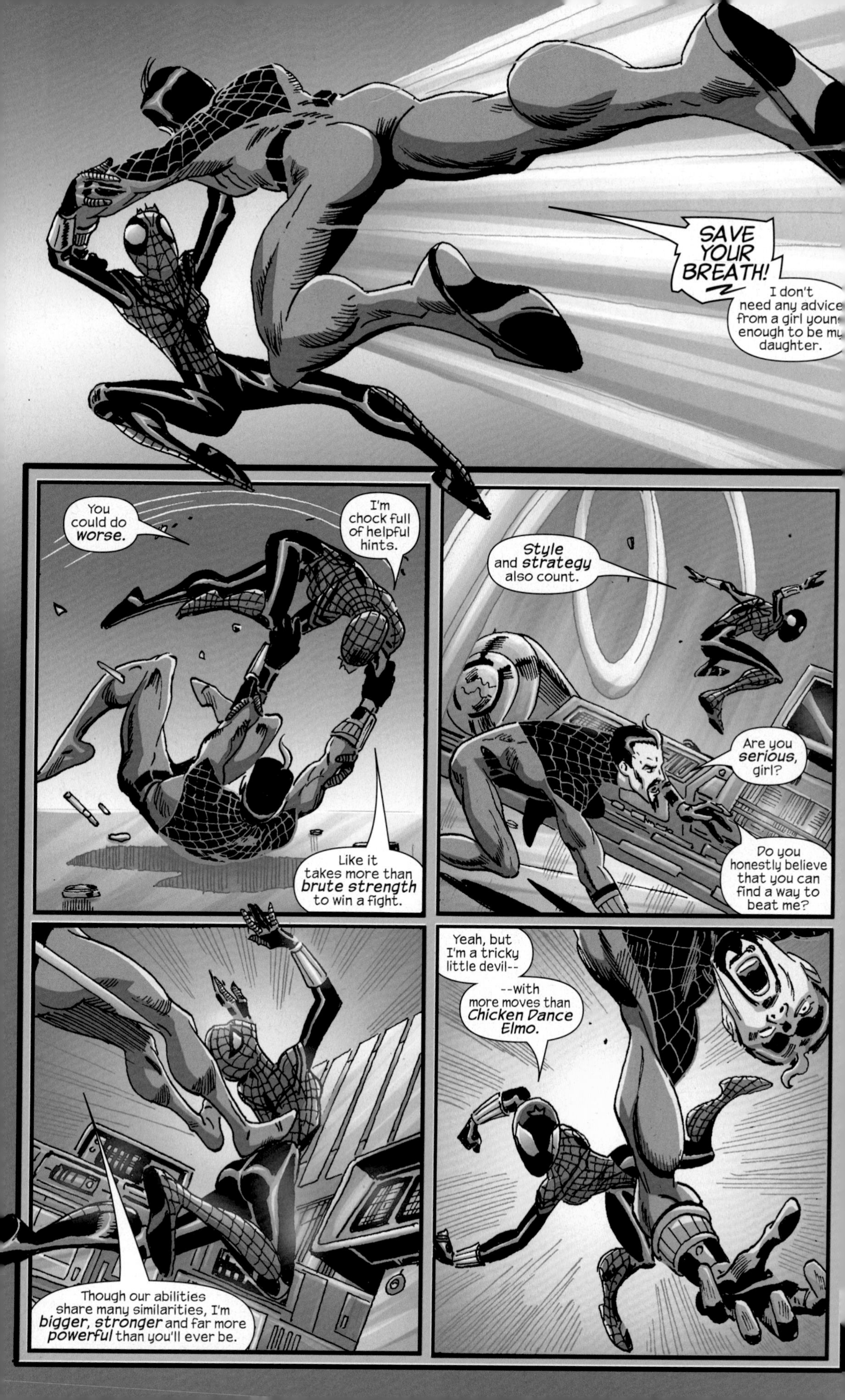
SAVE YOUR BREATH!
I don't need any advice from a girl young enough to be my daughter.
You could do *worse.*
I'm chock full of helpful hints.
Like it takes more than *brute strength* to win a fight.
Style and *strategy* also count.
Are you *serious,* girl?
Do you honestly believe that you can find a way to beat me?
Though our abilities share many similarities, I'm *bigger, stronger* and far more *powerful* than you'll ever be.
Yeah, but I'm a tricky little devil--
--with more moves than *Chicken Dance Elmo.*

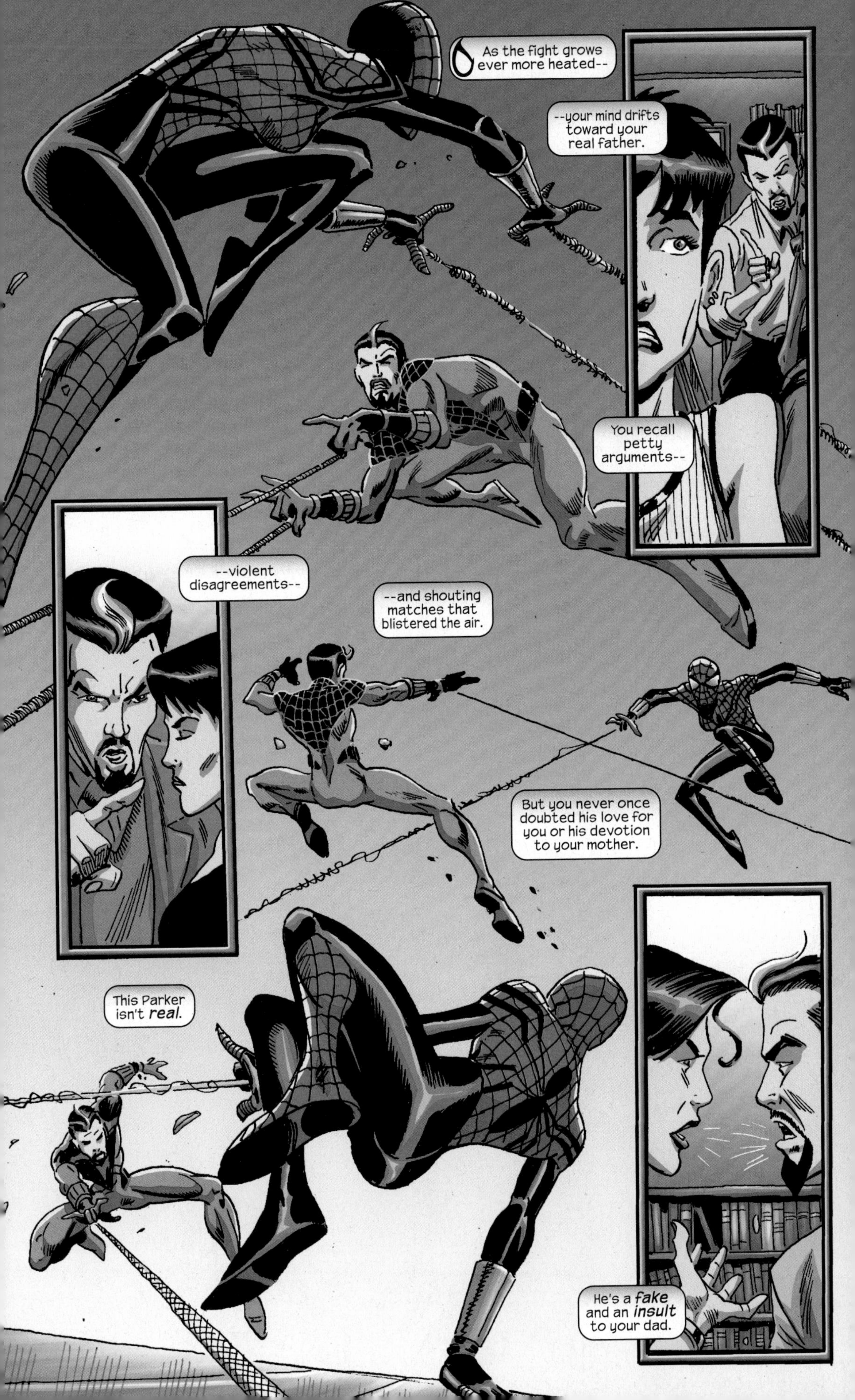
As the fight grows ever more heated--
--your mind drifts toward your real father.
You recall petty arguments--
--violent disagreements--
--and shouting matches that blistered the air.
But you never once doubted his love for you or his devotion to your mother.
This Parker isn't *real*.
He's a *fake* and an *insult* to your dad.

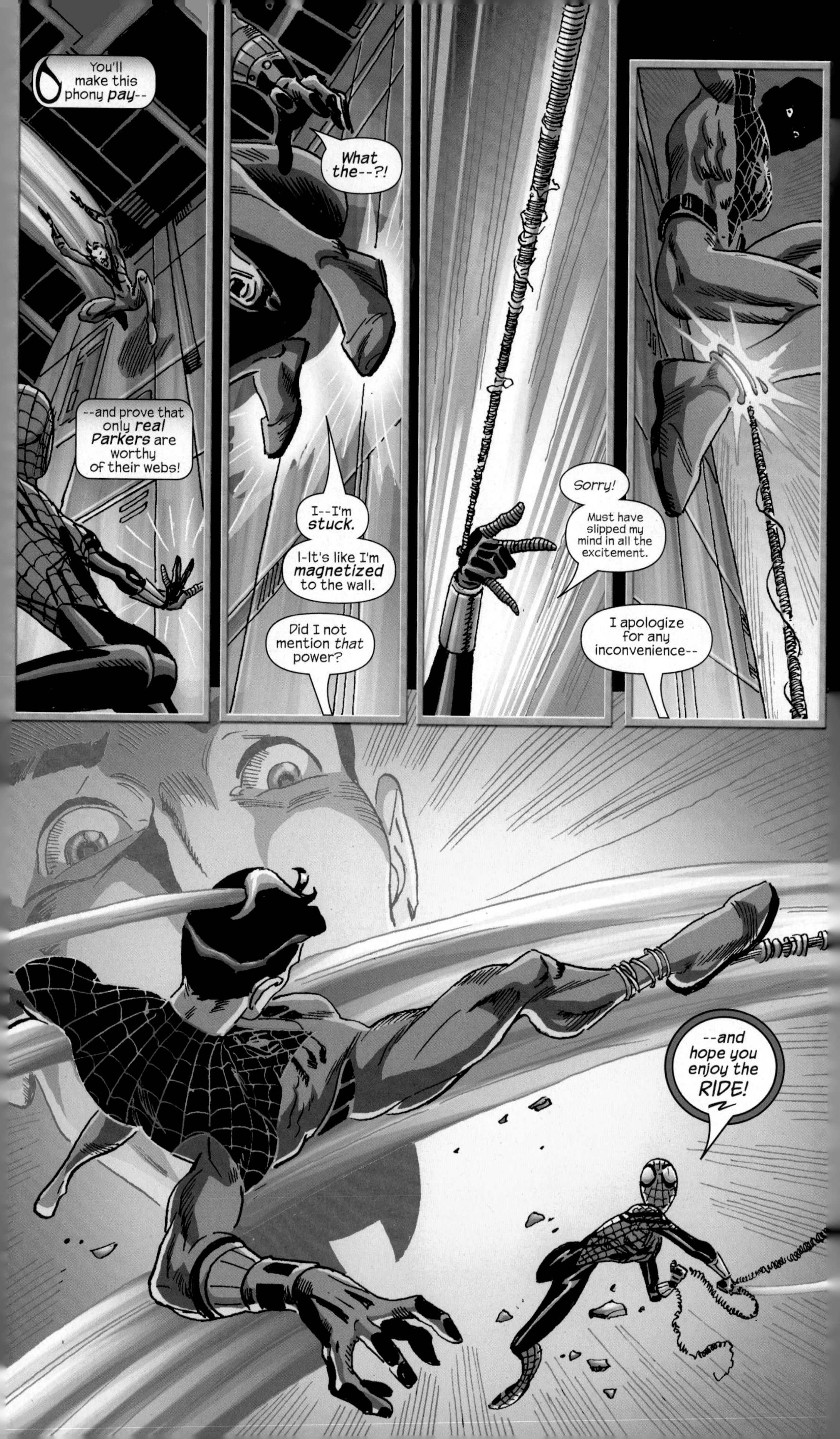
You'll make this phony *pay*--
--and prove that only *real* *Parkers* are worthy of their webs!
What the--?!
I--I'm *stuck.*
I-It's like I'm *magnetized* to the wall.
Did I not mention *that* power?
Sorry!
Must have slipped my mind in all the excitement.
I apologize for any inconvenience--
--and hope you enjoy the *RIDE!*

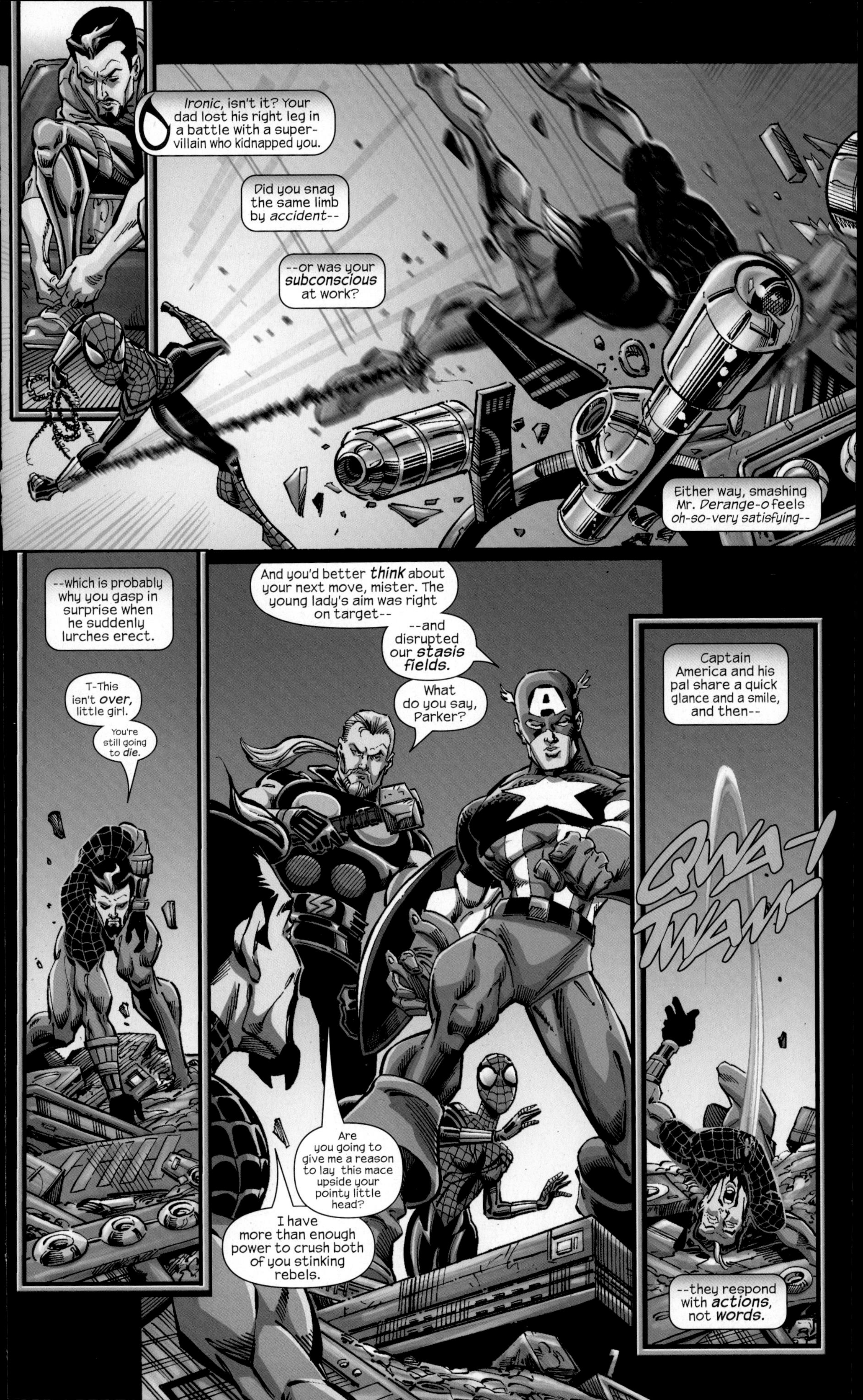
Ironic, isn't it? Your dad lost his right leg in a battle with a super-villain who kidnapped you.
Did you snag the same limb by accident--
--or was your subconscious at work?
Either way, smashing Mr. Derange-o feels oh-so-very satisfying--
--which is probably why you gasp in surprise when he suddenly lurches erect.
T-This isn't over, little girl.
You're still going to die.
And you'd better think about your next move, mister. The young lady's aim was right on target--
--and disrupted our stasis fields.
What do you say, Parker?
Are you going to give me a reason to lay this mace upside your pointy little head?
I have more than enough power to crush both of you stinking rebels.
Captain America and his pal share a quick glance and a smile, and then--
QWA-TWAW!
--they respond with actions, not words.

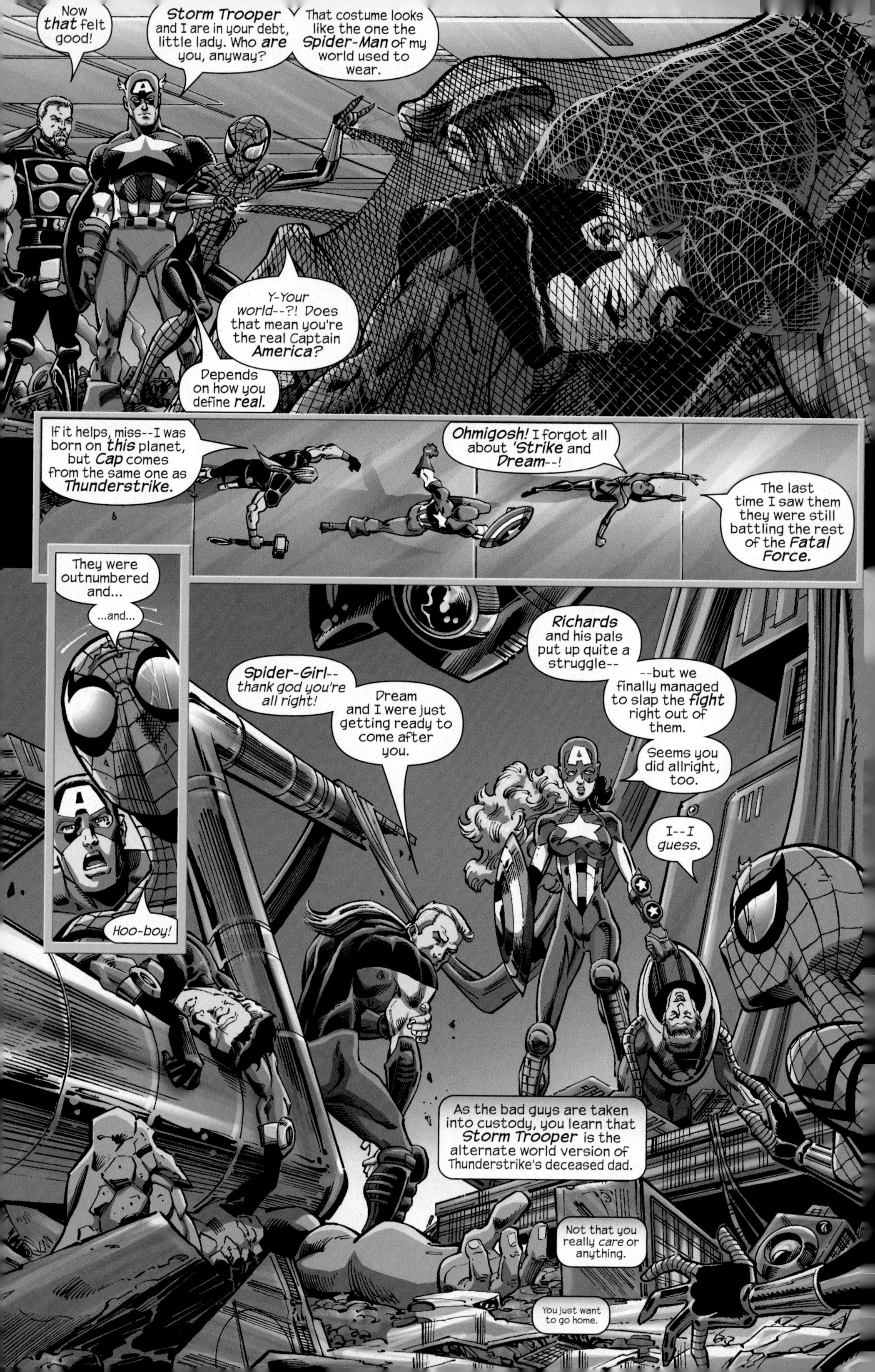

Now *that* felt good!
Storm Trooper and I are in your debt, little lady. Who *are* you, anyway?
That costume looks like the one the *Spider-Man* of my world used to wear.
Y-Your world--?! Does that mean you're the real Captain *America?*
Depends on how you define *real*.
If it helps, miss--I was born on *this* planet, but *Cap* comes from the same one as *Thunderstrike.*
Ohmigosh! I forgot all about *'Strike* and *Dream*--!
The last time I saw them they were still battling the rest of the *Fatal Force.*
They were outnumbered and...
...and...
Hoo-boy!
Spider-Girl-- *thank god you're all right!*
Dream and I were just getting ready to come after you.
Richards and his pals put up quite a struggle--
--but we finally managed to slap the *fight* right out of them.
Seems you did allright, too.
I--I *guess.*
As the bad guys are taken into custody, you learn that *Storm Trooper* is the alternate world version of Thunderstrike's deceased dad.
Not that you really *care* or anything.
You just want to go home.

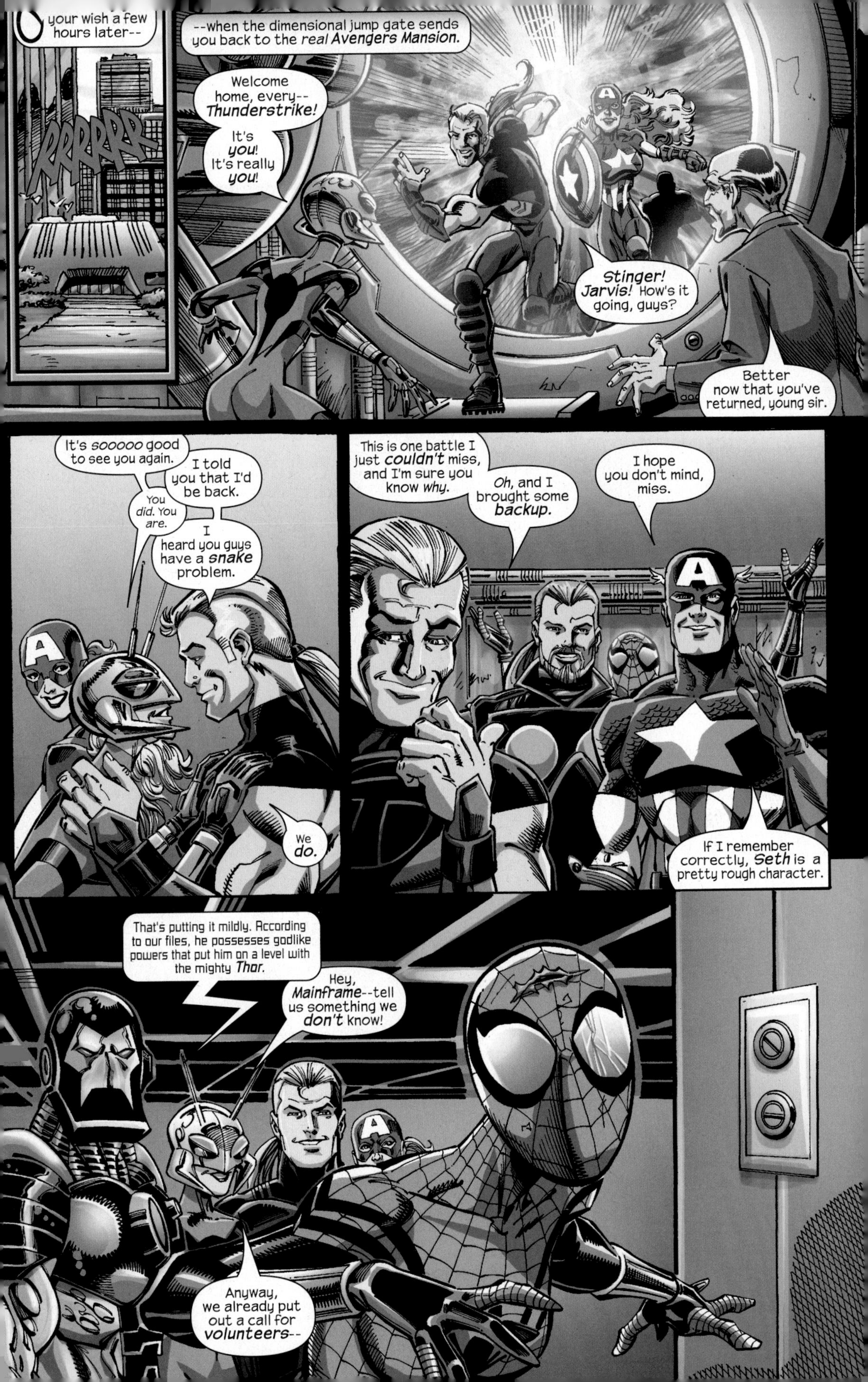

your wish a few hours later--
RRRRR
--when the dimensional jump gate sends you back to the real Avengers Mansion.
Welcome home, every-- Thunderstrike!
It's you! It's really you!
Stinger! Jarvis! How's it going, guys?
Better now that you've returned, young sir.
It's sooooo good to see you again.
I told you that I'd be back.
You did. You are.
I heard you guys have a snake problem.
We do.
This is one battle I just couldn't miss, and I'm sure you know why.
Oh, and I brought some backup.
I hope you don't mind, miss.
If I remember correctly, Seth is a pretty rough character.
That's putting it mildly. According to our files, he possesses godlike powers that put him on a level with the mighty Thor.
Hey, Mainframe--tell us something we don't know!
Anyway, we already put out a call for volunteers--

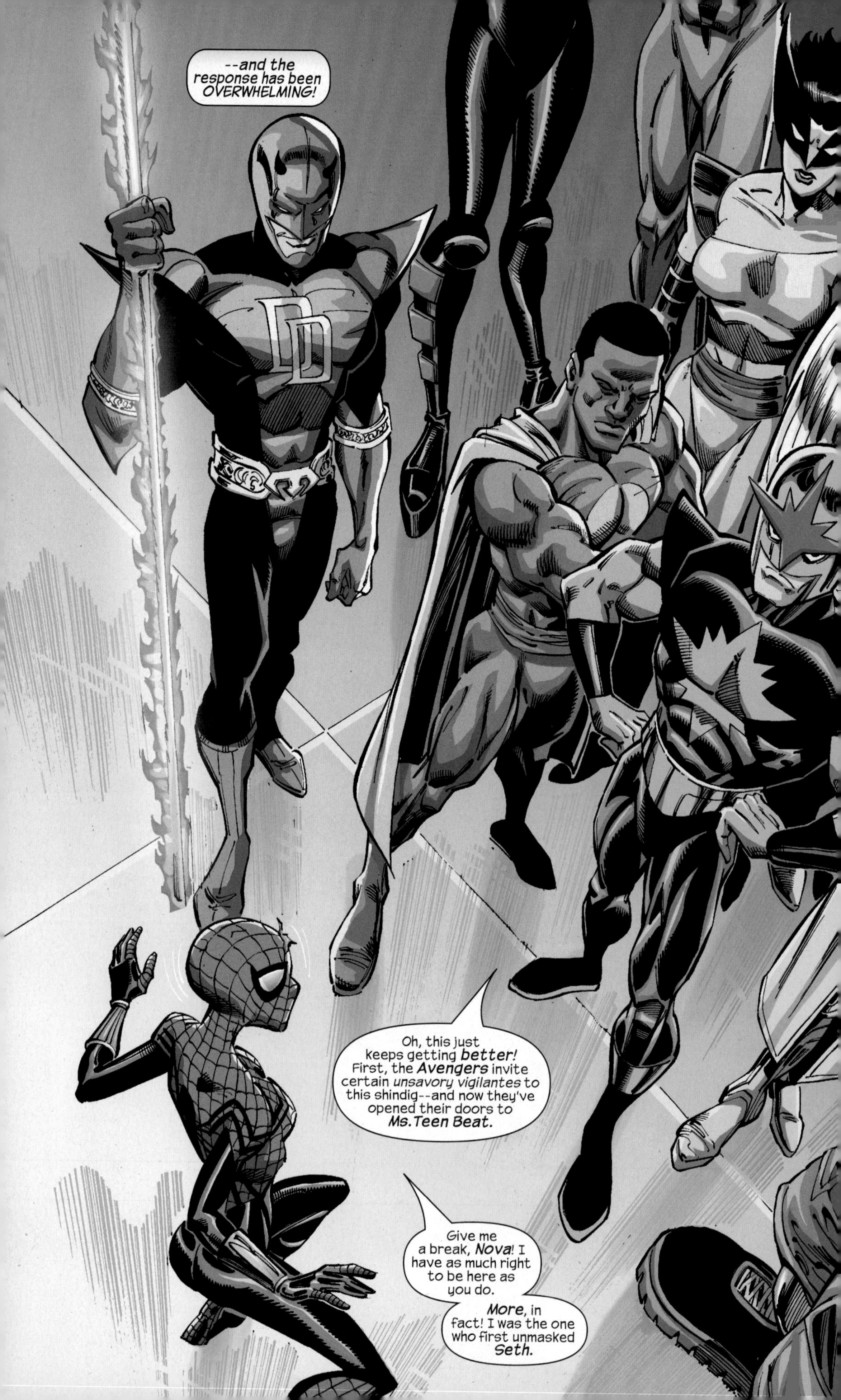
--and the response has been OVERWHELMING!
Oh, this just keeps getting better! First, the Avengers invite certain unsavory vigilantes to this shindig--and now they've opened their doors to Ms. Teen Beat.
Give me a break, Nova! I have as much right to be here as you do.
More, in fact! I was the one who first unmasked Seth.

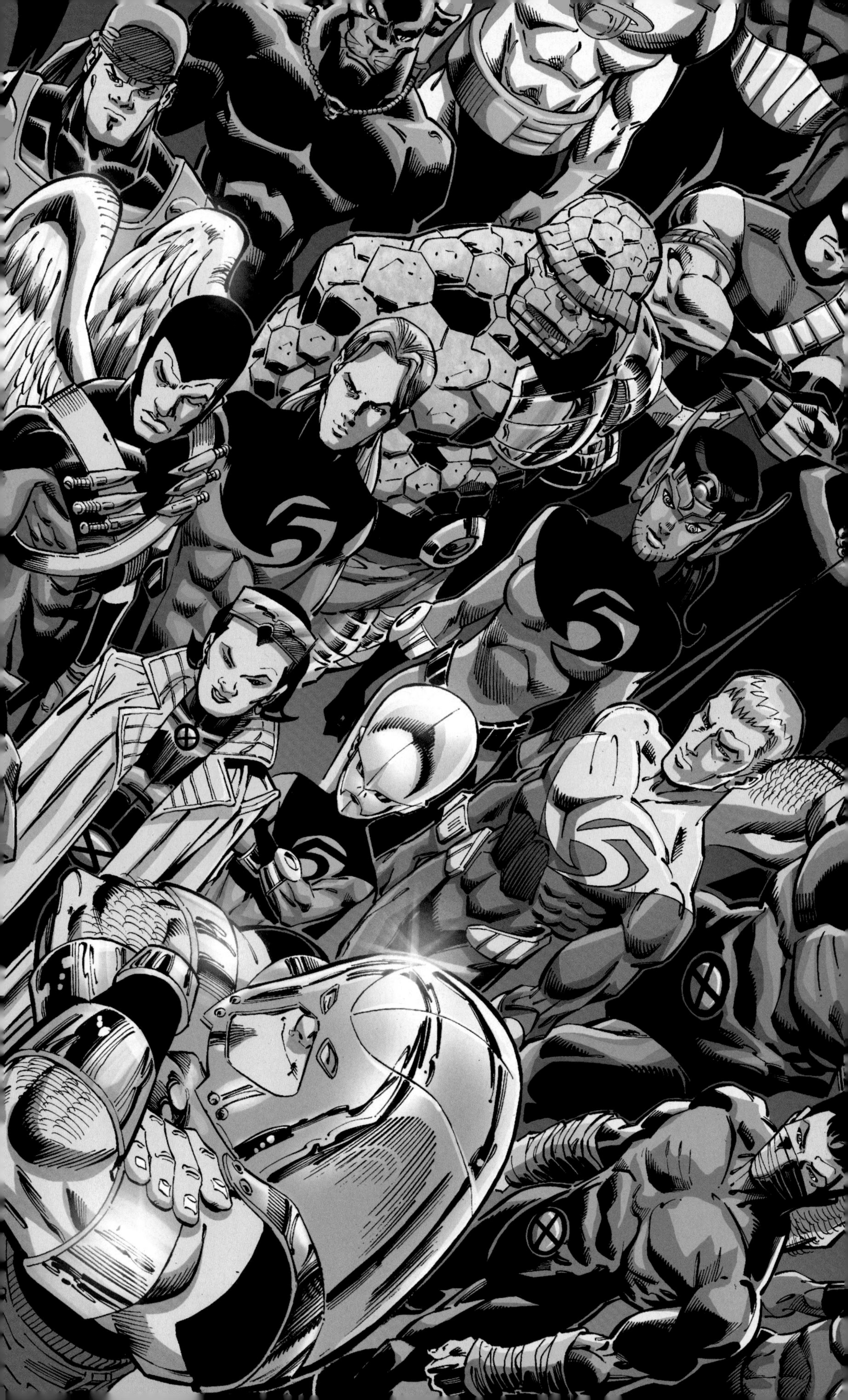

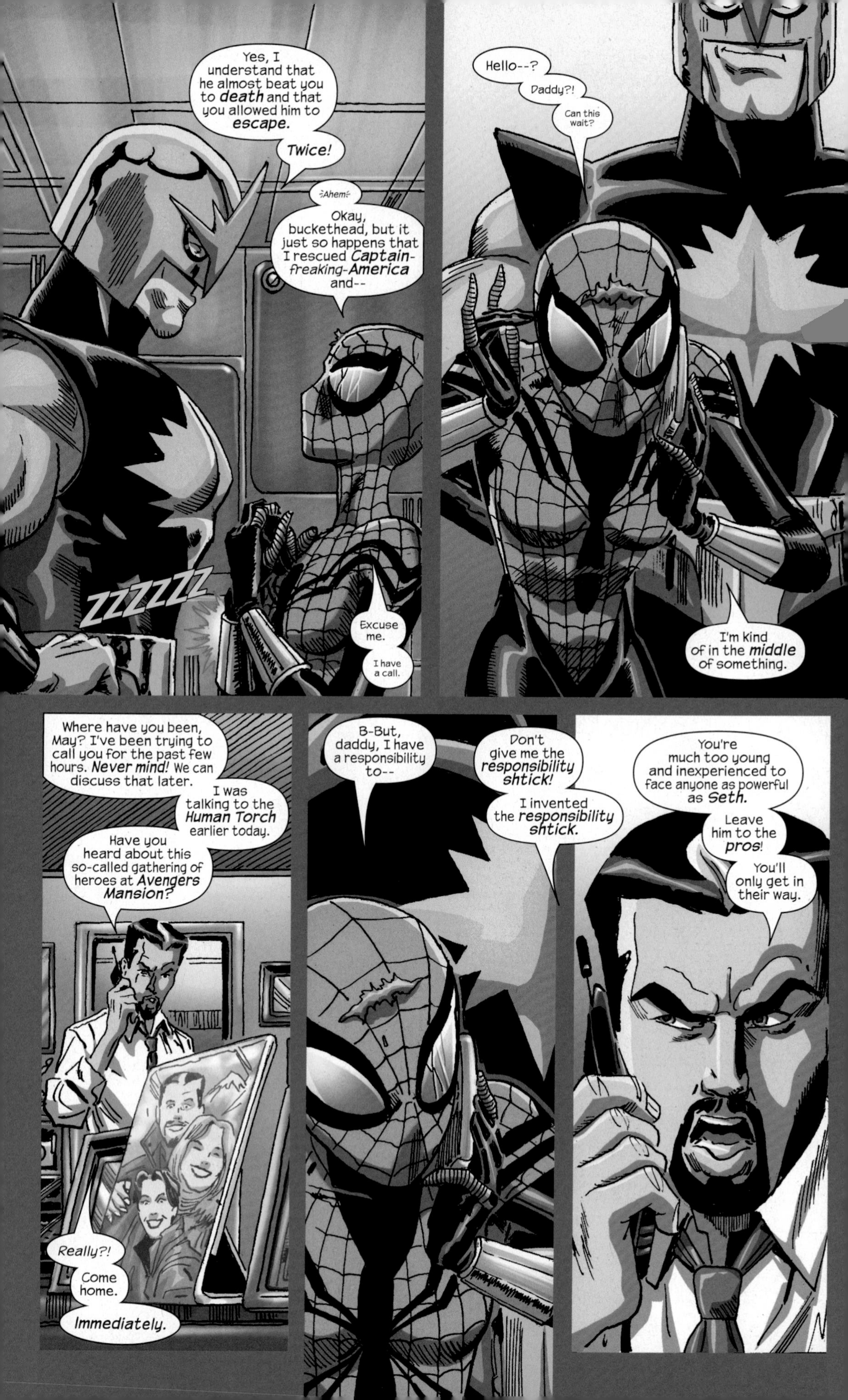
Yes, I understand that he almost beat you to death and that you allowed him to escape.
Twice!
Ahem
Okay, buckethead, but it just so happens that I rescued Captain-freaking-America and--
ZZZZZZ
Excuse me.
I have a call.
Hello--?
Daddy?!
Can this wait?
I'm kind of in the middle of something.
Where have you been, May? I've been trying to call you for the past few hours. Never mind! We can discuss that later.
I was talking to the Human Torch earlier today.
Have you heard about this so-called gathering of heroes at Avengers Mansion?
Really?!
Come home.
Immediately.
B-But, daddy, I have a responsibility to--
Don't give me the responsibility shtick!
I invented the responsibility shtick.
You're much too young and inexperienced to face anyone as powerful as Seth.
Leave him to the pros!
You'll only get in their way.

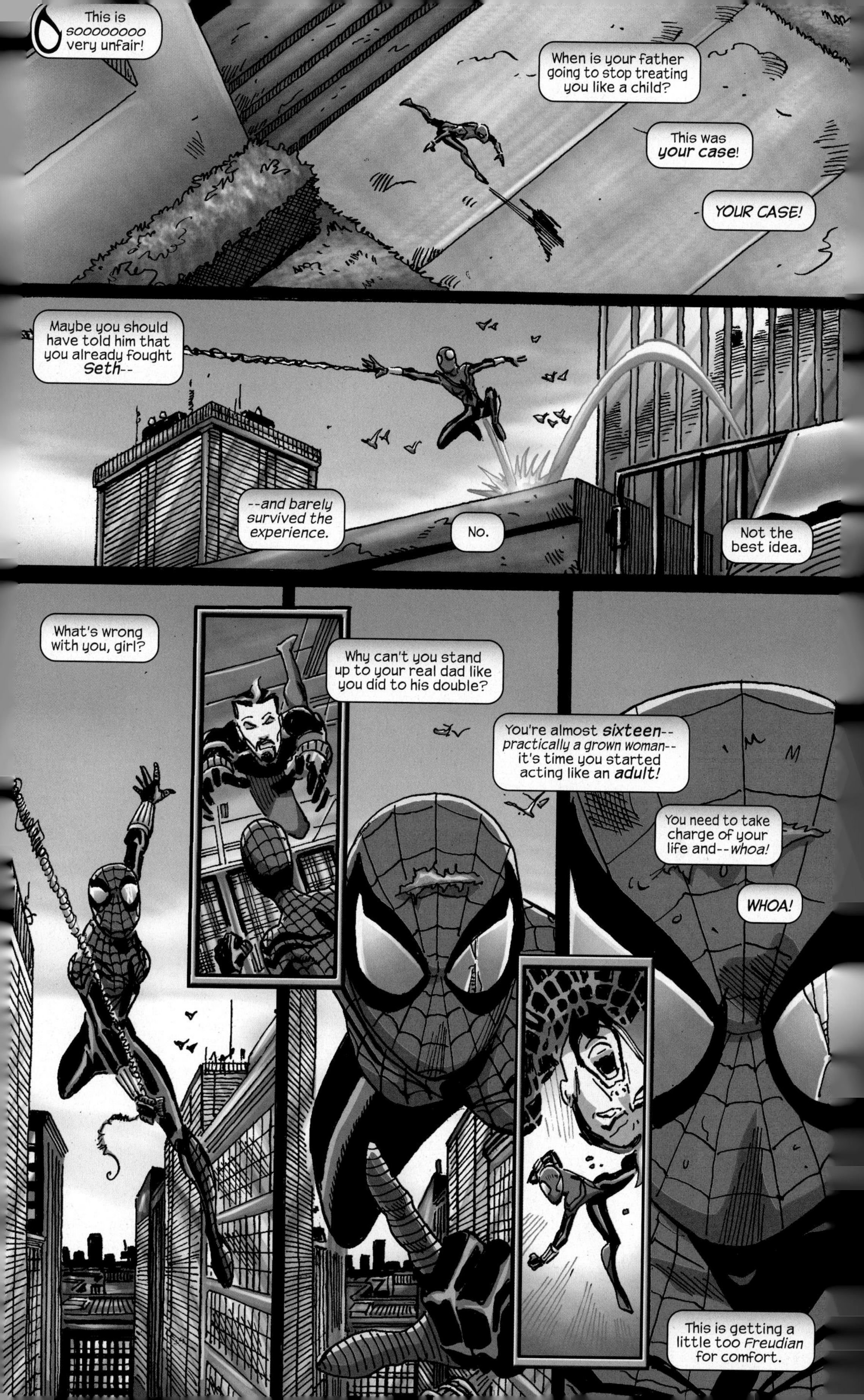
This is soooooooo very unfair!
When is your father going to stop treating you like a child?
This was your case!
YOUR CASE!
Maybe you should have told him that you already fought Seth--
--and barely survived the experience.
No.
Not the best idea.
What's wrong with you, girl?
Why can't you stand up to your real dad like you did to his double?
You're almost sixteen-- practically a grown woman-- it's time you started acting like an adult!
You need to take charge of your life and--whoa!
WHOA!
This is getting a little too Freudian for comfort.

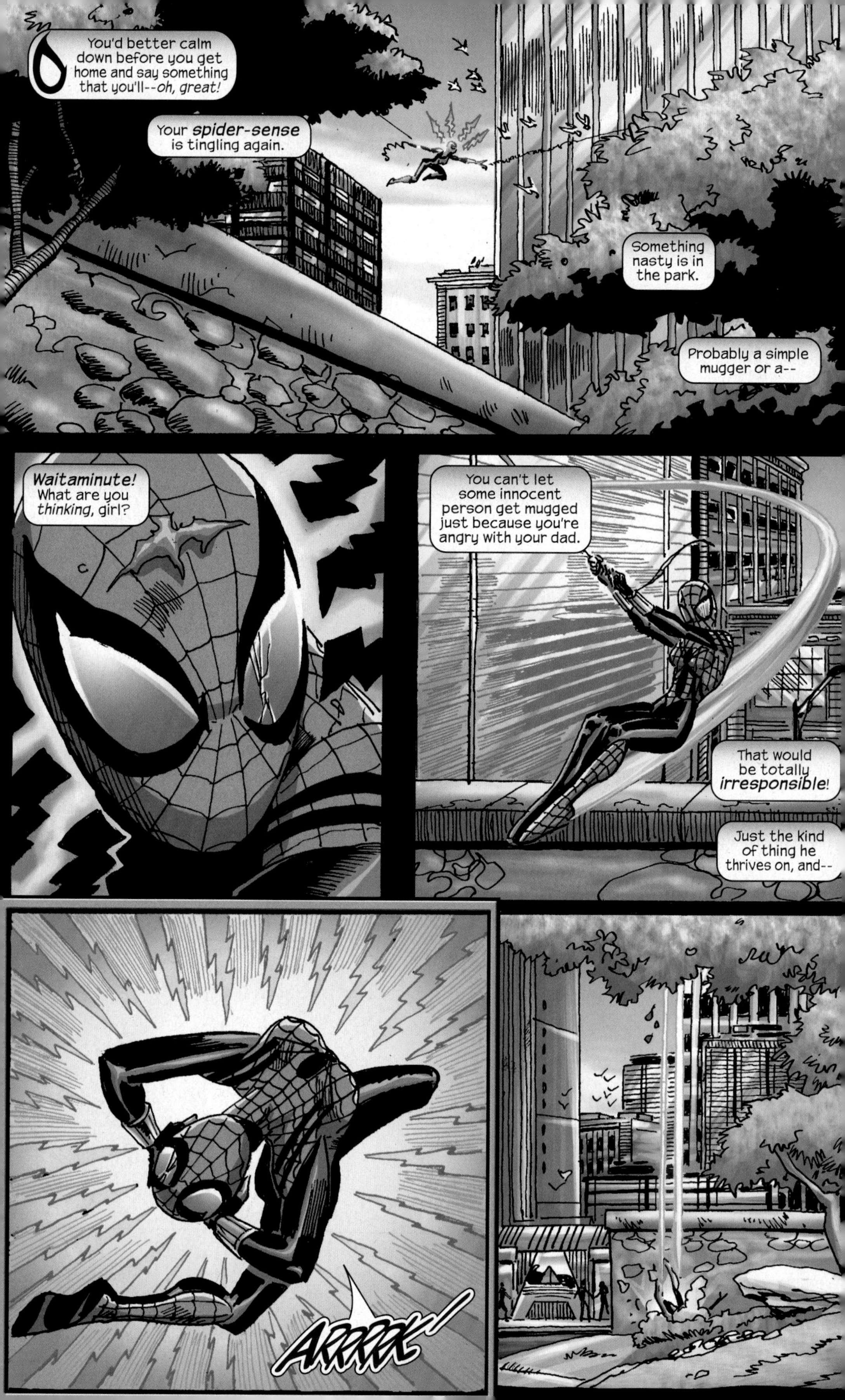
You'd better calm down before you get home and say something that you'll--oh, great!
Your spider-sense is tingling again.
Something nasty is in the park.
Probably a simple mugger or a--
Waitaminute! What are you thinking, girl?
You can't let some innocent person get mugged just because you're angry with your dad.
That would be totally irresponsible!
Just the kind of thing he thrives on, and--
ARRRRK!

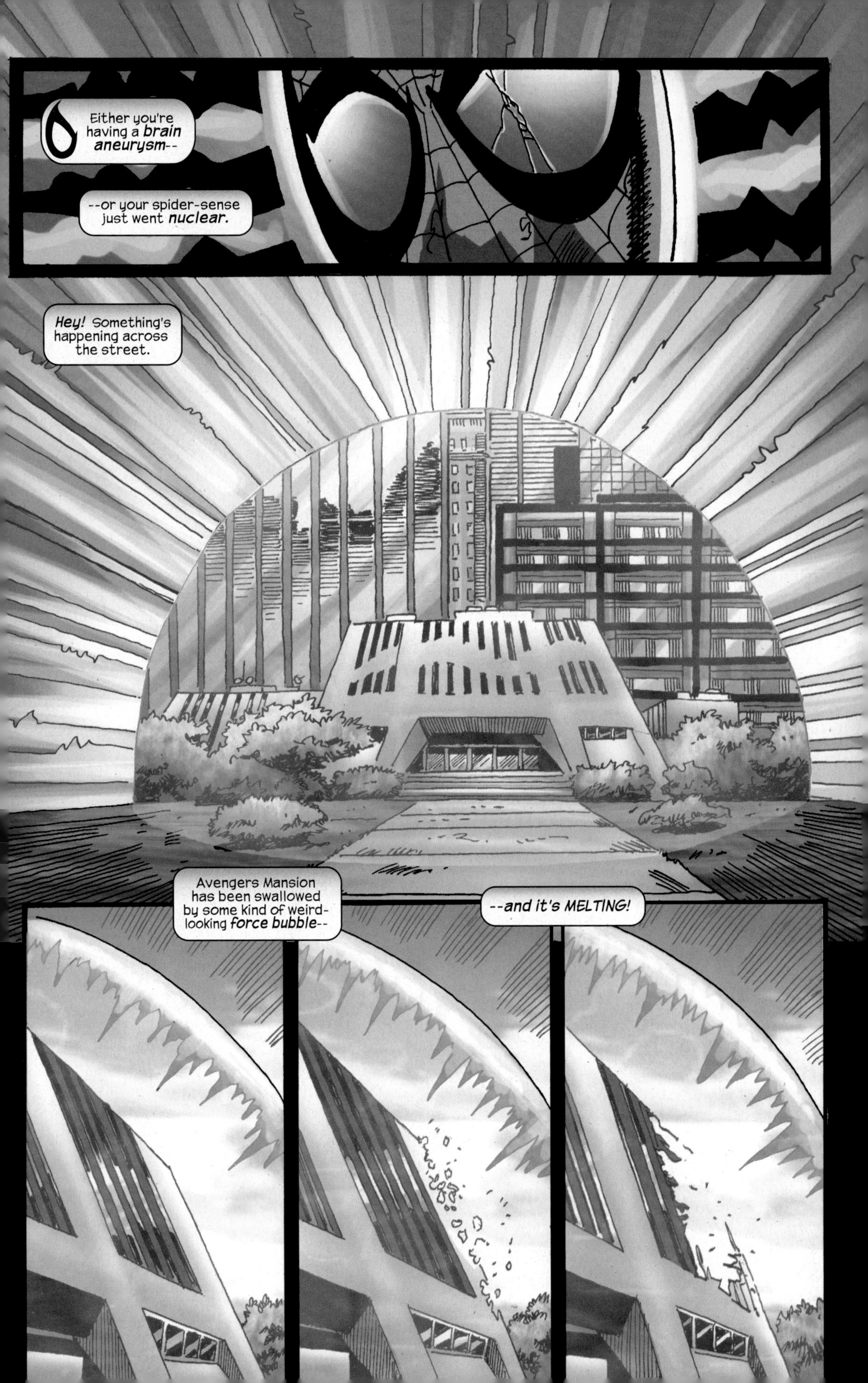

Either you're having a brain aneurysm--
--or your spider-sense just went nuclear.
Hey! Something's happening across the street.
Avengers Mansion has been swallowed by some kind of weird-looking force bubble--
--and it's MELTING!

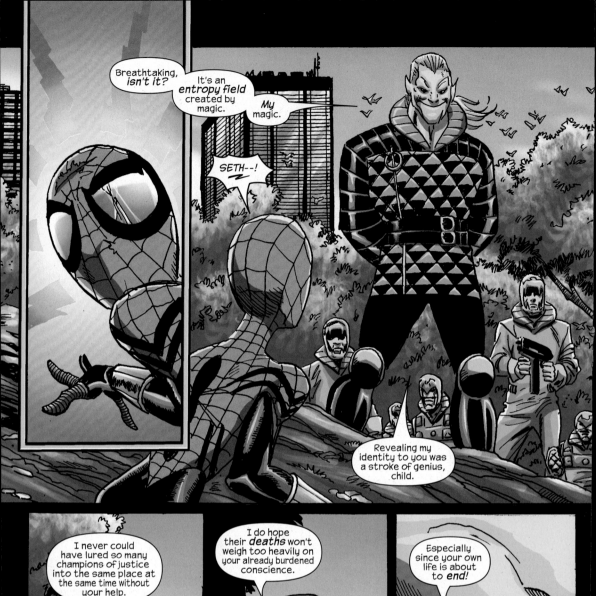

Breathtaking, **isn't it?**

It's an **entropy field** created by magic.

My magic.

SETH--!

Revealing my identity to you was a stroke of genius, child.

I never could have lured so many champions of justice into the same place at the same time without your help.

I do hope their **deaths** won't weigh too heavily on your already burdened conscience.

Especially since your own life is about to **end!**

2 B CONCLUDED!

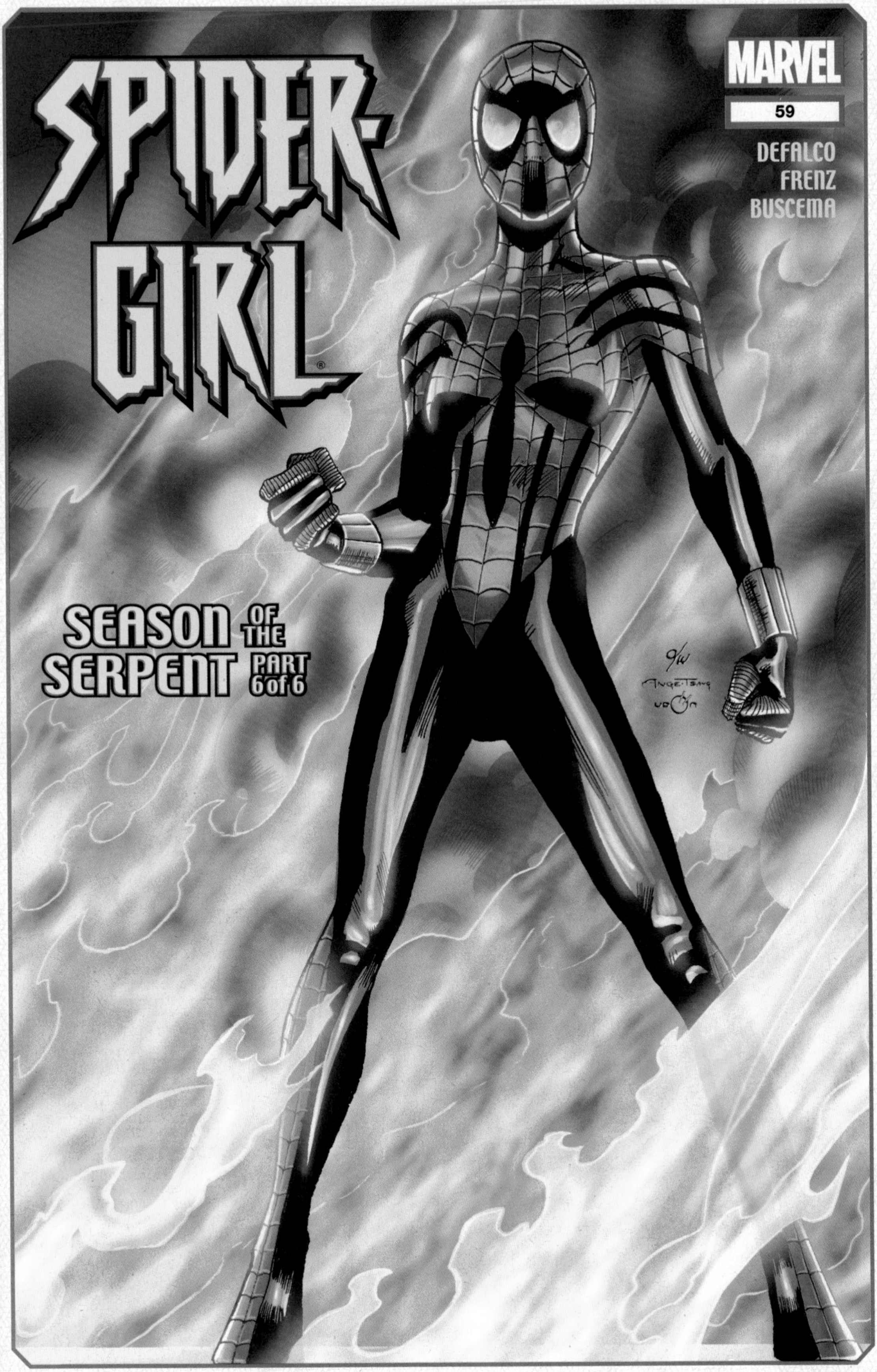
SPIDER-GIRL
MARVEL
59
DEFALCO
FRENZ
BUSCEMA
SEASON OF THE SERPENT PART 6 of 6

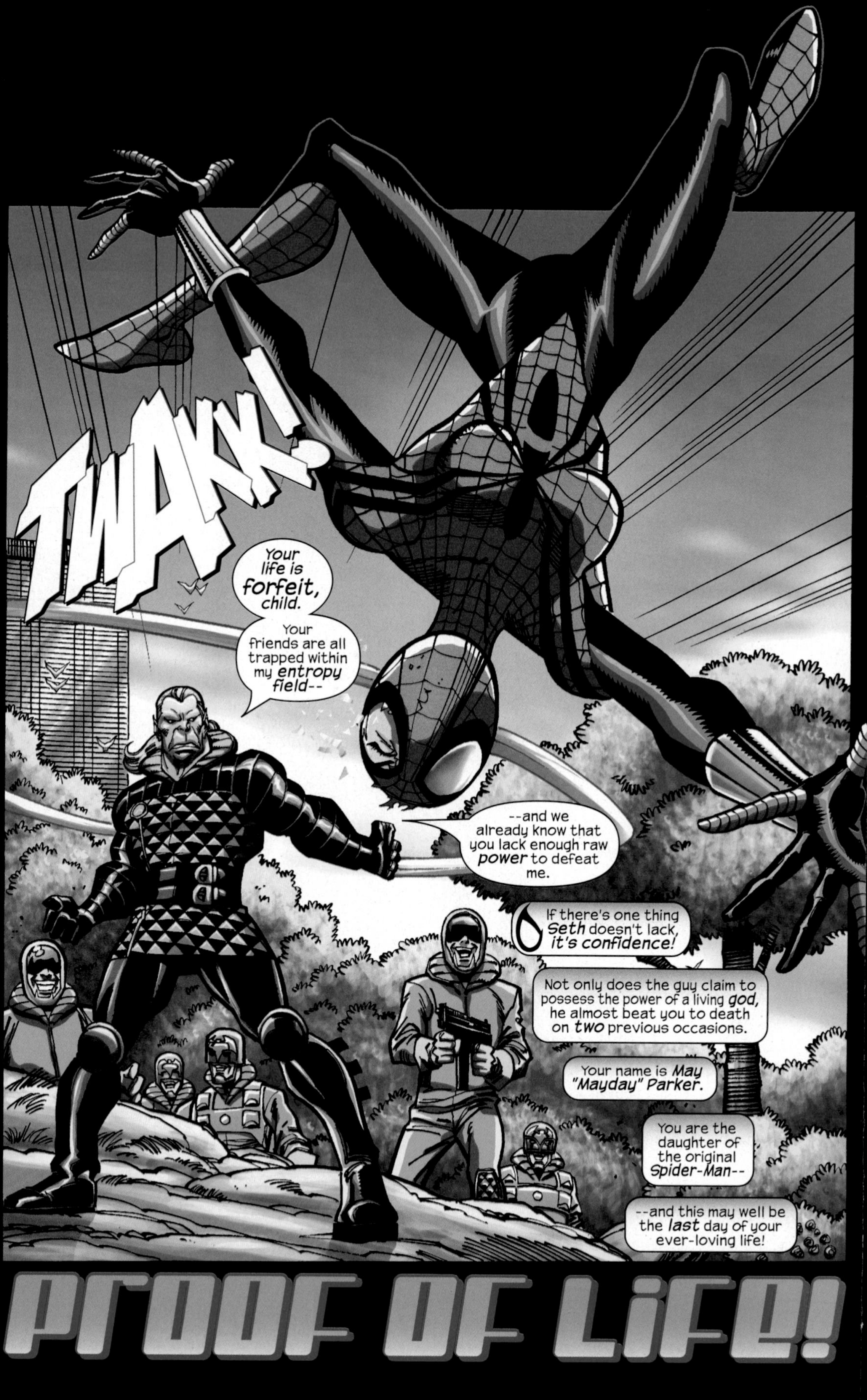
TWAKK!
Your life is forfeit, child.
Your friends are all trapped within my entropy field--
--and we already know that you lack enough raw power to defeat me.
If there's one thing Seth doesn't lack, it's confidence!
Not only does the guy claim to possess the power of a living god, he almost beat you to death on two previous occasions.
Your name is May "Mayday" Parker.
You are the daughter of the original Spider-Man--
--and this may well be the last day of your ever-loving life!
PROOF OF LIFE!

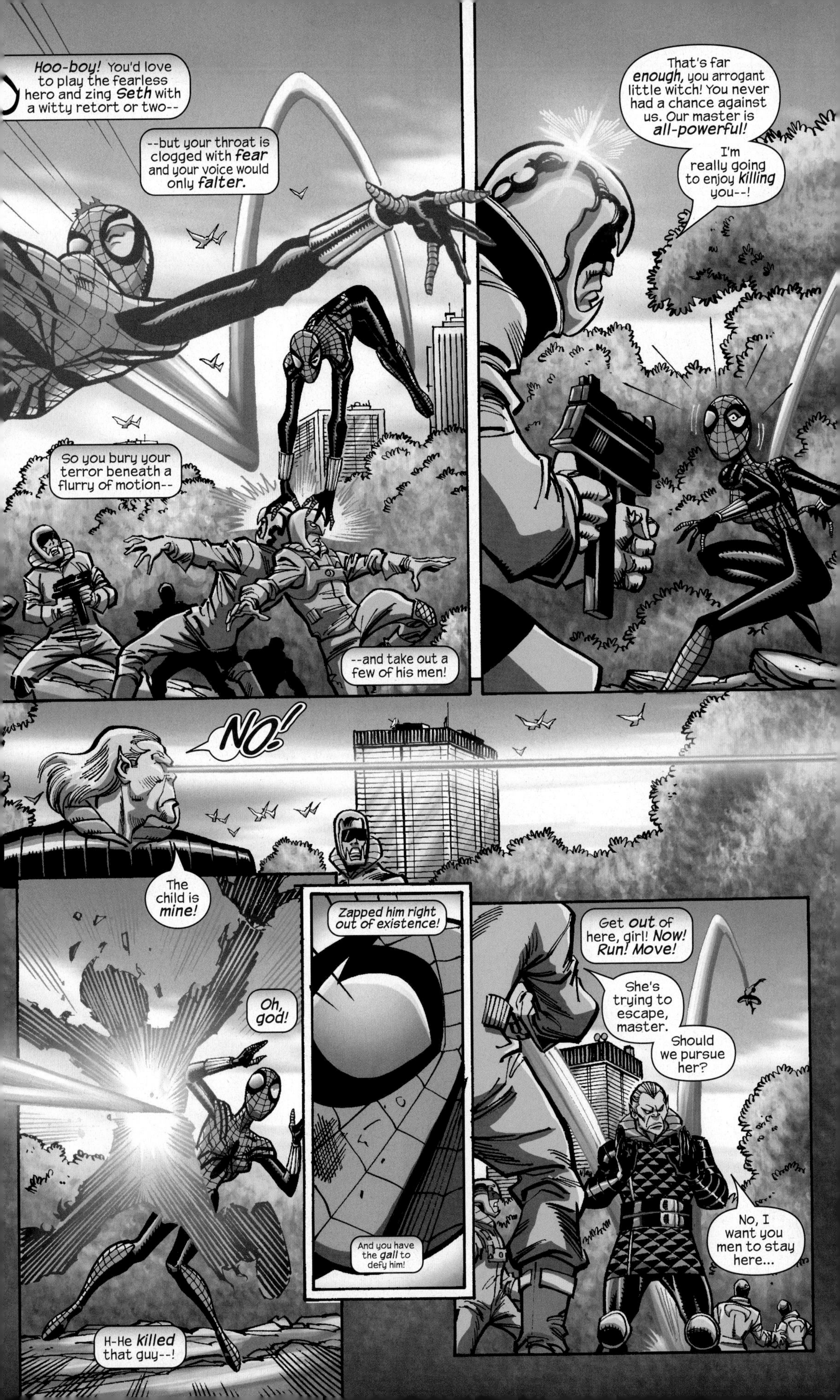

Hoo-boy! You'd love to play the fearless hero and zing Seth with a witty retort or two--
--but your throat is clogged with fear and your voice would only falter.
So you bury your terror beneath a flurry of motion--
--and take out a few of his men!
That's far enough, you arrogant little witch! You never had a chance against us. Our master is all-powerful!
I'm really going to enjoy killing you--!
NO!
The child is mine!
Oh, god!
H-He killed that guy--!
Zapped him right out of existence!
And you have the gall to defy him!
Get out of here, girl! Now! Run! Move!
She's trying to escape, master.
Should we pursue her?
No, I want you men to stay here...

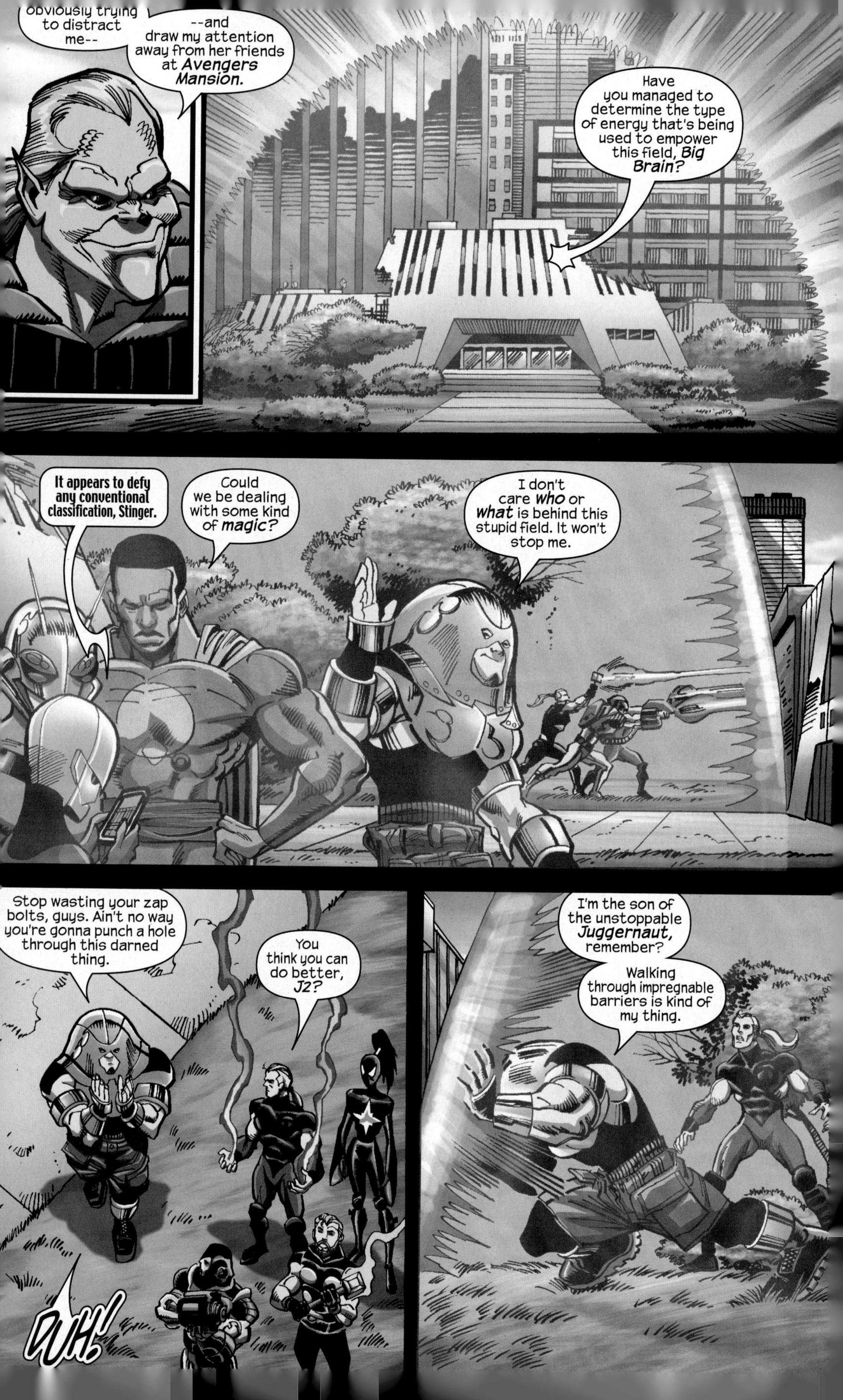
obviously trying to distract me--
--and draw my attention away from her friends at Avengers Mansion.
Have you managed to determine the type of energy that's being used to empower this field, Big Brain?
It appears to defy any conventional classification, Stinger.
Could we be dealing with some kind of magic?
I don't care who or what is behind this stupid field. It won't stop me.
Stop wasting your zap bolts, guys. Ain't no way you're gonna punch a hole through this darned thing.
You think you can do better, J2?
DUH!
I'm the son of the unstoppable Juggernaut, remember?
Walking through impregnable barriers is kind of my thing.

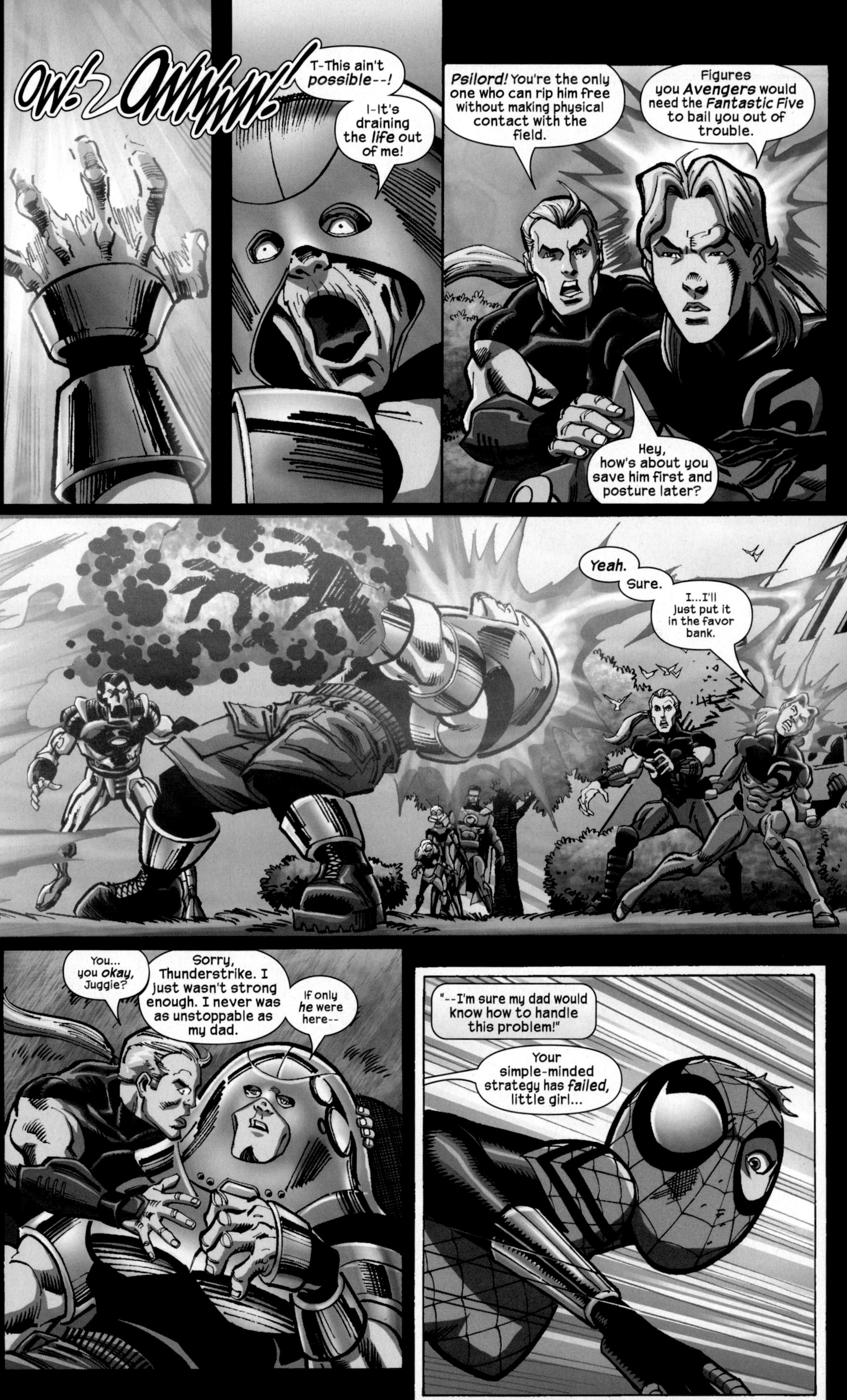
OW! AWWW!
T-This ain't possible--!
I-It's draining the life out of me!
Psilord! You're the only one who can rip him free without making physical contact with the field.
Figures you Avengers would need the Fantastic Five to bail you out of trouble.
Hey, how's about you save him first and posture later?
Yeah.
Sure.
I...I'll just put it in the favor bank.
You... you okay, Juggie?
Sorry, Thunderstrike. I just wasn't strong enough. I never was as unstoppable as my dad.
If only he were here--
"--I'm sure my dad would know how to handle this problem!"
Your simple-minded strategy has failed, little girl...

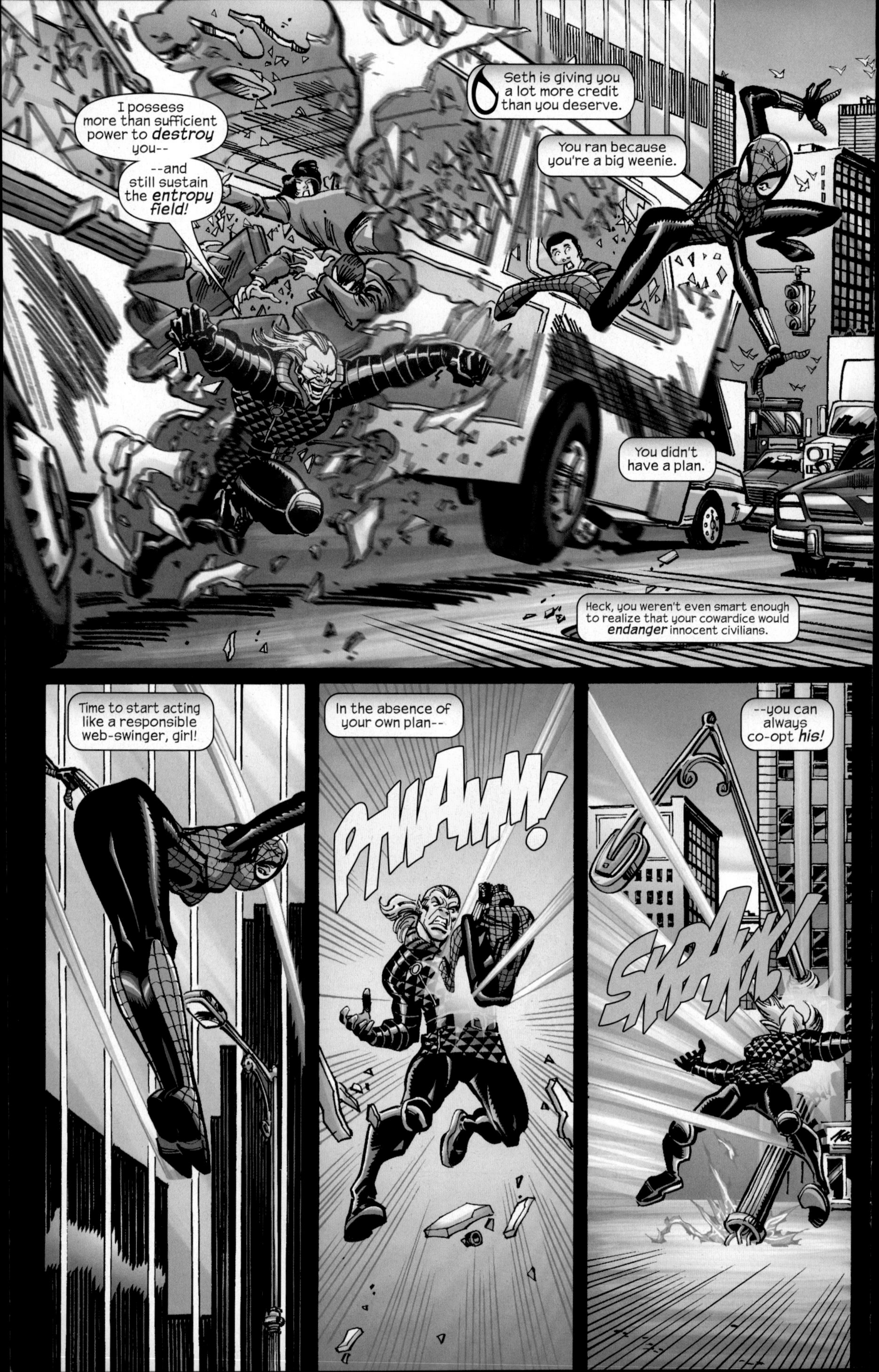
I possess more than sufficient power to destroy you--
--and still sustain the entropy field!
Seth is giving you a lot more credit than you deserve.
You ran because you're a big weenie.
You didn't have a plan.
Heck, you weren't even smart enough to realize that your cowardice would endanger innocent civilians.
Time to start acting like a responsible web-swinger, girl!
In the absence of your own plan--
PTHAMM!
--you can always co-opt his!
SHPANK!

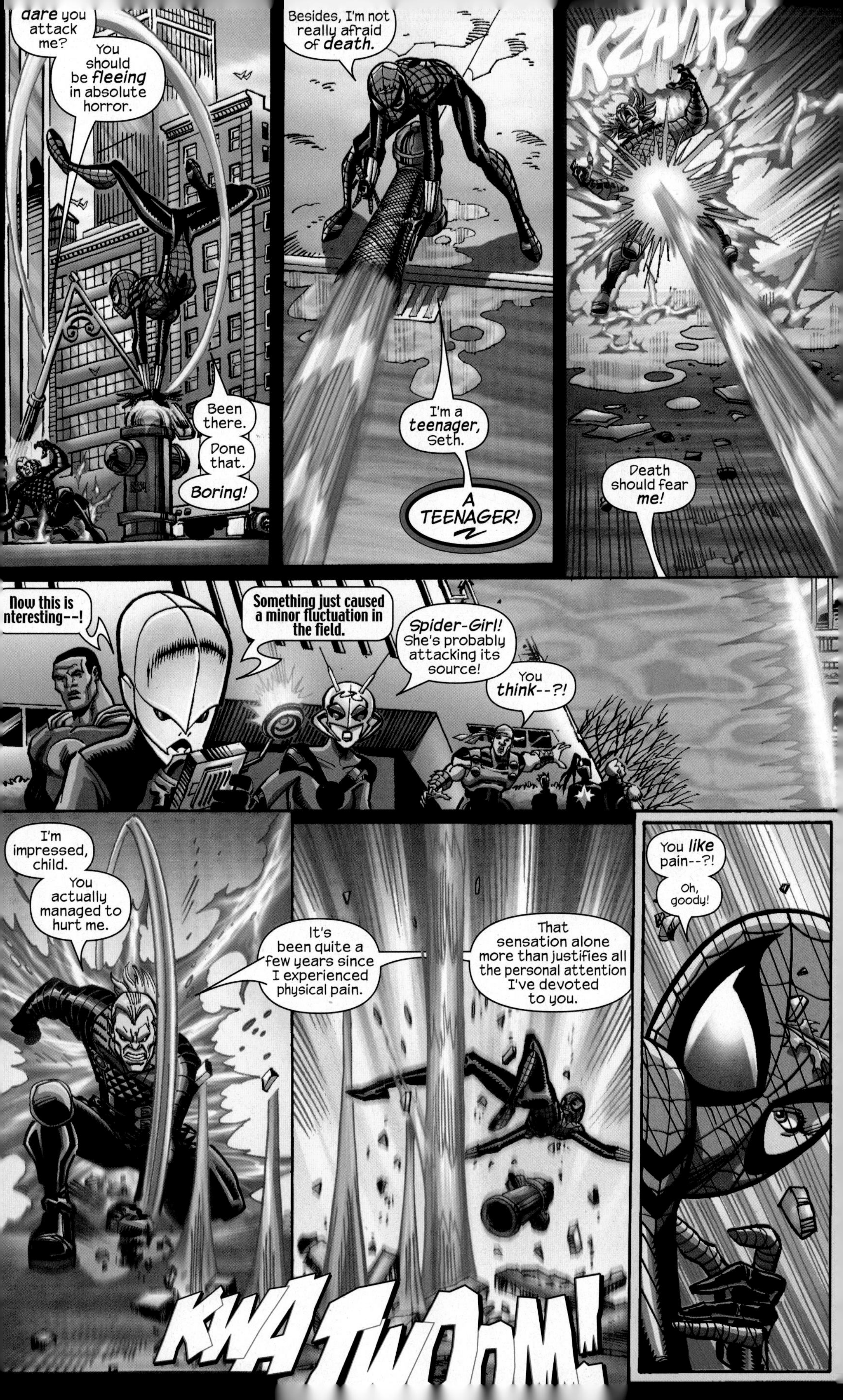
dare you attack me?
You should be fleeing in absolute horror.
Been there.
Done that.
Boring!
Besides, I'm not really afraid of death.
I'm a teenager, Seth.
A TEENAGER!
KZHAK!
Death should fear me!
Now this is interesting--!
Something just caused a minor fluctuation in the field.
Spider-Girl! She's probably attacking its source!
You think--?!
I'm impressed, child.
You actually managed to hurt me.
It's been quite a few years since I experienced physical pain.
That sensation alone more than justifies all the personal attention I've devoted to you.
KWATWOOM!
You like pain--?!
Oh, goody!

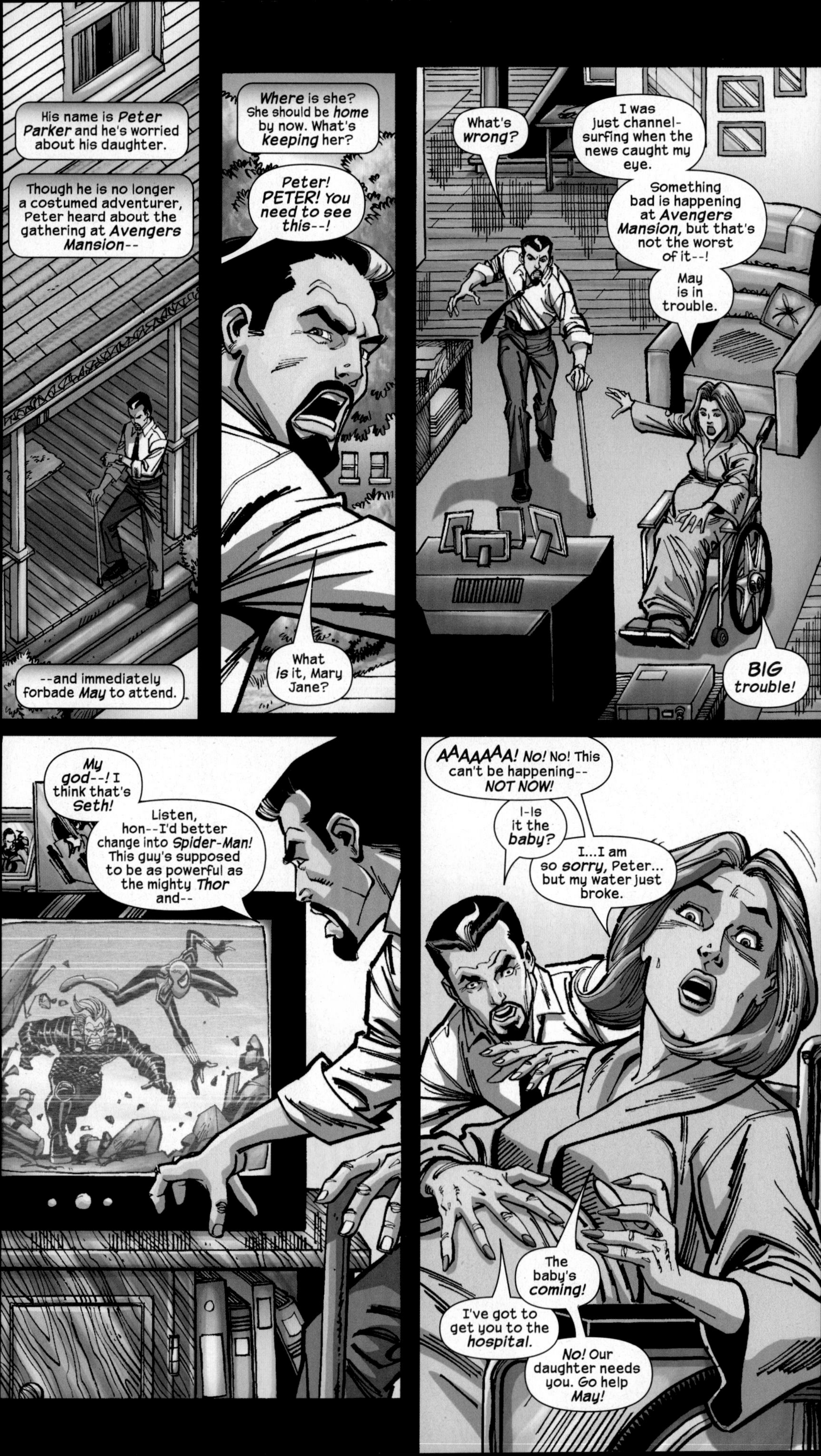
His name is Peter Parker and he's worried about his daughter.
Though he is no longer a costumed adventurer, Peter heard about the gathering at Avengers Mansion--
--and immediately forbade May to attend.
Where is she? She should be home by now. What's keeping her?
Peter! PETER! You need to see this--!
What is it, Mary Jane?
What's wrong?
I was just channel-surfing when the news caught my eye.
Something bad is happening at Avengers Mansion, but that's not the worst of it--!
May is in trouble.
BIG trouble!
My god--! I think that's Seth!
Listen, hon--I'd better change into Spider-Man! This guy's supposed to be as powerful as the mighty Thor and--
AAAAAA! No! No! This can't be happening-- NOT NOW!
I-Is it the baby?
I...I am so sorry, Peter... but my water just broke.
The baby's coming!
I've got to get you to the hospital.
No! Our daughter needs you. Go help May!

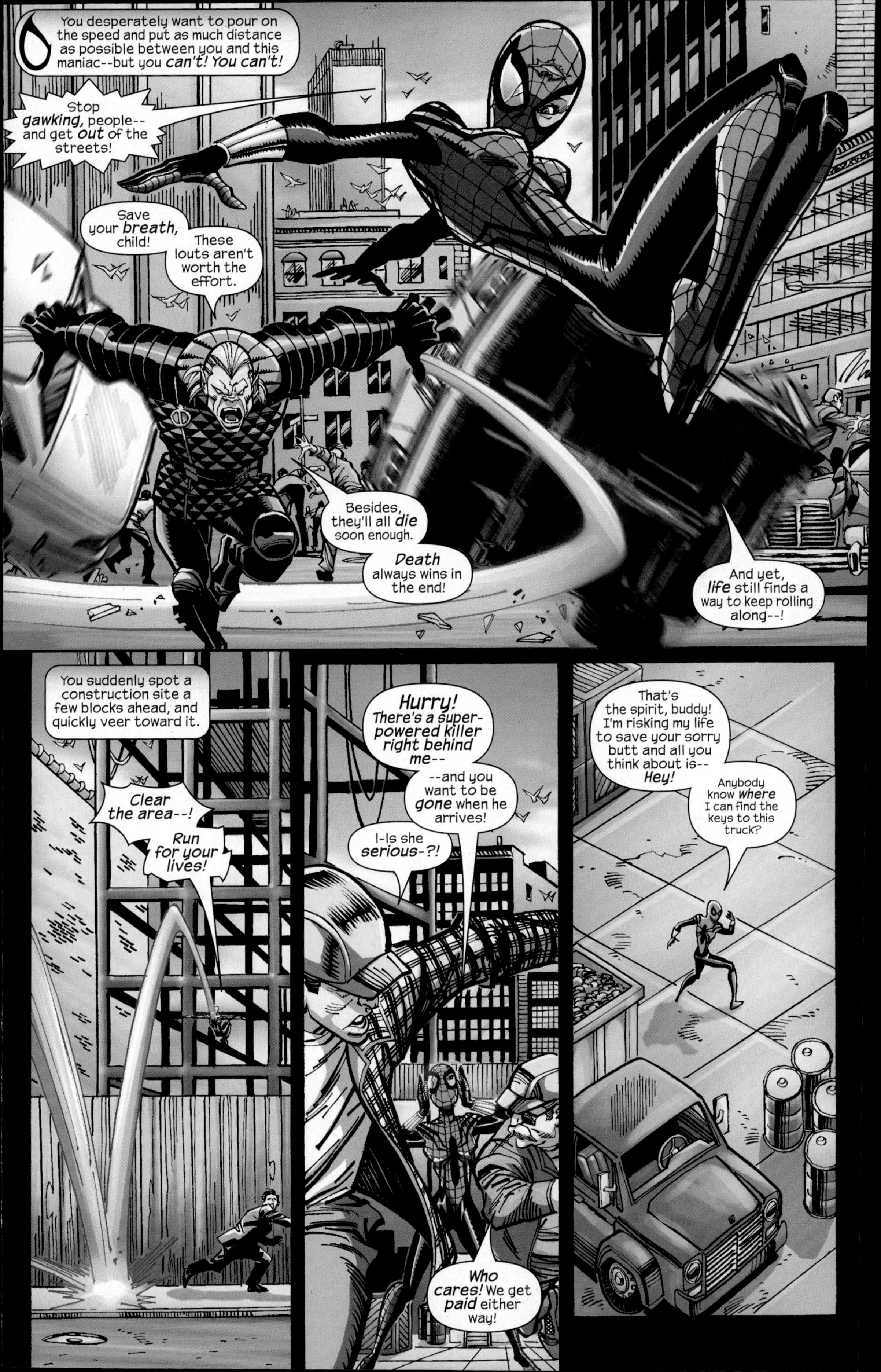
You desperately want to pour on the speed and put as much distance as possible between you and this maniac--but you *can't! You can't!*
Stop *gawking,* people--and get *out* of the streets!
Save your *breath,* child!
These louts aren't worth the effort.
Besides, they'll all *die* soon enough.
Death always wins in the end!
And yet, *life* still finds a way to keep rolling along--!
You suddenly spot a construction site a few blocks ahead, and quickly veer toward it.
Clear the area--!
Run for your lives!
Hurry! There's a super-powered killer right behind me--
--and you want to be *gone* when he arrives!
I-Is she *serious*-?!
Who *cares!* We get *paid* either way!
That's the spirit, buddy! I'm risking my life to save your sorry butt and all you think about is-- *Hey!*
Anybody know *where* I can find the keys to this truck?

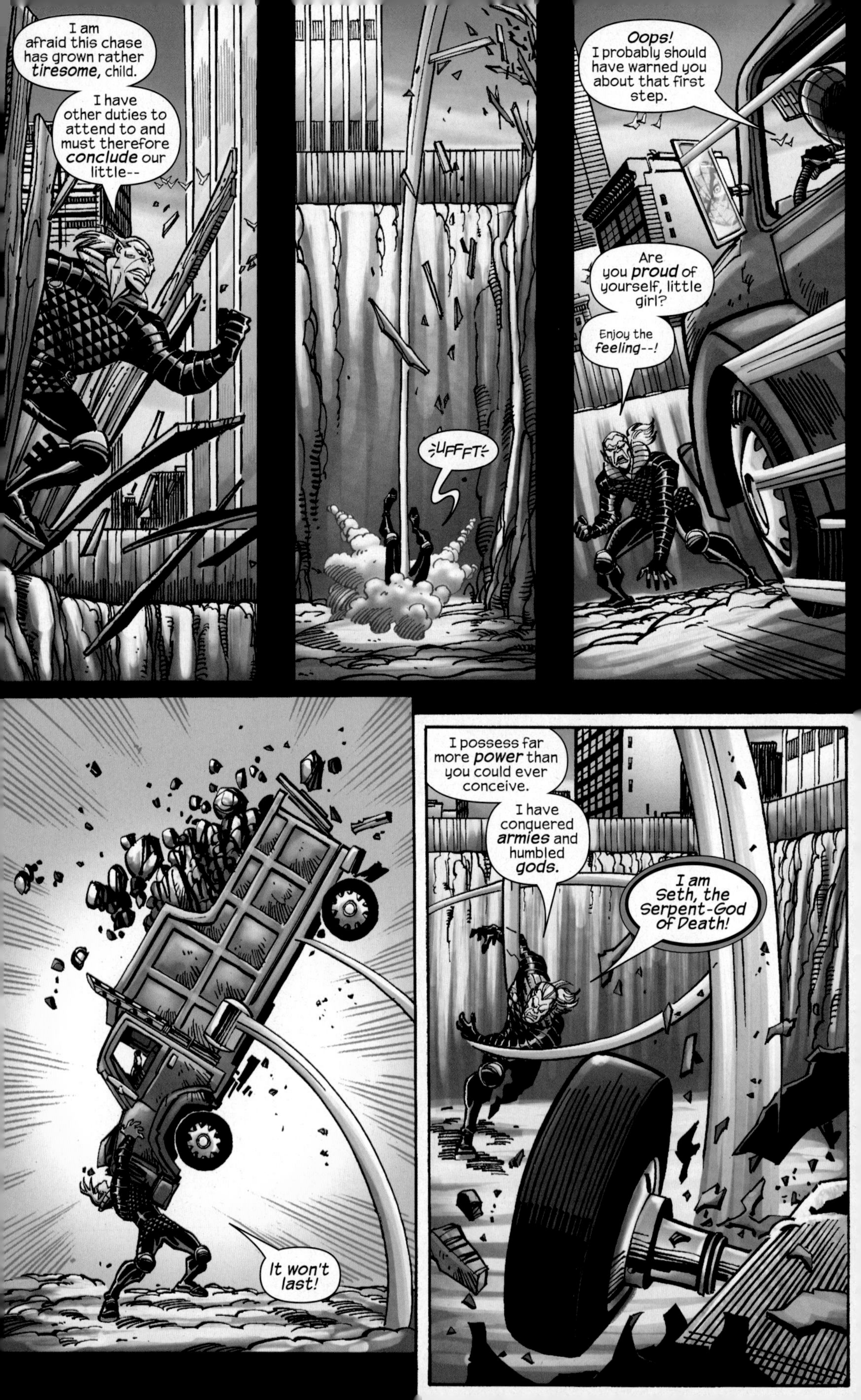
I am afraid this chase has grown rather *tiresome,* child.
I have other duties to attend to and must therefore *conclude* our little--
UFFFT!
Oops! I probably should have warned you about that first step.
Are you *proud* of yourself, little girl?
Enjoy the *feeling--!*
It won't last!
I possess far more *power* than you could ever conceive.
I have conquered *armies* and humbled *gods.*
I am Seth, the Serpent-God of Death!

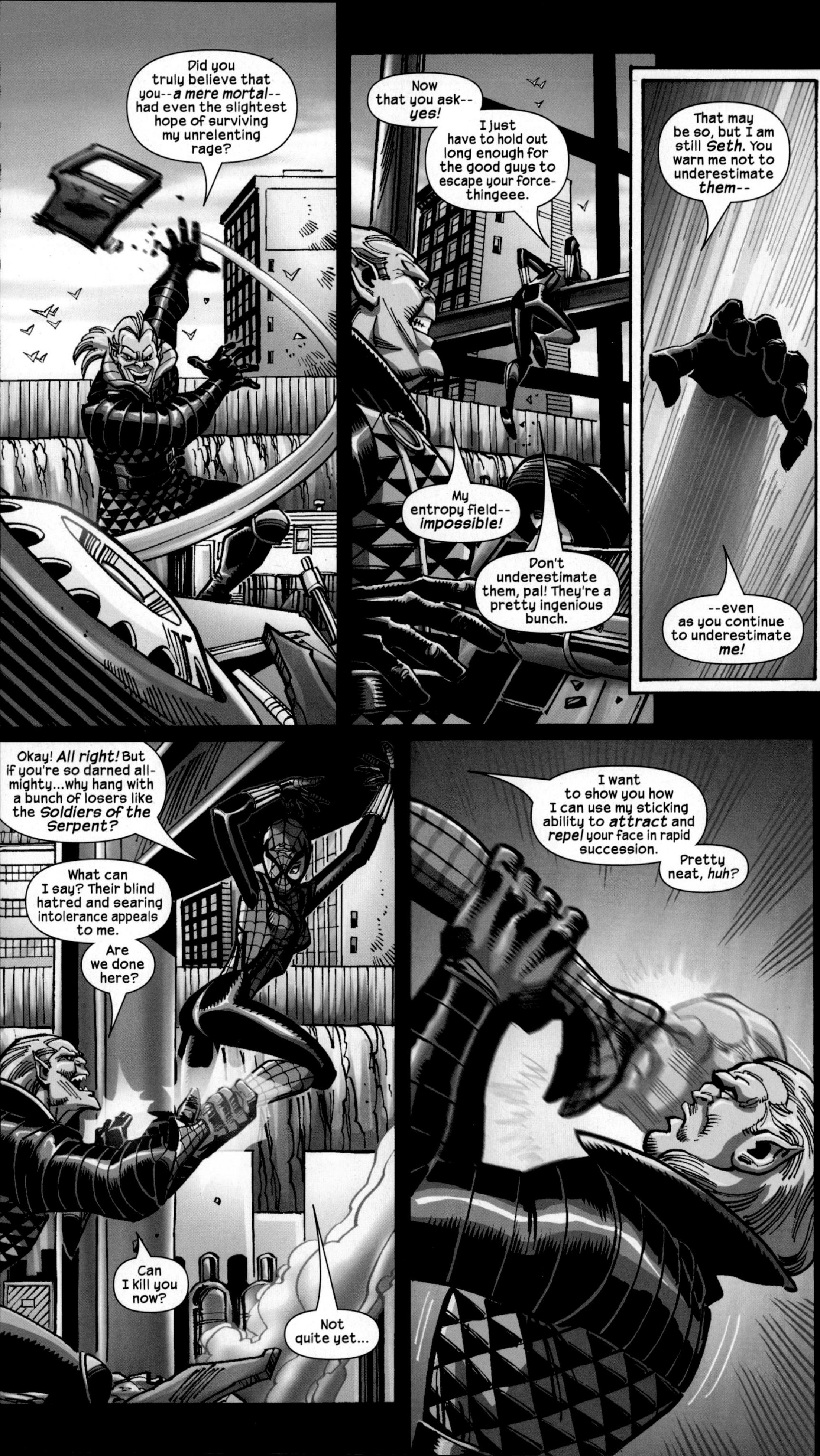

Did you truly believe that you--*a mere mortal*--had even the slightest hope of surviving my unrelenting rage?
Now that you ask--*yes!*
I just have to hold out long enough for the good guys to escape your force-thingeee.
My entropy field--*impossible!*
Don't underestimate them, pal! They're a pretty ingenious bunch.
That may be so, but I am still *Seth.* You warn me not to underestimate *them*--
--even as you continue to underestimate *me!*
Okay! *All right!* But if you're so darned all-mighty...why hang with a bunch of losers like the *Soldiers of the Serpent?*
What can I say? Their blind hatred and searing intolerance appeals to me.
Are we done here?
Can I kill you now?
Not quite yet...
I want to show you how I can use my sticking ability to *attract* and *repel* your face in rapid succession.
Pretty neat, *huh?*

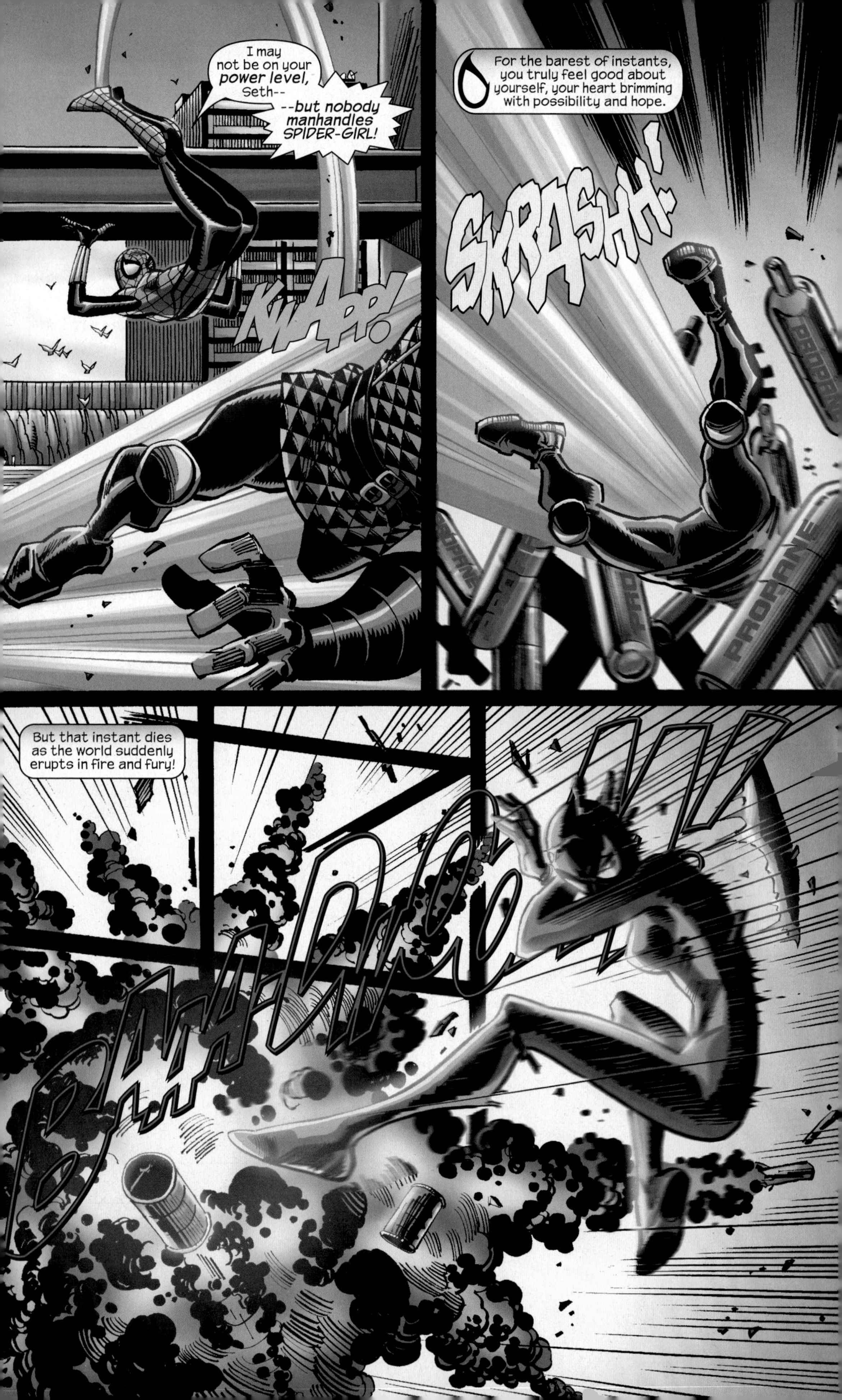
I may not be on your power level, Seth--
--but nobody manhandles SPIDER-GIRL!
KWAPP!
For the barest of instants, you truly feel good about yourself, your heart brimming with possibility and hope.
SKRASHH!
PROPANE
PROPANE
But that instant dies as the world suddenly erupts in fire and fury!

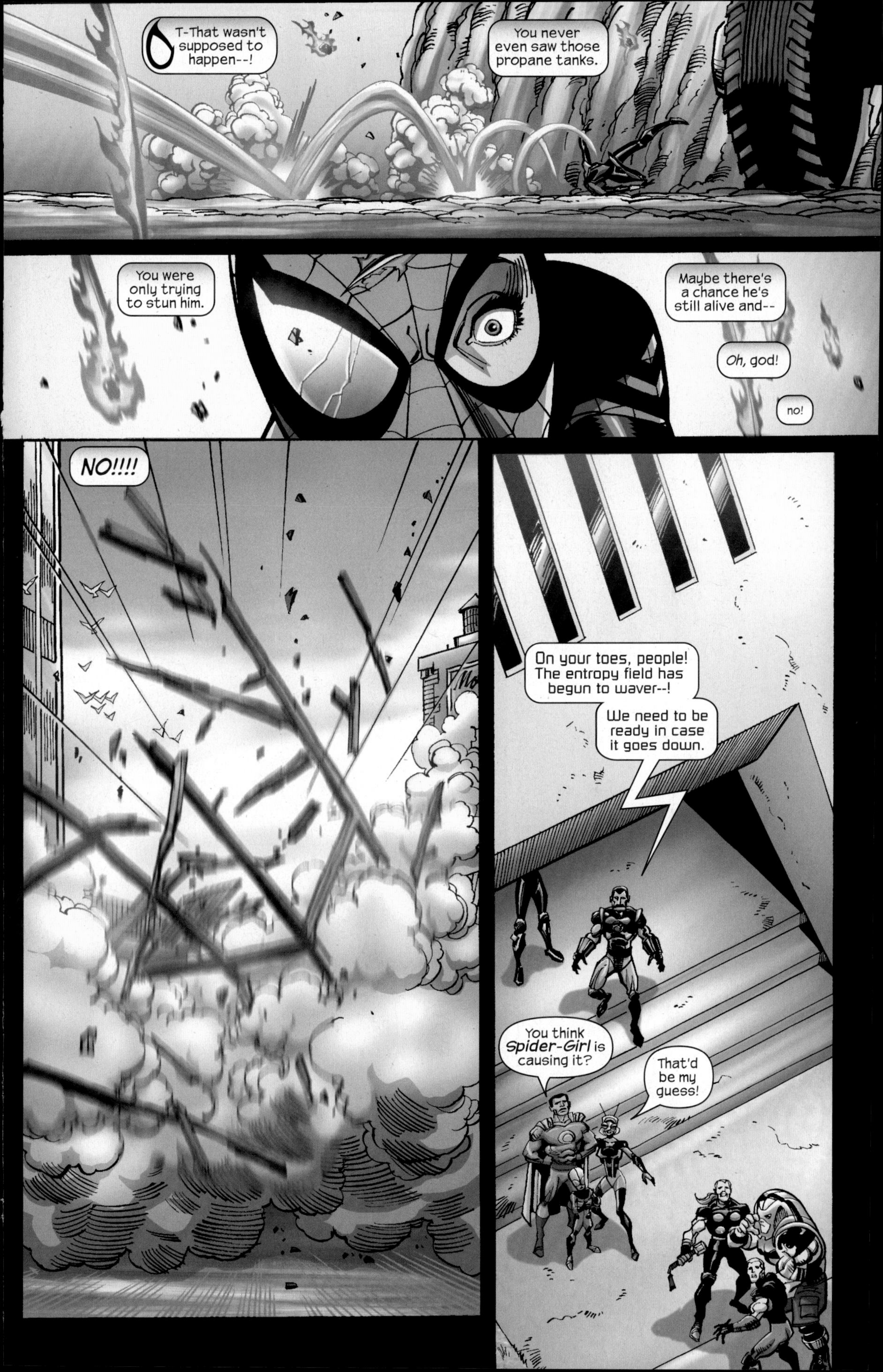

T-That wasn't supposed to happen--!
You never even saw those propane tanks.
You were only trying to stun him.
Maybe there's a chance he's still alive and--
Oh, god!
no!
NO!!!!
On your toes, people! The entropy field has begun to waver--!
We need to be ready in case it goes down.
You think Spider-Girl is causing it?
That'd be my guess!

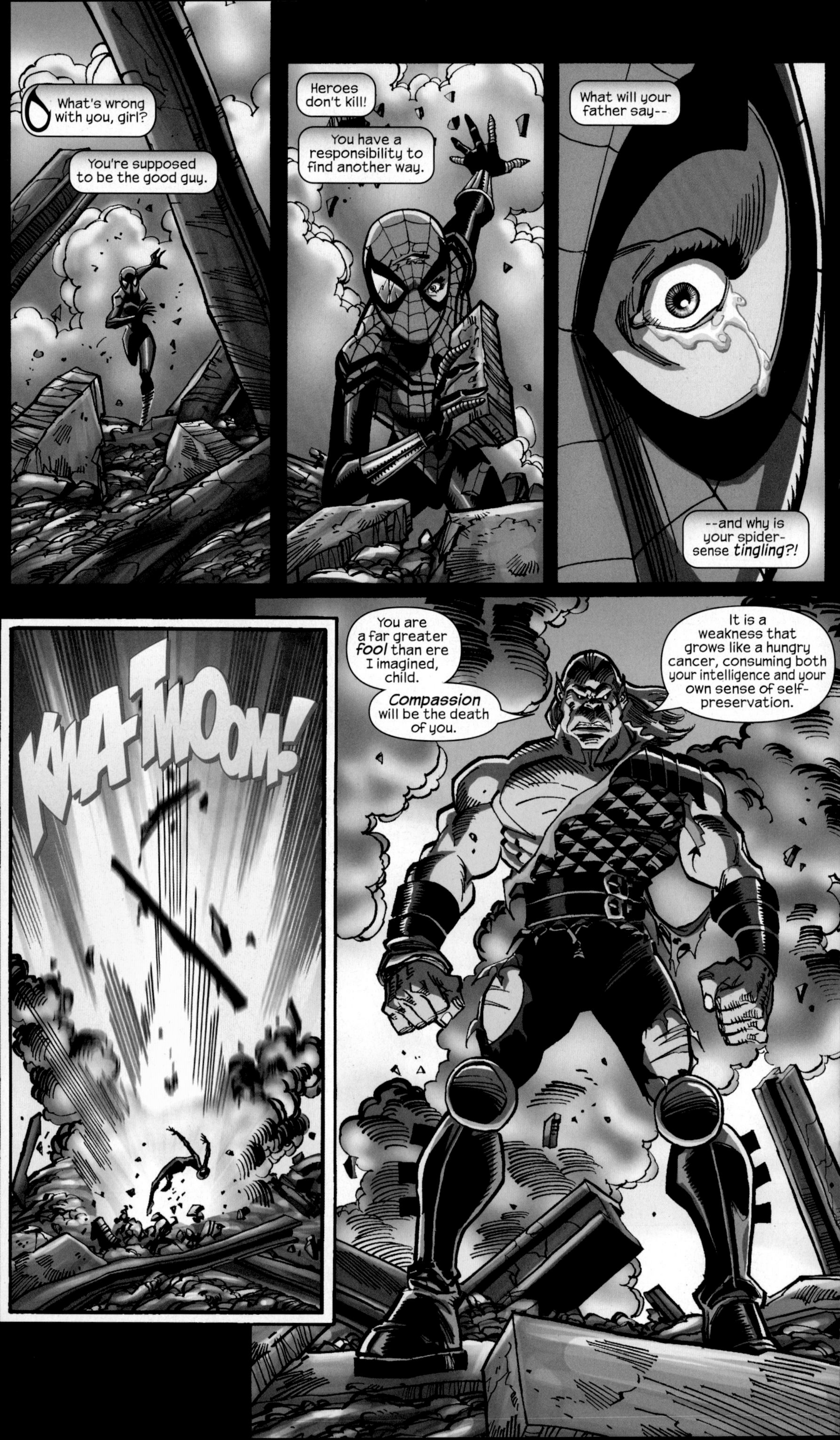

What's wrong with you, girl?
You're supposed to be the good guy.
Heroes don't kill!
You have a responsibility to find another way.
What will your father say--
--and why is your spider-sense *tingling?!*
KWA-TWOOM!
You are a far greater *fool* than ere I imagined, child.
Compassion will be the death of you.
It is a weakness that grows like a hungry cancer, consuming both your intelligence and your own sense of self-preservation.

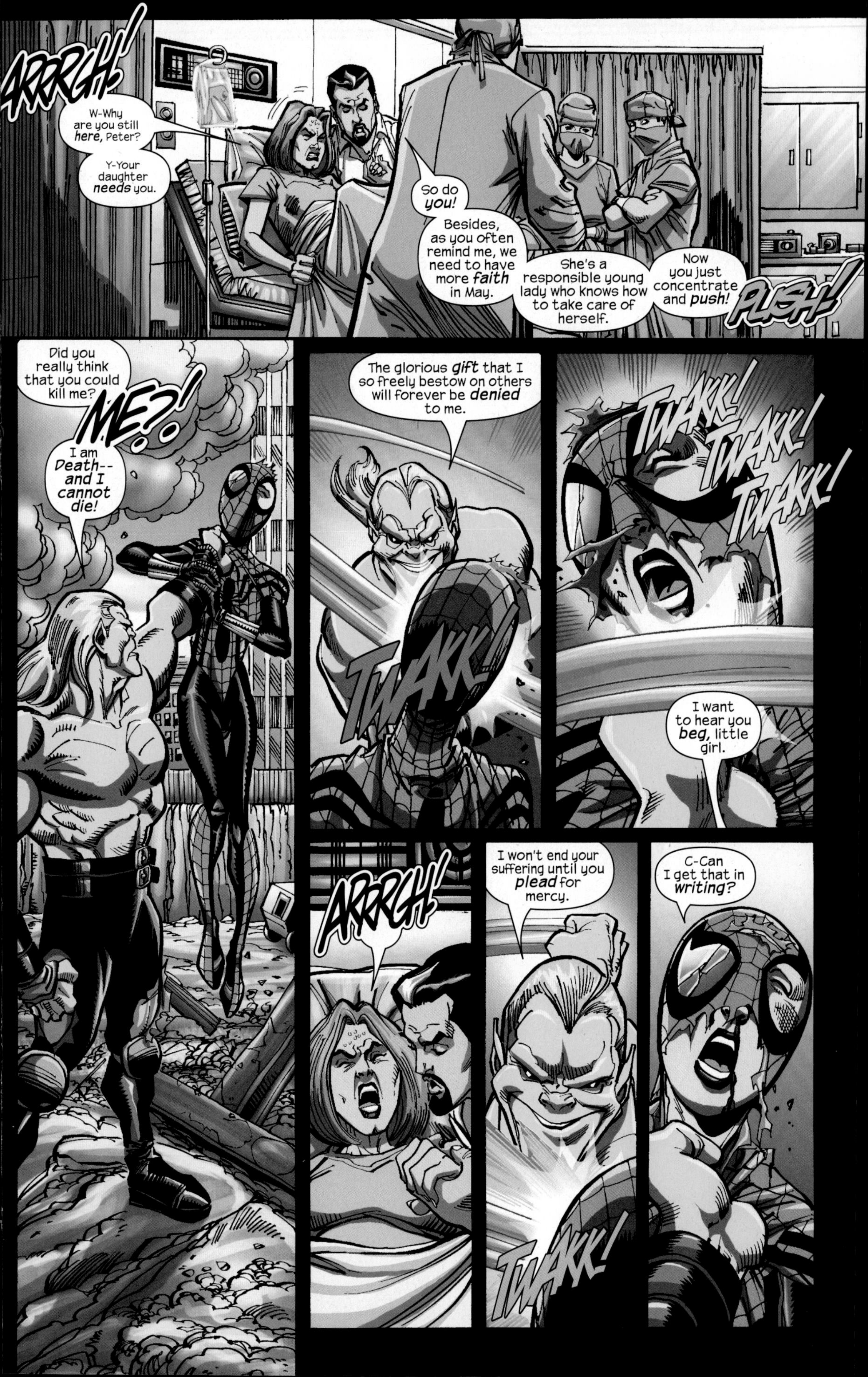
ARRRGH!
W-Why are you still here, Peter?
Y-Your daughter needs you.
So do you!
Besides, as you often remind me, we need to have more faith in May.
She's a responsible young lady who knows how to take care of herself.
Now you just concentrate and push!
PUSH!
Did you really think that you could kill me?
ME?!
I am Death-- and I cannot die!
The glorious gift that I so freely bestow on others will forever be denied to me.
TWAKK!
TWAKK! TWAKK! TWAKK!
I want to hear you beg, little girl.
ARRRGH!
I won't end your suffering until you plead for mercy.
C-Can I get that in writing?
TWAKK!

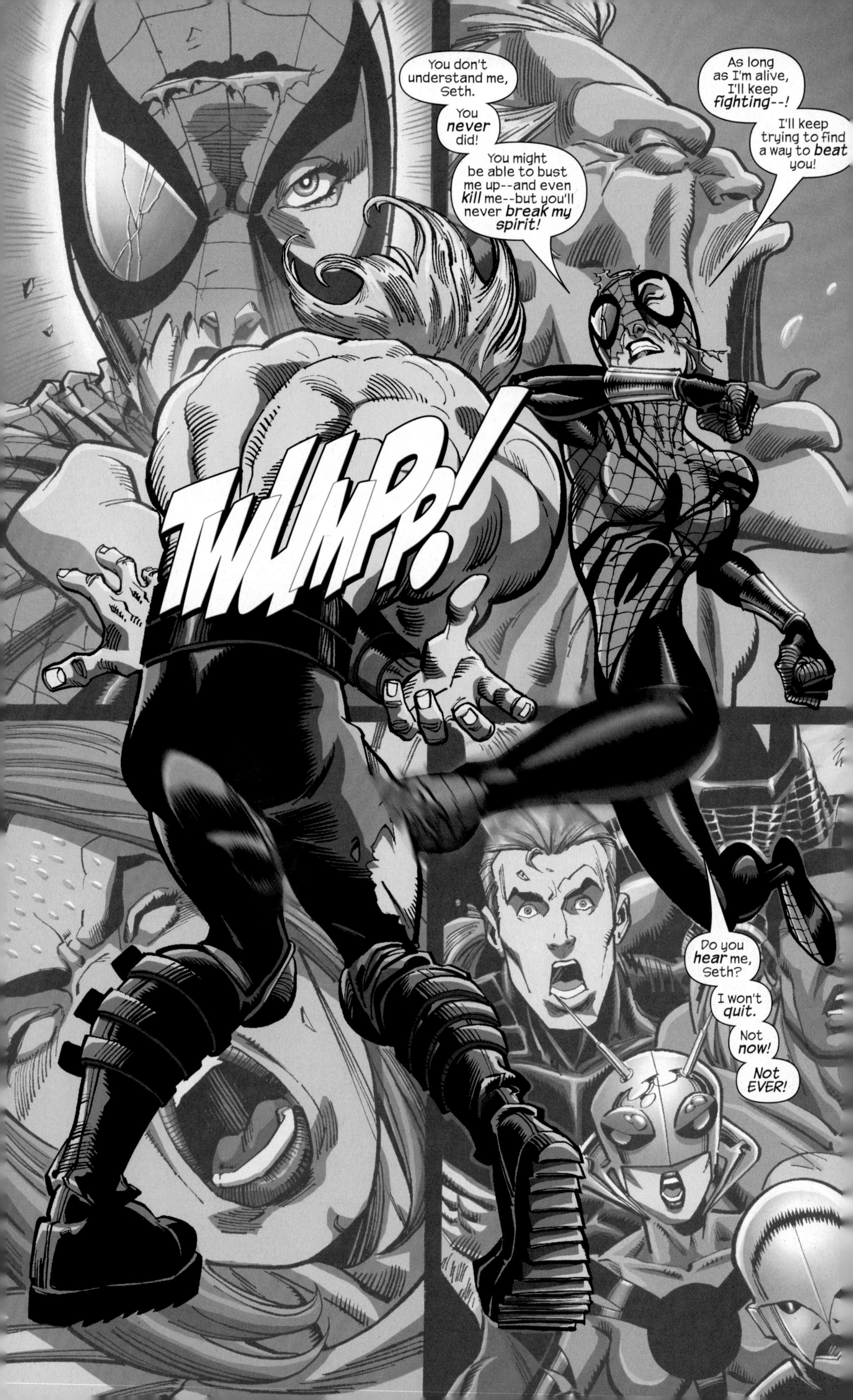

You don't understand me, Seth.
You *never* did!
You might be able to bust me up--and even *kill* me--but you'll never *break my spirit!*
As long as I'm alive, I'll keep *fighting*--!
I'll keep trying to find a way to *beat* you!
THWUMP!
Do you *hear* me, Seth?
I won't *quit.*
Not *now!*
Not *EVER!*

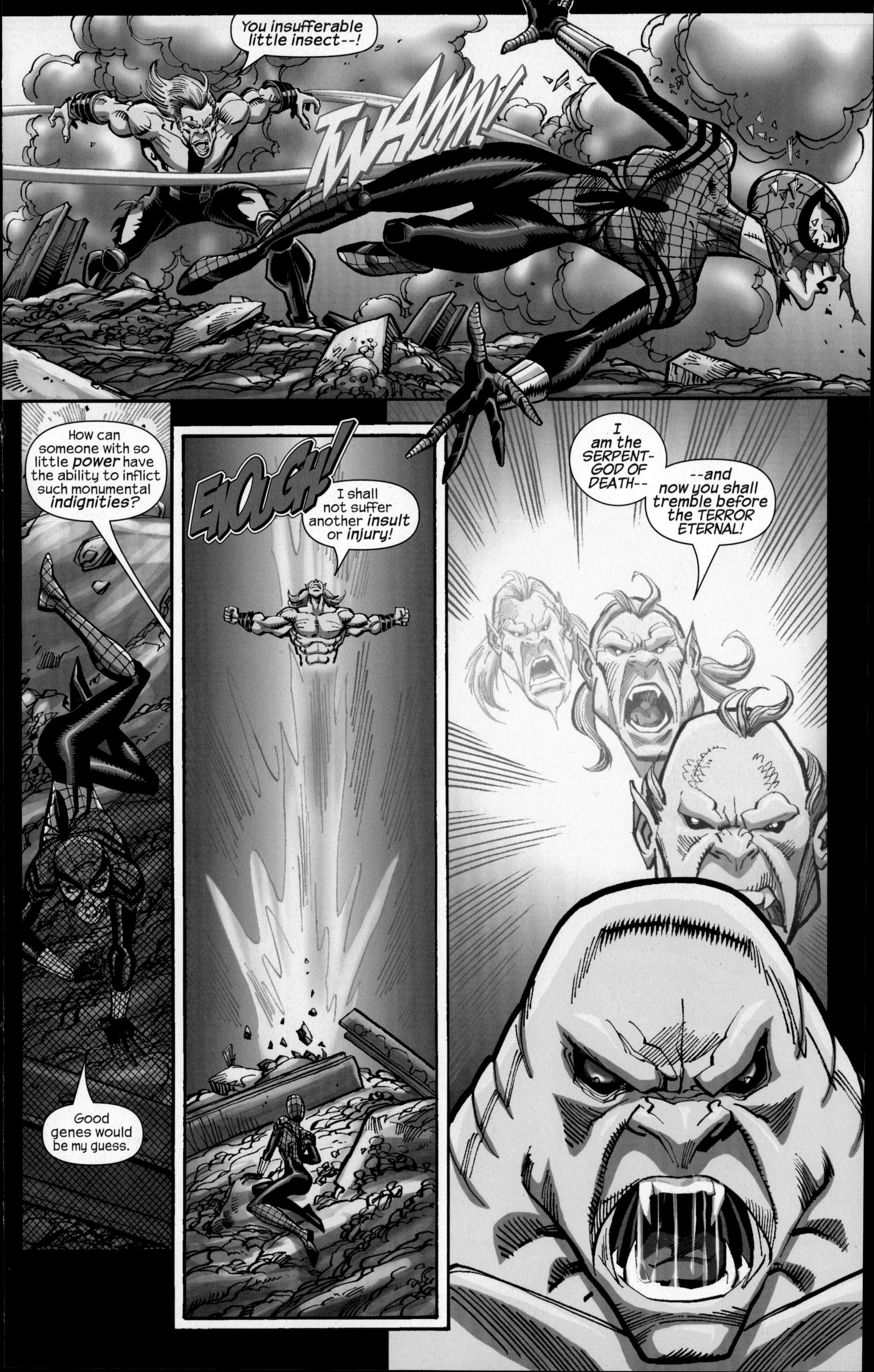
You insufferable little insect--!
TWAMM!
How can someone with so little power have the ability to inflict such monumental indignities?
Good genes would be my guess.
ENOUGH!
I shall not suffer another insult or injury!
I am the SERPENT-GOD OF DEATH--
--and now you shall tremble before the TERROR ETERNAL!

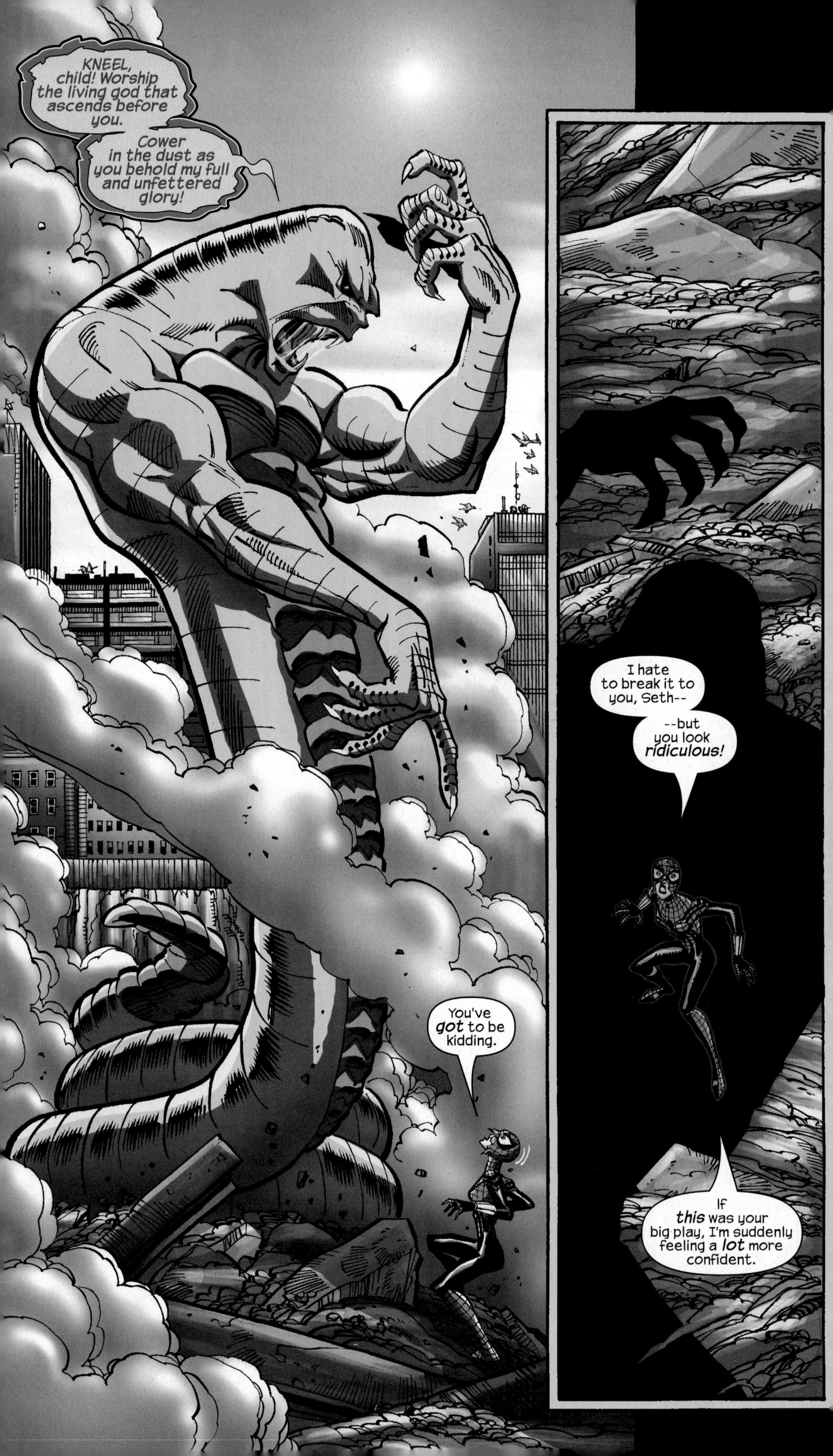
KNEEL, child! Worship the living god that ascends before you.
Cower in the dust as you behold my full and unfettered glory!
You've got to be kidding.
I hate to break it to you, Seth--
--but you look ridiculous!
If this was your big play, I'm suddenly feeling a lot more confident.

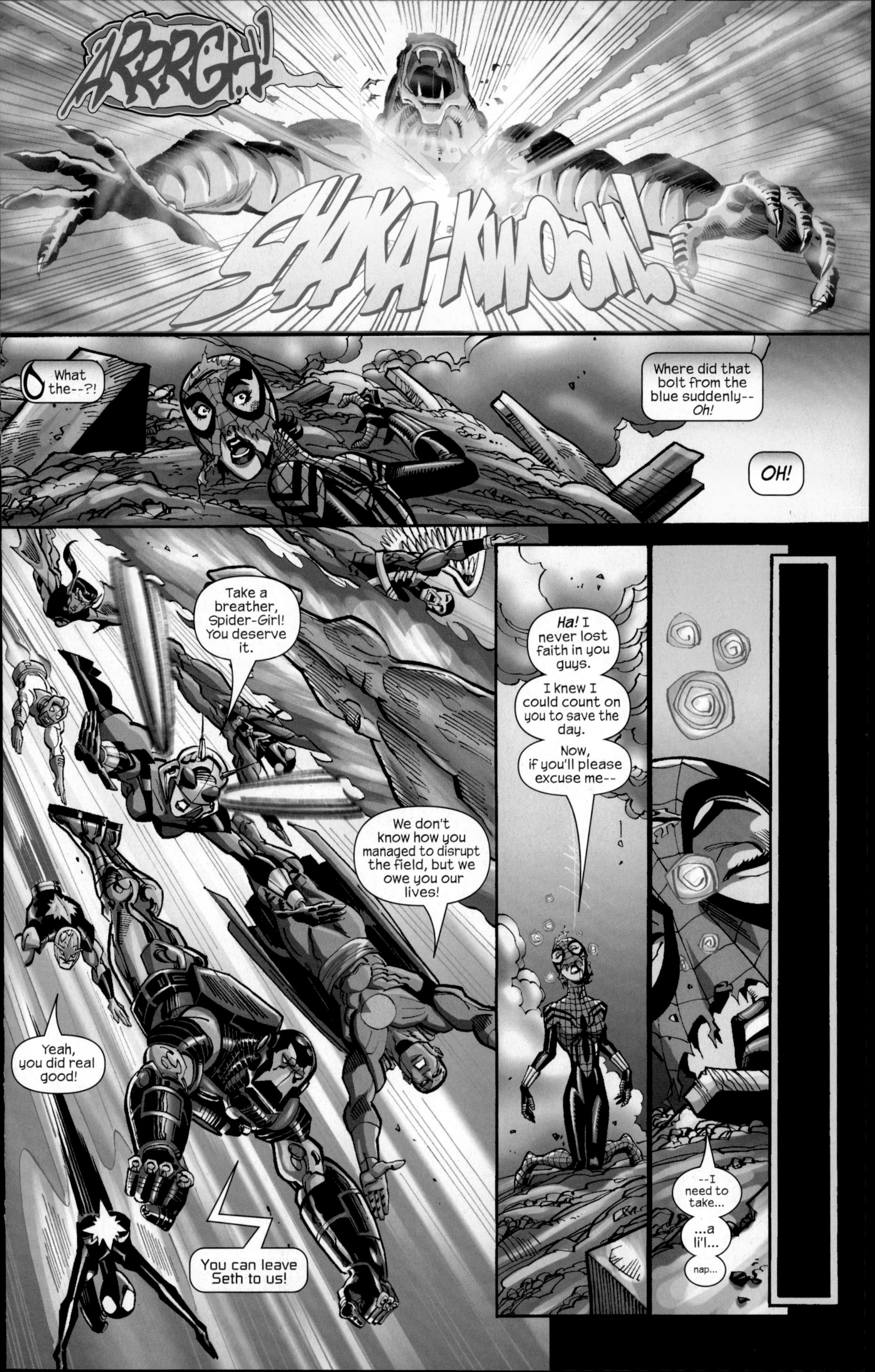
ARRRGH!
SHAKA-KWOOM!
What the--?!
Where did that bolt from the blue suddenly-- Oh!
OH!
Take a breather, Spider-Girl! You deserve it.
We don't know how you managed to disrupt the field, but we owe you our lives!
Yeah, you did real good!
You can leave Seth to us!
Ha! I never lost faith in you guys.
I knew I could count on you to save the day.
Now, if you'll please excuse me--
--I need to take...
...a li'l...
nap...

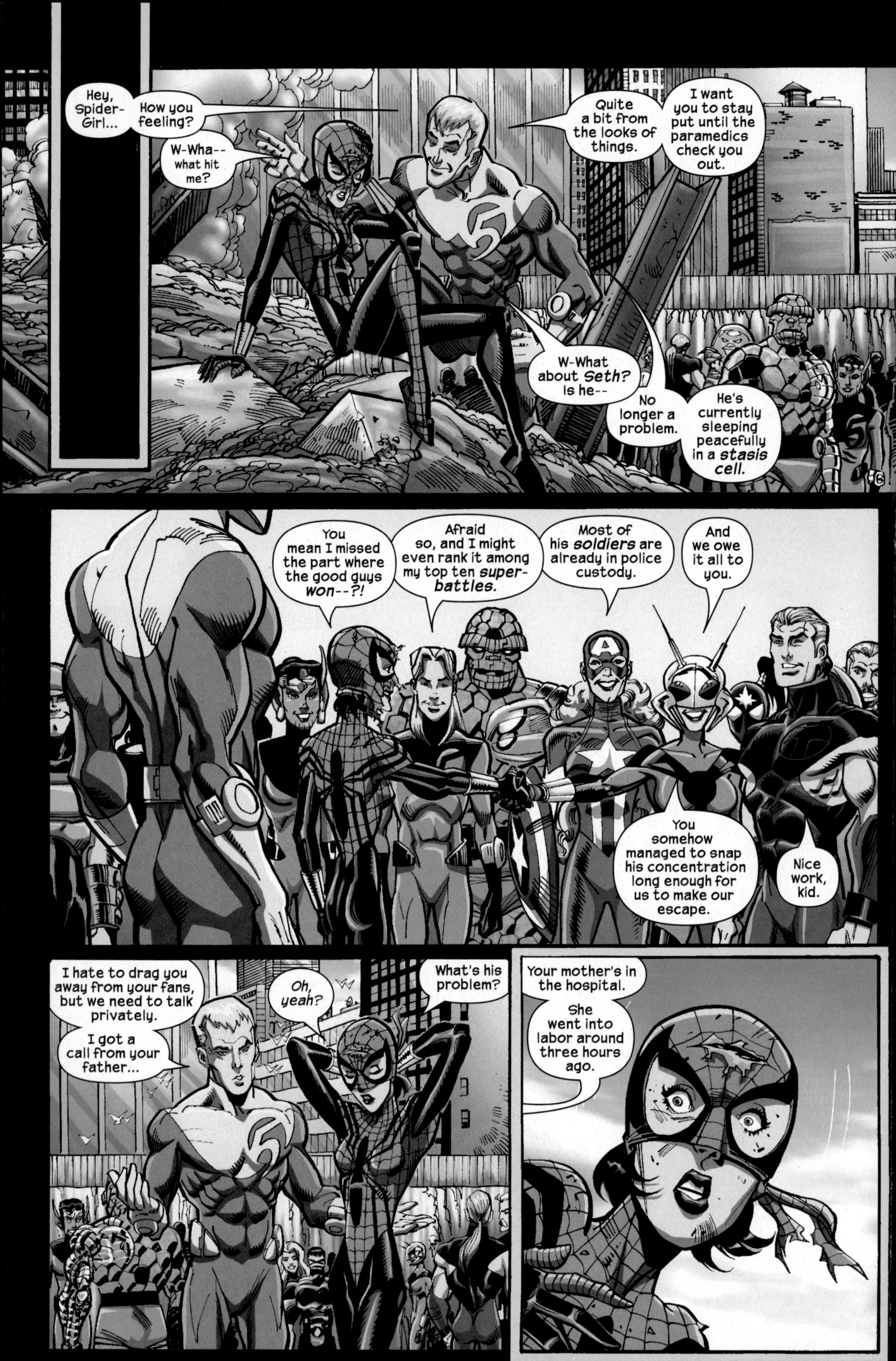
Hey, Spider-Girl...
How you feeling?
W-Wha-- what hit me?
Quite a bit from the looks of things.
I want you to stay put until the paramedics check you out.
W-What about Seth? Is he--
No longer a problem.
He's currently sleeping peacefully in a stasis cell.
You mean I missed the part where the good guys won--?!
Afraid so, and I might even rank it among my top ten super-battles.
Most of his soldiers are already in police custody.
And we owe it all to you.
You somehow managed to snap his concentration long enough for us to make our escape.
Nice work, kid.
I hate to drag you away from your fans, but we need to talk privately.
I got a call from your father...
Oh, yeah?
What's his problem?
Your mother's in the hospital.
She went into labor around three hours ago.

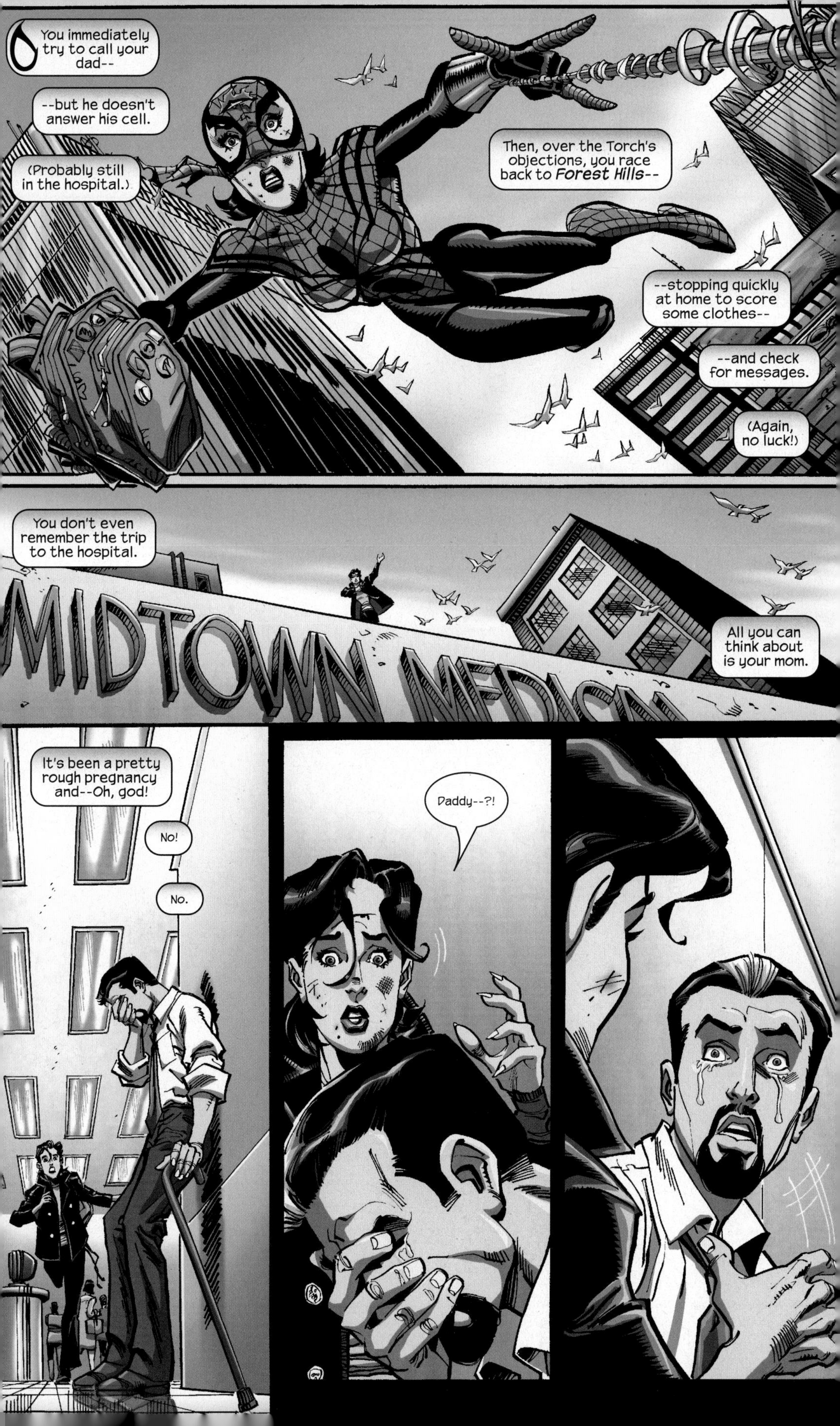

You immediately try to call your dad--
--but he doesn't answer his cell.
(Probably still in the hospital.)
Then, over the Torch's objections, you race back to Forest Hills--
--stopping quickly at home to score some clothes--
--and check for messages.
(Again, no luck!)
You don't even remember the trip to the hospital.
MIDTOWN MEDIC
All you can think about is your mom.
It's been a pretty rough pregnancy and--Oh, god!
No!
No.
Daddy--?!

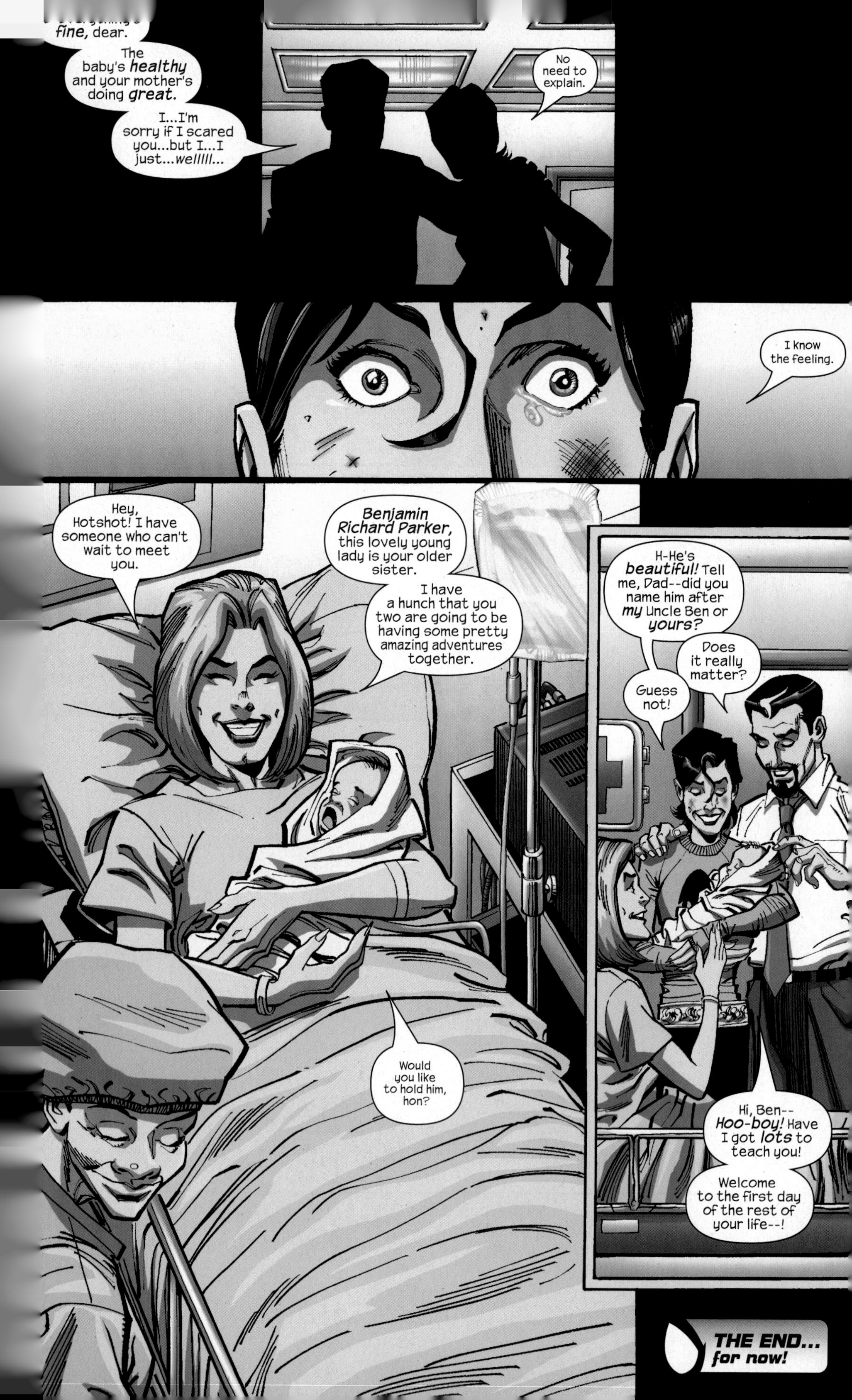

fine, dear.
The baby's healthy and your mother's doing great.
I...I'm sorry if I scared you...but I...I just...wellll...
No need to explain.
I know the feeling.
Hey, Hotshot! I have someone who can't wait to meet you.
Benjamin Richard Parker, this lovely young lady is your older sister.
I have a hunch that you two are going to be having some pretty amazing adventures together.
Would you like to hold him, hon?
H-He's beautiful! Tell me, Dad--did you name him after my Uncle Ben or yours?
Does it really matter?
Guess not!
Hi, Ben-- Hoo-boy! Have I got lots to teach you!
Welcome to the first day of the rest of your life--!
THE END... for now!

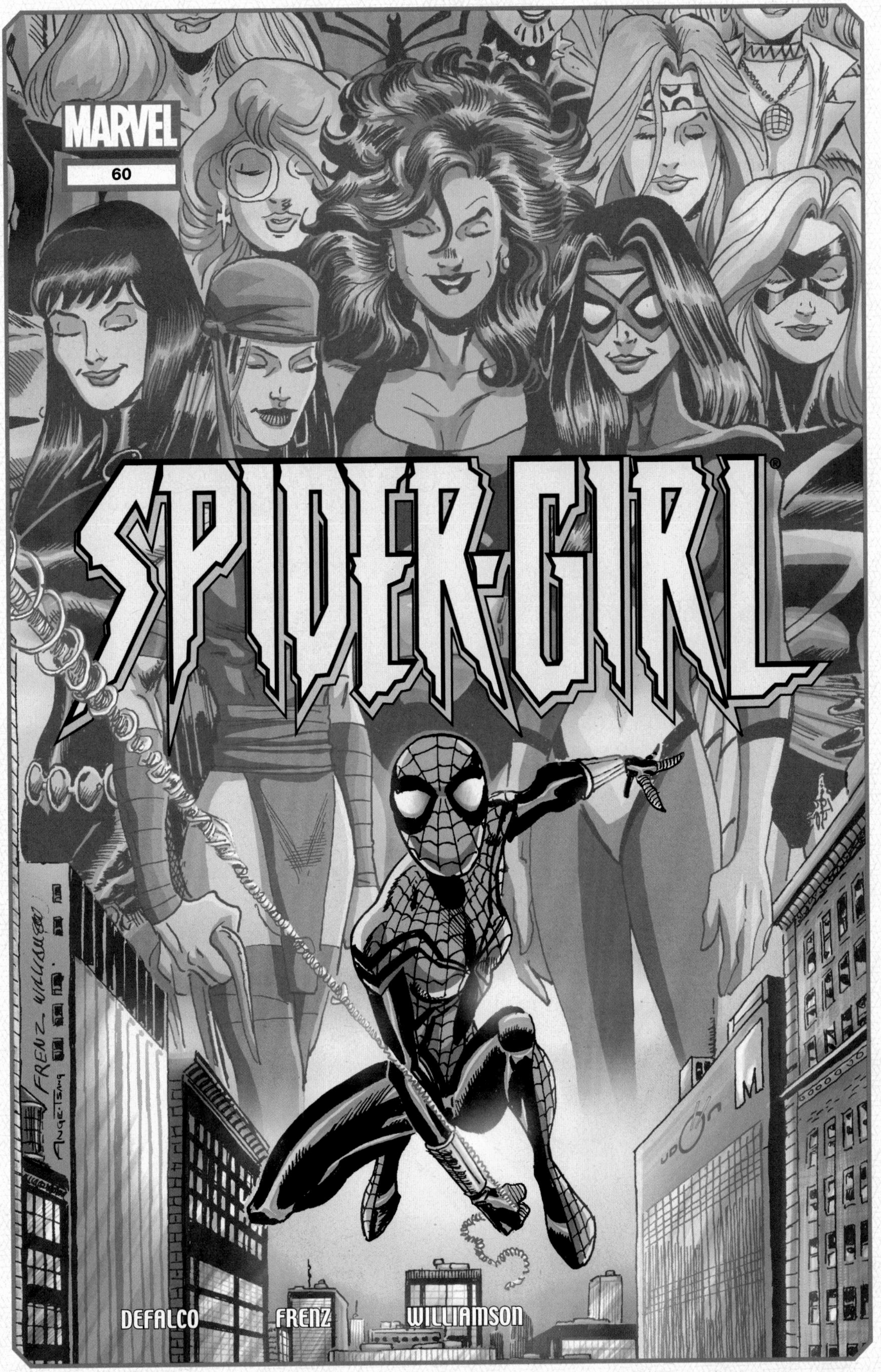

MARVEL
60
SPIDER-GIRL
DEFALCO
FRENZ
WILLIAMSON

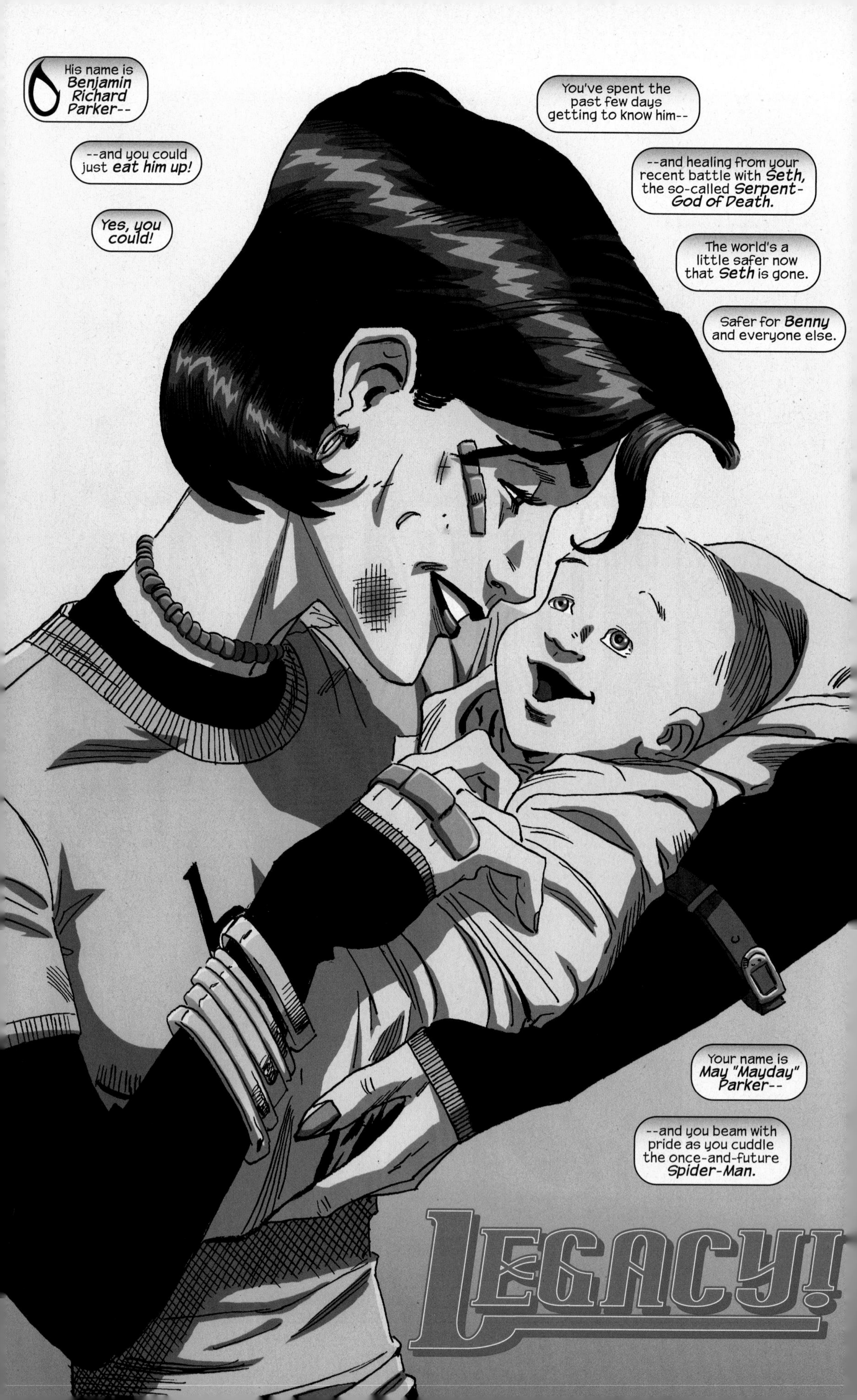
His name is Benjamin Richard Parker--
--and you could just eat him up!
Yes, you could!
You've spent the past few days getting to know him--
--and healing from your recent battle with Seth, the so-called Serpent-God of Death.
The world's a little safer now that Seth is gone.
Safer for Benny and everyone else.
Your name is May "Mayday" Parker--
--and you beam with pride as you cuddle the once-and-future Spider-Man.
LEGACY!

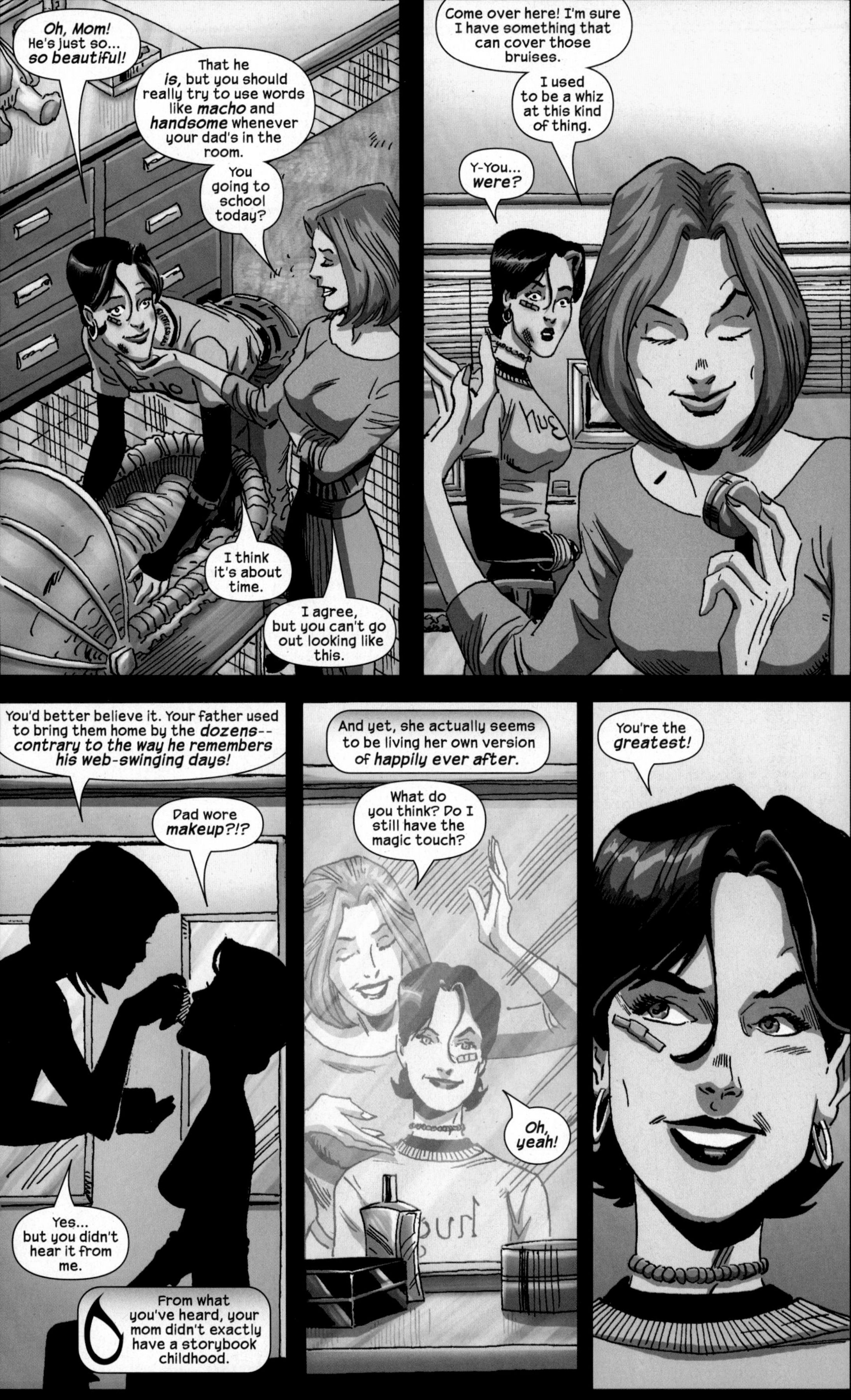

Oh, Mom! He's just so... so beautiful!
That he is, but you should really try to use words like macho and handsome whenever your dad's in the room.
You going to school today?
I think it's about time.
I agree, but you can't go out looking like this.
Come over here! I'm sure I have something that can cover those bruises.
I used to be a whiz at this kind of thing.
Y-You... were?
You'd better believe it. Your father used to bring them home by the dozens-- contrary to the way he remembers his web-swinging days!
Dad wore makeup?!?
Yes... but you didn't hear it from me.
From what you've heard, your mom didn't exactly have a storybook childhood.
And yet, she actually seems to be living her own version of happily ever after.
What do you think? Do I still have the magic touch?
Oh, yeah!
You're the greatest!

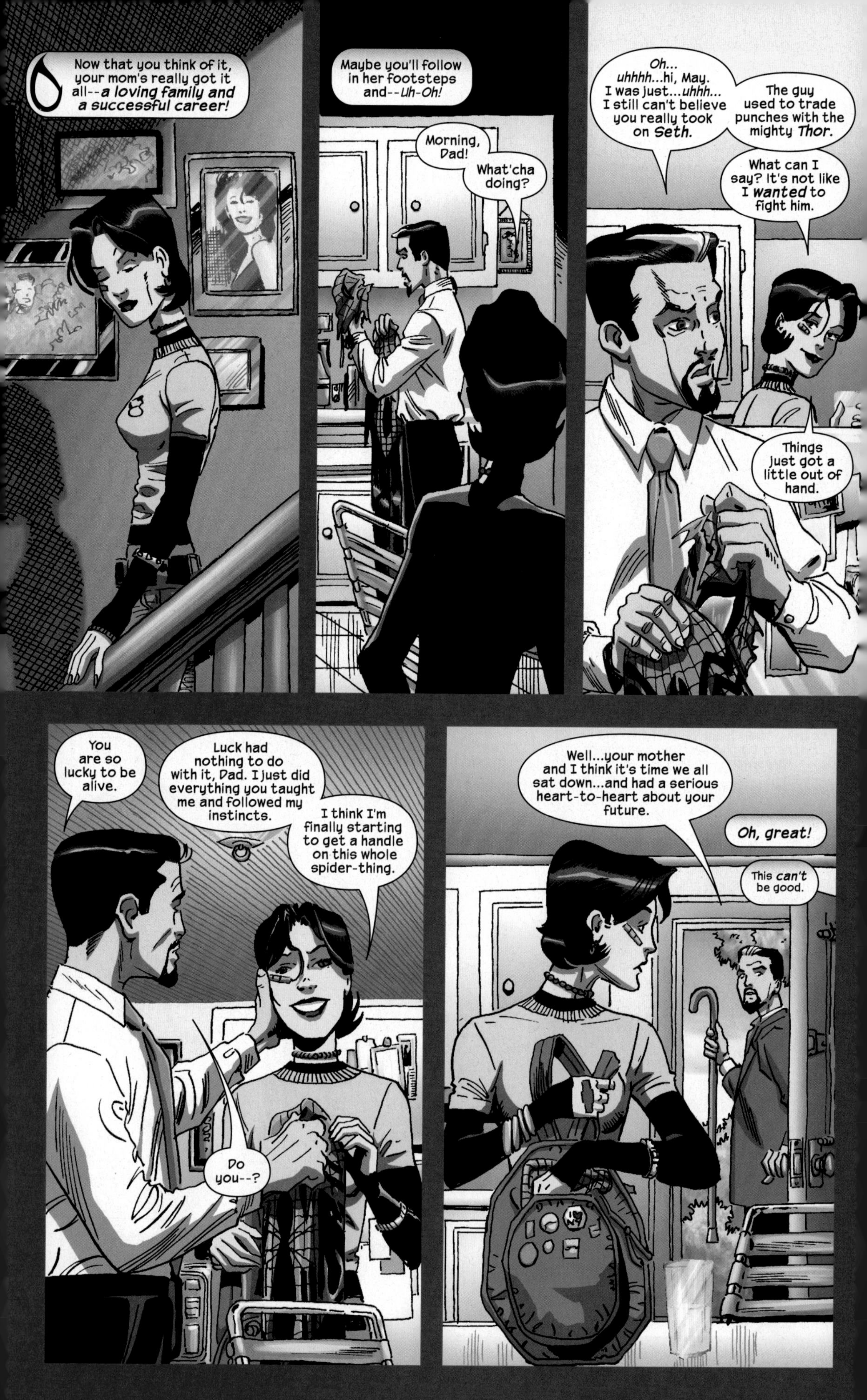
Now that you think of it, your mom's really got it all--a loving family and a successful career!
Maybe you'll follow in her footsteps and--Uh-Oh!
Morning, Dad!
What'cha doing?
Oh... uhhhh...hi, May. I was just...uhhh... I still can't believe you really took on Seth.
The guy used to trade punches with the mighty Thor.
What can I say? It's not like I wanted to fight him.
Things just got a little out of hand.
You are so lucky to be alive.
Luck had nothing to do with it, Dad. I just did everything you taught me and followed my instincts.
I think I'm finally starting to get a handle on this whole spider-thing.
Do you--?
Well...your mother and I think it's time we all sat down...and had a serious heart-to-heart about your future.
Oh, great!
This can't be good.

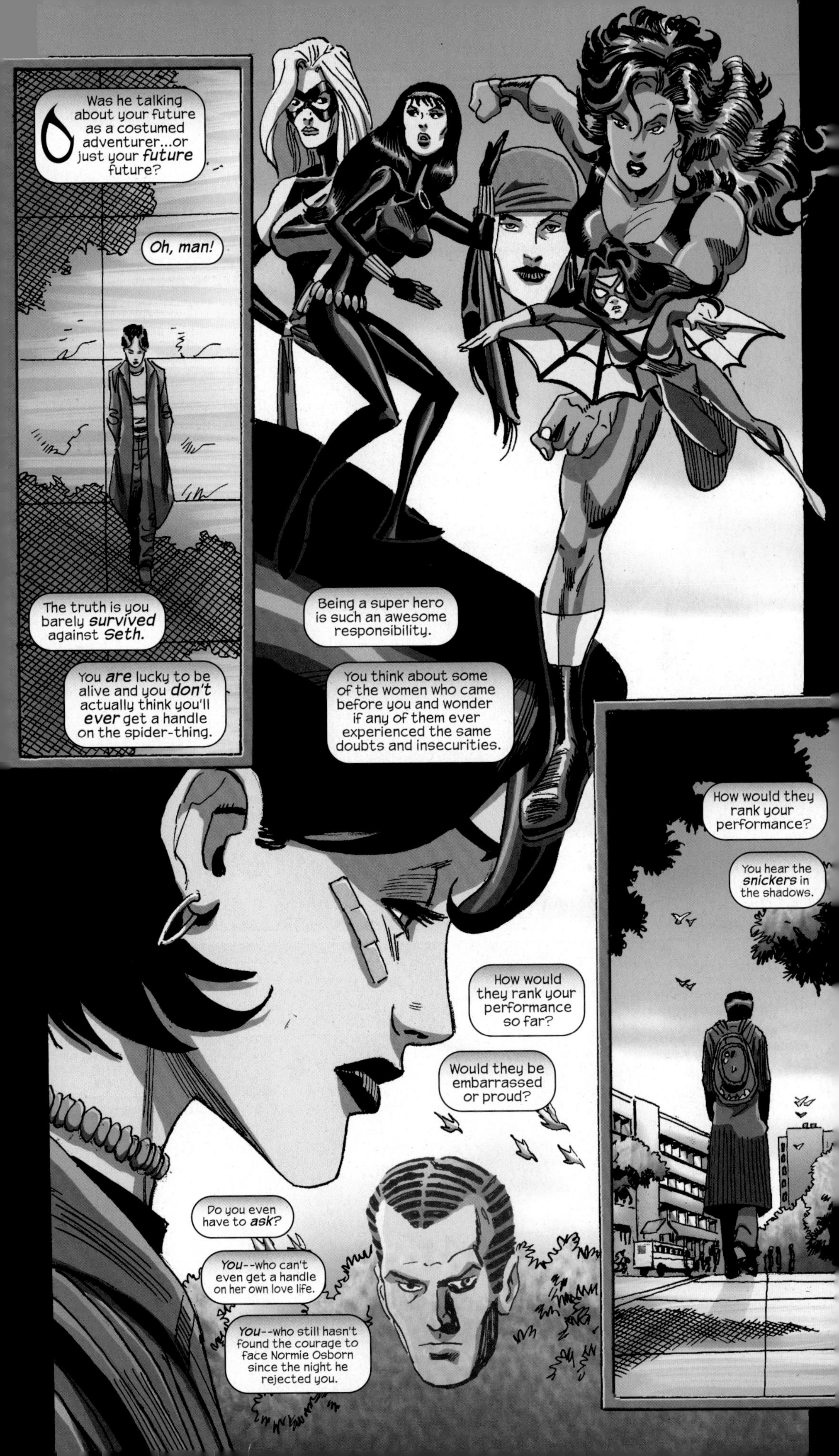
Was he talking about your future as a costumed adventurer...or just your *future* future?
Oh, man!
The truth is you barely *survived* against *Seth.*
You *are* lucky to be alive and you *don't* actually think you'll *ever* get a handle on the spider-thing.
Being a super hero is such an awesome responsibility.
You think about some of the women who came before you and wonder if any of them ever experienced the same doubts and insecurities.
How would they rank your performance?
You hear the *snickers* in the shadows.
How would they rank your performance so far?
Would they be embarrassed or proud?
Do you even have to *ask?*
You--who can't even get a handle on her own love life.
You--who still hasn't found the courage to face Normie Osborn since the night he rejected you.

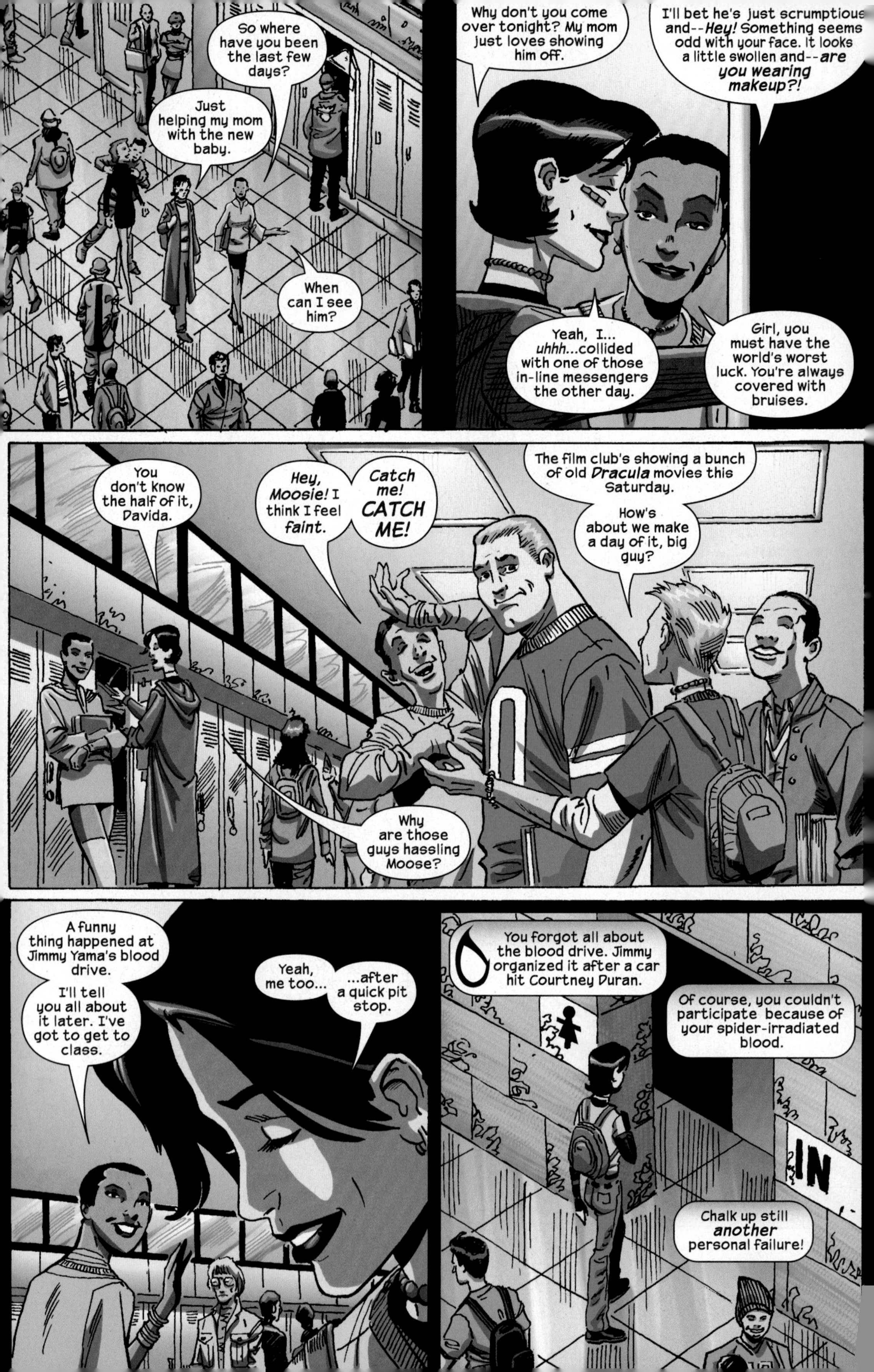
So where have you been the last few days?
Just helping my mom with the new baby.
When can I see him?
Why don't you come over tonight? My mom just loves showing him off.
I'll bet he's just scrumptious and--Hey! Something seems odd with your face. It looks a little swollen and--are you wearing makeup?!
Yeah, I... uhhh...collided with one of those in-line messengers the other day.
Girl, you must have the world's worst luck. You're always covered with bruises.
You don't know the half of it, Davida.
Hey, Moosie! I think I feel faint.
Catch me! CATCH ME!
The film club's showing a bunch of old Dracula movies this Saturday.
How's about we make a day of it, big guy?
Why are those guys hassling Moose?
A funny thing happened at Jimmy Yama's blood drive.
I'll tell you all about it later. I've got to get to class.
Yeah, me too...
...after a quick pit stop.
You forgot all about the blood drive. Jimmy organized it after a car hit Courtney Duran.
Of course, you couldn't participate because of your spider-irradiated blood.
IN
Chalk up still another personal failure!

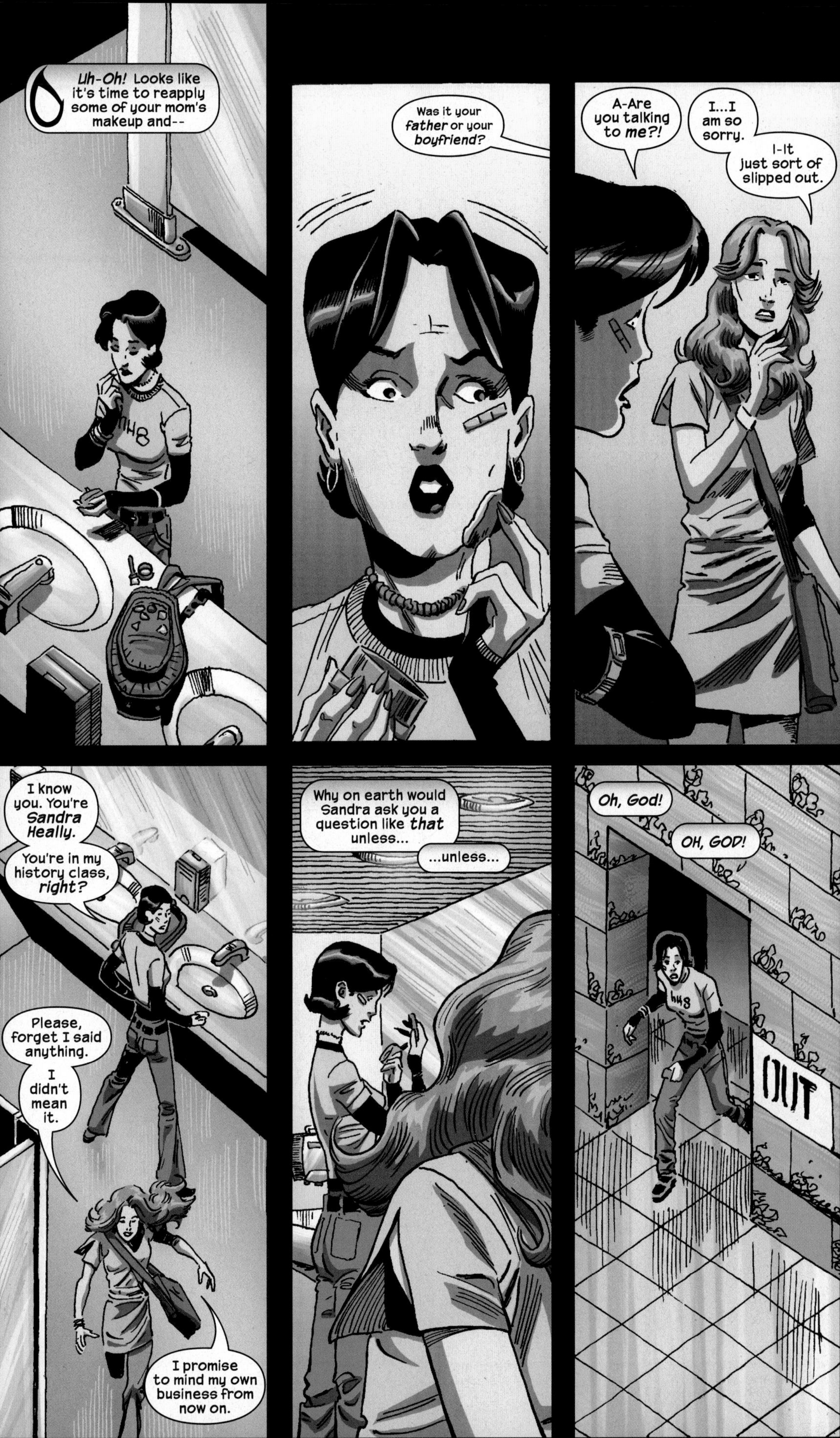
Uh-Oh! Looks like it's time to reapply some of your mom's makeup and--
Was it your father or your boyfriend?
A-Are you talking to me?!
I...I am so sorry.
I-It just sort of slipped out.
I know you. You're Sandra Heally.
You're in my history class, right?
Please, forget I said anything.
I didn't mean it.
I promise to mind my own business from now on.
Why on earth would Sandra ask you a question like that unless...
...unless...
Oh, God!
OH, GOD!
OUT

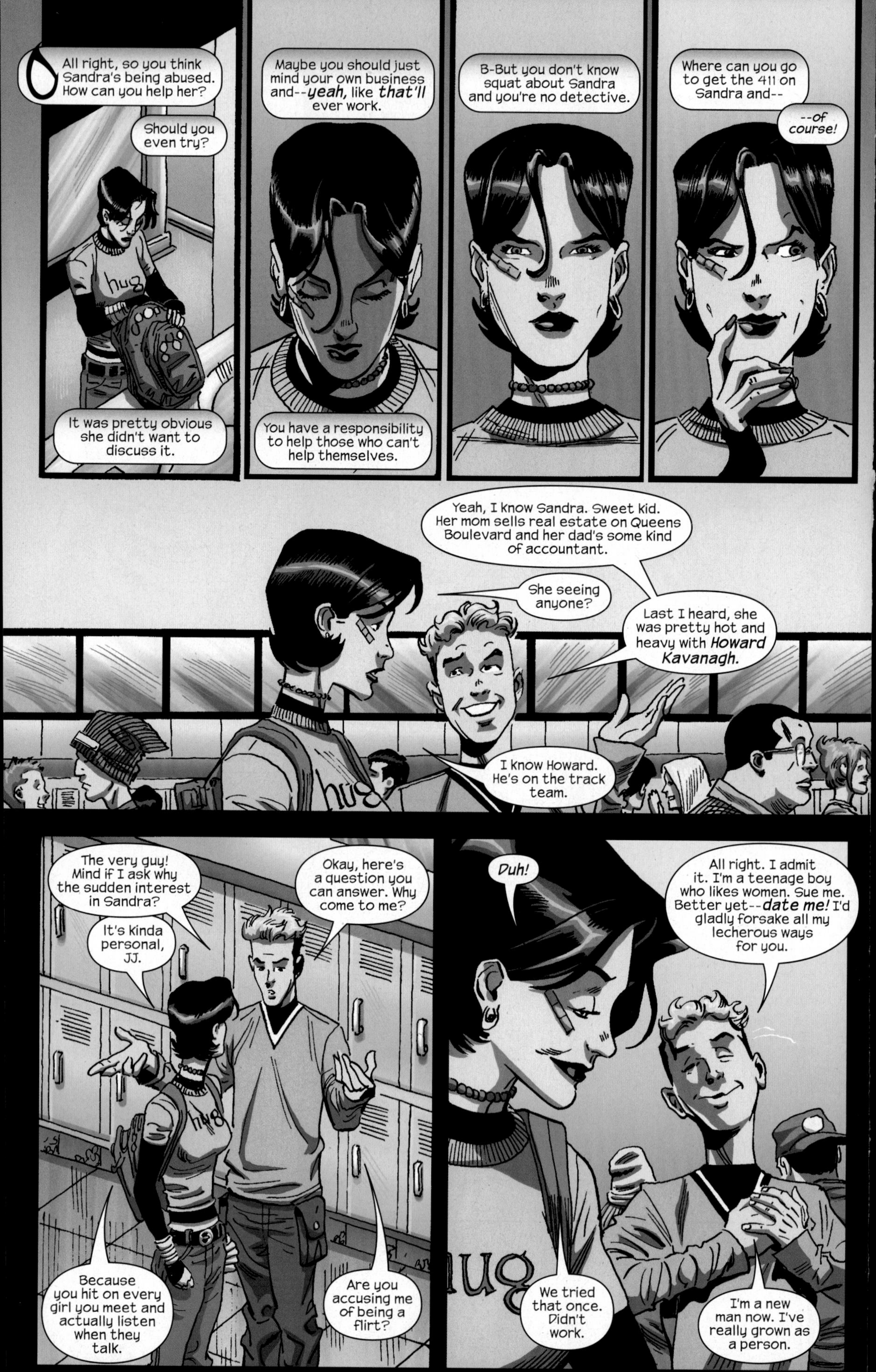

All right, so you think Sandra's being abused. How can you help her?
Should you even try?
It was pretty obvious she didn't want to discuss it.
Maybe you should just mind your own business and--*yeah,* like *that'll* ever work.
You have a responsibility to help those who can't help themselves.
B-But you don't know squat about Sandra and you're no detective.
Where can you go to get the 411 on Sandra and--
--*of course!*
Yeah, I know Sandra. Sweet kid. Her mom sells real estate on Queens Boulevard and her dad's some kind of accountant.
She seeing anyone?
Last I heard, she was pretty hot and heavy with *Howard Kavanagh.*
I know Howard. He's on the track team.
The very guy! Mind if I ask why the sudden interest in Sandra?
It's kinda personal, JJ.
Okay, here's a question you can answer. Why come to me?
Because you hit on every girl you meet and actually listen when they talk.
Are you accusing me of being a flirt?
Duh!
All right. I admit it. I'm a teenage boy who likes women. Sue me. Better yet--*date me!* I'd gladly forsake all my lecherous ways for you.
We tried that once. Didn't work.
I'm a new man now. I've really grown as a person.

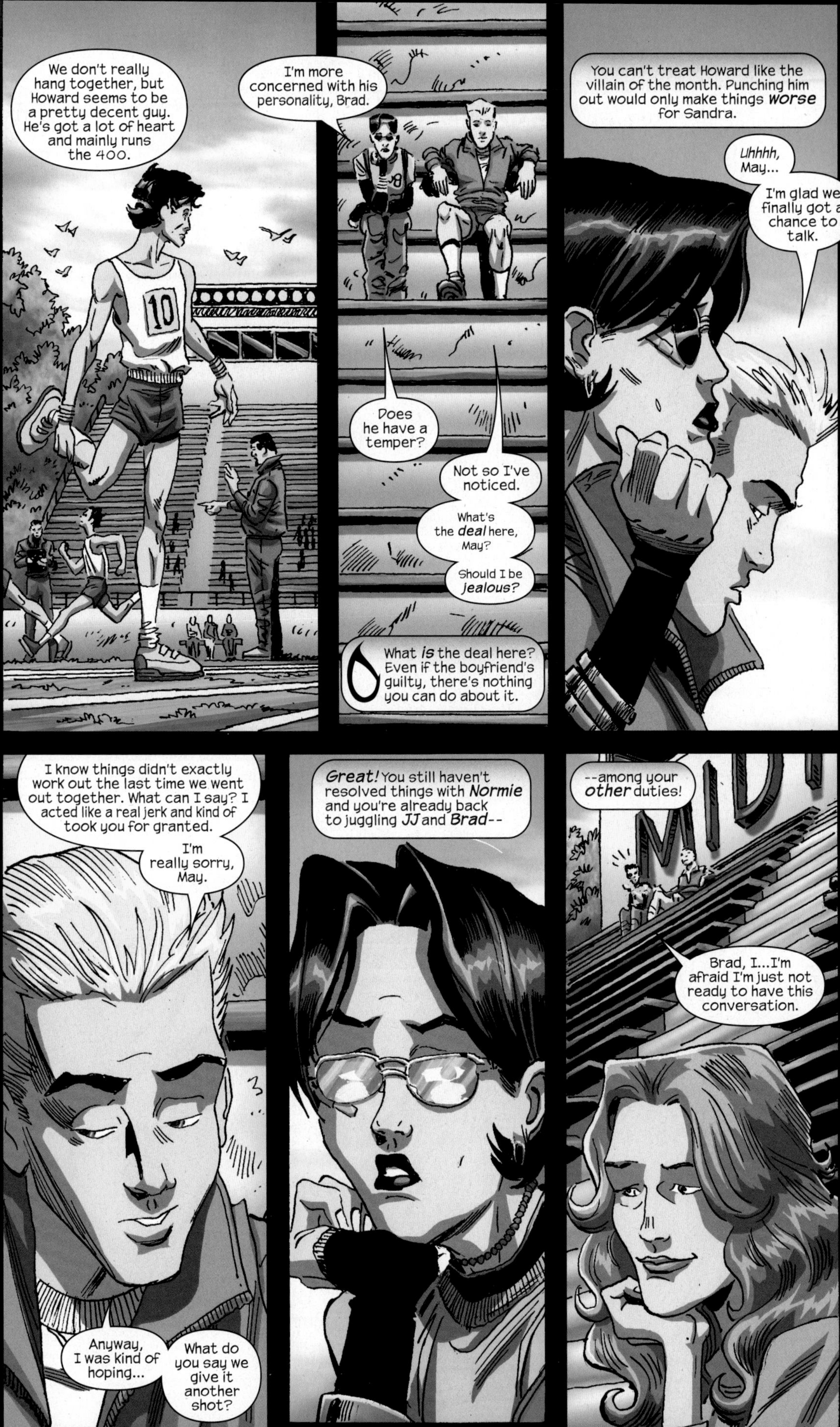
We don't really hang together, but Howard seems to be a pretty decent guy. He's got a lot of heart and mainly runs the 400.
10
I'm more concerned with his personality, Brad.
Does he have a temper?
Not so I've noticed.
What's the *deal* here, May?
Should I be *jealous?*
What *is* the deal here? Even if the boyfriend's guilty, there's nothing you can do about it.
You can't treat Howard like the villain of the month. Punching him out would only make things *worse* for Sandra.
Uhhhh, May...
I'm glad we finally got a chance to talk.
I know things didn't exactly work out the last time we went out together. What can I say? I acted like a real jerk and kind of took you for granted.
I'm really sorry, May.
Anyway, I was kind of hoping...
What do you say we give it another shot?
Great! You still haven't resolved things with *Normie* and you're already back to juggling *JJ* and *Brad*--
--among your *other* duties!
Brad, I...I'm afraid I'm just not ready to have this conversation.

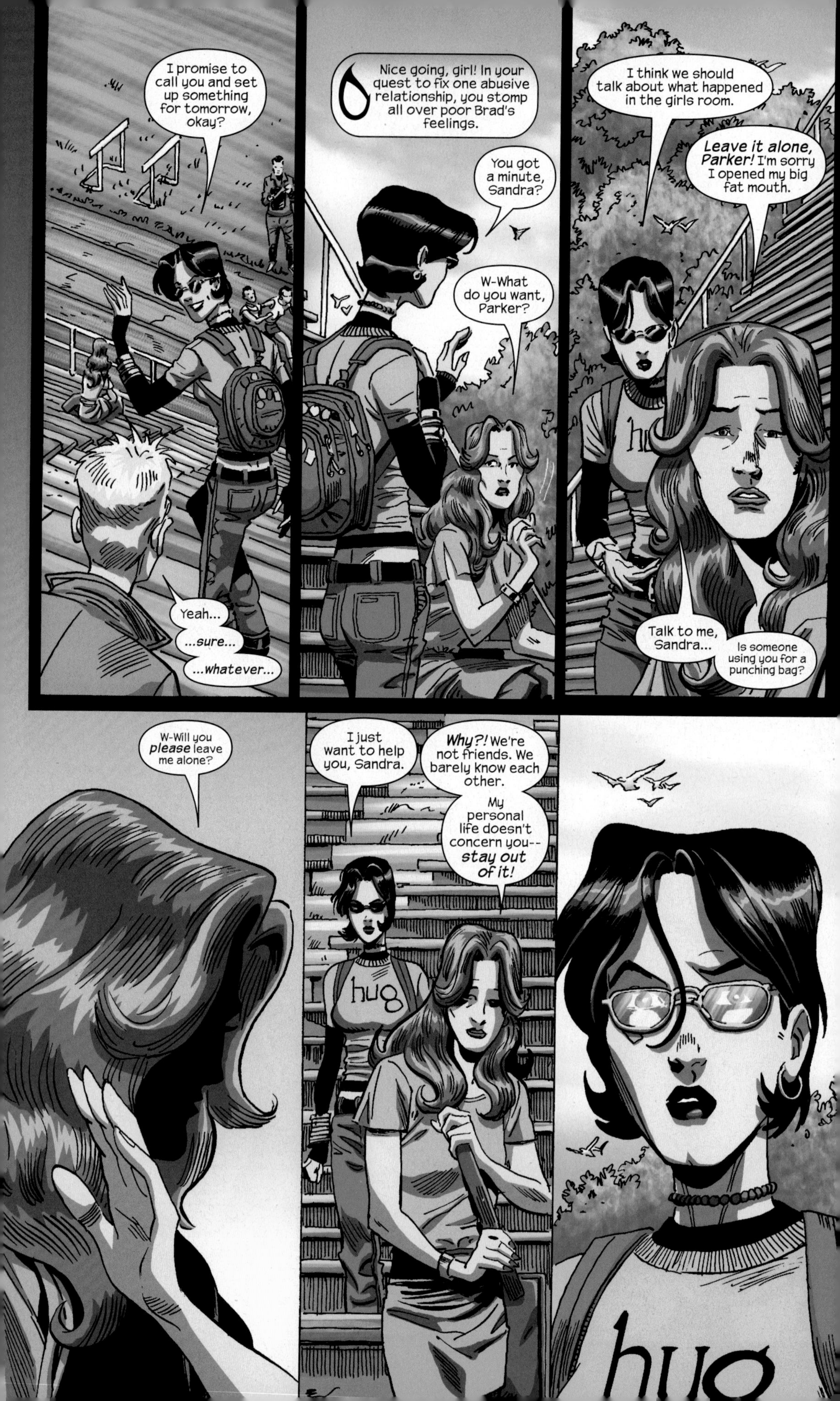
I promise to call you and set up something for tomorrow, okay?
Yeah...
...sure...
...whatever...
Nice going, girl! In your quest to fix one abusive relationship, you stomp all over poor Brad's feelings.
You got a minute, Sandra?
W-What do you want, Parker?
I think we should talk about what happened in the girls room.
Leave it alone, Parker! I'm sorry I opened my big fat mouth.
Talk to me, Sandra...
Is someone using you for a punching bag?
W-Will you please leave me alone?
I just want to help you, Sandra.
Why?! We're not friends. We barely know each other.
My personal life doesn't concern you-- stay out of it!
hug

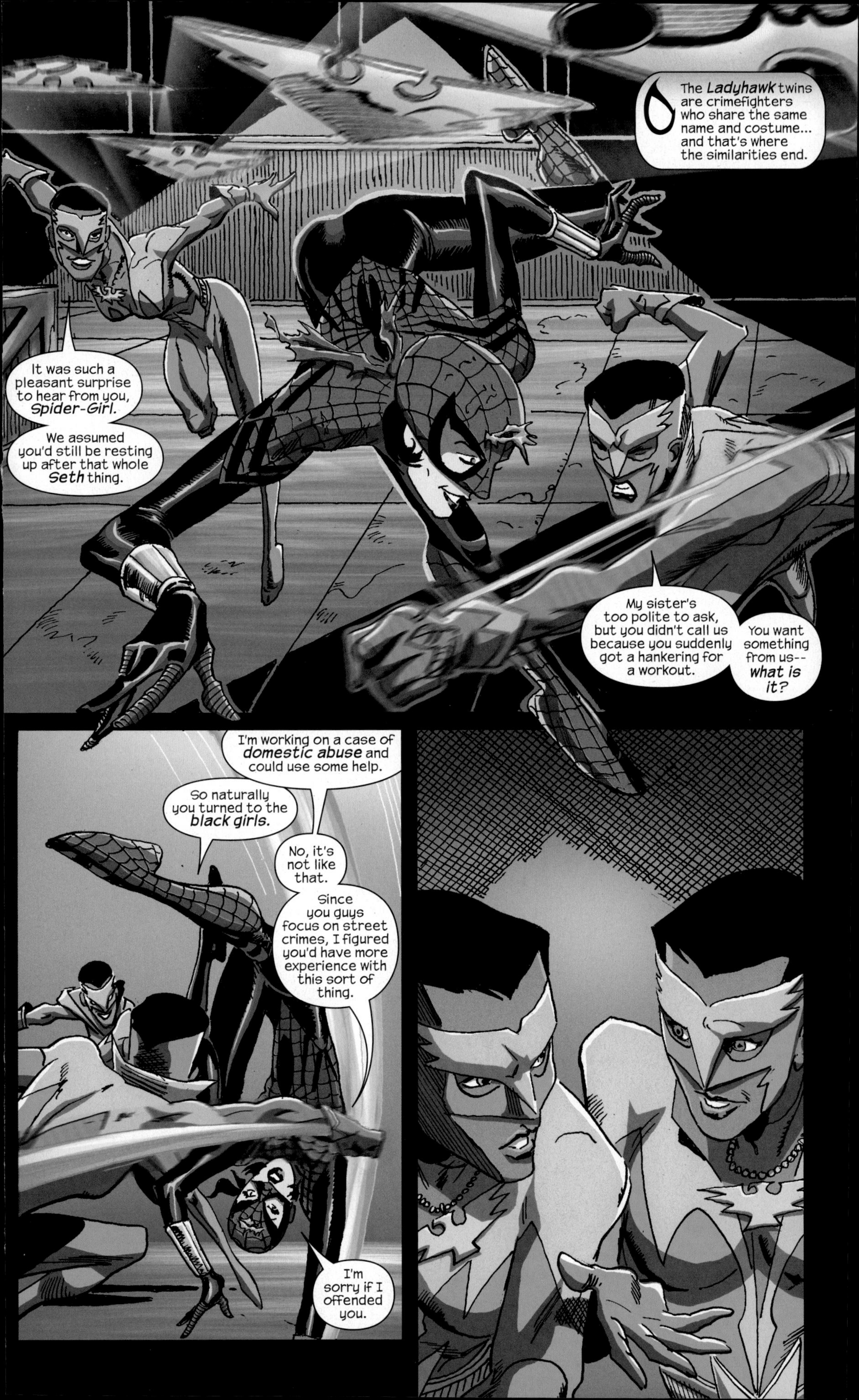
The *Ladyhawk* twins are crimefighters who share the same name and costume... and that's where the similarities end.
It was such a pleasant surprise to hear from you, *Spider-Girl*.
We assumed you'd still be resting up after that whole *Seth* thing.
My sister's too polite to ask, but you didn't call us because you suddenly got a hankering for a workout.
You want something from us-- *what is it?*
I'm working on a case of *domestic abuse* and could use some help.
So naturally you turned to the *black girls.*
No, it's not like that.
Since you guys focus on street crimes, I figured you'd have more experience with this sort of thing.
I'm sorry if I offended you.

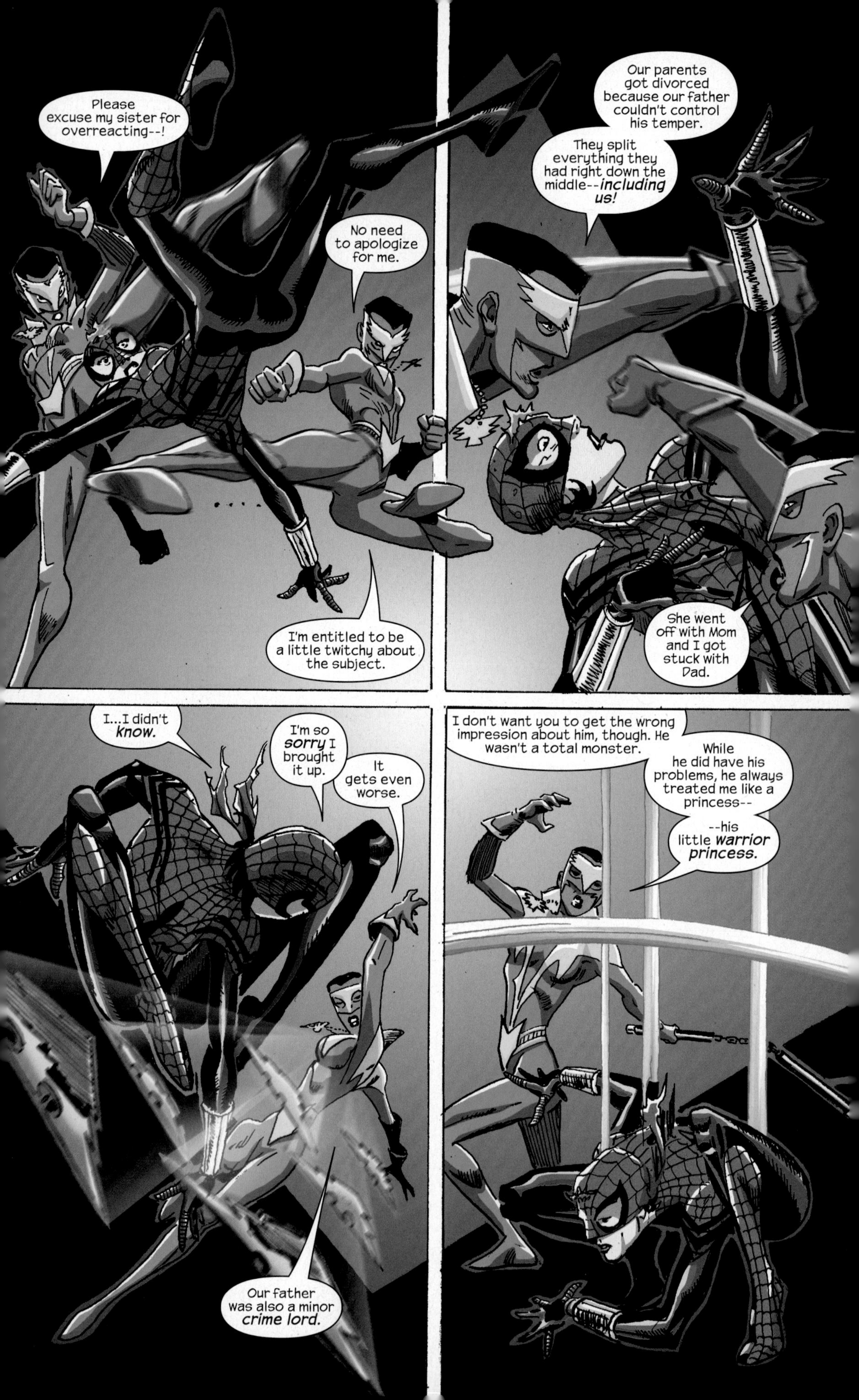

Please excuse my sister for overreacting--!
No need to apologize for me.
I'm entitled to be a little twitchy about the subject.
Our parents got divorced because our father couldn't control his temper.
They split everything they had right down the middle--*including us!*
She went off with Mom and I got stuck with Dad.
I...I didn't *know.*
I'm so *sorry* I brought it up.
It gets even worse.
Our father was also a minor *crime lord.*
I don't want you to get the wrong impression about him, though. He wasn't a total monster.
While he did have his problems, he always treated me like a princess--
--his little *warrior princess.*

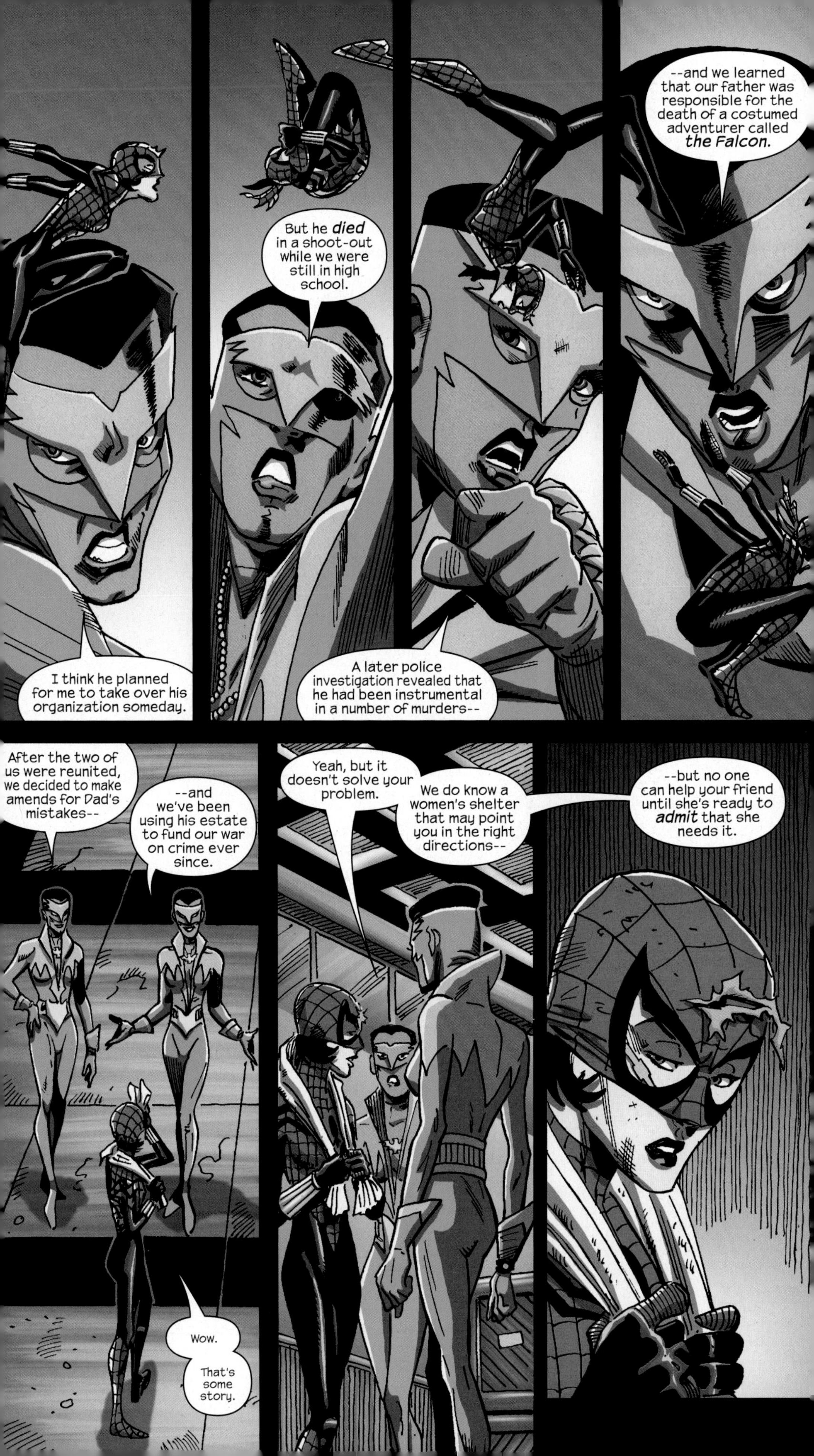
I think he planned for me to take over his organization someday.
But he *died* in a shoot-out while we were still in high school.
A later police investigation revealed that he had been instrumental in a number of murders--
--and we learned that our father was responsible for the death of a costumed adventurer called **the Falcon.**
After the two of us were reunited, we decided to make amends for Dad's mistakes--
--and we've been using his estate to fund our war on crime ever since.
Wow.
That's some story.
Yeah, but it doesn't solve your problem.
We do know a women's shelter that may point you in the right directions--
--but no one can help your friend until she's ready to *admit* that she needs it.

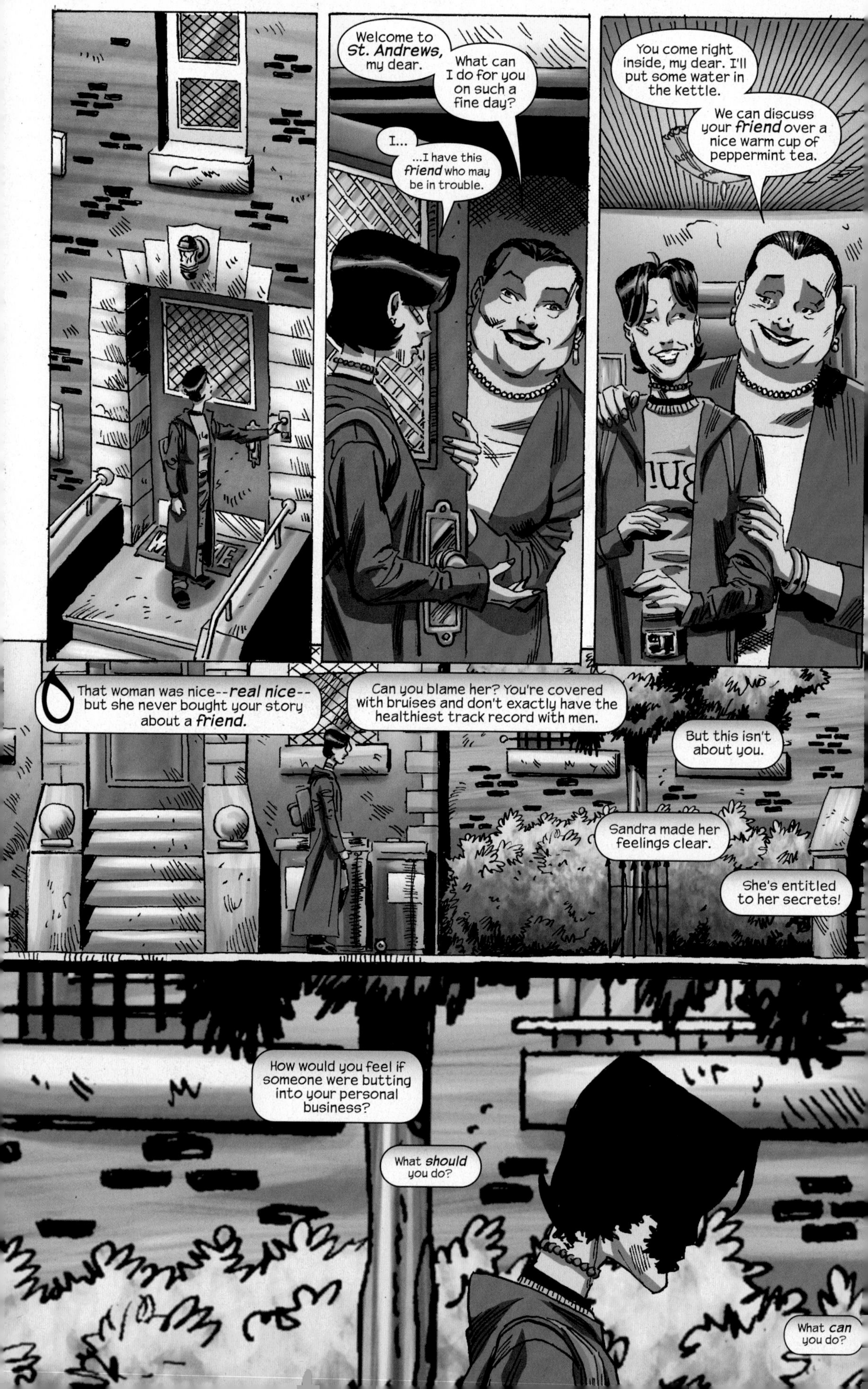
Welcome to St. Andrews, my dear.
What can I do for you on such a fine day?
I...
...I have this friend who may be in trouble.
You come right inside, my dear. I'll put some water in the kettle.
We can discuss your friend over a nice warm cup of peppermint tea.
That woman was nice--real nice--but she never bought your story about a friend.
Can you blame her? You're covered with bruises and don't exactly have the healthiest track record with men.
But this isn't about you.
Sandra made her feelings clear.
She's entitled to her secrets!
How would you feel if someone were butting into your personal business?
What should you do?
What can you do?

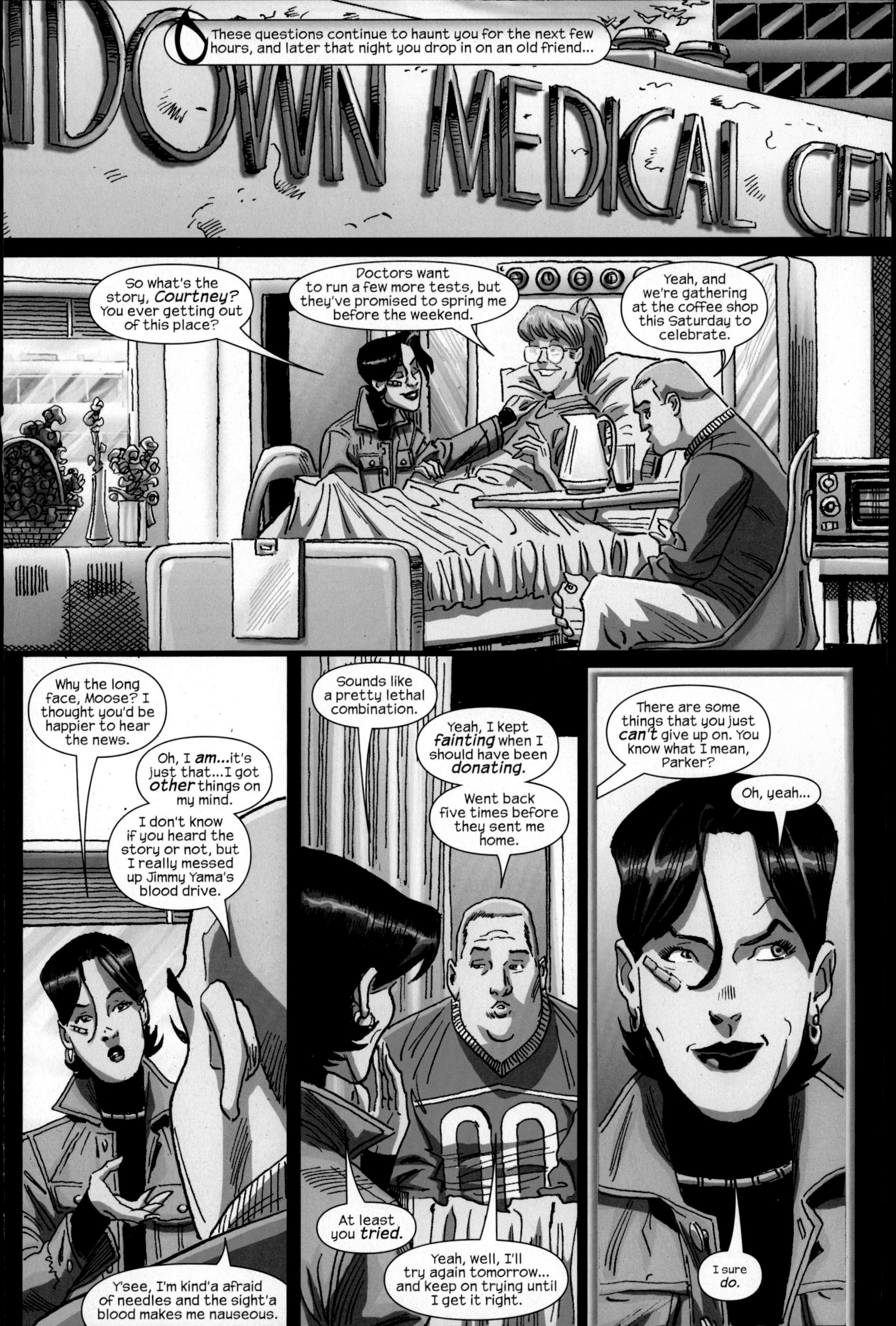

These questions continue to haunt you for the next few hours, and later that night you drop in on an old friend...
DOWN MEDICAL CEN
So what's the story, Courtney? You ever getting out of this place?
Doctors want to run a few more tests, but they've promised to spring me before the weekend.
Yeah, and we're gathering at the coffee shop this Saturday to celebrate.
Why the long face, Moose? I thought you'd be happier to hear the news.
Oh, I am...it's just that...I got other things on my mind.
I don't know if you heard the story or not, but I really messed up Jimmy Yama's blood drive.
Y'see, I'm kind'a afraid of needles and the sight'a blood makes me nauseous.
Sounds like a pretty lethal combination.
Yeah, I kept fainting when I should have been donating.
Went back five times before they sent me home.
At least you tried.
Yeah, well, I'll try again tomorrow... and keep on trying until I get it right.
There are some things that you just can't give up on. You know what I mean, Parker?
Oh, yeah...
I sure do.

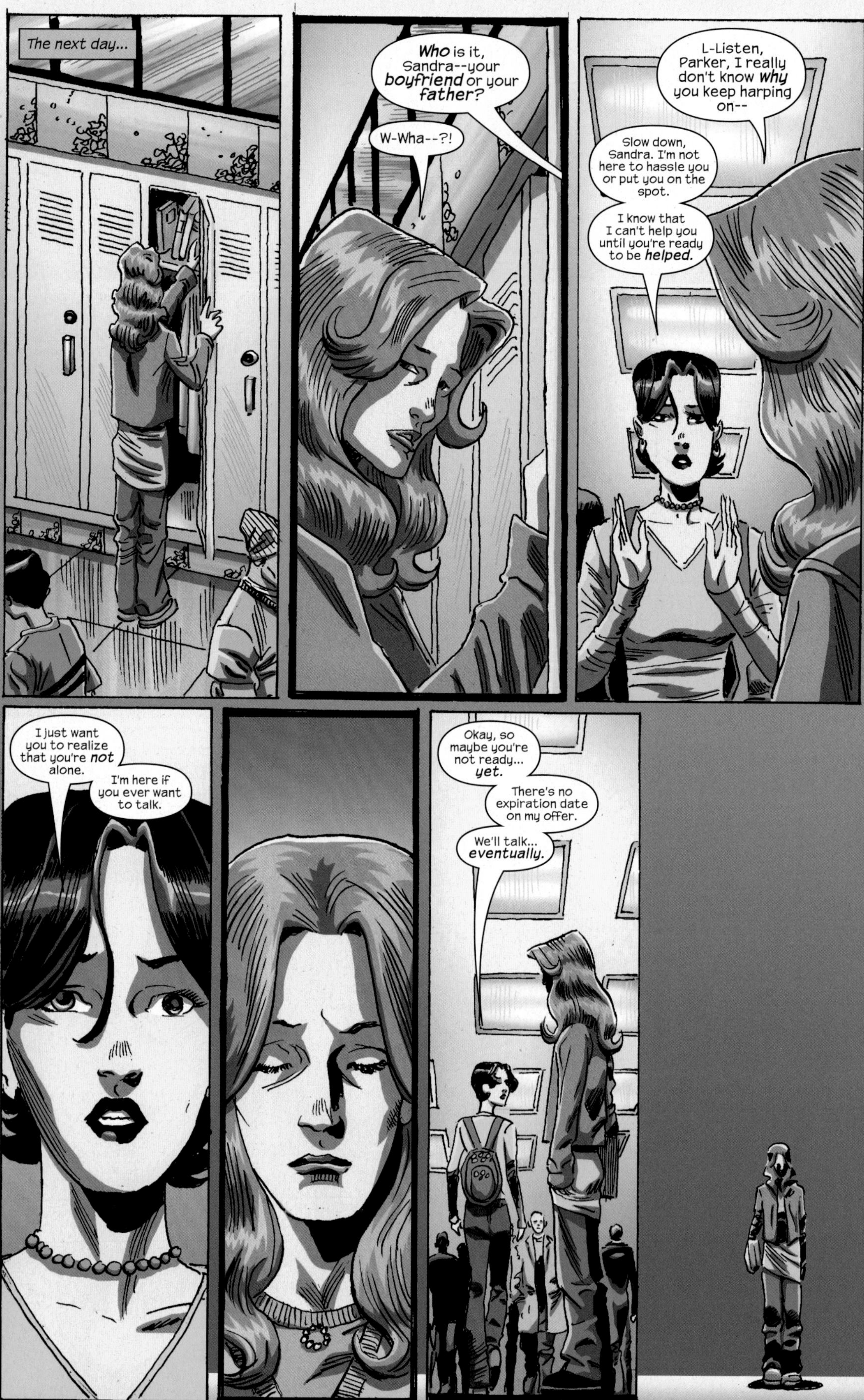
The next day...
Who is it, Sandra--your boyfriend or your father?
W-Wha--?!
L-Listen, Parker, I really don't know why you keep harping on--
Slow down, Sandra. I'm not here to hassle you or put you on the spot.
I know that I can't help you until you're ready to be helped.
I just want you to realize that you're not alone.
I'm here if you ever want to talk.
Okay, so maybe you're not ready... yet.
There's no expiration date on my offer.
We'll talk... eventually.

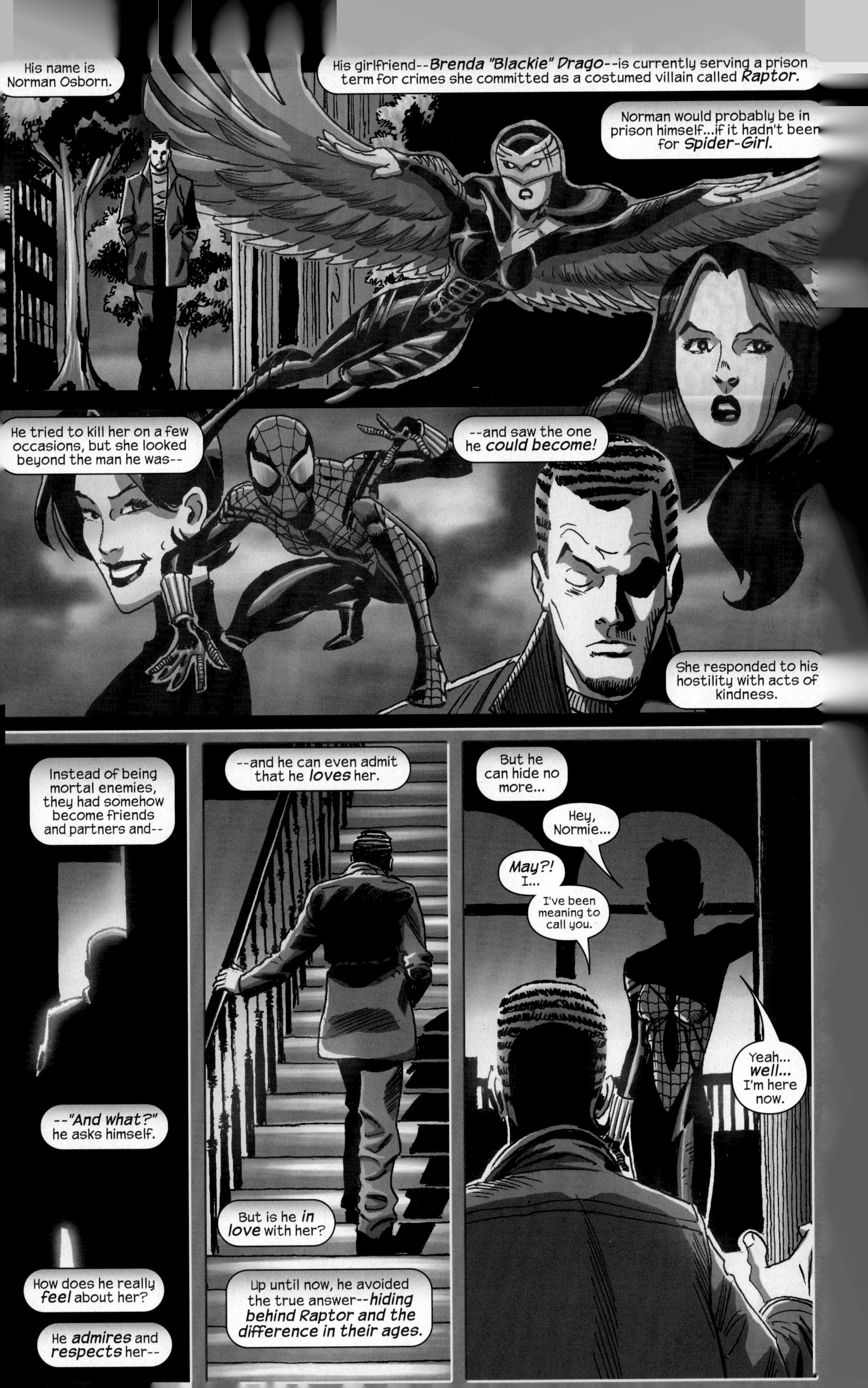
His name is Norman Osborn.
His girlfriend--Brenda "Blackie" Drago--is currently serving a prison term for crimes she committed as a costumed villain called Raptor.
Norman would probably be in prison himself...if it hadn't been for Spider-Girl.
He tried to kill her on a few occasions, but she looked beyond the man he was--
--and saw the one he could become!
She responded to his hostility with acts of kindness.
Instead of being mortal enemies, they had somehow become friends and partners and--
--"And what?" he asks himself.
How does he really feel about her?
He admires and respects her--
--and he can even admit that he loves her.
But is he in love with her?
Up until now, he avoided the true answer--hiding behind Raptor and the difference in their ages.
But he can hide no more...
Hey, Normie...
May?! I...
I've been meaning to call you.
Yeah... well... I'm here now.

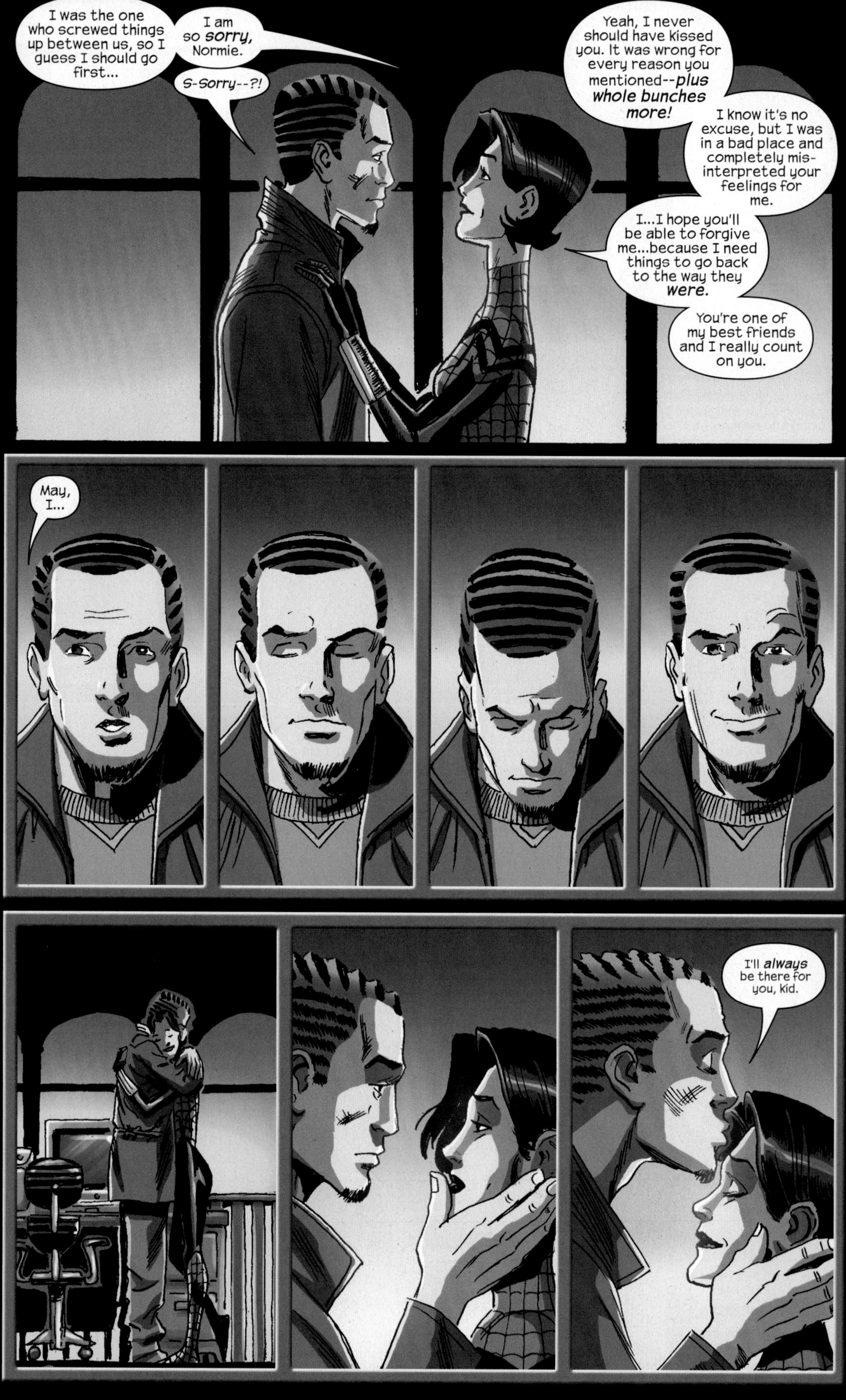
I was the one who screwed things up between us, so I guess I should go first...
I am so *sorry,* Normie.
S-Sorry--?!
Yeah, I never should have kissed you. It was wrong for every reason you mentioned--*plus whole bunches more!*
I know it's no excuse, but I was in a bad place and completely mis-interpreted your feelings for me.
I...I hope you'll be able to forgive me...because I need things to go back to the way they *were.*
You're one of my best friends and I really count on you.
May, I...
I'll *always* be there for you, kid.

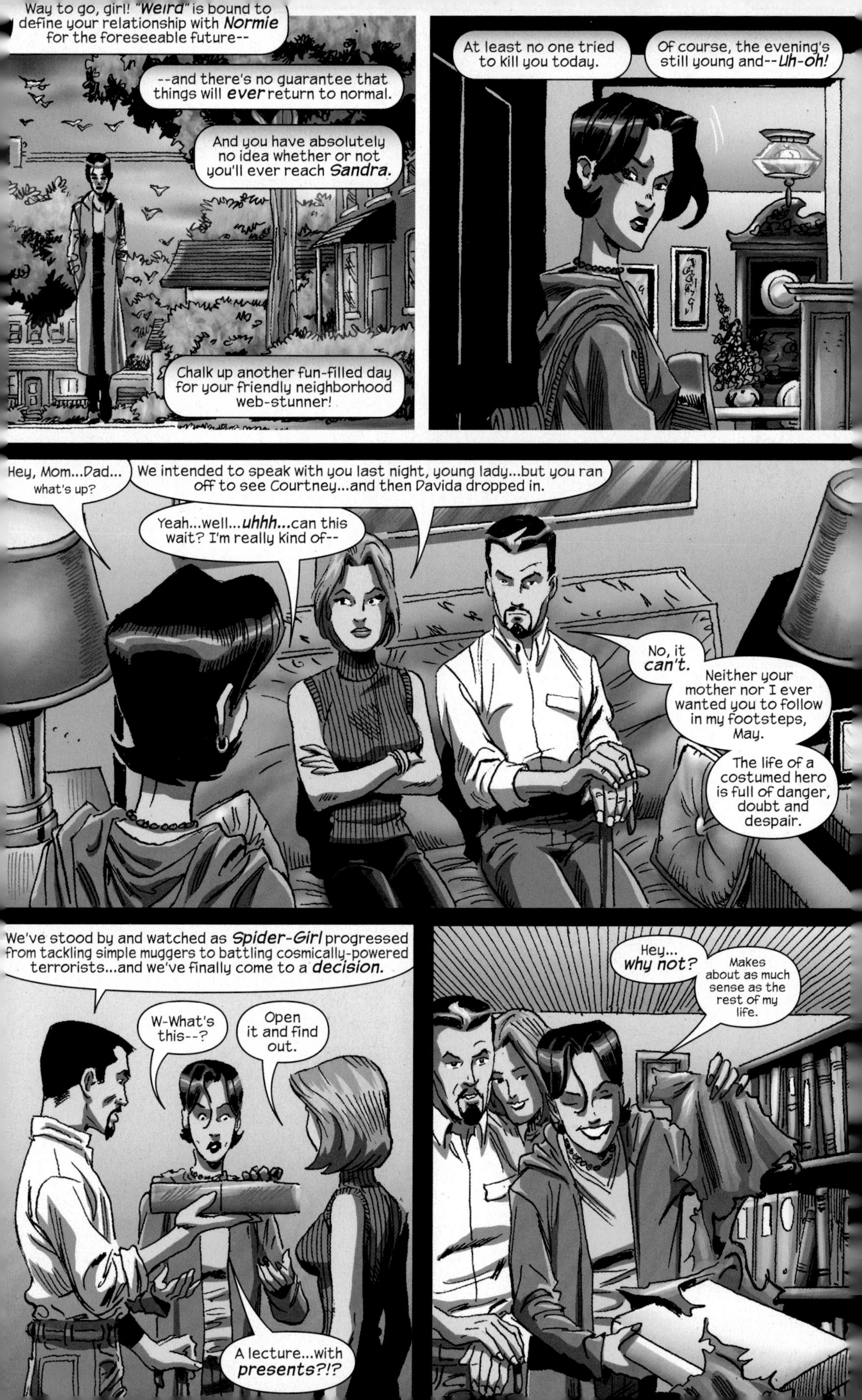
Way to go, girl! "Weird" is bound to define your relationship with Normie for the foreseeable future--
--and there's no guarantee that things will ever return to normal.
And you have absolutely no idea whether or not you'll ever reach Sandra.
Chalk up another fun-filled day for your friendly neighborhood web-stunner!
At least no one tried to kill you today.
Of course, the evening's still young and--Uh-oh!
Hey, Mom...Dad... what's up?
We intended to speak with you last night, young lady...but you ran off to see Courtney...and then Davida dropped in.
Yeah...well...uhhh...can this wait? I'm really kind of--
No, it can't.
Neither your mother nor I ever wanted you to follow in my footsteps, May.
The life of a costumed hero is full of danger, doubt and despair.
We've stood by and watched as Spider-Girl progressed from tackling simple muggers to battling cosmically-powered terrorists...and we've finally come to a decision.
W-What's this--?
Open it and find out.
A lecture...with presents?!?
Hey... why not?
Makes about as much sense as the rest of my life.

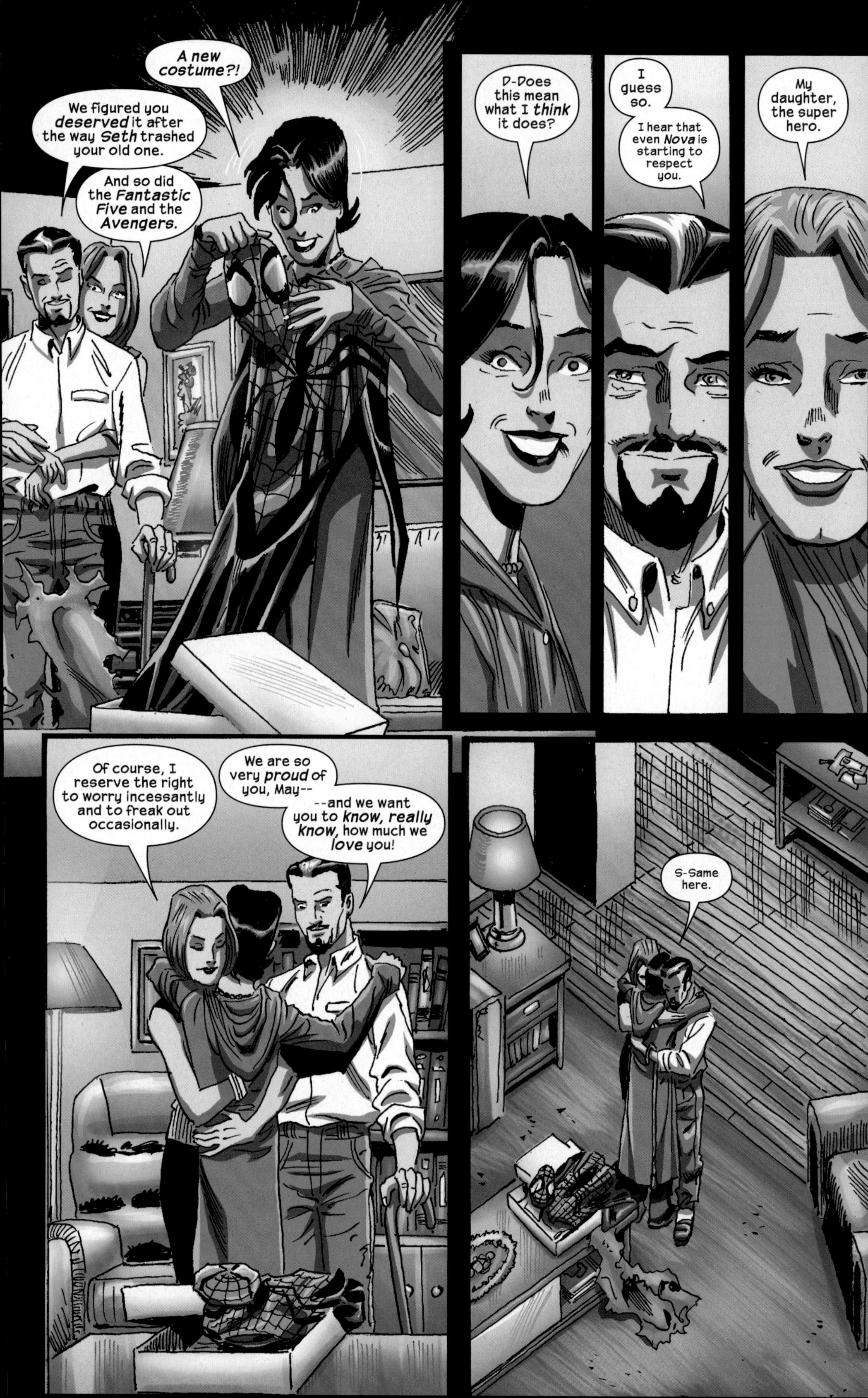
A new costume?!
We figured you deserved it after the way Seth trashed your old one.
And so did the Fantastic Five and the Avengers.
D-Does this mean what I think it does?
I guess so.
I hear that even Nova is starting to respect you.
My daughter, the super hero.
Of course, I reserve the right to worry incessantly and to freak out occasionally.
We are so very proud of you, May--
--and we want you to know, really know, how much we love you!
S-Same here.

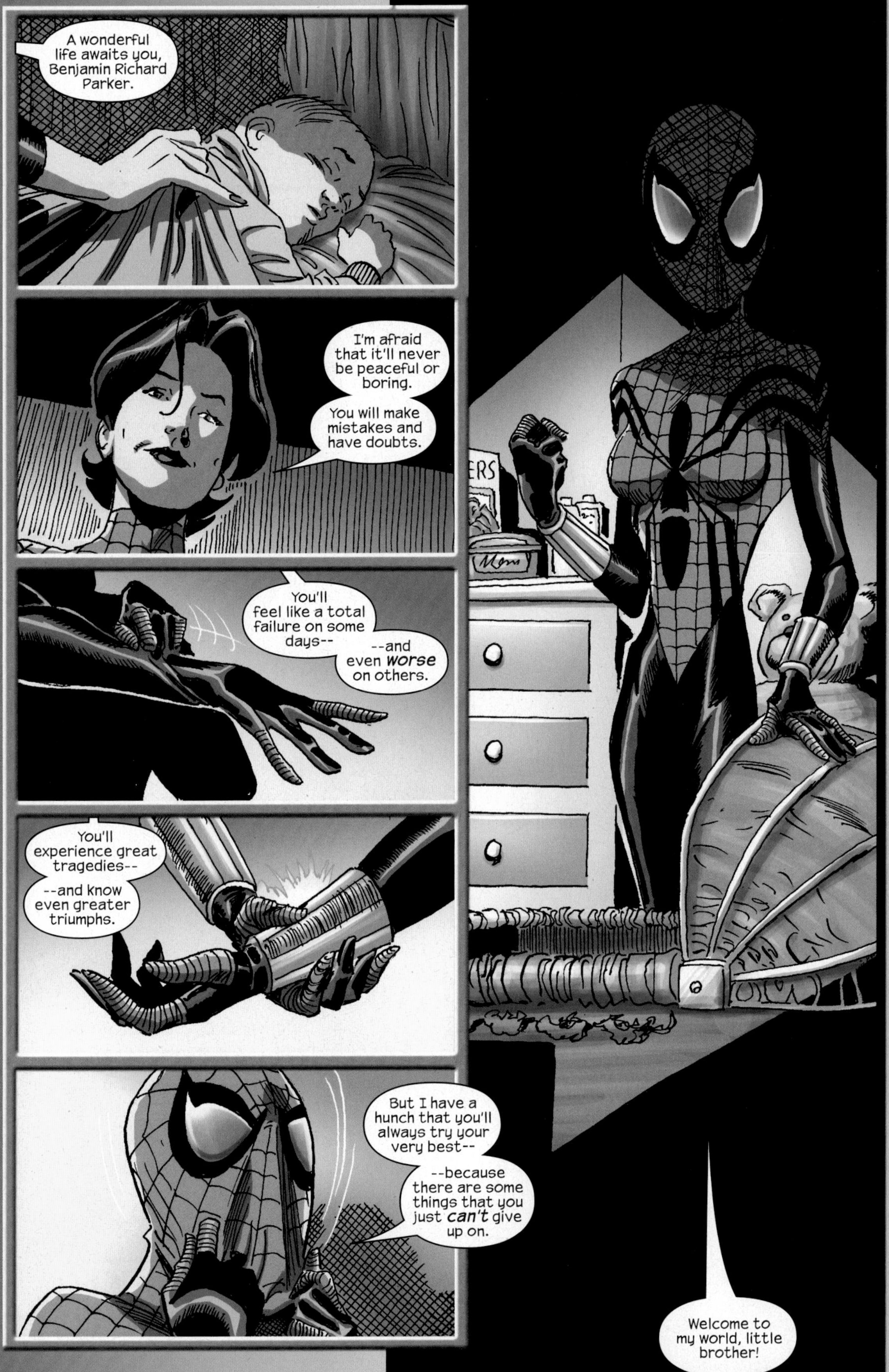
A wonderful life awaits you, Benjamin Richard Parker.
I'm afraid that it'll never be peaceful or boring.
You will make mistakes and have doubts.
You'll feel like a total failure on some days--
--and even *worse* on others.
You'll experience great tragedies--
--and know even greater triumphs.
But I have a hunch that you'll always try your very best--
--because there are some things that you just *can't* give up on.
Welcome to my world, little brother!

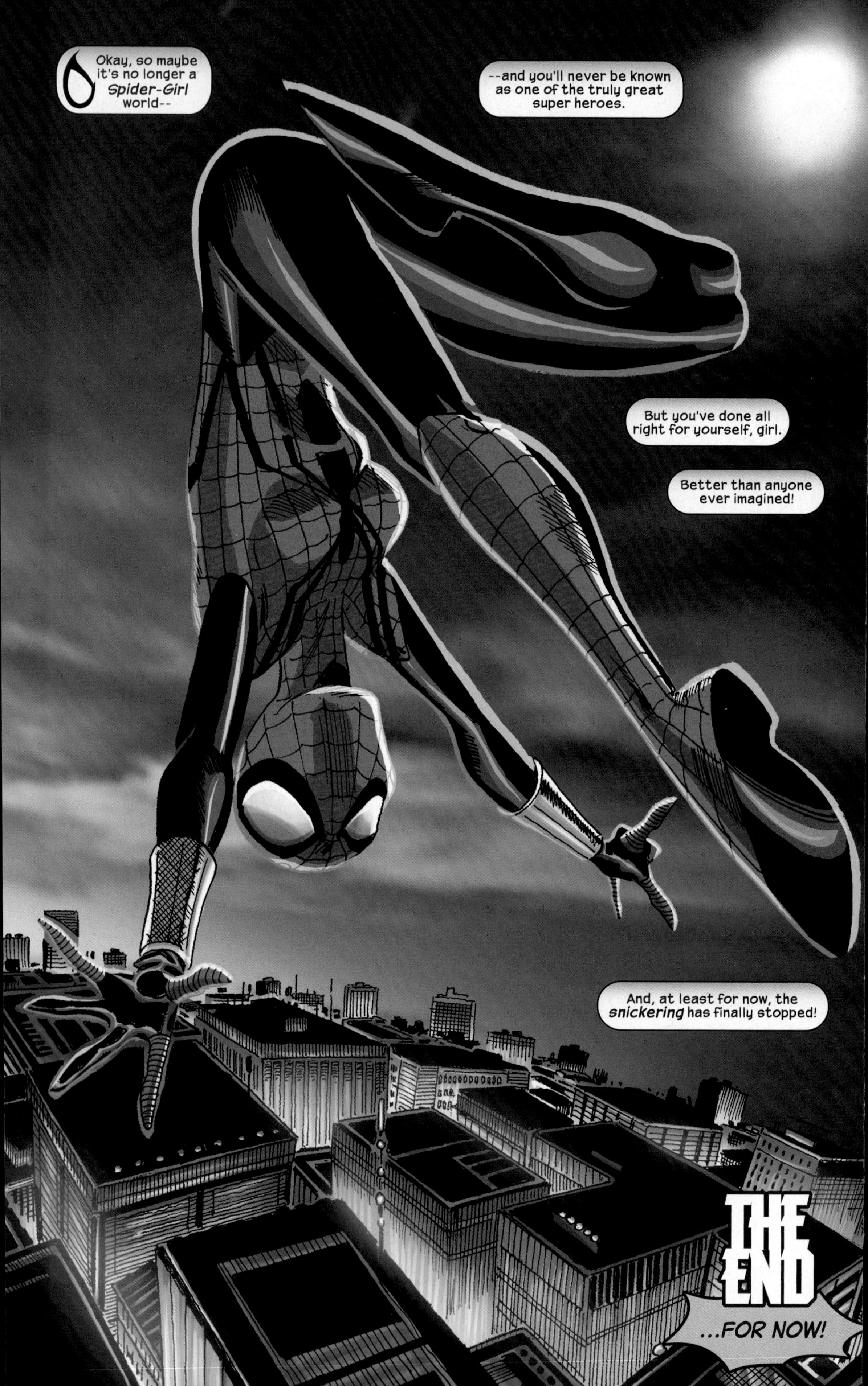
Okay, so maybe it's no longer a *Spider-Girl* world--
--and you'll never be known as one of the truly great super heroes.
But you've done all right for yourself, girl.
Better than anyone ever imagined!
And, at least for now, the *snickering* has finally stopped!
THE END
...FOR NOW!

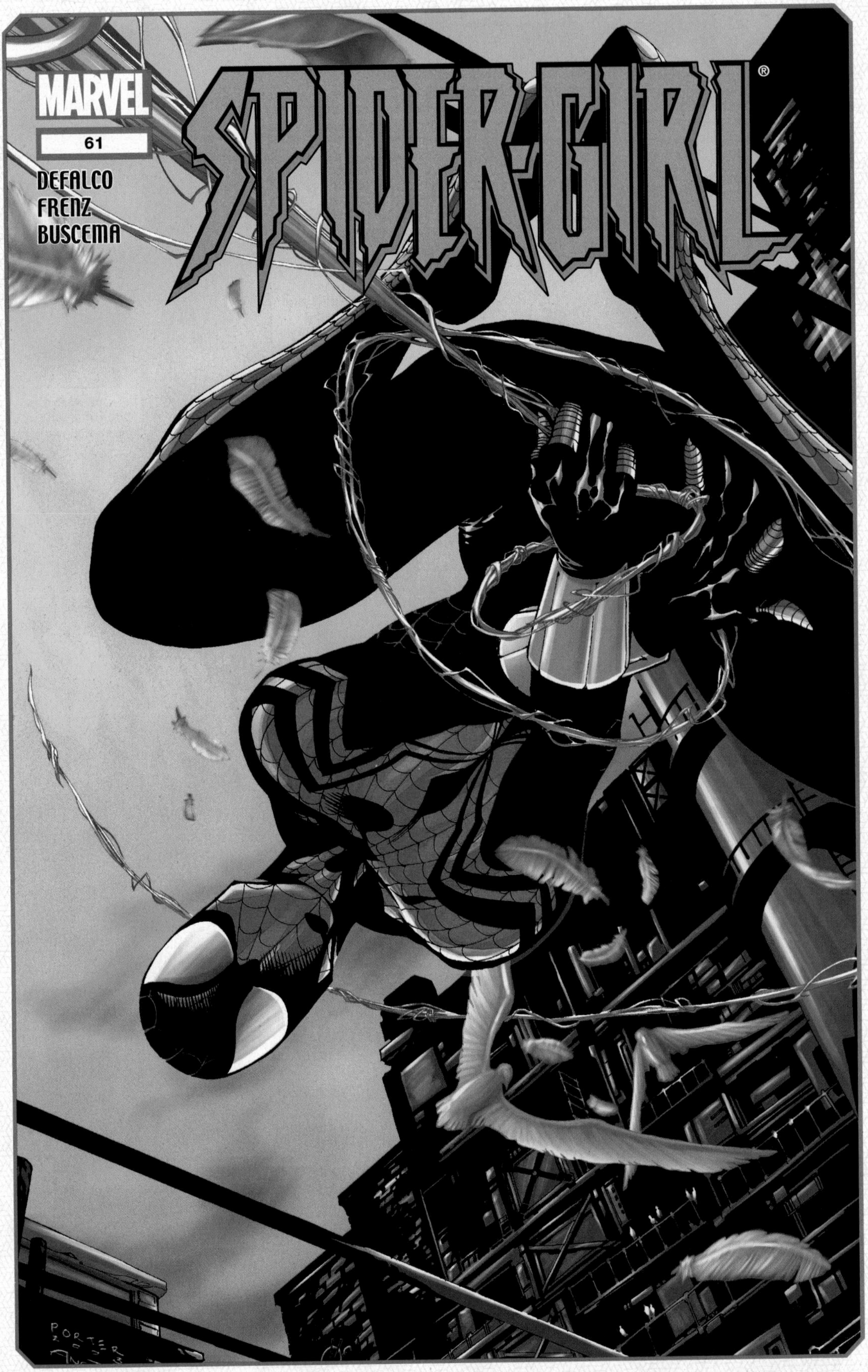

MARVEL
61
SPIDER-GIRL®
DEFALCO
FRENZ
BUSCEMA

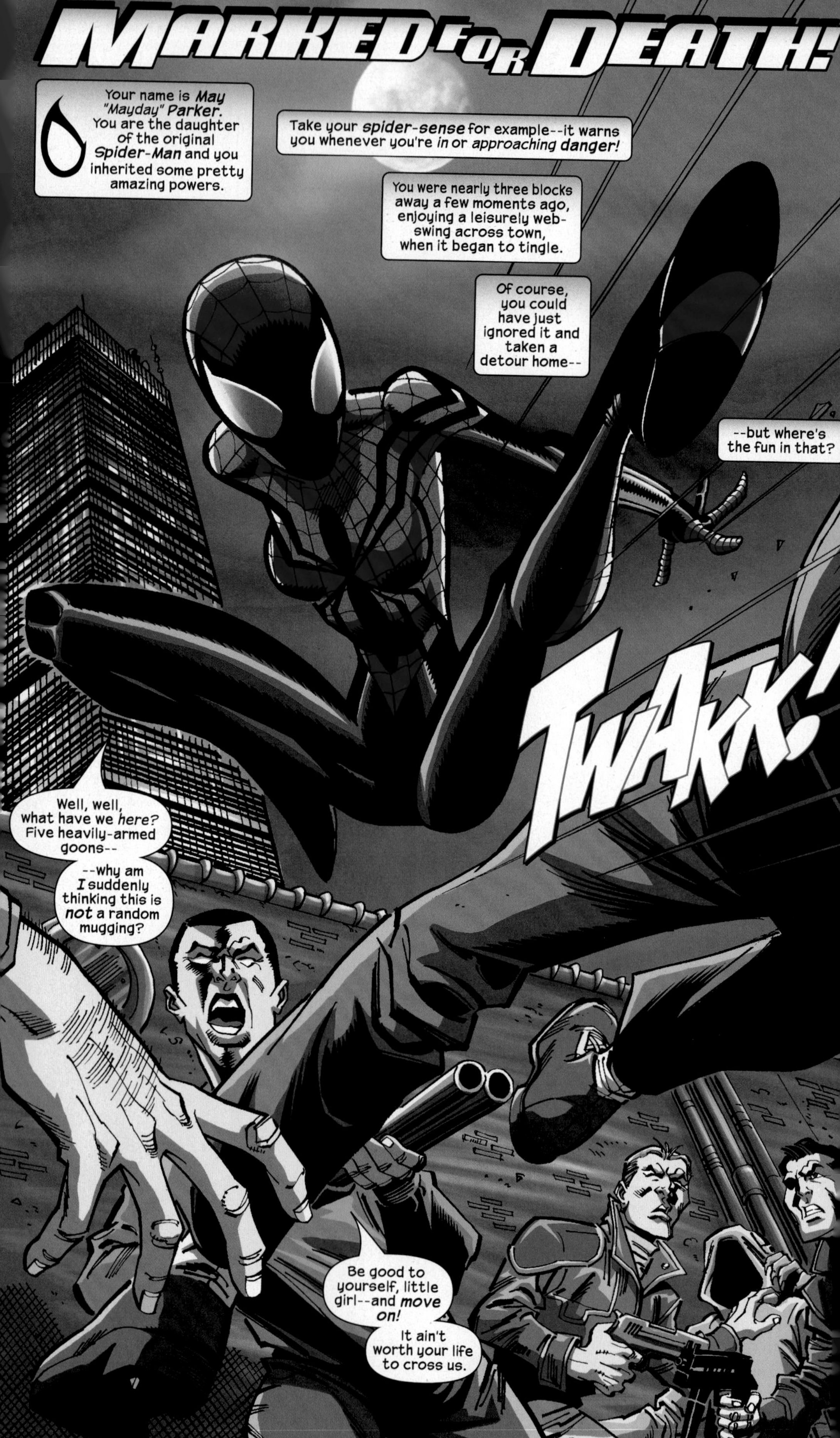
MARKED FOR DEATH!
Your name is May "Mayday" Parker. You are the daughter of the original Spider-Man and you inherited some pretty amazing powers.
Take your spider-sense for example--it warns you whenever you're in or approaching danger!
You were nearly three blocks away a few moments ago, enjoying a leisurely web-swing across town, when it began to tingle.
Of course, you could have just ignored it and taken a detour home--
--but where's the fun in that?
TWAKK!
Well, well, what have we here? Five heavily-armed goons--
--why am I suddenly thinking this is not a random mugging?
Be good to yourself, little girl--and move on!
It ain't worth your life to cross us.

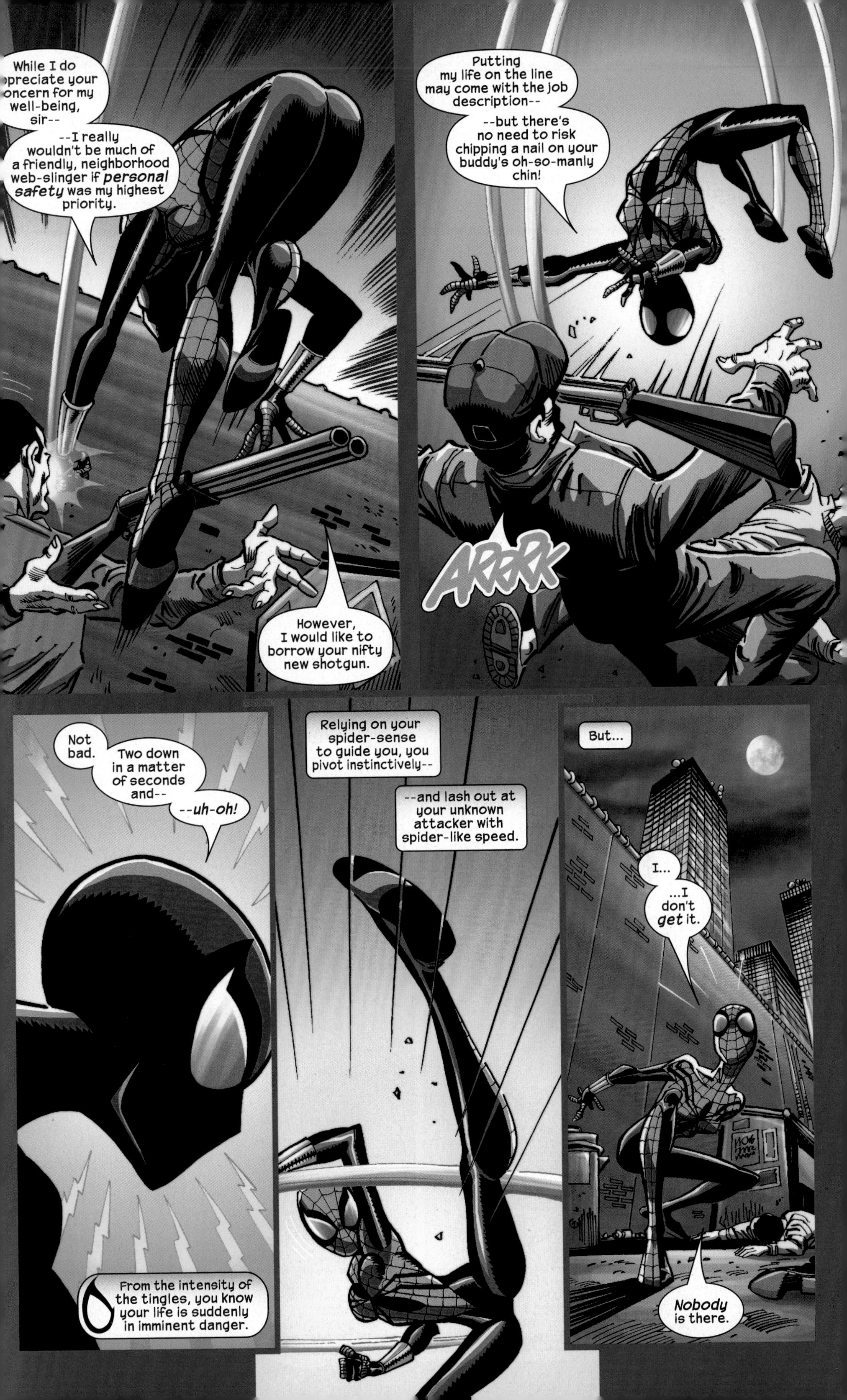
While I do ppreciate your oncern for my well-being, sir--
--I really wouldn't be much of a friendly, neighborhood web-slinger if *personal safety* was my highest priority.
However, I would like to borrow your nifty new shotgun.
Putting my life on the line may come with the job description--
--but there's no need to risk chipping a nail on your buddy's oh-so-manly chin!
ARRRK
Not bad.
Two down in a matter of seconds and--
--*uh-oh!*
From the intensity of the tingles, you know your life is suddenly in imminent danger.
Relying on your spider-sense to guide you, you pivot instinctively--
--and lash out at your unknown attacker with spider-like speed.
But...
I...
...I don't *get* it.
Nobody is there.

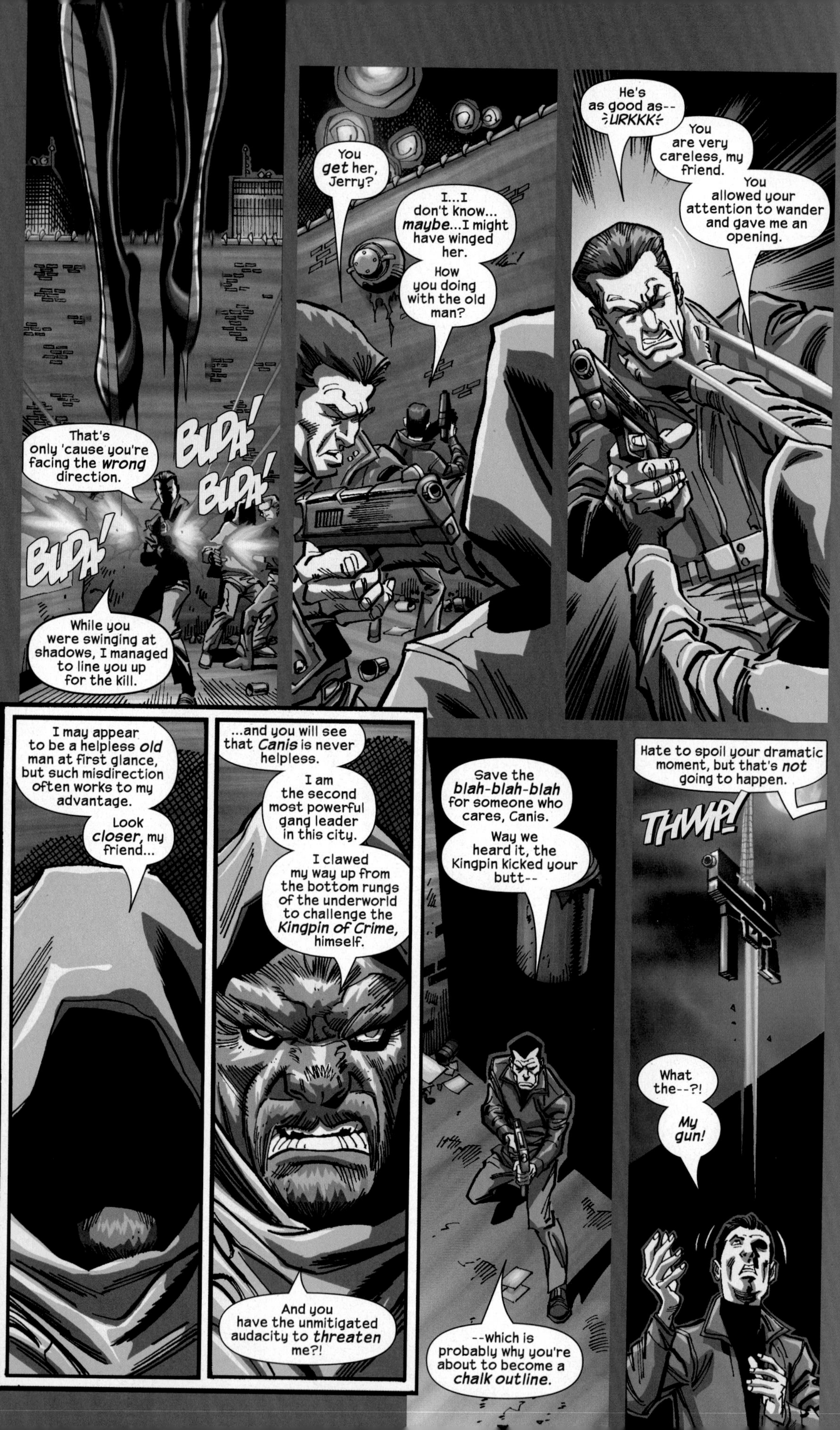
That's only 'cause you're facing the wrong direction.
BUDA! BUDA! BUDA!
While you were swinging at shadows, I managed to line you up for the kill.
You get her, Jerry?
I...I don't know... maybe...I might have winged her.
How you doing with the old man?
He's as good as-- URKKK
You are very careless, my friend.
You allowed your attention to wander and gave me an opening.
I may appear to be a helpless old man at first glance, but such misdirection often works to my advantage.
Look closer, my friend...
...and you will see that Canis is never helpless.
I am the second most powerful gang leader in this city.
I clawed my way up from the bottom rungs of the underworld to challenge the Kingpin of Crime, himself.
And you have the unmitigated audacity to threaten me?!
Save the blah-blah-blah for someone who cares, Canis.
Way we heard it, the Kingpin kicked your butt--
--which is probably why you're about to become a chalk outline.
Hate to spoil your dramatic moment, but that's not going to happen.
THWIP!
What the--?!
My gun!

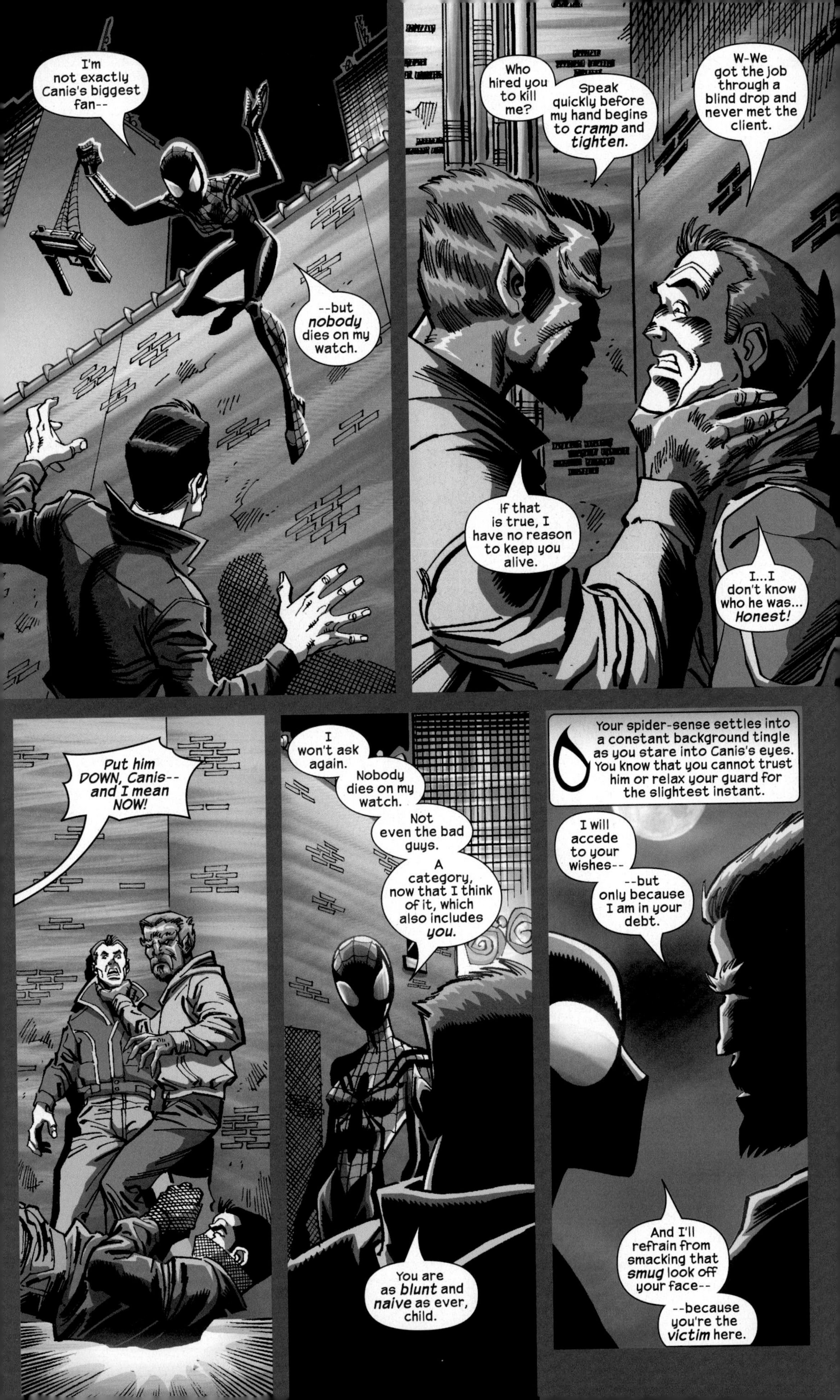
I'm not exactly Canis's biggest fan--
--but nobody dies on my watch.
Who hired you to kill me?
Speak quickly before my hand begins to cramp and tighten.
W-We got the job through a blind drop and never met the client.
If that is true, I have no reason to keep you alive.
I...I don't know who he was... Honest!
Put him DOWN, Canis-- and I mean NOW!
I won't ask again.
Nobody dies on my watch.
Not even the bad guys.
A category, now that I think of it, which also includes you.
You are as blunt and naive as ever, child.
Your spider-sense settles into a constant background tingle as you stare into Canis's eyes. You know that you cannot trust him or relax your guard for the slightest instant.
I will accede to your wishes--
--but only because I am in your debt.
And I'll refrain from smacking that smug look off your face--
--because you're the victim here.

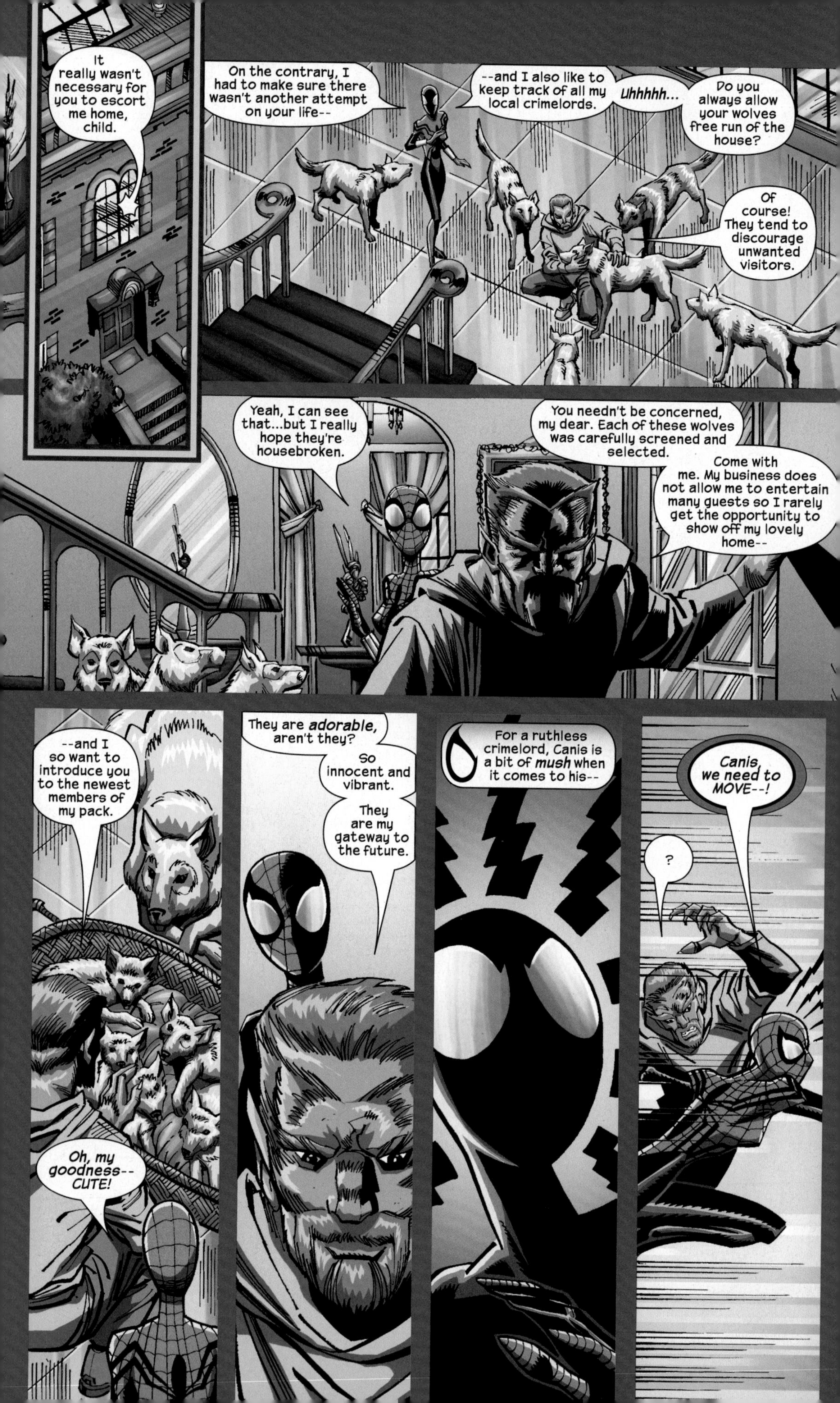

It really wasn't necessary for you to escort me home, child.
On the contrary, I had to make sure there wasn't another attempt on your life--
--and I also like to keep track of all my local crimelords.
Uhhhhh...
Do you always allow your wolves free run of the house?
Of course! They tend to discourage unwanted visitors.
Yeah, I can see that...but I really hope they're housebroken.
You needn't be concerned, my dear. Each of these wolves was carefully screened and selected.
Come with me. My business does not allow me to entertain many guests so I rarely get the opportunity to show off my lovely home--
--and I so want to introduce you to the newest members of my pack.
Oh, my goodness-- CUTE!
They are adorable, aren't they?
So innocent and vibrant.
They are my gateway to the future.
For a ruthless crimelord, Canis is a bit of mush when it comes to his--
Canis, we need to MOVE--!
?

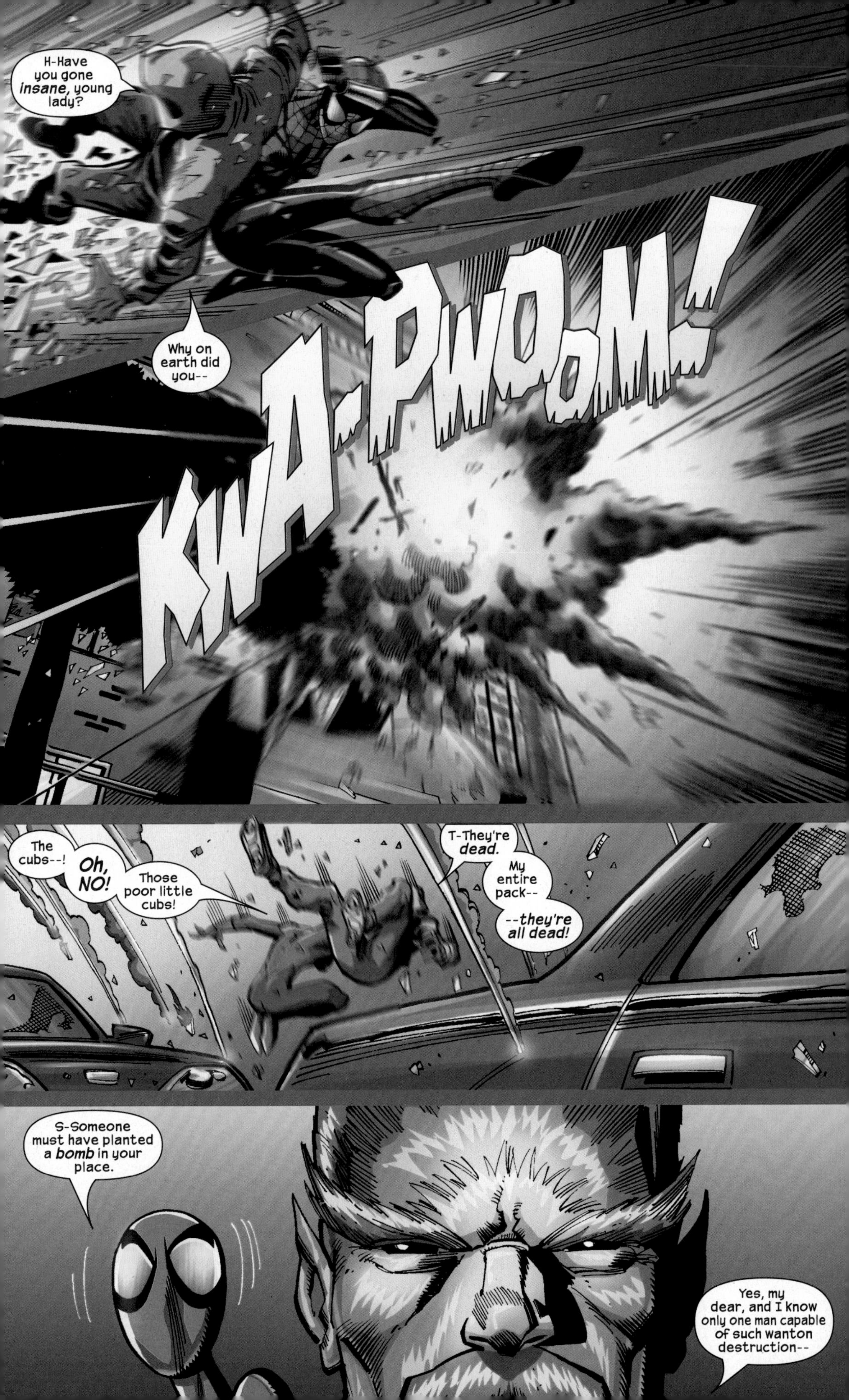
H-Have you gone *insane*, young lady?
Why on earth did you--
KWA-PWOOM!
The cubs--!
Oh, NO!
Those poor little cubs!
T-They're *dead.*
My entire pack--
--they're all dead!
S-Someone must have planted a *bomb* in your place.
Yes, my dear, and I know only one man capable of such wanton destruction--

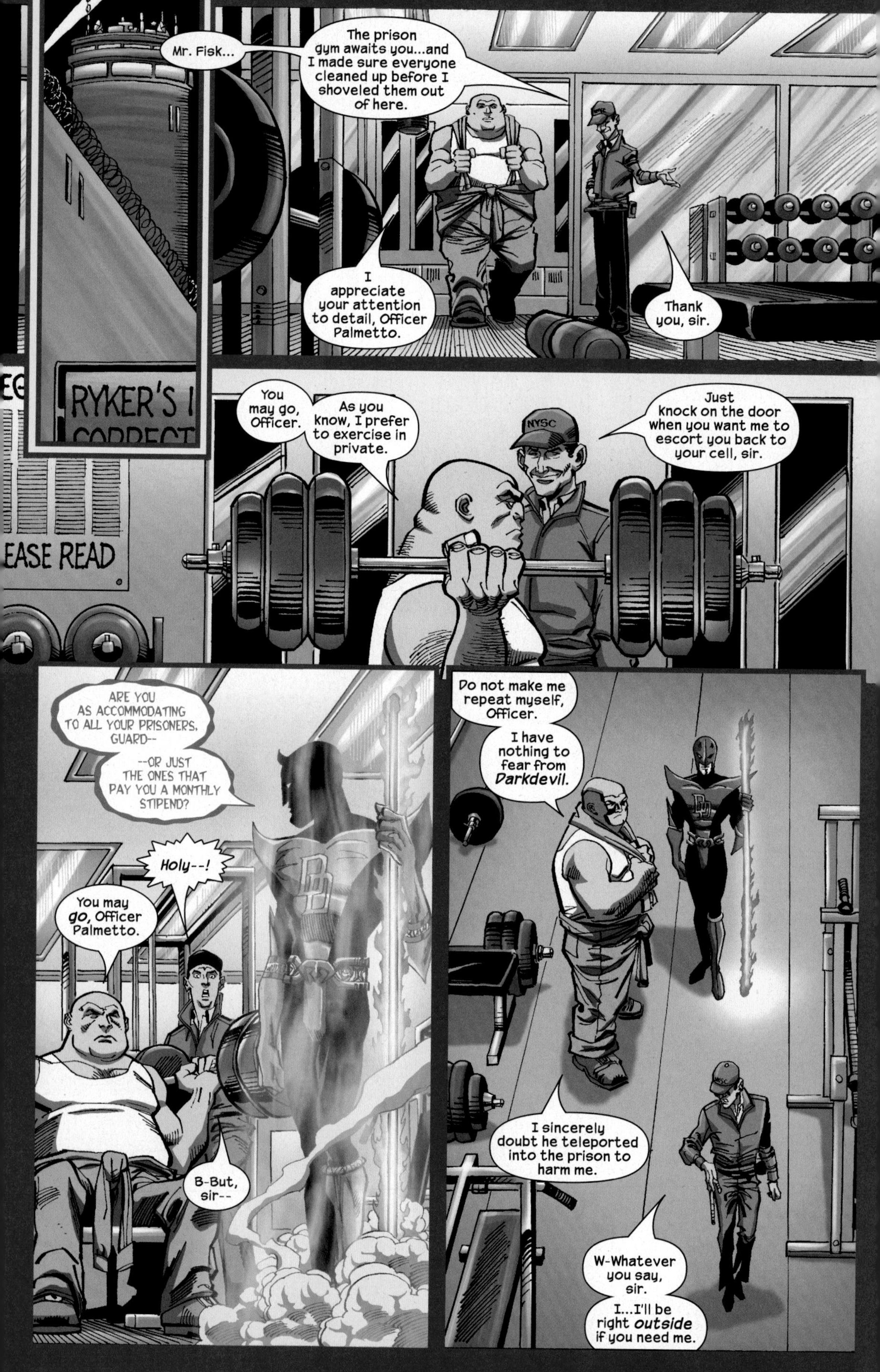
Mr. Fisk...
The prison gym awaits you...and I made sure everyone cleaned up before I shoveled them out of here.
I appreciate your attention to detail, Officer Palmetto.
Thank you, sir.
RYKER'S I
CORRECT
EASE READ
You may go, Officer.
As you know, I prefer to exercise in private.
NYSC
Just knock on the door when you want me to escort you back to your cell, sir.
ARE YOU AS ACCOMMODATING TO ALL YOUR PRISONERS, GUARD--
--OR JUST THE ONES THAT PAY YOU A MONTHLY STIPEND?
Holy--!
You may *go*, Officer Palmetto.
B-But, sir--
Do not make me repeat myself, Officer.
I have nothing to fear from *Darkdevil*.
I sincerely doubt he teleported into the prison to harm me.
W-Whatever you say, sir.
I...I'll be right *outside* if you need me.

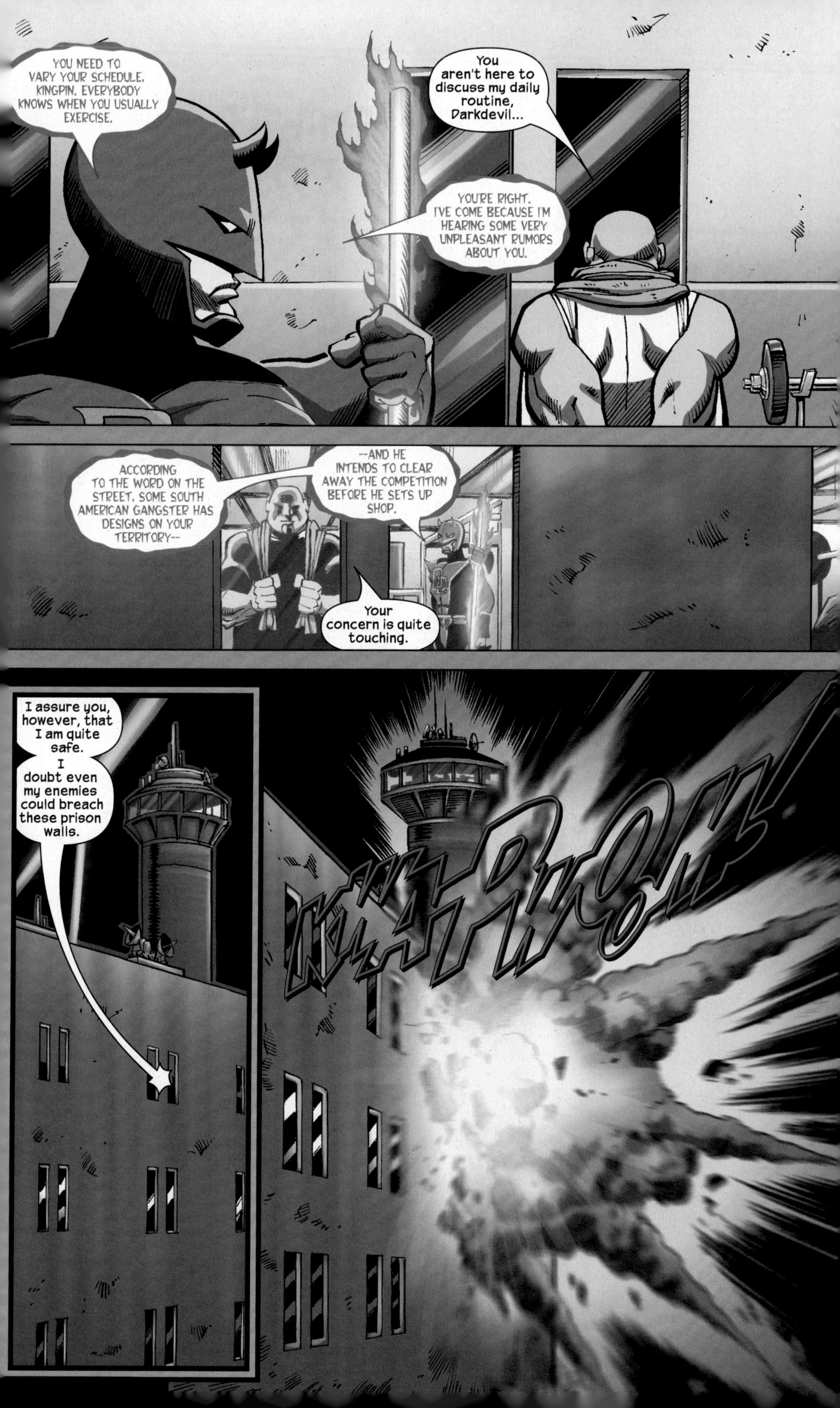
YOU NEED TO VARY YOUR SCHEDULE, KINGPIN. EVERYBODY KNOWS WHEN YOU USUALLY EXERCISE.
You aren't here to discuss my daily routine, Darkdevil...
YOU'RE RIGHT. I'VE COME BECAUSE I'M HEARING SOME VERY UNPLEASANT RUMORS ABOUT YOU.
ACCORDING TO THE WORD ON THE STREET, SOME SOUTH AMERICAN GANGSTER HAS DESIGNS ON YOUR TERRITORY--
--AND HE INTENDS TO CLEAR AWAY THE COMPETITION BEFORE HE SETS UP SHOP.
Your concern is quite touching.
I assure you, however, that I am quite safe.
I doubt even my enemies could breach these prison walls.
KRAKOOM

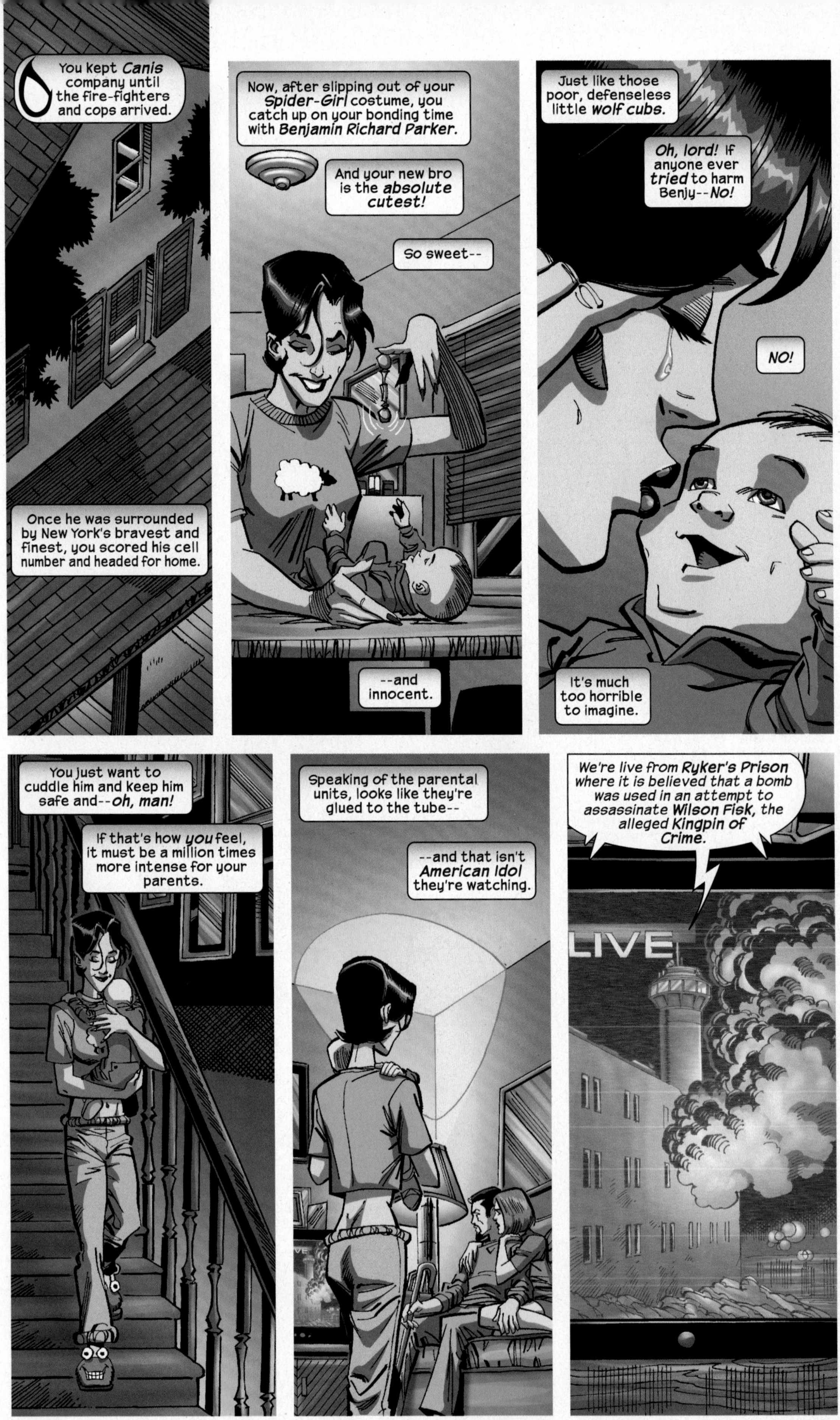

You kept *Canis* company until the fire-fighters and cops arrived.
Once he was surrounded by New York's bravest and finest, you scored his cell number and headed for home.
Now, after slipping out of your *Spider-Girl* costume, you catch up on your bonding time with *Benjamin Richard Parker.*
And your new bro is the ***absolute cutest!***
So sweet--
--and innocent.
Just like those poor, defenseless little ***wolf cubs.***
Oh, lord! If anyone ever *tried* to harm Benjy--*No!*
NO!
It's much too horrible to imagine.
You just want to cuddle him and keep him safe and--*oh, man!*
If that's how *you* feel, it must be a million times more intense for your parents.
Speaking of the parental units, looks like they're glued to the tube--
--and that isn't *American Idol* they're watching.
*We're live from **Ryker's Prison** where it is believed that a bomb was used in an attempt to assassinate **Wilson Fisk**, the alleged **Kingpin of Crime.***
LIVE

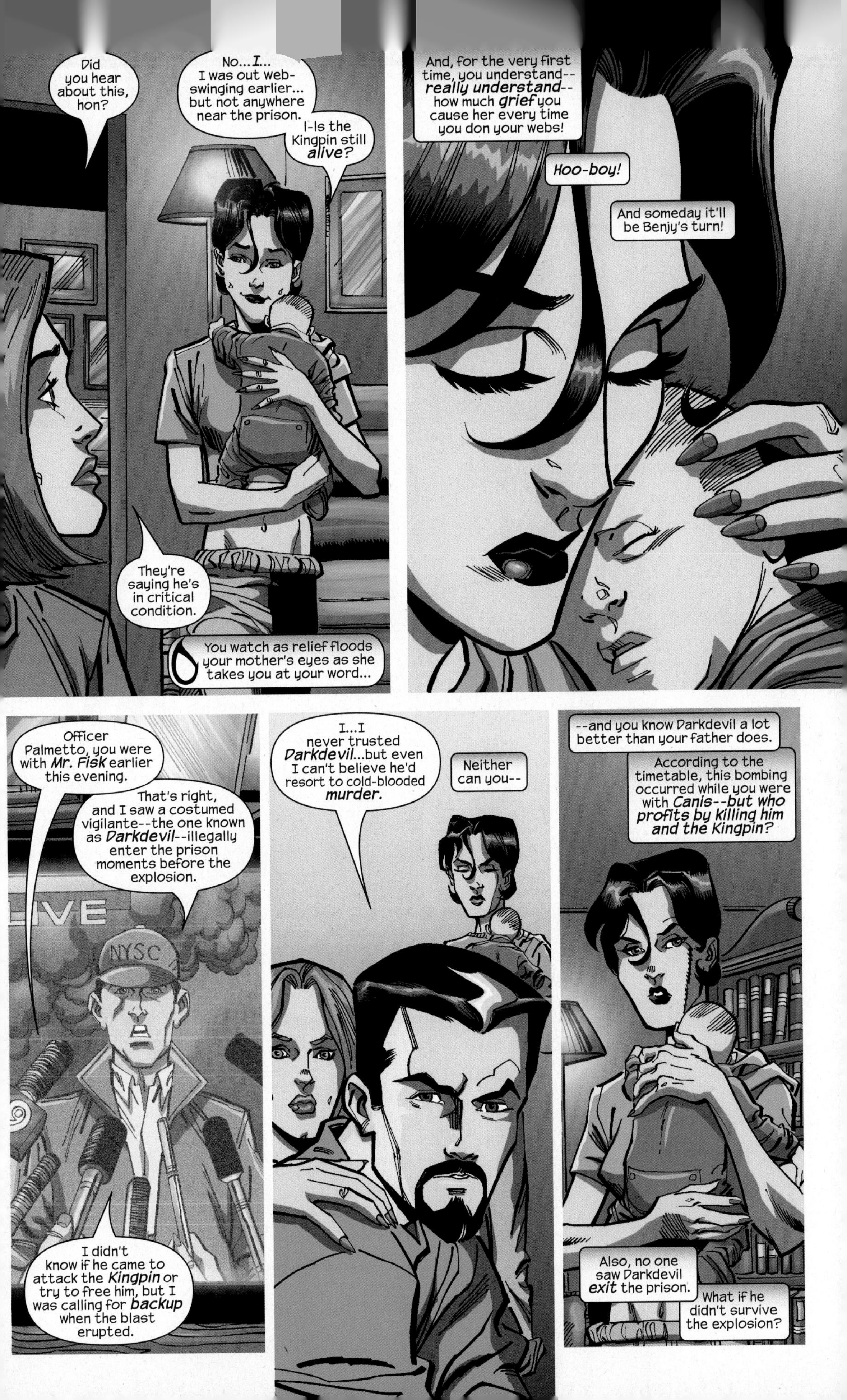
Did you hear about this, hon?
No... I... I was out web-swinging earlier... but not anywhere near the prison.
I-Is the Kingpin still alive?
They're saying he's in critical condition.
You watch as relief floods your mother's eyes as she takes you at your word...
And, for the very first time, you understand-- really understand-- how much grief you cause her every time you don your webs!
Hoo-boy!
And someday it'll be Benjy's turn!
Officer Palmetto, you were with Mr. Fisk earlier this evening.
That's right, and I saw a costumed vigilante--the one known as Darkdevil--illegally enter the prison moments before the explosion.
LIVE
NYSC
I didn't know if he came to attack the Kingpin or try to free him, but I was calling for backup when the blast erupted.
I...I never trusted Darkdevil...but even I can't believe he'd resort to cold-blooded murder.
Neither can you--
--and you know Darkdevil a lot better than your father does.
According to the timetable, this bombing occurred while you were with Canis--but who profits by killing him and the Kingpin?
Also, no one saw Darkdevil exit the prison.
What if he didn't survive the explosion?

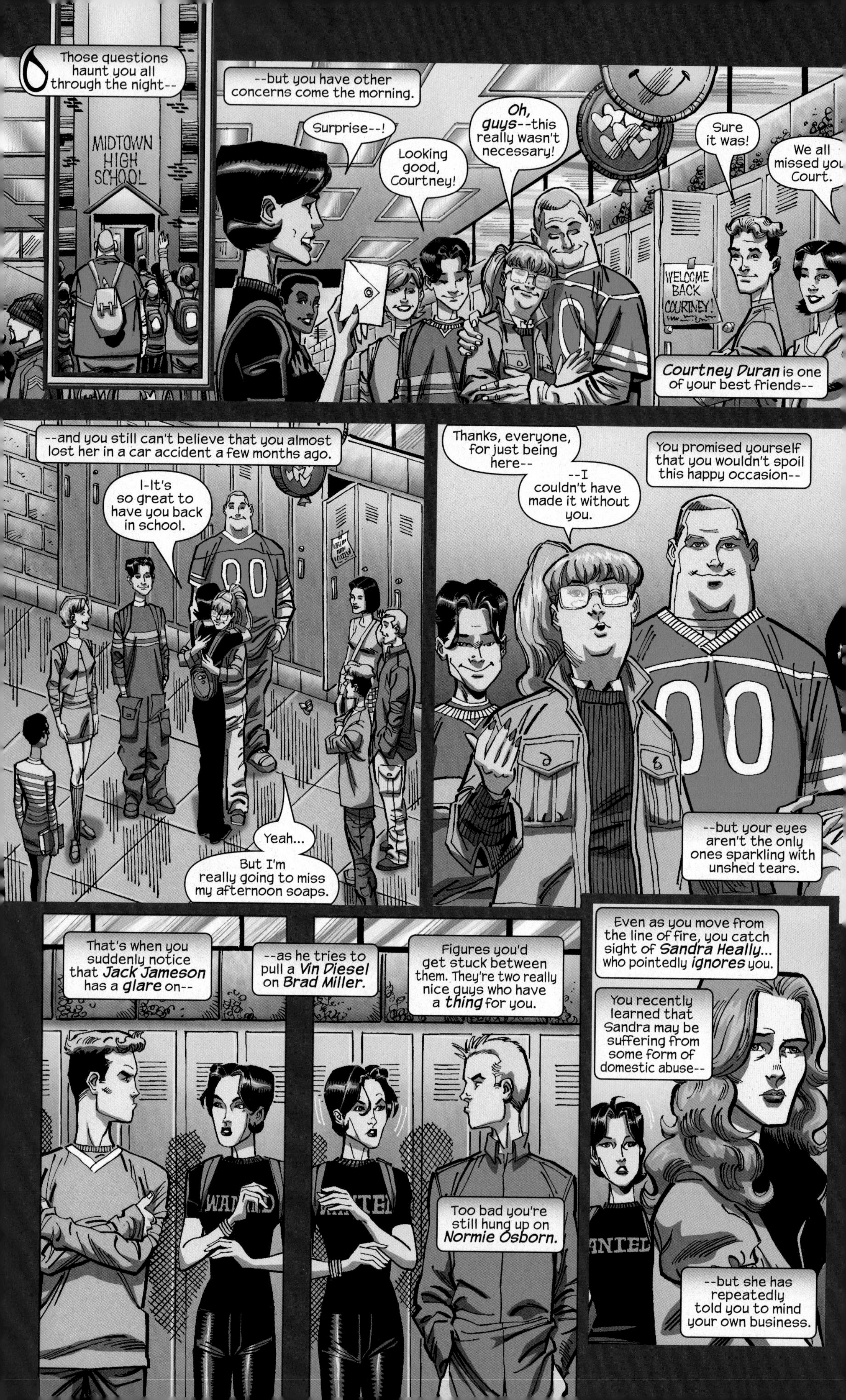

Those questions haunt you all through the night--
MIDTOWN HIGH SCHOOL
--but you have other concerns come the morning.
Surprise--!
Looking good, Courtney!
Oh, guys--this really wasn't necessary!
Sure it was!
We all missed you Court.
WELCOME BACK COURTNEY!
Courtney Duran is one of your best friends--
--and you still can't believe that you almost lost her in a car accident a few months ago.
I-It's so great to have you back in school.
Yeah...
But I'm really going to miss my afternoon soaps.
Thanks, everyone, for just being here--
--I couldn't have made it without you.
You promised yourself that you wouldn't spoil this happy occasion--
--but your eyes aren't the only ones sparkling with unshed tears.
That's when you suddenly notice that Jack Jameson has a glare on--
--as he tries to pull a Vin Diesel on Brad Miller.
Figures you'd get stuck between them. They're two really nice guys who have a thing for you.
Too bad you're still hung up on Normie Osborn.
Even as you move from the line of fire, you catch sight of Sandra Heally... who pointedly ignores you.
You recently learned that Sandra may be suffering from some form of domestic abuse--
--but she has repeatedly told you to mind your own business.

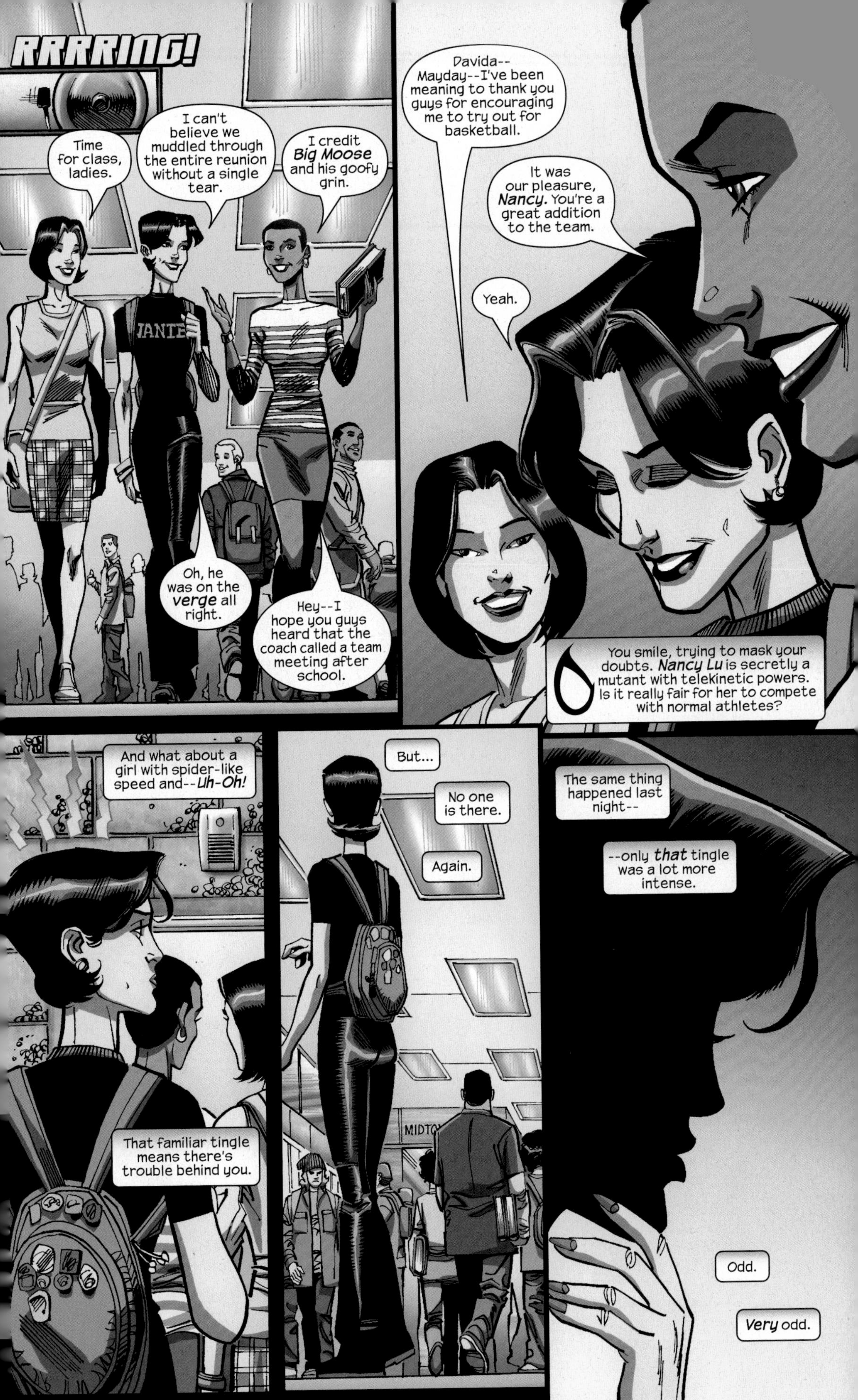
RRRRING!
Time for class, ladies.
I can't believe we muddled through the entire reunion without a single tear.
I credit Big Moose and his goofy grin.
Oh, he was on the verge all right.
Hey--I hope you guys heard that the coach called a team meeting after school.
Davida--Mayday--I've been meaning to thank you guys for encouraging me to try out for basketball.
It was our pleasure, Nancy. You're a great addition to the team.
Yeah.
You smile, trying to mask your doubts. Nancy Lu is secretly a mutant with telekinetic powers. Is it really fair for her to compete with normal athletes?
And what about a girl with spider-like speed and--Uh-Oh!
That familiar tingle means there's trouble behind you.
But...
No one is there.
Again.
The same thing happened last night--
--only that tingle was a lot more intense.
Odd.
Very odd.

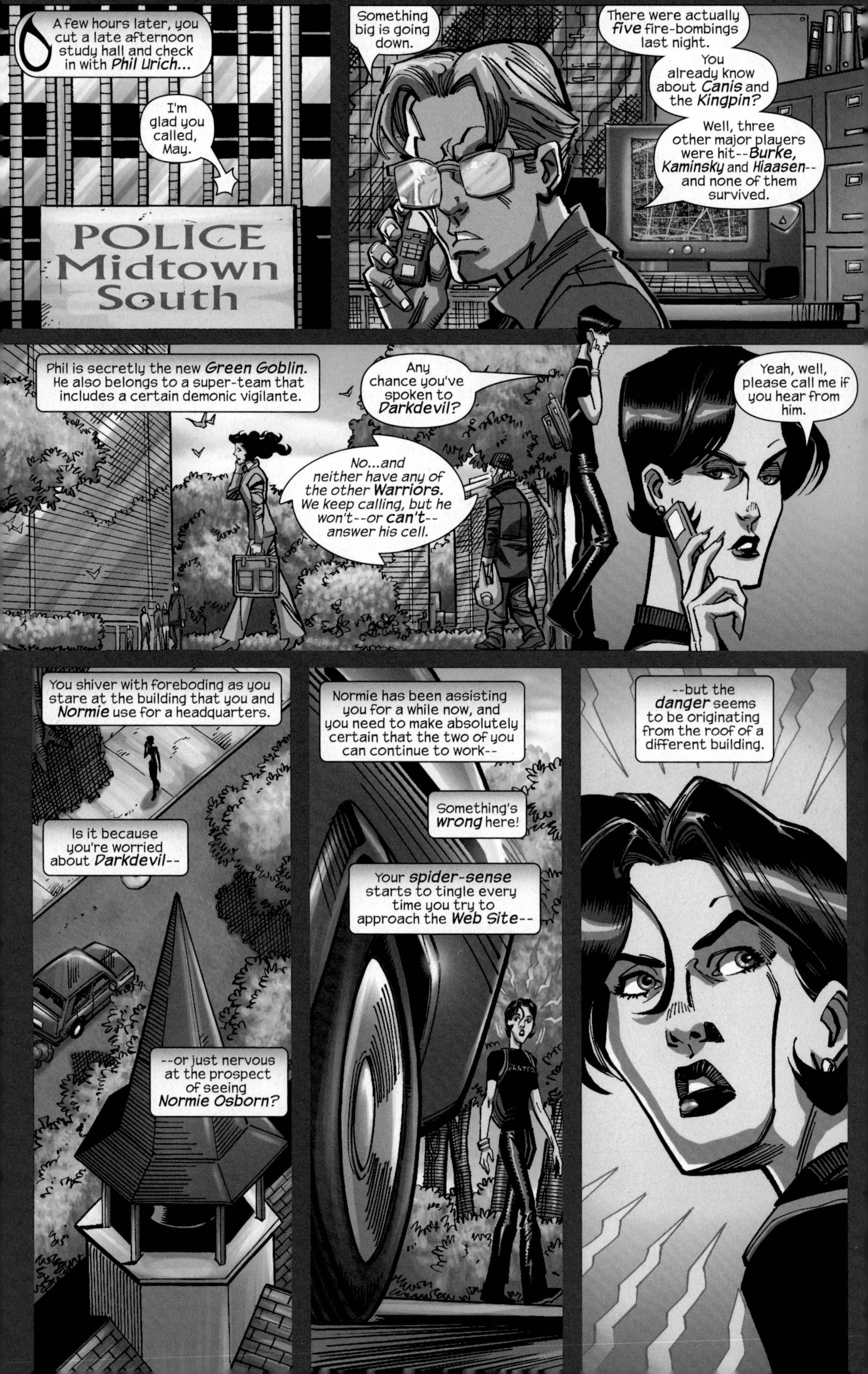
A few hours later, you cut a late afternoon study hall and check in with Phil Urich...
I'm glad you called, May.
POLICE Midtown South
Something big is going down.
There were actually five fire-bombings last night.
You already know about Canis and the Kingpin?
Well, three other major players were hit--Burke, Kaminsky and Hiaasen--and none of them survived.
Phil is secretly the new Green Goblin. He also belongs to a super-team that includes a certain demonic vigilante.
Any chance you've spoken to Darkdevil?
No...and neither have any of the other Warriors. We keep calling, but he won't--or can't--answer his cell.
Yeah, well, please call me if you hear from him.
You shiver with foreboding as you stare at the building that you and Normie use for a headquarters.
Is it because you're worried about Darkdevil--
--or just nervous at the prospect of seeing Normie Osborn?
Normie has been assisting you for a while now, and you need to make absolutely certain that the two of you can continue to work--
Something's wrong here!
Your spider-sense starts to tingle every time you try to approach the Web Site--
--but the danger seems to be originating from the roof of a different building.

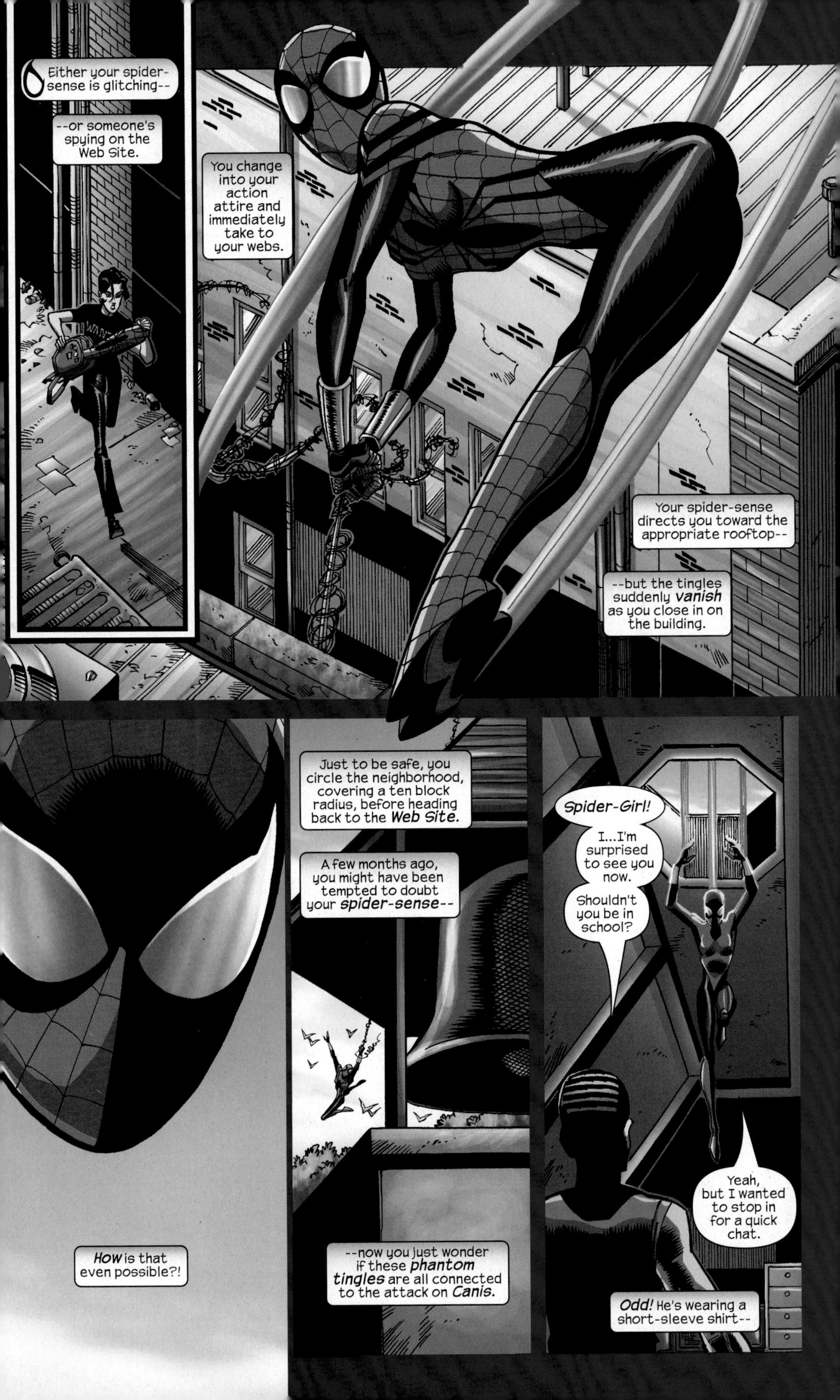
Either your spider-sense is glitching--
--or someone's spying on the Web Site.
You change into your action attire and immediately take to your webs.
Your spider-sense directs you toward the appropriate rooftop--
--but the tingles suddenly *vanish* as you close in on the building.
HOW is that even possible?!
Just to be safe, you circle the neighborhood, covering a ten block radius, before heading back to the *Web Site*.
A few months ago, you might have been tempted to doubt your *spider-sense*--
--now you just wonder if these *phantom tingles* are all connected to the attack on *Canis*.
Spider-Girl!
I...I'm surprised to see you now.
Shouldn't you be in school?
Yeah, but I wanted to stop in for a quick chat.
Odd! He's wearing a short-sleeve shirt--

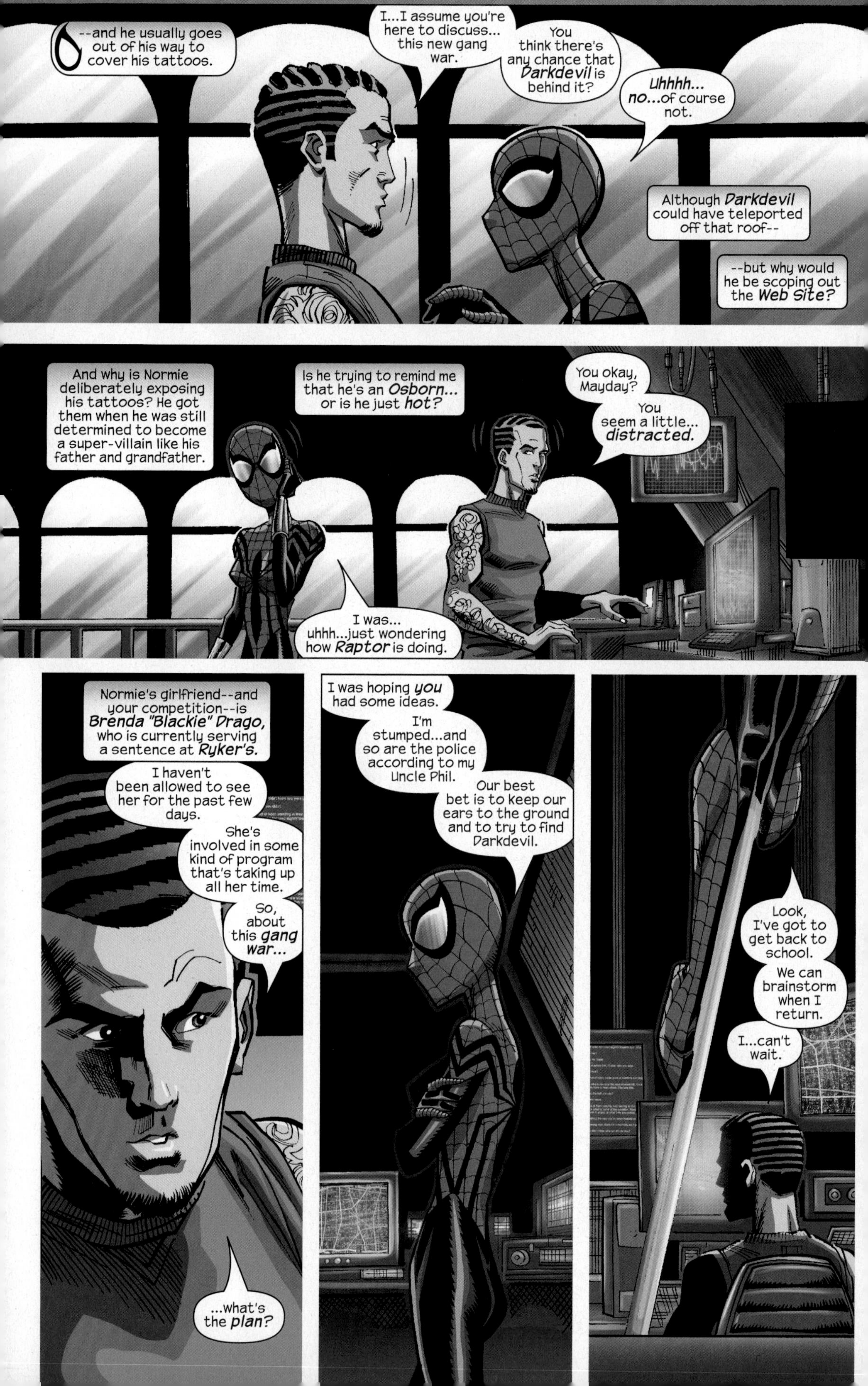

--and he usually goes out of his way to cover his tattoos.
I...I assume you're here to discuss... this new gang war.
You think there's any chance that Darkdevil is behind it?
Uhhhh... no...of course not.
Although Darkdevil could have teleported off that roof--
--but why would he be scoping out the Web Site?
And why is Normie deliberately exposing his tattoos? He got them when he was still determined to become a super-villain like his father and grandfather.
Is he trying to remind me that he's an Osborn... or is he just hot?
You okay, Mayday?
You seem a little... distracted.
I was... uhhh...just wondering how Raptor is doing.
Normie's girlfriend--and your competition--is Brenda "Blackie" Drago, who is currently serving a sentence at Ryker's.
I haven't been allowed to see her for the past few days.
She's involved in some kind of program that's taking up all her time.
So, about this gang war...
...what's the plan?
I was hoping you had some ideas.
I'm stumped...and so are the police according to my Uncle Phil.
Our best bet is to keep our ears to the ground and to try to find Darkdevil.
Look, I've got to get back to school.
We can brainstorm when I return.
I...can't wait.

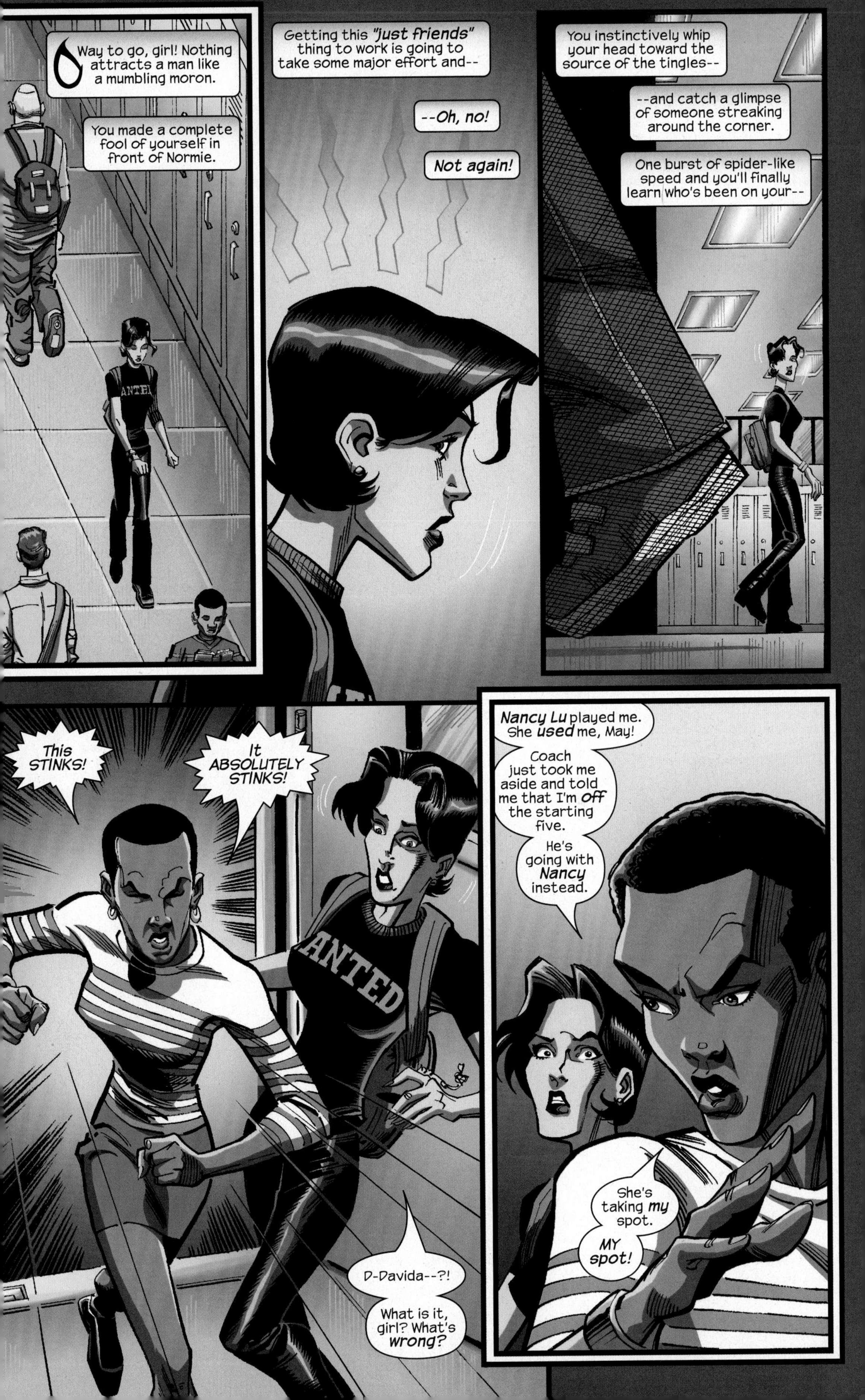

Way to go, girl! Nothing attracts a man like a mumbling moron.
You made a complete fool of yourself in front of Normie.
Getting this "just friends" thing to work is going to take some major effort and--
--Oh, no!
Not again!
You instinctively whip your head toward the source of the tingles--
--and catch a glimpse of someone streaking around the corner.
One burst of spider-like speed and you'll finally learn who's been on your--
This STINKS!
It ABSOLUTELY STINKS!
D-Davida--?!
What is it, girl? What's wrong?
Nancy Lu played me. She used me, May!
Coach just took me aside and told me that I'm off the starting five.
He's going with Nancy instead.
She's taking my spot.
MY spot!

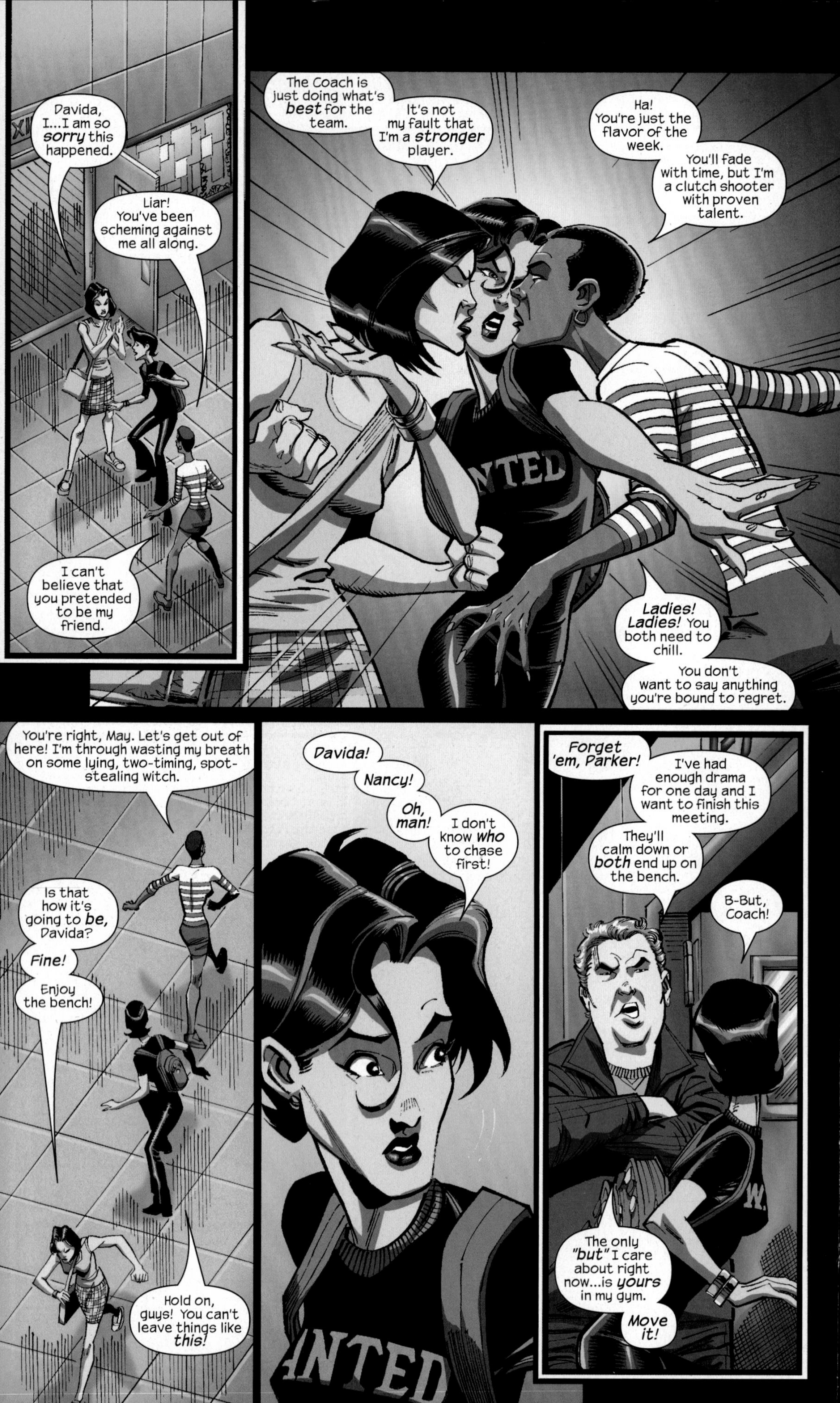

Davida, I...I am so *sorry* this happened.
Liar! You've been scheming against me all along.
I can't believe that you pretended to be my friend.
The Coach is just doing what's *best* for the team.
It's not my fault that I'm a *stronger* player.
Ha! You're just the flavor of the week.
You'll fade with time, but I'm a clutch shooter with proven talent.
Ladies! Ladies! You both need to chill.
You don't want to say anything you're bound to regret.
You're right, May. Let's get out of here! I'm through wasting my breath on some lying, two-timing, spot-stealing witch.
Is that how it's going to *be,* Davida?
Fine!
Enjoy the bench!
Hold on, guys! You can't leave things like *this!*
Davida!
Nancy!
Oh, man!
I don't know *who* to chase first!
Forget 'em, Parker!
I've had enough drama for one day and I want to finish this meeting.
They'll calm down or *both* end up on the bench.
B-But, Coach!
The only *"but"* I care about right now...is *yours* in my gym.
Move it!

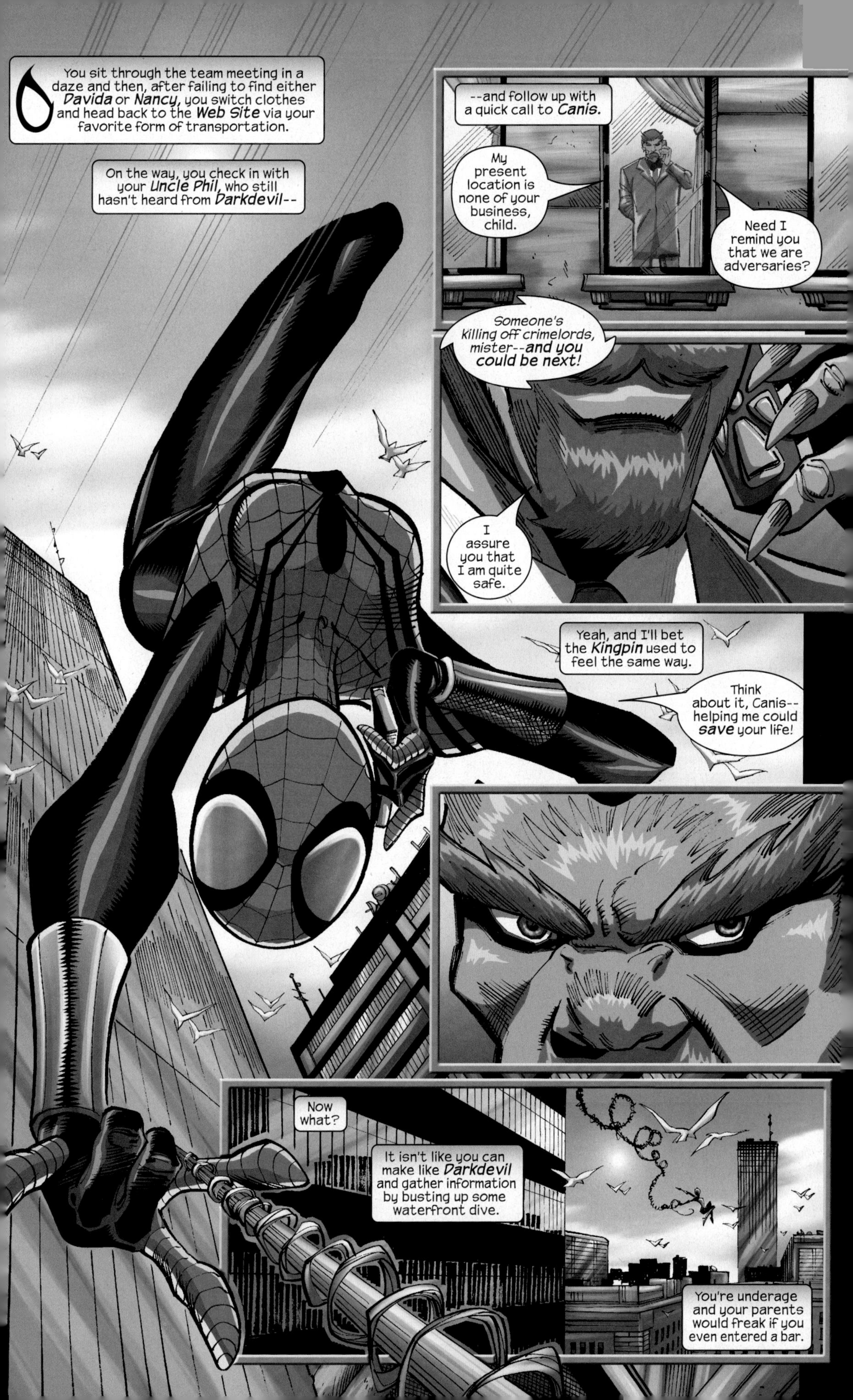
You sit through the team meeting in a daze and then, after failing to find either Davida or Nancy, you switch clothes and head back to the Web Site via your favorite form of transportation.
On the way, you check in with your Uncle Phil, who still hasn't heard from Darkdevil--
--and follow up with a quick call to Canis.
My present location is none of your business, child.
Need I remind you that we are adversaries?
Someone's killing off crimelords, mister--and you could be next!
I assure you that I am quite safe.
Yeah, and I'll bet the Kingpin used to feel the same way.
Think about it, Canis-- helping me could save your life!
Now what?
It isn't like you can make like Darkdevil and gather information by busting up some waterfront dive.
You're underage and your parents would freak if you even entered a bar.

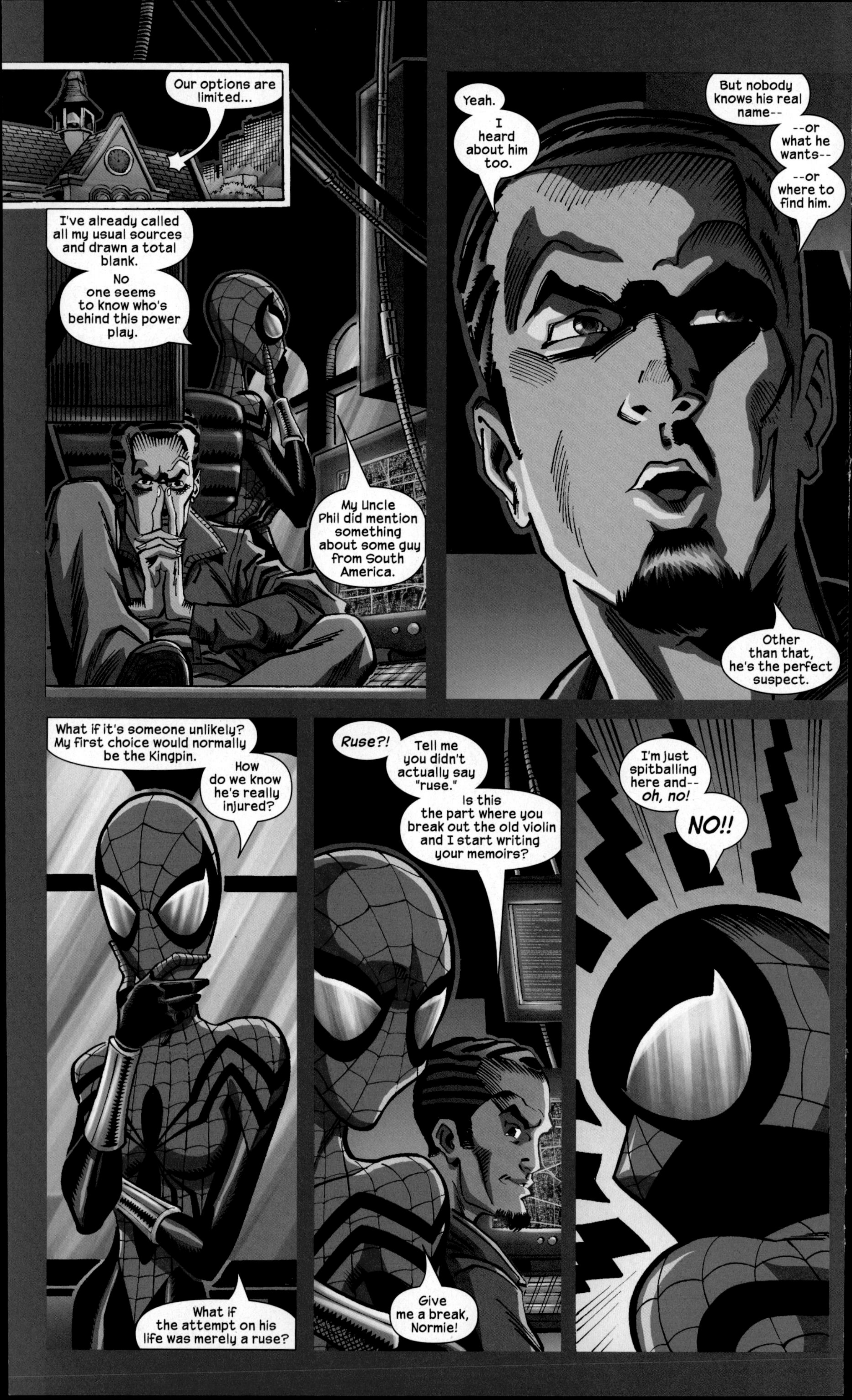

Our options are limited...
I've already called all my usual sources and drawn a total blank.
No one seems to know who's behind this power play.
My Uncle Phil did mention something about some guy from South America.
Yeah.
I heard about him too.
But nobody knows his real name--
--or what he wants--
--or where to find him.
Other than that, he's the perfect suspect.
What if it's someone unlikely? My first choice would normally be the Kingpin.
How do we know he's really injured?
What if the attempt on his life was merely a ruse?
Ruse?!
Tell me you didn't actually say "ruse."
Is this the part where you break out the old violin and I start writing your memoirs?
Give me a break, Normie!
I'm just spitballing here and-- oh, no!
NO!!

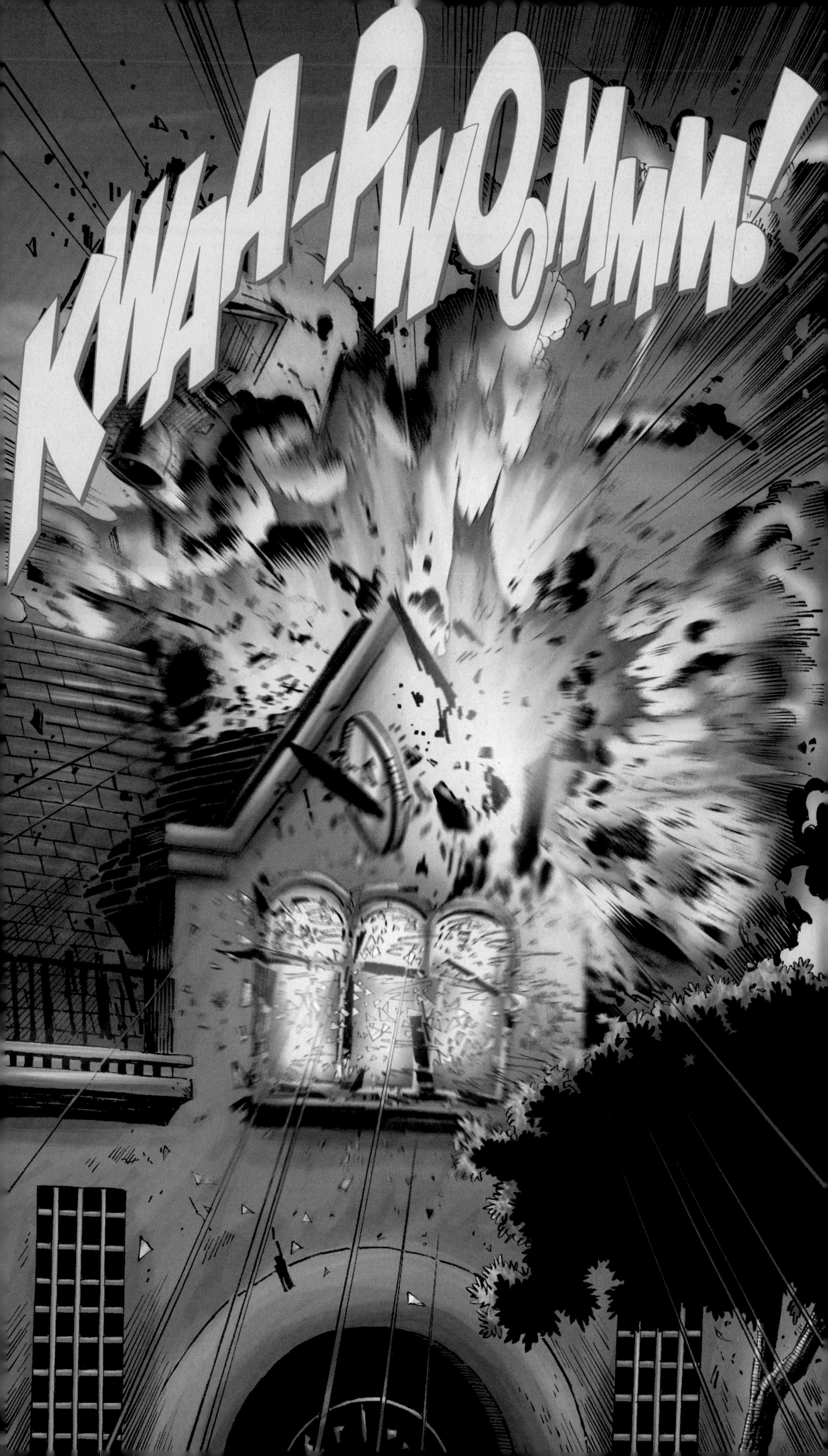
KWAA-PWOOMMM!

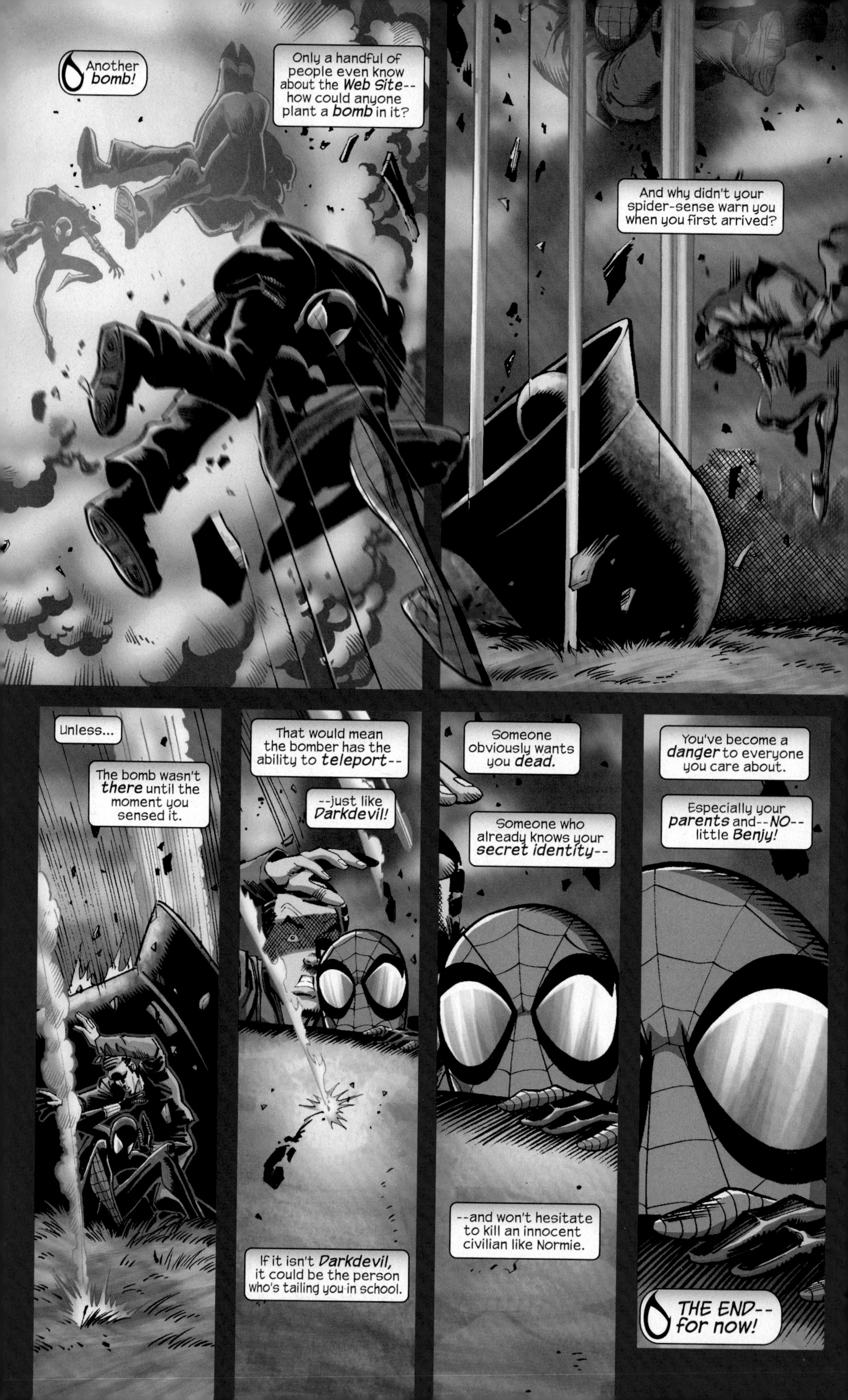

Another bomb!
Only a handful of people even know about the Web Site-- how could anyone plant a bomb in it?
And why didn't your spider-sense warn you when you first arrived?
Unless...
The bomb wasn't there until the moment you sensed it.
That would mean the bomber has the ability to teleport--
--just like Darkdevil!
If it isn't Darkdevil, it could be the person who's tailing you in school.
Someone obviously wants you dead.
Someone who already knows your secret identity--
--and won't hesitate to kill an innocent civilian like Normie.
You've become a danger to everyone you care about.
Especially your parents and--NO-- little Benjy!
THE END-- for now!

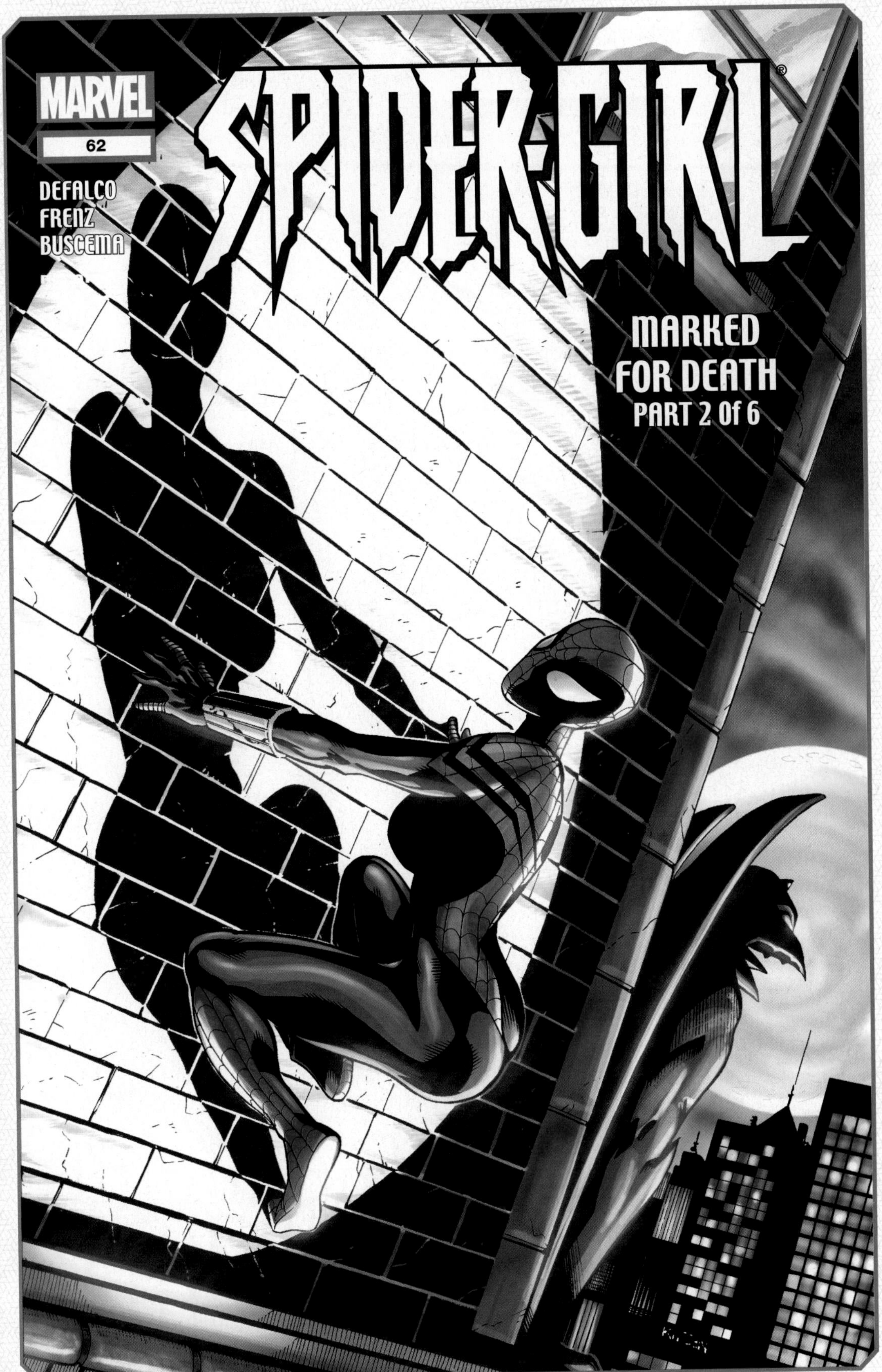

MARVEL
62
DEFALCO
FRENZ
BUSCEMA
SPIDER-GIRL
MARKED
FOR DEATH
PART 2 Of 6

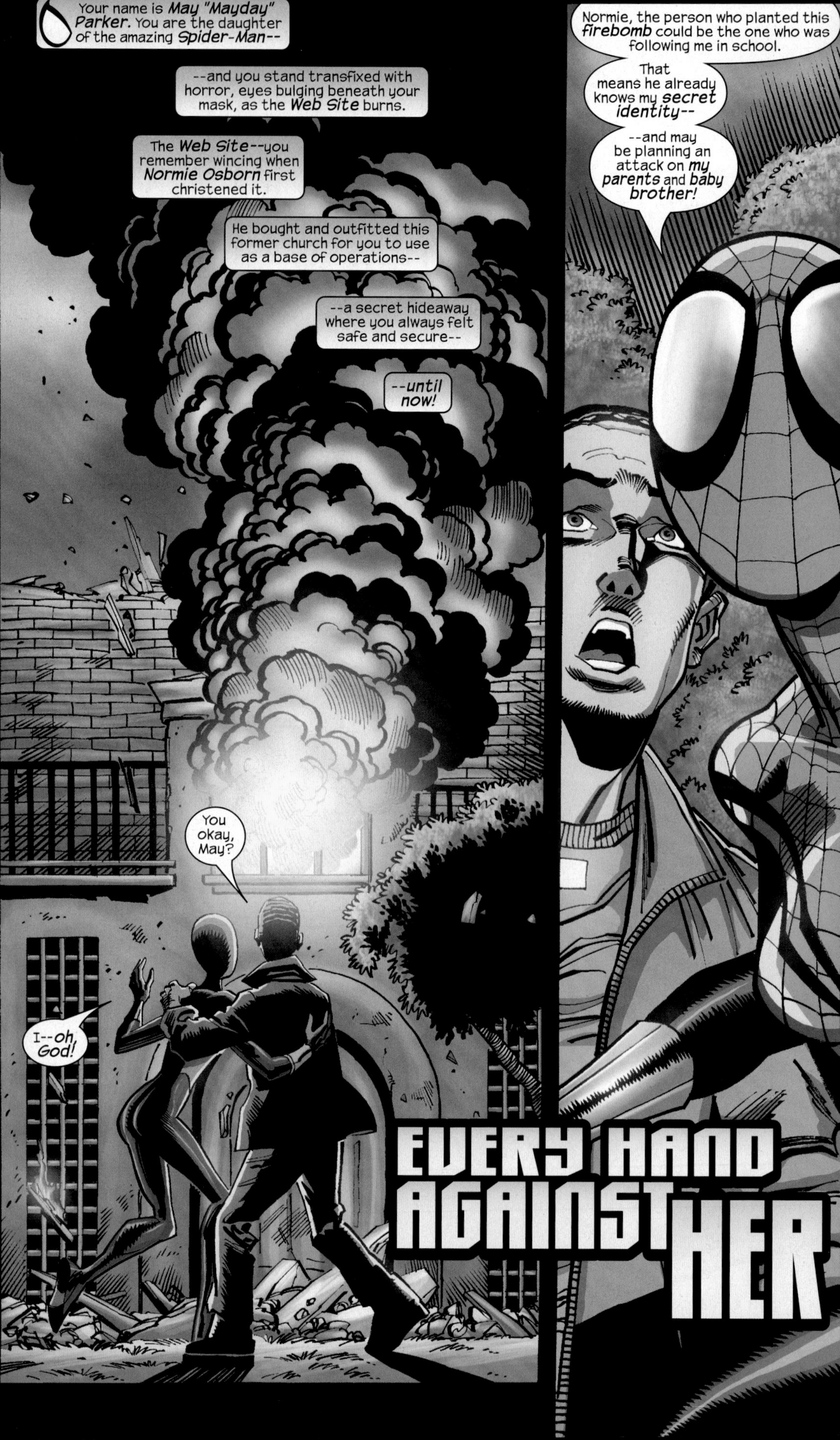
Your name is May "Mayday" Parker. You are the daughter of the amazing Spider-Man--
--and you stand transfixed with horror, eyes bulging beneath your mask, as the Web Site burns.
The Web Site--you remember wincing when Normie Osborn first christened it.
He bought and outfitted this former church for you to use as a base of operations--
--a secret hideaway where you always felt safe and secure--
--until now!
You okay, May?
I--oh, God!
Normie, the person who planted this firebomb could be the one who was following me in school.
That means he already knows my secret identity--
--and may be planning an attack on my parents and baby brother!
EVERY HAND AGAINST HER

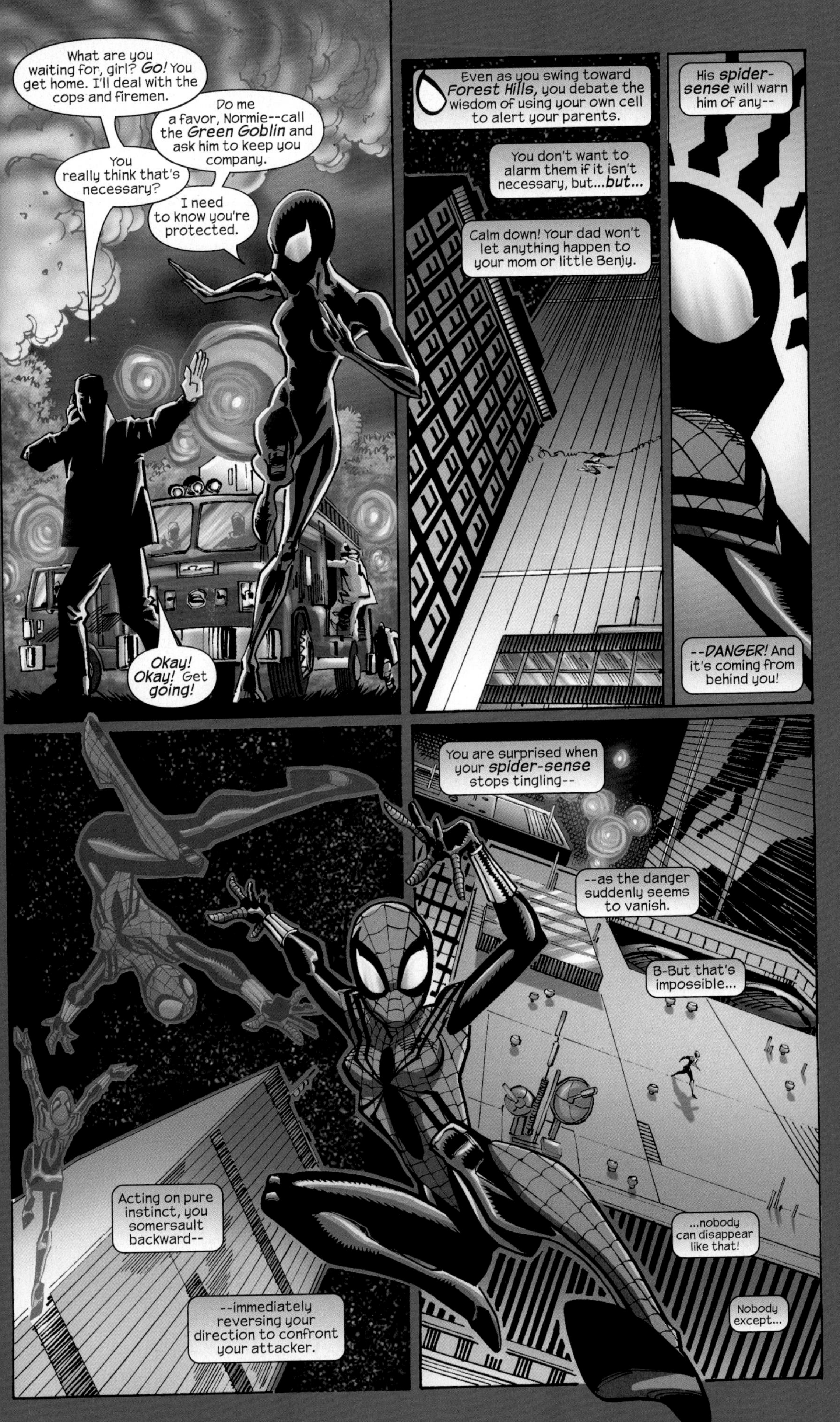
What are you waiting for, girl? Go! You get home. I'll deal with the cops and firemen.
Do me a favor, Normie--call the Green Goblin and ask him to keep you company.
You really think that's necessary?
I need to know you're protected.
Okay! Okay! Get going!
Even as you swing toward Forest Hills, you debate the wisdom of using your own cell to alert your parents.
You don't want to alarm them if it isn't necessary, but...but...
Calm down! Your dad won't let anything happen to your mom or little Benjy.
His spider-sense will warn him of any--
--DANGER! And it's coming from behind you!
Acting on pure instinct, you somersault backward--
--immediately reversing your direction to confront your attacker.
You are surprised when your spider-sense stops tingling--
--as the danger suddenly seems to vanish.
B-But that's impossible...
...nobody can disappear like that!
Nobody except...

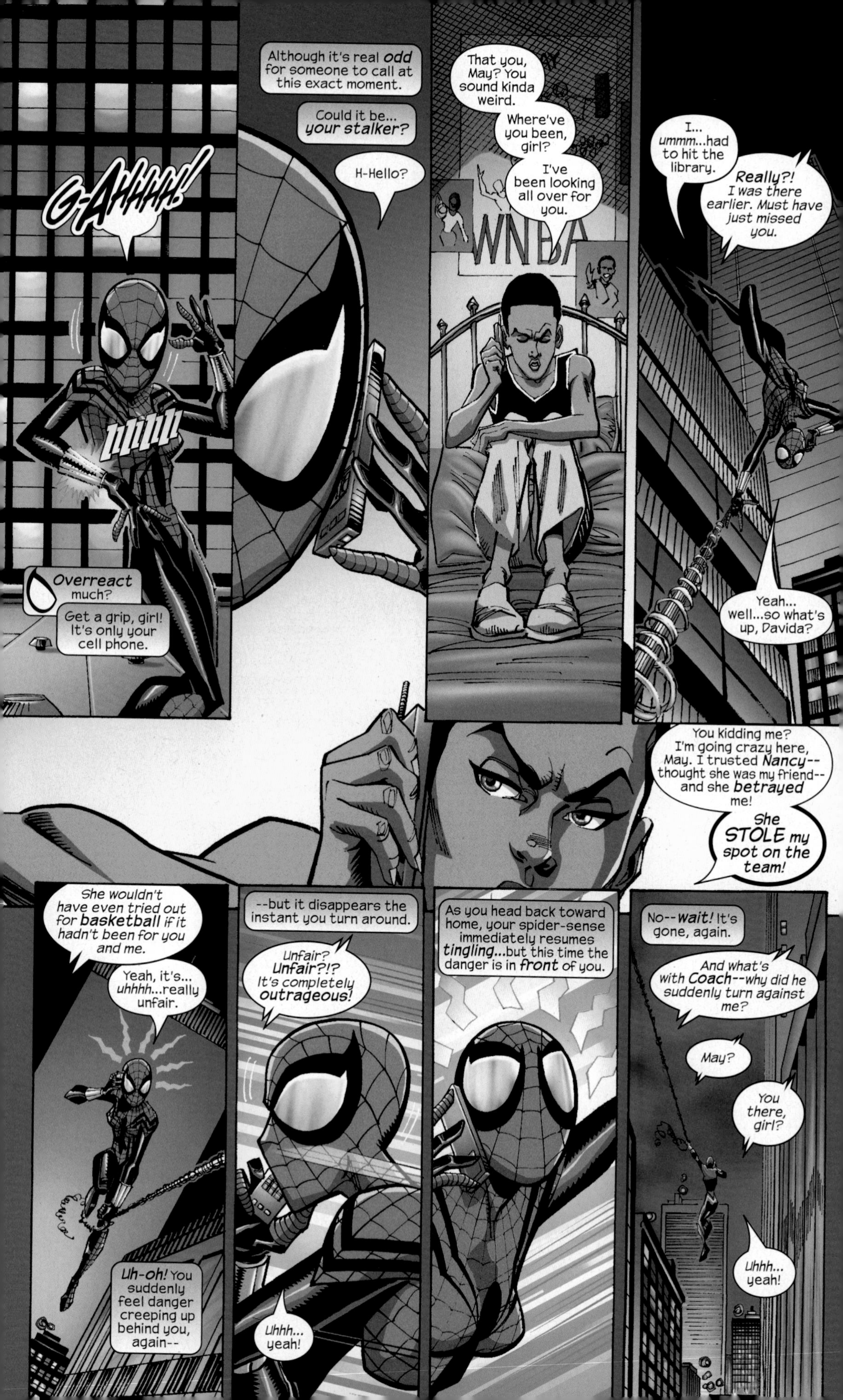

G-AHHHH!
BZZZZ
Overreact much?
Get a grip, girl! It's only your cell phone.
Although it's real odd for someone to call at this exact moment.
Could it be... your stalker?
H-Hello?
That you, May? You sound kinda weird.
Where've you been, girl?
I've been looking all over for you.
WNBA
I... ummm...had to hit the library.
Really?! I was there earlier. Must have just missed you.
Yeah... well...so what's up, Davida?
You kidding me? I'm going crazy here, May. I trusted Nancy--thought she was my friend--and she betrayed me!
She STOLE my spot on the team!
She wouldn't have even tried out for basketball if it hadn't been for you and me.
Yeah, it's... uhhhh...really unfair.
Uh-oh! You suddenly feel danger creeping up behind you, again--
--but it disappears the instant you turn around.
Unfair? Unfair?!? It's completely outrageous!
Uhhh... yeah!
As you head back toward home, your spider-sense immediately resumes tingling...but this time the danger is in front of you.
No--wait! It's gone, again.
And what's with Coach--why did he suddenly turn against me?
May?
You there, girl?
Uhhh... yeah!

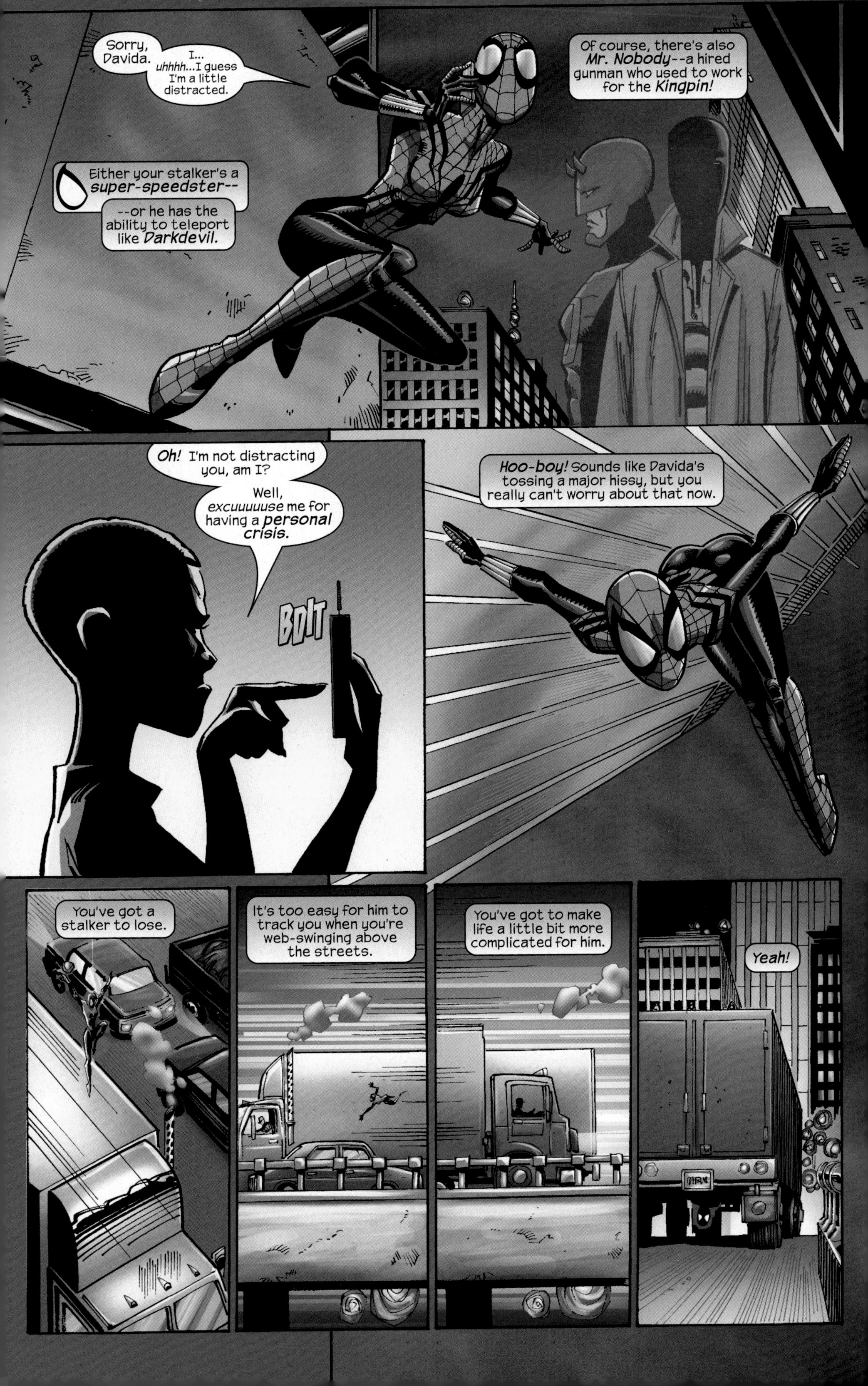
Sorry, Davida.
I... uhhhh...I guess I'm a little distracted.
Of course, there's also Mr. Nobody--a hired gunman who used to work for the Kingpin!
Either your stalker's a super-speedster--
--or he has the ability to teleport like Darkdevil.
Oh! I'm not distracting you, am I?
Well, excuuuuuse me for having a personal crisis.
BDIT
Hoo-boy! Sounds like Davida's tossing a major hissy, but you really can't worry about that now.
You've got a stalker to lose.
It's too easy for him to track you when you're web-swinging above the streets.
You've got to make life a little bit more complicated for him.
Yeah!

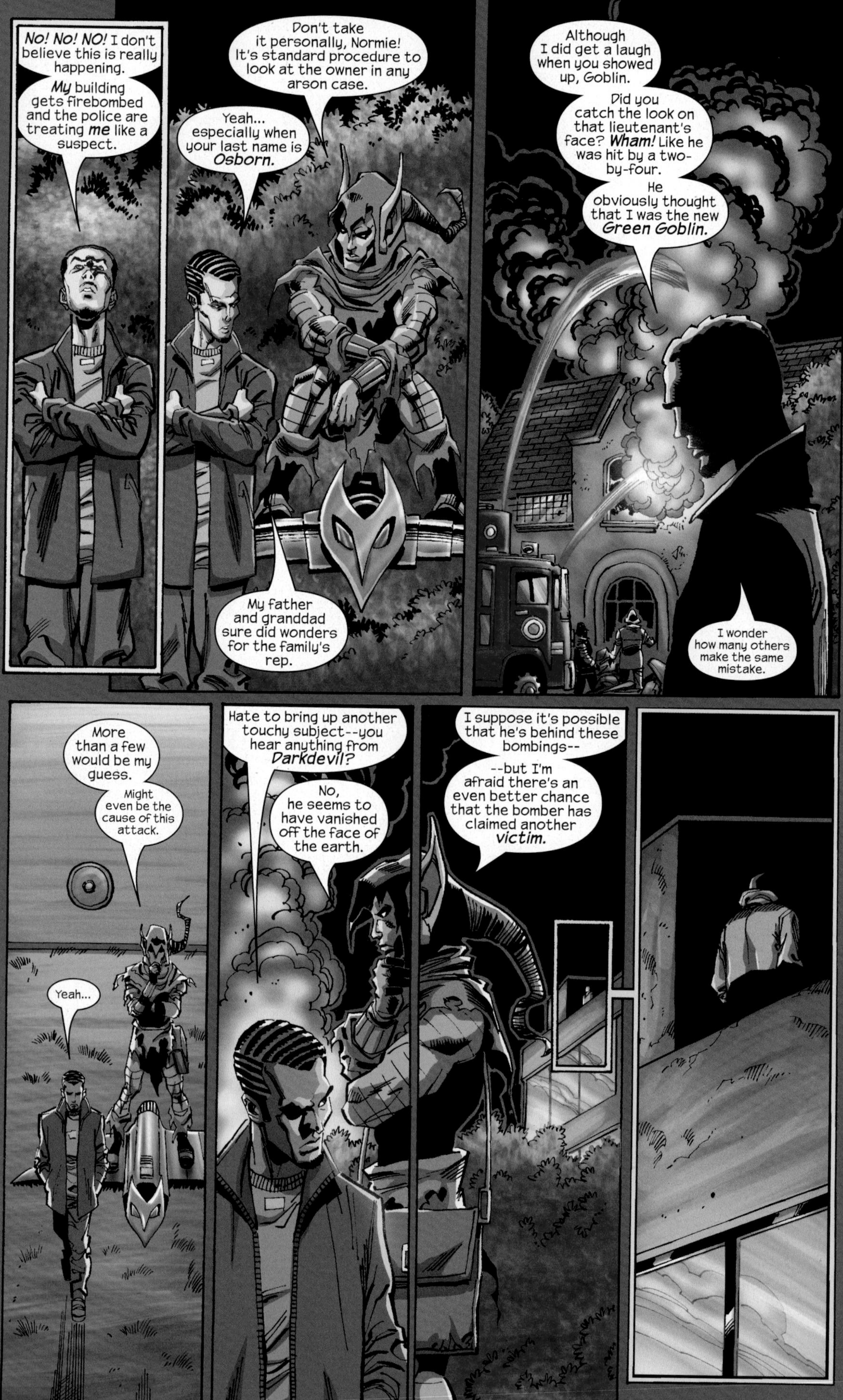
NO! NO! NO! I don't believe this is really happening.
My building gets firebombed and the police are treating me like a suspect.
Don't take it personally, Normie! It's standard procedure to look at the owner in any arson case.
Yeah... especially when your last name is Osborn.
My father and granddad sure did wonders for the family's rep.
Although I did get a laugh when you showed up, Goblin.
Did you catch the look on that lieutenant's face? Wham! Like he was hit by a two-by-four.
He obviously thought that I was the new Green Goblin.
I wonder how many others make the same mistake.
More than a few would be my guess.
Might even be the cause of this attack.
Yeah...
Hate to bring up another touchy subject--you hear anything from Darkdevil?
No, he seems to have vanished off the face of the earth.
I suppose it's possible that he's behind these bombings--
--but I'm afraid there's an even better chance that the bomber has claimed another victim.

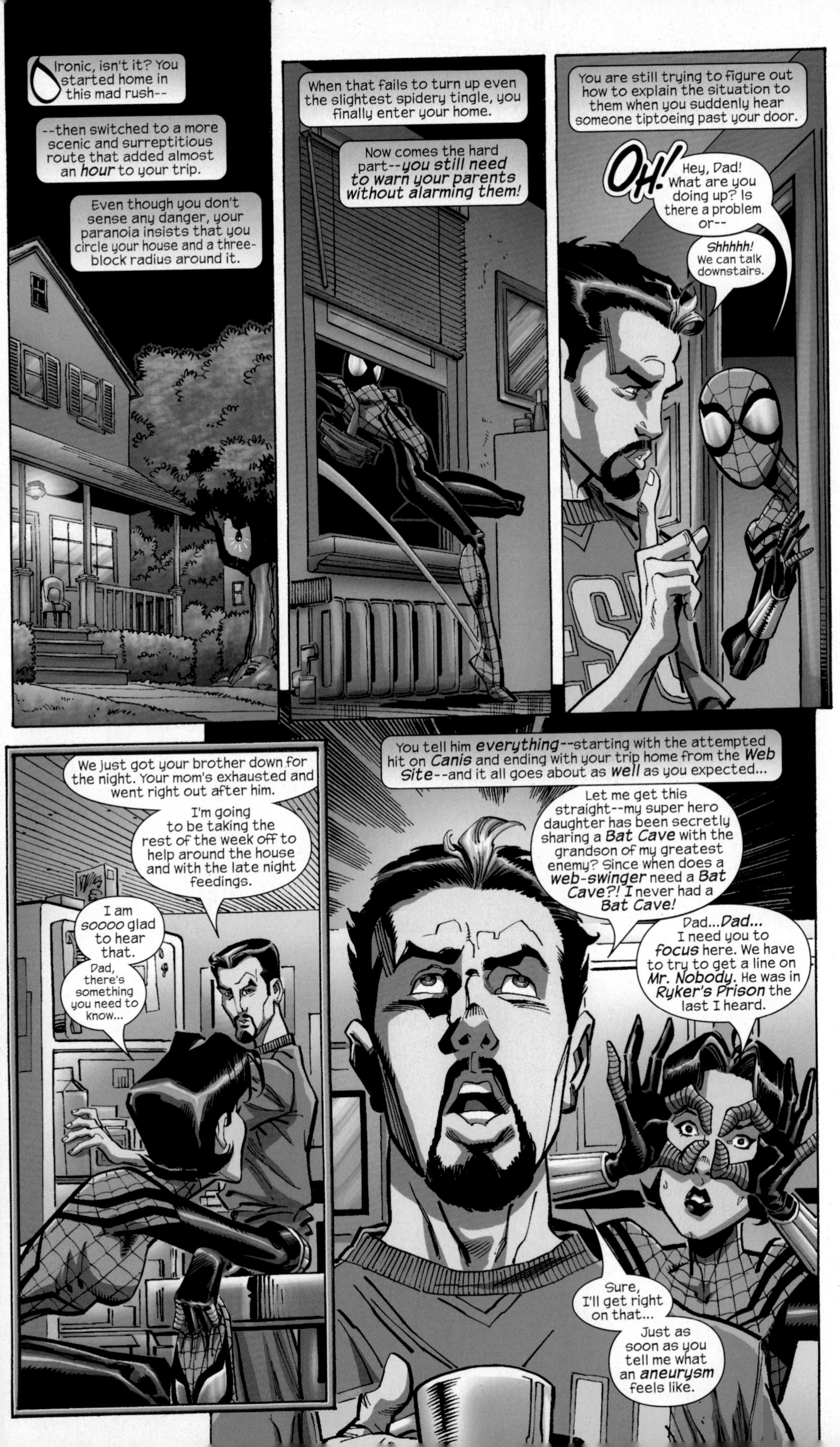

Ironic, isn't it? You started home in this mad rush--
--then switched to a more scenic and surreptitious route that added almost an *hour* to your trip.
Even though you don't sense any danger, your paranoia insists that you circle your house and a three-block radius around it.
When that fails to turn up even the slightest spidery tingle, you finally enter your home.
Now comes the hard part--*you still need to warn your parents without alarming them!*
You are still trying to figure out how to explain the situation to them when you suddenly hear someone tiptoeing past your door.
OH!
Hey, Dad! What are you doing up? Is there a problem or--
Shhhhh! We can talk downstairs.
We just got your brother down for the night. Your mom's exhausted and went right out after him.
I'm going to be taking the rest of the week off to help around the house and with the late night feedings.
I am *soooo* glad to hear that.
Dad, there's something you need to know...
You tell him *everything*--starting with the attempted hit on *Canis* and ending with your trip home from the *Web Site*--and it all goes about as *well* as you expected...
Let me get this straight--my super hero daughter has been secretly sharing a *Bat Cave* with the grandson of my greatest enemy? Since when does a *web-swinger* need a *Bat Cave?! I* never had a *Bat Cave!*
Dad...*Dad...* I need you to *focus* here. We have to try to get a line on *Mr. Nobody.* He was in *Ryker's Prison* the last I heard.
Sure, I'll get right on that...
Just as soon as you tell me what an *aneurysm* feels like.

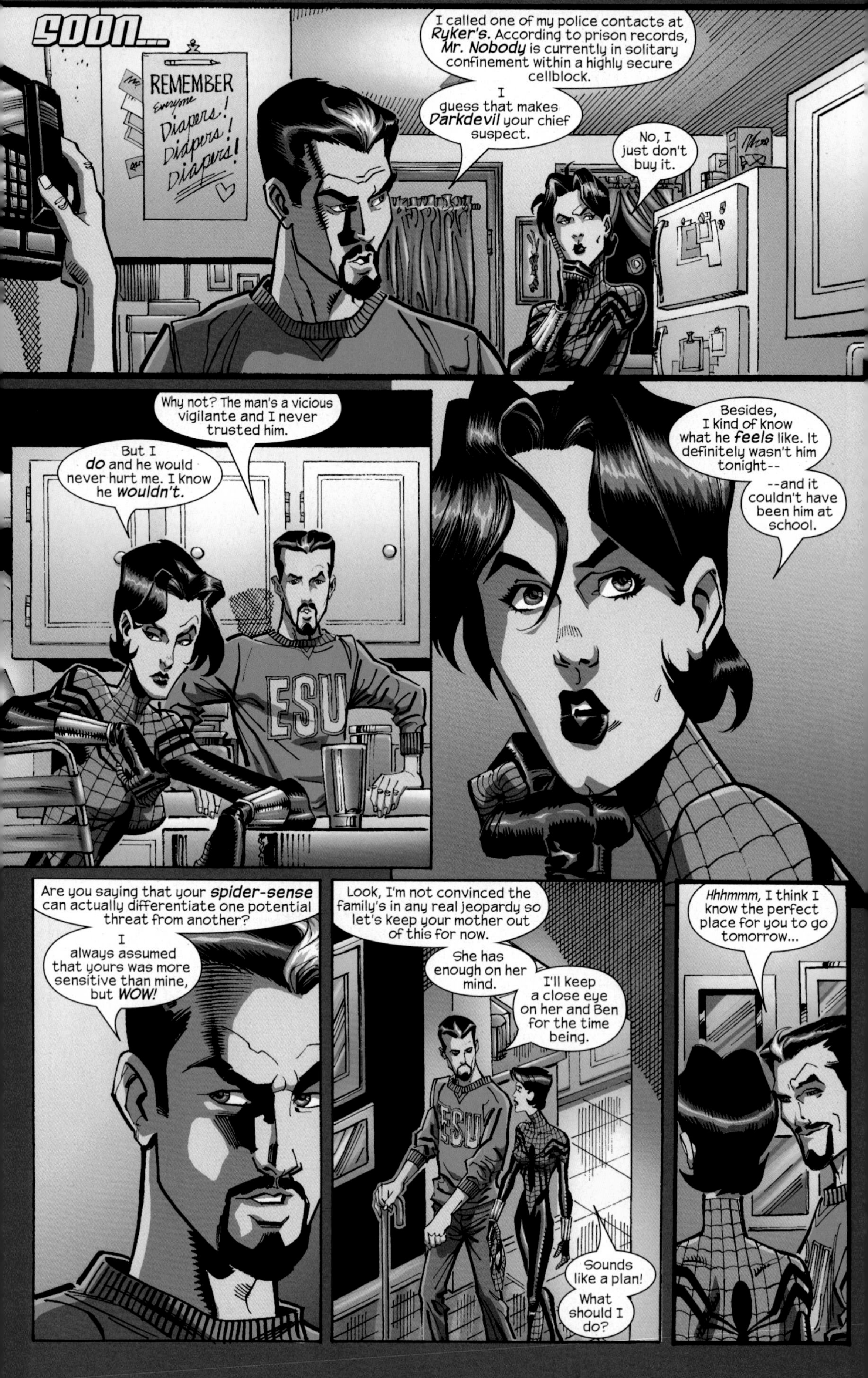
SOON...
REMEMBER Everyone Diapers! Diapers! Diapers!
I called one of my police contacts at Ryker's. According to prison records, Mr. Nobody is currently in solitary confinement within a highly secure cellblock.
I guess that makes Darkdevil your chief suspect.
No, I just don't buy it.
Why not? The man's a vicious vigilante and I never trusted him.
But I do and he would never hurt me. I know he wouldn't.
ESU
Besides, I kind of know what he feels like. It definitely wasn't him tonight--
--and it couldn't have been him at school.
Are you saying that your spider-sense can actually differentiate one potential threat from another?
I always assumed that yours was more sensitive than mine, but WOW!
Look, I'm not convinced the family's in any real jeopardy so let's keep your mother out of this for now.
She has enough on her mind.
I'll keep a close eye on her and Ben for the time being.
ESU
Sounds like a plan!
What should I do?
Hhhmmm, I think I know the perfect place for you to go tomorrow...

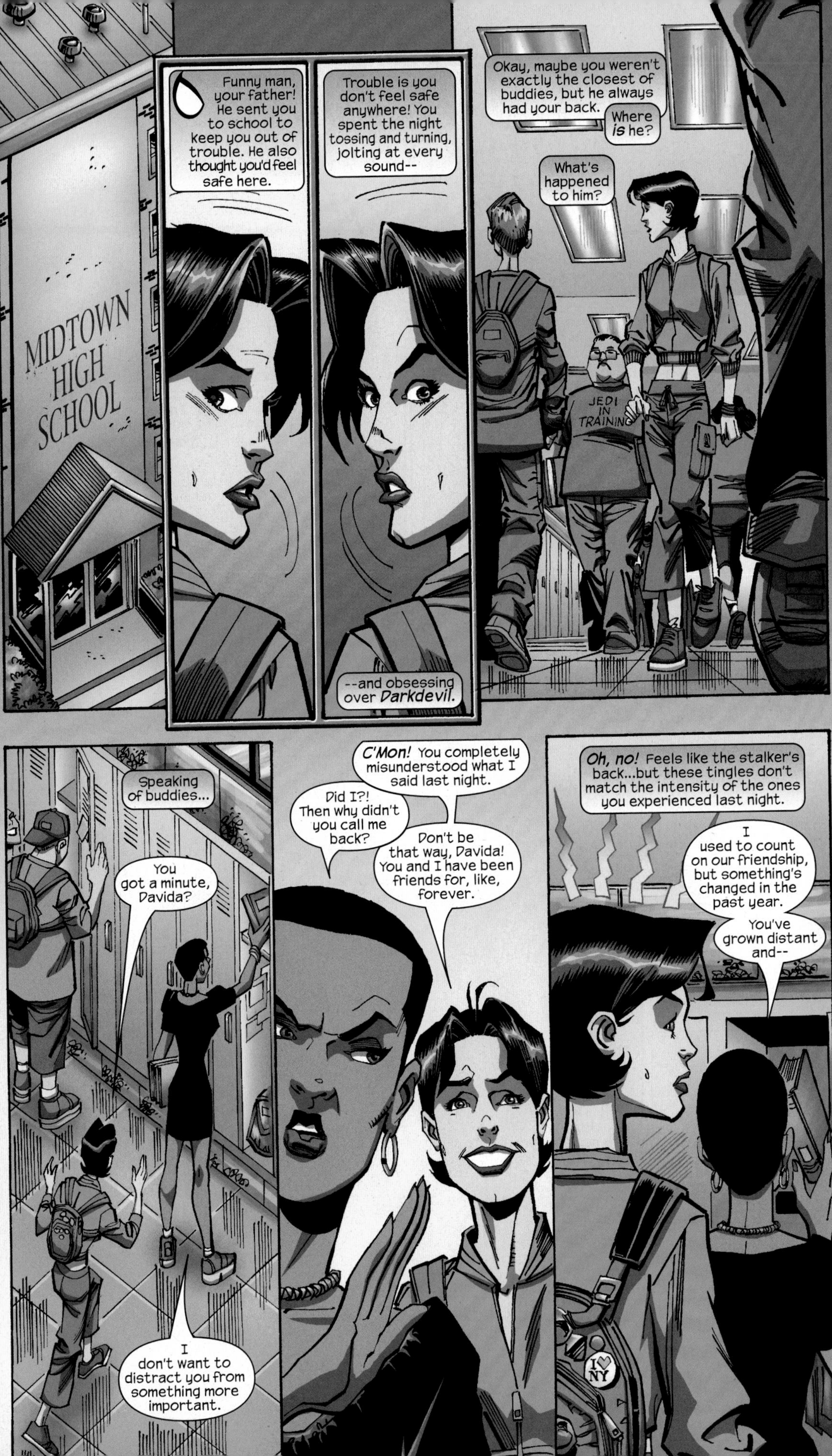
MIDTOWN HIGH SCHOOL
Funny man, your father! He sent you to school to keep you out of trouble. He also thought you'd feel safe here.
Trouble is you don't feel safe anywhere! You spent the night tossing and turning, jolting at every sound--
--and obsessing over Darkdevil.
Okay, maybe you weren't exactly the closest of buddies, but he always had your back.
Where is he?
What's happened to him?
JEDI IN TRAINING
Speaking of buddies...
You got a minute, Davida?
I don't want to distract you from something more important.
C'Mon! You completely misunderstood what I said last night.
Did I?! Then why didn't you call me back?
Don't be that way, Davida! You and I have been friends for, like, forever.
Oh, no! Feels like the stalker's back...but these tingles don't match the intensity of the ones you experienced last night.
I used to count on our friendship, but something's changed in the past year.
You've grown distant and--
I ♥ NY

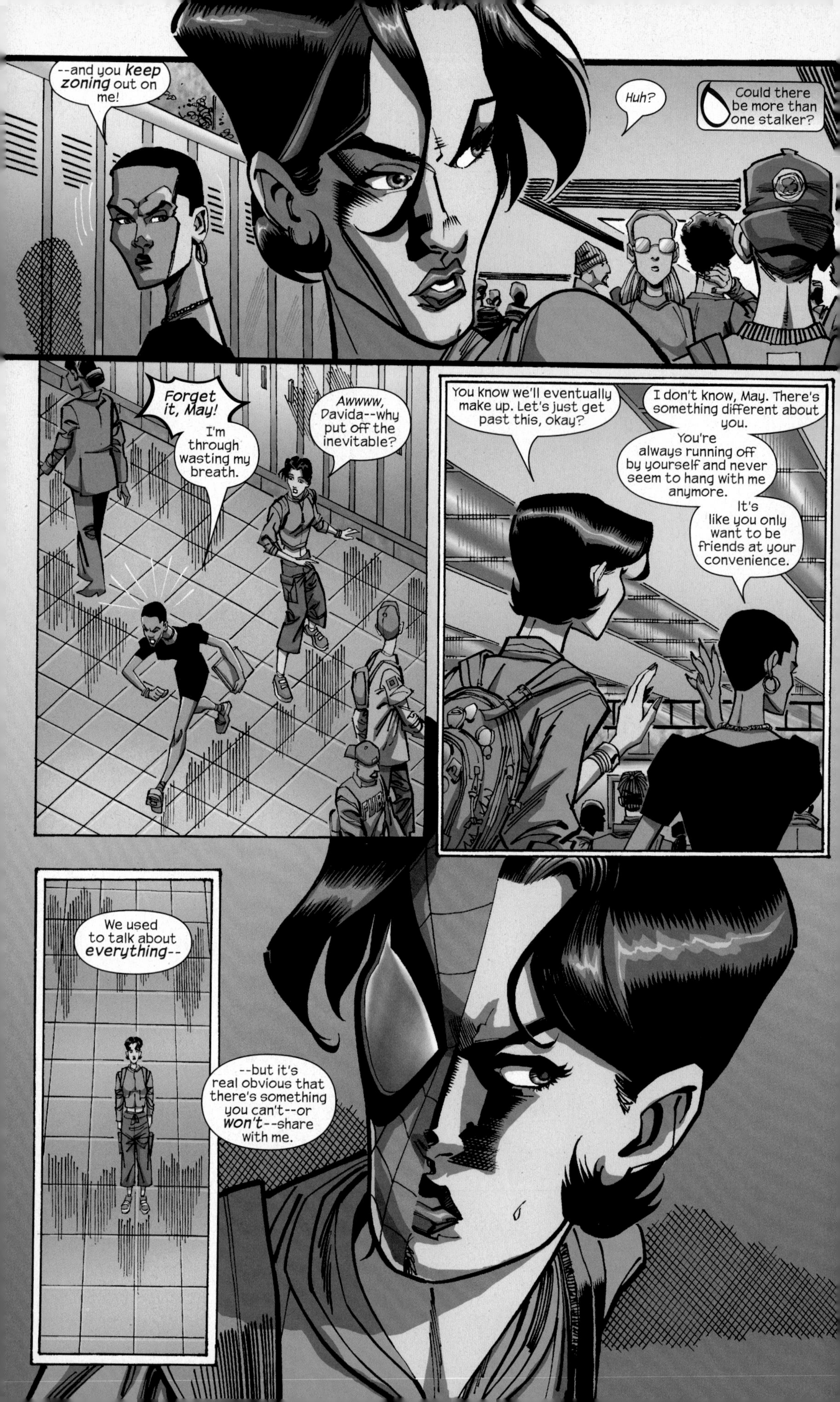
--and you keep zoning out on me!
Huh?
Could there be more than one stalker?
Forget it, May! I'm through wasting my breath.
Awwww, Davida--why put off the inevitable?
You know we'll eventually make up. Let's just get past this, okay?
I don't know, May. There's something different about you.
You're always running off by yourself and never seem to hang with me anymore.
It's like you only want to be friends at your convenience.
We used to talk about everything--
--but it's real obvious that there's something you can't--or won't--share with me.

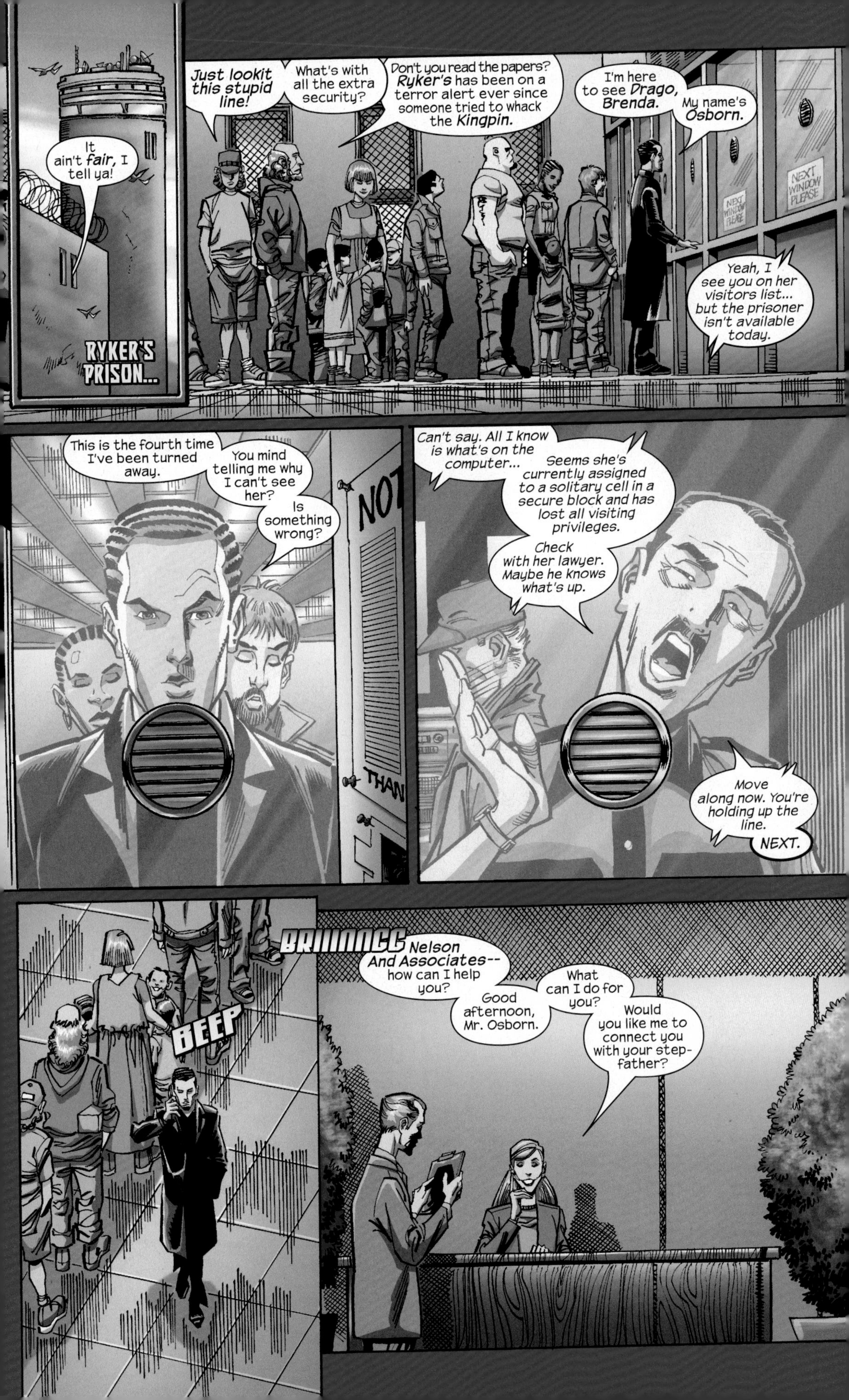

RYKER'S PRISON...
It ain't fair, I tell ya!
Just lookit this stupid line!
What's with all the extra security?
Don't you read the papers? Ryker's has been on a terror alert ever since someone tried to whack the Kingpin.
I'm here to see Drago, Brenda.
My name's Osborn.
NEXT WINDOW PLEASE
NEXT WINDOW PLEASE
Yeah, I see you on her visitors list... but the prisoner isn't available today.
This is the fourth time I've been turned away.
You mind telling me why I can't see her?
Is something wrong?
Can't say. All I know is what's on the computer...
Seems she's currently assigned to a solitary cell in a secure block and has lost all visiting privileges.
Check with her lawyer. Maybe he knows what's up.
Move along now. You're holding up the line.
NEXT.
BRIIINNGG
BEEP
Nelson And Associates-- how can I help you?
Good afternoon, Mr. Osborn.
What can I do for you?
Would you like me to connect you with your step-father?

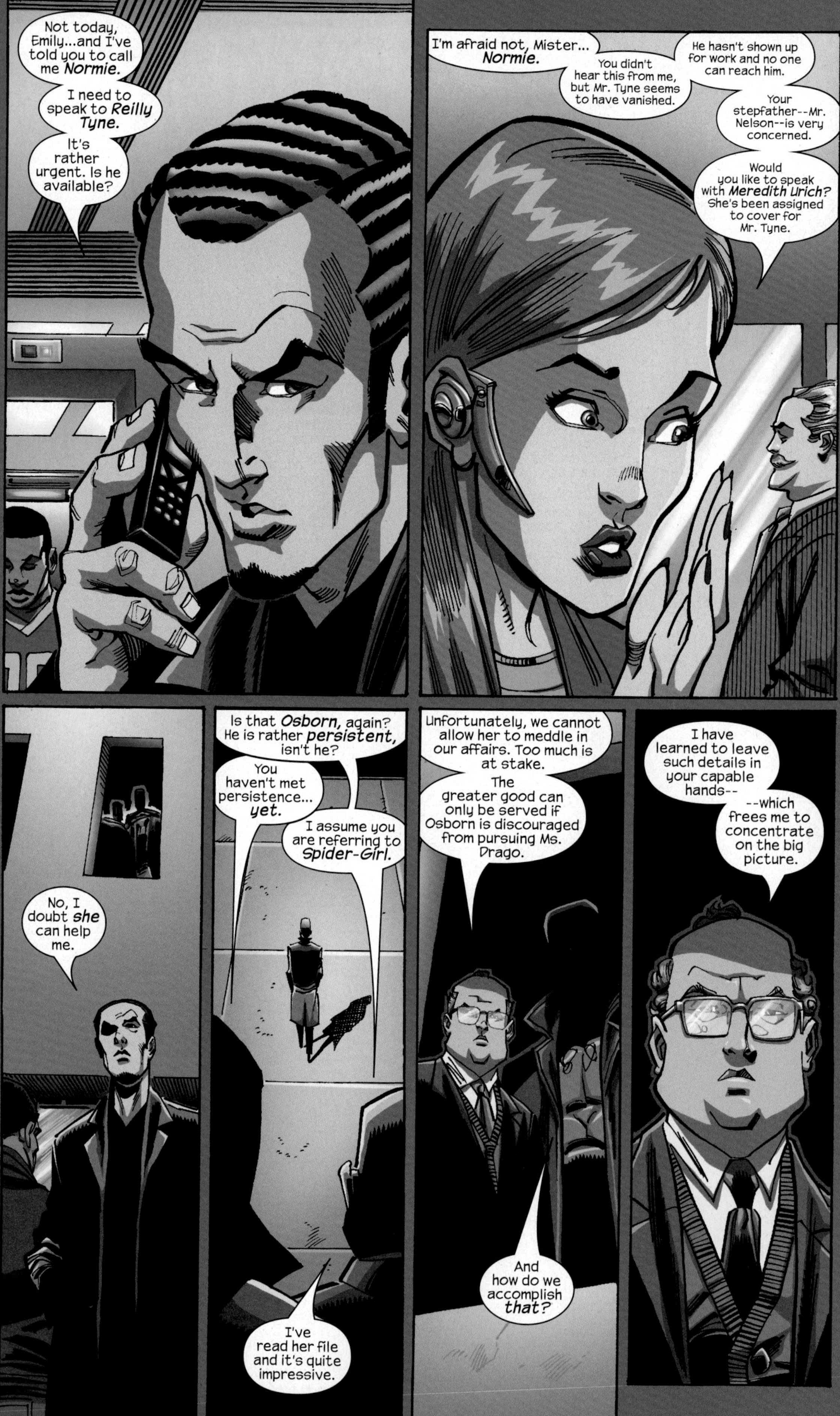
Not today, Emily...and I've told you to call me Normie.
I need to speak to Reilly Tyne.
It's rather urgent. Is he available?
I'm afraid not, Mister... Normie.
You didn't hear this from me, but Mr. Tyne seems to have vanished.
He hasn't shown up for work and no one can reach him.
Your stepfather--Mr. Nelson--is very concerned.
Would you like to speak with Meredith Urich? She's been assigned to cover for Mr. Tyne.
No, I doubt she can help me.
Is that Osborn, again? He is rather persistent, isn't he?
You haven't met persistence... yet.
I assume you are referring to Spider-Girl.
I've read her file and it's quite impressive.
Unfortunately, we cannot allow her to meddle in our affairs. Too much is at stake.
The greater good can only be served if Osborn is discouraged from pursuing Ms. Drago.
And how do we accomplish that?
I have learned to leave such details in your capable hands--
--which frees me to concentrate on the big picture.

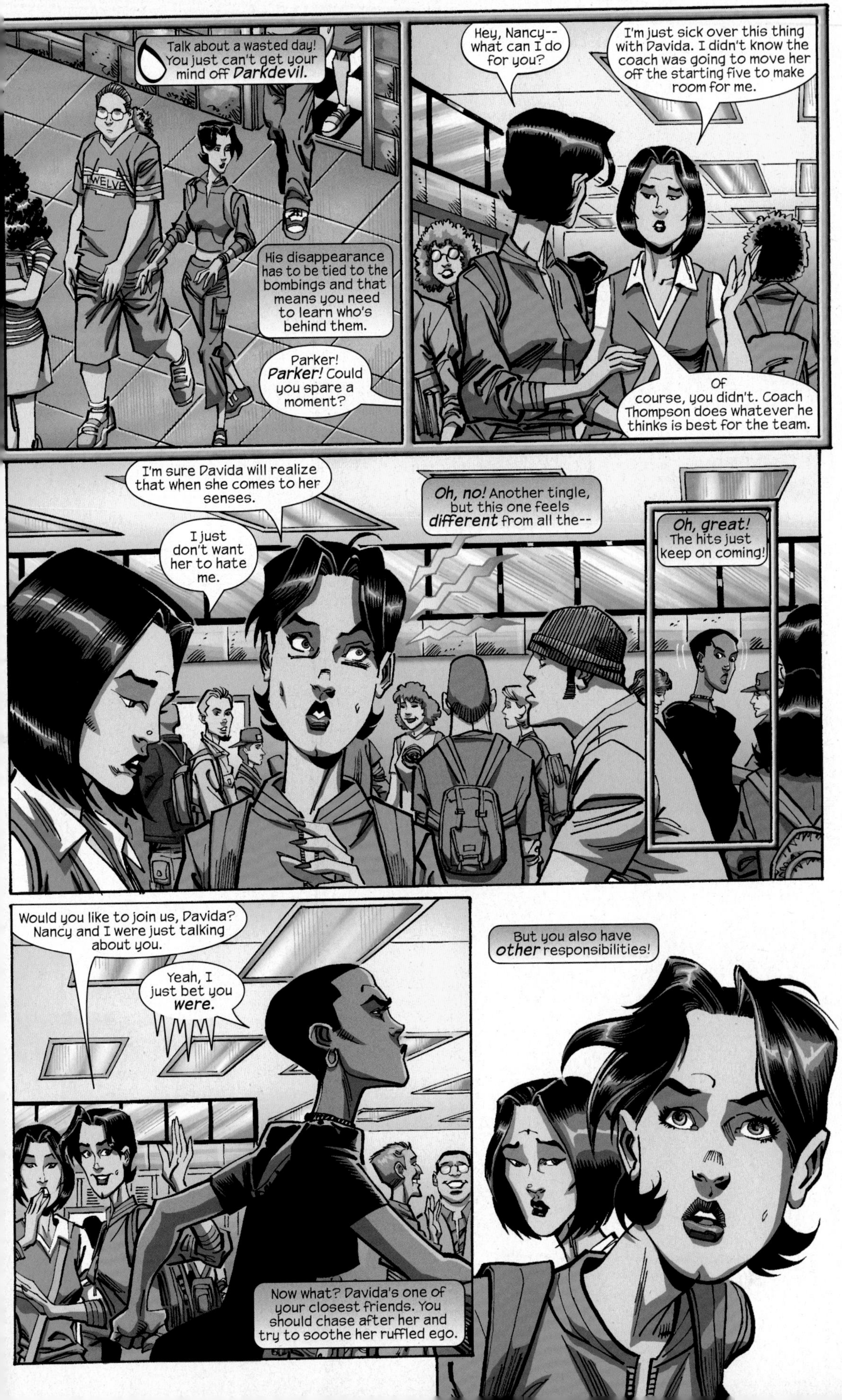

Talk about a wasted day! You just can't get your mind off Darkdevil.
TWELVE
His disappearance has to be tied to the bombings and that means you need to learn who's behind them.
Parker! Parker! Could you spare a moment?
Hey, Nancy-- what can I do for you?
I'm just sick over this thing with Davida. I didn't know the coach was going to move her off the starting five to make room for me.
Of course, you didn't. Coach Thompson does whatever he thinks is best for the team.
I'm sure Davida will realize that when she comes to her senses.
I just don't want her to hate me.
Oh, no! Another tingle, but this one feels different from all the--
Oh, great! The hits just keep on coming!
Would you like to join us, Davida? Nancy and I were just talking about you.
Yeah, I just bet you were.
But you also have other responsibilities!
Now what? Davida's one of your closest friends. You should chase after her and try to soothe her ruffled ego.

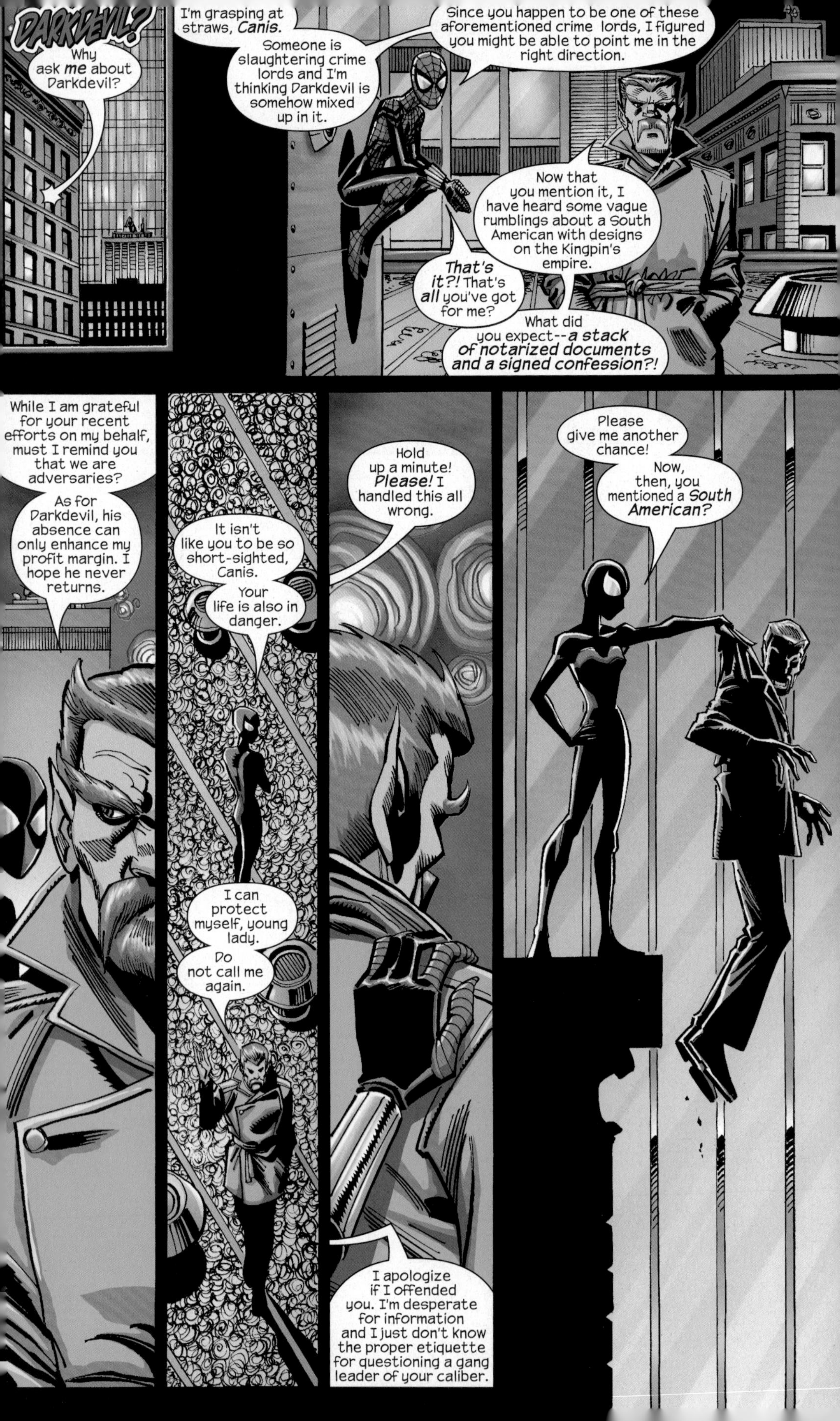
DARKDEVIL?
Why ask me about Darkdevil?
I'm grasping at straws, Canis.
Someone is slaughtering crime lords and I'm thinking Darkdevil is somehow mixed up in it.
Since you happen to be one of these aforementioned crime lords, I figured you might be able to point me in the right direction.
Now that you mention it, I have heard some vague rumblings about a South American with designs on the Kingpin's empire.
That's it?! That's all you've got for me?
What did you expect--a stack of notarized documents and a signed confession?!
While I am grateful for your recent efforts on my behalf, must I remind you that we are adversaries?
As for Darkdevil, his absence can only enhance my profit margin. I hope he never returns.
It isn't like you to be so short-sighted, Canis.
Your life is also in danger.
I can protect myself, young lady.
Do not call me again.
Hold up a minute! Please! I handled this all wrong.
I apologize if I offended you. I'm desperate for information and I just don't know the proper etiquette for questioning a gang leader of your caliber.
Please give me another chance!
Now, then, you mentioned a South American?

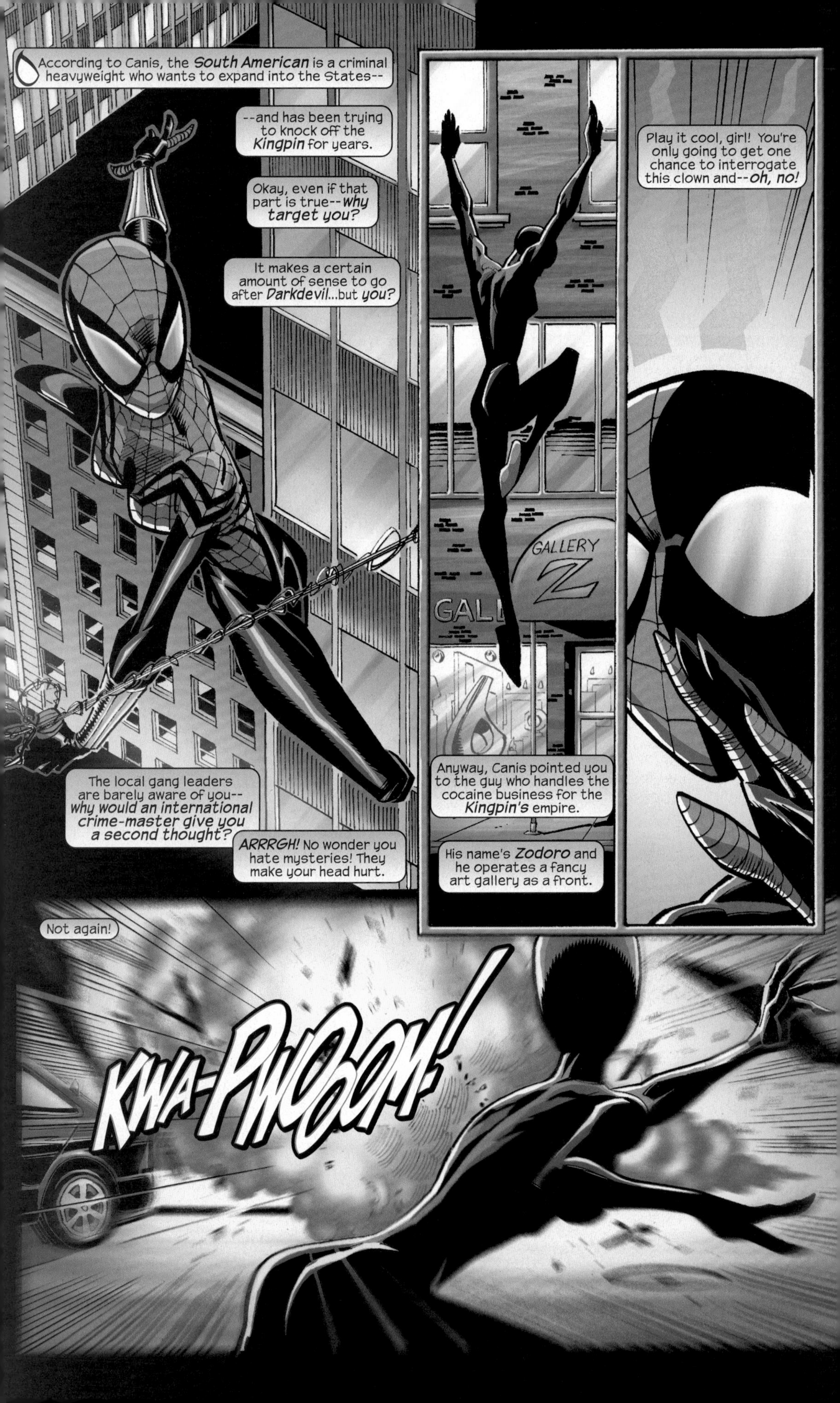

According to Canis, the South American is a criminal heavyweight who wants to expand into the States--
--and has been trying to knock off the Kingpin for years.
Okay, even if that part is true--why target you?
It makes a certain amount of sense to go after Darkdevil...but you?
The local gang leaders are barely aware of you--why would an international crime-master give you a second thought?
ARRRGH! No wonder you hate mysteries! They make your head hurt.
GALLERY Z
GALL
Anyway, Canis pointed you to the guy who handles the cocaine business for the Kingpin's empire.
His name's Zodoro and he operates a fancy art gallery as a front.
Play it cool, girl! You're only going to get one chance to interrogate this clown and--oh, no!
Not again!
KWA-PWOOM!

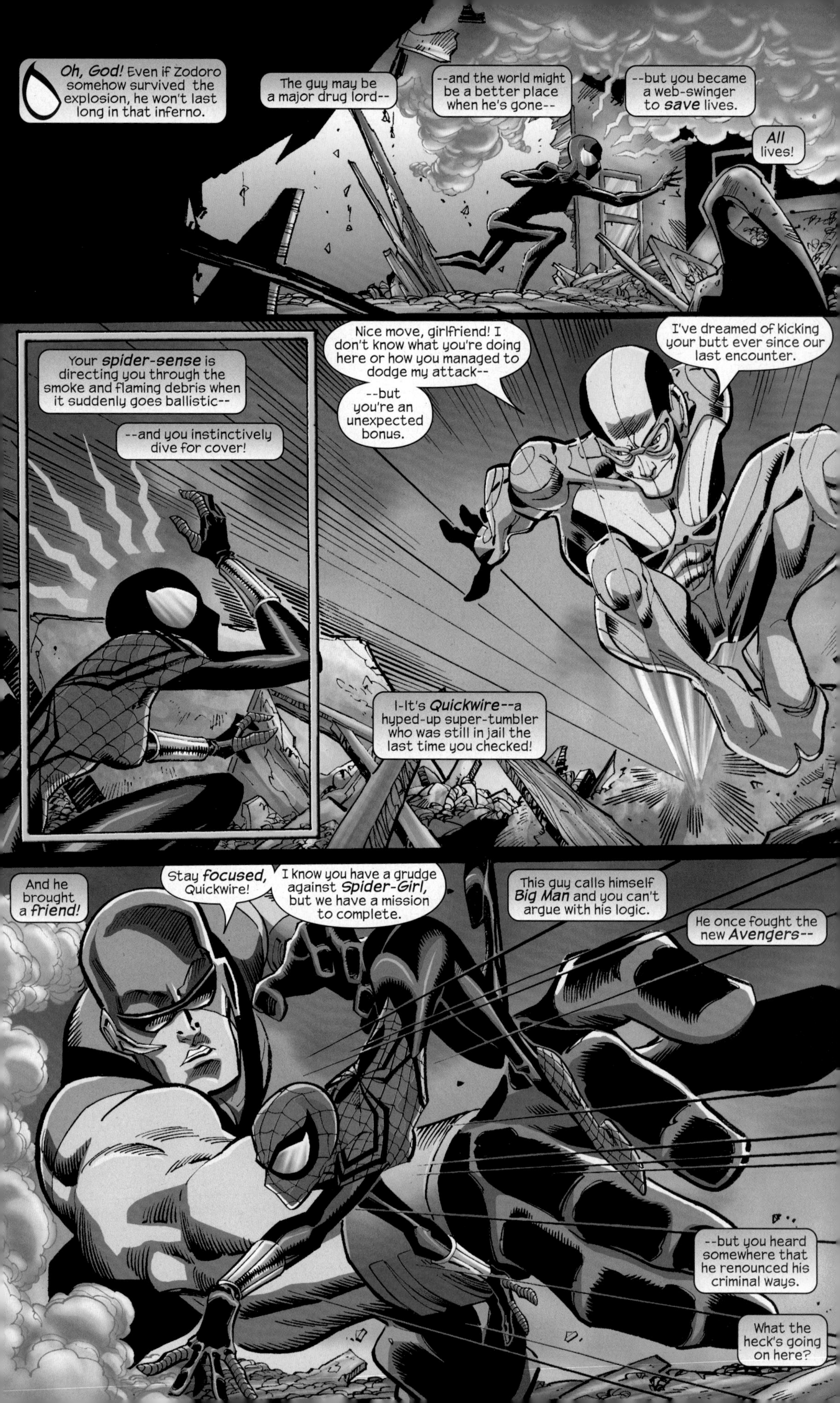

Oh, God! Even if Zodoro somehow survived the explosion, he won't last long in that inferno.
The guy may be a major drug lord--
--and the world might be a better place when he's gone--
--but you became a web-swinger to save lives.
All lives!
Your spider-sense is directing you through the smoke and flaming debris when it suddenly goes ballistic--
--and you instinctively dive for cover!
Nice move, girlfriend! I don't know what you're doing here or how you managed to dodge my attack--
--but you're an unexpected bonus.
I've dreamed of kicking your butt ever since our last encounter.
I-It's Quickwire--a hyped-up super-tumbler who was still in jail the last time you checked!
And he brought a friend!
Stay focused, Quickwire!
I know you have a grudge against Spider-Girl, but we have a mission to complete.
This guy calls himself Big Man and you can't argue with his logic.
He once fought the new Avengers--
--but you heard somewhere that he renounced his criminal ways.
What the heck's going on here?

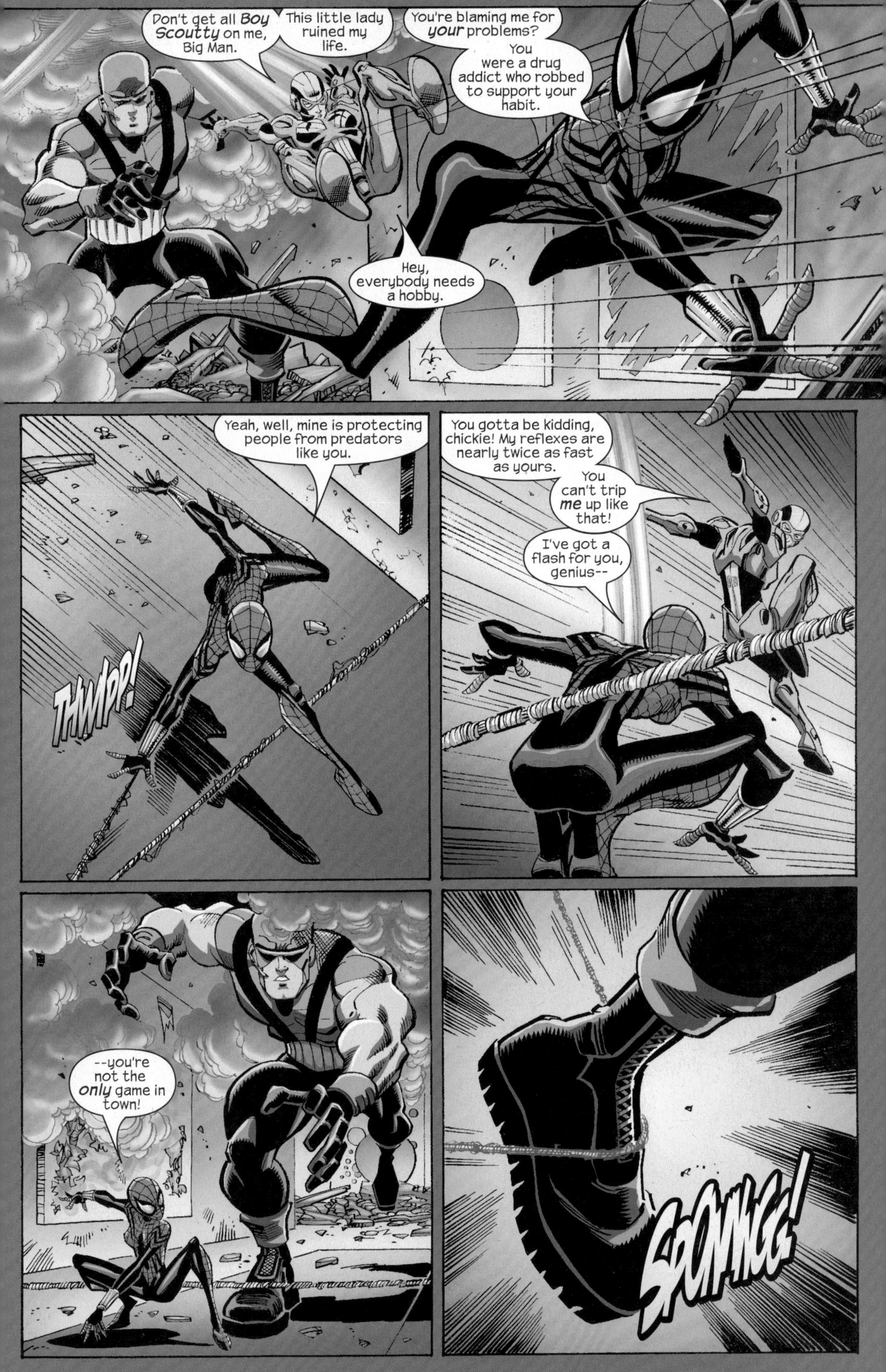

Don't get all Boy Scoutty on me, Big Man.
This little lady ruined my life.
You're blaming me for your problems?
You were a drug addict who robbed to support your habit.
Hey, everybody needs a hobby.
Yeah, well, mine is protecting people from predators like you.
THWIPP!
You gotta be kidding, chickie! My reflexes are nearly twice as fast as yours.
You can't trip me up like that!
I've got a flash for you, genius--
--you're not the only game in town!
SPONNGG!

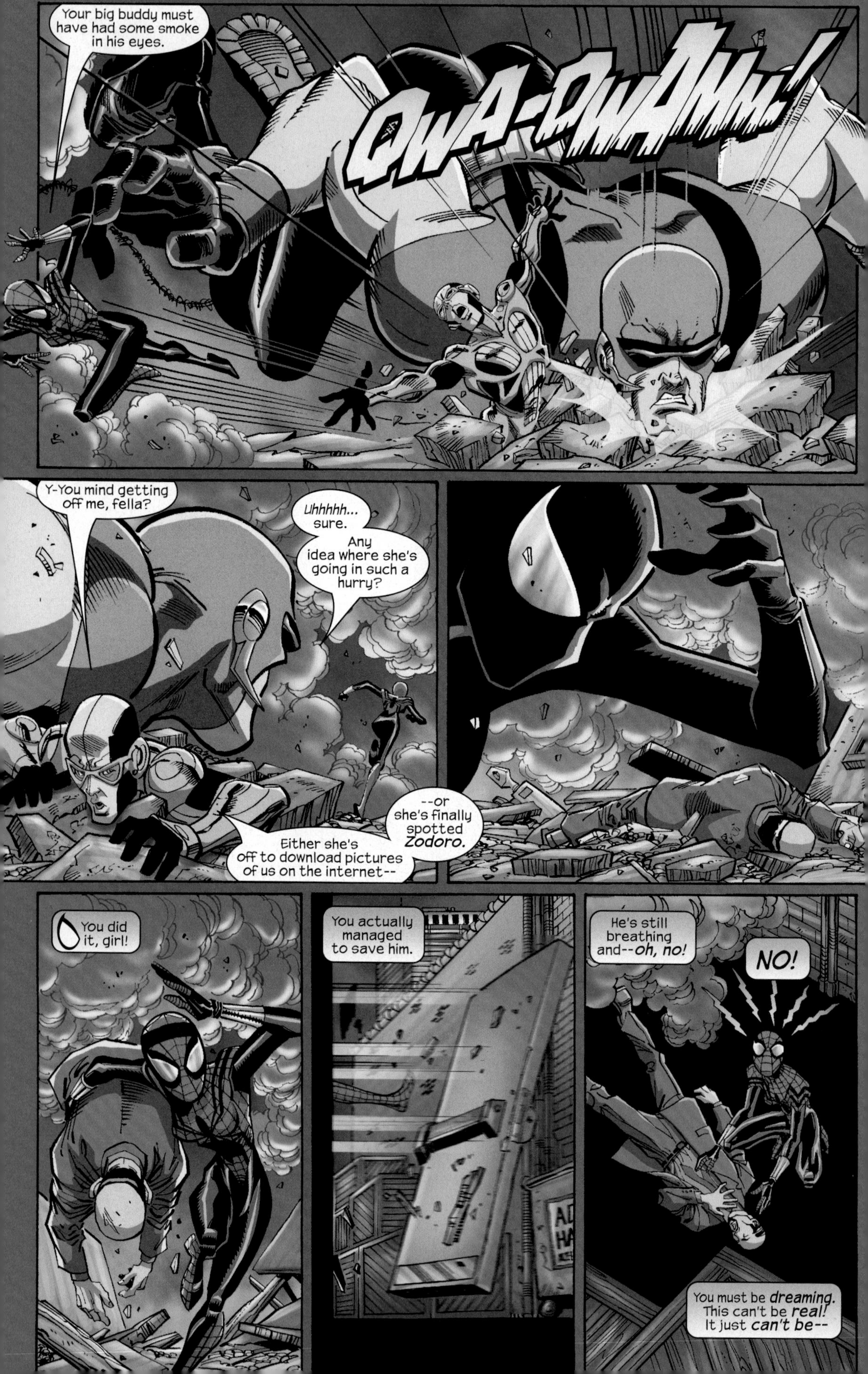
Your big buddy must have had some smoke in his eyes.
QWA-QWAMM!
Y-You mind getting off me, fella?
Uhhhhh... sure.
Any idea where she's going in such a hurry?
Either she's off to download pictures of us on the internet--
--or she's finally spotted Zodoro.
You did it, girl!
You actually managed to save him.
He's still breathing and--oh, no!
NO!
You must be dreaming. This can't be real! It just can't be--

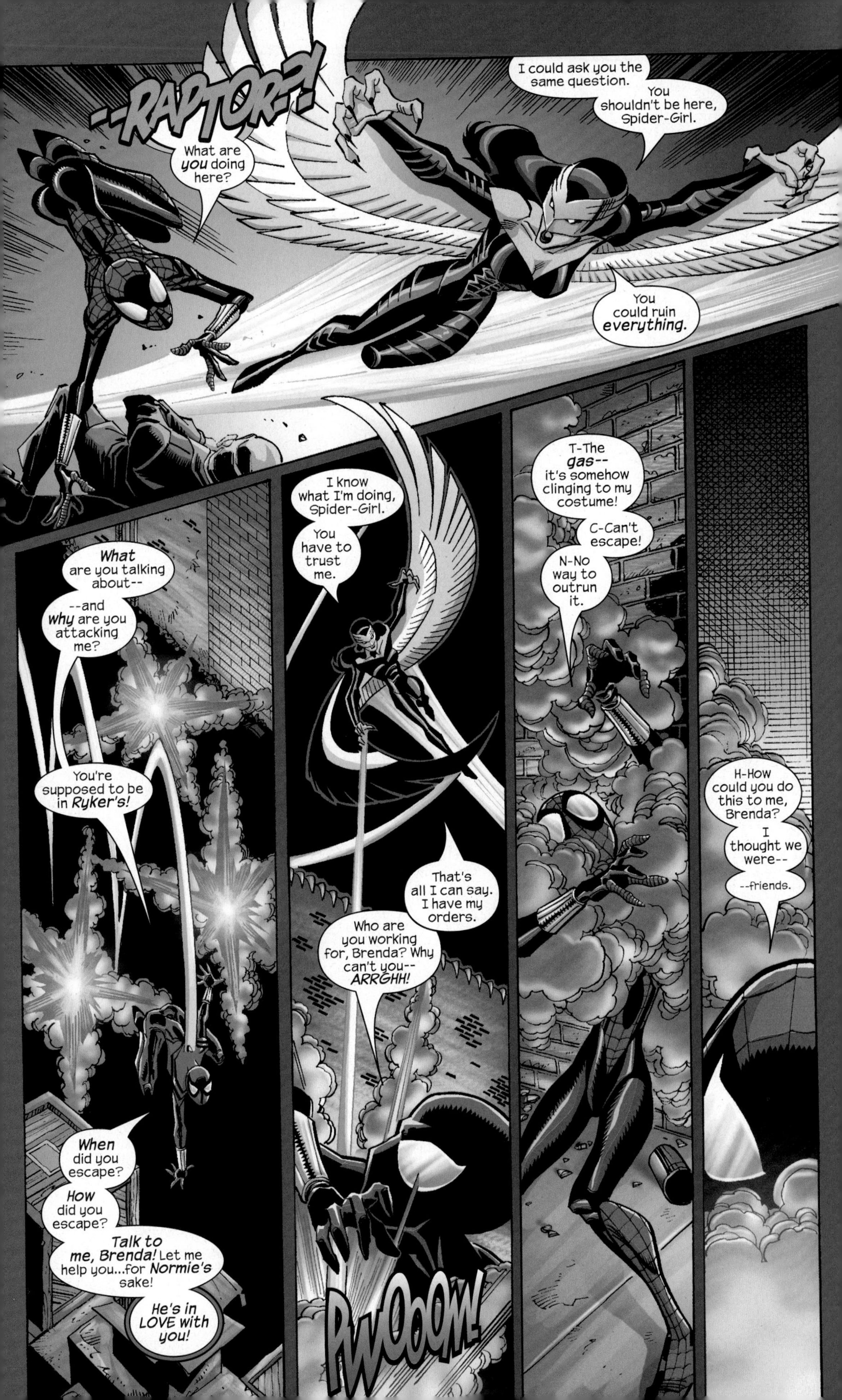
--RAPTOR--?!
What are you doing here?
I could ask you the same question.
You shouldn't be here, Spider-Girl.
You could ruin everything.
What are you talking about--
--and why are you attacking me?
You're supposed to be in Ryker's!
When did you escape?
How did you escape?
Talk to me, Brenda! Let me help you...for Normie's sake!
He's in LOVE with you!
I know what I'm doing, Spider-Girl.
You have to trust me.
That's all I can say. I have my orders.
Who are you working for, Brenda? Why can't you-- ARRGHH!
PWOOOM!
T-The gas-- it's somehow clinging to my costume!
C-Can't escape!
N-No way to outrun it.
H-How could you do this to me, Brenda?
I thought we were--
--friends.

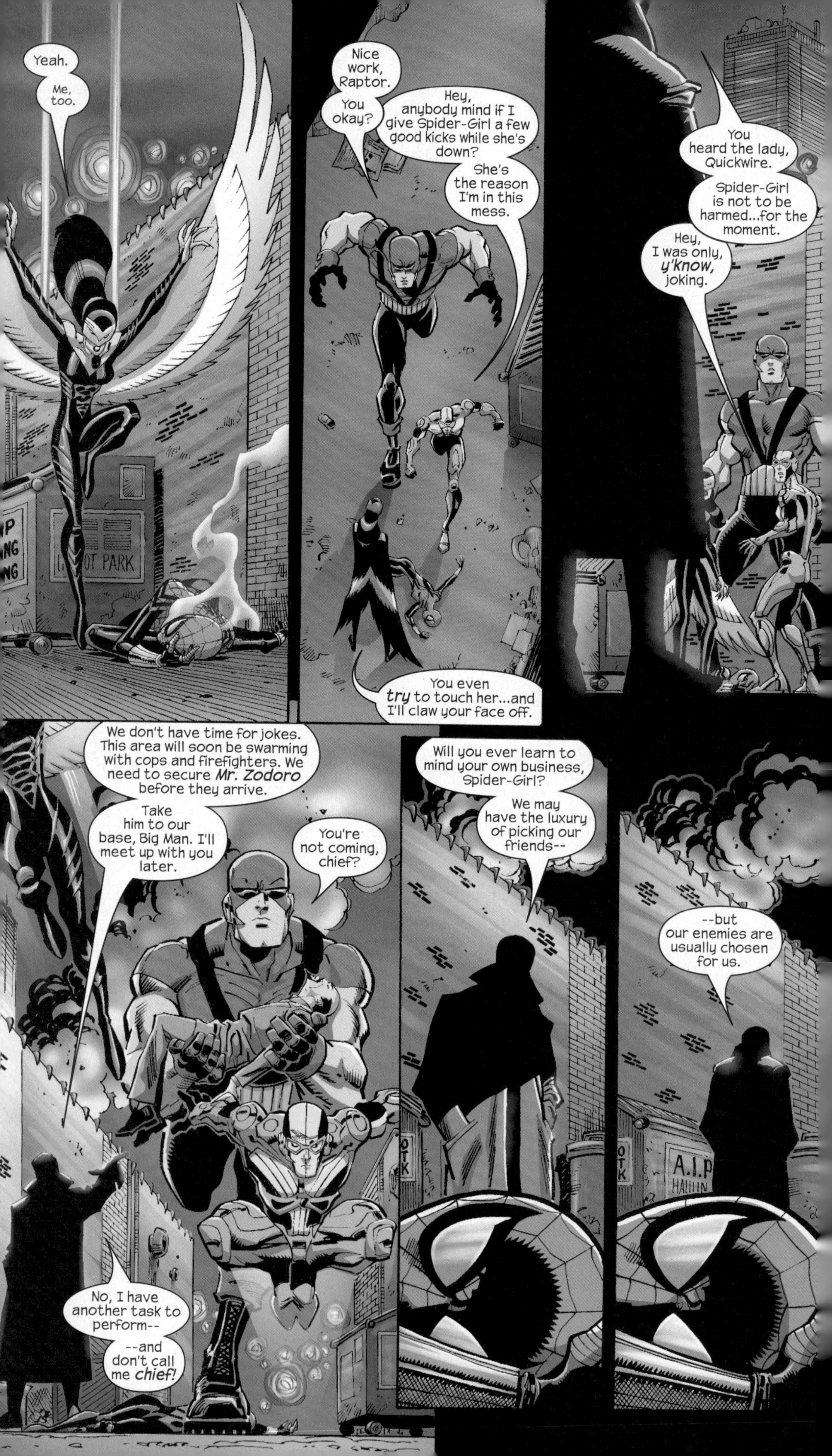

Yeah.
Me, too.
Nice work, Raptor.
You okay?
Hey, anybody mind if I give Spider-Girl a few good kicks while she's down?
She's the reason I'm in this mess.
You even *try* to touch her...and I'll claw your face off.
You heard the lady, Quickwire.
Spider-Girl is not to be harmed...for the moment.
Hey, I was only, *y'know,* joking.
We don't have time for jokes. This area will soon be swarming with cops and firefighters. We need to secure *Mr. Zodoro* before they arrive.
Take him to our base, Big Man. I'll meet up with you later.
You're not coming, chief?
No, I have another task to perform--
--and don't call me *chief!*
Will you ever learn to mind your own business, Spider-Girl?
We may have the luxury of picking our friends--
--but our enemies are usually chosen for us.

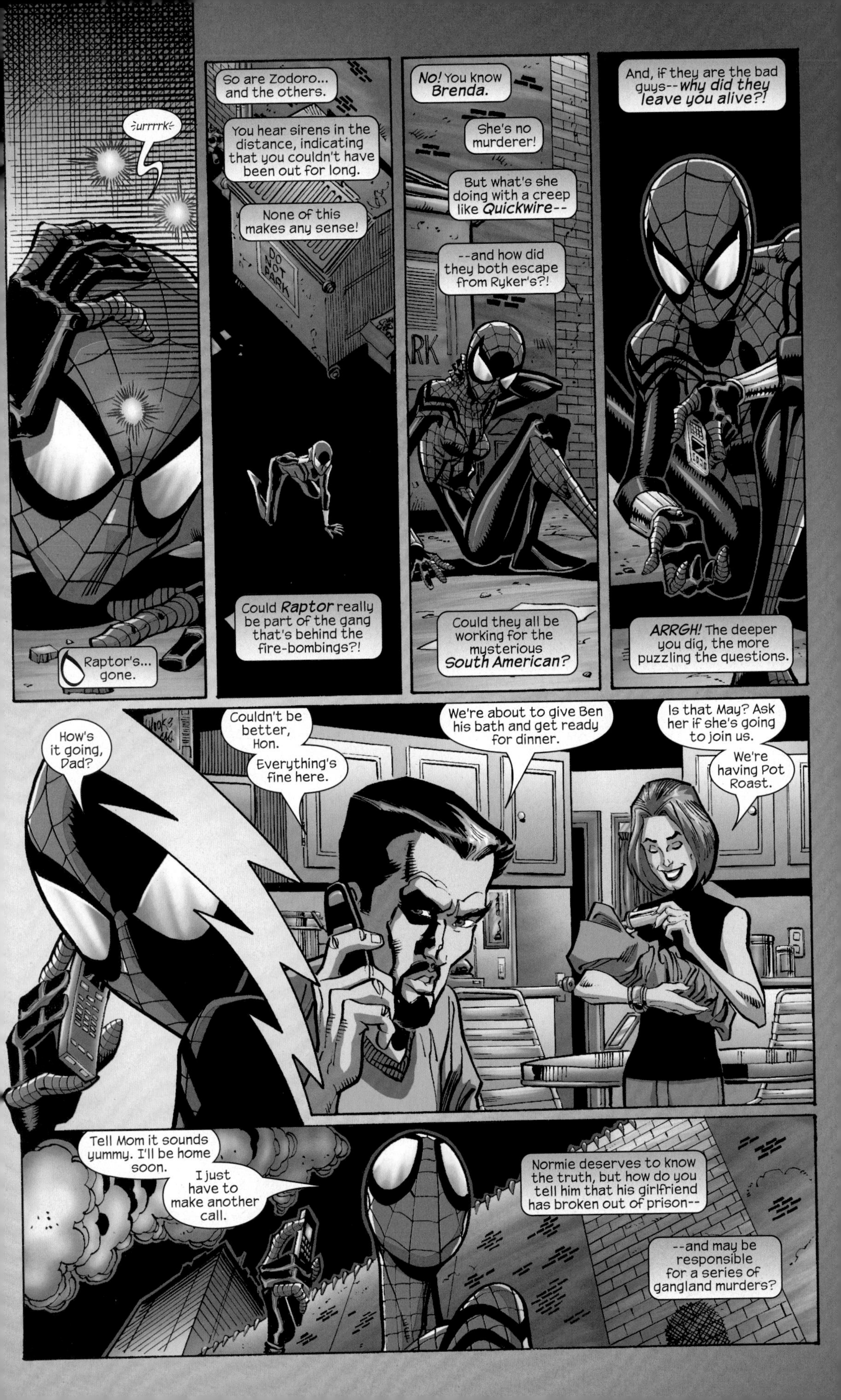

urrrrk
Raptor's... gone.
So are Zodoro... and the others.
You hear sirens in the distance, indicating that you couldn't have been out for long.
None of this makes any sense!
DO NOT PARK
Could Raptor really be part of the gang that's behind the fire-bombings?!
No! You know Brenda.
She's no murderer!
But what's she doing with a creep like Quickwire--
--and how did they both escape from Ryker's?!
Could they all be working for the mysterious South American?
And, if they are the bad guys--why did they leave you alive?!
ARRGH! The deeper you dig, the more puzzling the questions.
How's it going, Dad?
Couldn't be better, Hon.
Everything's fine here.
We're about to give Ben his bath and get ready for dinner.
Is that May? Ask her if she's going to join us.
We're having Pot Roast.
Tell Mom it sounds yummy. I'll be home soon.
I just have to make another call.
Normie deserves to know the truth, but how do you tell him that his girlfriend has broken out of prison--
--and may be responsible for a series of gangland murders?

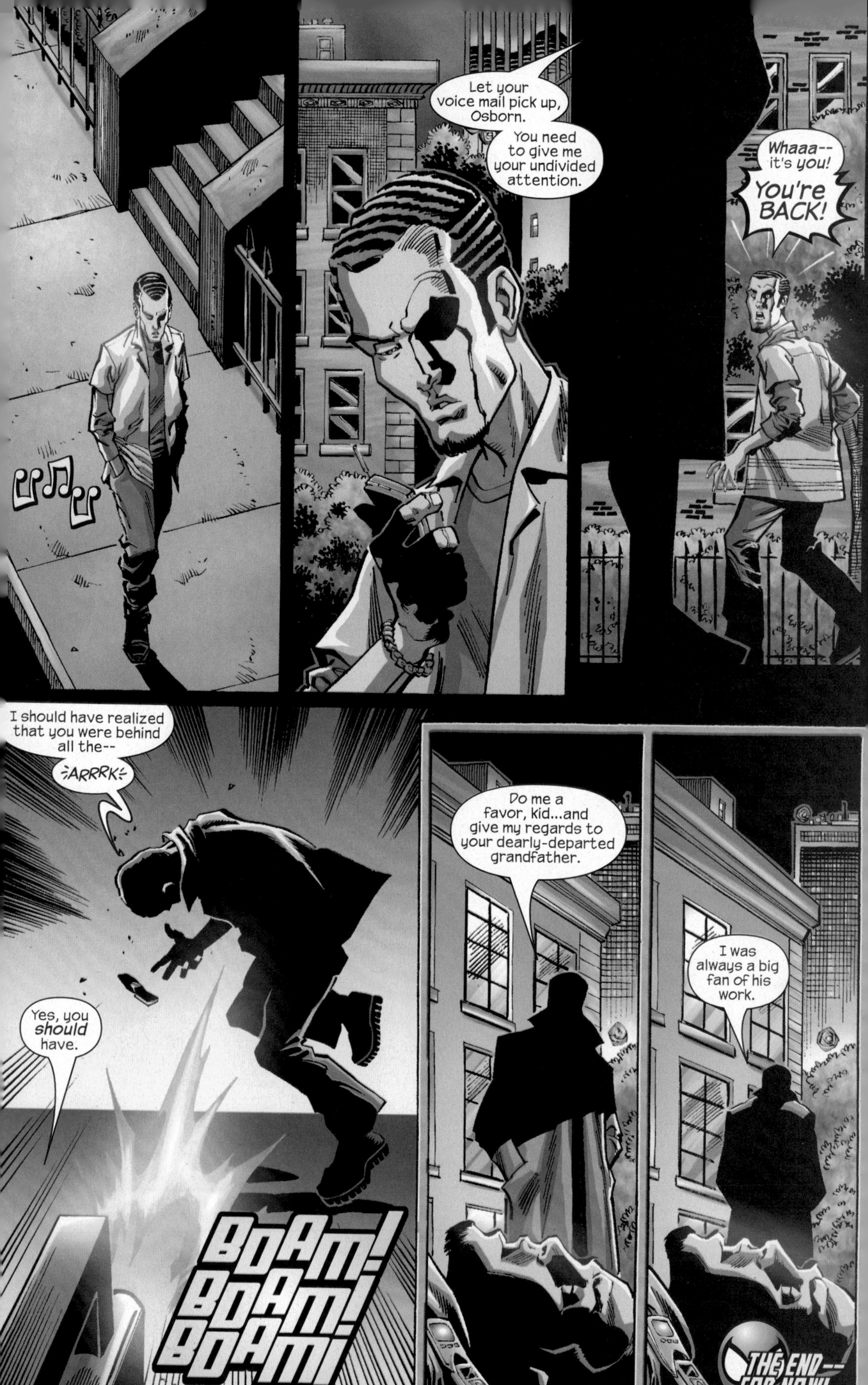

Let your voice mail pick up, Osborn.
You need to give me your undivided attention.
Whaaa-- it's you! You're BACK!
I should have realized that you were behind all the--
ARRRK
Yes, you *should* have.
BOAM! BOAM! BOAM!
Do me a favor, kid...and give my regards to your dearly-departed grandfather.
I was always a big fan of his work.
THE END-- FOR NOW!

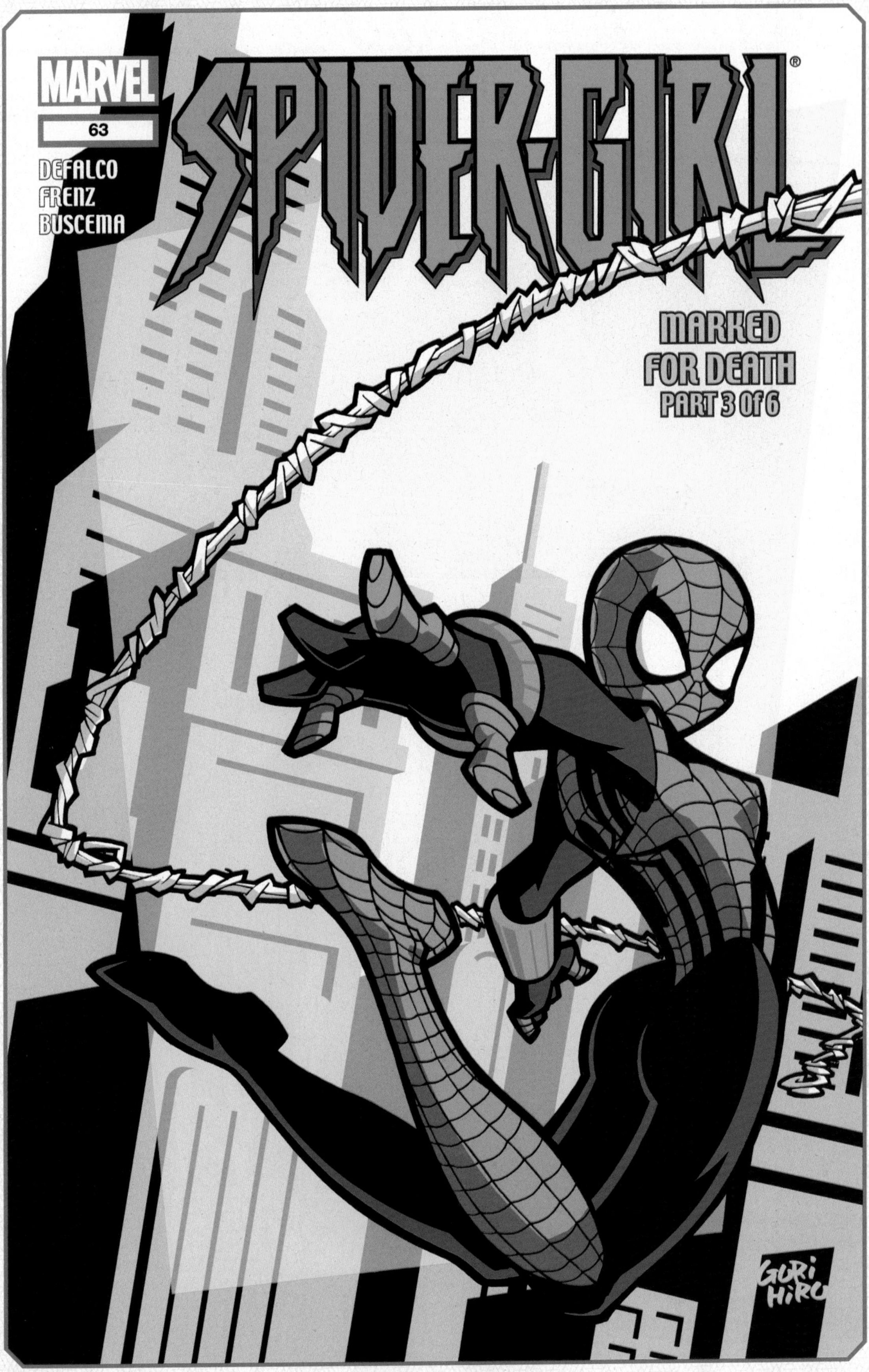
MARVEL
63
DEFALCO
FRENZ
BUSCEMA
SPIDER-GIRL®
MARKED
FOR DEATH
PART 3 OF 6
GURIHIRU

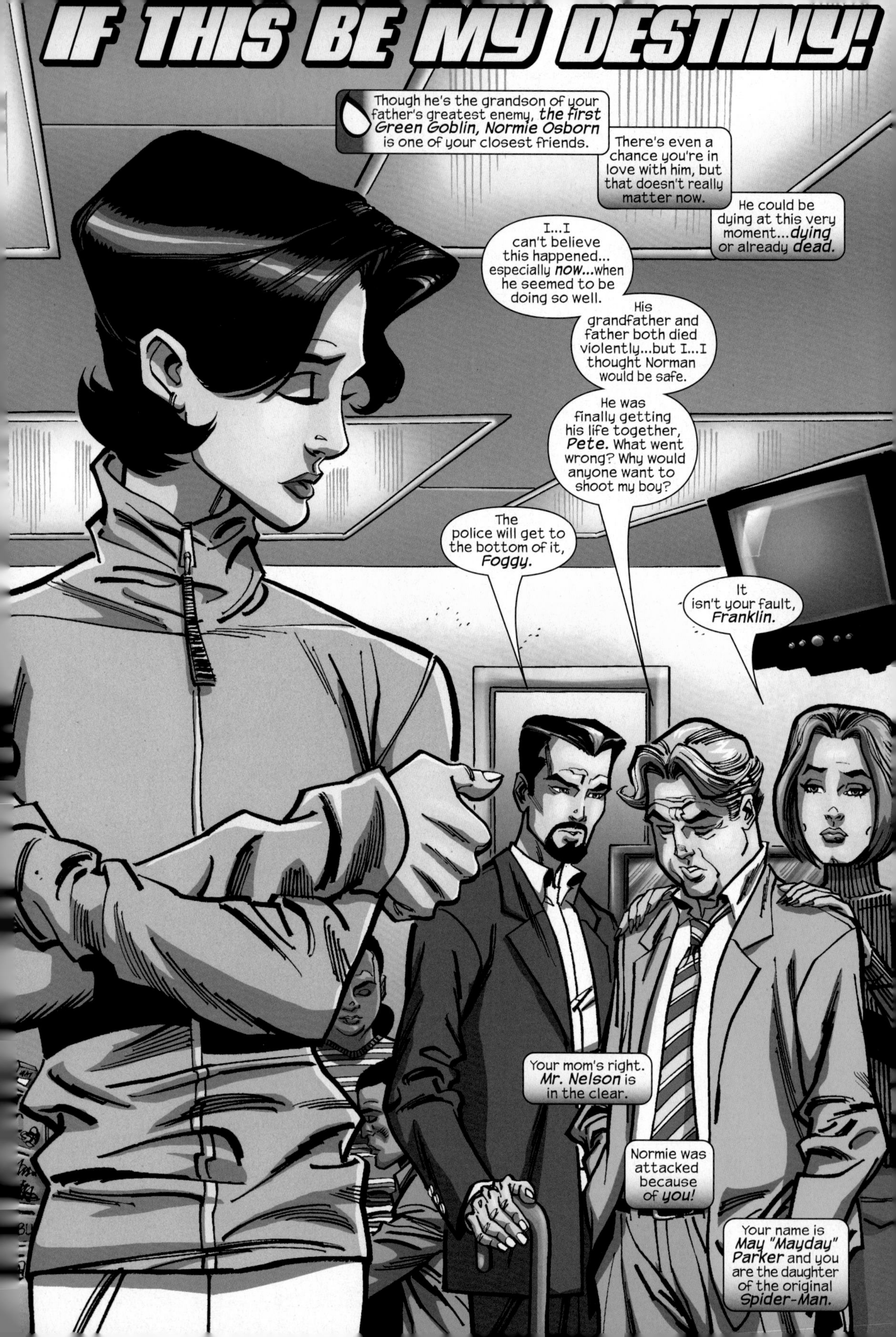
IF THIS BE MY DESTINY!
Though he's the grandson of your father's greatest enemy, the first Green Goblin, Normie Osborn is one of your closest friends.
There's even a chance you're in love with him, but that doesn't really matter now.
He could be dying at this very moment...dying or already dead.
I...I can't believe this happened... especially now...when he seemed to be doing so well.
His grandfather and father both died violently...but I...I thought Norman would be safe.
He was finally getting his life together, Pete. What went wrong? Why would anyone want to shoot my boy?
The police will get to the bottom of it, Foggy.
It isn't your fault, Franklin.
Your mom's right. Mr. Nelson is in the clear.
Normie was attacked because of you!
Your name is May "Mayday" Parker and you are the daughter of the original Spider-Man.

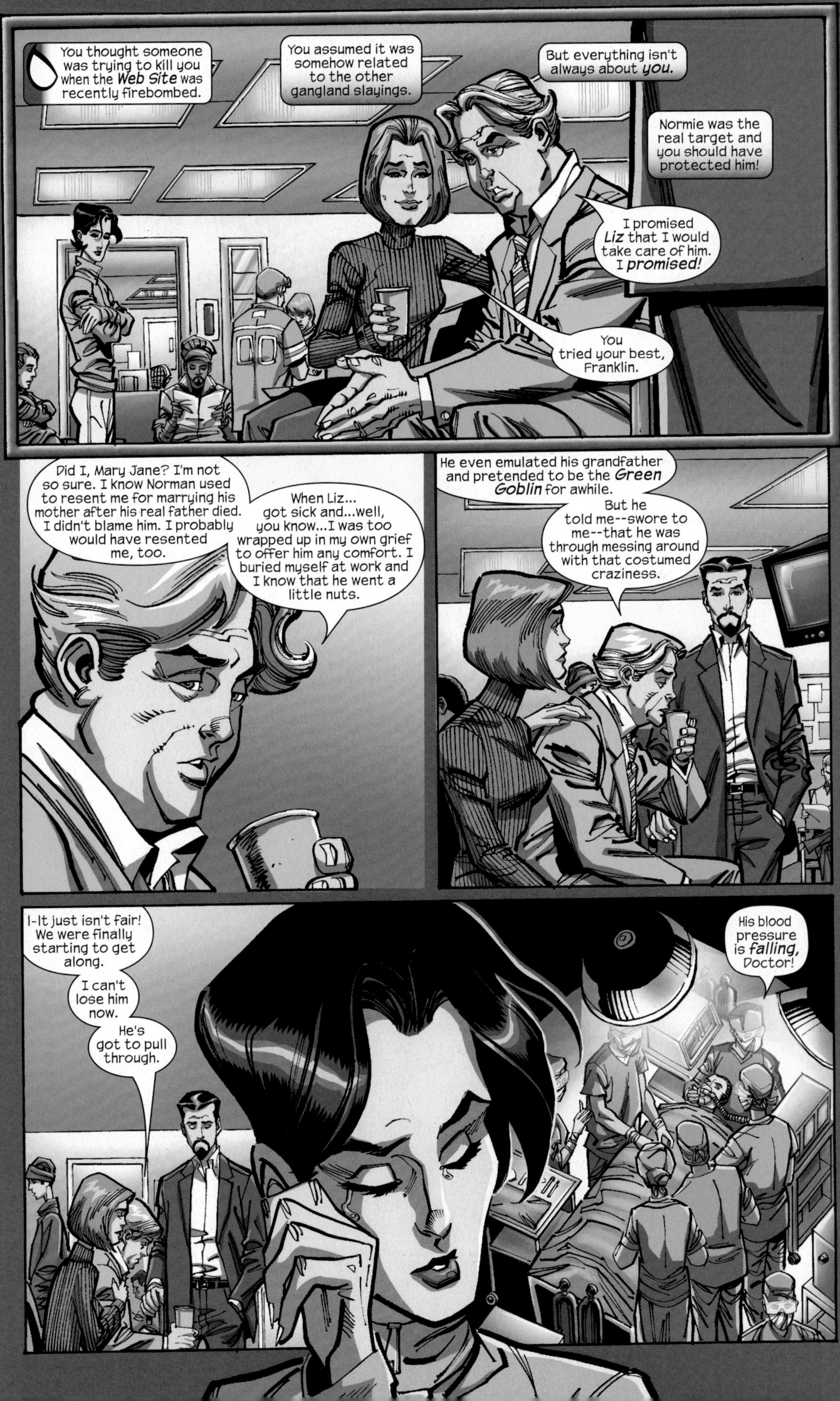

You thought someone was trying to kill you when the Web Site was recently firebombed.
You assumed it was somehow related to the other gangland slayings.
But everything isn't always about you.
Normie was the real target and you should have protected him!
I promised Liz that I would take care of him. I promised!
You tried your best, Franklin.
Did I, Mary Jane? I'm not so sure. I know Norman used to resent me for marrying his mother after his real father died. I didn't blame him. I probably would have resented me, too.
When Liz... got sick and...well, you know...I was too wrapped up in my own grief to offer him any comfort. I buried myself at work and I know that he went a little nuts.
He even emulated his grandfather and pretended to be the Green Goblin for awhile.
But he told me--swore to me--that he was through messing around with that costumed craziness.
I-It just isn't fair! We were finally starting to get along.
I can't lose him now.
He's got to pull through.
His blood pressure is falling, Doctor!

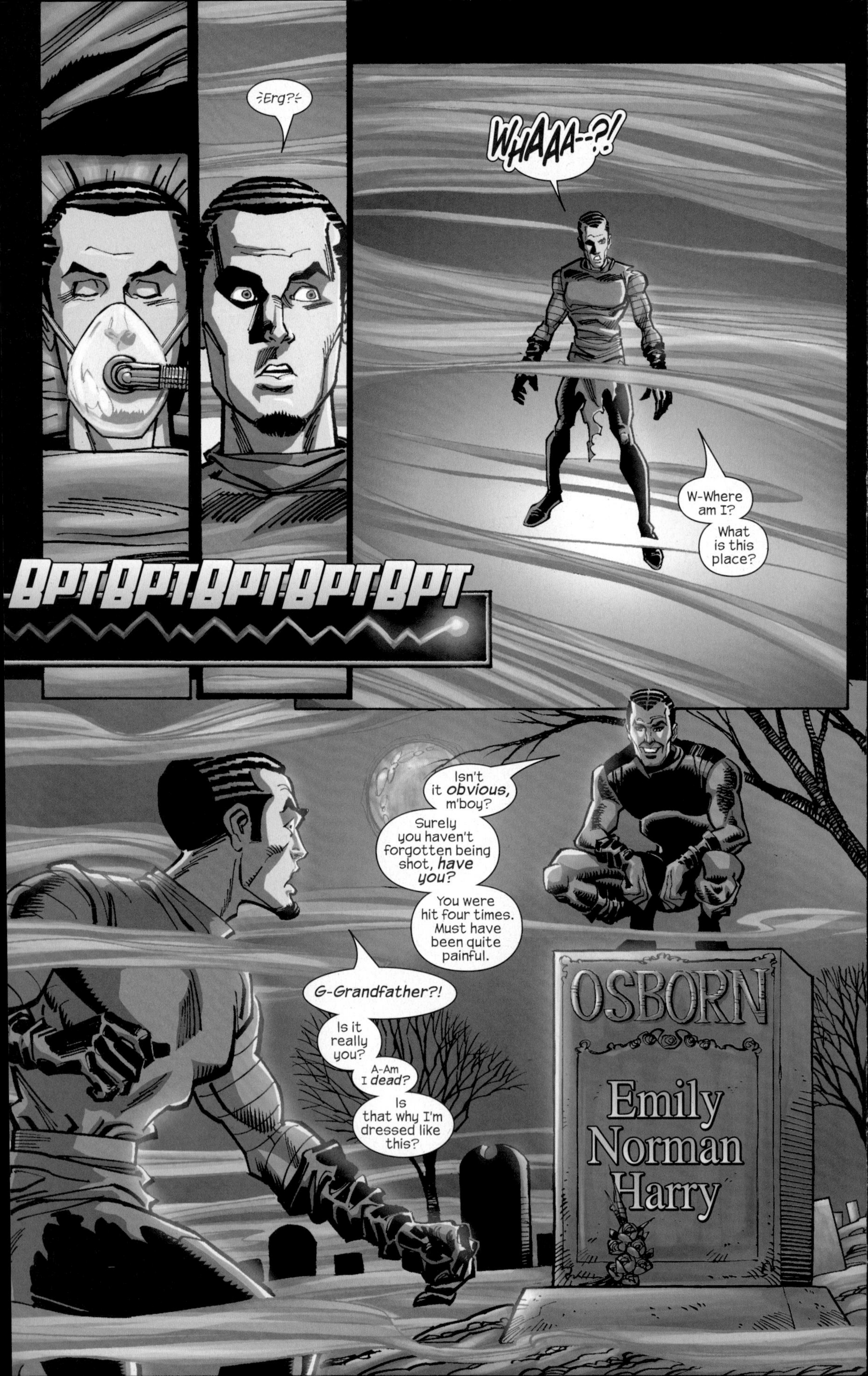

Erg?
WHAAA--?!
W-Where am I?
What is this place?
BPT BPT BPT BPT BPT
Isn't it obvious, m'boy?
Surely you haven't forgotten being shot, have you?
You were hit four times. Must have been quite painful.
G-Grandfather?!
Is it really you?
A-Am I dead?
Is that why I'm dressed like this?
OSBORN
Emily
Norman
Harry

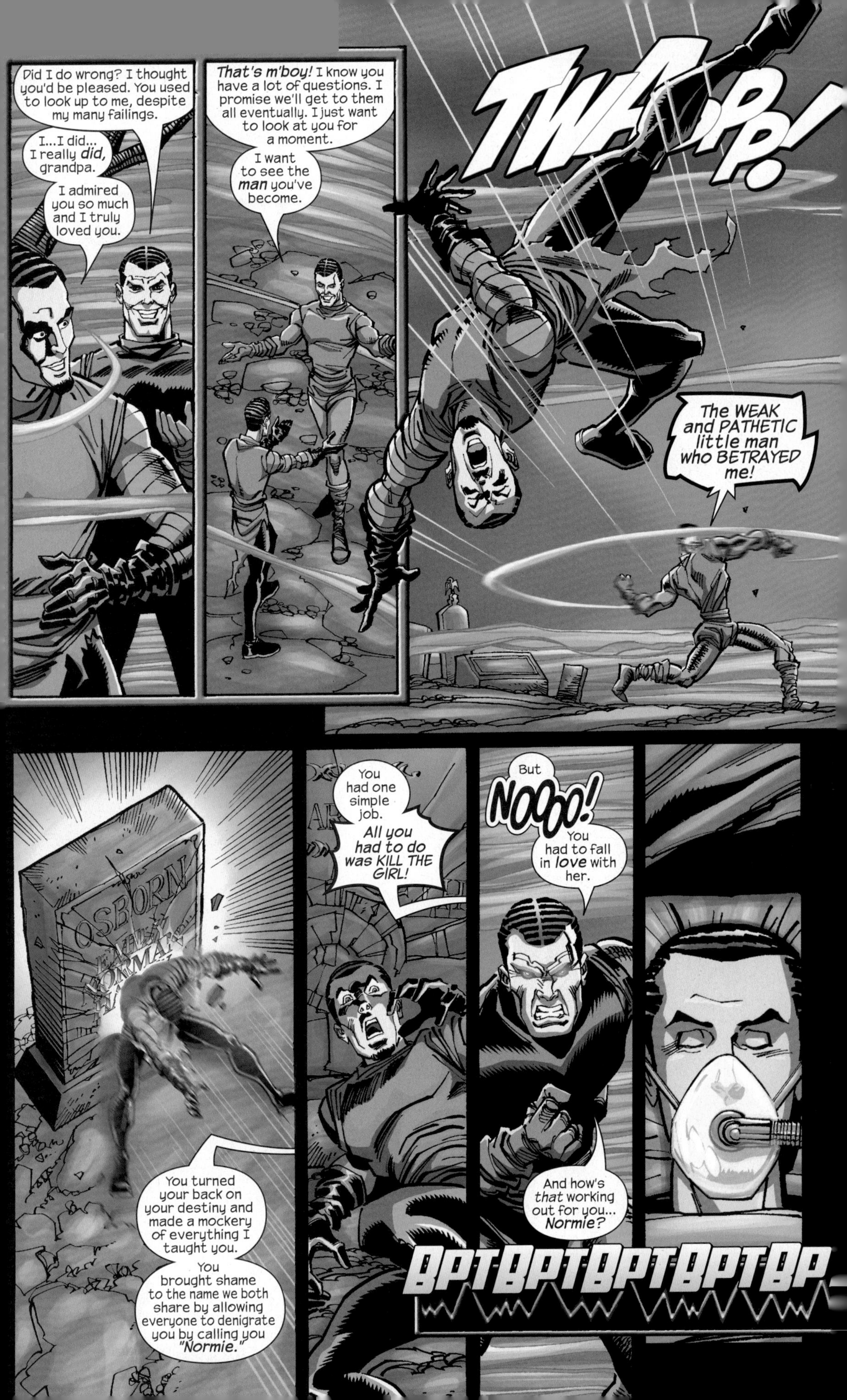

Did I do wrong? I thought you'd be pleased. You used to look up to me, despite my many failings.
I...I did... I really *did,* grandpa.
I admired you so much and I truly loved you.
That's m'boy! I know you have a lot of questions. I promise we'll get to them all eventually. I just want to look at you for a moment.
I want to see the *man* you've become.
TWAPP!
The WEAK and PATHETIC little man who BETRAYED me!
You turned your back on your destiny and made a mockery of everything I taught you.
You brought shame to the name we both share by allowing everyone to denigrate you by calling you *"Normie."*
You had one simple job.
All you had to do was KILL THE GIRL!
But
NOOOO!
You had to fall in *love* with her.
And how's *that* working out for you... *Normie?*
BPTBPTBPTBPTBP

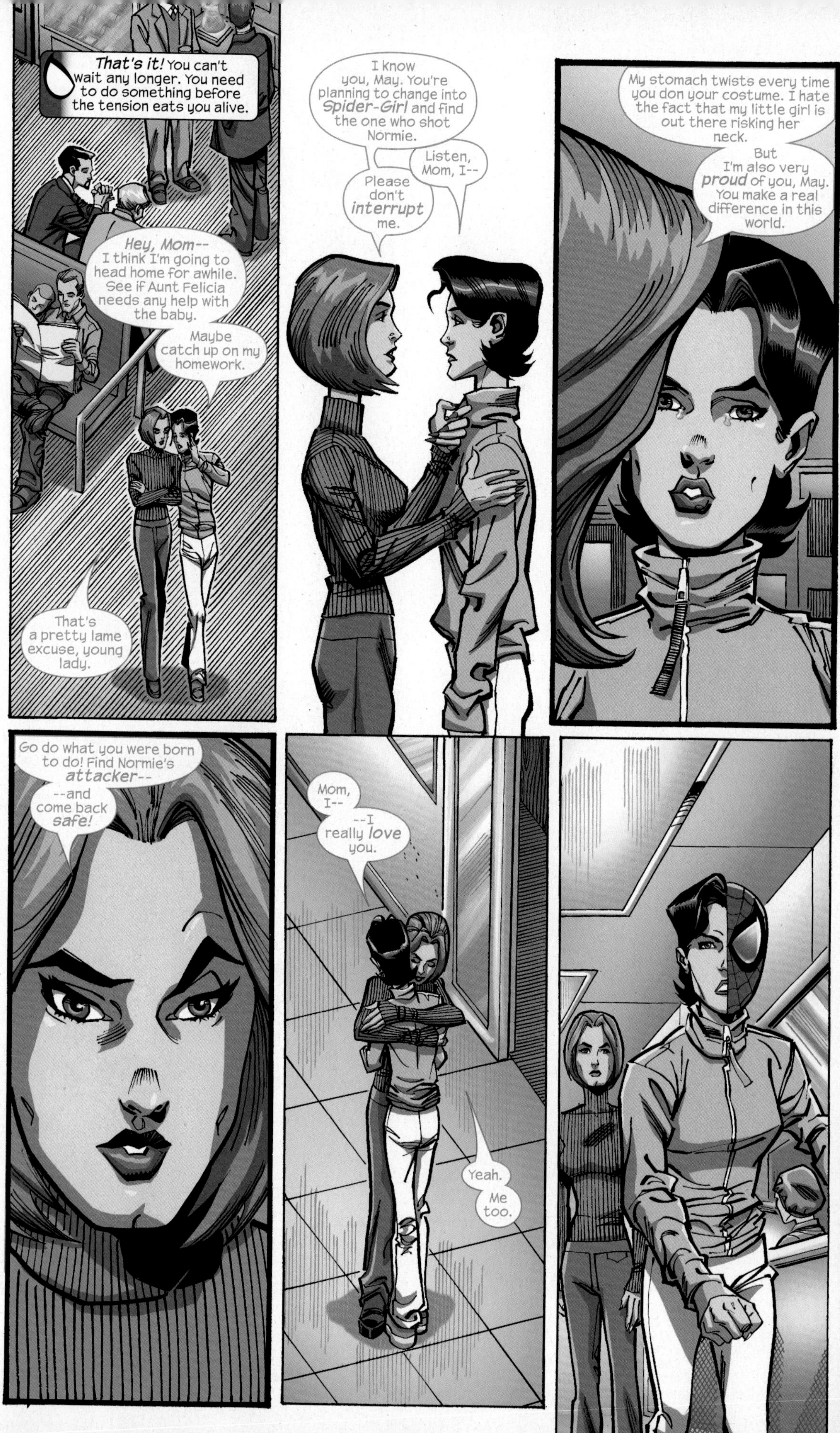
That's it! You can't wait any longer. You need to do something before the tension eats you alive.
Hey, Mom-- I think I'm going to head home for awhile. See if Aunt Felicia needs any help with the baby.
Maybe catch up on my homework.
That's a pretty lame excuse, young lady.
I know you, May. You're planning to change into Spider-Girl and find the one who shot Normie.
Listen, Mom, I--
Please don't interrupt me.
My stomach twists every time you don your costume. I hate the fact that my little girl is out there risking her neck.
But I'm also very proud of you, May. You make a real difference in this world.
Go do what you were born to do! Find Normie's attacker--
--and come back safe!
Mom, I--
--I really love you.
Yeah.
Me too.

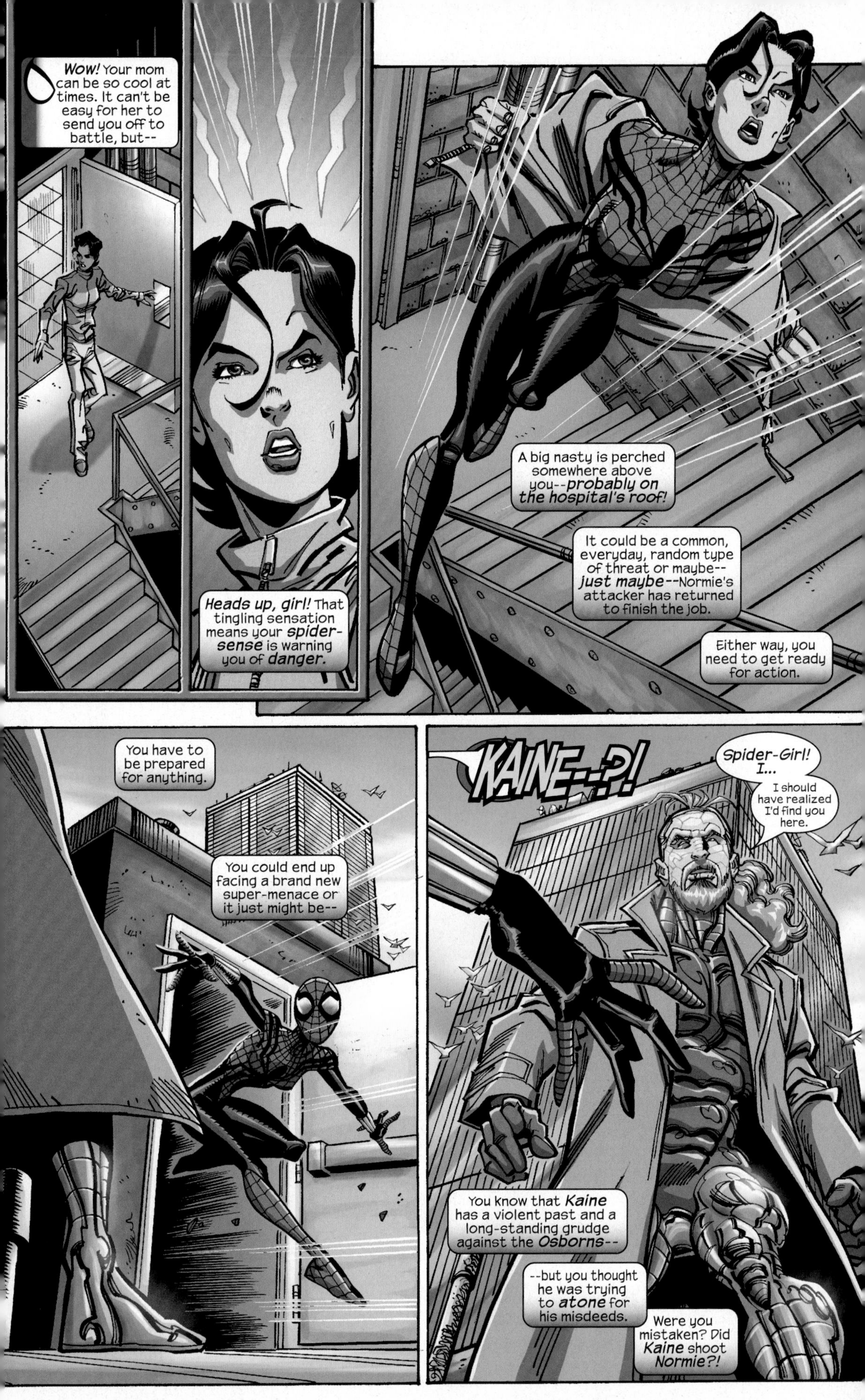
Wow! Your mom can be so cool at times. It can't be easy for her to send you off to battle, but--
Heads up, girl! That tingling sensation means your spider-sense is warning you of danger.
A big nasty is perched somewhere above you--probably on the hospital's roof!
It could be a common, everyday, random type of threat or maybe--just maybe--Normie's attacker has returned to finish the job.
Either way, you need to get ready for action.
You have to be prepared for anything.
You could end up facing a brand new super-menace or it just might be--
KAINE--?!
Spider-Girl! I...
I should have realized I'd find you here.
You know that Kaine has a violent past and a long-standing grudge against the Osborns--
--but you thought he was trying to atone for his misdeeds.
Were you mistaken? Did Kaine shoot Normie?!

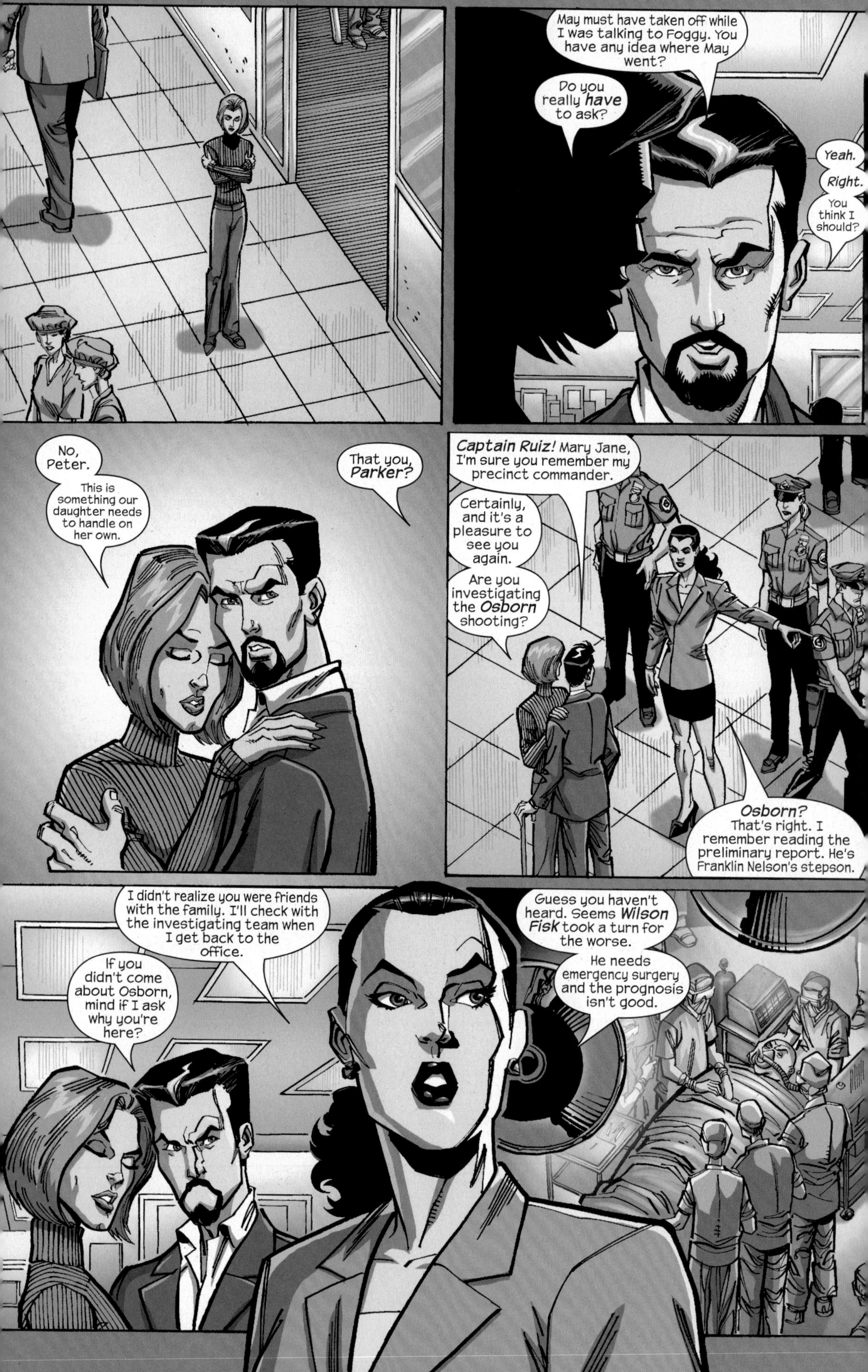
May must have taken off while I was talking to Foggy. You have any idea where May went?
Do you really *have* to ask?
Yeah.
Right.
You think I should?
No, Peter.
This is something our daughter needs to handle on her own.
That you, *Parker?*
Captain Ruiz! Mary Jane, I'm sure you remember my precinct commander.
Certainly, and it's a pleasure to see you again.
Are you investigating the *Osborn* shooting?
Osborn? That's right. I remember reading the preliminary report. He's Franklin Nelson's stepson.
I didn't realize you were friends with the family. I'll check with the investigating team when I get back to the office.
If you didn't come about Osborn, mind if I ask why you're here?
Guess you haven't heard. Seems *Wilson Fisk* took a turn for the worse.
He needs emergency surgery and the prognosis isn't good.

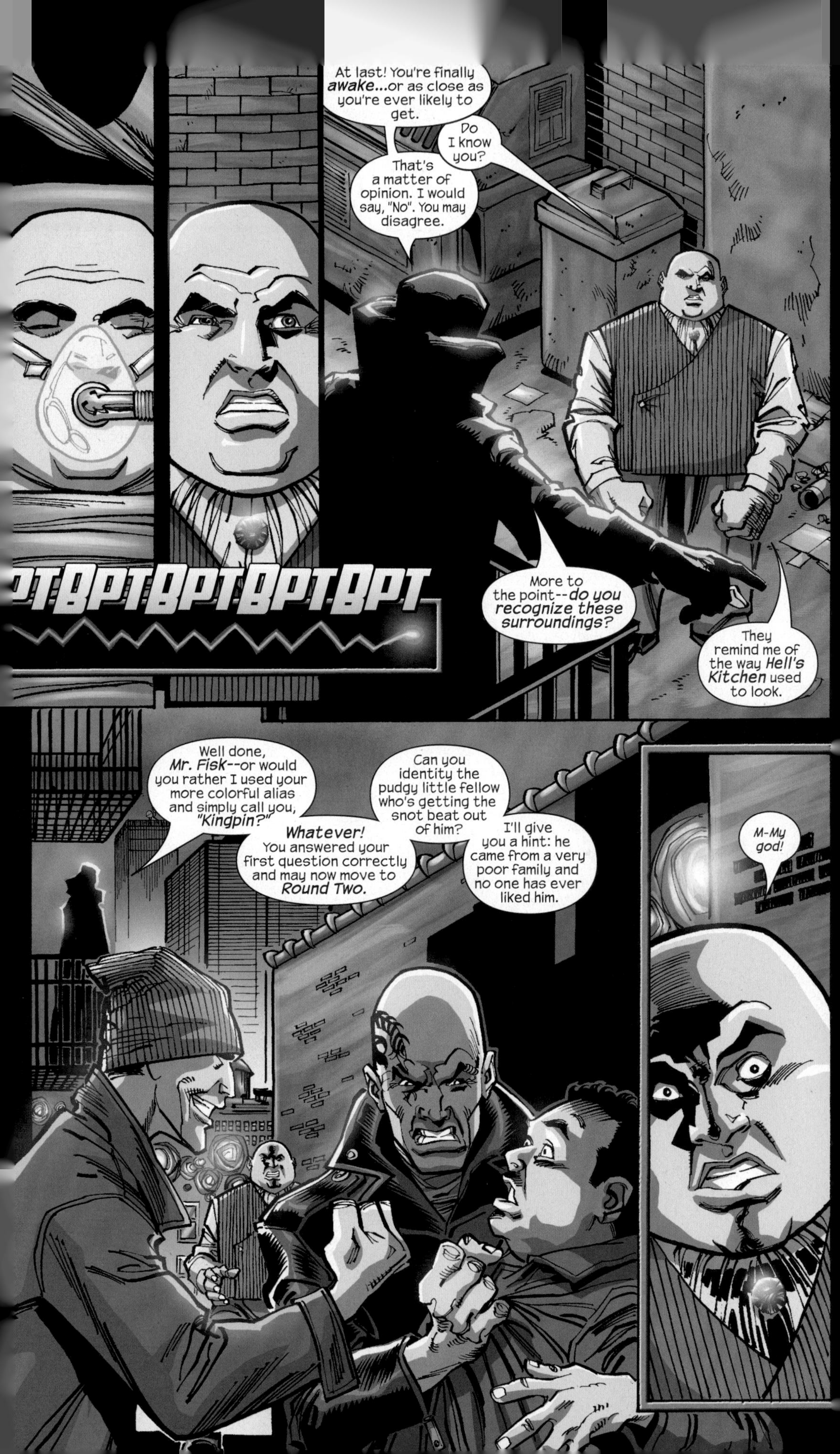
At last! You're finally *awake*...or as close as you're ever likely to get.
Do I know you?
That's a matter of opinion. I would say, "No". You may disagree.
BPTBPTBPTBPTBPT
More to the point--*do you recognize these surroundings?*
They remind me of the way *Hell's Kitchen* used to look.
Well done, *Mr. Fisk*--or would you rather I used your more colorful alias and simply call you, *"Kingpin?"*
Whatever! You answered your first question correctly and may now move to *Round Two.*
Can you identity the pudgy little fellow who's getting the snot beat out of him?
I'll give you a hint: he came from a very poor family and no one has ever liked him.
M-My god!

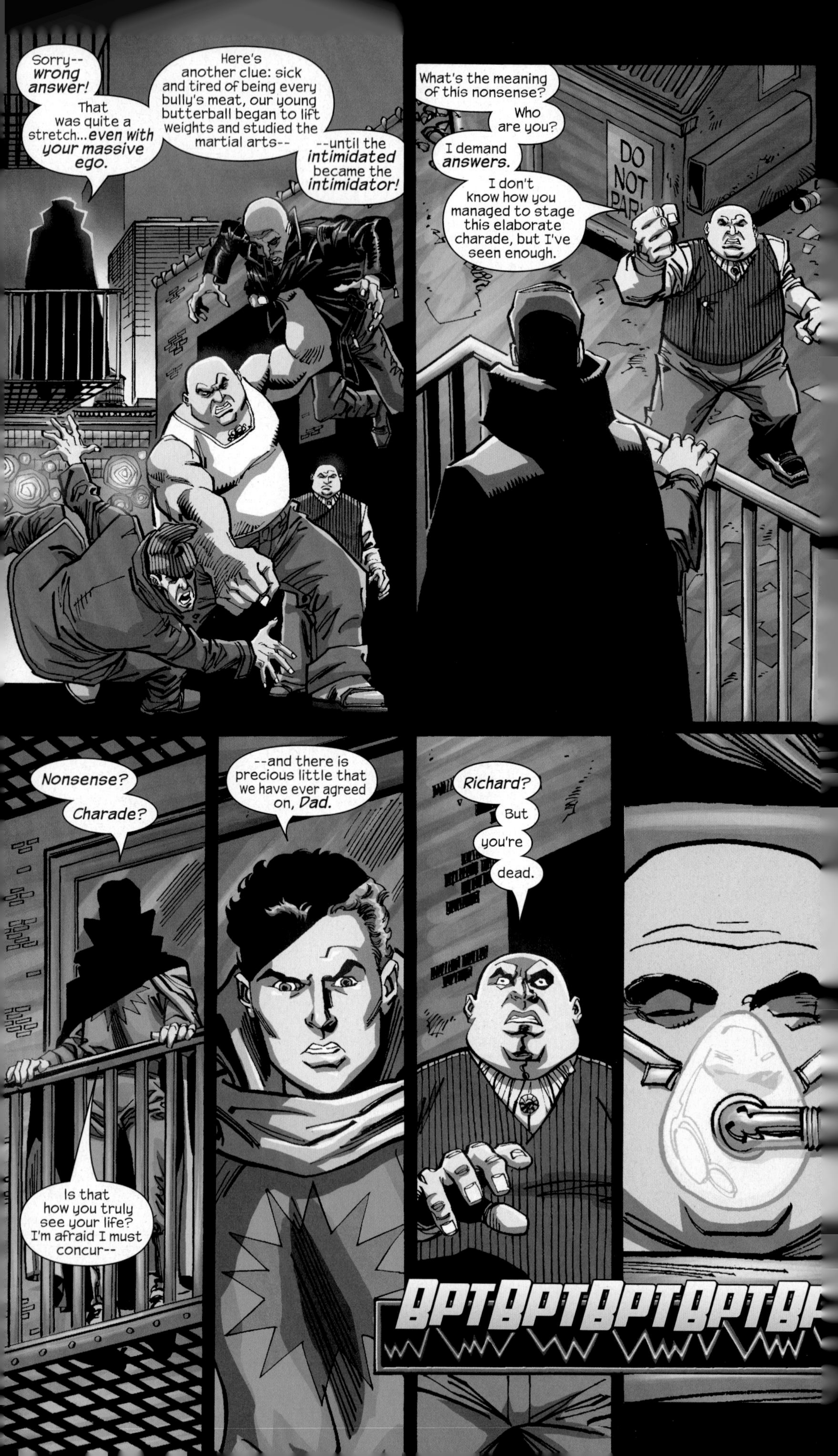
Sorry-- *wrong answer!*
That was quite a stretch...*even with your massive ego.*
Here's another clue: sick and tired of being every bully's meat, our young butterball began to lift weights and studied the martial arts--
--until the *intimidated* became the *intimidator!*
What's the meaning of this nonsense?
Who are you?
I demand *answers.*
I don't know how you managed to stage this elaborate charade, but I've seen enough.
DO NOT PAR
Nonsense?
Charade?
Is that how you truly see your life? I'm afraid I must concur--
--and there is precious little that we have ever agreed on, *Dad.*
Richard?
But
you're
dead.
BPTBPTBPTBPTBP

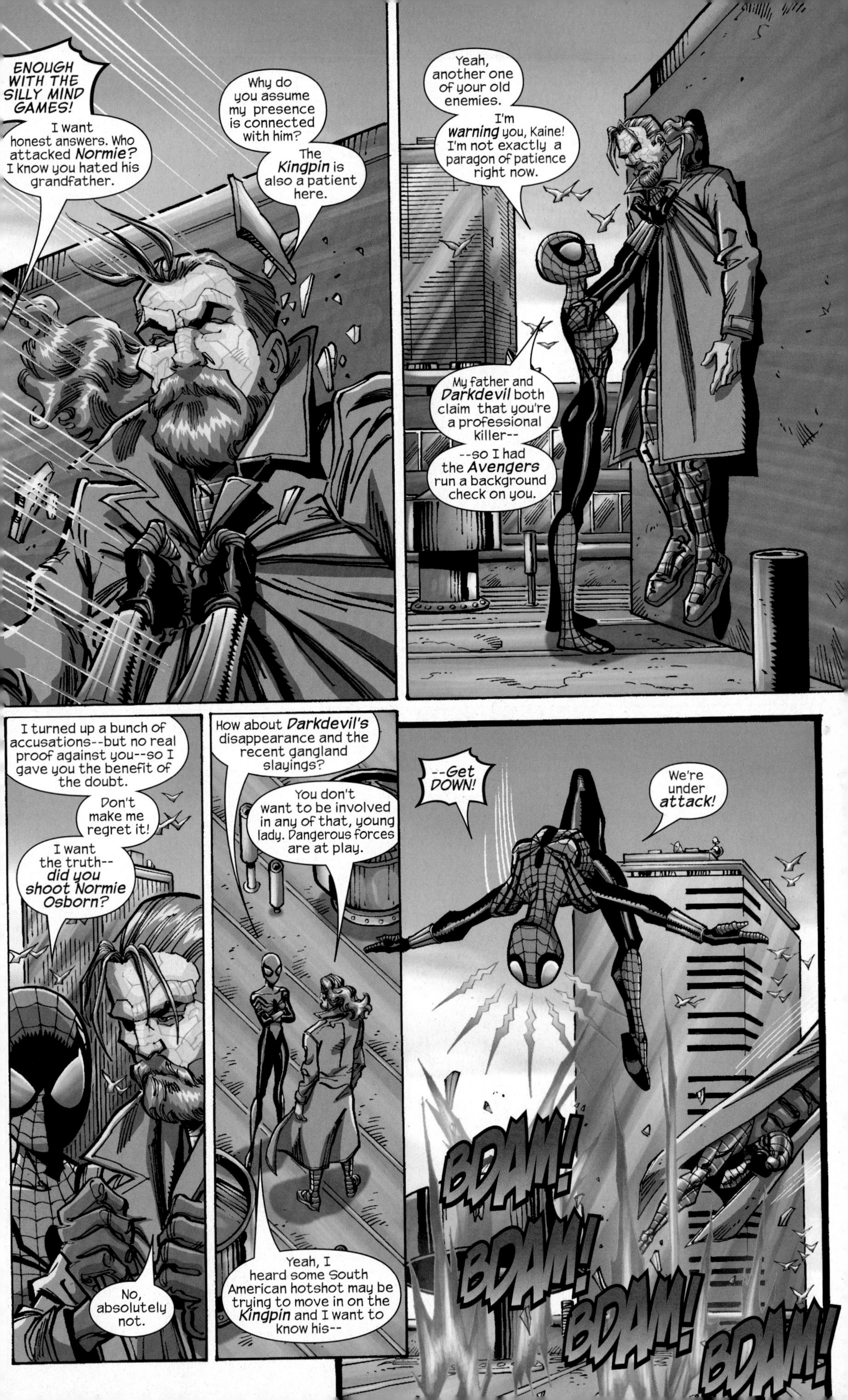

ENOUGH WITH THE SILLY MIND GAMES!
I want honest answers. Who attacked Normie? I know you hated his grandfather.
Why do you assume my presence is connected with him?
The Kingpin is also a patient here.
Yeah, another one of your old enemies.
I'm warning you, Kaine! I'm not exactly a paragon of patience right now.
My father and Darkdevil both claim that you're a professional killer--
--so I had the Avengers run a background check on you.
I turned up a bunch of accusations--but no real proof against you--so I gave you the benefit of the doubt.
Don't make me regret it!
I want the truth-- did you shoot Normie Osborn?
No, absolutely not.
How about Darkdevil's disappearance and the recent gangland slayings?
You don't want to be involved in any of that, young lady. Dangerous forces are at play.
Yeah, I heard some South American hotshot may be trying to move in on the Kingpin and I want to know his--
--Get DOWN!
We're under attack!
BDAM!
BDAM!
BDAM!
BDAM!

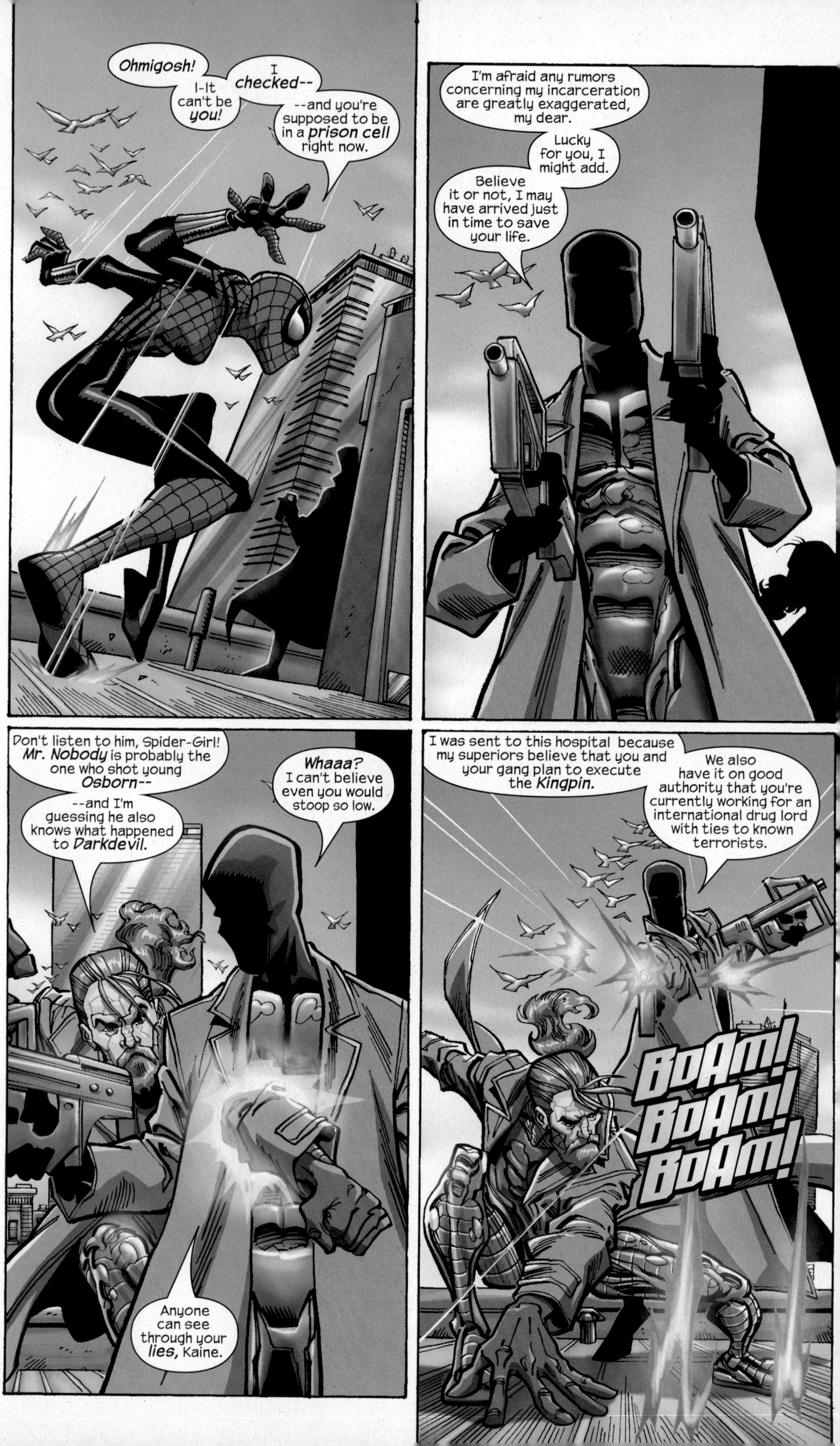

Ohmigosh!
I-It can't be you!
I checked--
--and you're supposed to be in a prison cell right now.
I'm afraid any rumors concerning my incarceration are greatly exaggerated, my dear.
Lucky for you, I might add.
Believe it or not, I may have arrived just in time to save your life.
Don't listen to him, Spider-Girl! Mr. Nobody is probably the one who shot young Osborn--
--and I'm guessing he also knows what happened to Darkdevil.
Whaaa? I can't believe even you would stoop so low.
Anyone can see through your lies, Kaine.
I was sent to this hospital because my superiors believe that you and your gang plan to execute the Kingpin.
We also have it on good authority that you're currently working for an international drug lord with ties to known terrorists.
BOAM! BOAM! BOAM!

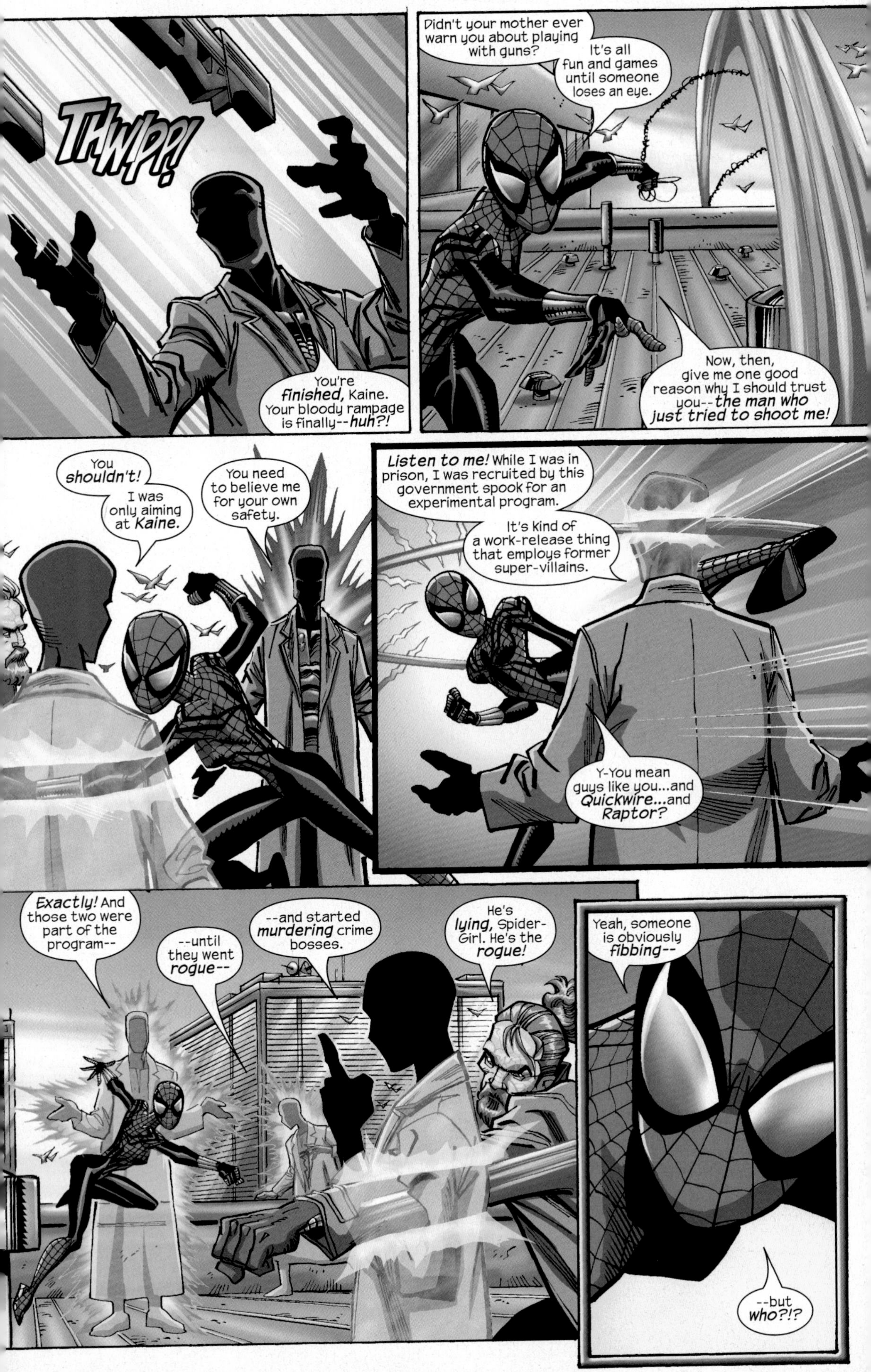
THWIPP!
You're finished, Kaine. Your bloody rampage is finally--huh?!
Didn't your mother ever warn you about playing with guns?
It's all fun and games until someone loses an eye.
Now, then, give me one good reason why I should trust you--the man who just tried to shoot me!
You shouldn't!
I was only aiming at Kaine.
You need to believe me for your own safety.
Listen to me! While I was in prison, I was recruited by this government spook for an experimental program.
It's kind of a work-release thing that employs former super-villains.
Y-You mean guys like you...and Quickwire...and Raptor?
Exactly! And those two were part of the program--
--until they went rogue--
--and started murdering crime bosses.
He's lying, Spider-Girl. He's the rogue!
Yeah, someone is obviously fibbing--
--but who?!?

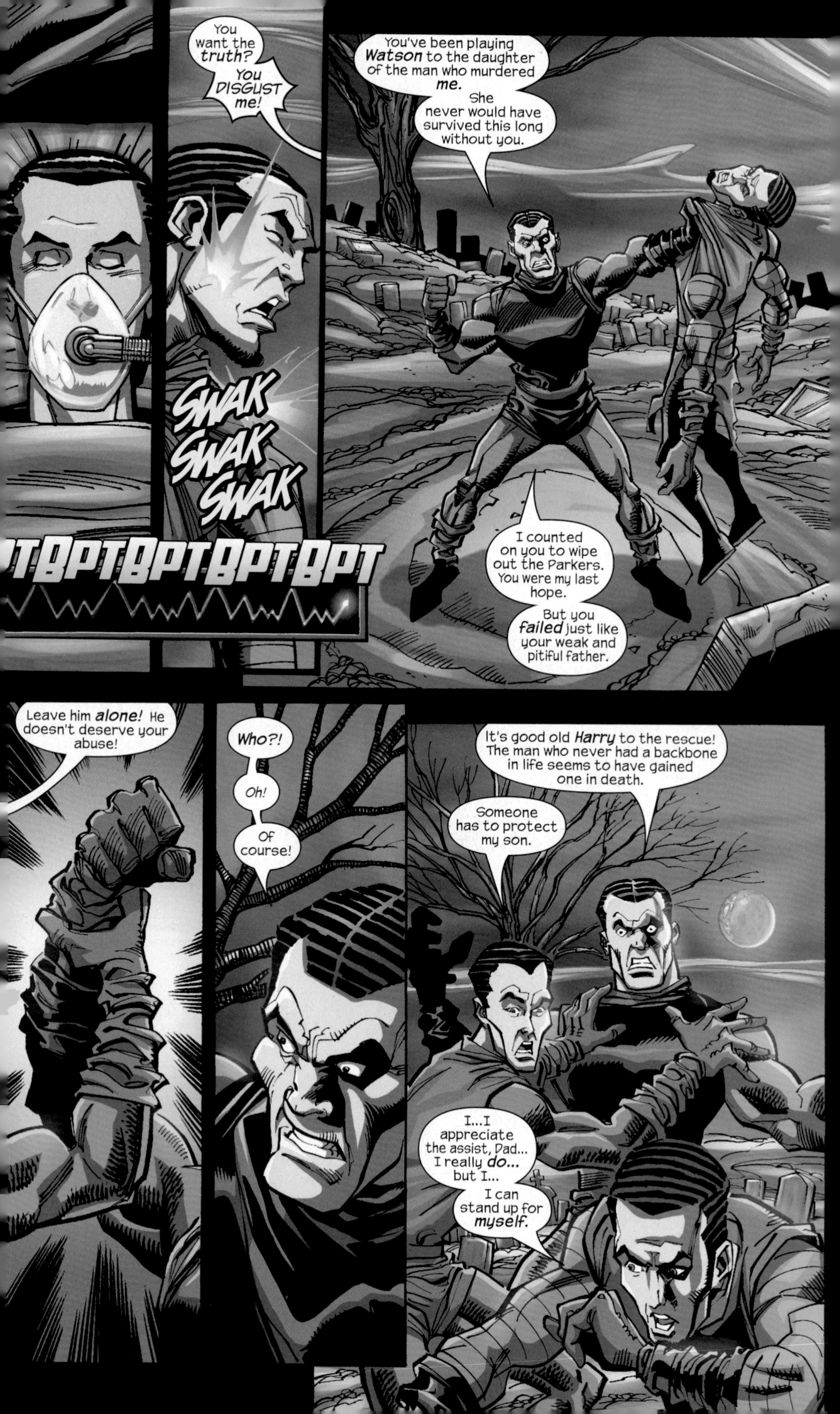
You want the truth? You DISGUST me!
SWAK SWAK SWAK
BPTBPTBPTBPT
You've been playing Watson to the daughter of the man who murdered me.
She never would have survived this long without you.
I counted on you to wipe out the Parkers. You were my last hope.
But you failed just like your weak and pitiful father.
Leave him alone! He doesn't deserve your abuse!
Who?!
Oh!
Of course!
It's good old Harry to the rescue! The man who never had a backbone in life seems to have gained one in death.
Someone has to protect my son.
I...I appreciate the assist, Dad... I really do... but I...
I can stand up for myself.

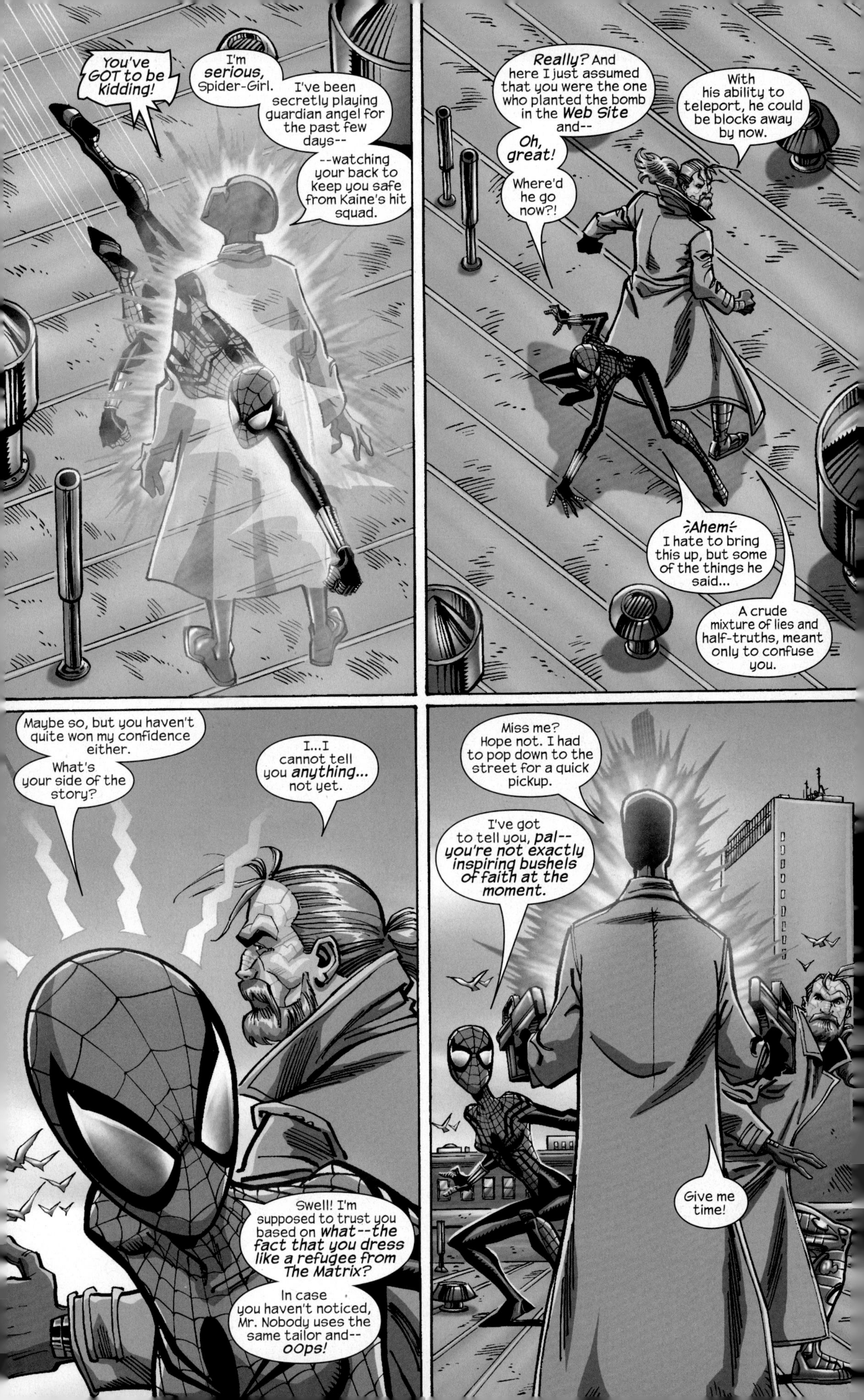
You've GOT to be kidding!
I'm serious, Spider-Girl.
I've been secretly playing guardian angel for the past few days--
--watching your back to keep you safe from Kaine's hit squad.
Really? And here I just assumed that you were the one who planted the bomb in the Web Site and--
Oh, great!
Where'd he go now?!
With his ability to teleport, he could be blocks away by now.
Ahem
I hate to bring this up, but some of the things he said...
A crude mixture of lies and half-truths, meant only to confuse you.
Maybe so, but you haven't quite won my confidence either.
What's your side of the story?
I...I cannot tell you anything... not yet.
Swell! I'm supposed to trust you based on what--the fact that you dress like a refugee from The Matrix?
In case you haven't noticed, Mr. Nobody uses the same tailor and--
oops!
Miss me? Hope not. I had to pop down to the street for a quick pickup.
I've got to tell you, pal--you're not exactly inspiring bushels of faith at the moment.
Give me time!

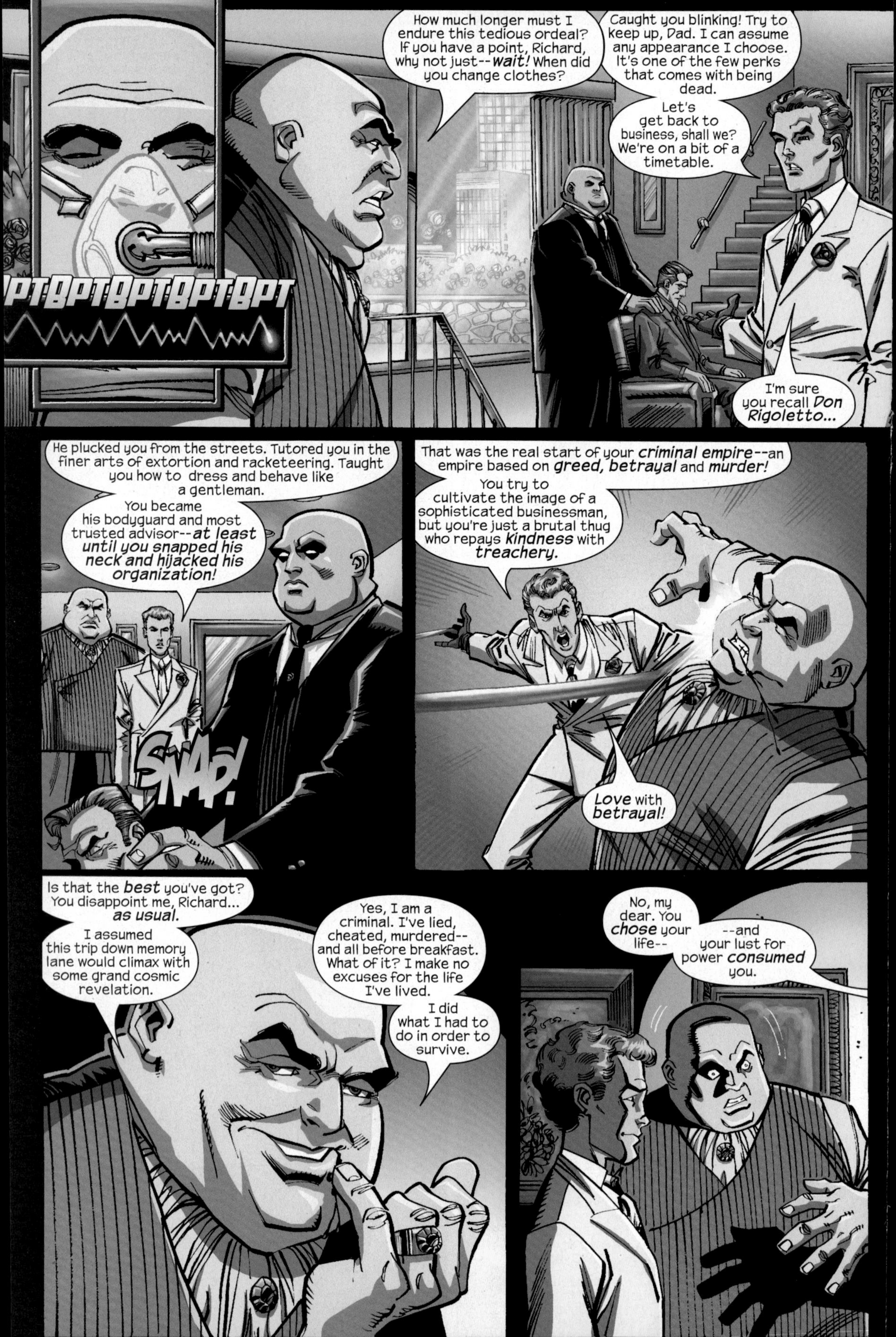

How much longer must I endure this tedious ordeal? If you have a point, Richard, why not just--wait! When did you change clothes?
Caught you blinking! Try to keep up, Dad. I can assume any appearance I choose. It's one of the few perks that comes with being dead.
Let's get back to business, shall we? We're on a bit of a timetable.
BPTBPTBPTBPTBPT
I'm sure you recall Don Rigoletto...
He plucked you from the streets. Tutored you in the finer arts of extortion and racketeering. Taught you how to dress and behave like a gentleman.
You became his bodyguard and most trusted advisor--at least until you snapped his neck and hijacked his organization!
SNAP!
That was the real start of your criminal empire--an empire based on greed, betrayal and murder!
You try to cultivate the image of a sophisticated businessman, but you're just a brutal thug who repays kindness with treachery.
Love with betrayal!
Is that the best you've got? You disappoint me, Richard... as usual.
I assumed this trip down memory lane would climax with some grand cosmic revelation.
Yes, I am a criminal. I've lied, cheated, murdered-- and all before breakfast. What of it? I make no excuses for the life I've lived.
I did what I had to do in order to survive.
No, my dear. You chose your life--
--and your lust for power consumed you.

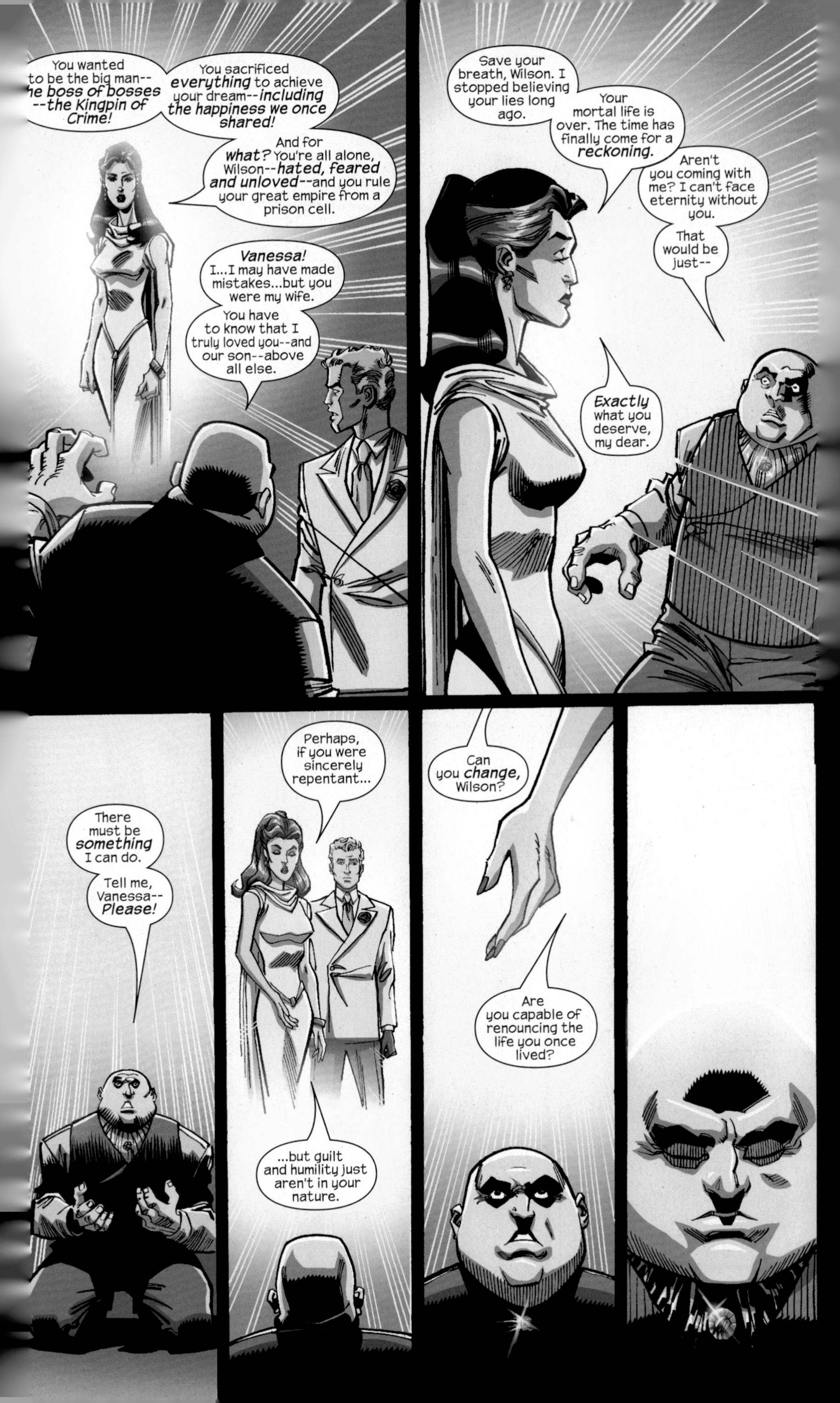

You wanted to be the big man--the boss of bosses--the Kingpin of Crime!
You sacrificed everything to achieve your dream--including the happiness we once shared!
And for what? You're all alone, Wilson--hated, feared and unloved--and you rule your great empire from a prison cell.
Vanessa! I...I may have made mistakes...but you were my wife.
You have to know that I truly loved you--and our son--above all else.
Save your breath, Wilson. I stopped believing your lies long ago.
Your mortal life is over. The time has finally come for a reckoning.
Aren't you coming with me? I can't face eternity without you.
That would be just--
Exactly what you deserve, my dear.
There must be something I can do.
Tell me, Vanessa--Please!
Perhaps, if you were sincerely repentant...
...but guilt and humility just aren't in your nature.
Can you change, Wilson?
Are you capable of renouncing the life you once lived?

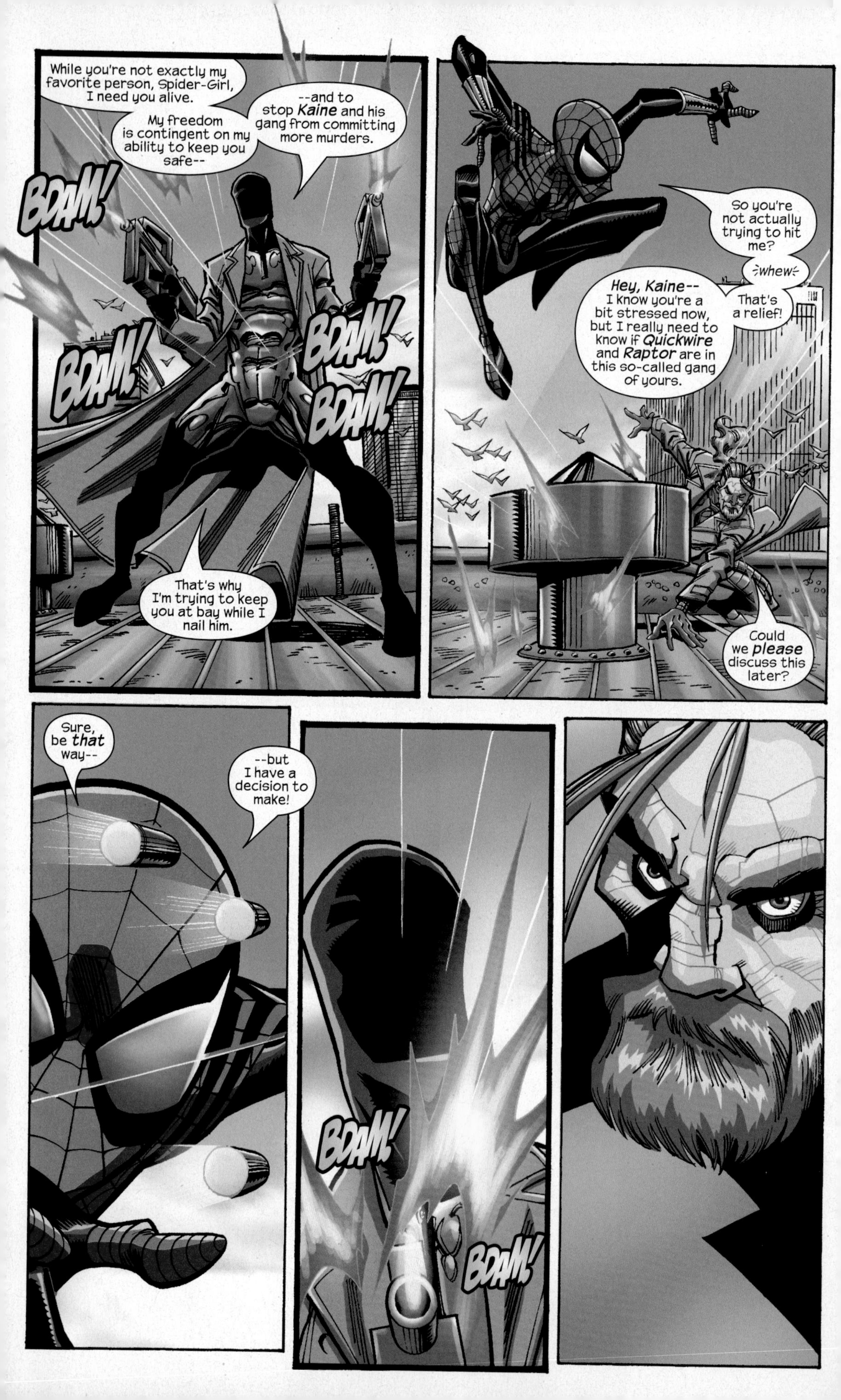
While you're not exactly my favorite person, Spider-Girl, I need you alive.
My freedom is contingent on my ability to keep you safe--
--and to stop Kaine and his gang from committing more murders.
BDAM!
BDAM!
BDAM!
BDAM!
That's why I'm trying to keep you at bay while I nail him.
So you're not actually trying to hit me?
whew
That's a relief!
Hey, Kaine-- I know you're a bit stressed now, but I really need to know if Quickwire and Raptor are in this so-called gang of yours.
Could we please discuss this later?
Sure, be that way--
--but I have a decision to make!
BDAM!
BDAM!

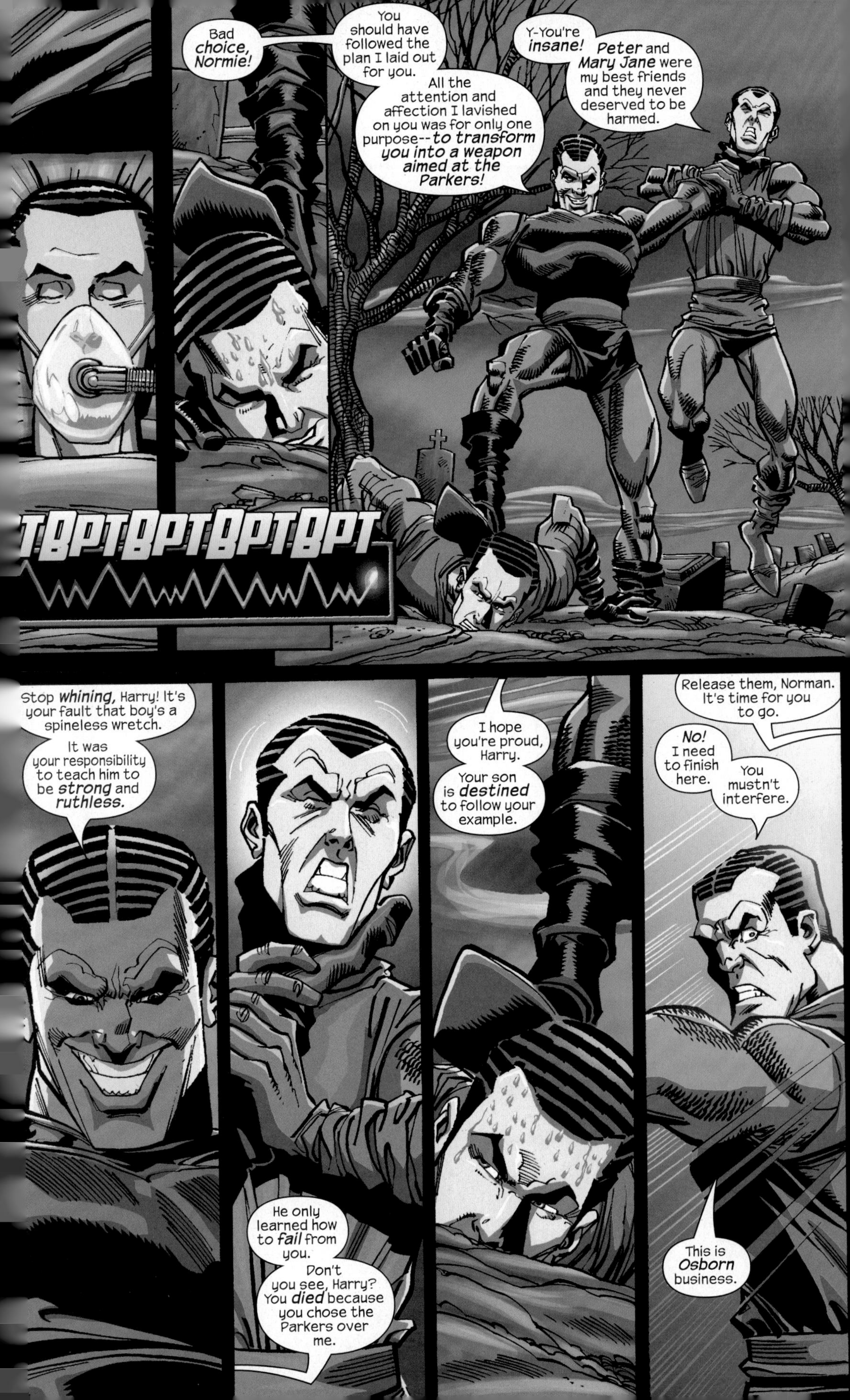

Bad choice, Normie!
You should have followed the plan I laid out for you.
All the attention and affection I lavished on you was for only one purpose--to transform you into a weapon aimed at the Parkers!
Y-You're insane! Peter and Mary Jane were my best friends and they never deserved to be harmed.
TBPTBPTBPTBPT
Stop whining, Harry! It's your fault that boy's a spineless wretch.
It was your responsibility to teach him to be strong and ruthless.
He only learned how to fail from you.
Don't you see, Harry? You died because you chose the Parkers over me.
I hope you're proud, Harry.
Your son is destined to follow your example.
Release them, Norman. It's time for you to go.
No! I need to finish here.
You mustn't interfere.
This is Osborn business.

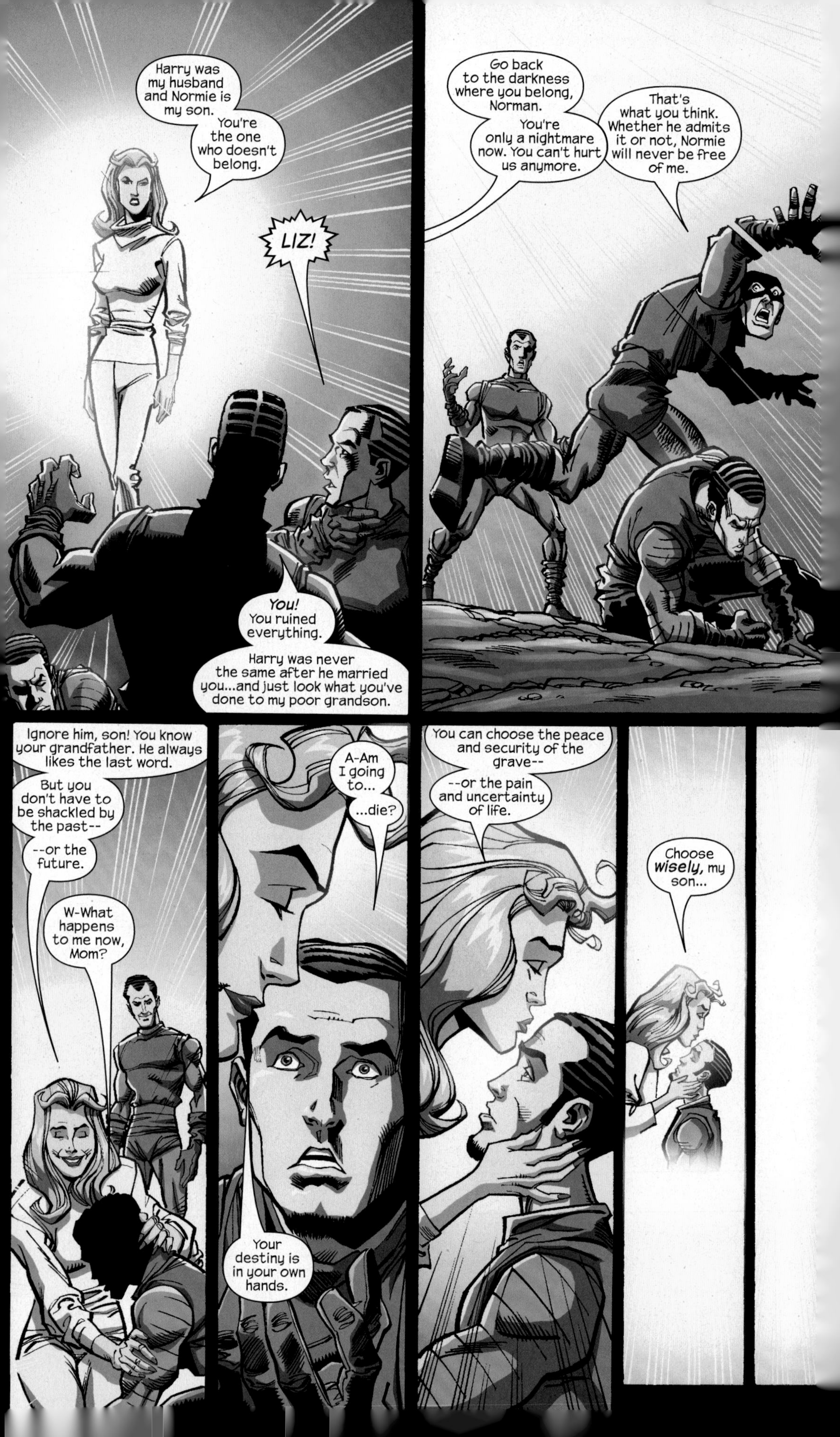
Harry was my husband and Normie is my son.
You're the one who doesn't belong.
LIZ!
You! You ruined everything.
Harry was never the same after he married you...and just look what you've done to my poor grandson.
Go back to the darkness where you belong, Norman.
You're only a nightmare now. You can't hurt us anymore.
That's what you think. Whether he admits it or not, Normie will never be free of me.
Ignore him, son! You know your grandfather. He always likes the last word.
But you don't have to be shackled by the past--
--or the future.
W-What happens to me now, Mom?
A-Am I going to...
...die?
Your destiny is in your own hands.
You can choose the peace and security of the grave--
--or the pain and uncertainty of life.
Choose *wisely,* my son...

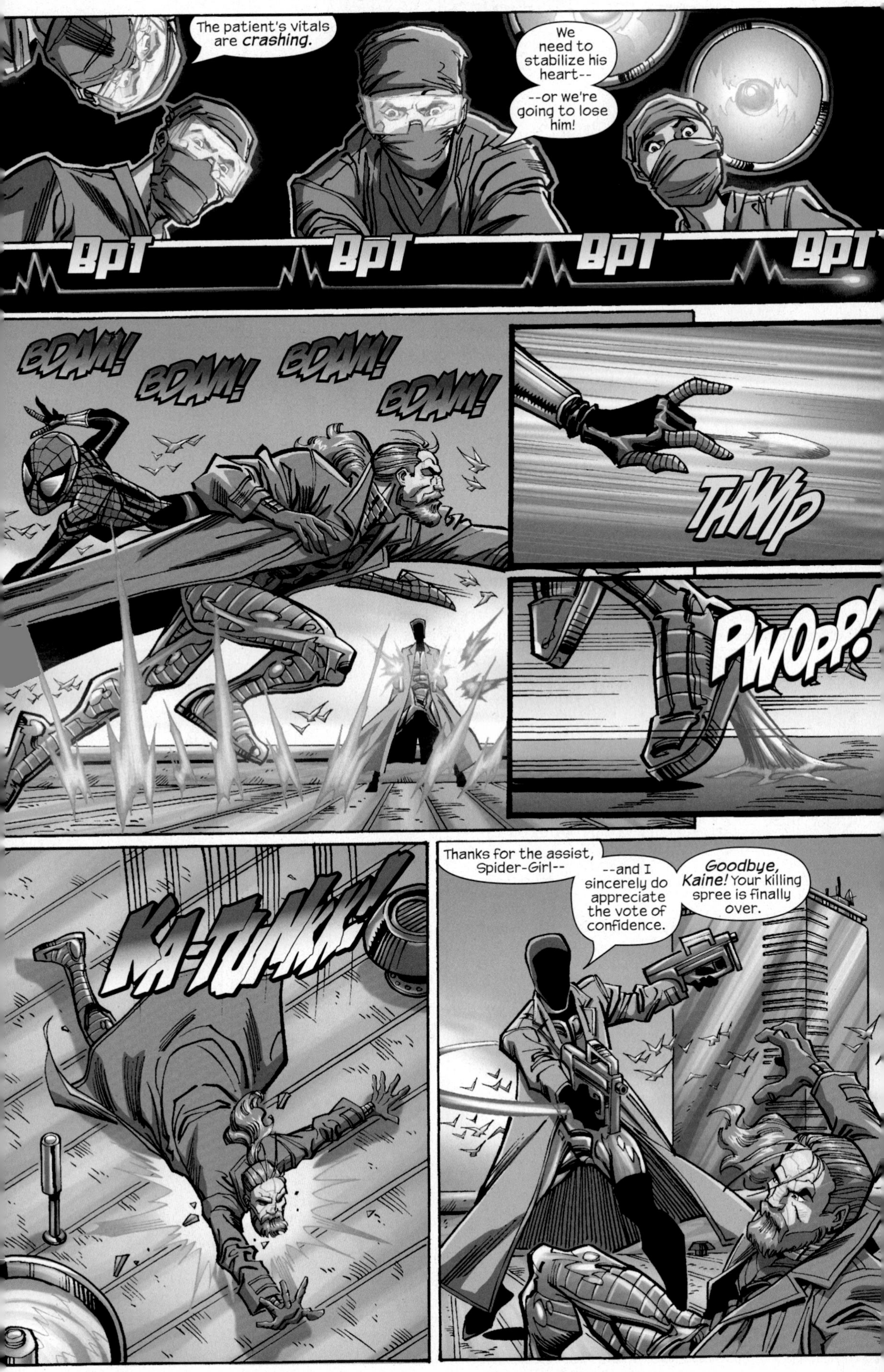
The patient's vitals are *crashing*.
We need to stabilize his heart--
--or we're going to lose him!
BPT
BPT
BPT
BPT
BDAM!
BDAM!
BDAM!
BDAM!
THWIP
PWOPP!
KA-TUNKK!
Thanks for the assist, Spider-Girl--
--and I sincerely do appreciate the vote of confidence.
Goodbye, Kaine! Your killing spree is finally over.

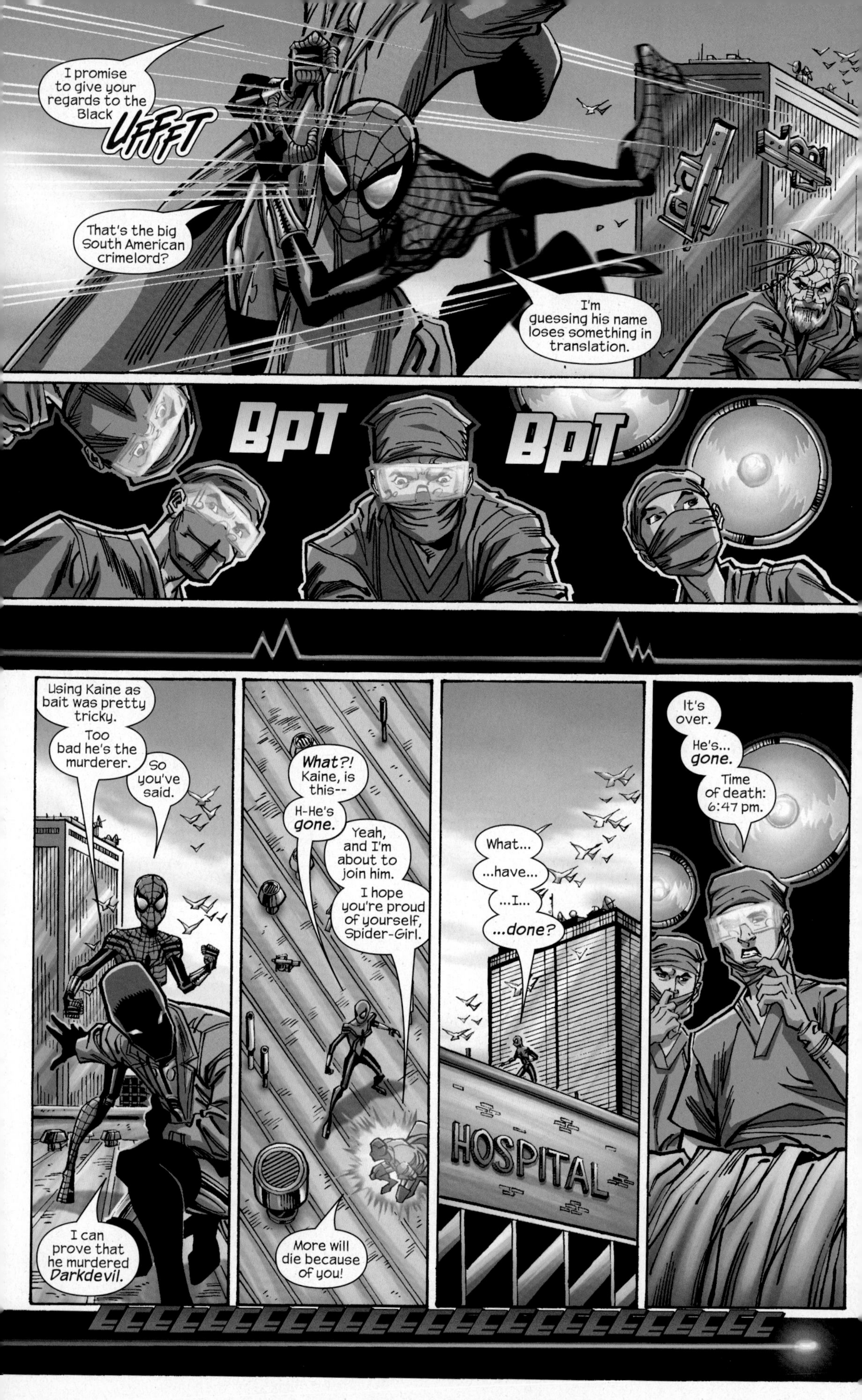
I promise to give your regards to the Black
UFFFT
That's the big South American crimelord?
I'm guessing his name loses something in translation.
BPT
BPT
Using Kaine as bait was pretty tricky.
Too bad he's the murderer.
So you've said.
I can prove that he murdered Darkdevil.
What?! Kaine, is this--
H-He's gone.
Yeah, and I'm about to join him.
I hope you're proud of yourself, Spider-Girl.
More will die because of you!
What...
...have...
...I...
...done?
HOSPITAL
It's over.
He's... gone.
Time of death: 6:47 pm.

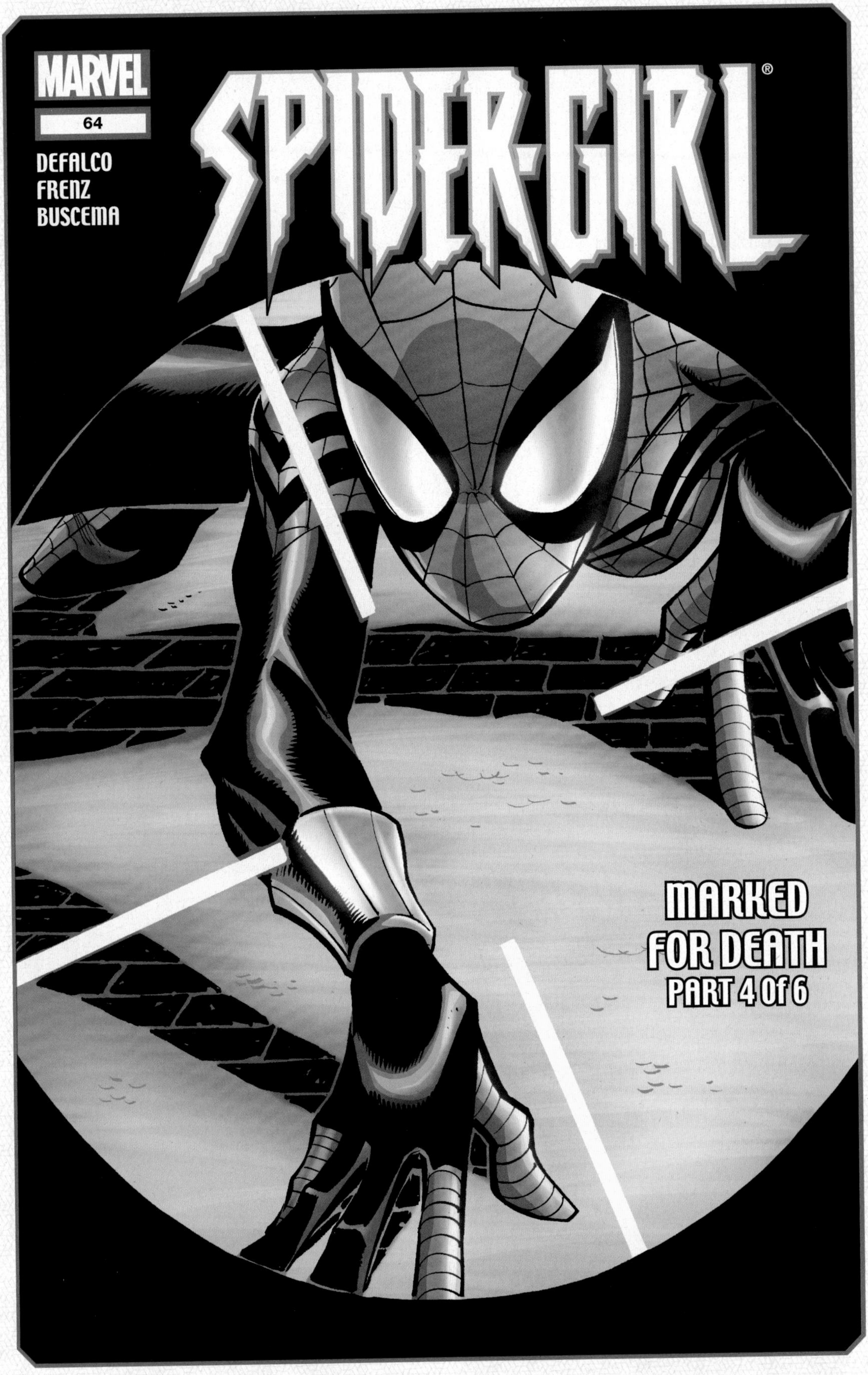
MARVEL
64
DEFALCO
FRENZ
BUSCEMA
SPIDER-GIRL
MARKED
FOR DEATH
PART 4 Of 6

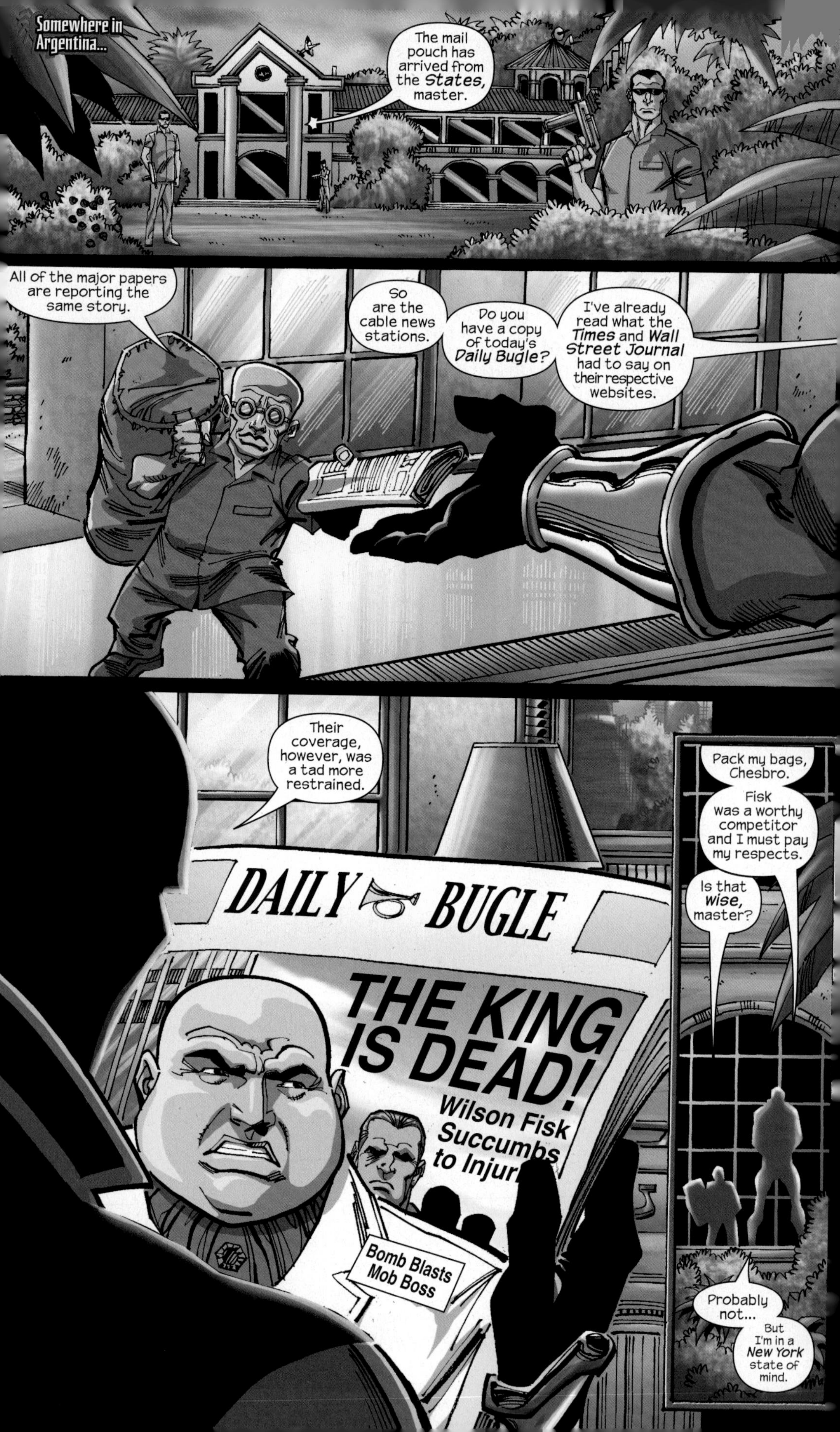
Somewhere in Argentina...
The mail pouch has arrived from the States, master.
All of the major papers are reporting the same story.
So are the cable news stations.
Do you have a copy of today's Daily Bugle?
I've already read what the Times and Wall Street Journal had to say on their respective websites.
Their coverage, however, was a tad more restrained.
DAILY BUGLE
THE KING IS DEAD!
Wilson Fisk Succumbs to Injur
Bomb Blasts Mob Boss
Pack my bags, Chesbro.
Fisk was a worthy competitor and I must pay my respects.
Is that wise, master?
Probably not...
But I'm in a New York state of mind.

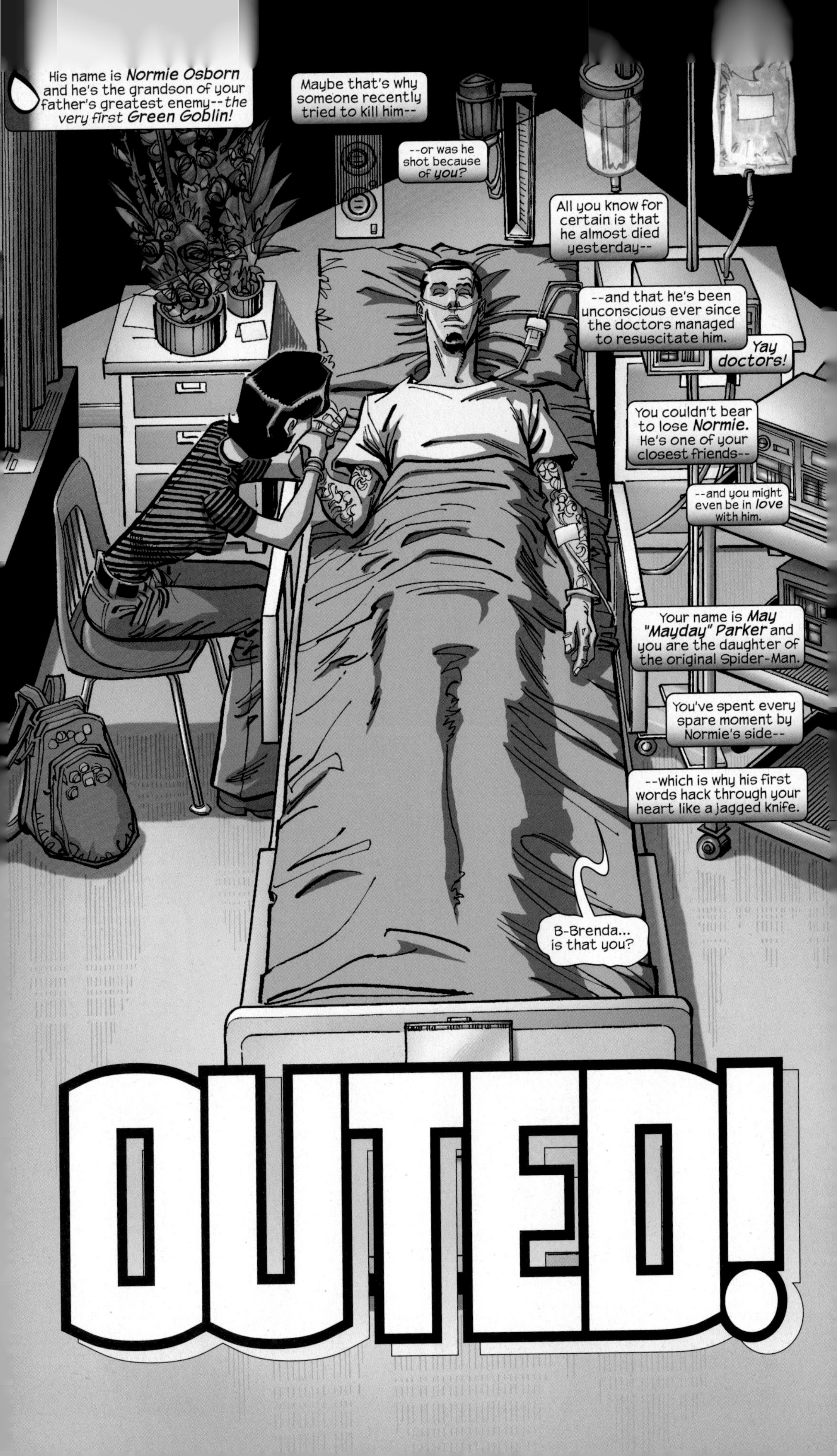

His name is Normie Osborn and he's the grandson of your father's greatest enemy--the very first Green Goblin!
Maybe that's why someone recently tried to kill him--
--or was he shot because of you?
All you know for certain is that he almost died yesterday--
--and that he's been unconscious ever since the doctors managed to resuscitate him.
Yay doctors!
You couldn't bear to lose Normie. He's one of your closest friends--
--and you might even be in love with him.
Your name is May "Mayday" Parker and you are the daughter of the original Spider-Man.
You've spent every spare moment by Normie's side--
--which is why his first words hack through your heart like a jagged knife.
B-Brenda... is that you?
OUTED!

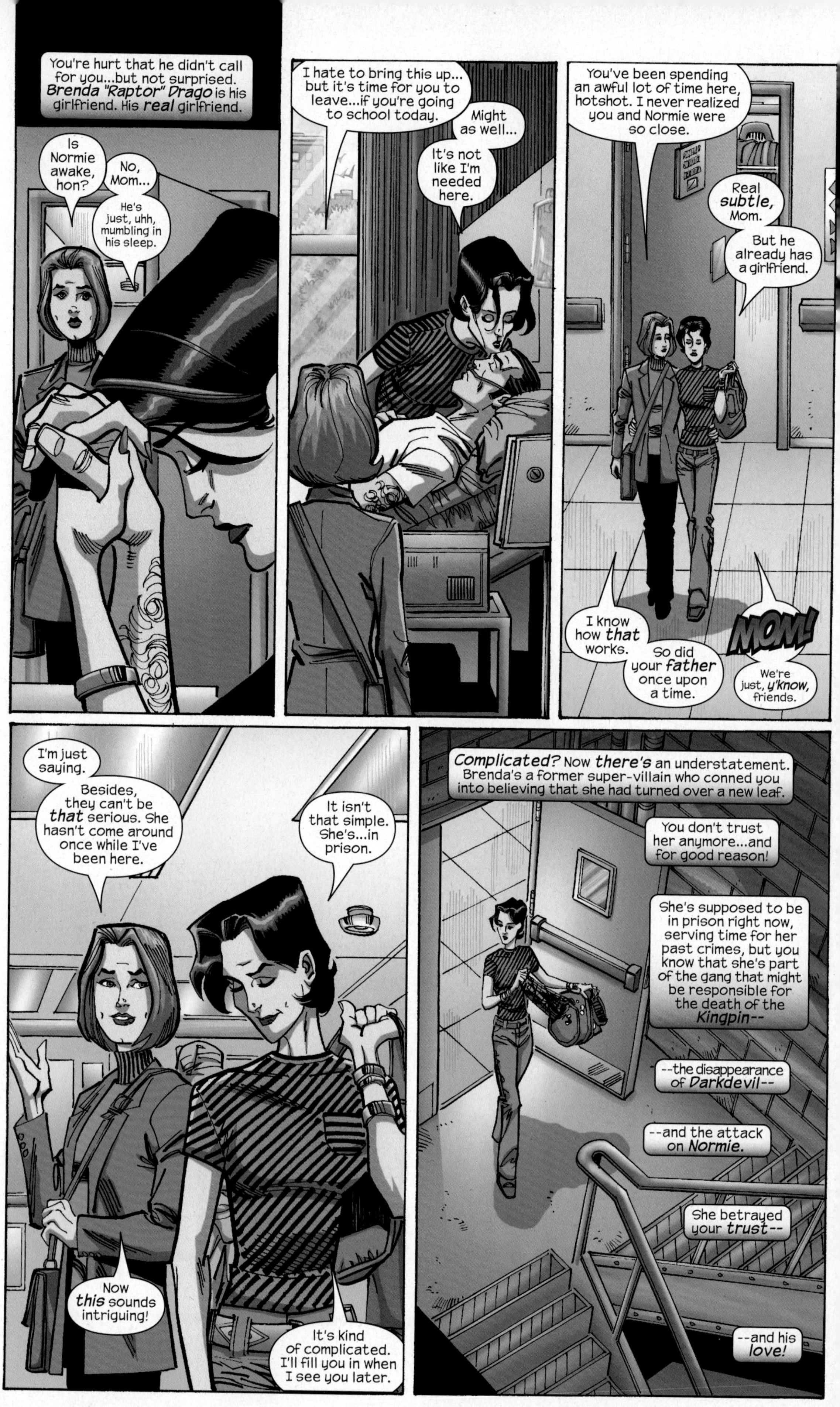
You're hurt that he didn't call for you...but not surprised. Brenda "Raptor" Drago is his girlfriend. His real girlfriend.
Is Normie awake, hon?
No, Mom...
He's just, uhh, mumbling in his sleep.
I hate to bring this up... but it's time for you to leave...if you're going to school today.
Might as well...
It's not like I'm needed here.
You've been spending an awful lot of time here, hotshot. I never realized you and Normie were so close.
Real subtle, Mom.
But he already has a girlfriend.
I know how that works.
So did your father once upon a time.
MOM!
We're just, y'know, friends.
I'm just saying.
Besides, they can't be that serious. She hasn't come around once while I've been here.
It isn't that simple. She's...in prison.
Now this sounds intriguing!
It's kind of complicated. I'll fill you in when I see you later.
Complicated? Now there's an understatement. Brenda's a former super-villain who conned you into believing that she had turned over a new leaf.
You don't trust her anymore...and for good reason!
She's supposed to be in prison right now, serving time for her past crimes, but you know that she's part of the gang that might be responsible for the death of the Kingpin--
--the disappearance of Darkdevil--
--and the attack on Normie.
She betrayed your trust--
--and his love!

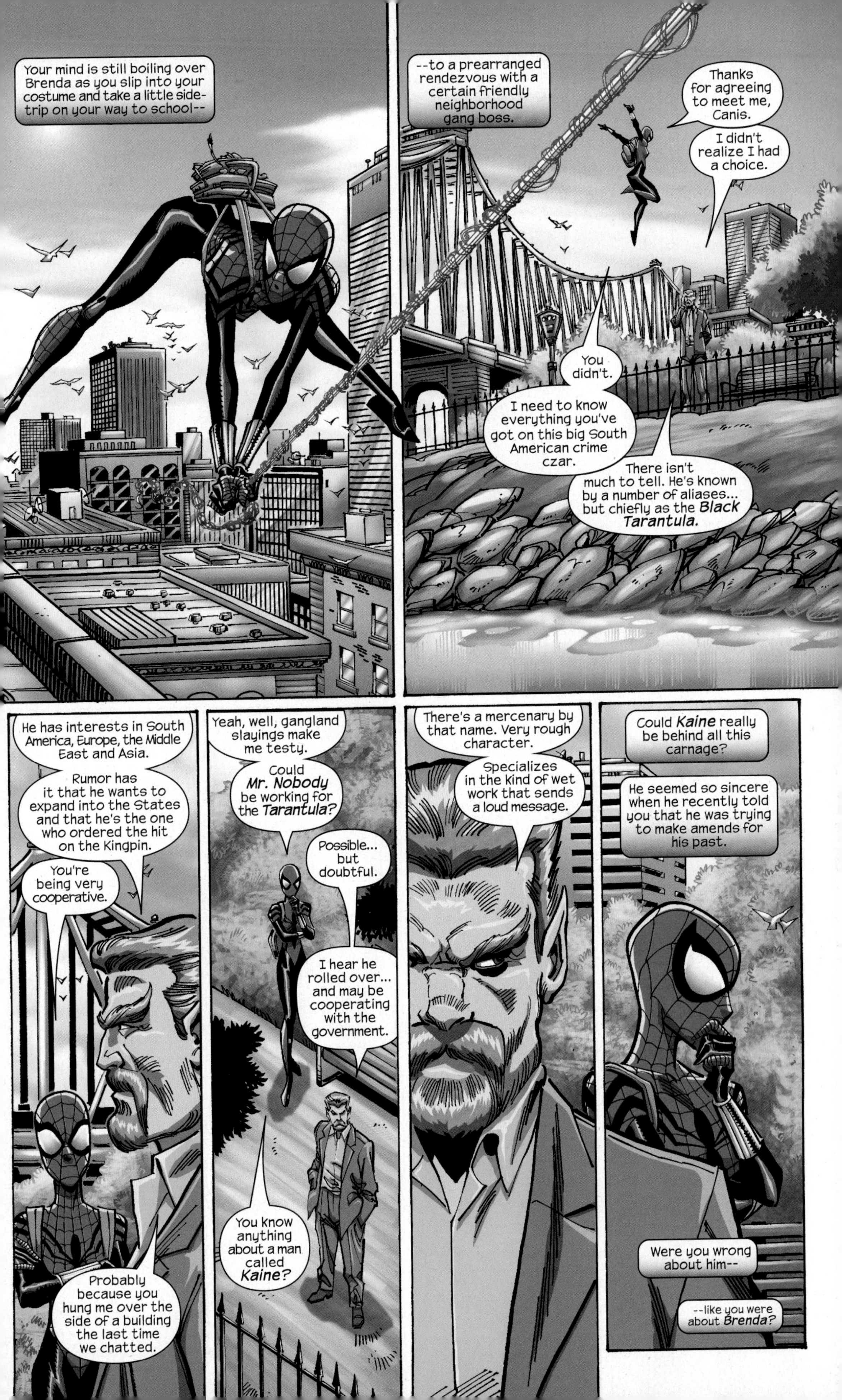

Your mind is still boiling over Brenda as you slip into your costume and take a little side-trip on your way to school--
--to a prearranged rendezvous with a certain friendly neighborhood gang boss.
Thanks for agreeing to meet me, Canis.
I didn't realize I had a choice.
You didn't.
I need to know everything you've got on this big South American crime czar.
There isn't much to tell. He's known by a number of aliases... but chiefly as the *Black Tarantula.*
He has interests in South America, Europe, the Middle East and Asia.
Rumor has it that he wants to expand into the States and that he's the one who ordered the hit on the Kingpin.
You're being very cooperative.
Probably because you hung me over the side of a building the last time we chatted.
Yeah, well, gangland slayings make me testy.
Could *Mr. Nobody* be working for the *Tarantula?*
Possible... but doubtful.
I hear he rolled over... and may be cooperating with the government.
You know anything about a man called *Kaine?*
There's a mercenary by that name. Very rough character.
Specializes in the kind of wet work that sends a loud message.
Could *Kaine* really be behind all this carnage?
He seemed so sincere when he recently told you that he was trying to make amends for his past.
Were you wrong about him--
--like you were about *Brenda?*

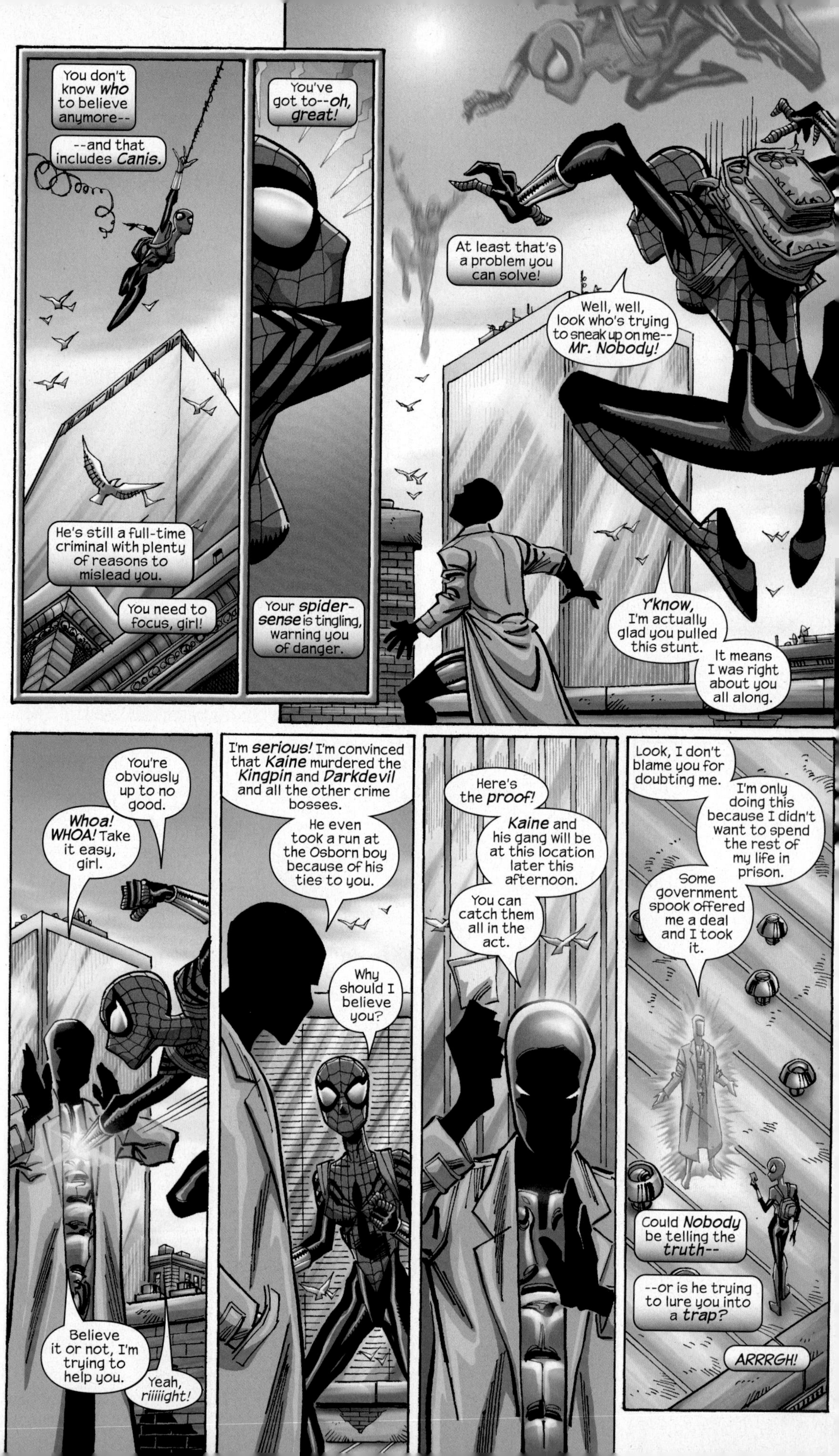

You don't know *who* to believe anymore--
--and that includes *Canis.*
He's still a full-time criminal with plenty of reasons to mislead you.
You need to focus, girl!
You've got to--*oh, great!*
Your *spider-sense* is tingling, warning you of danger.
At least that's a problem you can solve!
Well, well, look who's trying to sneak up on me-- *Mr. Nobody!*
Y'know, I'm actually glad you pulled this stunt.
It means I was right about you all along.
You're obviously up to no good.
Whoa! WHOA! Take it easy, girl.
Believe it or not, I'm trying to help you.
Yeah, *riiiiight!*
I'm *serious!* I'm convinced that *Kaine* murdered the *Kingpin* and *Darkdevil* and all the other crime bosses.
He even took a run at the Osborn boy because of his ties to you.
Why should I believe you?
Here's the *proof!*
Kaine and his gang will be at this location later this afternoon.
You can catch them all in the act.
Look, I don't blame you for doubting me.
I'm only doing this because I didn't want to spend the rest of my life in prison.
Some government spook offered me a deal and I took it.
Could *Nobody* be telling the *truth--*
--or is he trying to lure you into a *trap?*
ARRRGH!

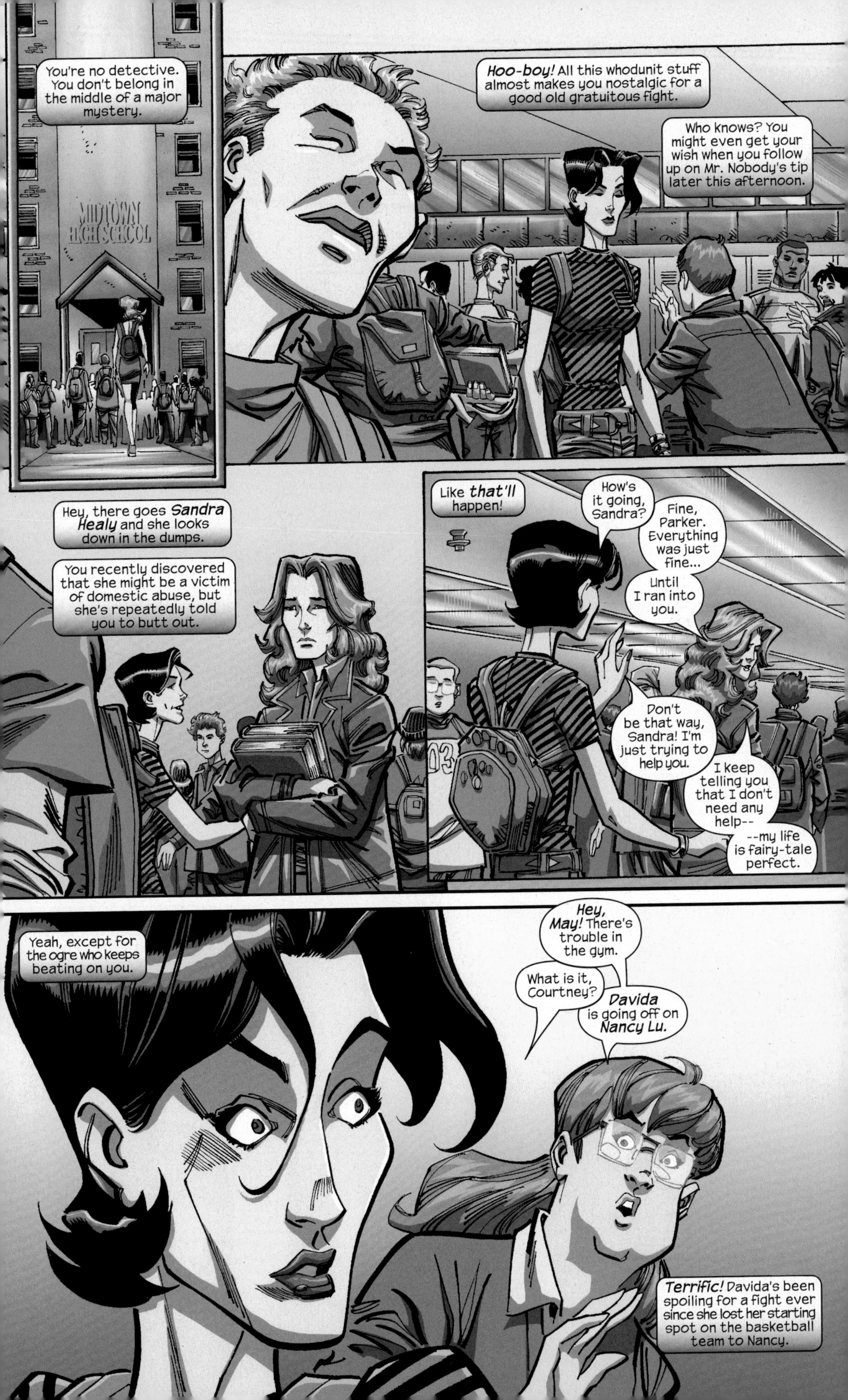
You're no detective. You don't belong in the middle of a major mystery.
MIDTOWN HIGH SCHOOL
Hoo-boy! All this whodunit stuff almost makes you nostalgic for a good old gratuitous fight.
Who knows? You might even get your wish when you follow up on Mr. Nobody's tip later this afternoon.
Hey, there goes Sandra Healy and she looks down in the dumps.
You recently discovered that she might be a victim of domestic abuse, but she's repeatedly told you to butt out.
Like that'll happen!
How's it going, Sandra?
Fine, Parker. Everything was just fine...
Until I ran into you.
Don't be that way, Sandra! I'm just trying to help you.
I keep telling you that I don't need any help--
--my life is fairy-tale perfect.
Yeah, except for the ogre who keeps beating on you.
Hey, May! There's trouble in the gym.
What is it, Courtney?
Davida is going off on Nancy Lu.
Terrific! Davida's been spoiling for a fight ever since she lost her starting spot on the basketball team to Nancy.

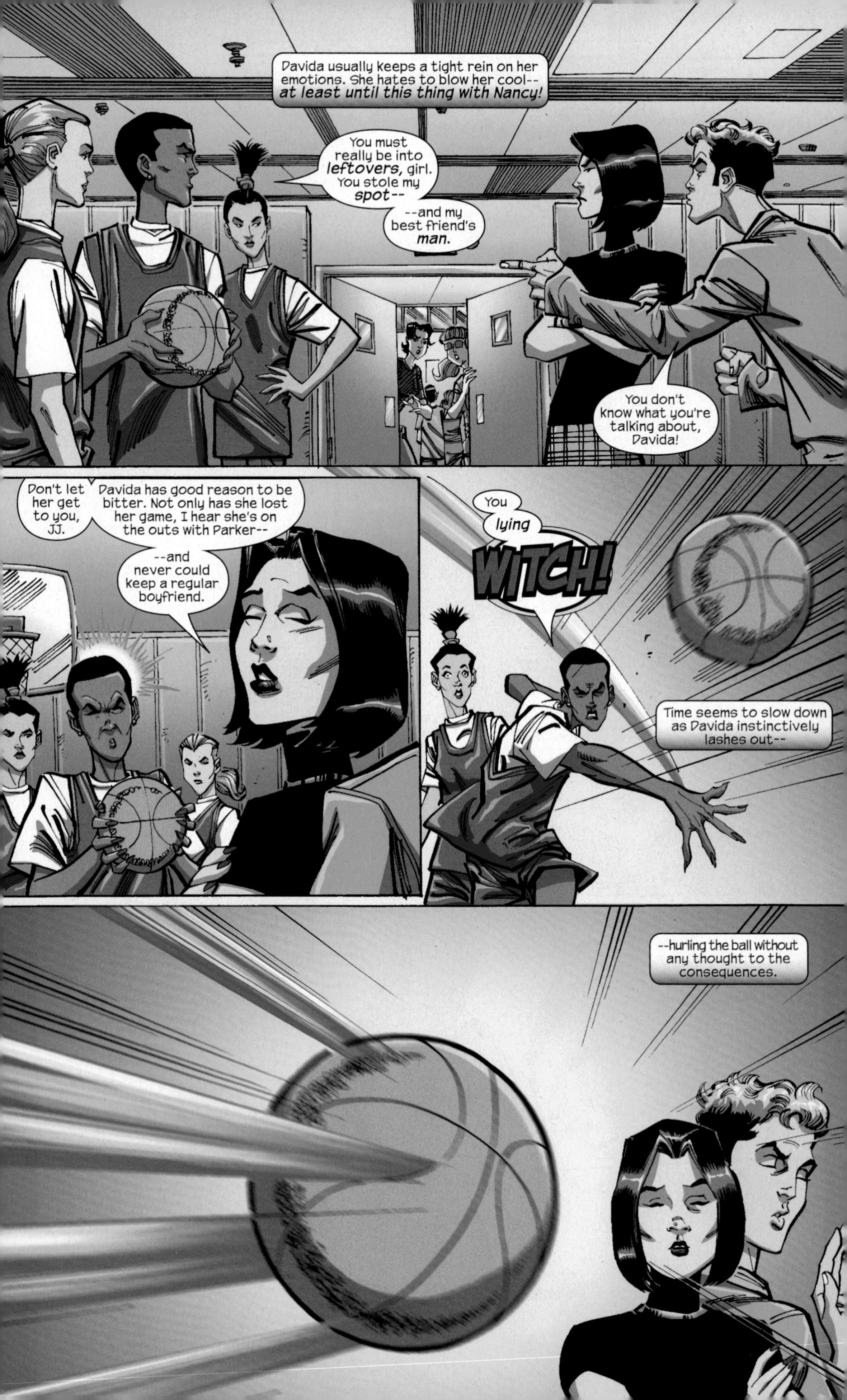
Davida usually keeps a tight rein on her emotions. She hates to blow her cool-- at least until this thing with Nancy!
You must really be into leftovers, girl. You stole my spot--
--and my best friend's man.
You don't know what you're talking about, Davida!
Don't let her get to you, JJ.
Davida has good reason to be bitter. Not only has she lost her game, I hear she's on the outs with Parker--
--and never could keep a regular boyfriend.
You lying WITCH!
Time seems to slow down as Davida instinctively lashes out--
--hurling the ball without any thought to the consequences.

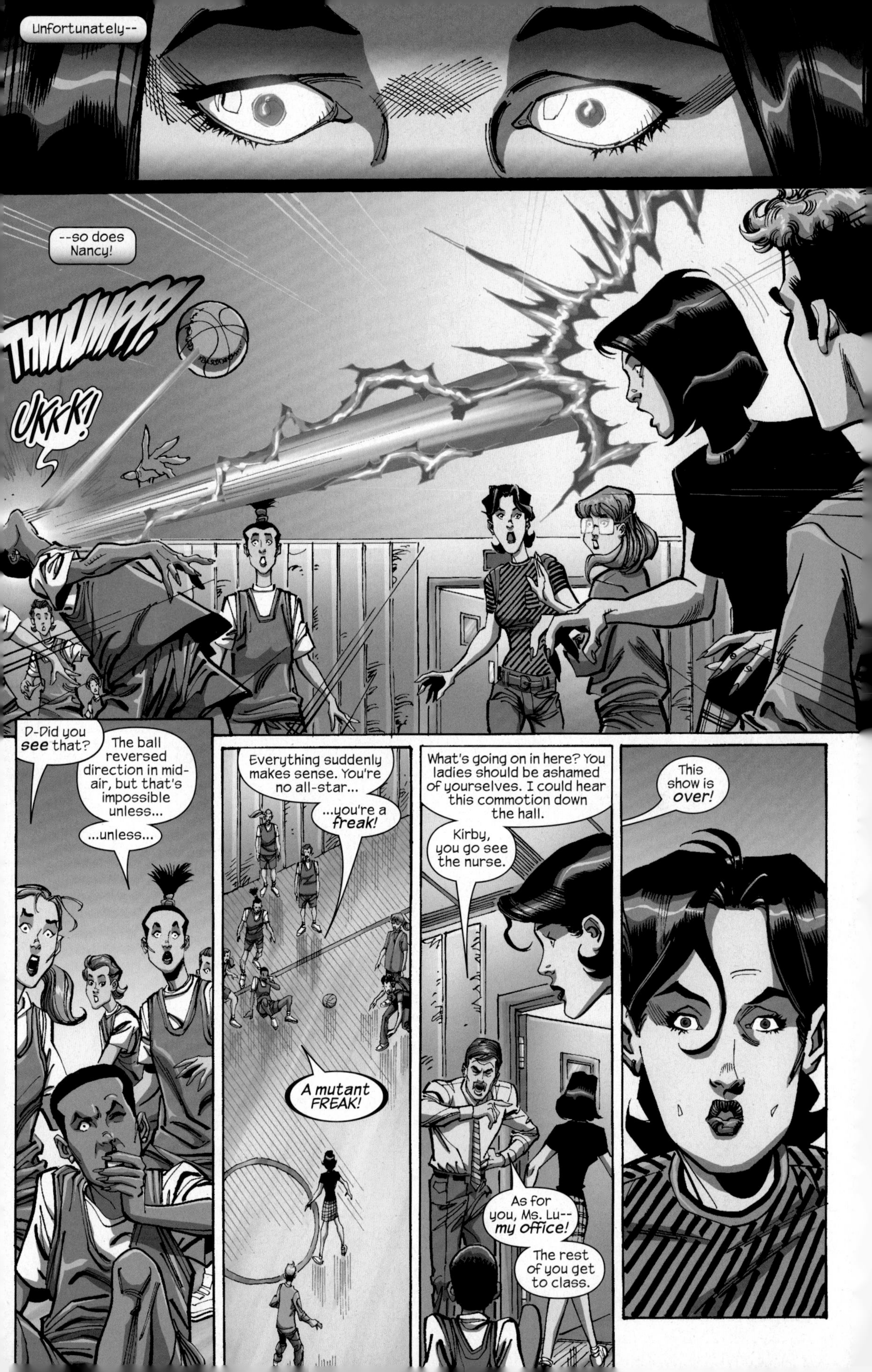
Unfortunately--
--so does Nancy!
THWUMPP!
UKK-K!
D-Did you see that?
The ball reversed direction in mid-air, but that's impossible unless...
...unless...
Everything suddenly makes sense. You're no all-star...
...you're a freak!
A mutant FREAK!
What's going on in here? You ladies should be ashamed of yourselves. I could hear this commotion down the hall.
Kirby, you go see the nurse.
As for you, Ms. Lu-- my office!
The rest of you get to class.
This show is over!

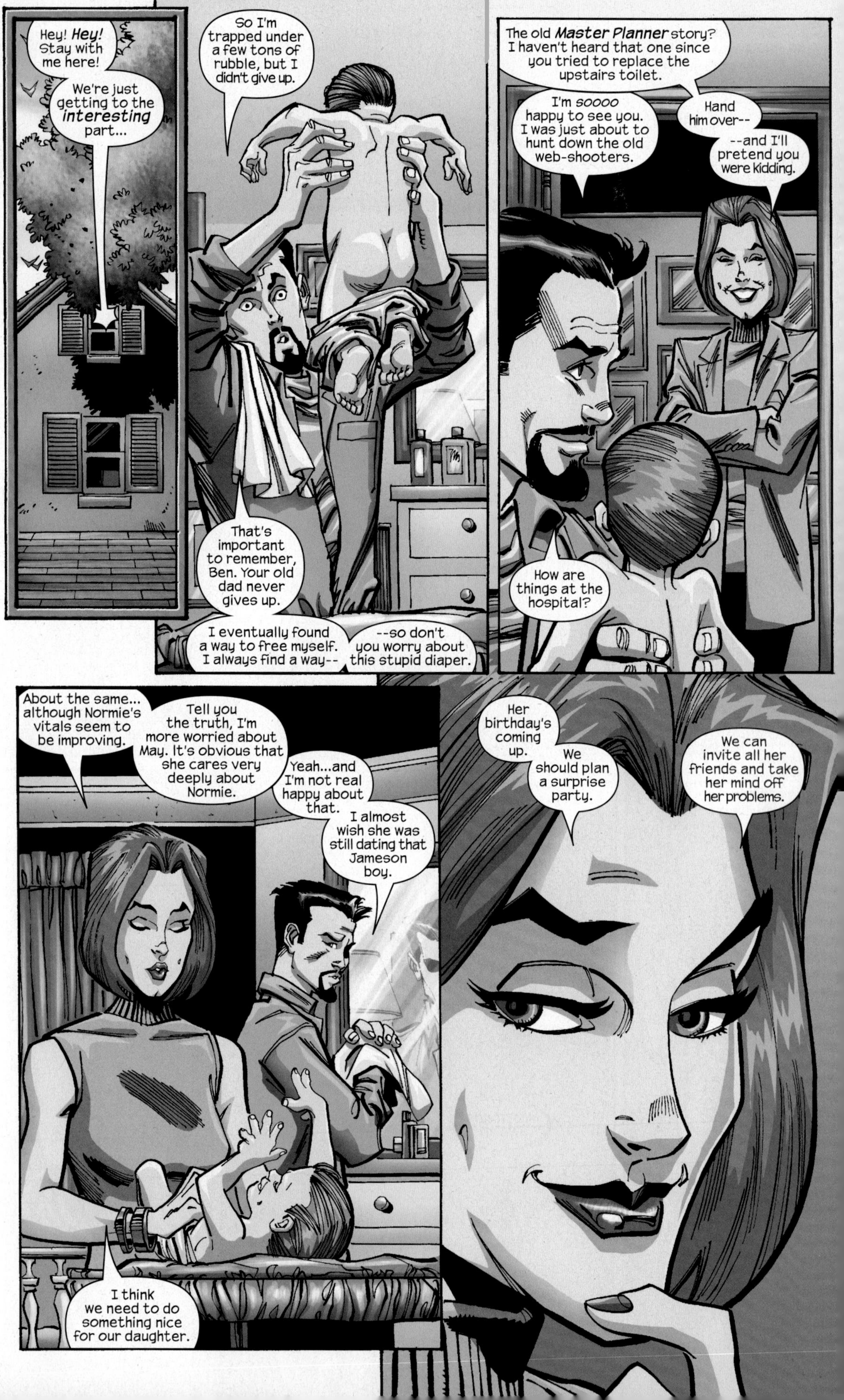

Hey! Hey! Stay with me here!
We're just getting to the interesting part...
So I'm trapped under a few tons of rubble, but I didn't give up.
That's important to remember, Ben. Your old dad never gives up.
I eventually found a way to free myself. I always find a way--
--so don't you worry about this stupid diaper.
The old Master Planner story? I haven't heard that one since you tried to replace the upstairs toilet.
I'm soooo happy to see you. I was just about to hunt down the old web-shooters.
Hand him over--
--and I'll pretend you were kidding.
How are things at the hospital?
About the same... although Normie's vitals seem to be improving.
Tell you the truth, I'm more worried about May. It's obvious that she cares very deeply about Normie.
Yeah...and I'm not real happy about that.
I almost wish she was still dating that Jameson boy.
I think we need to do something nice for our daughter.
Her birthday's coming up.
We should plan a surprise party.
We can invite all her friends and take her mind off her problems.

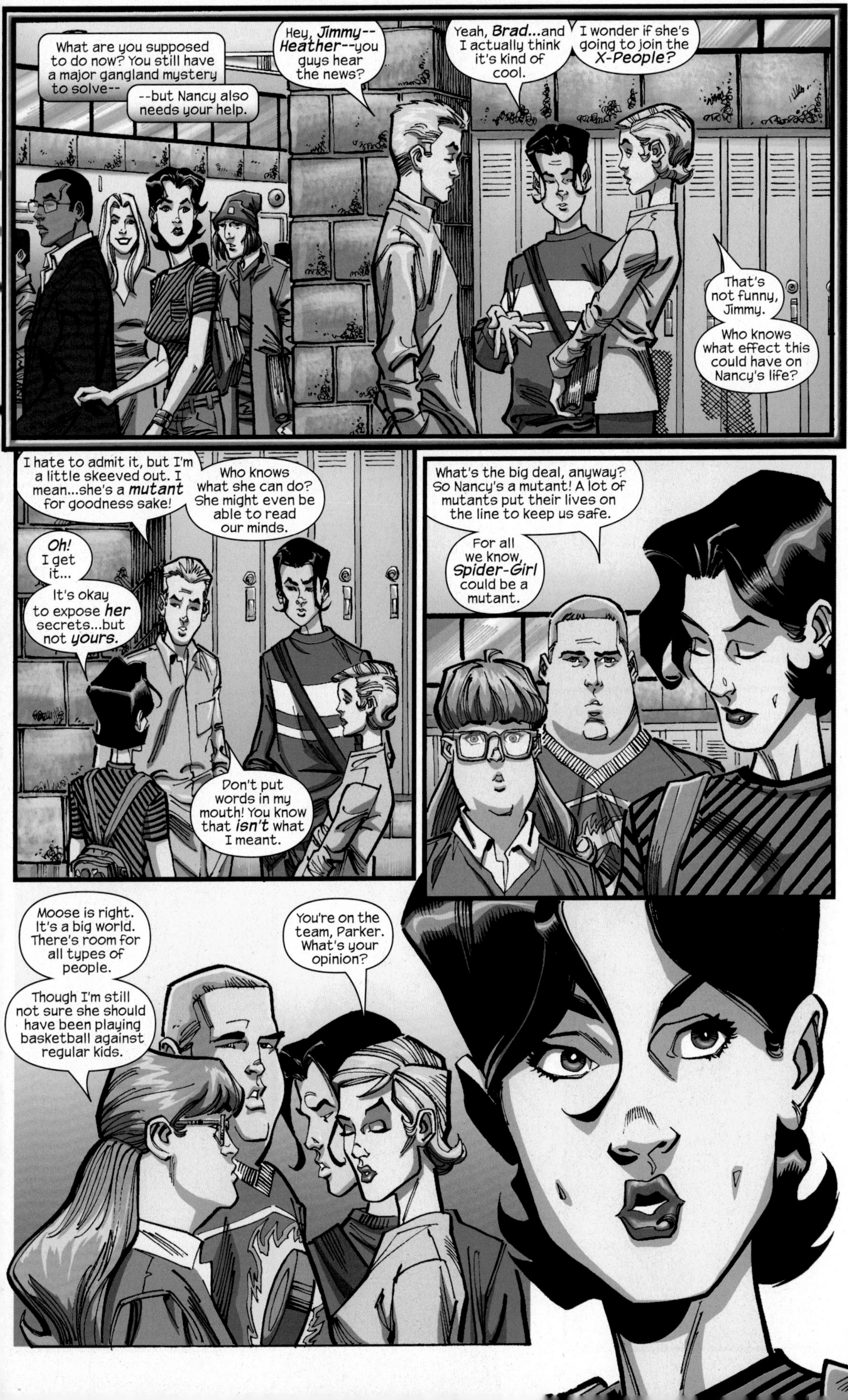
What are you supposed to do now? You still have a major gangland mystery to solve--
--but Nancy also needs your help.
Hey, Jimmy-- Heather--you guys hear the news?
Yeah, Brad...and I actually think it's kind of cool.
I wonder if she's going to join the X-People?
That's not funny, Jimmy.
Who knows what effect this could have on Nancy's life?
I hate to admit it, but I'm a little skeeved out. I mean...she's a mutant for goodness sake!
Who knows what she can do? She might even be able to read our minds.
Oh! I get it...
It's okay to expose her secrets...but not yours.
Don't put words in my mouth! You know that isn't what I meant.
What's the big deal, anyway? So Nancy's a mutant! A lot of mutants put their lives on the line to keep us safe.
For all we know, Spider-Girl could be a mutant.
Moose is right. It's a big world. There's room for all types of people.
Though I'm still not sure she should have been playing basketball against regular kids.
You're on the team, Parker. What's your opinion?

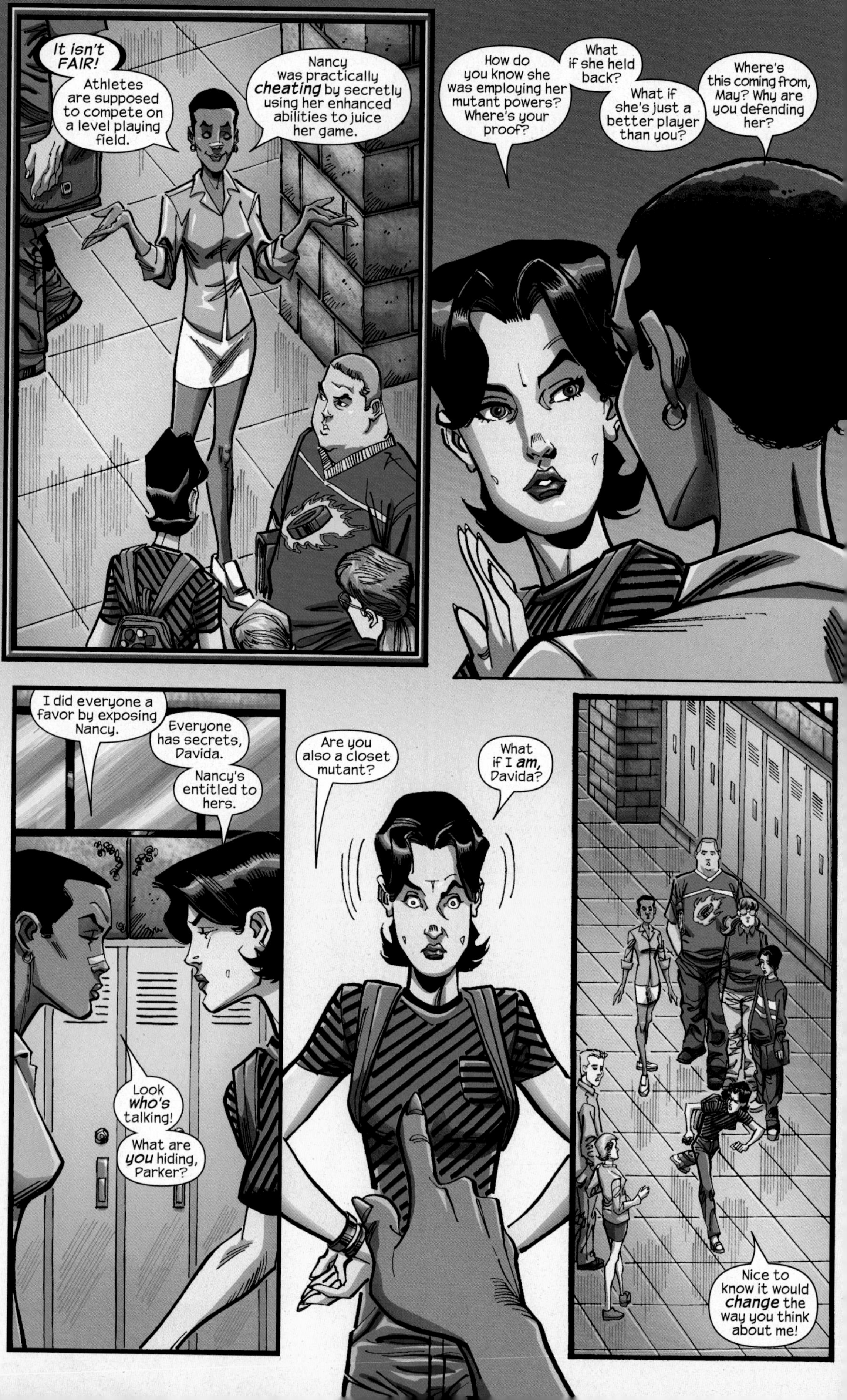
It isn't FAIR!
Athletes are supposed to compete on a level playing field.
Nancy was practically *cheating* by secretly using her enhanced abilities to juice her game.
How do you know she was employing her mutant powers? Where's your proof?
What if she held back?
What if she's just a better player than you?
Where's this coming from, May? Why are you defending her?
I did everyone a favor by exposing Nancy.
Everyone has secrets, Davida.
Nancy's entitled to hers.
Look *who's* talking!
What are *you* hiding, Parker?
Are you also a closet mutant?
What if I *am*, Davida?
Nice to know it would *change* the way you think about me!

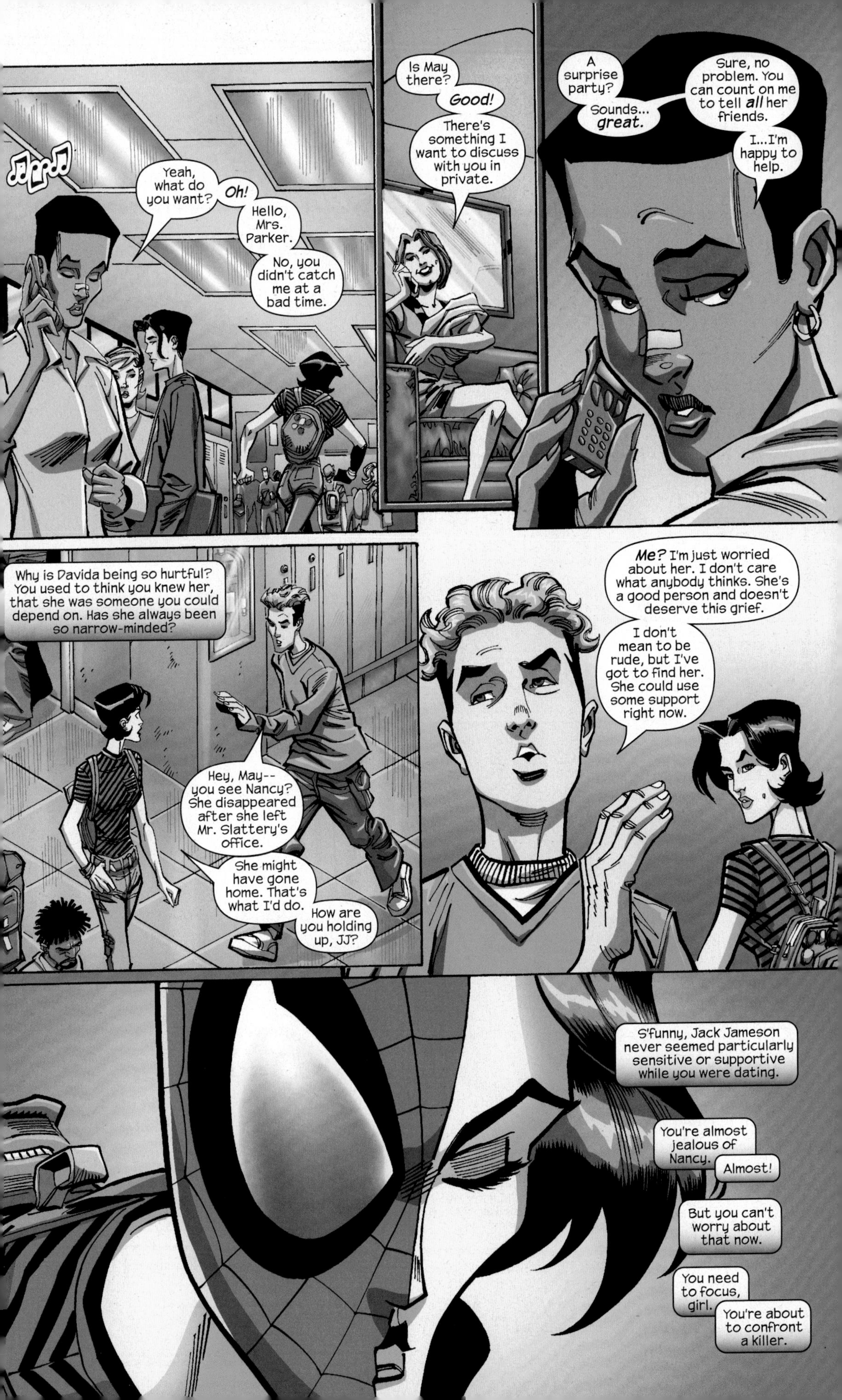

Yeah, what do you want?
Oh!
Hello, Mrs. Parker.
No, you didn't catch me at a bad time.
Is May there?
Good!
There's something I want to discuss with you in private.
A surprise party?
Sounds... great.
Sure, no problem. You can count on me to tell all her friends.
I...I'm happy to help.
Why is Davida being so hurtful? You used to think you knew her, that she was someone you could depend on. Has she always been so narrow-minded?
Hey, May-- you see Nancy? She disappeared after she left Mr. Slattery's office.
She might have gone home. That's what I'd do.
How are you holding up, JJ?
Me? I'm just worried about her. I don't care what anybody thinks. She's a good person and doesn't deserve this grief.
I don't mean to be rude, but I've got to find her. She could use some support right now.
S'funny, Jack Jameson never seemed particularly sensitive or supportive while you were dating.
You're almost jealous of Nancy.
Almost!
But you can't worry about that now.
You need to focus, girl.
You're about to confront a killer.

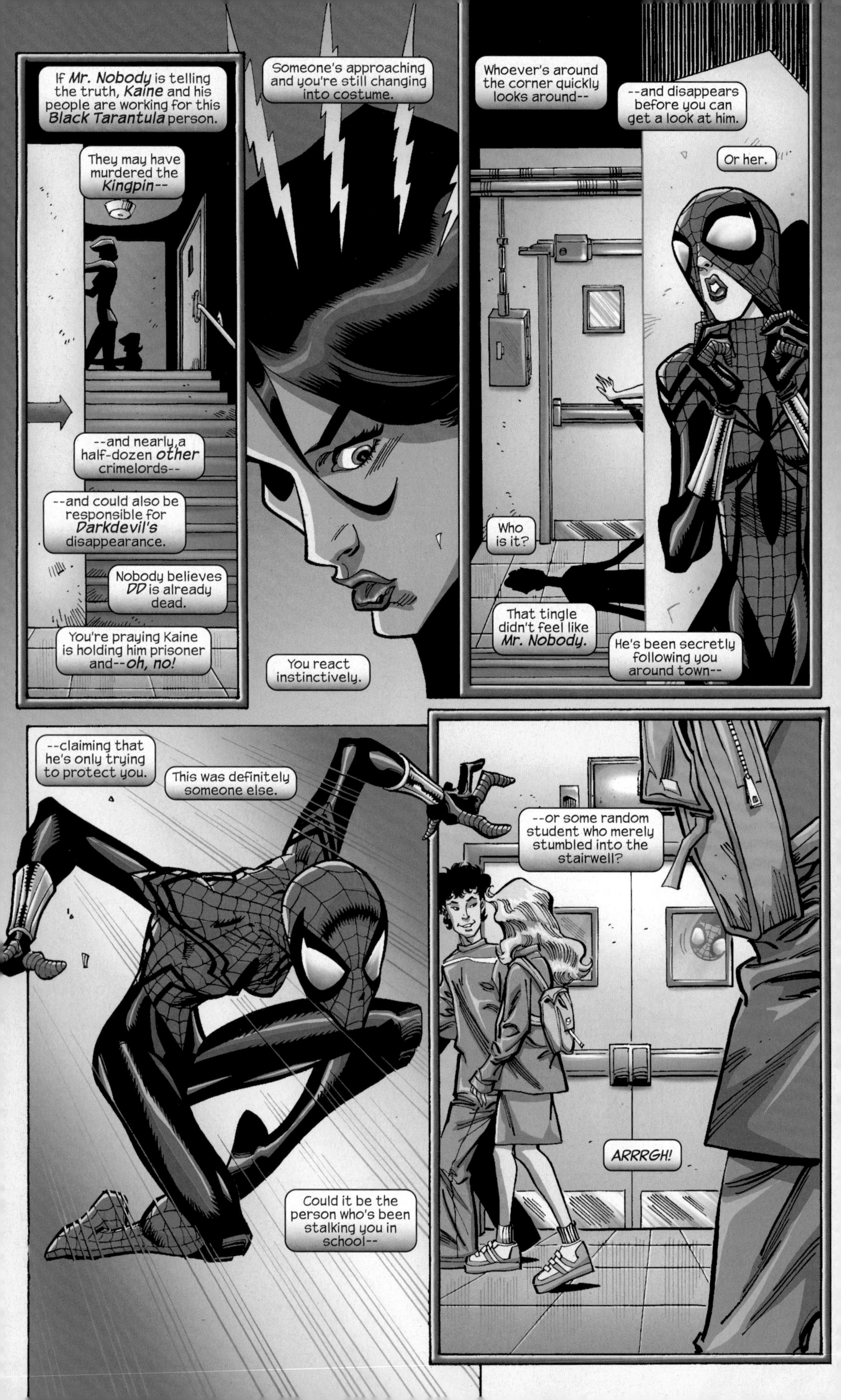
If Mr. Nobody is telling the truth, Kaine and his people are working for this Black Tarantula person.
They may have murdered the Kingpin--
--and nearly a half-dozen other crimelords--
--and could also be responsible for Darkdevil's disappearance.
Nobody believes DD is already dead.
You're praying Kaine is holding him prisoner and--oh, no!
Someone's approaching and you're still changing into costume.
You react instinctively.
Whoever's around the corner quickly looks around--
--and disappears before you can get a look at him.
Or her.
Who is it?
That tingle didn't feel like Mr. Nobody.
He's been secretly following you around town--
--claiming that he's only trying to protect you.
This was definitely someone else.
Could it be the person who's been stalking you in school--
--or some random student who merely stumbled into the stairwell?
ARRRGH!

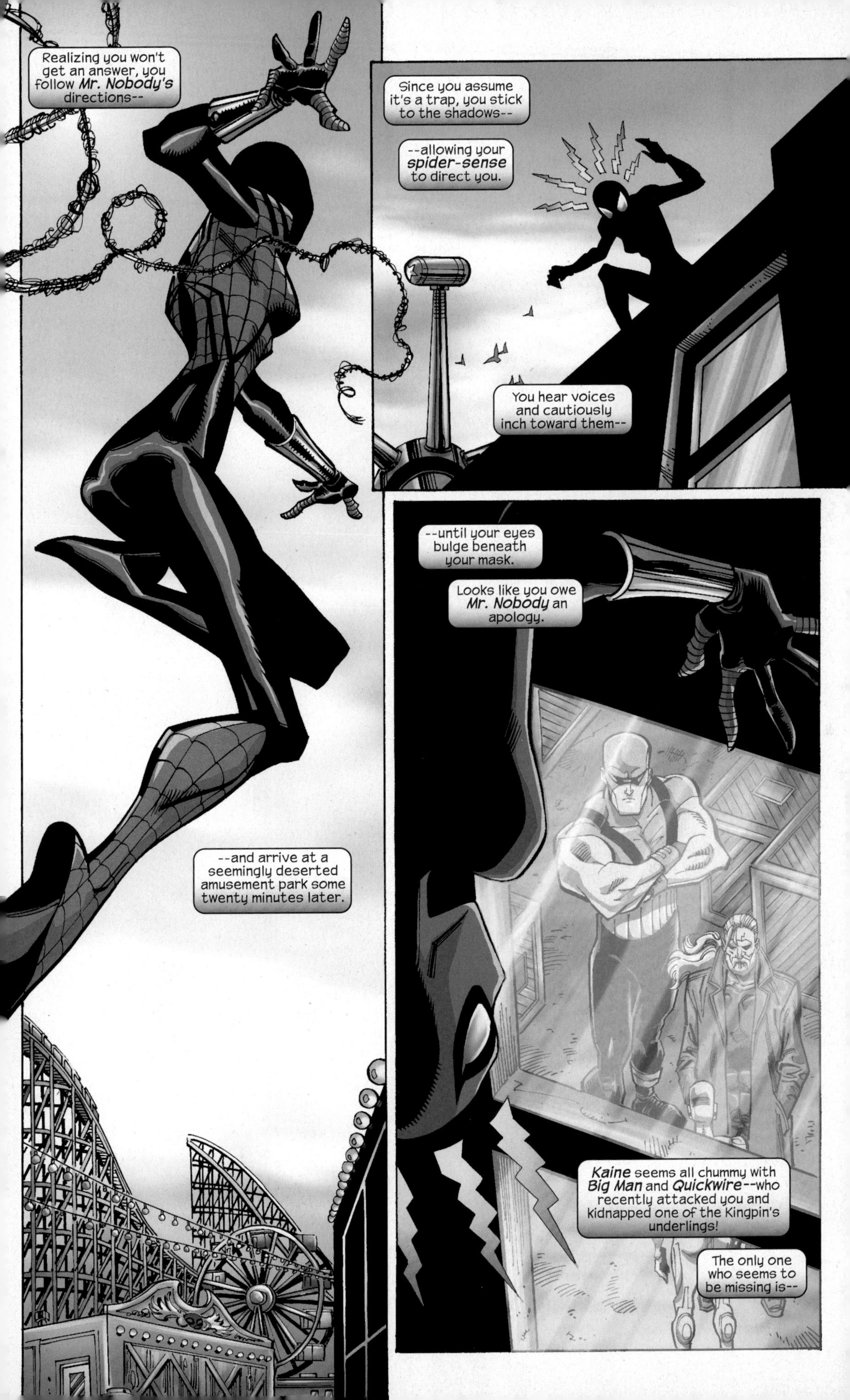

Realizing you won't get an answer, you follow Mr. Nobody's directions--
--and arrive at a seemingly deserted amusement park some twenty minutes later.
Since you assume it's a trap, you stick to the shadows--
--allowing your spider-sense to direct you.
You hear voices and cautiously inch toward them--
--until your eyes bulge beneath your mask.
Looks like you owe Mr. Nobody an apology.
Kaine seems all chummy with Big Man and Quickwire--who recently attacked you and kidnapped one of the Kingpin's underlings!
The only one who seems to be missing is--

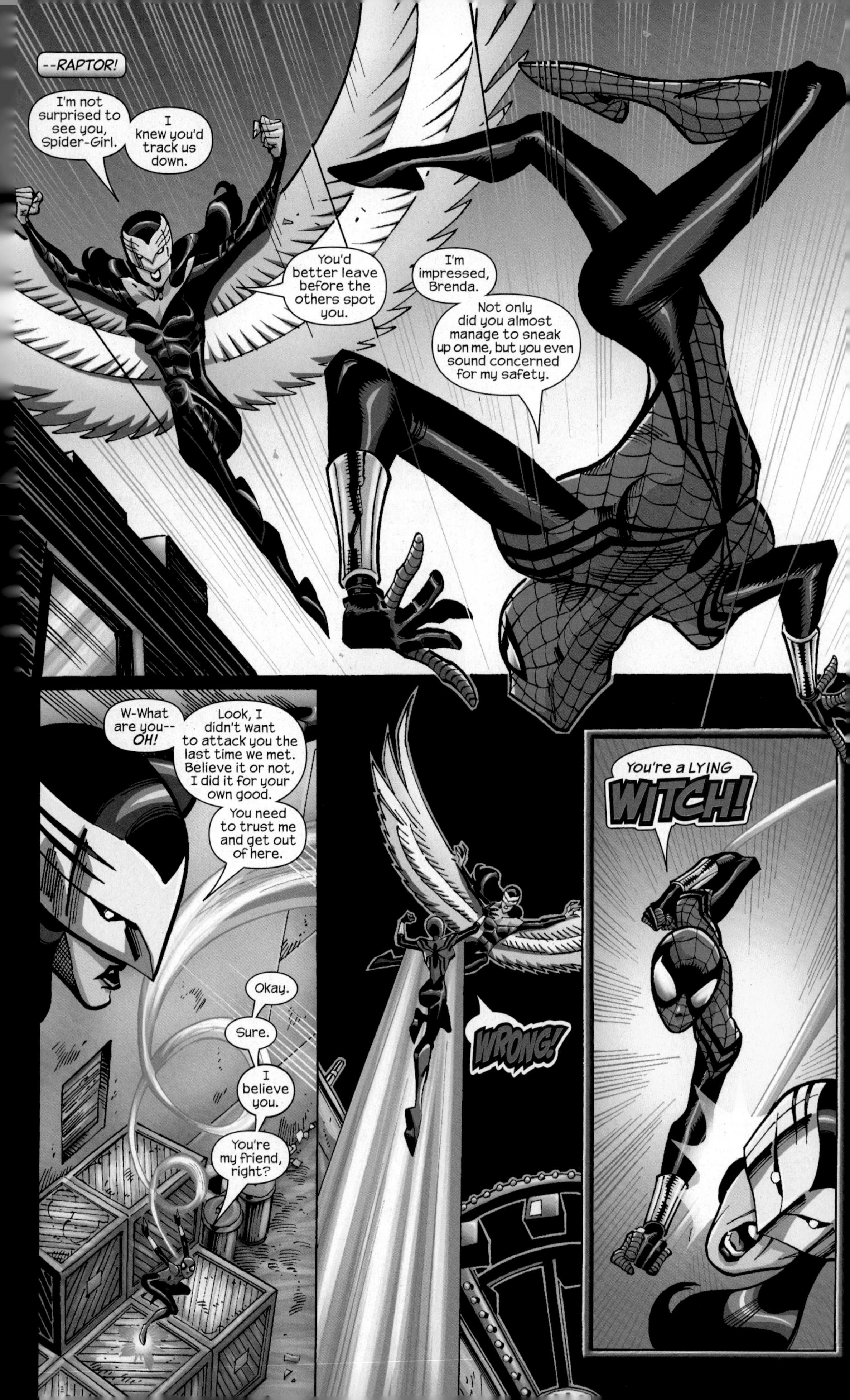
--RAPTOR!
I'm not surprised to see you, Spider-Girl.
I knew you'd track us down.
You'd better leave before the others spot you.
I'm impressed, Brenda.
Not only did you almost manage to sneak up on me, but you even sound concerned for my safety.
W-What are you-- OH!
Look, I didn't want to attack you the last time we met. Believe it or not, I did it for your own good.
You need to trust me and get out of here.
Okay.
Sure.
I believe you.
You're my friend, right?
WRONG!
You're a LYING WITCH!

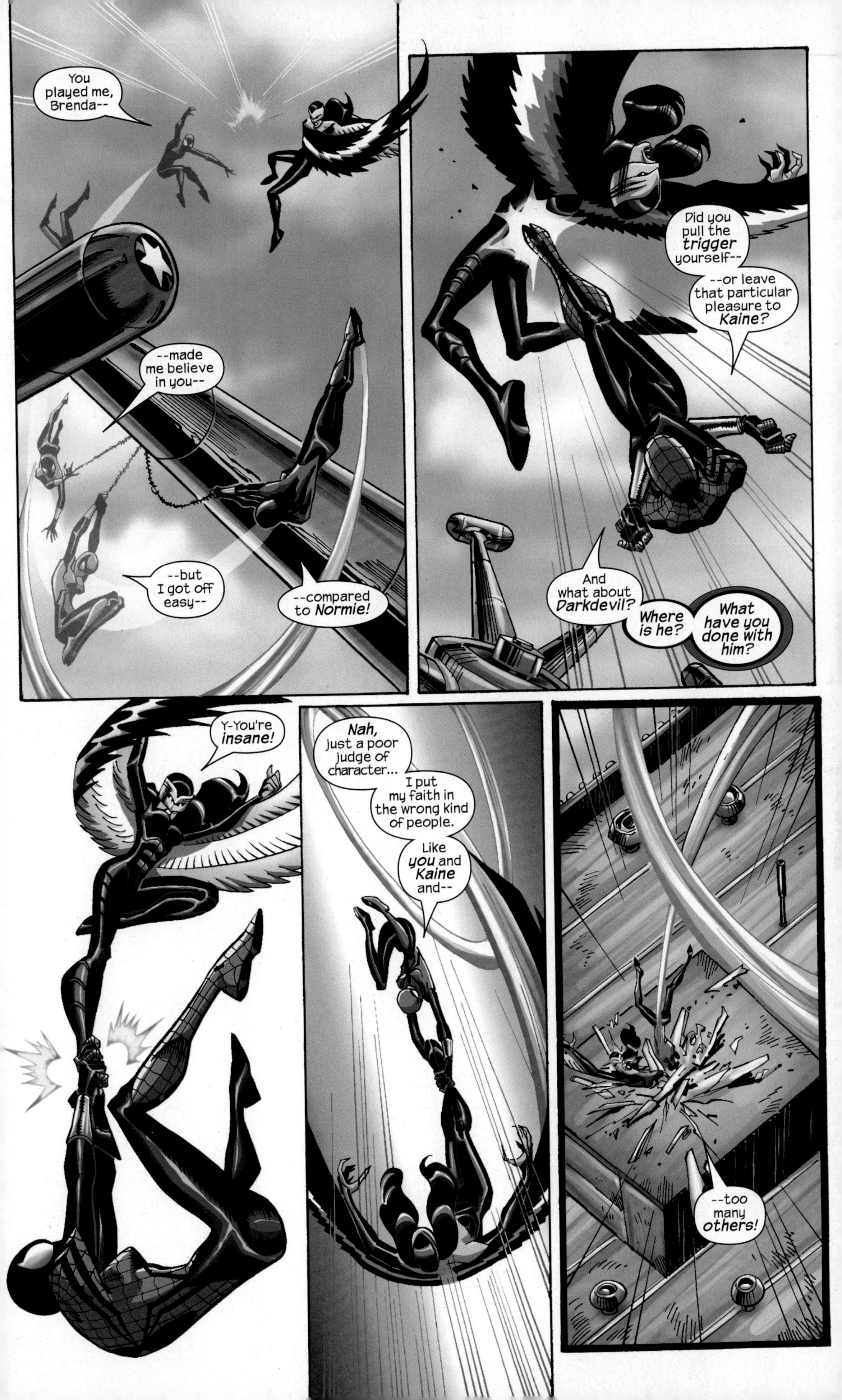
You played me, Brenda--
--made me believe in you--
--but I got off easy--
--compared to Normie!
Did you pull the trigger yourself--
--or leave that particular pleasure to Kaine?
And what about Darkdevil?
Where is he?
What have you done with him?
Y-You're insane!
Nah, just a poor judge of character... I put my faith in the wrong kind of people.
Like you and Kaine and--
--too many others!

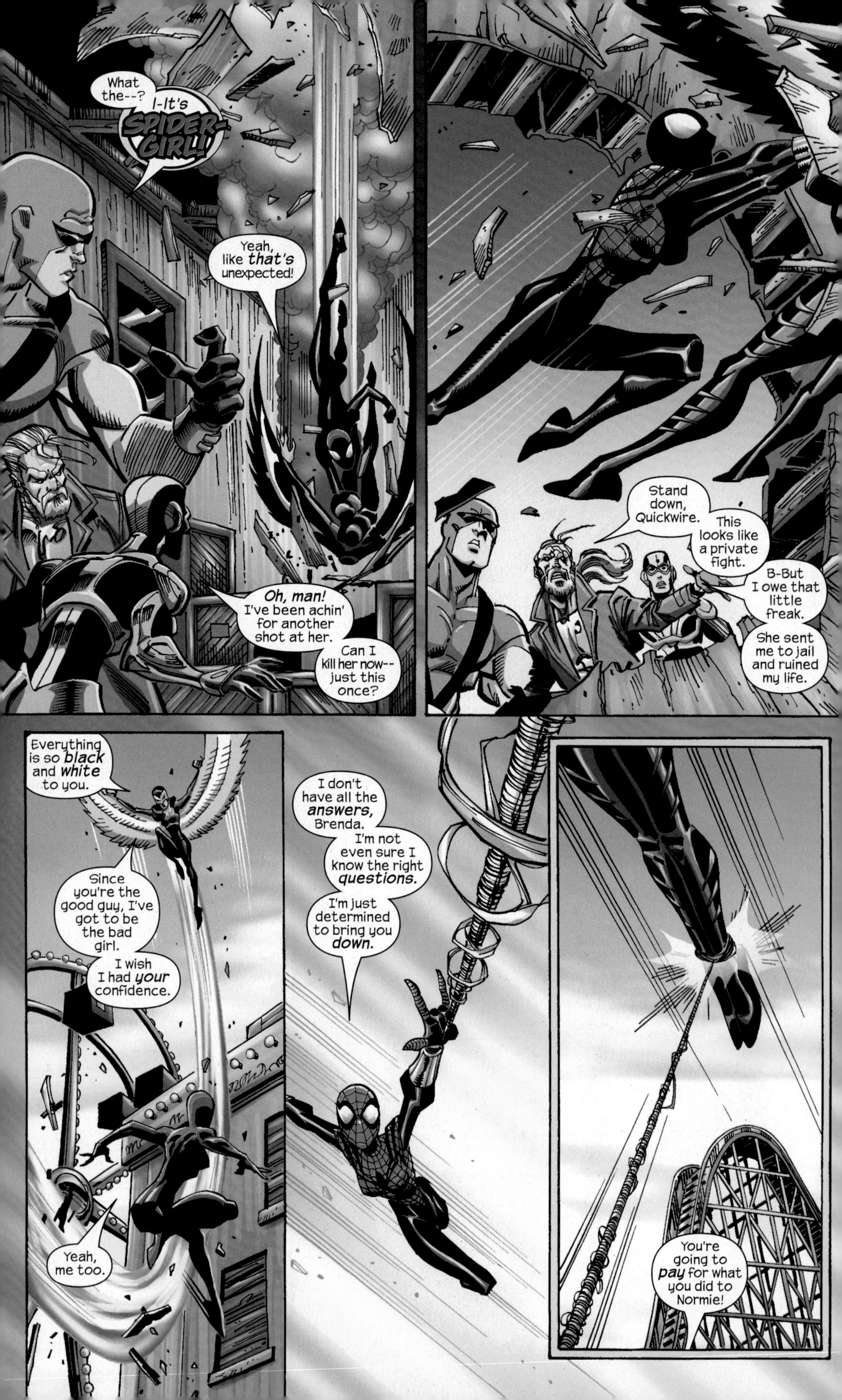
What the--? I-It's SPIDER-GIRL!
Yeah, like that's unexpected!
Oh, man! I've been achin' for another shot at her.
Can I kill her now-- just this once?
Stand down, Quickwire.
This looks like a private fight.
B-But I owe that little freak.
She sent me to jail and ruined my life.
Everything is so black and white to you.
Since you're the good guy, I've got to be the bad girl.
I wish I had your confidence.
Yeah, me too.
I don't have all the answers, Brenda.
I'm not even sure I know the right questions.
I'm just determined to bring you down.
You're going to pay for what you did to Normie!

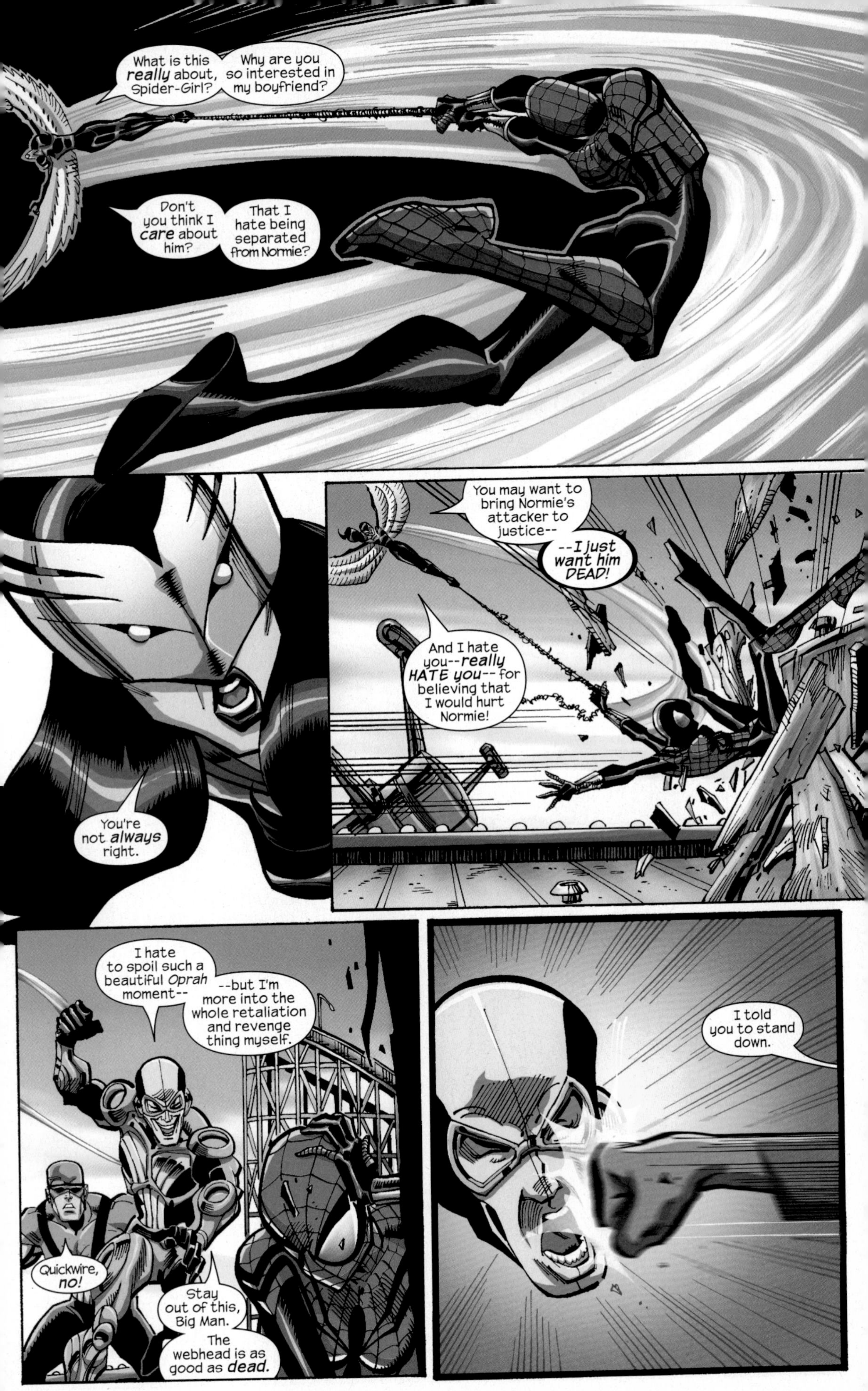
What is this really about, Spider-Girl?
Why are you so interested in my boyfriend?
Don't you think I care about him?
That I hate being separated from Normie?
You're not always right.
You may want to bring Normie's attacker to justice--
--I just want him DEAD!
And I hate you--really HATE you--for believing that I would hurt Normie!
I hate to spoil such a beautiful Oprah moment--
--but I'm more into the whole retaliation and revenge thing myself.
Quickwire, no!
Stay out of this, Big Man.
The webhead is as good as dead.
I told you to stand down.

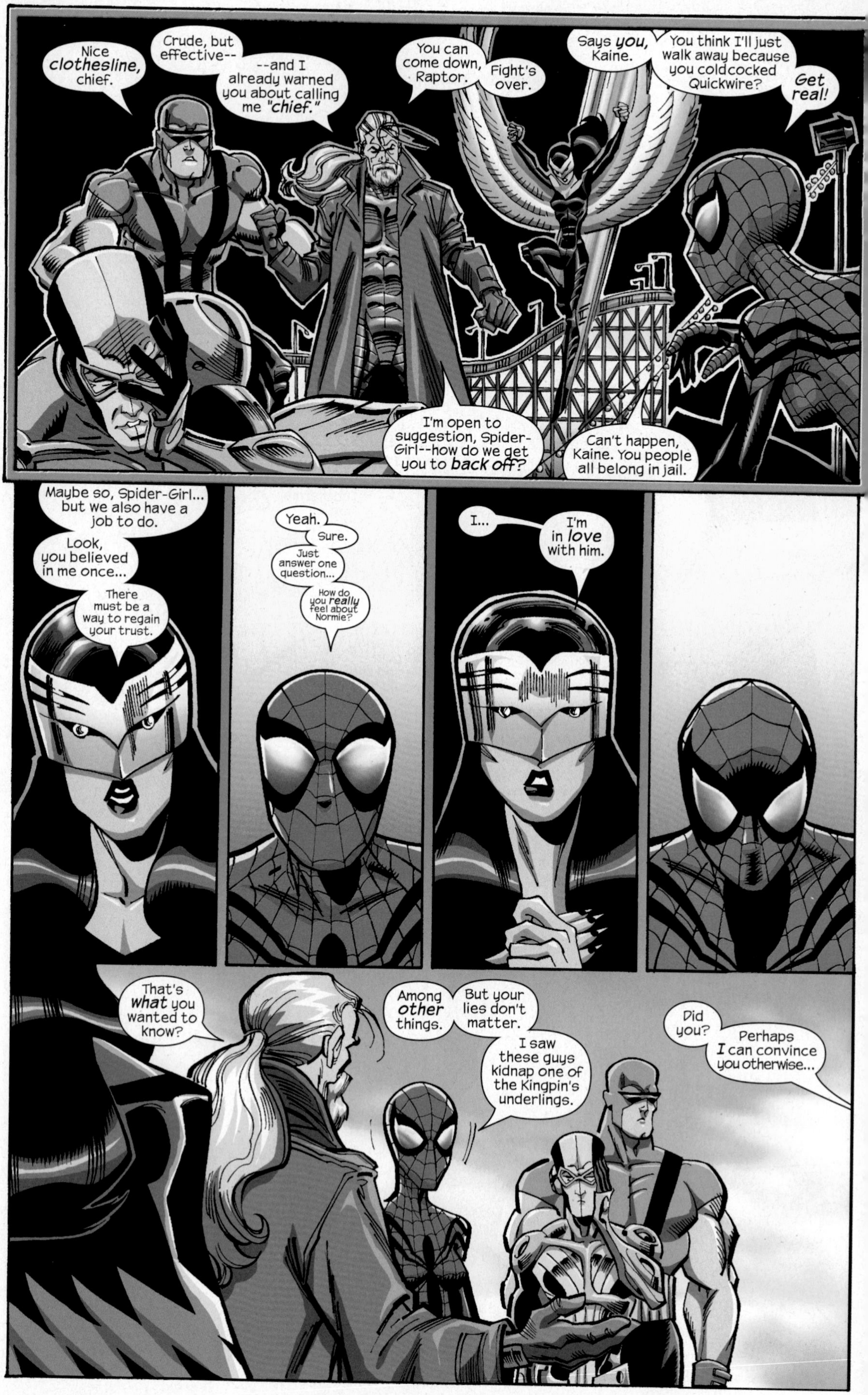
Nice clothesline, chief.
Crude, but effective--
--and I already warned you about calling me "chief."
You can come down, Raptor.
Fight's over.
Says you, Kaine.
You think I'll just walk away because you coldcocked Quickwire?
Get real!
I'm open to suggestion, Spider-Girl--how do we get you to back off?
Can't happen, Kaine. You people all belong in jail.
Maybe so, Spider-Girl... but we also have a job to do.
Look, you believed in me once...
There must be a way to regain your trust.
Yeah.
Sure.
Just answer one question...
How do you really feel about Normie?
I...
I'm in love with him.
That's what you wanted to know?
Among other things.
But your lies don't matter.
I saw these guys kidnap one of the Kingpin's underlings.
Did you?
Perhaps I can convince you otherwise...

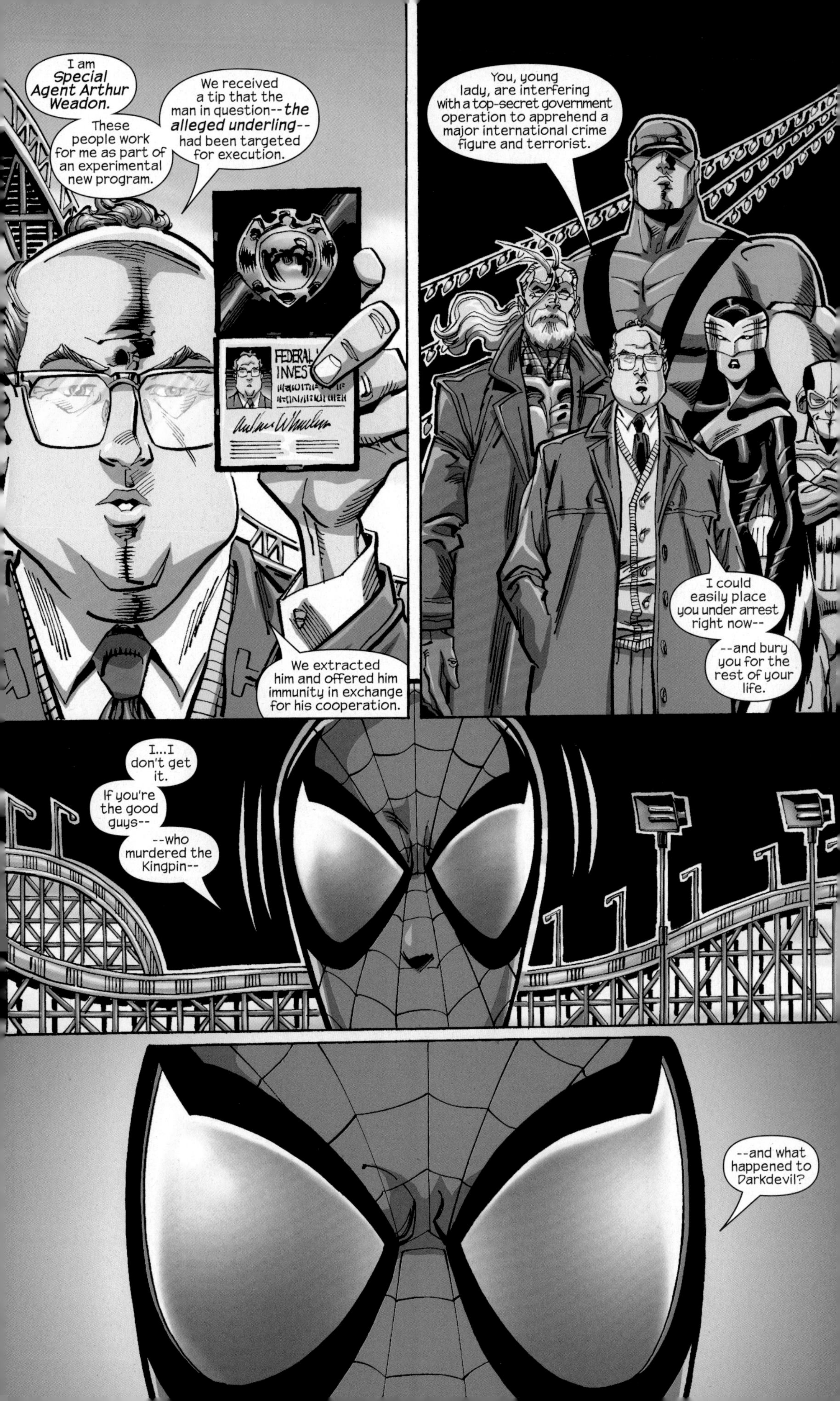

I am *Special Agent Arthur Weadon.*
These people work for me as part of an experimental new program.
We received a tip that the man in question-- *the alleged underling*-- had been targeted for execution.
We extracted him and offered him immunity in exchange for his cooperation.
You, young lady, are interfering with a top-secret government operation to apprehend a major international crime figure and terrorist.
I could easily place you under arrest right now--
--and bury you for the rest of your life.
I...I don't get it.
If you're the good guys--
--who murdered the Kingpin--
--and what happened to Darkdevil?

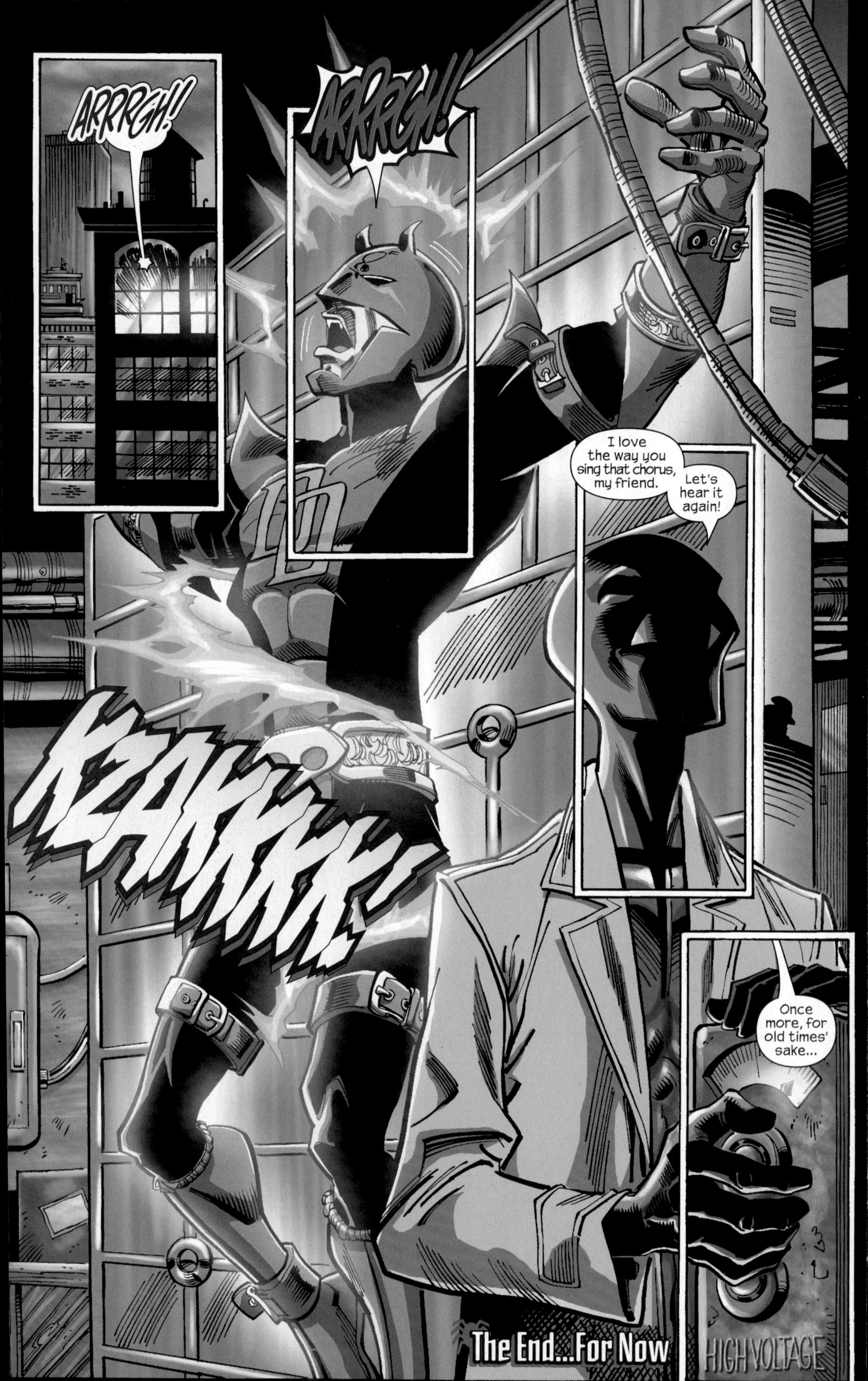
ARRRGH!!
ARRRGH!!
I love the way you sing that chorus, my friend.
Let's hear it again!
KZAKKK!
Once more, for old times' sake...
HIGH VOLTAGE

The End...For Now

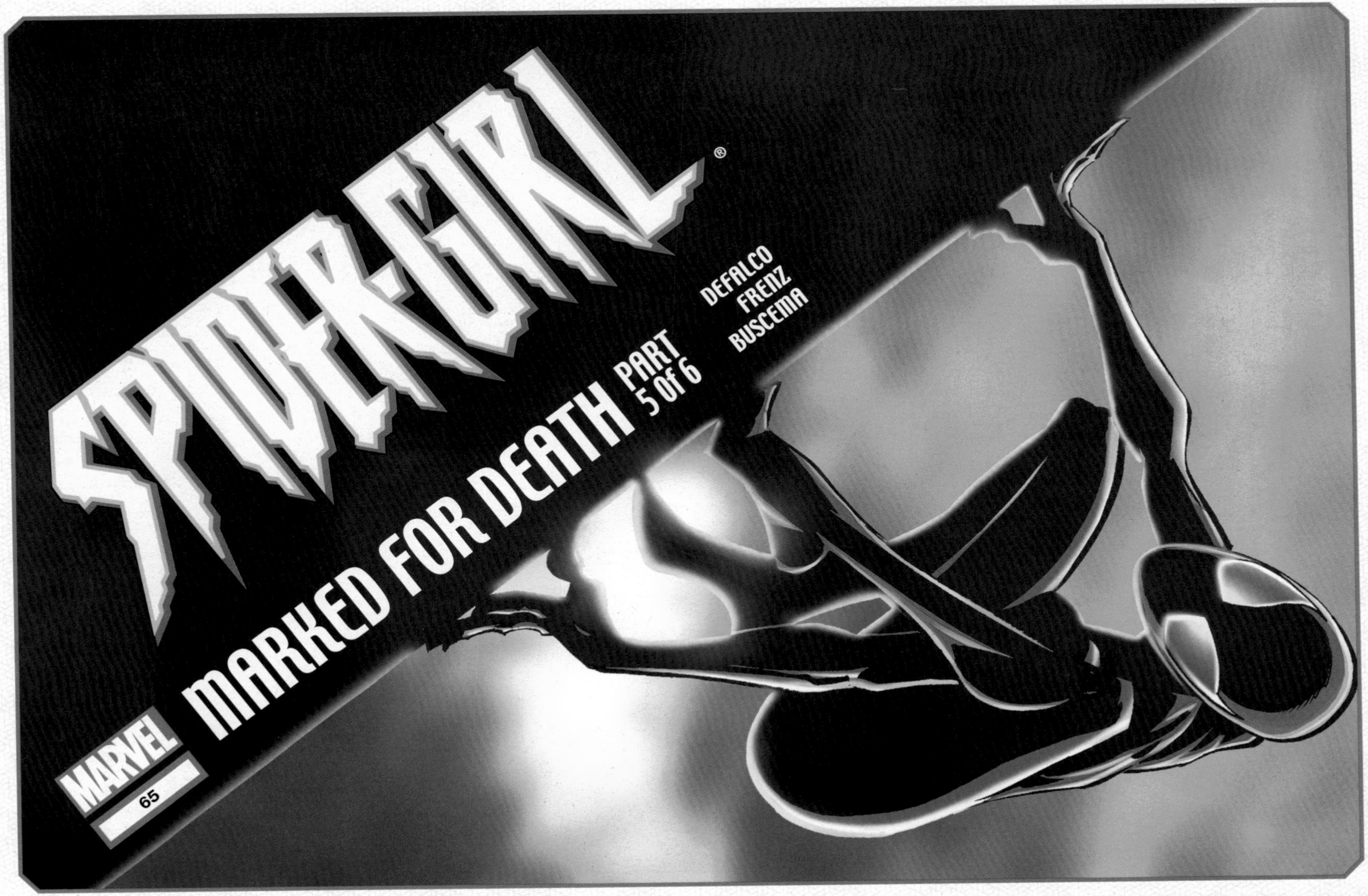
SPIDER-GIRL®
MARKED FOR DEATH PART 5 OF 6
DEFALCO
FRENZ
BUSCEMA
MARVEL
65

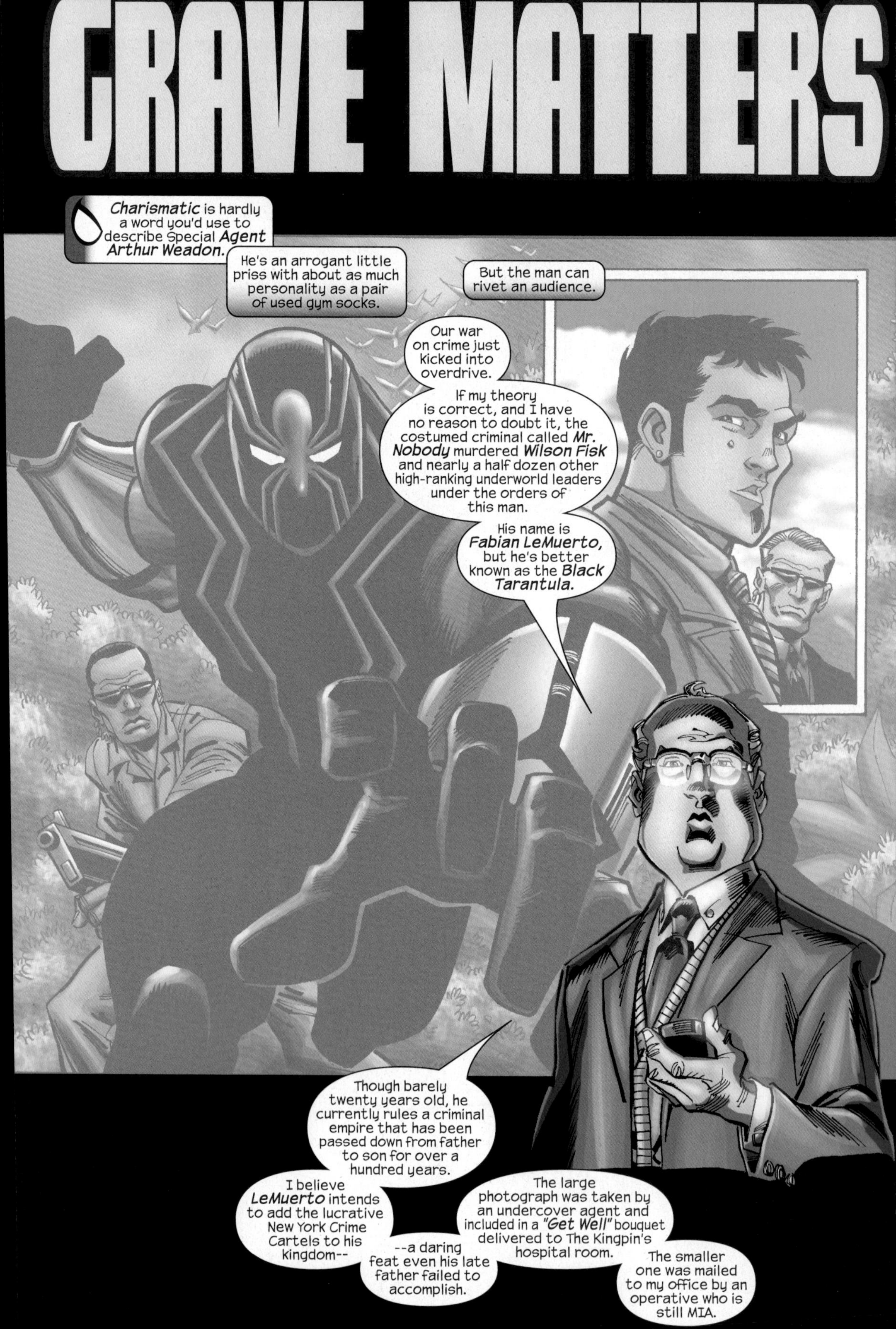
GRAVE MATTERS
Charismatic is hardly a word you'd use to describe Special Agent Arthur Weadon.
He's an arrogant little priss with about as much personality as a pair of used gym socks.
But the man can rivet an audience.
Our war on crime just kicked into overdrive.
If my theory is correct, and I have no reason to doubt it, the costumed criminal called Mr. Nobody murdered Wilson Fisk and nearly a half dozen other high-ranking underworld leaders under the orders of this man.
His name is Fabian LeMuerto, but he's better known as the Black Tarantula.
Though barely twenty years old, he currently rules a criminal empire that has been passed down from father to son for over a hundred years.
I believe LeMuerto intends to add the lucrative New York Crime Cartels to his kingdom--
--a daring feat even his late father failed to accomplish.
The large photograph was taken by an undercover agent and included in a "Get Well" bouquet delivered to The Kingpin's hospital room.
The smaller one was mailed to my office by an operative who is still MIA.

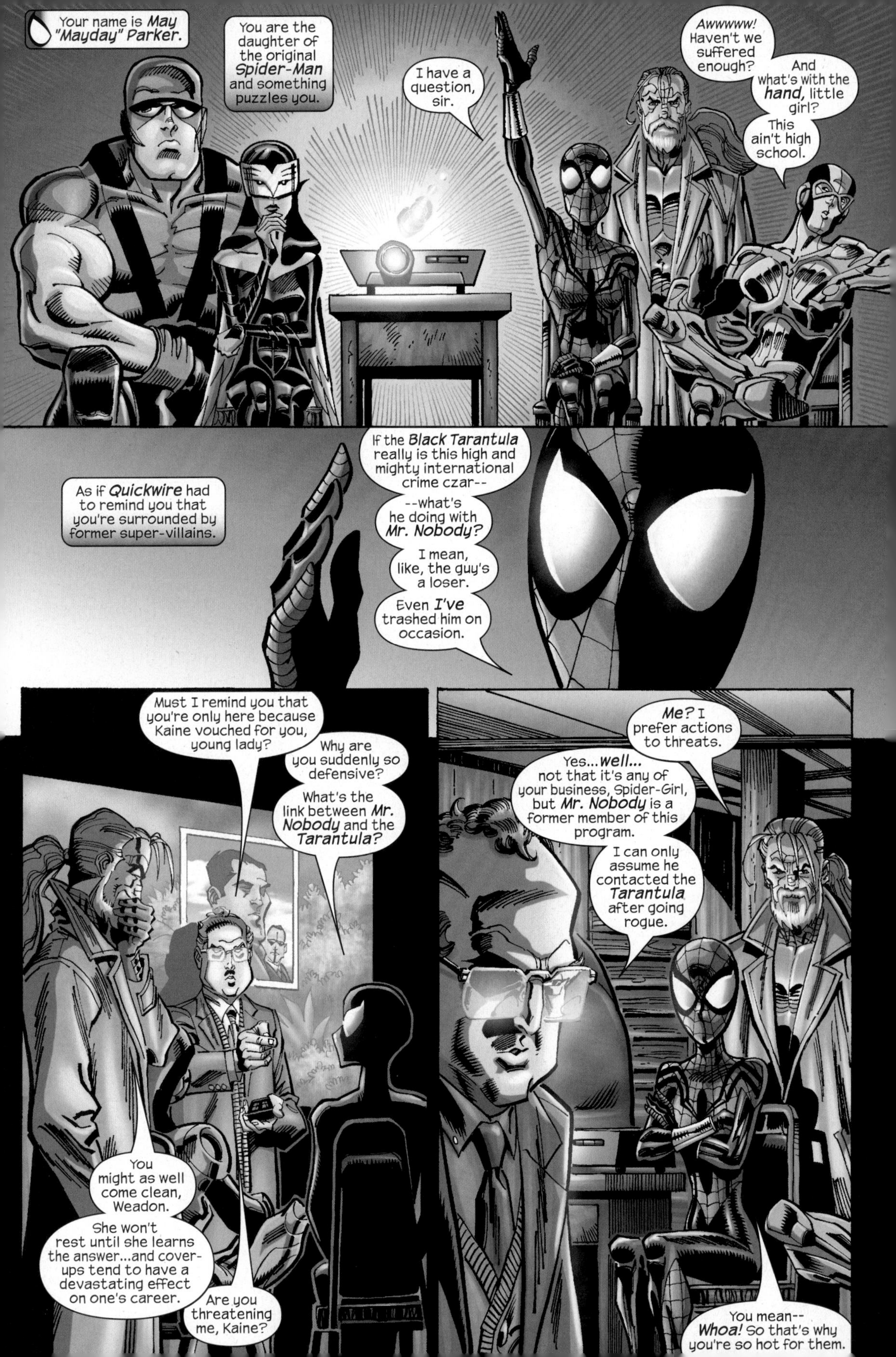
Your name is May "Mayday" Parker.
You are the daughter of the original Spider-Man and something puzzles you.
I have a question, sir.
Awwwww! Haven't we suffered enough?
And what's with the hand, little girl?
This ain't high school.
As if Quickwire had to remind you that you're surrounded by former super-villains.
If the Black Tarantula really is this high and mighty international crime czar--
--what's he doing with Mr. Nobody?
I mean, like, the guy's a loser.
Even I've trashed him on occasion.
Must I remind you that you're only here because Kaine vouched for you, young lady?
Why are you suddenly so defensive?
What's the link between Mr. Nobody and the Tarantula?
You might as well come clean, Weadon.
She won't rest until she learns the answer...and cover-ups tend to have a devastating effect on one's career.
Are you threatening me, Kaine?
Me? I prefer actions to threats.
Yes...well... not that it's any of your business, Spider-Girl, but Mr. Nobody is a former member of this program.
I can only assume he contacted the Tarantula after going rogue.
You mean-- Whoa! So that's why you're so hot for them.

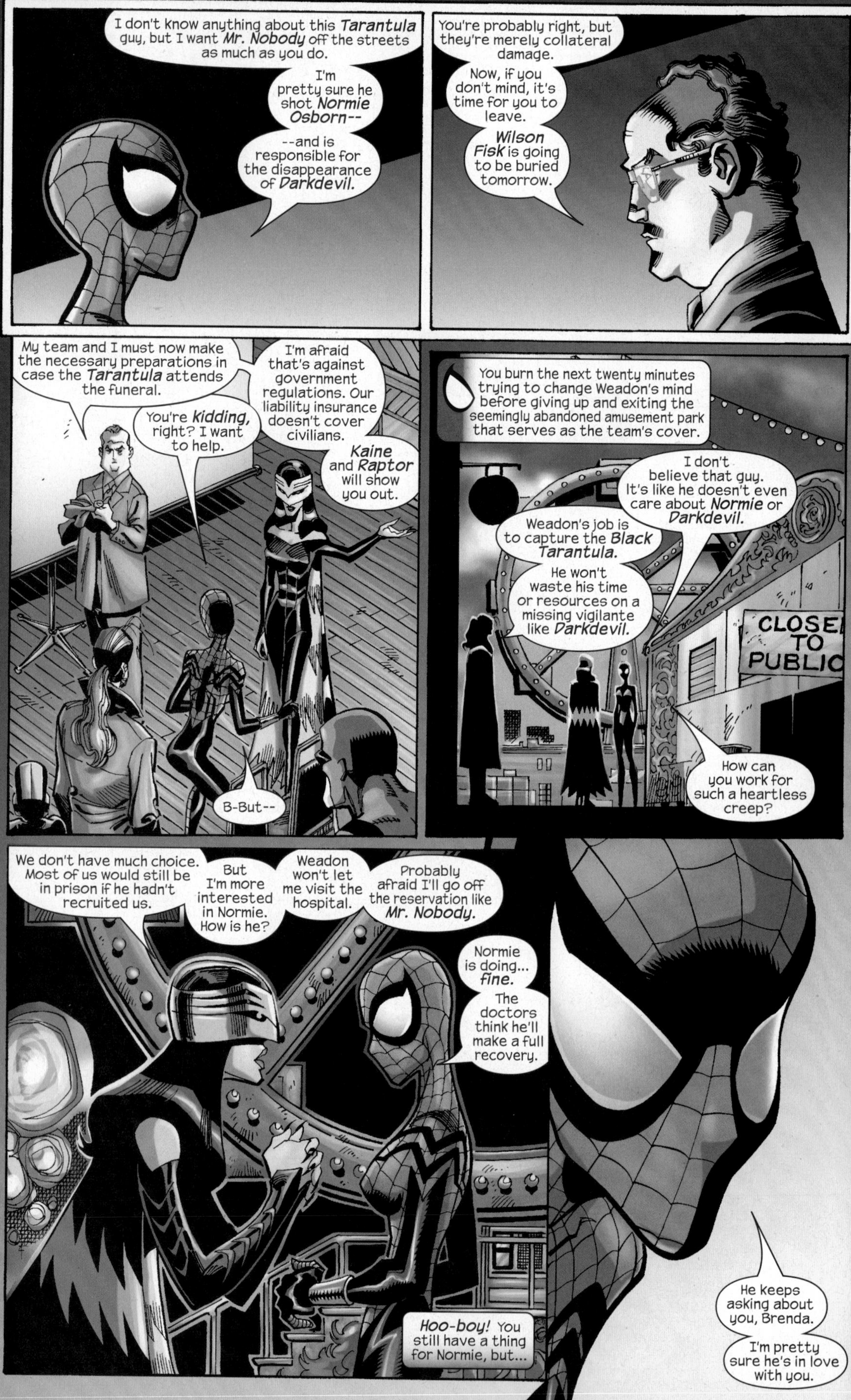

I don't know anything about this Tarantula guy, but I want Mr. Nobody off the streets as much as you do.
I'm pretty sure he shot Normie Osborn--
--and is responsible for the disappearance of Darkdevil.
You're probably right, but they're merely collateral damage.
Now, if you don't mind, it's time for you to leave.
Wilson Fisk is going to be buried tomorrow.
My team and I must now make the necessary preparations in case the Tarantula attends the funeral.
You're kidding, right? I want to help.
I'm afraid that's against government regulations. Our liability insurance doesn't cover civilians.
Kaine and Raptor will show you out.
B-But--
You burn the next twenty minutes trying to change Weadon's mind before giving up and exiting the seemingly abandoned amusement park that serves as the team's cover.
I don't believe that guy. It's like he doesn't even care about Normie or Darkdevil.
Weadon's job is to capture the Black Tarantula.
He won't waste his time or resources on a missing vigilante like Darkdevil.
CLOSE TO PUBLIC
How can you work for such a heartless creep?
We don't have much choice. Most of us would still be in prison if he hadn't recruited us.
But I'm more interested in Normie. How is he?
Weadon won't let me visit the hospital.
Probably afraid I'll go off the reservation like Mr. Nobody.
Normie is doing... fine.
The doctors think he'll make a full recovery.
Hoo-boy! You still have a thing for Normie, but...
He keeps asking about you, Brenda.
I'm pretty sure he's in love with you.

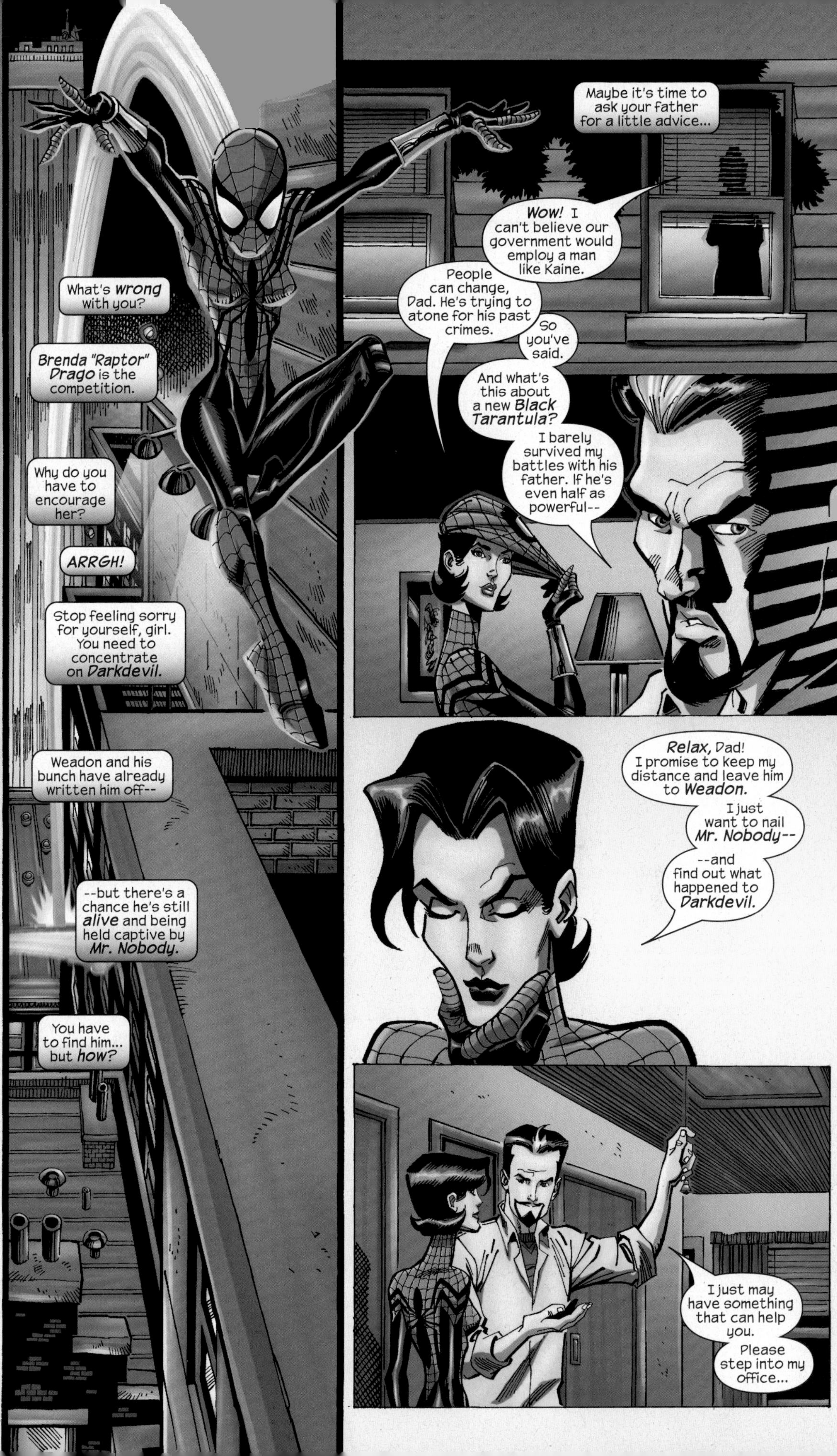
What's wrong with you?
Brenda "Raptor" Drago is the competition.
Why do you have to encourage her?
ARRGH!
Stop feeling sorry for yourself, girl. You need to concentrate on Darkdevil.
Weadon and his bunch have already written him off--
--but there's a chance he's still alive and being held captive by Mr. Nobody.
You have to find him... but how?
Maybe it's time to ask your father for a little advice...
Wow! I can't believe our government would employ a man like Kaine.
People can change, Dad. He's trying to atone for his past crimes.
So you've said.
And what's this about a new Black Tarantula?
I barely survived my battles with his father. If he's even half as powerful--
Relax, Dad! I promise to keep my distance and leave him to Weadon.
I just want to nail Mr. Nobody--
--and find out what happened to Darkdevil.
I just may have something that can help you.
Please step into my office...

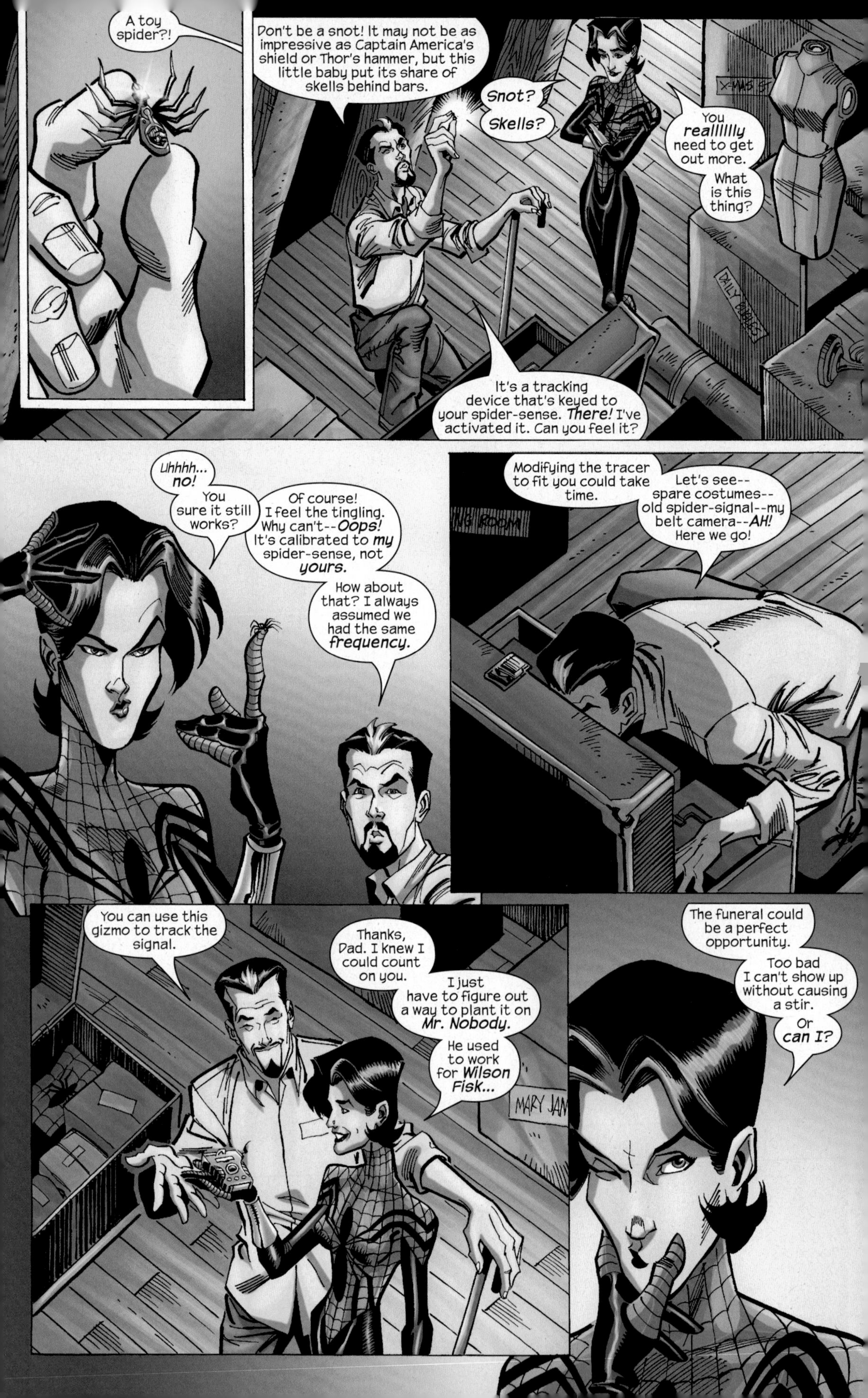
A toy spider?!
Don't be a snot! It may not be as impressive as Captain America's shield or Thor's hammer, but this little baby put its share of skells behind bars.
Snot?
Skells?
You reallllly need to get out more.
What is this thing?
It's a tracking device that's keyed to your spider-sense. There! I've activated it. Can you feel it?
Uhhhh... no!
You sure it still works?
Of course! I feel the tingling. Why can't--Oops! It's calibrated to my spider-sense, not yours.
How about that? I always assumed we had the same frequency.
Modifying the tracer to fit you could take time.
Let's see-- spare costumes-- old spider-signal--my belt camera--AH! Here we go!
You can use this gizmo to track the signal.
Thanks, Dad. I knew I could count on you.
I just have to figure out a way to plant it on Mr. Nobody.
He used to work for Wilson Fisk...
The funeral could be a perfect opportunity.
Too bad I can't show up without causing a stir.
Or can I?

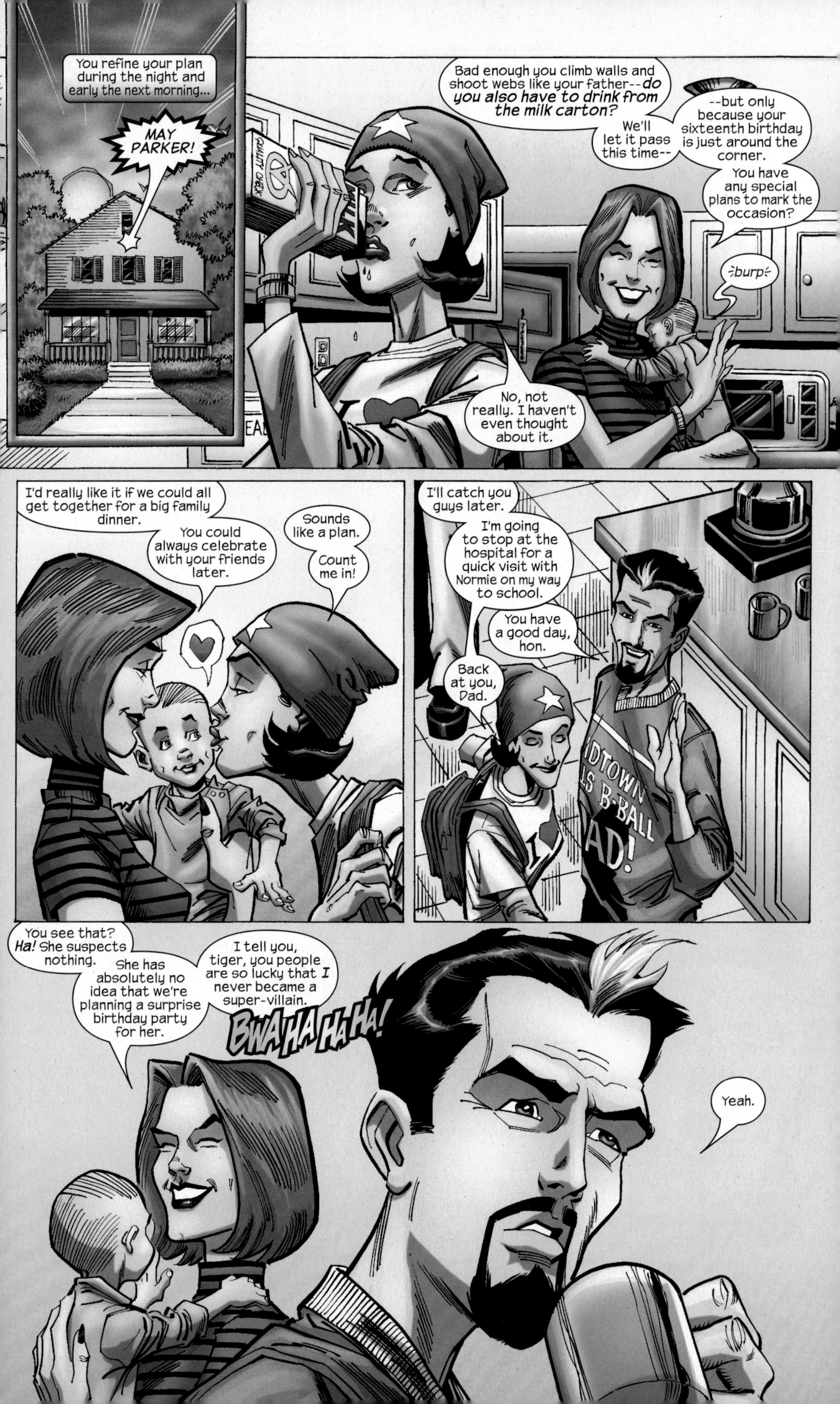
You refine your plan during the night and early the next morning...
MAY PARKER!
Bad enough you climb walls and shoot webs like your father--*do you also have to drink from the milk carton?*
We'll let it pass this time--
--but only because your sixteenth birthday is just around the corner.
You have any special plans to mark the occasion?
burp
No, not really. I haven't even thought about it.
I'd really like it if we could all get together for a big family dinner.
You could always celebrate with your friends later.
Sounds like a plan.
Count me in!
I'll catch you guys later.
I'm going to stop at the hospital for a quick visit with Normie on my way to school.
You have a good day, hon.
Back at you, Dad.
You see that? *Ha!* She suspects nothing.
She has absolutely no idea that we're planning a surprise birthday party for her.
I tell you, tiger, you people are so lucky that *I* never became a super-villain.
BWAHAHAHA!
Yeah.

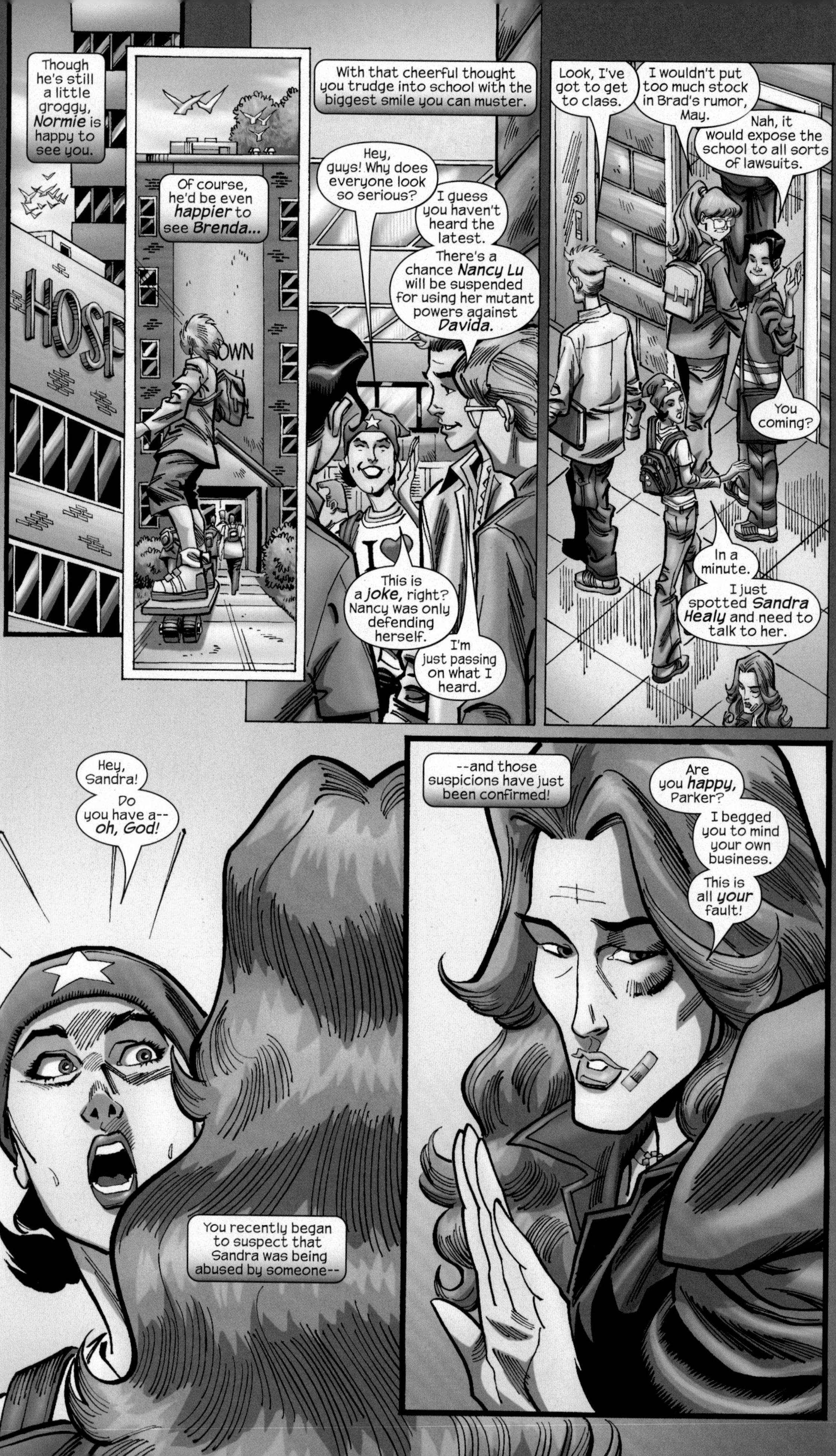

Though he's still a little groggy, Normie is happy to see you.
Of course, he'd be even happier to see Brenda...
With that cheerful thought you trudge into school with the biggest smile you can muster.
Hey, guys! Why does everyone look so serious?
I guess you haven't heard the latest.
There's a chance Nancy Lu will be suspended for using her mutant powers against Davida.
This is a joke, right? Nancy was only defending herself.
I'm just passing on what I heard.
Look, I've got to get to class.
I wouldn't put too much stock in Brad's rumor, May.
Nah, it would expose the school to all sorts of lawsuits.
You coming?
In a minute.
I just spotted Sandra Healy and need to talk to her.
Hey, Sandra!
Do you have a-- oh, God!
You recently began to suspect that Sandra was being abused by someone--
--and those suspicions have just been confirmed!
Are you happy, Parker?
I begged you to mind your own business.
This is all your fault!

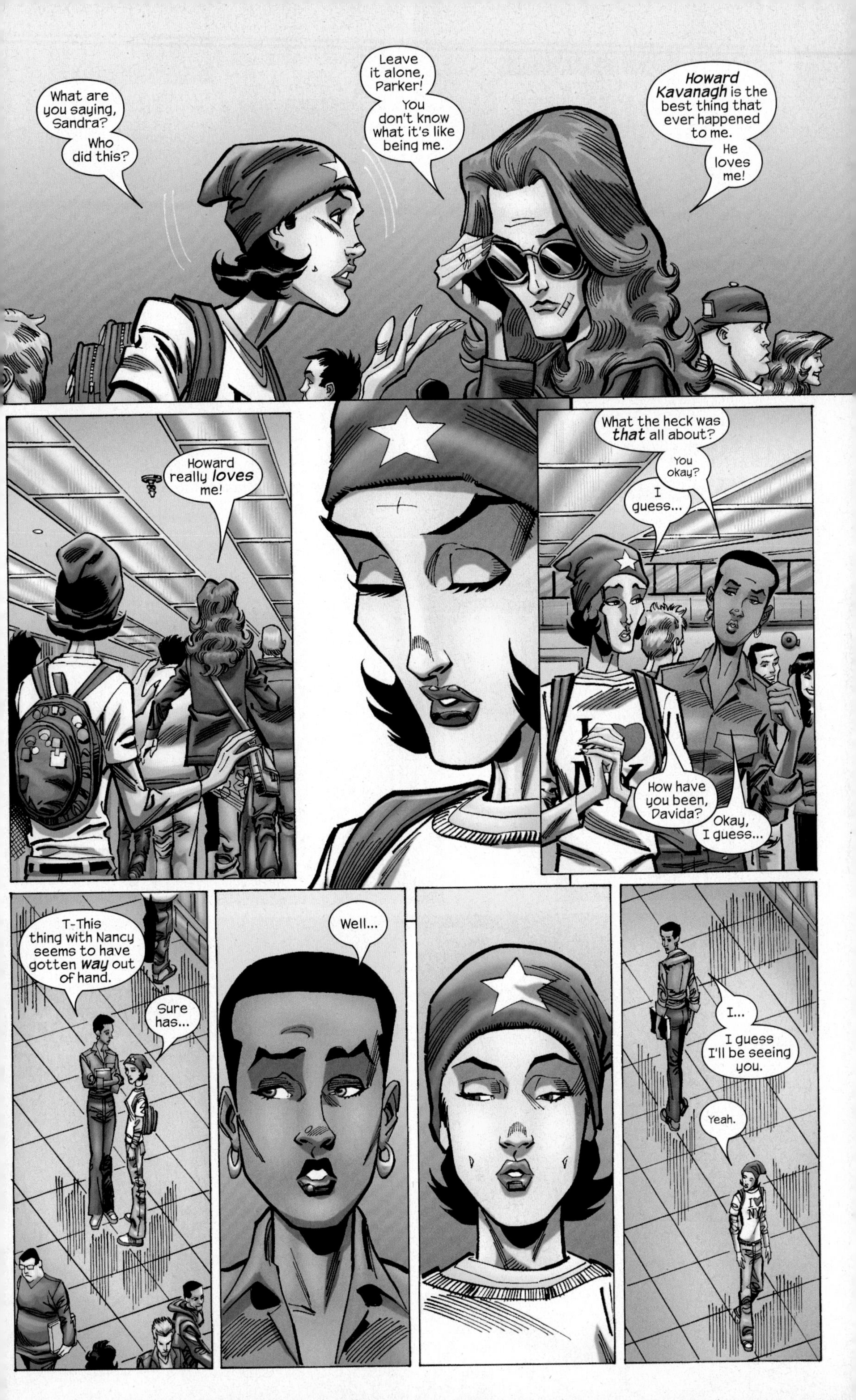
What are you saying, Sandra?
Who did this?
Leave it alone, Parker!
You don't know what it's like being me.
Howard Kavanagh is the best thing that ever happened to me.
He loves me!
Howard really loves me!
What the heck was that all about?
You okay?
I guess...
How have you been, Davida?
Okay, I guess...
T-This thing with Nancy seems to have gotten way out of hand.
Sure has...
Well...
I...
I guess I'll be seeing you.
Yeah.

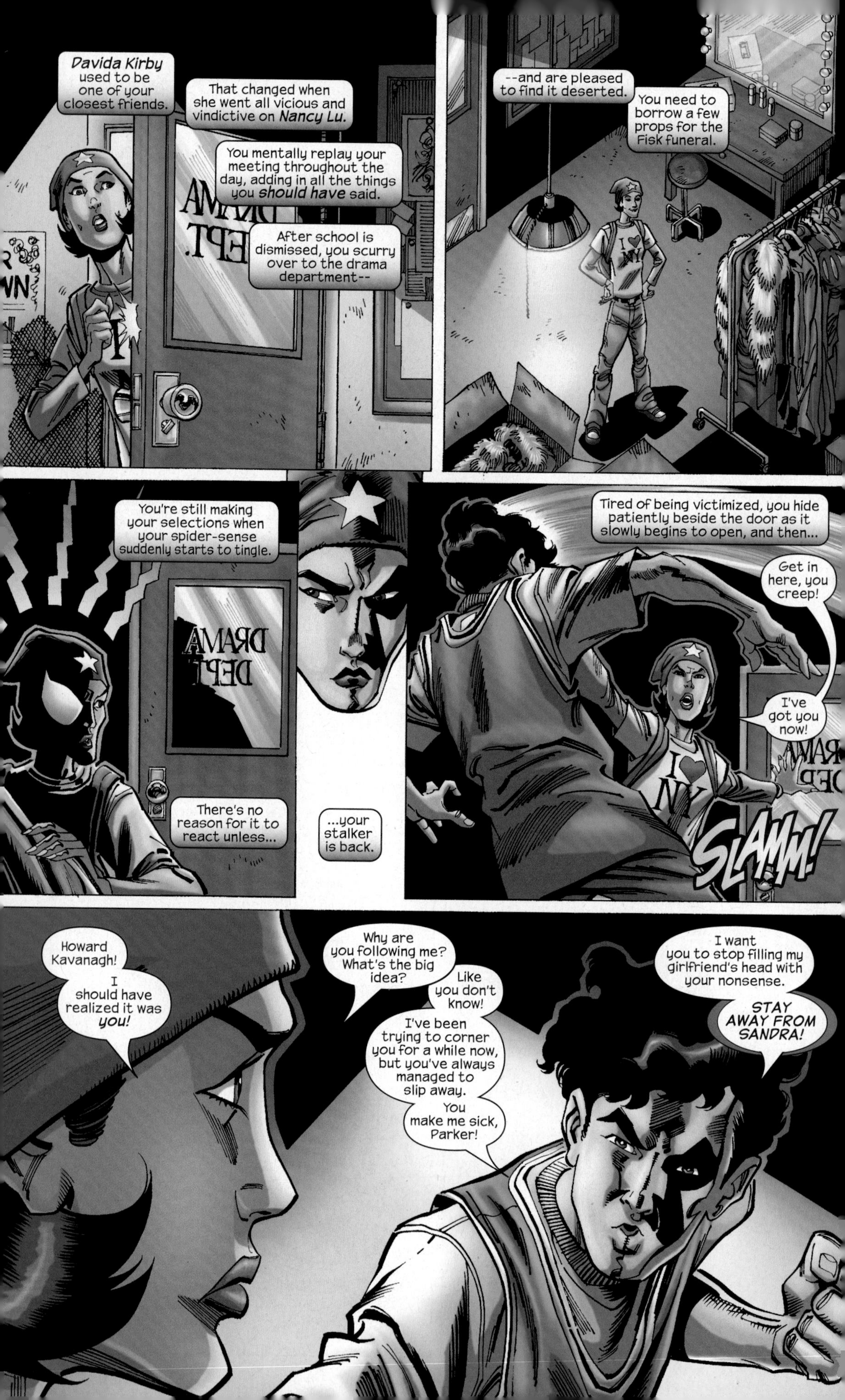
Davida Kirby used to be one of your closest friends.
That changed when she went all vicious and vindictive on Nancy Lu.
You mentally replay your meeting throughout the day, adding in all the things you should have said.
After school is dismissed, you scurry over to the drama department--
--and are pleased to find it deserted.
You need to borrow a few props for the Fisk funeral.
You're still making your selections when your spider-sense suddenly starts to tingle.
There's no reason for it to react unless...
...your stalker is back.
Tired of being victimized, you hide patiently beside the door as it slowly begins to open, and then...
Get in here, you creep!
I've got you now!
SLAMM!
Howard Kavanagh!
I should have realized it was you!
Why are you following me? What's the big idea?
Like you don't know!
I've been trying to corner you for a while now, but you've always managed to slip away.
You make me sick, Parker!
I want you to stop filling my girlfriend's head with your nonsense.
STAY AWAY FROM SANDRA!

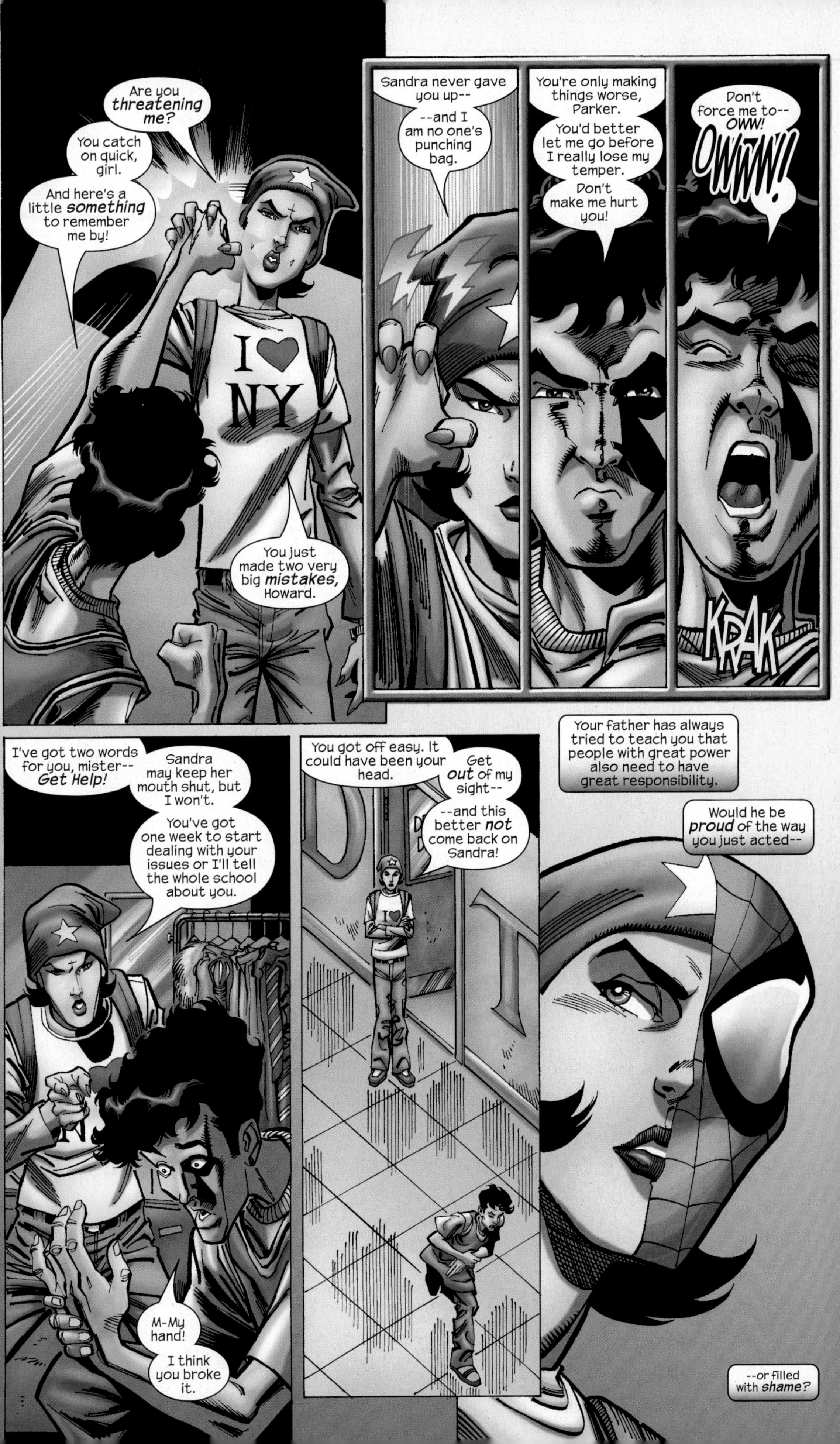
Are you threatening me?
You catch on quick, girl.
And here's a little something to remember me by!
You just made two very big mistakes, Howard.
Sandra never gave you up--
--and I am no one's punching bag.
You're only making things worse, Parker.
You'd better let me go before I really lose my temper.
Don't make me hurt you!
Don't force me to-- OWW!
OWWW!
KRAK
I've got two words for you, mister-- Get Help!
Sandra may keep her mouth shut, but I won't.
You've got one week to start dealing with your issues or I'll tell the whole school about you.
M-My hand!
I think you broke it.
You got off easy. It could have been your head.
Get out of my sight--
--and this better not come back on Sandra!
Your father has always tried to teach you that people with great power also need to have great responsibility.
Would he be proud of the way you just acted--
--or filled with shame?

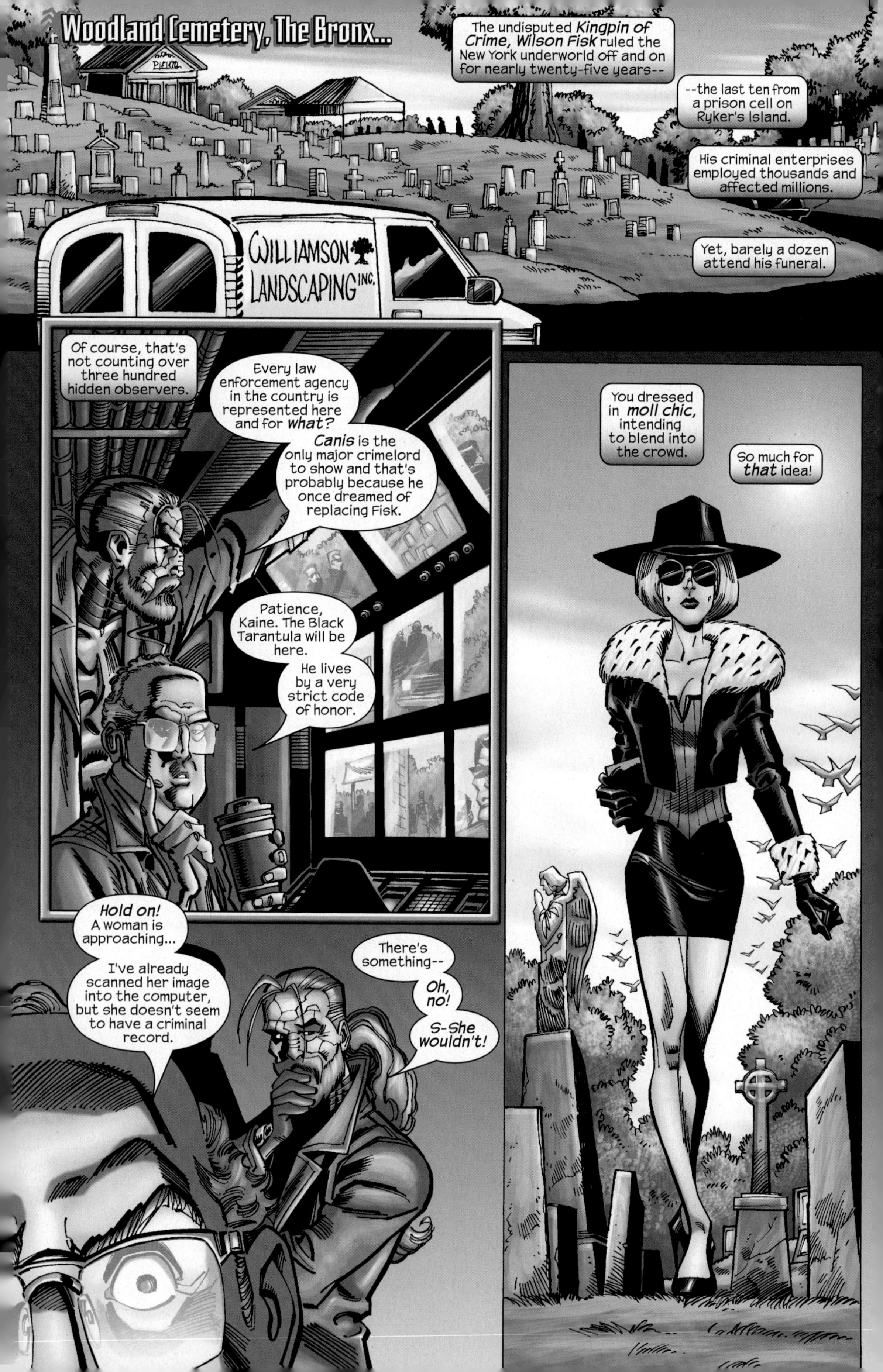
Woodland Cemetery, The Bronx...
The undisputed Kingpin of Crime, Wilson Fisk ruled the New York underworld off and on for nearly twenty-five years--
--the last ten from a prison cell on Ryker's Island.
His criminal enterprises employed thousands and affected millions.
Yet, barely a dozen attend his funeral.
WILLIAMSON LANDSCAPING INC.
Of course, that's not counting over three hundred hidden observers.
Every law enforcement agency in the country is represented here and for what?
Canis is the only major crimelord to show and that's probably because he once dreamed of replacing Fisk.
Patience, Kaine. The Black Tarantula will be here.
He lives by a very strict code of honor.
Hold on! A woman is approaching...
I've already scanned her image into the computer, but she doesn't seem to have a criminal record.
There's something--
Oh, no!
S-She wouldn't!
You dressed in moll chic, intending to blend into the crowd.
So much for that idea!

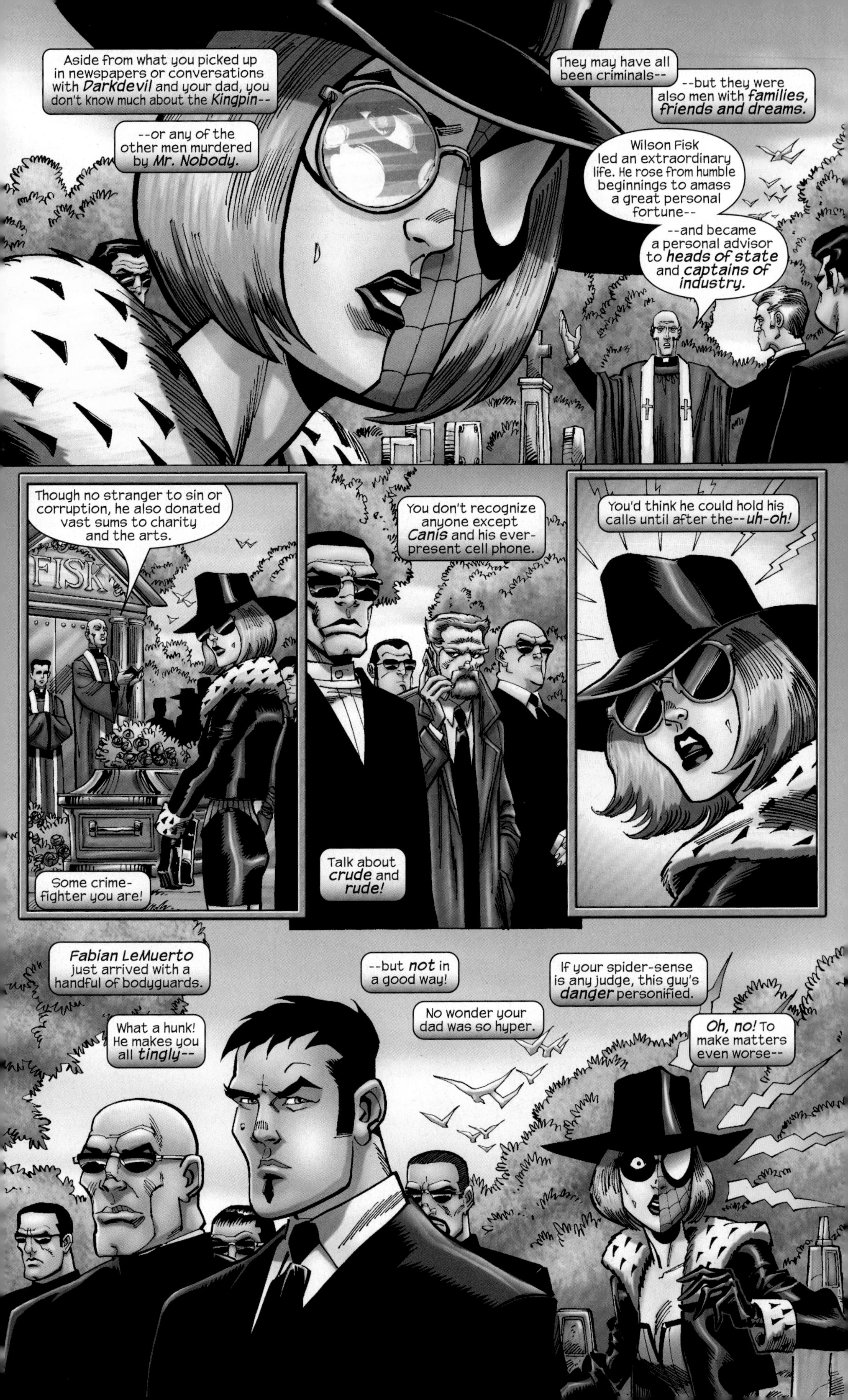
Aside from what you picked up in newspapers or conversations with *Darkdevil* and your dad, you don't know much about the *Kingpin*--
--or any of the other men murdered by *Mr. Nobody.*
They may have all been criminals--
--but they were also men with *families, friends and dreams.*
Wilson Fisk led an extraordinary life. He rose from humble beginnings to amass a great personal fortune--
--and became a personal advisor to *heads of state* and *captains of industry.*
Though no stranger to sin or corruption, he also donated vast sums to charity and the arts.
FISK
Some crime-fighter you are!
You don't recognize anyone except *Canis* and his ever-present cell phone.
Talk about *crude* and *rude!*
You'd think he could hold his calls until after the--*uh-oh!*
Fabian LeMuerto just arrived with a handful of bodyguards.
What a hunk! He makes you all *tingly*--
--but *not* in a good way!
No wonder your dad was so hyper.
If your spider-sense is any judge, this guy's *danger* personified.
Oh, no! To make matters even worse--

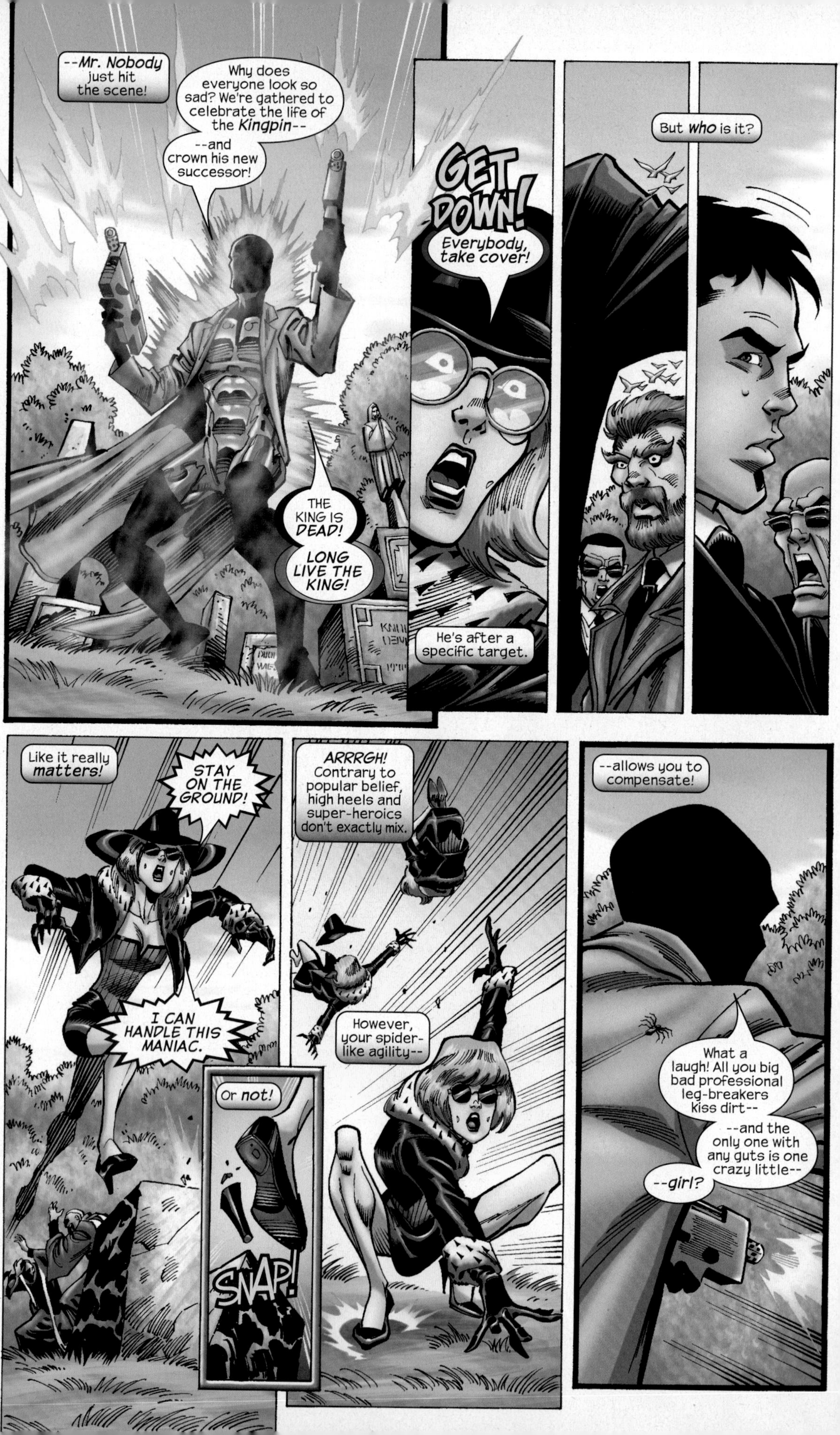
--Mr. Nobody just hit the scene!
Why does everyone look so sad? We're gathered to celebrate the life of the Kingpin--
--and crown his new successor!
THE KING IS DEAD!
LONG LIVE THE KING!
GET DOWN!
Everybody, take cover!
He's after a specific target.
But who is it?
Like it really matters!
STAY ON THE GROUND!
I CAN HANDLE THIS MANIAC.
Or not!
SNAP!
ARRRGH! Contrary to popular belief, high heels and super-heroics don't exactly mix.
However, your spider-like agility--
--allows you to compensate!
What a laugh! All you big bad professional leg-breakers kiss dirt--
--and the only one with any guts is one crazy little--
--girl?

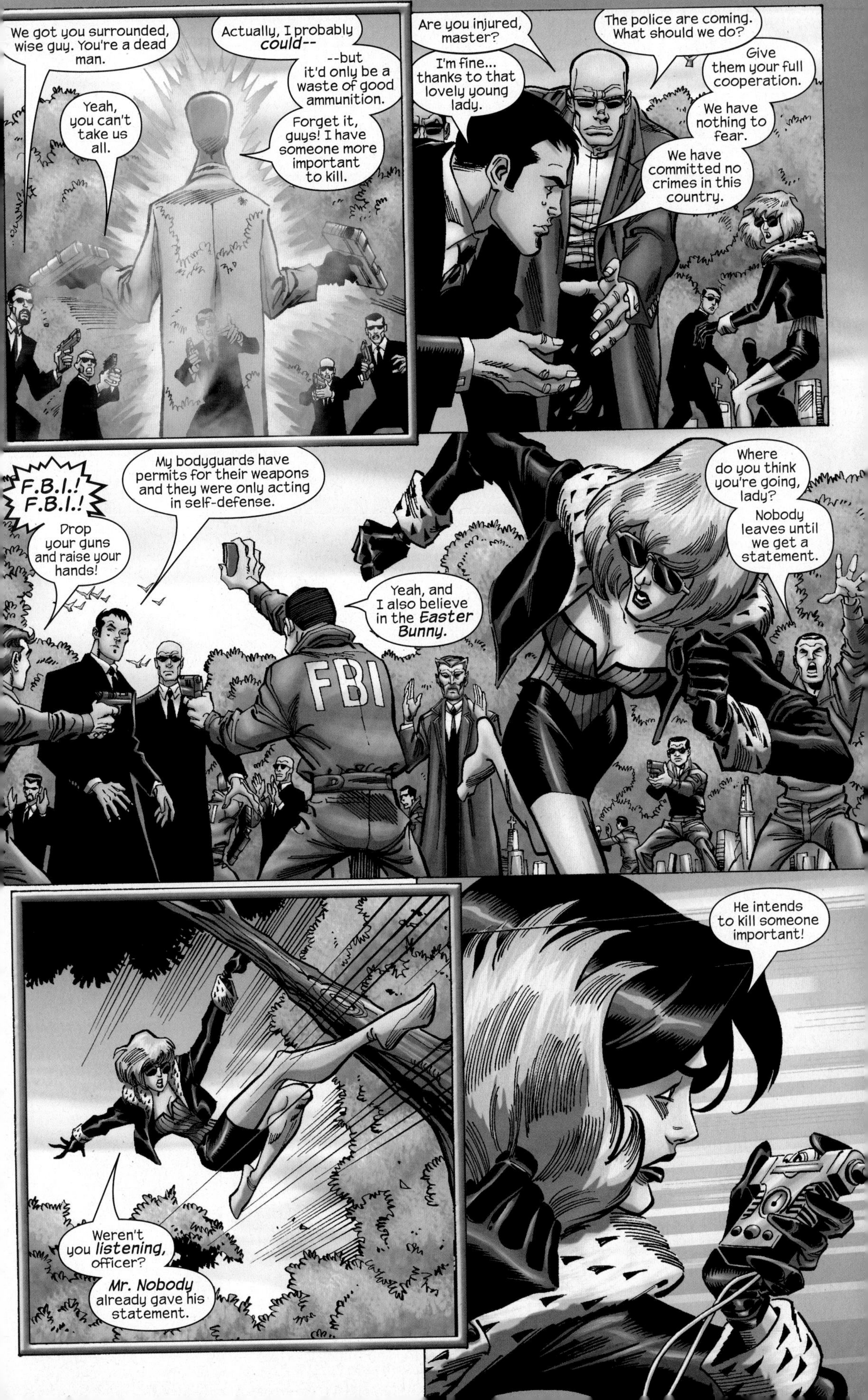
We got you surrounded, wise guy. You're a dead man.
Yeah, you can't take us all.
Actually, I probably *could*--
--but it'd only be a waste of good ammunition.
Forget it, guys! I have someone more important to kill.
Are you injured, master?
I'm fine... thanks to that lovely young lady.
The police are coming. What should we do?
Give them your full cooperation.
We have nothing to fear.
We have committed no crimes in this country.
F.B.I.! F.B.I.!
Drop your guns and raise your hands!
My bodyguards have permits for their weapons and they were only acting in self-defense.
Yeah, and I also believe in the *Easter Bunny.*
FBI
Where do you think you're going, lady?
Nobody leaves until we get a statement.
Weren't you *listening,* officer?
Mr. Nobody already gave his statement.
He intends to kill someone important!

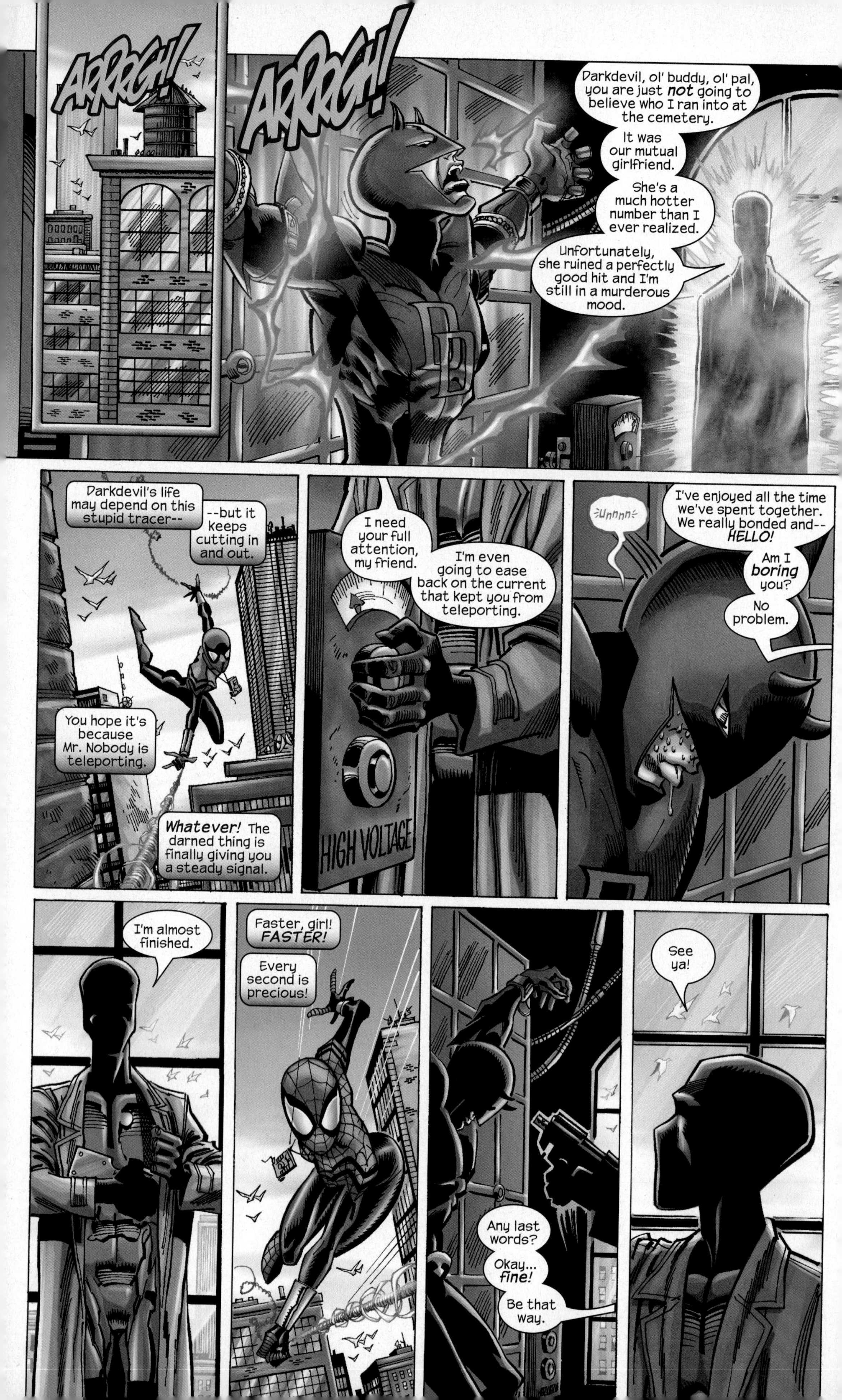
ARRRGH!
ARRRGH!
Darkdevil, ol' buddy, ol' pal, you are just **not** going to believe who I ran into at the cemetery.
It was our mutual girlfriend.
She's a much hotter number than I ever realized.
Unfortunately, she ruined a perfectly good hit and I'm still in a murderous mood.
Darkdevil's life may depend on this stupid tracer--
--but it keeps cutting in and out.
You hope it's because Mr. Nobody is teleporting.
Whatever! The darned thing is finally giving you a steady signal.
I need your full attention, my friend.
I'm even going to ease back on the current that kept you from teleporting.
HIGH VOLTAGE
Unnnn
I've enjoyed all the time we've spent together. We really bonded and-- ***HELLO!***
Am I ***boring*** you?
No problem.
I'm almost finished.
Faster, girl! ***FASTER!***
Every second is precious!
Any last words?
Okay... ***fine!***
Be that way.
See ya!

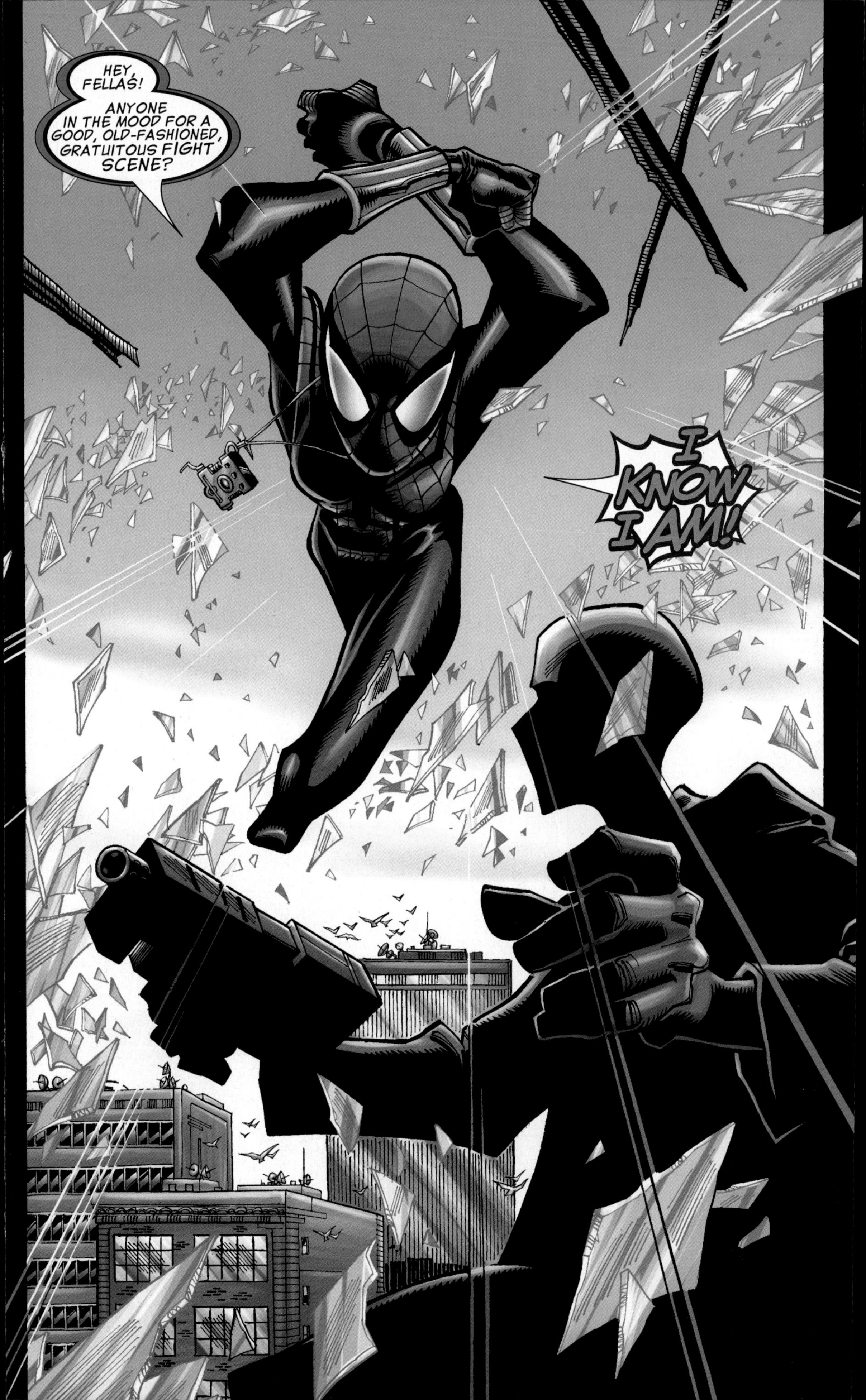
HEY, FELLAS! ANYONE IN THE MOOD FOR A GOOD, OLD-FASHIONED, GRATUITOUS FIGHT SCENE?
I KNOW I AM!

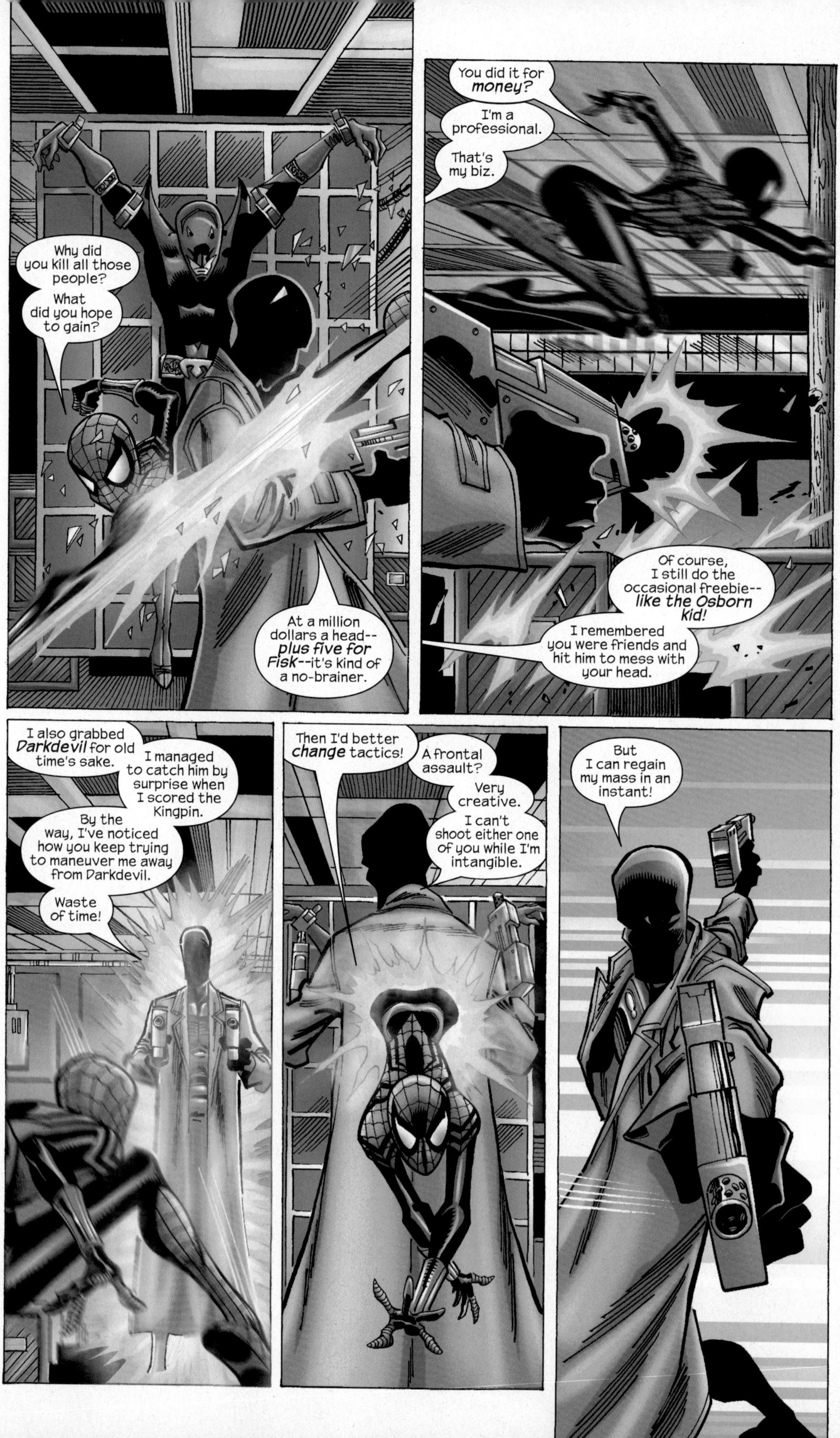
Why did you kill all those people?
What did you hope to gain?
At a million dollars a head-- plus five for Fisk--it's kind of a no-brainer.
You did it for money?
I'm a professional.
That's my biz.
Of course, I still do the occasional freebie-- like the Osborn kid!
I remembered you were friends and hit him to mess with your head.
I also grabbed Darkdevil for old time's sake.
I managed to catch him by surprise when I scored the Kingpin.
By the way, I've noticed how you keep trying to maneuver me away from Darkdevil.
Waste of time!
Then I'd better change tactics!
A frontal assault?
Very creative.
I can't shoot either one of you while I'm intangible.
But I can regain my mass in an instant!

KA-TWAKK

Is that a fact?

Nicely played, kid.

I didn't expect you to react so quickly.

I won't underestimate you again.

How did you first make contact with the *Black Tarantula?*

What if he reneges on your deal?

Why are you suddenly so interested in the-- *Oh!*

Of course. You're trying to distract me again.

Too bad I'm already facing *Darkdevil--*

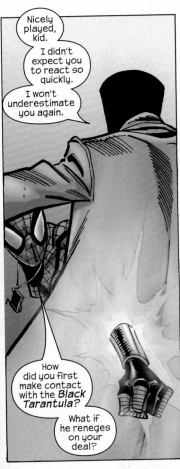

--and back in *firing position!*

No! DON'T!

BOAM! BOAM! BOAM!

KZAK!

HIGH VOLTAGE

ARRRGH!

Talk about hilarious! You threw off my aim when you made me flinch--

--and now *Darkdevil* is going to *fry!*

BOAM! BOAM! BOAM!

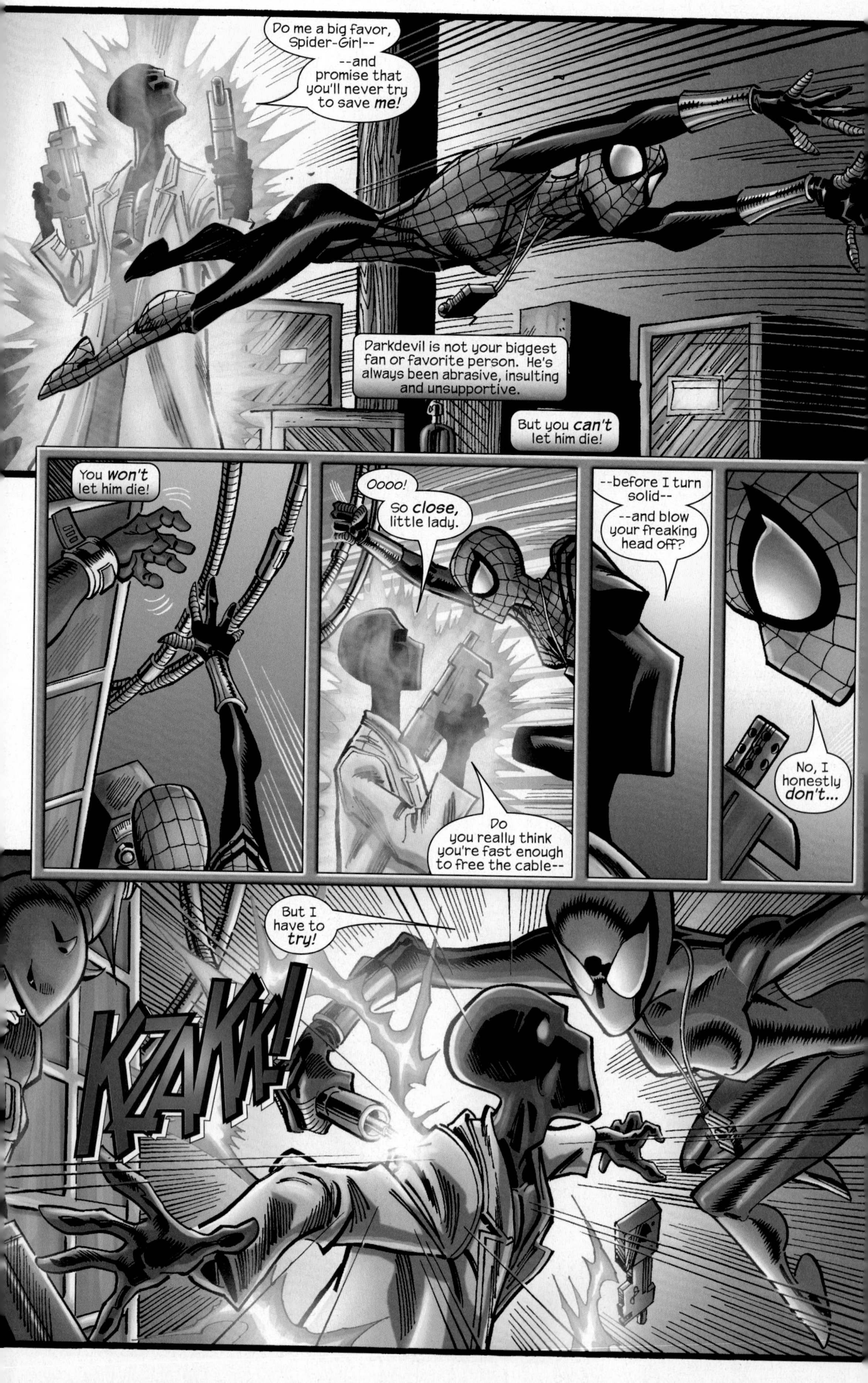
Do me a big favor, Spider-Girl--
--and promise that you'll never try to save *me!*
Darkdevil is not your biggest fan or favorite person. He's always been abrasive, insulting and unsupportive.
But you *can't* let him die!
You *won't* let him die!
Oooo!
So *close,* little lady.
Do you really think you're fast enough to free the cable--
--before I turn solid--
--and blow your freaking head off?
No, I honestly *don't...*
But I have to *try!*
KZAKK!

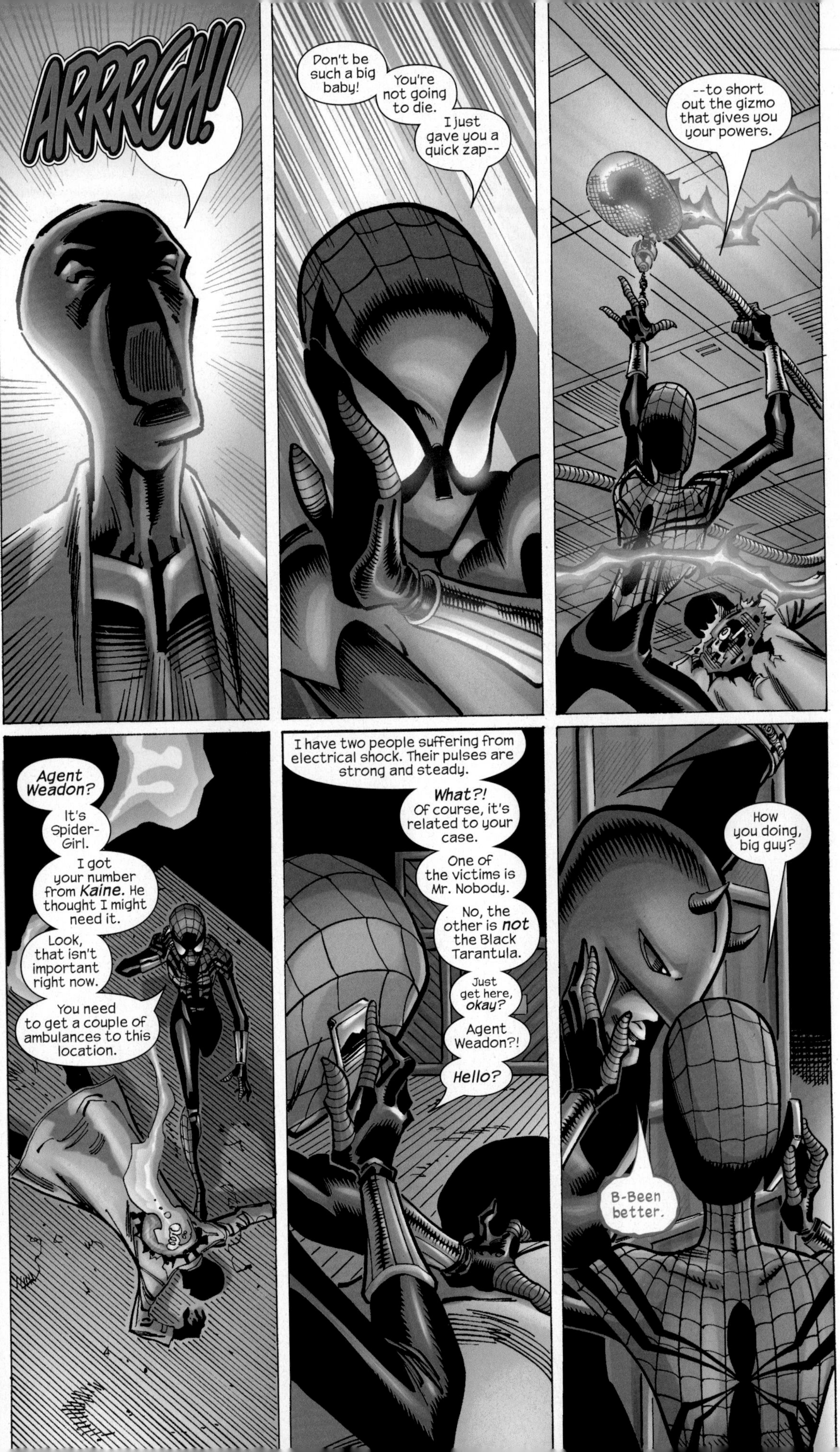
ARRRGH!
Don't be such a big baby!
You're not going to die.
I just gave you a quick zap--
--to short out the gizmo that gives you your powers.
Agent Weadon?
It's Spider-Girl.
I got your number from Kaine. He thought I might need it.
Look, that isn't important right now.
You need to get a couple of ambulances to this location.
I have two people suffering from electrical shock. Their pulses are strong and steady.
What?! Of course, it's related to your case.
One of the victims is Mr. Nobody.
No, the other is not the Black Tarantula.
Just get here, okay?
Agent Weadon?!
Hello?
How you doing, big guy?
B-Been better.

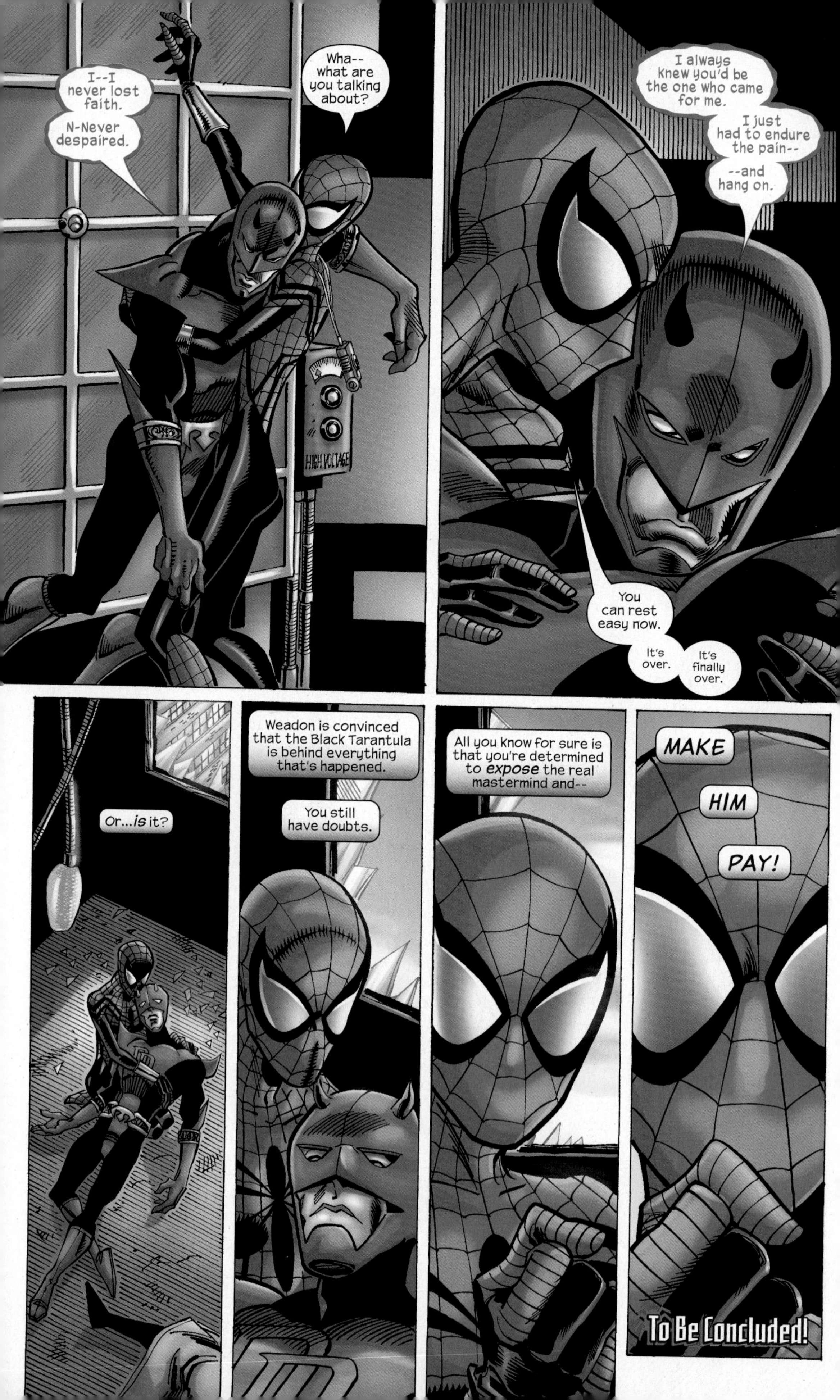
I--I never lost faith.
N-Never despaired.
Wha-- what are you talking about?
I always knew you'd be the one who came for me.
I just had to endure the pain--
--and hang on.
You can rest easy now.
It's over.
It's finally over.
Or...*is* it?
Weadon is convinced that the Black Tarantula is behind everything that's happened.
You still have doubts.
All you know for sure is that you're determined to *expose* the real mastermind and--
MAKE
HIM
PAY!
HIGH VOLTAGE
To Be Concluded!

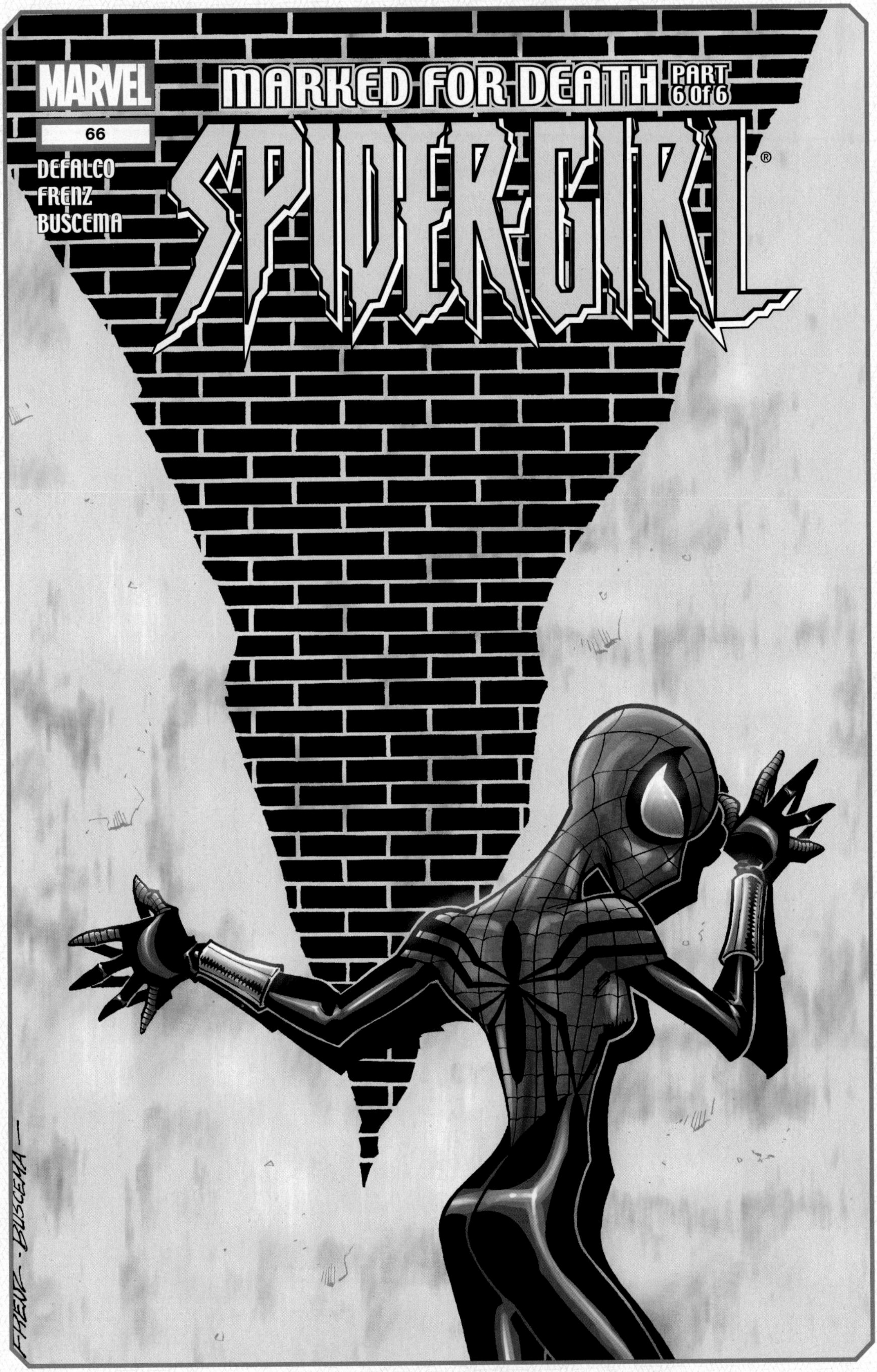
MARVEL
66
DEFALCO
FRENZ
BUSCEMA
MARKED FOR DEATH PART 6 OF 6
SPIDER-GIRL®
FRENZ · BUSCEMA

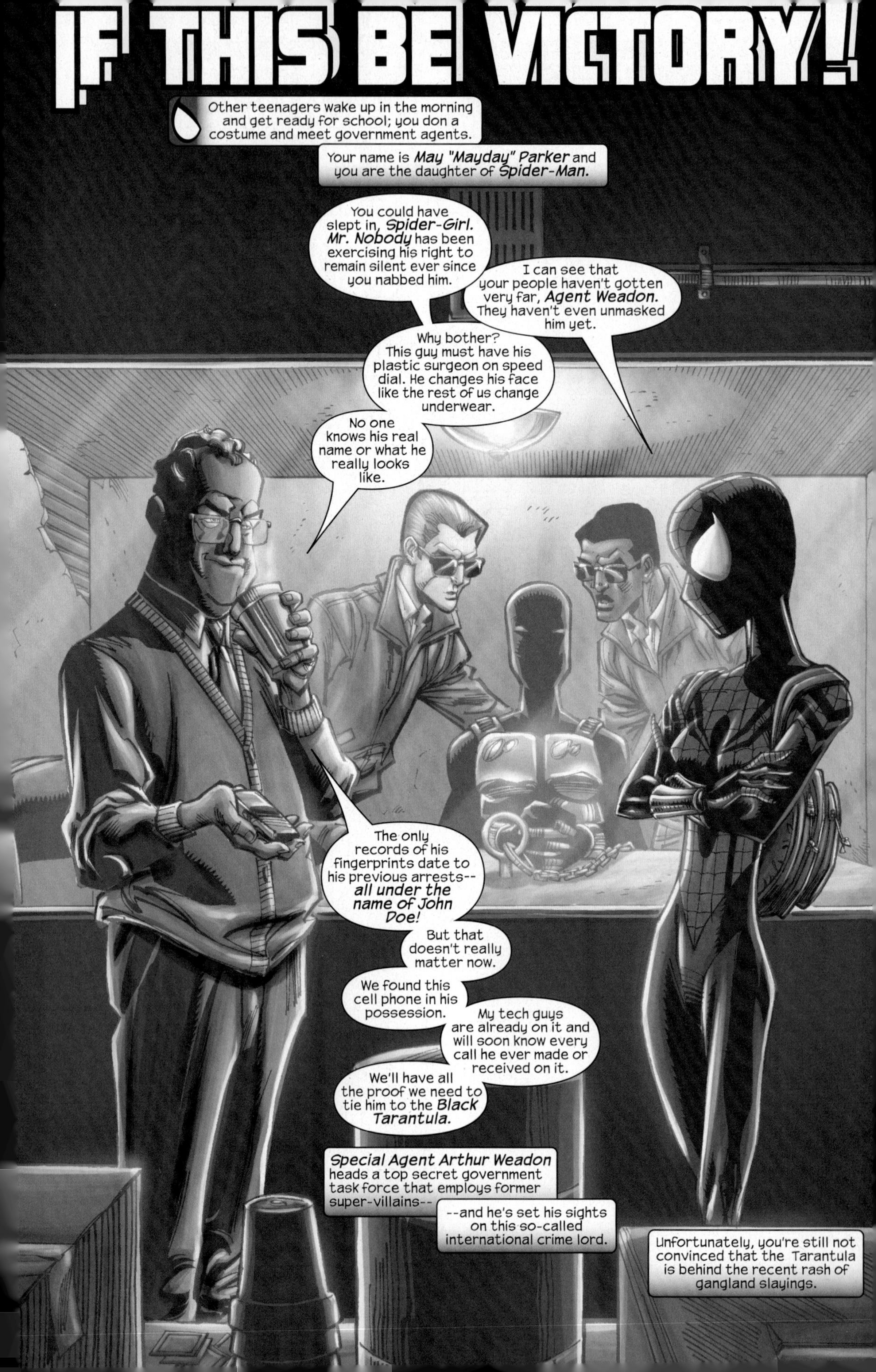
IF THIS BE VICTORY!
Other teenagers wake up in the morning and get ready for school; you don a costume and meet government agents.
Your name is May "Mayday" Parker and you are the daughter of Spider-Man.
You could have slept in, Spider-Girl. Mr. Nobody has been exercising his right to remain silent ever since you nabbed him.
I can see that your people haven't gotten very far, Agent Weadon. They haven't even unmasked him yet.
Why bother? This guy must have his plastic surgeon on speed dial. He changes his face like the rest of us change underwear.
No one knows his real name or what he really looks like.
The only records of his fingerprints date to his previous arrests-- all under the name of John Doe!
But that doesn't really matter now.
We found this cell phone in his possession.
My tech guys are already on it and will soon know every call he ever made or received on it.
We'll have all the proof we need to tie him to the Black Tarantula.
Special Agent Arthur Weadon heads a top secret government task force that employs former super-villains--
--and he's set his sights on this so-called international crime lord.
Unfortunately, you're still not convinced that the Tarantula is behind the recent rash of gangland slayings.

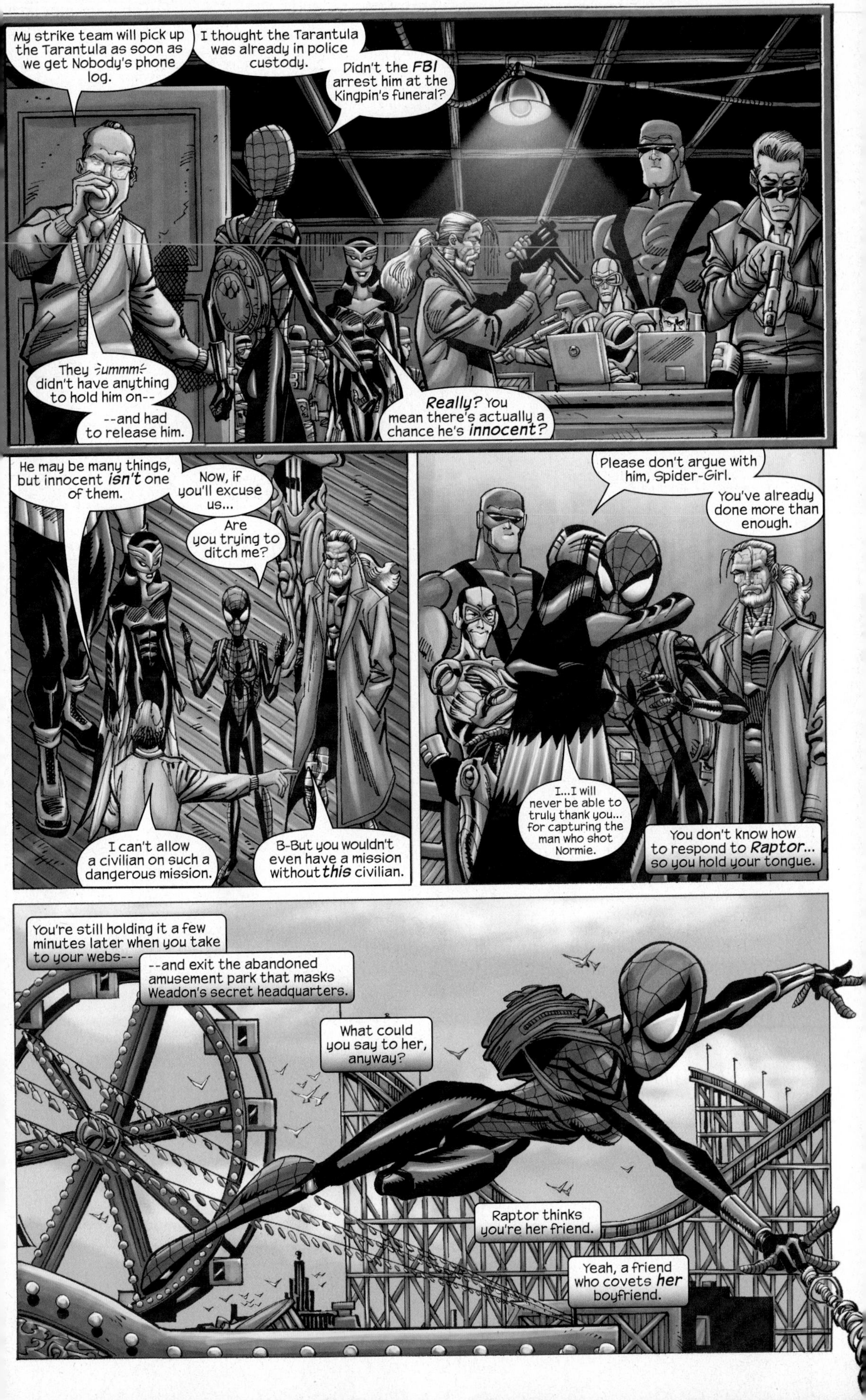

My strike team will pick up the Tarantula as soon as we get Nobody's phone log.
I thought the Tarantula was already in police custody.
Didn't the FBI arrest him at the Kingpin's funeral?
They ~ummm~ didn't have anything to hold him on--
--and had to release him.
Really? You mean there's actually a chance he's innocent?
He may be many things, but innocent isn't one of them.
Now, if you'll excuse us...
Are you trying to ditch me?
I can't allow a civilian on such a dangerous mission.
B-But you wouldn't even have a mission without this civilian.
Please don't argue with him, Spider-Girl.
You've already done more than enough.
I...I will never be able to truly thank you... for capturing the man who shot Normie.
You don't know how to respond to Raptor... so you hold your tongue.
You're still holding it a few minutes later when you take to your webs--
--and exit the abandoned amusement park that masks Weadon's secret headquarters.
What could you say to her, anyway?
Raptor thinks you're her friend.
Yeah, a friend who covets her boyfriend.

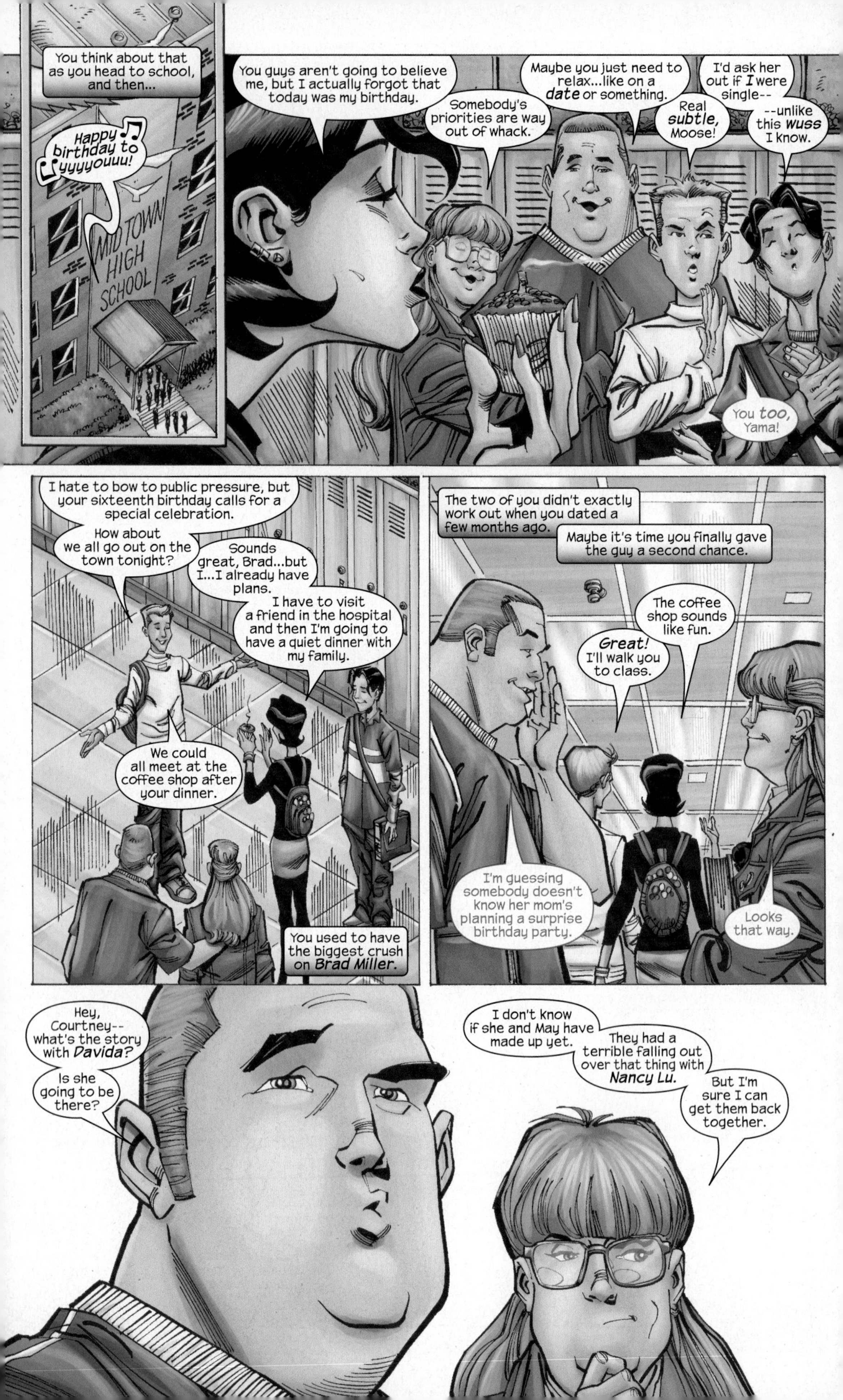

You think about that as you head to school, and then...
Happy birthday to yyyyouuu!
MID TOWN HIGH SCHOOL
You guys aren't going to believe me, but I actually forgot that today was my birthday.
Somebody's priorities are way out of whack.
Maybe you just need to relax...like on a date or something.
Real subtle, Moose!
I'd ask her out if I were single--
--unlike this wuss I know.
You too, Yama!
I hate to bow to public pressure, but your sixteenth birthday calls for a special celebration.
How about we all go out on the town tonight?
Sounds great, Brad...but I...I already have plans.
I have to visit a friend in the hospital and then I'm going to have a quiet dinner with my family.
We could all meet at the coffee shop after your dinner.
You used to have the biggest crush on Brad Miller.
The two of you didn't exactly work out when you dated a few months ago.
Maybe it's time you finally gave the guy a second chance.
The coffee shop sounds like fun.
Great! I'll walk you to class.
I'm guessing somebody doesn't know her mom's planning a surprise birthday party.
Looks that way.
Hey, Courtney-- what's the story with Davida?
Is she going to be there?
I don't know if she and May have made up yet.
They had a terrible falling out over that thing with Nancy Lu.
But I'm sure I can get them back together.

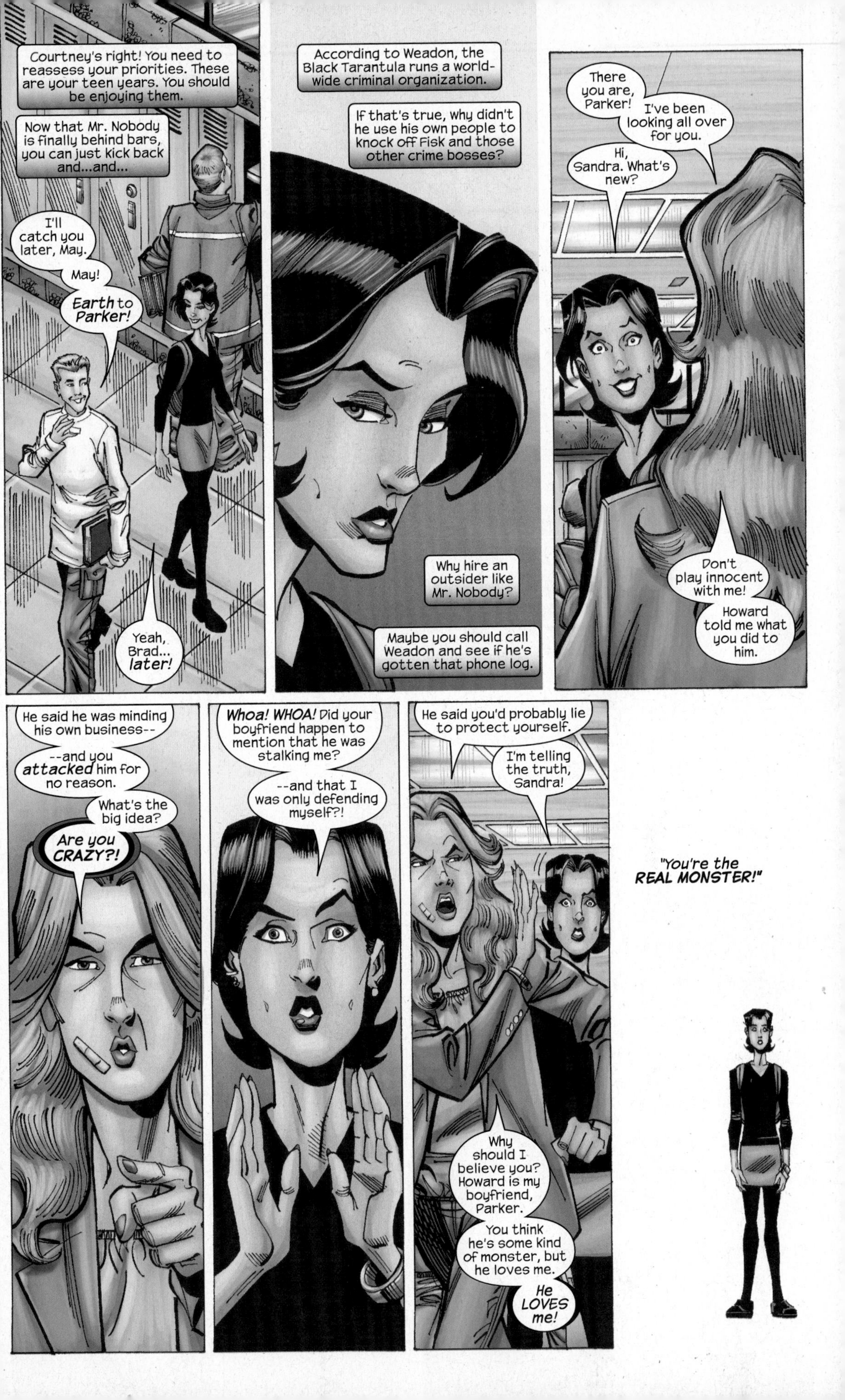
Courtney's right! You need to reassess your priorities. These are your teen years. You should be enjoying them.
Now that Mr. Nobody is finally behind bars, you can just kick back and...and...
I'll catch you later, May.
May!
Earth to Parker!
Yeah, Brad... later!
According to Weadon, the Black Tarantula runs a world-wide criminal organization.
If that's true, why didn't he use his own people to knock off Fisk and those other crime bosses?
Why hire an outsider like Mr. Nobody?
Maybe you should call Weadon and see if he's gotten that phone log.
There you are, Parker!
I've been looking all over for you.
Hi, Sandra. What's new?
Don't play innocent with me!
Howard told me what you did to him.
He said he was minding his own business--
--and you attacked him for no reason.
What's the big idea?
Are you CRAZY?!
Whoa! WHOA! Did your boyfriend happen to mention that he was stalking me?
--and that I was only defending myself?!
He said you'd probably lie to protect yourself.
I'm telling the truth, Sandra!
Why should I believe you? Howard is my boyfriend, Parker.
You think he's some kind of monster, but he loves me.
He LOVES me!
"You're the REAL MONSTER!"

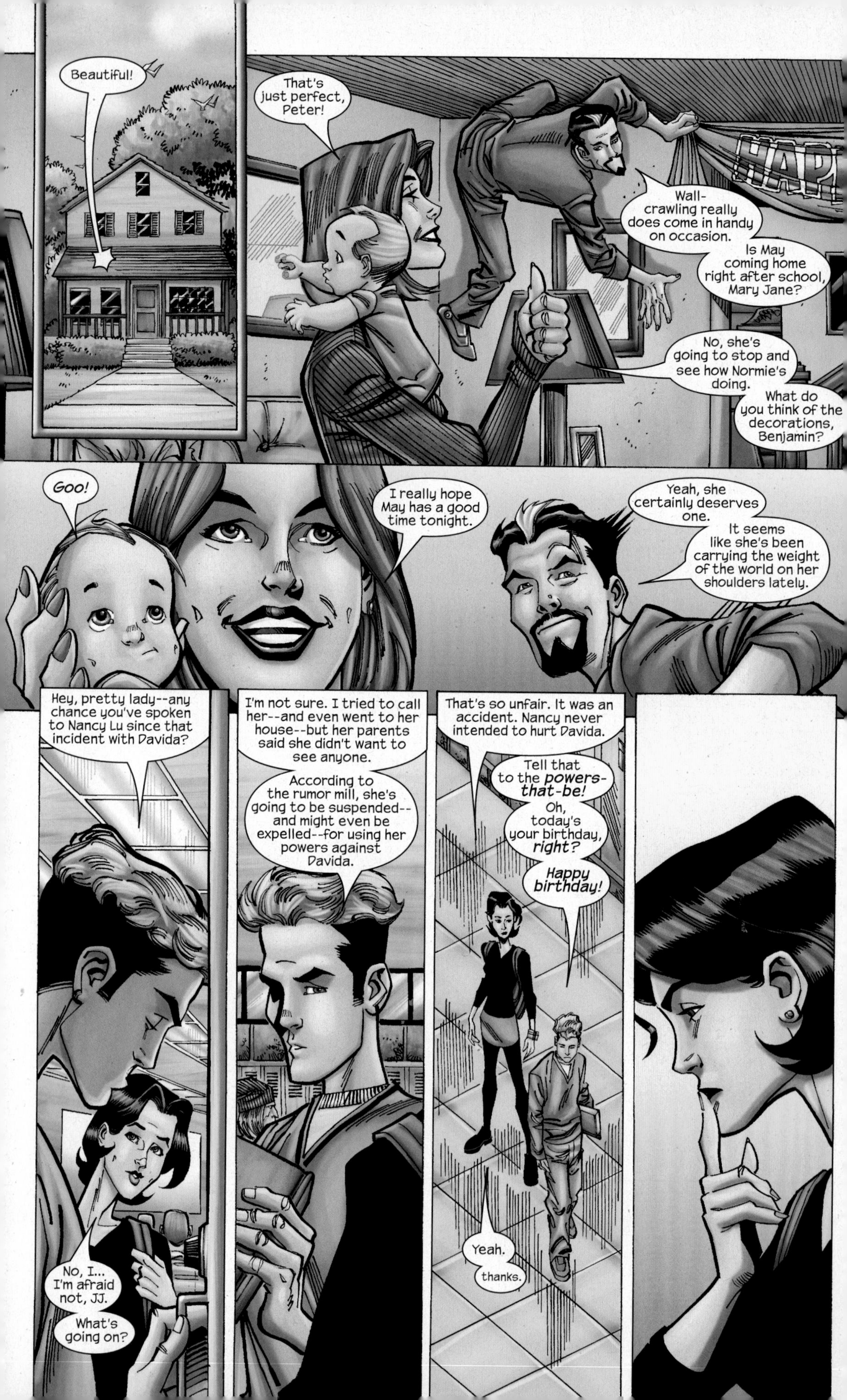
Beautiful!
That's just perfect, Peter!
Wall-crawling really does come in handy on occasion.
Is May coming home right after school, Mary Jane?
No, she's going to stop and see how Normie's doing.
What do you think of the decorations, Benjamin?
Goo!
I really hope May has a good time tonight.
Yeah, she certainly deserves one.
It seems like she's been carrying the weight of the world on her shoulders lately.
Hey, pretty lady--any chance you've spoken to Nancy Lu since that incident with Davida?
No, I... I'm afraid not, JJ.
What's going on?
I'm not sure. I tried to call her--and even went to her house--but her parents said she didn't want to see anyone.
According to the rumor mill, she's going to be suspended--and might even be expelled--for using her powers against Davida.
That's so unfair. It was an accident. Nancy never intended to hurt Davida.
Tell that to the *powers-that-be!*
Oh, today's your birthday, *right?*
Happy birthday!
Yeah.
thanks.

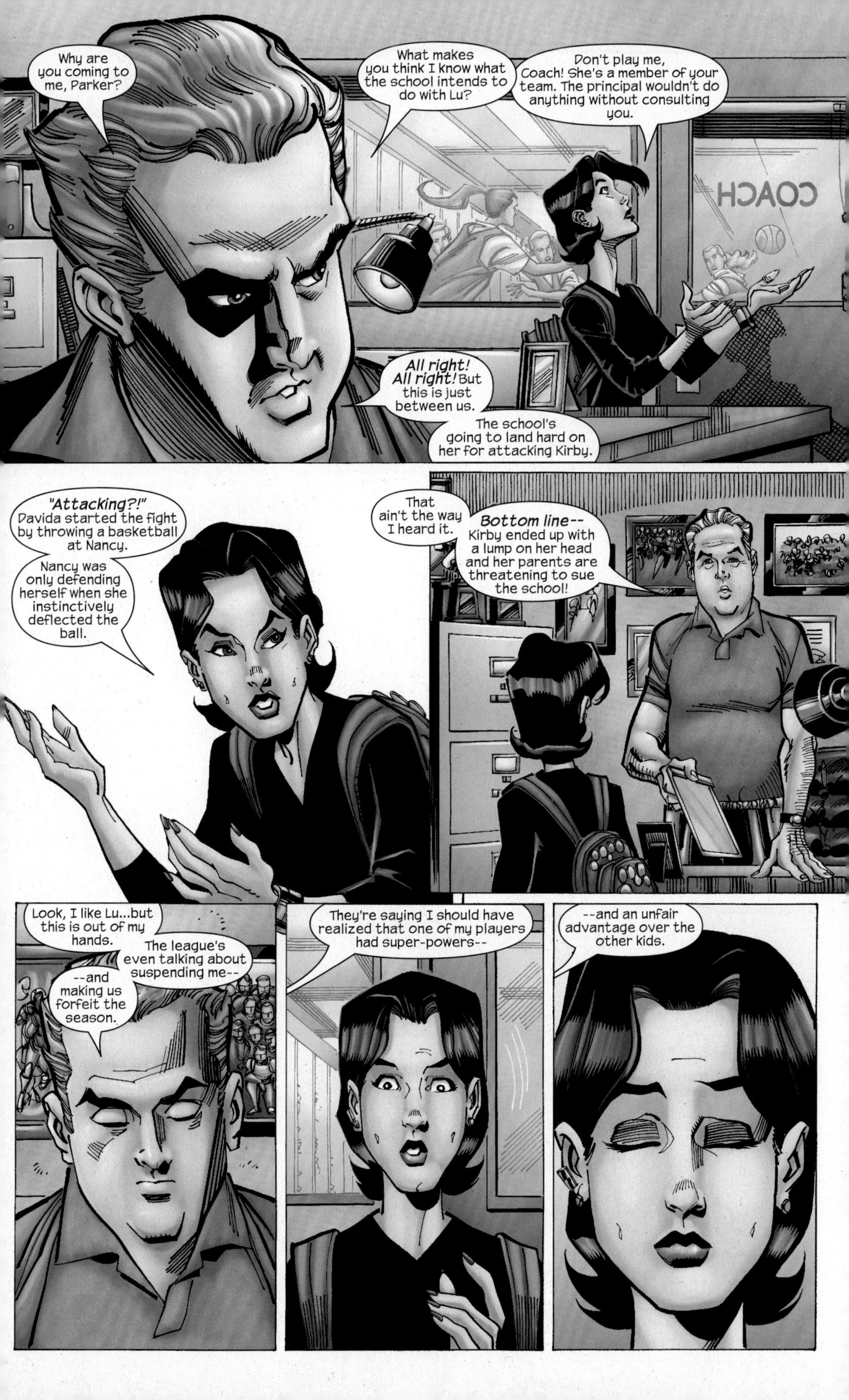
Why are you coming to me, Parker?
What makes you think I know what the school intends to do with Lu?
Don't play me, Coach! She's a member of your team. The principal wouldn't do anything without consulting you.
COACH
All right! All right! But this is just between us.
The school's going to land hard on her for attacking Kirby.
"Attacking?!" Davida started the fight by throwing a basketball at Nancy.
Nancy was only defending herself when she instinctively deflected the ball.
That ain't the way I heard it.
Bottom line-- Kirby ended up with a lump on her head and her parents are threatening to sue the school!
Look, I like Lu...but this is out of my hands.
The league's even talking about suspending me--
--and making us forfeit the season.
They're saying I should have realized that one of my players had super-powers--
--and an unfair advantage over the other kids.

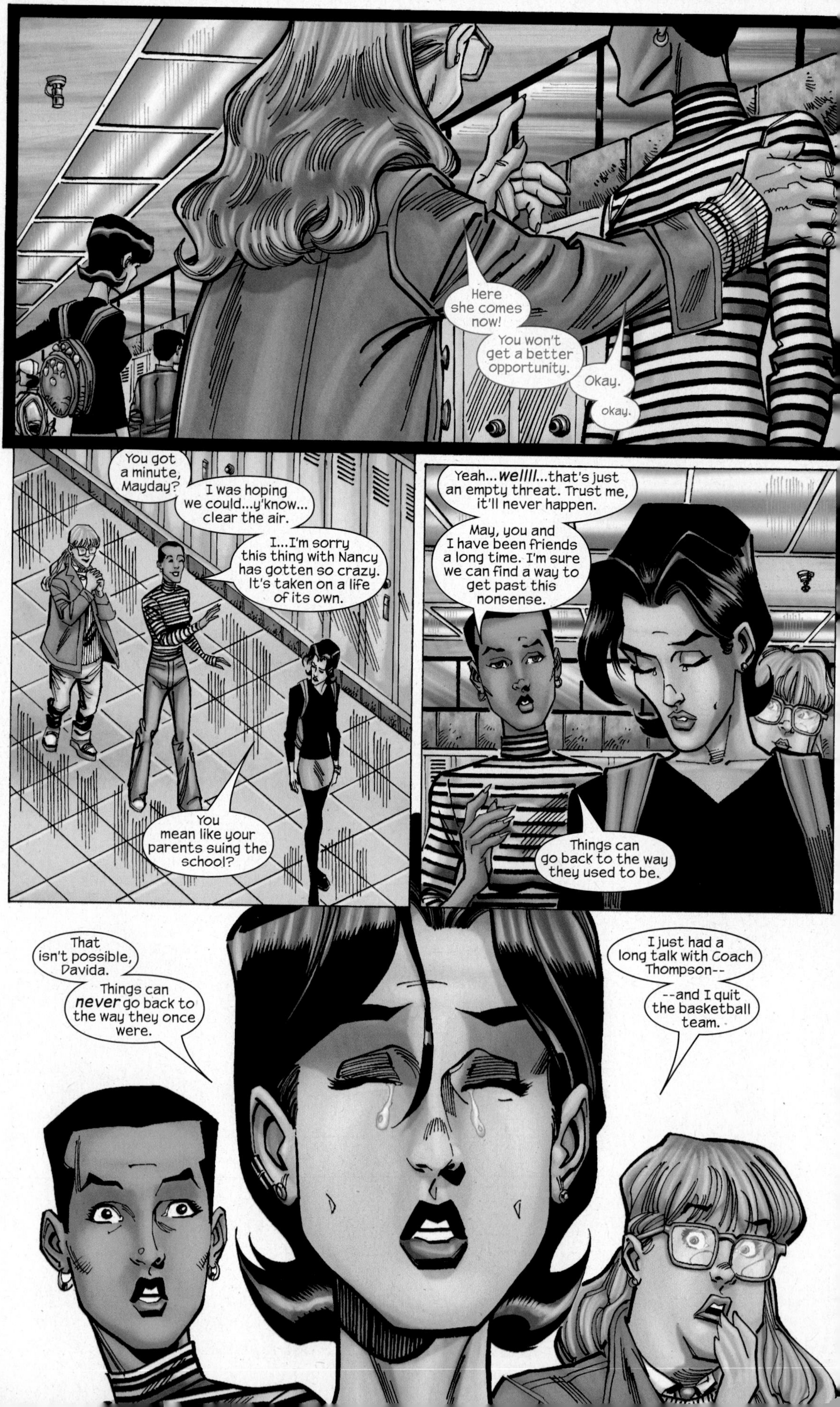
Here she comes now!
You won't get a better opportunity.
Okay.
okay.
You got a minute, Mayday?
I was hoping we could...y'know... clear the air.
I...I'm sorry this thing with Nancy has gotten so crazy. It's taken on a life of its own.
You mean like your parents suing the school?
Yeah...wellll...that's just an empty threat. Trust me, it'll never happen.
May, you and I have been friends a long time. I'm sure we can find a way to get past this nonsense.
Things can go back to the way they used to be.
That isn't possible, Davida.
Things can never go back to the way they once were.
I just had a long talk with Coach Thompson--
--and I quit the basketball team.

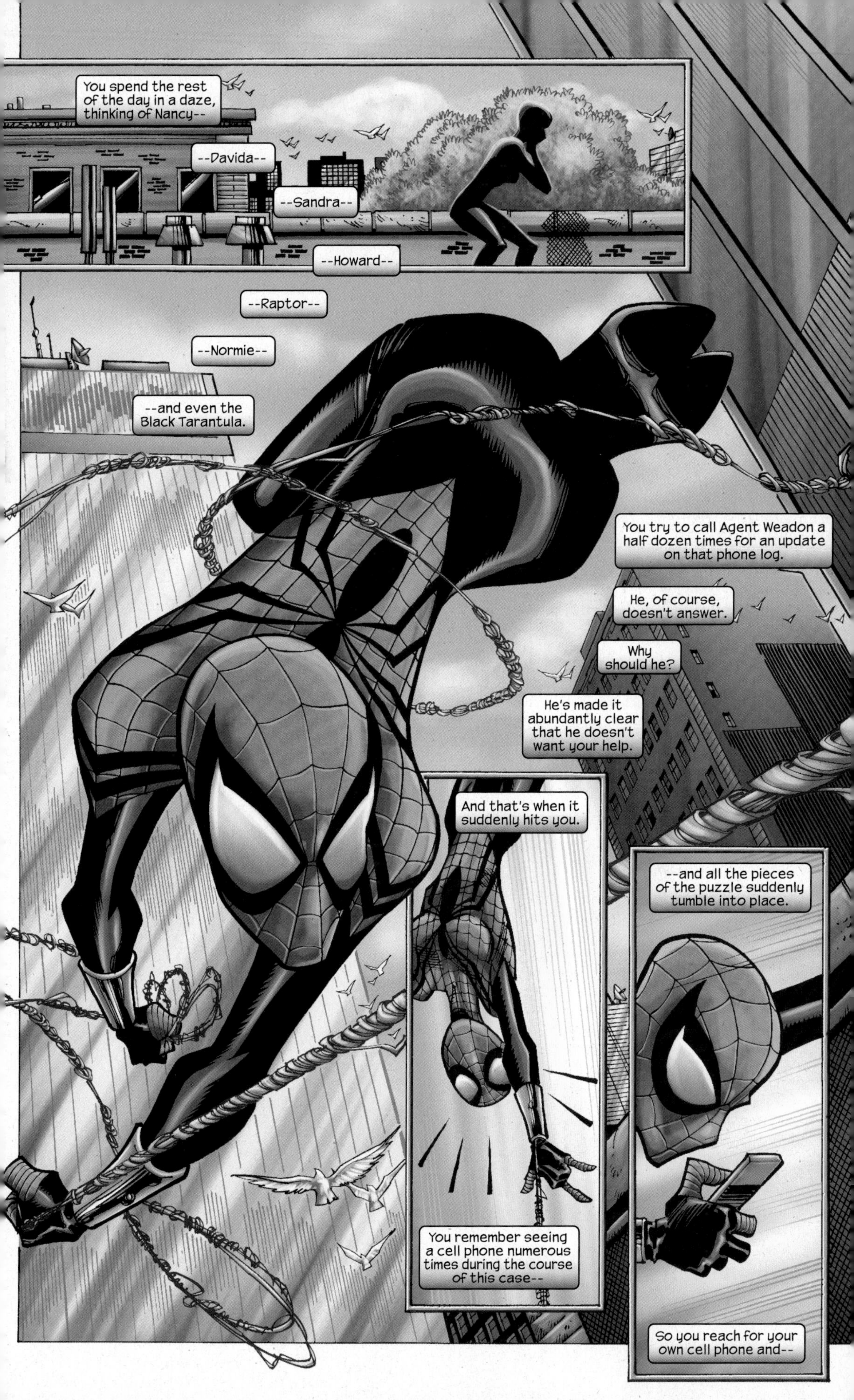
You spend the rest of the day in a daze, thinking of Nancy--
--Davida--
--Sandra--
--Howard--
--Raptor--
--Normie--
--and even the Black Tarantula.
You try to call Agent Weadon a half dozen times for an update on that phone log.
He, of course, doesn't answer.
Why should he?
He's made it abundantly clear that he doesn't want your help.
And that's when it suddenly hits you.
You remember seeing a cell phone numerous times during the course of this case--
--and all the pieces of the puzzle suddenly tumble into place.
So you reach for your own cell phone and--

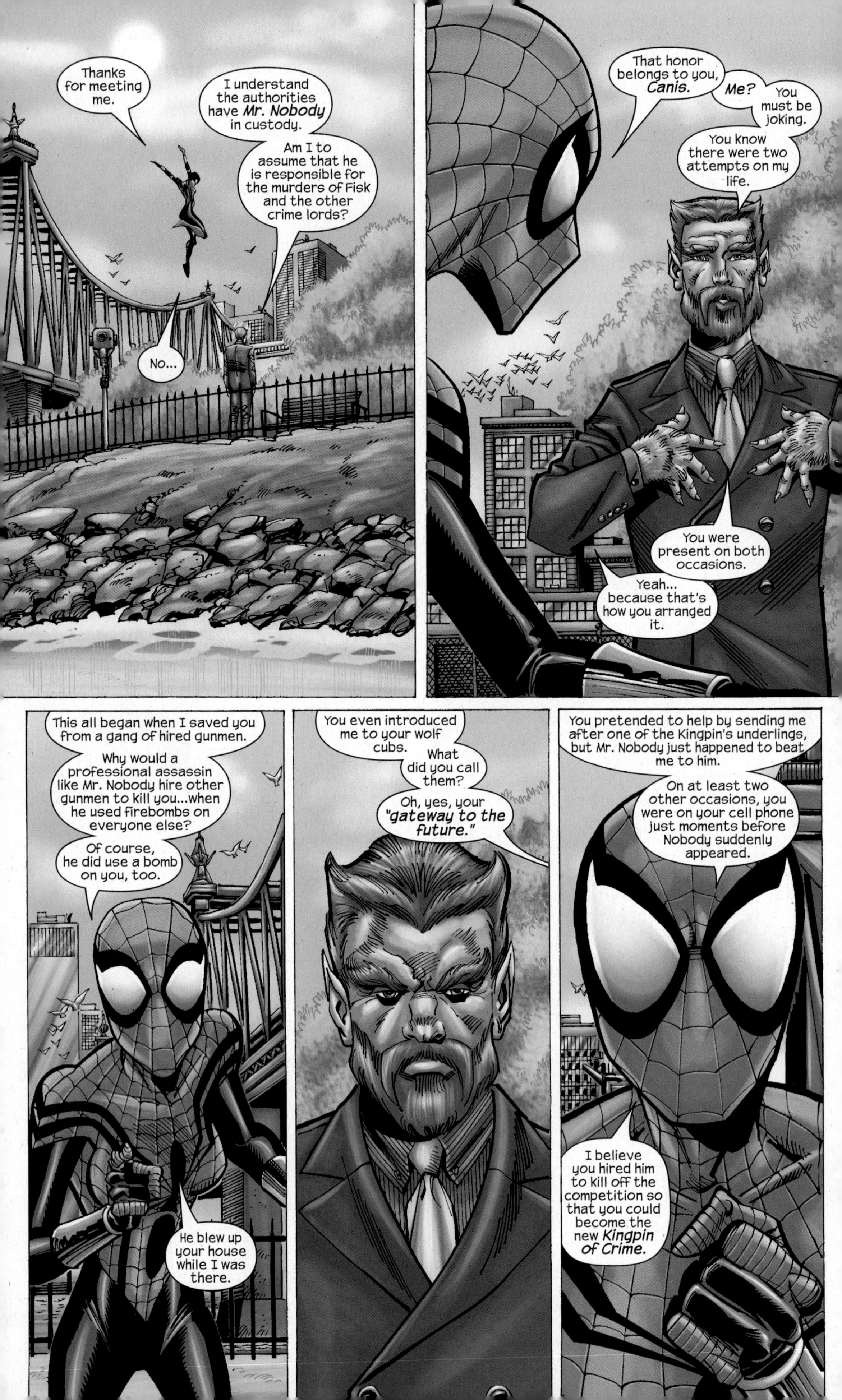
Thanks for meeting me.
I understand the authorities have Mr. Nobody in custody.
Am I to assume that he is responsible for the murders of Fisk and the other crime lords?
No...
That honor belongs to you, Canis.
Me?
You must be joking.
You know there were two attempts on my life.
You were present on both occasions.
Yeah... because that's how you arranged it.
This all began when I saved you from a gang of hired gunmen.
Why would a professional assassin like Mr. Nobody hire other gunmen to kill you...when he used firebombs on everyone else?
Of course, he did use a bomb on you, too.
He blew up your house while I was there.
You even introduced me to your wolf cubs.
What did you call them?
Oh, yes, your "gateway to the future."
You pretended to help by sending me after one of the Kingpin's underlings, but Mr. Nobody just happened to beat me to him.
On at least two other occasions, you were on your cell phone just moments before Nobody suddenly appeared.
I believe you hired him to kill off the competition so that you could become the new Kingpin of Crime.

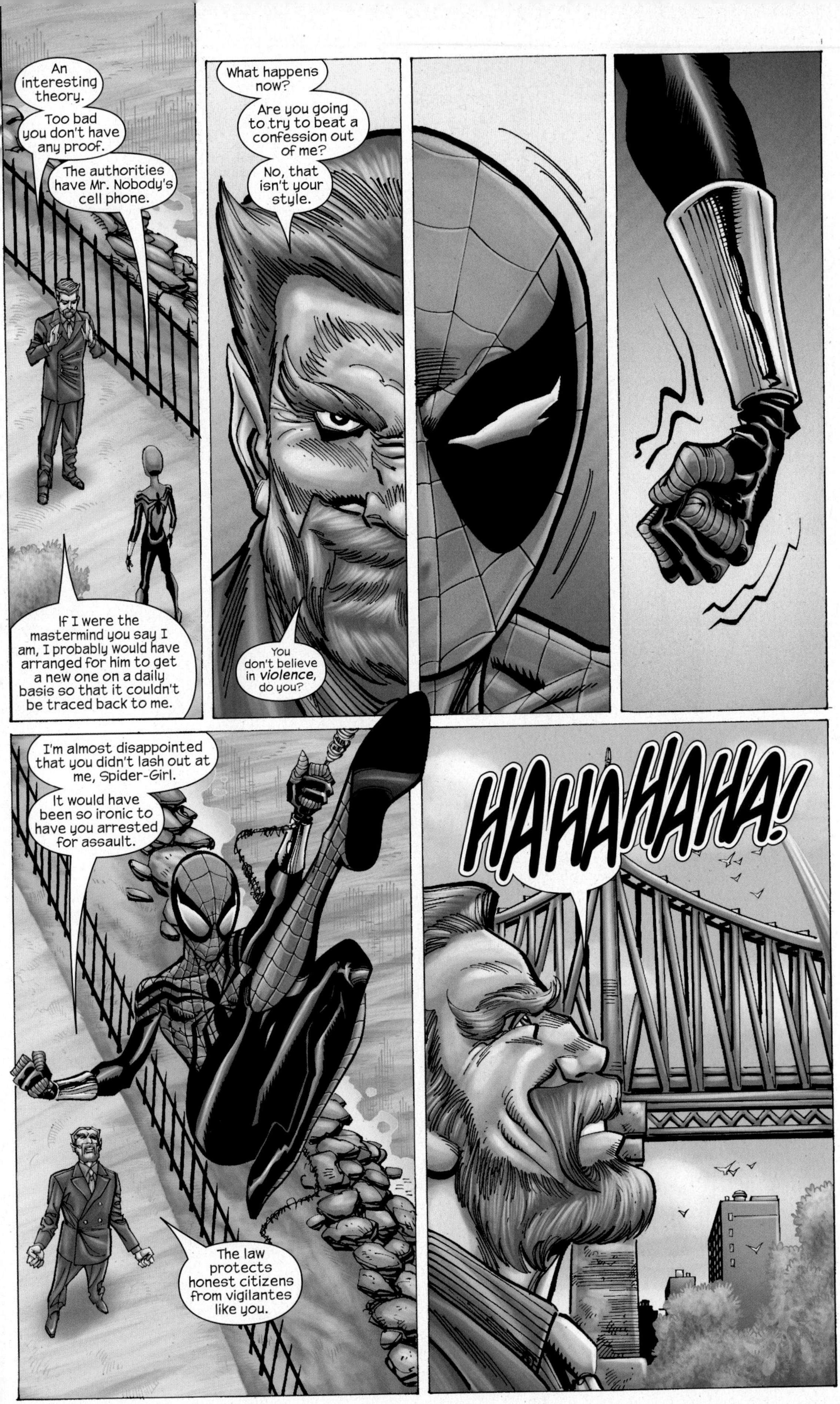

An interesting theory.
Too bad you don't have any proof.
The authorities have Mr. Nobody's cell phone.
If I were the mastermind you say I am, I probably would have arranged for him to get a new one on a daily basis so that it couldn't be traced back to me.
What happens now?
Are you going to try to beat a confession out of me?
No, that isn't your style.
You don't believe in violence, do you?
I'm almost disappointed that you didn't lash out at me, Spider-Girl.
It would have been so ironic to have you arrested for assault.
The law protects honest citizens from vigilantes like you.
HAHAHAHA!

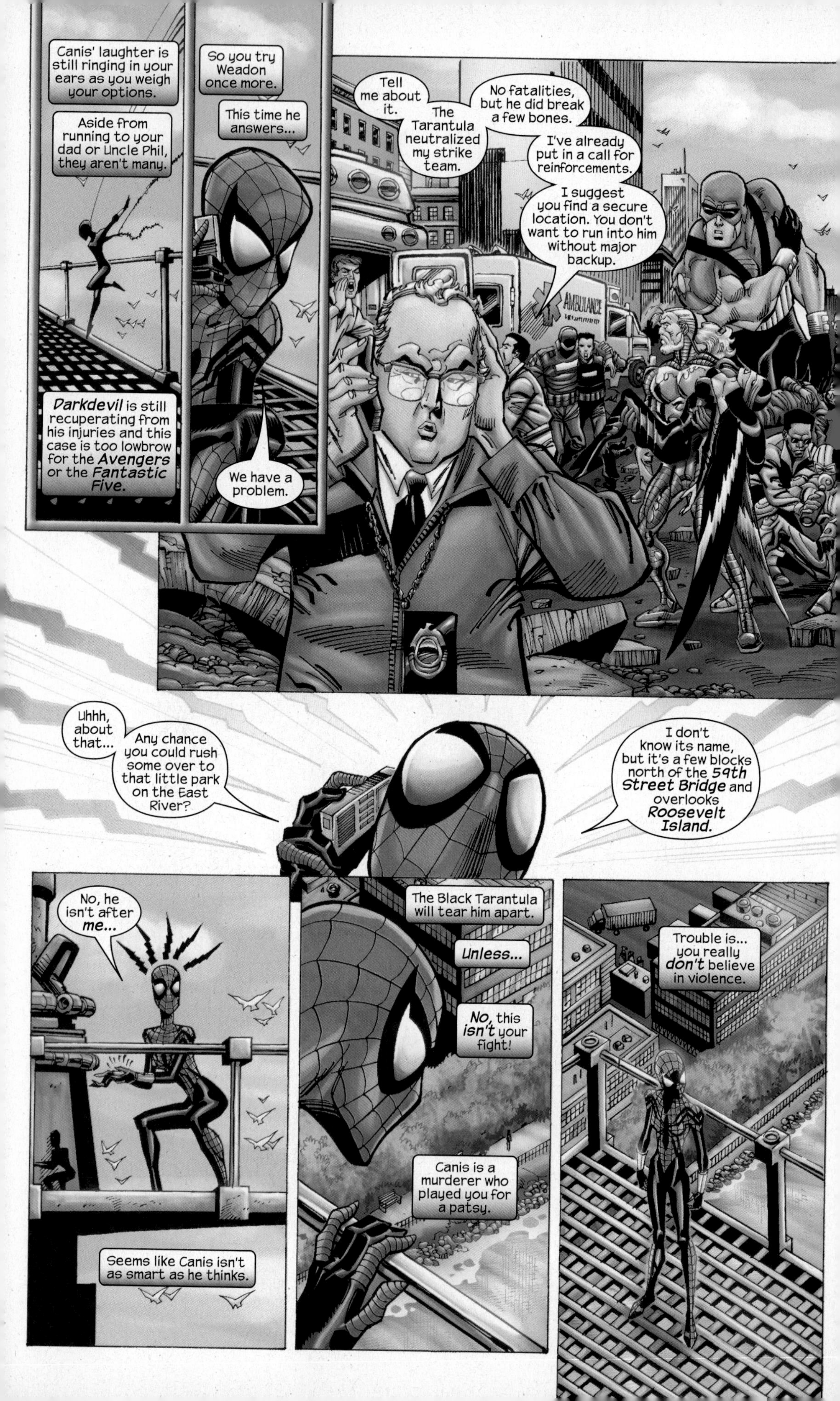

Canis' laughter is still ringing in your ears as you weigh your options.
Aside from running to your dad or Uncle Phil, they aren't many.
Darkdevil is still recuperating from his injuries and this case is too lowbrow for the Avengers or the Fantastic Five.
So you try Weadon once more.
This time he answers...
We have a problem.
Tell me about it.
The Tarantula neutralized my strike team.
No fatalities, but he did break a few bones.
I've already put in a call for reinforcements.
I suggest you find a secure location. You don't want to run into him without major backup.
AMBULANCE
Uhhh, about that...
Any chance you could rush some over to that little park on the East River?
I don't know its name, but it's a few blocks north of the 59th Street Bridge and overlooks Roosevelt Island.
No, he isn't after me...
Seems like Canis isn't as smart as he thinks.
The Black Tarantula will tear him apart.
Unless...
No, this isn't your fight!
Canis is a murderer who played you for a patsy.
Trouble is... you really don't believe in violence.

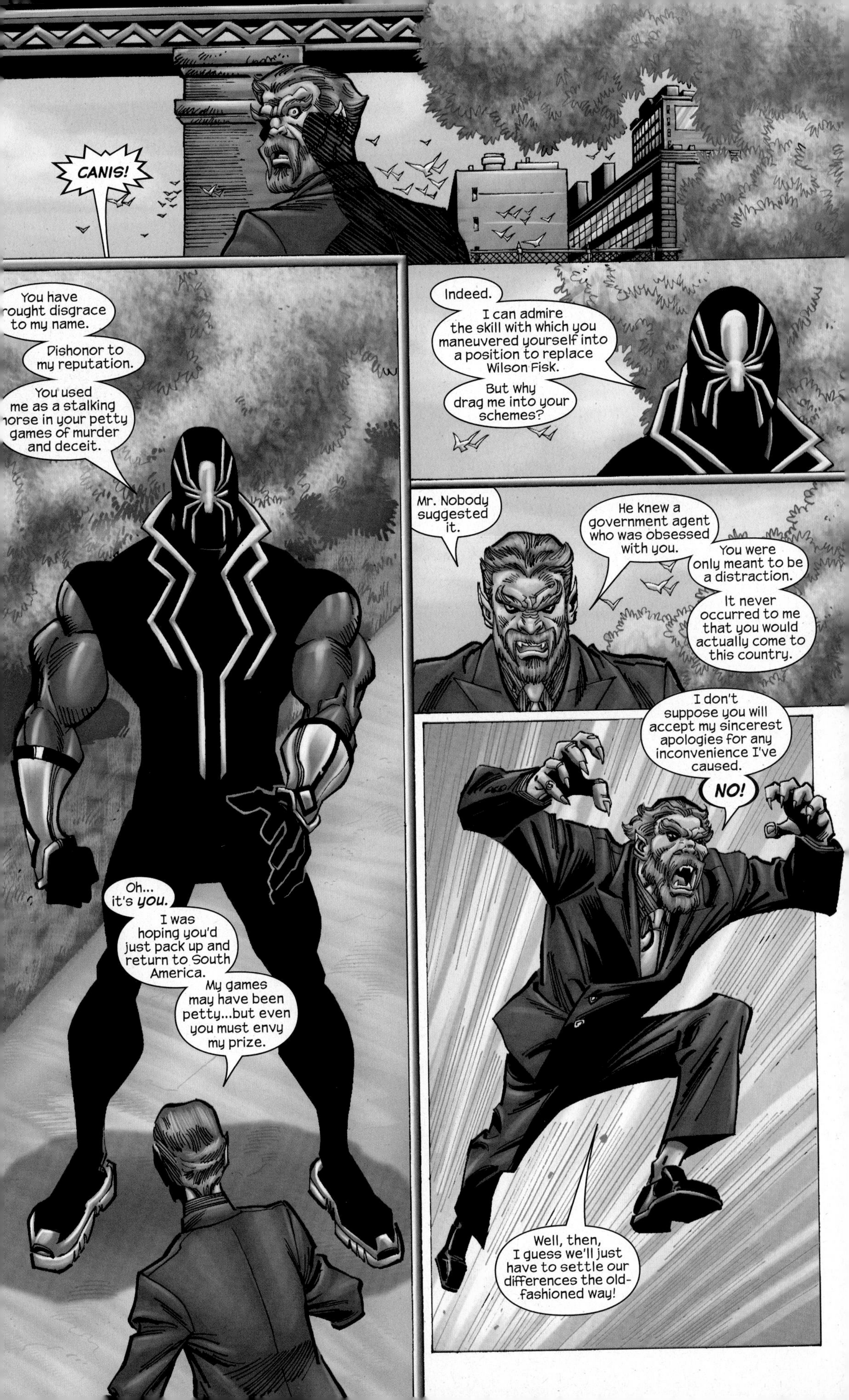
CANIS!
You have rought disgrace to my name.
Dishonor to my reputation.
You used me as a stalking horse in your petty games of murder and deceit.
Oh... it's YOU.
I was hoping you'd just pack up and return to South America.
My games may have been petty...but even you must envy my prize.
Indeed.
I can admire the skill with which you maneuvered yourself into a position to replace Wilson Fisk.
But why drag me into your schemes?
Mr. Nobody suggested it.
He knew a government agent who was obsessed with you.
You were only meant to be a distraction.
It never occurred to me that you would actually come to this country.
I don't suppose you will accept my sincerest apologies for any inconvenience I've caused.
NO!
Well, then, I guess we'll just have to settle our differences the old-fashioned way!

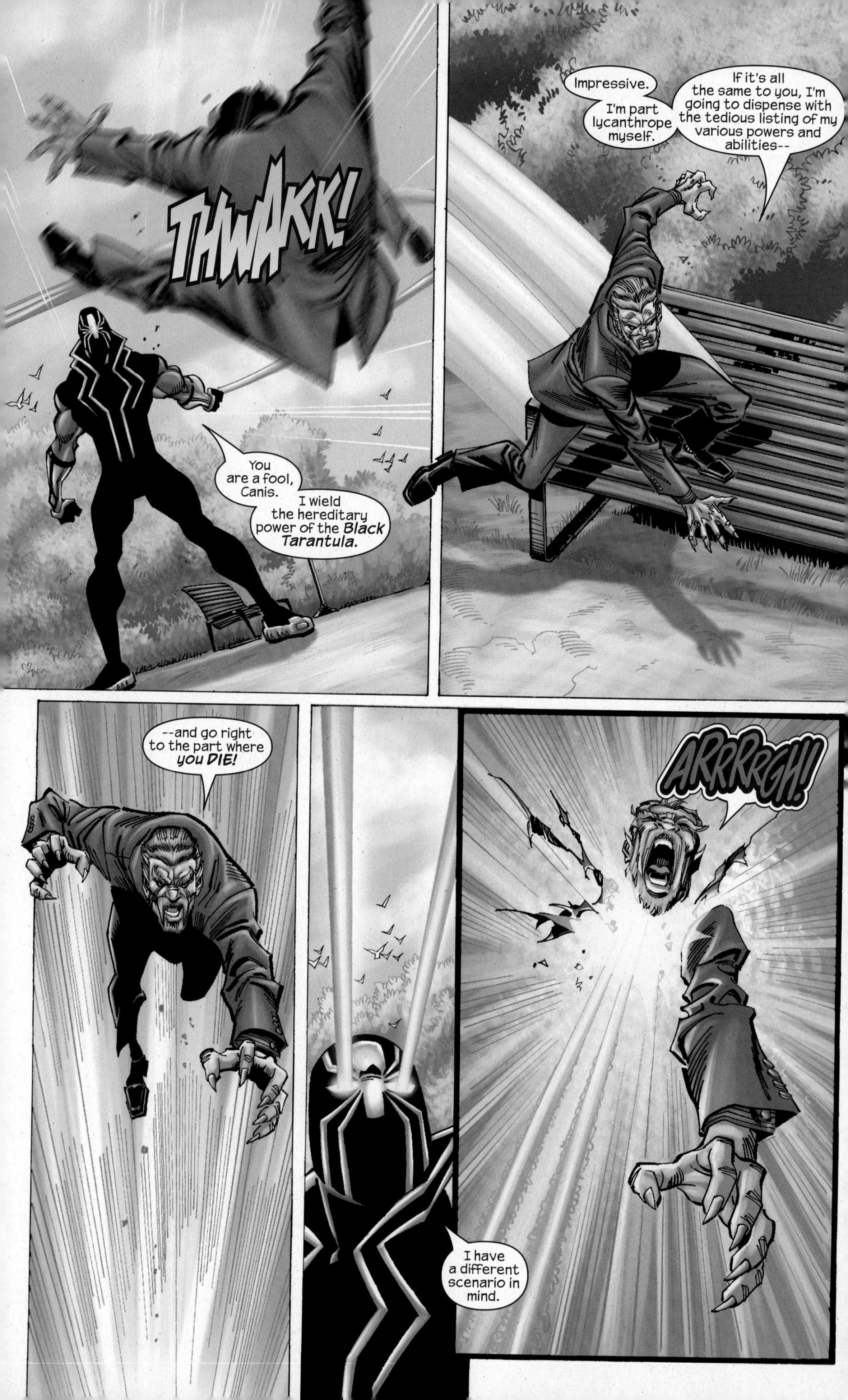
THWAKK!
You are a fool, Canis.
I wield the hereditary power of the Black Tarantula.
Impressive.
I'm part lycanthrope myself.
If it's all the same to you, I'm going to dispense with the tedious listing of my various powers and abilities--
--and go right to the part where you DIE!
ARRRRGH!
I have a different scenario in mind.

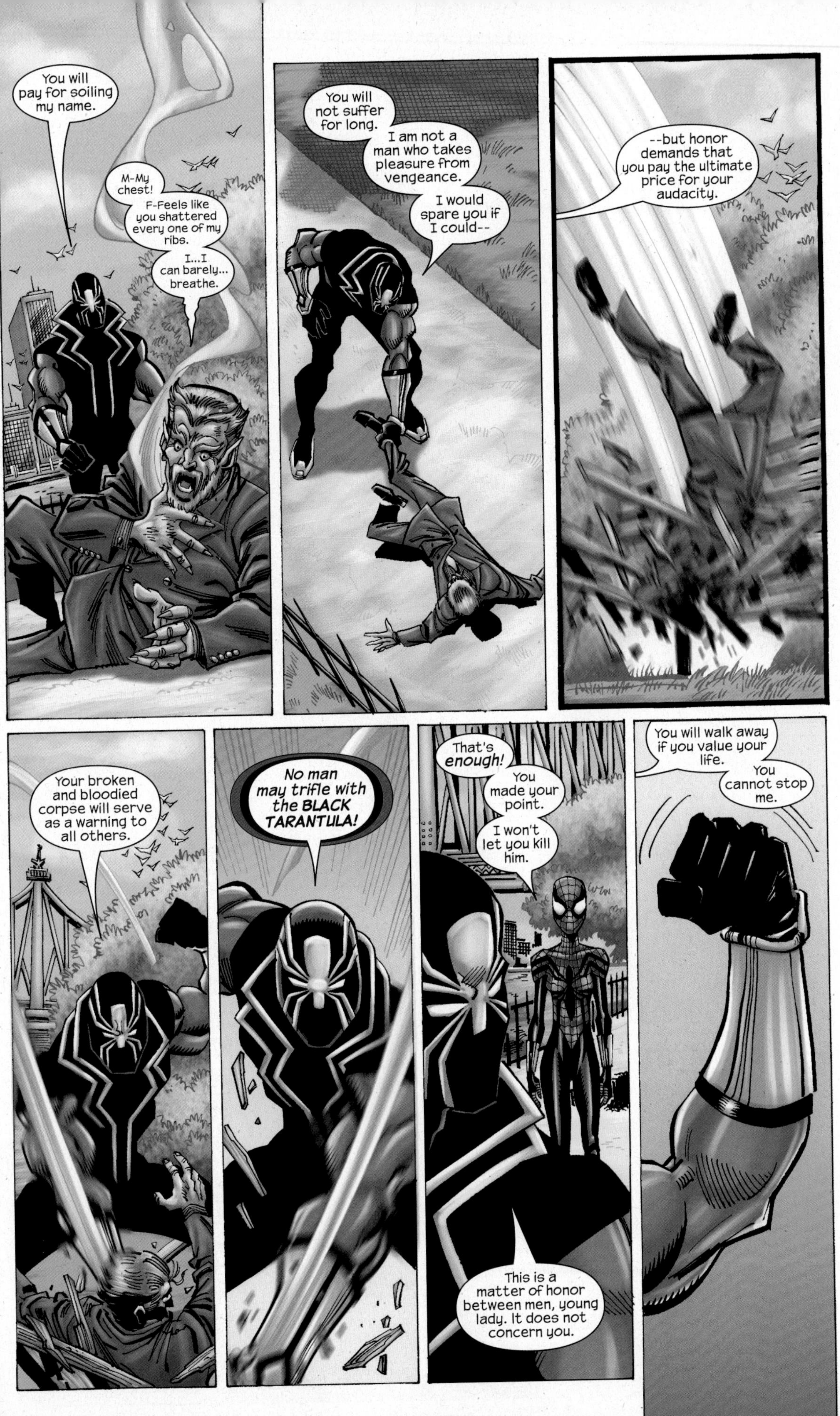
You will pay for soiling my name.
M-My chest!
F-Feels like you shattered every one of my ribs.
I...I can barely... breathe.
You will not suffer for long.
I am not a man who takes pleasure from vengeance.
I would spare you if I could--
--but honor demands that you pay the ultimate price for your audacity.
Your broken and bloodied corpse will serve as a warning to all others.
No man may trifle with the BLACK TARANTULA!
That's enough!
You made your point.
I won't let you kill him.
This is a matter of honor between men, young lady. It does not concern you.
You will walk away if you value your life.
You cannot stop me.

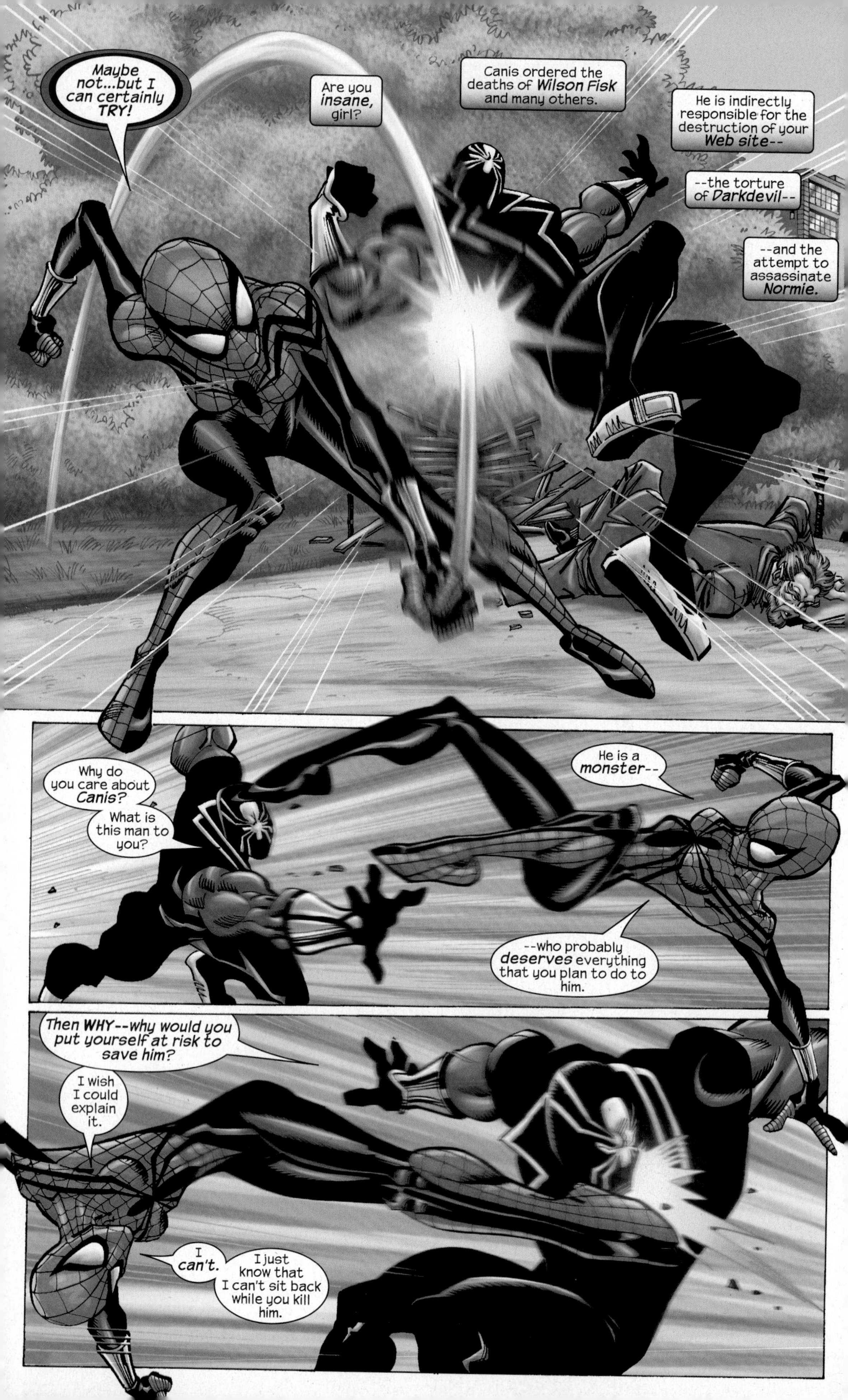

Maybe not...but I can certainly TRY!
Are you insane, girl?
Canis ordered the deaths of Wilson Fisk and many others.
He is indirectly responsible for the destruction of your Web site--
--the torture of Darkdevil--
--and the attempt to assassinate Normie.
Why do you care about Canis?
What is this man to you?
He is a monster--
--who probably deserves everything that you plan to do to him.
Then WHY--why would you put yourself at risk to save him?
I wish I could explain it.
I can't.
I just know that I can't sit back while you kill him.

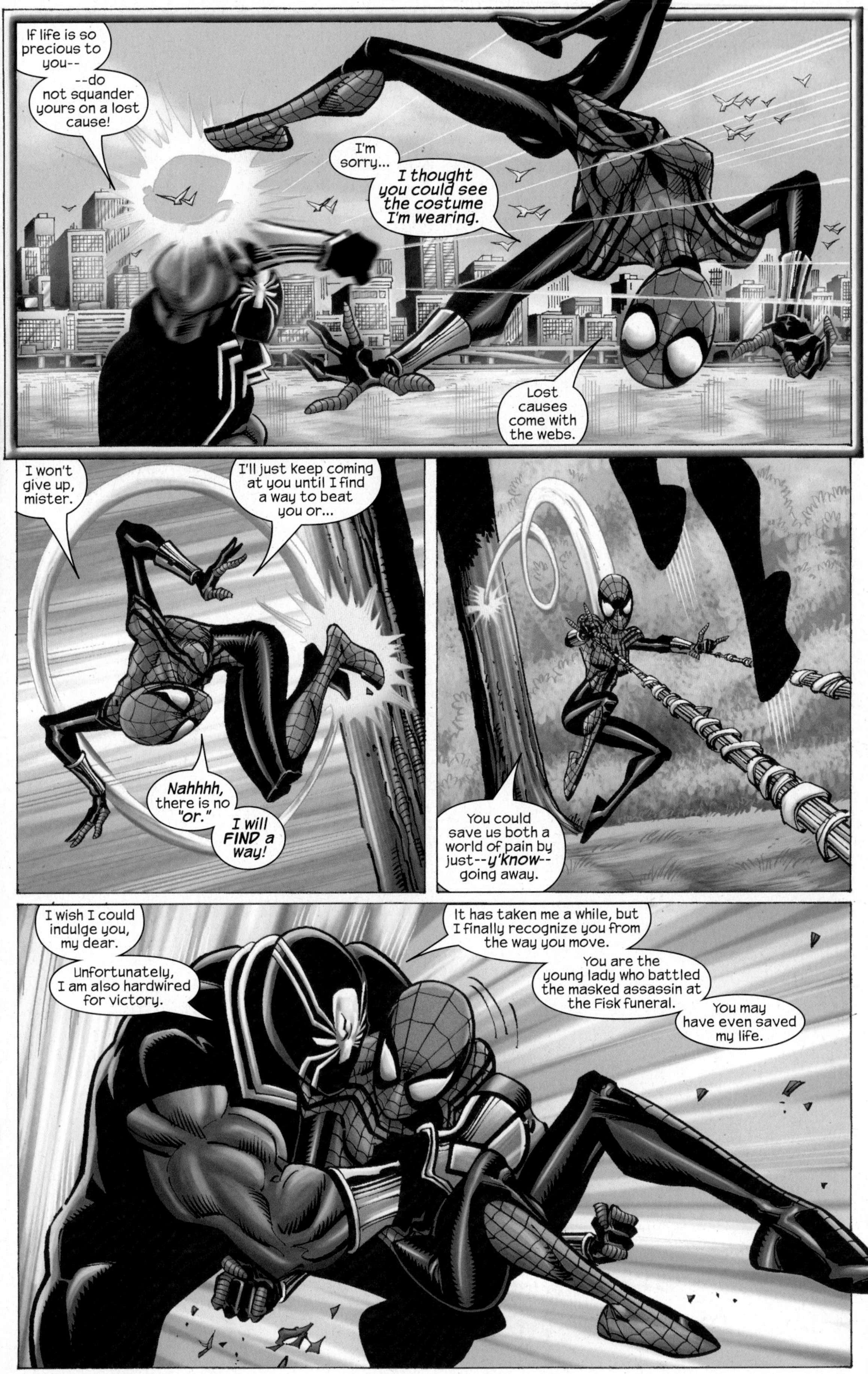
If life is so precious to you--
--do not squander yours on a lost cause!
I'm sorry... I thought you could see the costume I'm wearing.
Lost causes come with the webs.
I won't give up, mister.
I'll just keep coming at you until I find a way to beat you or...
Nahhhh, there is no "or." I will FIND a way!
You could save us both a world of pain by just--y'know--going away.
I wish I could indulge you, my dear.
Unfortunately, I am also hardwired for victory.
It has taken me a while, but I finally recognize you from the way you move.
You are the young lady who battled the masked assassin at the Fisk funeral.
You may have even saved my life.

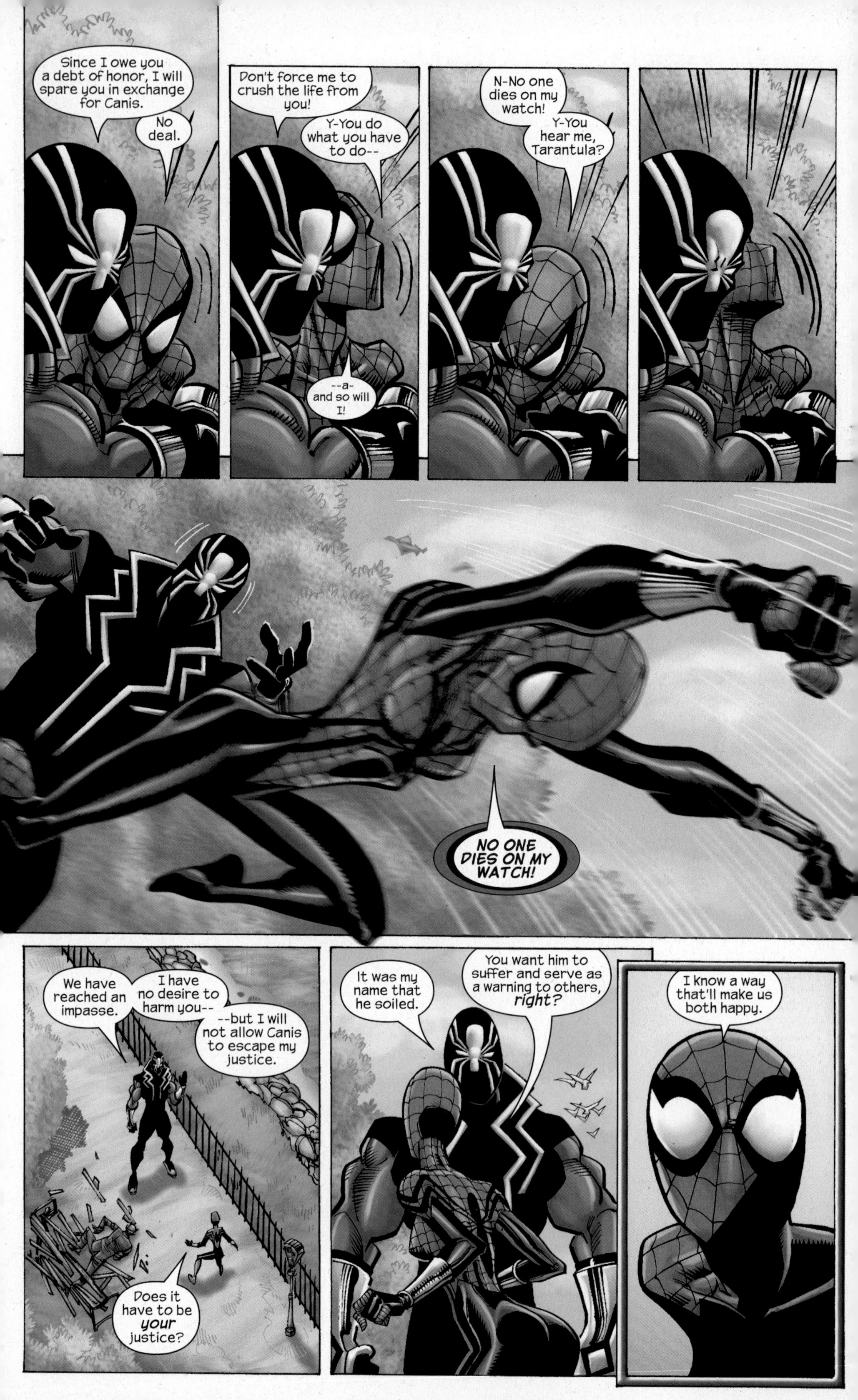
Since I owe you a debt of honor, I will spare you in exchange for Canis.
No deal.
Don't force me to crush the life from you!
Y-You do what you have to do--
--a-
and so will I!
N-No one dies on my watch!
Y-You hear me, Tarantula?
NO ONE DIES ON MY WATCH!
We have reached an impasse.
I have no desire to harm you--
--but I will not allow Canis to escape my justice.
Does it have to be *your* justice?
It was my name that he soiled.
You want him to suffer and serve as a warning to others, *right?*
I know a way that'll make us both happy.

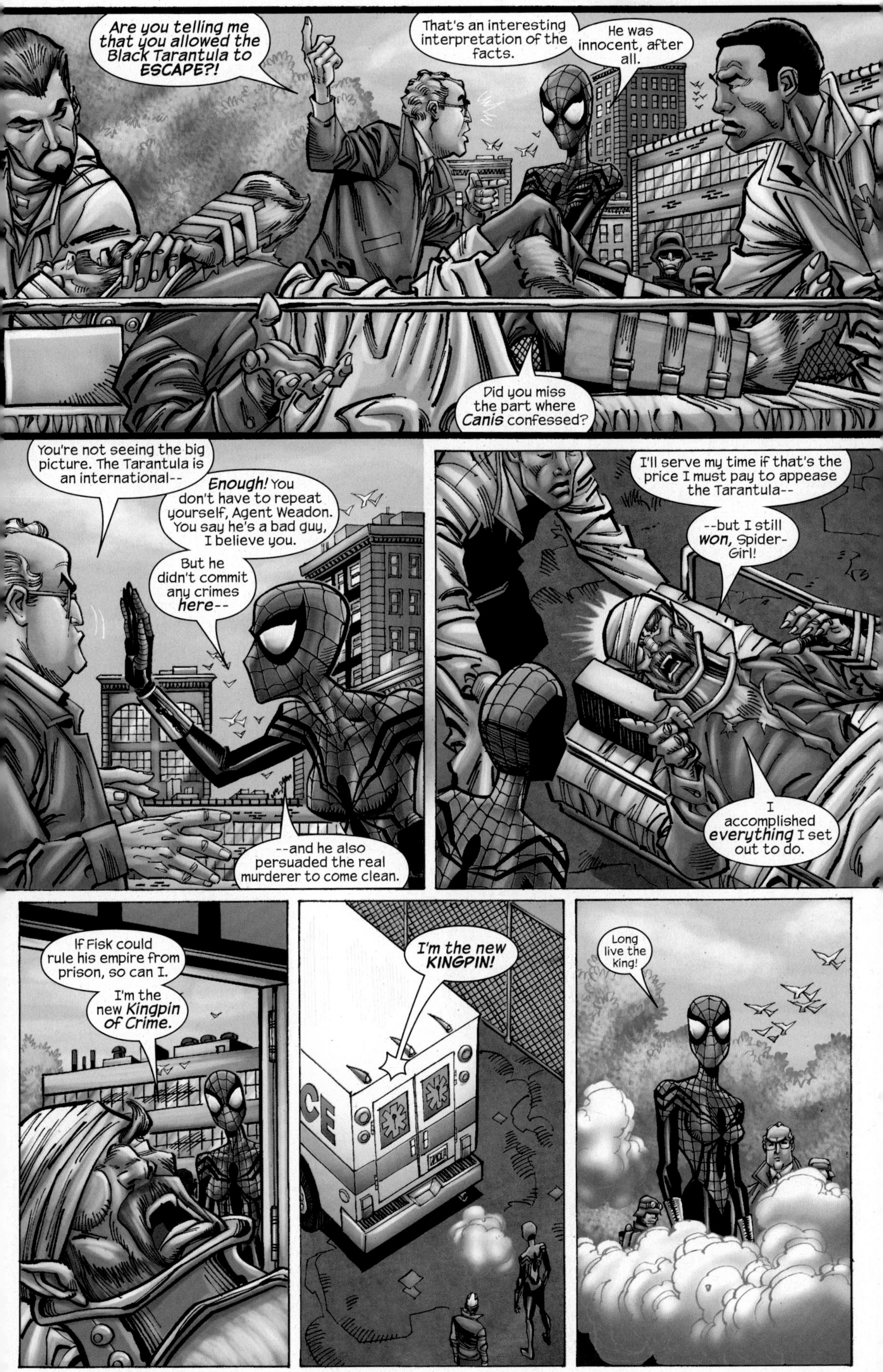

Are you telling me that you allowed the Black Tarantula to ESCAPE?!
That's an interesting interpretation of the facts.
He was innocent, after all.
Did you miss the part where Canis confessed?
You're not seeing the big picture. The Tarantula is an international--
Enough! You don't have to repeat yourself, Agent Weadon. You say he's a bad guy, I believe you.
But he didn't commit any crimes here--
--and he also persuaded the real murderer to come clean.
I'll serve my time if that's the price I must pay to appease the Tarantula--
--but I still won, Spider-Girl!
I accomplished everything I set out to do.
If Fisk could rule his empire from prison, so can I.
I'm the new Kingpin of Crime.
I'm the new KINGPIN!
Long live the king!

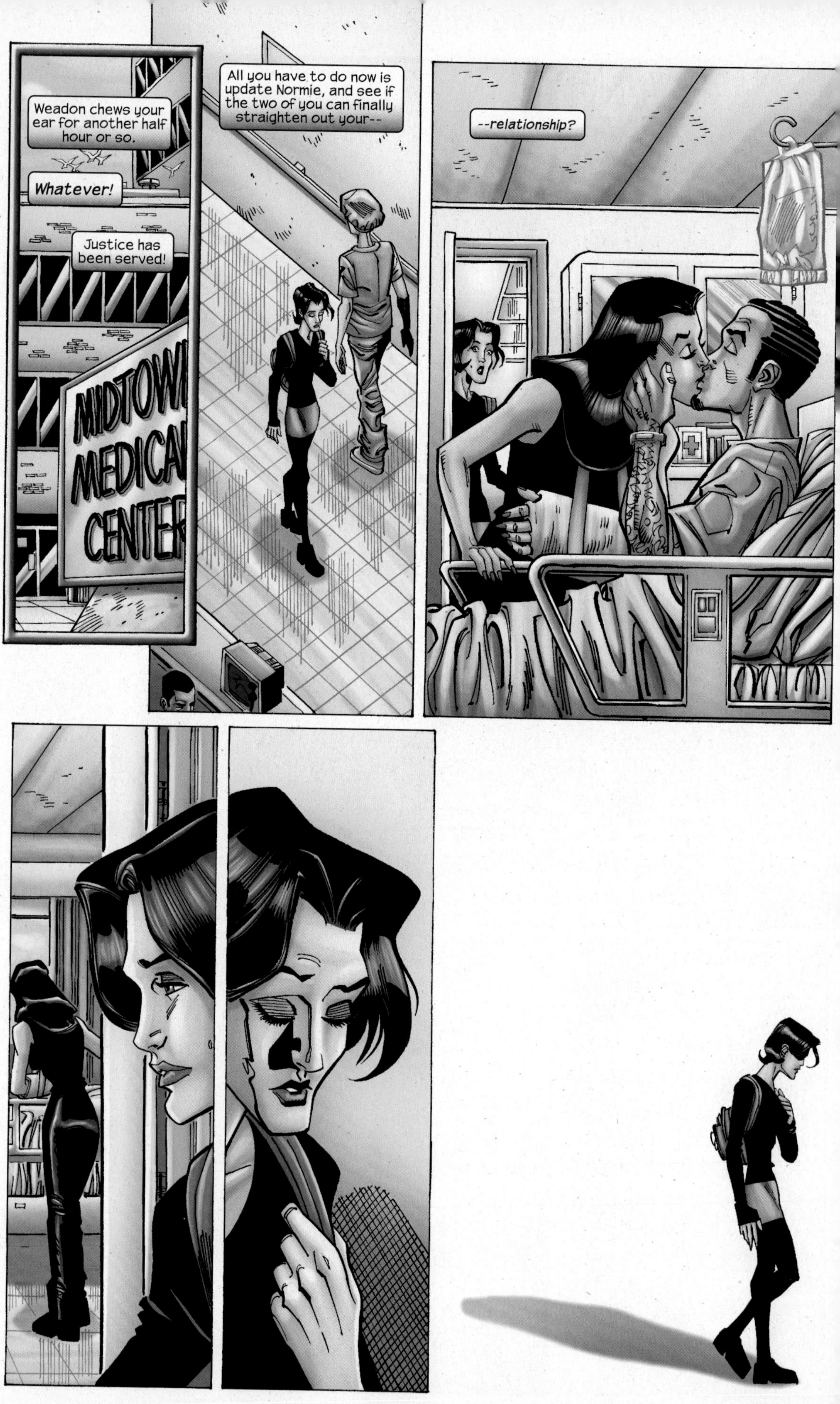
Weadon chews your ear for another half hour or so.
Whatever!
Justice has been served!
MIDTOWN MEDICAL CENTER
All you have to do now is update Normie, and see if the two of you can finally straighten out your--
--relationship?

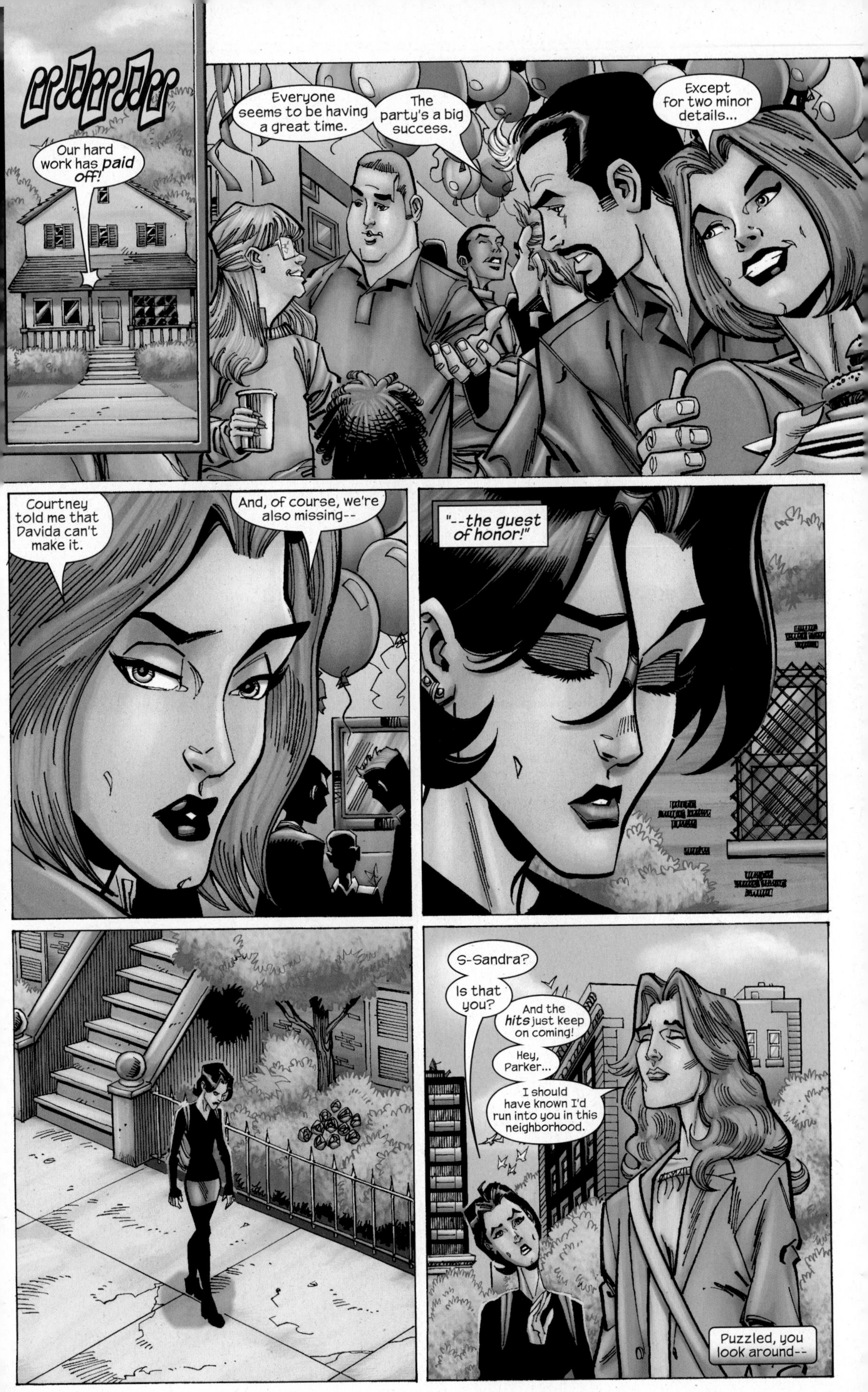
Our hard work has *paid* off!
Everyone seems to be having a great time.
The party's a big success.
Except for two minor details...
Courtney told me that Davida can't make it.
And, of course, we're also missing--
"--*the guest of honor!*"
S-Sandra?
Is that you?
And the *hits* just keep on coming!
Hey, Parker...
I should have known I'd run into you in this neighborhood.
Puzzled, you look around--

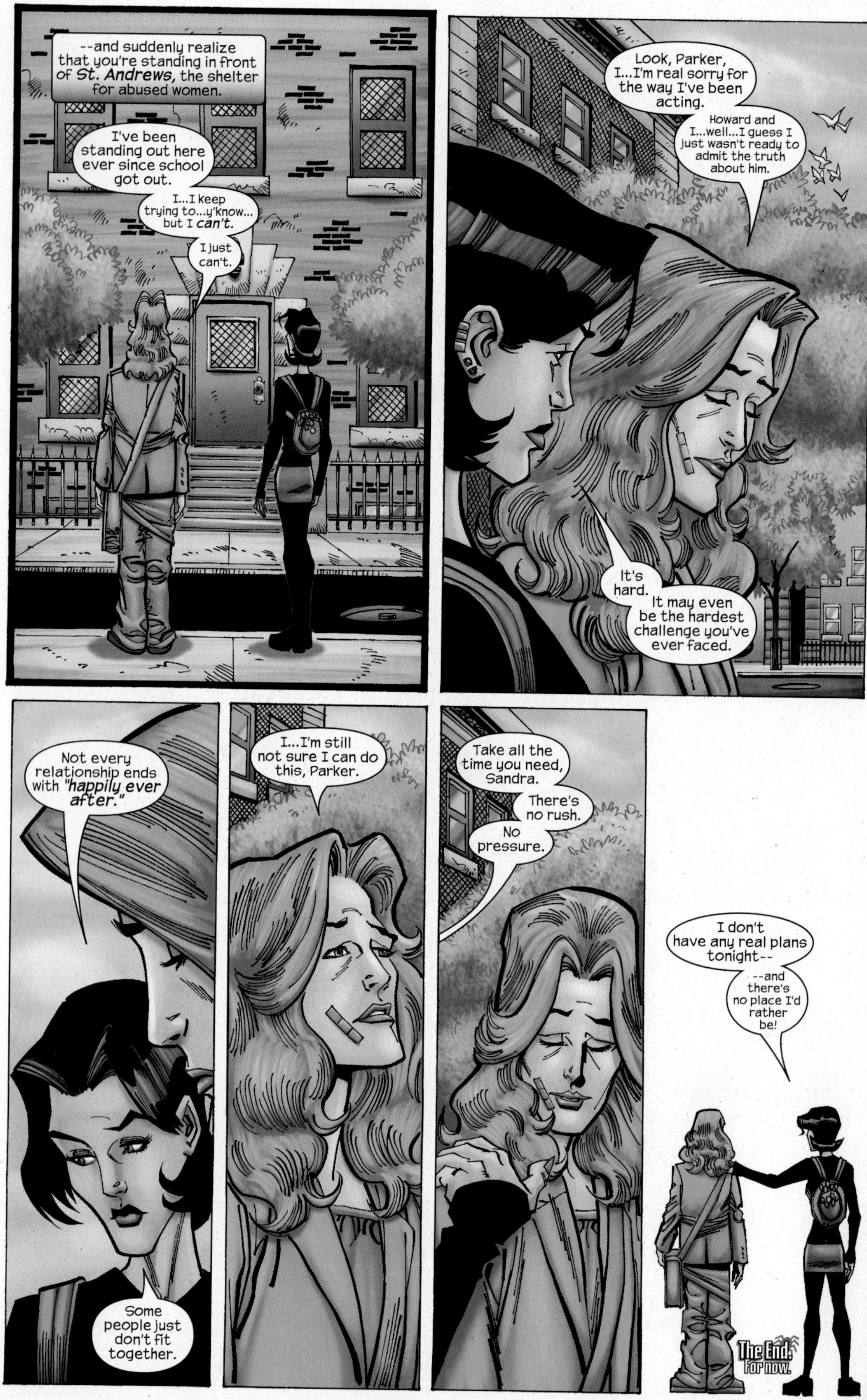
--and suddenly realize that you're standing in front of St. Andrews, the shelter for abused women.
I've been standing out here ever since school got out.
I...I keep trying to...y'know... but I can't.
I just can't.
Look, Parker, I...I'm real sorry for the way I've been acting.
Howard and I...well...I guess I just wasn't ready to admit the truth about him.
It's hard.
It may even be the hardest challenge you've ever faced.
Not every relationship ends with "happily ever after."
Some people just don't fit together.
I...I'm still not sure I can do this, Parker.
Take all the time you need, Sandra.
There's no rush.
No pressure.
I don't have any real plans tonight--
--and there's no place I'd rather be!
The End. For now.

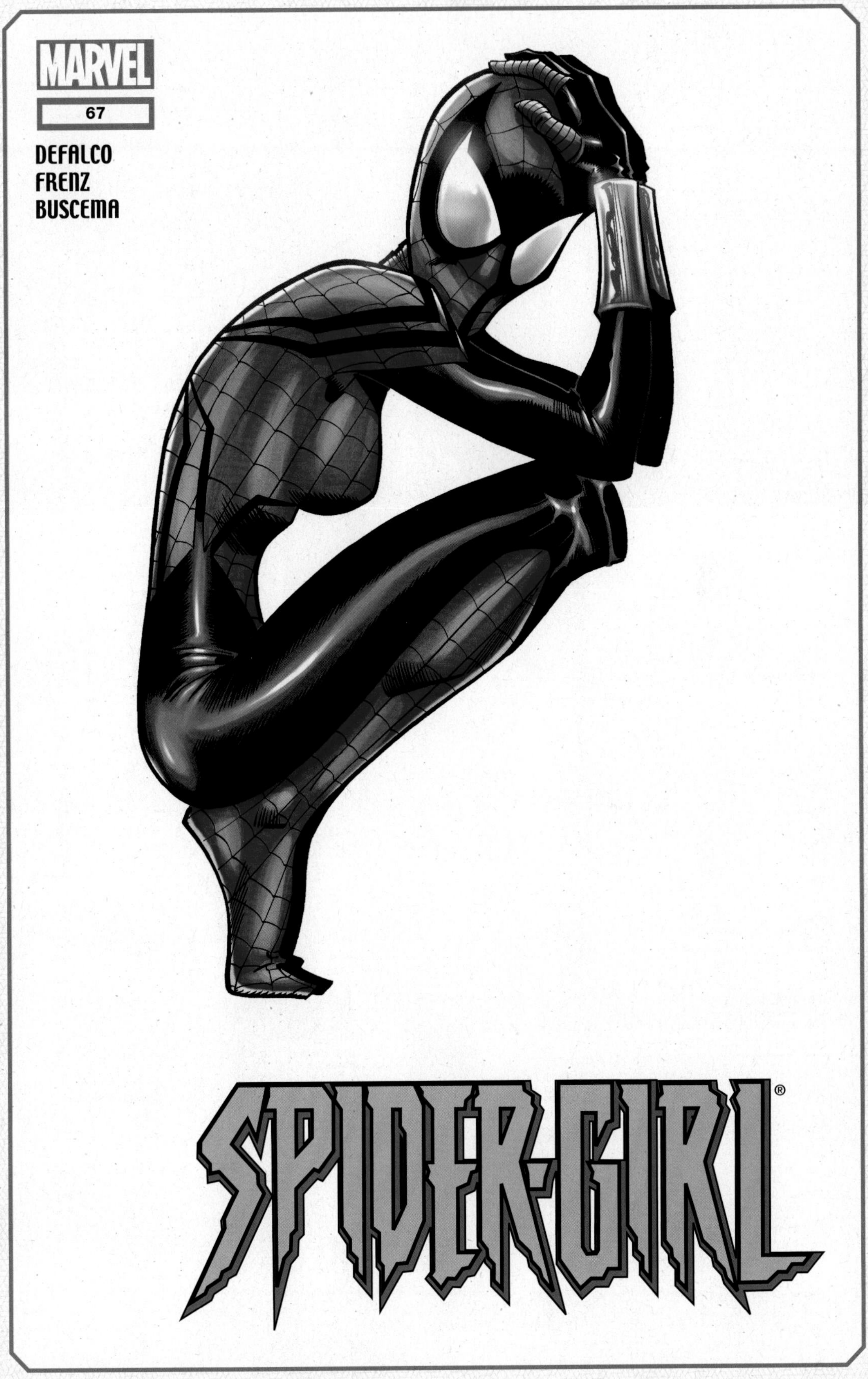
MARVEL
67
DEFALCO
FRENZ
BUSCEMA
SPIDER-GIRL®

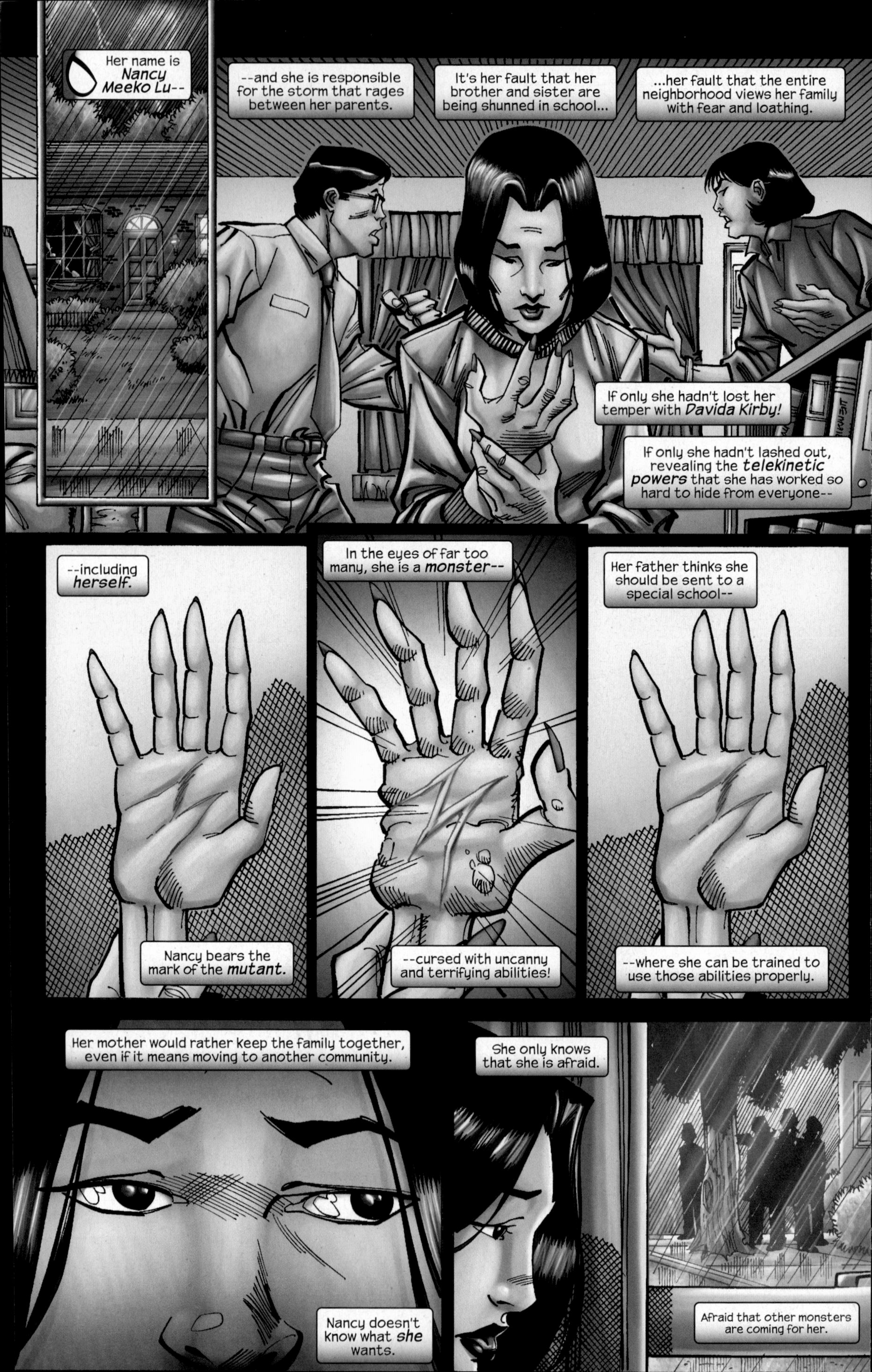

Her name is Nancy Meeko Lu--
--and she is responsible for the storm that rages between her parents.
It's her fault that her brother and sister are being shunned in school...
...her fault that the entire neighborhood views her family with fear and loathing.
If only she hadn't lost her temper with Davida Kirby!
If only she hadn't lashed out, revealing the telekinetic powers that she has worked so hard to hide from everyone--
--including herself.
Nancy bears the mark of the mutant.
In the eyes of far too many, she is a monster--
--cursed with uncanny and terrifying abilities!
Her father thinks she should be sent to a special school--
--where she can be trained to use those abilities properly.
Her mother would rather keep the family together, even if it means moving to another community.
Nancy doesn't know what she wants.
She only knows that she is afraid.
Afraid that other monsters are coming for her.

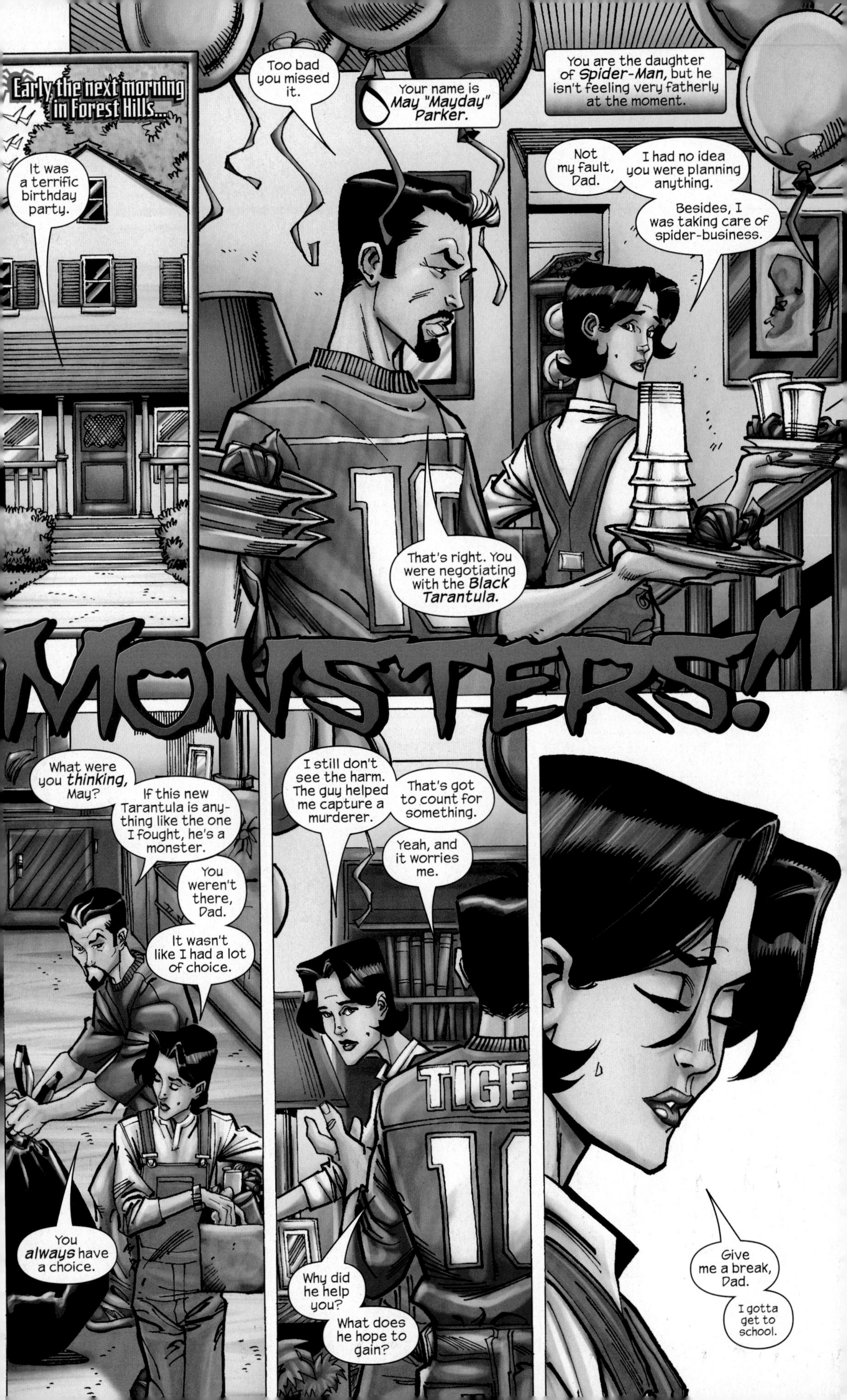

Early the next morning in Forest Hills...
It was a terrific birthday party.
Too bad you missed it.
Your name is May "Mayday" Parker.
You are the daughter of Spider-Man, but he isn't feeling very fatherly at the moment.
Not my fault, Dad.
I had no idea you were planning anything.
Besides, I was taking care of spider-business.
That's right. You were negotiating with the Black Tarantula.
MONSTERS!
What were you thinking, May?
If this new Tarantula is anything like the one I fought, he's a monster.
You weren't there, Dad.
It wasn't like I had a lot of choice.
You always have a choice.
I still don't see the harm. The guy helped me capture a murderer.
That's got to count for something.
Yeah, and it worries me.
Why did he help you?
What does he hope to gain?
Give me a break, Dad.
I gotta get to school.

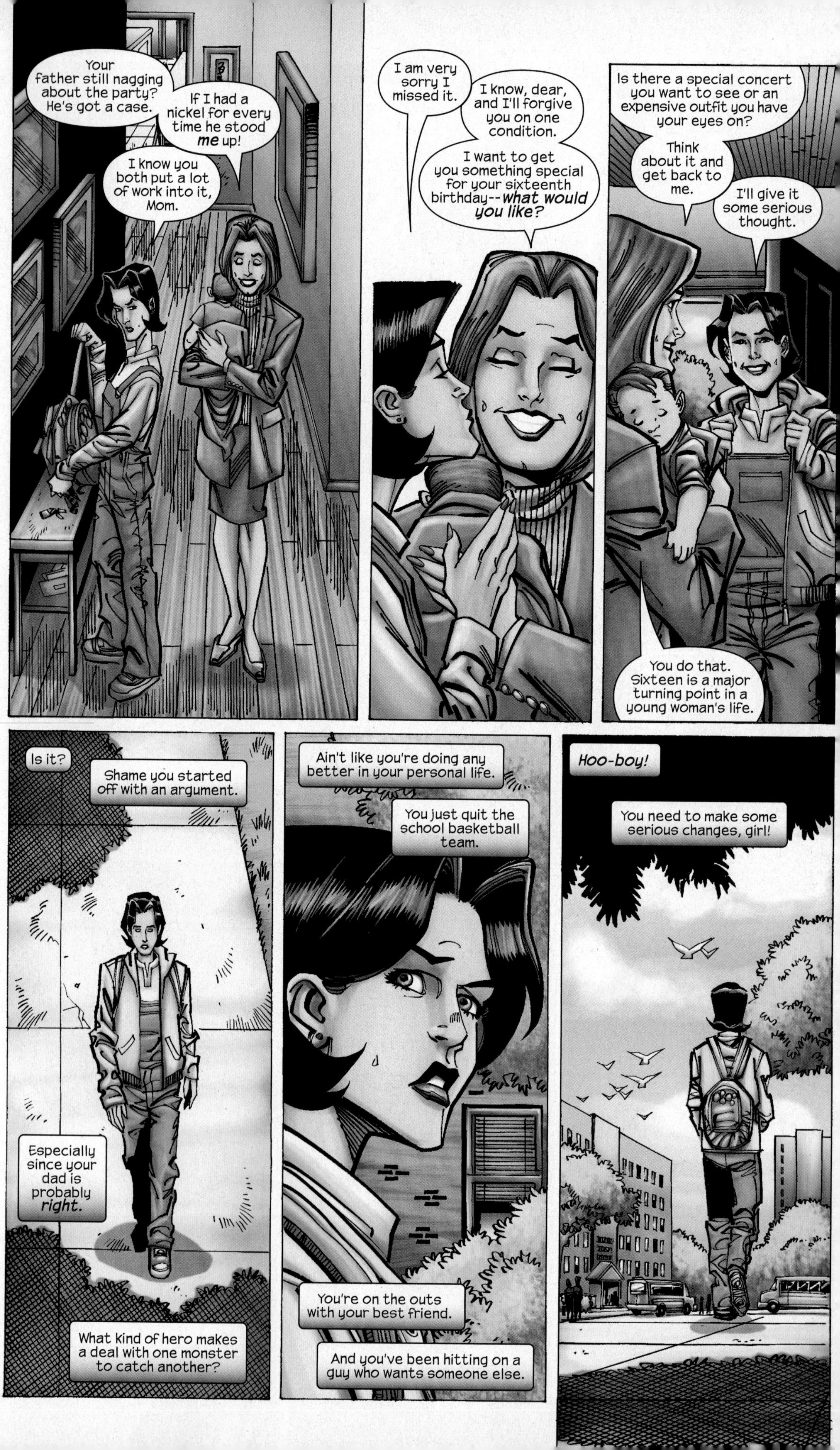
Your father still nagging about the party? He's got a case.
If I had a nickel for every time he stood *me* up!
I know you both put a lot of work into it, Mom.
I am very sorry I missed it.
I know, dear, and I'll forgive you on one condition.
I want to get you something special for your sixteenth birthday--*what would you like?*
Is there a special concert you want to see or an expensive outfit you have your eyes on?
Think about it and get back to me.
I'll give it some serious thought.
You do that. Sixteen is a major turning point in a young woman's life.
Is it?
Shame you started off with an argument.
Especially since your dad is probably *right.*
What kind of hero makes a deal with one monster to catch another?
Ain't like you're doing any better in your personal life.
You just quit the school basketball team.
You're on the outs with your best friend.
And you've been hitting on a guy who wants someone else.
Hoo-boy!
You need to make some serious changes, girl!

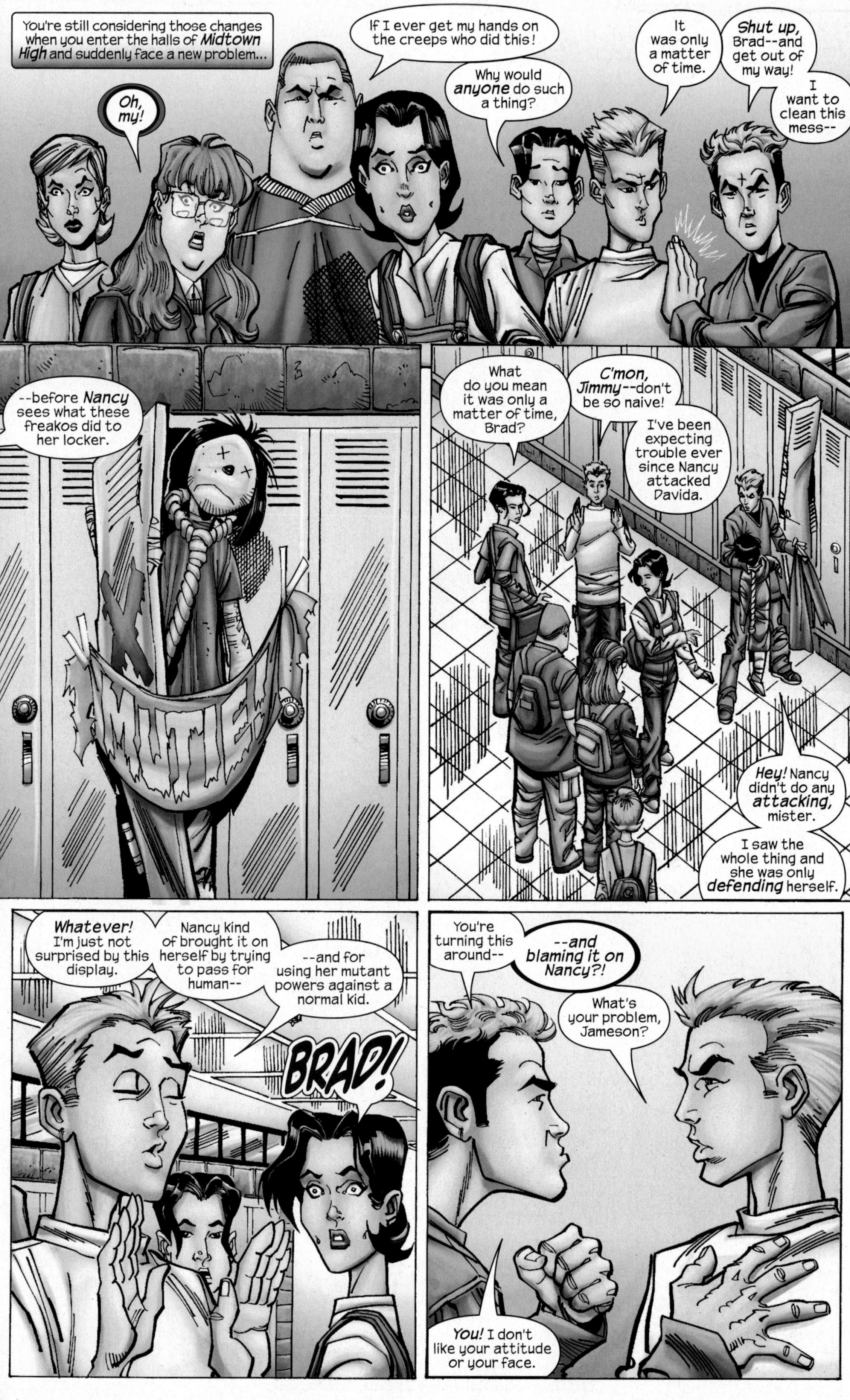
You're still considering those changes when you enter the halls of *Midtown High* and suddenly face a new problem...
Oh, my!
If I ever get my hands on the creeps who did this!
Why would *anyone* do such a thing?
It was only a matter of time.
Shut up, Brad--and get out of my way!
I want to clean this mess--
--before *Nancy* sees what these freakos did to her locker.
MUTIE
What do you mean it was only a matter of time, Brad?
C'mon, Jimmy--don't be so naive!
I've been expecting trouble ever since Nancy attacked Davida.
Hey! Nancy didn't do any *attacking,* mister.
I saw the whole thing and she was only *defending* herself.
Whatever! I'm just not surprised by this display.
Nancy kind of brought it on herself by trying to pass for human--
--and for using her mutant powers against a normal kid.
BRAD!
You're turning this around--
--*and blaming it on Nancy?!*
What's your problem, Jameson?
You! I don't like your attitude or your face.

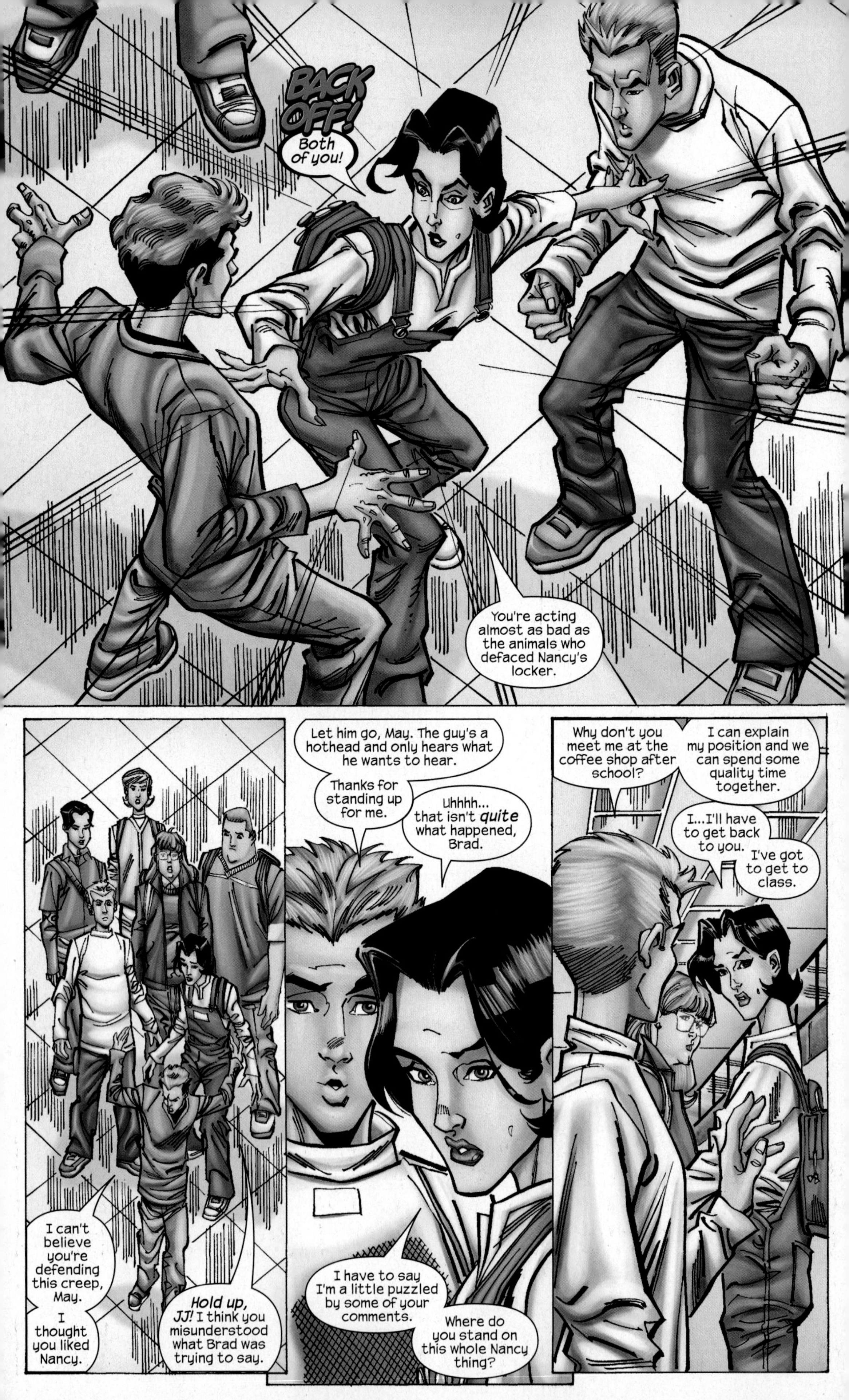
BACK OFF!
Both of you!
You're acting almost as bad as the animals who defaced Nancy's locker.
I can't believe you're defending this creep, May.
I thought you liked Nancy.
Hold up, JJ! I think you misunderstood what Brad was trying to say.
Let him go, May. The guy's a hothead and only hears what he wants to hear.
Thanks for standing up for me.
Uhhhh... that isn't quite what happened, Brad.
I have to say I'm a little puzzled by some of your comments.
Where do you stand on this whole Nancy thing?
Why don't you meet me at the coffee shop after school?
I can explain my position and we can spend some quality time together.
I...I'll have to get back to you.
I've got to get to class.

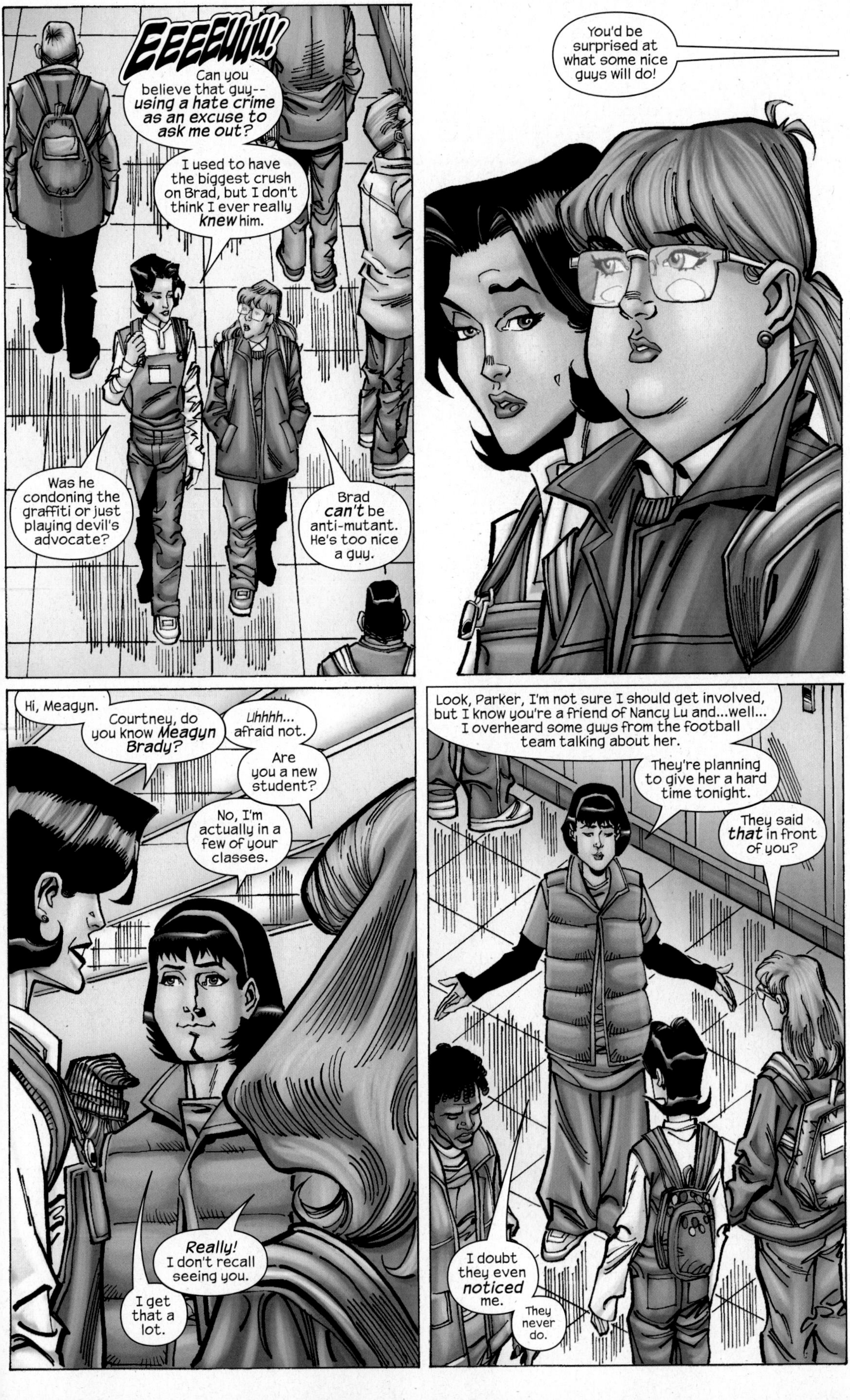
EEEEUUU!
Can you believe that guy-- using a hate crime as an excuse to ask me out?
I used to have the biggest crush on Brad, but I don't think I ever really knew him.
Was he condoning the graffiti or just playing devil's advocate?
Brad can't be anti-mutant. He's too nice a guy.
You'd be surprised at what some nice guys will do!
Hi, Meagyn.
Courtney, do you know Meagyn Brady?
Uhhhh... afraid not.
Are you a new student?
No, I'm actually in a few of your classes.
Really! I don't recall seeing you.
I get that a lot.
Look, Parker, I'm not sure I should get involved, but I know you're a friend of Nancy Lu and...well... I overheard some guys from the football team talking about her.
They're planning to give her a hard time tonight.
They said that in front of you?
I doubt they even noticed me.
They never do.

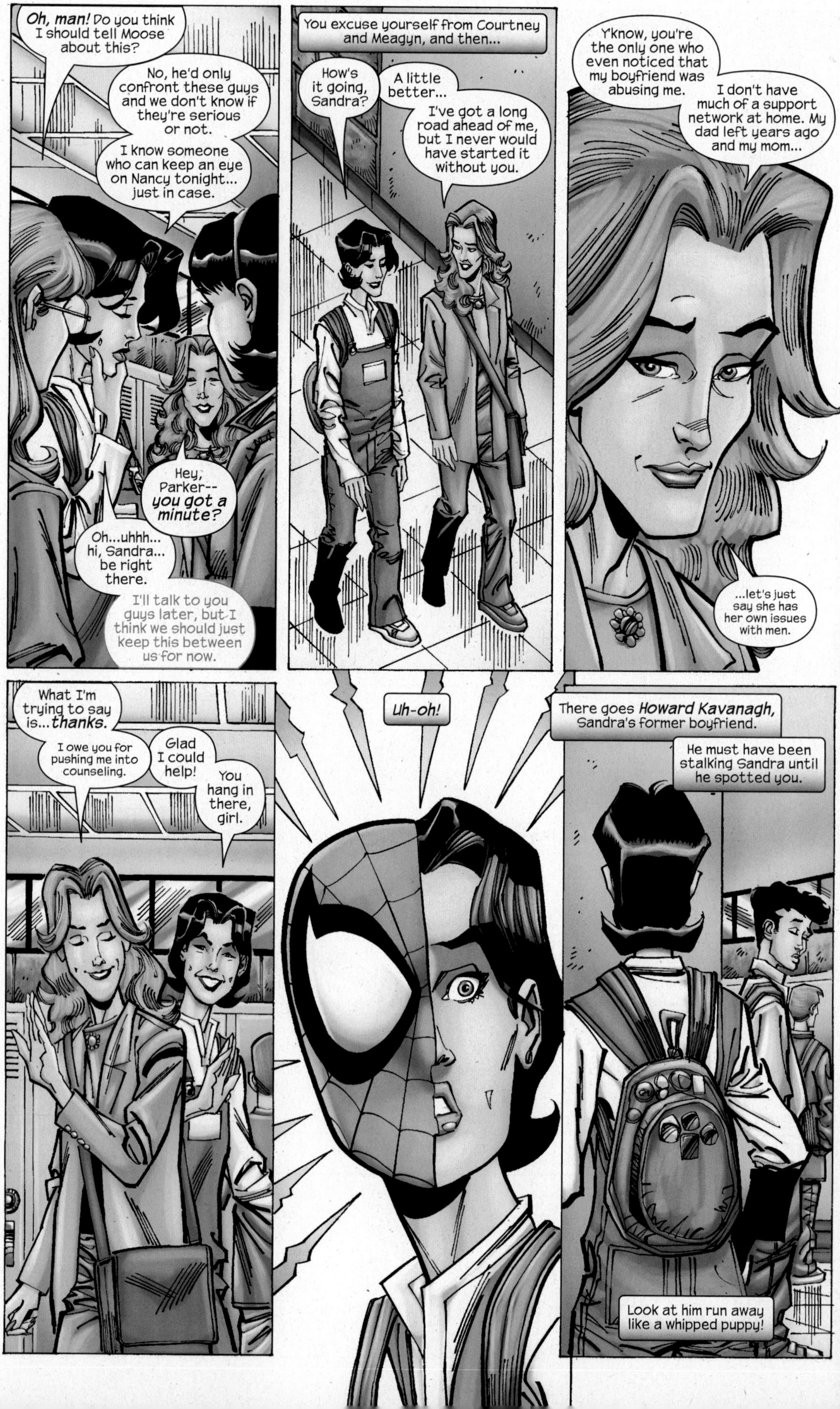
Oh, man! Do you think I should tell Moose about this?
No, he'd only confront these guys and we don't know if they're serious or not.
I know someone who can keep an eye on Nancy tonight... just in case.
Hey, Parker-- you got a minute?
Oh...uhhh... hi, Sandra... be right there.
I'll talk to you guys later, but I think we should just keep this between us for now.
You excuse yourself from Courtney and Meagyn, and then...
How's it going, Sandra?
A little better...
I've got a long road ahead of me, but I never would have started it without you.
Y'know, you're the only one who even noticed that my boyfriend was abusing me.
I don't have much of a support network at home. My dad left years ago and my mom...
...let's just say she has her own issues with men.
What I'm trying to say is...thanks.
I owe you for pushing me into counseling.
Glad I could help!
You hang in there, girl.
Uh-oh!
There goes Howard Kavanagh, Sandra's former boyfriend.
He must have been stalking Sandra until he spotted you.
Look at him run away like a whipped puppy!

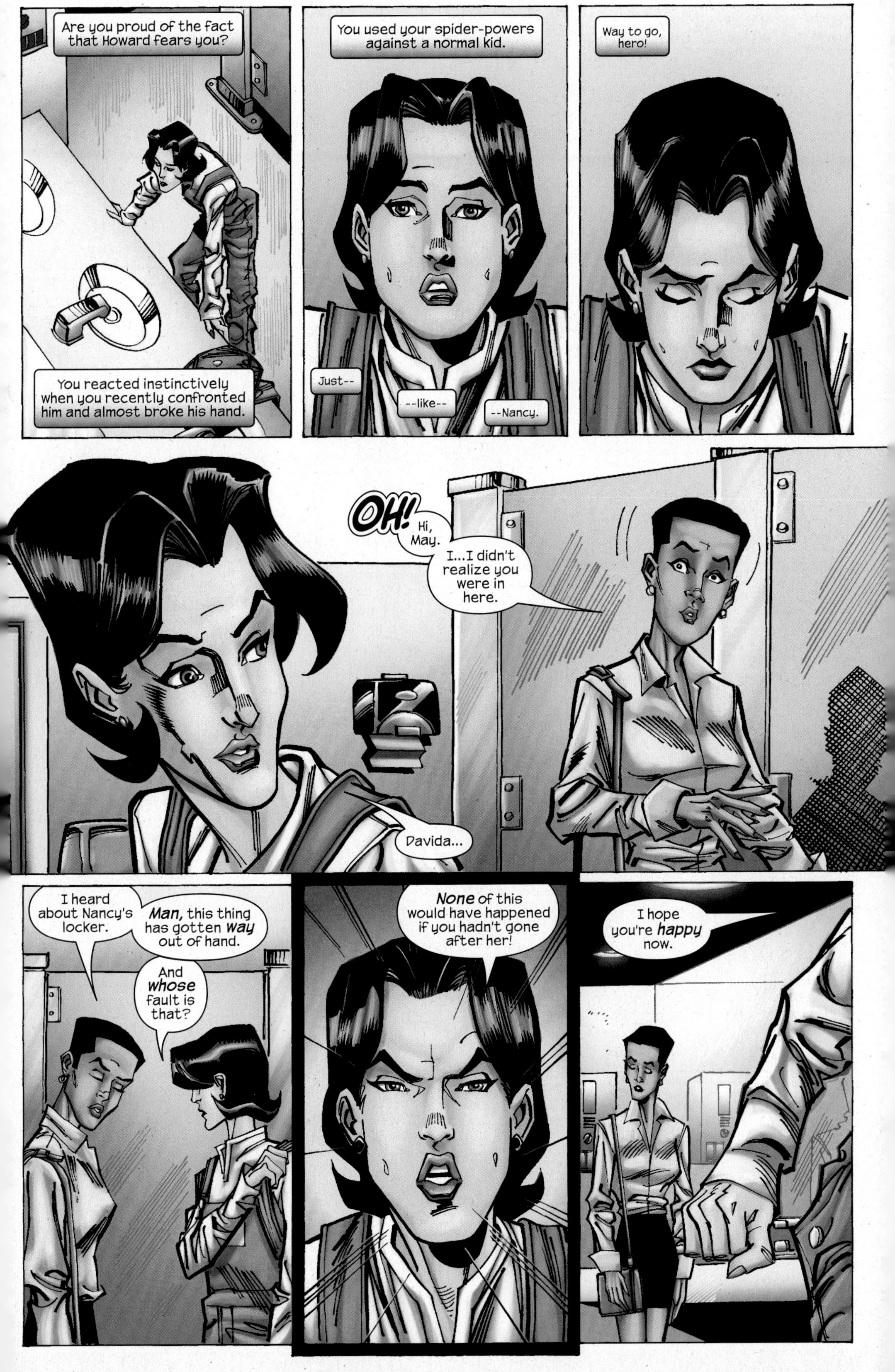

Are you proud of the fact that Howard fears you?
You reacted instinctively when you recently confronted him and almost broke his hand.
You used your spider-powers against a normal kid.
Just--
--like--
--Nancy.
Way to go, hero!
OH!
Hi, May.
I...I didn't realize you were in here.
Davida...
I heard about Nancy's locker.
Man, this thing has gotten *way* out of hand.
And *whose* fault is that?
None of this would have happened if you hadn't gone after her!
I hope you're *happy* now.

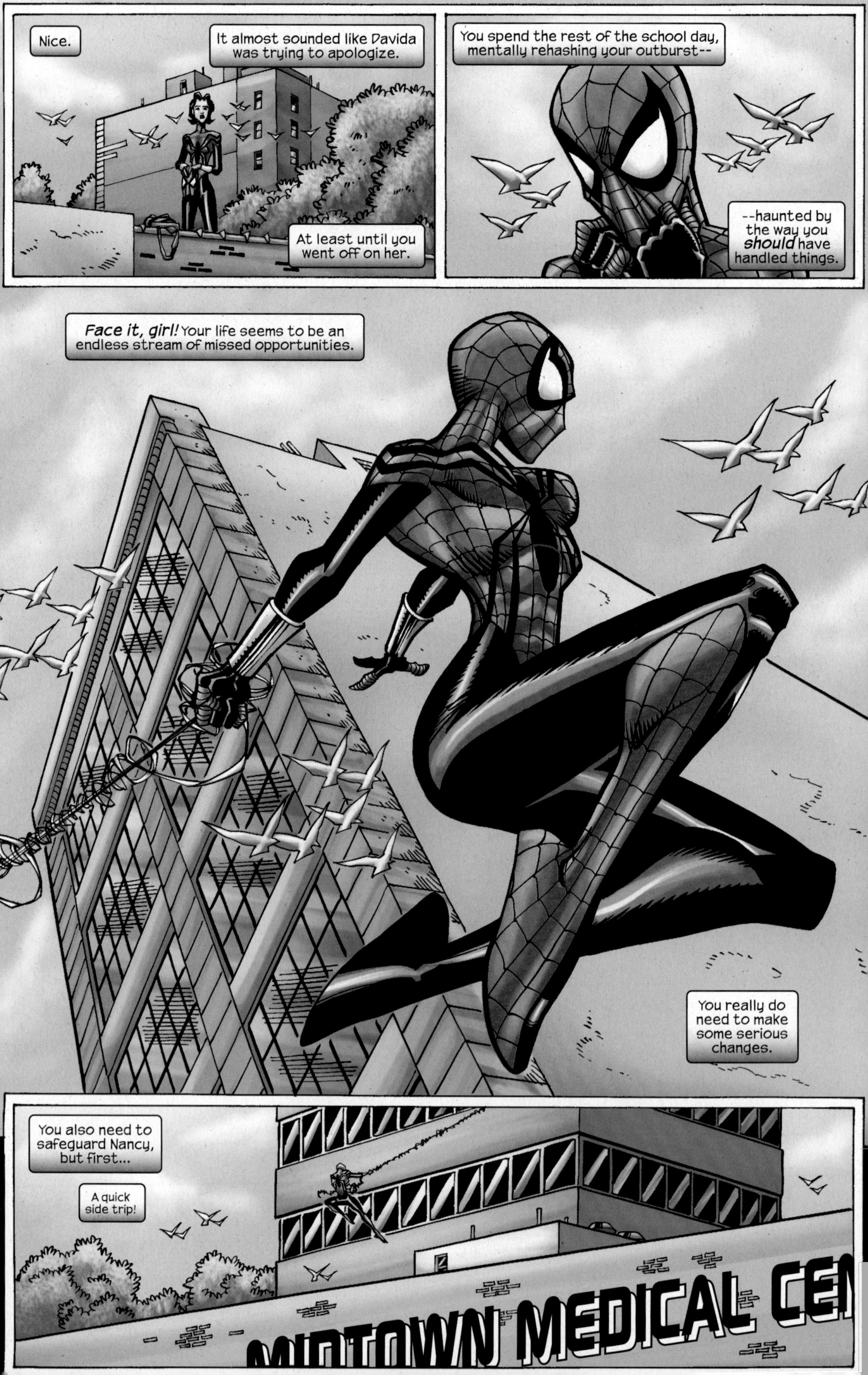
Nice.
It almost sounded like Davida was trying to apologize.
At least until you went off on her.
You spend the rest of the school day, mentally rehashing your outburst--
--haunted by the way you *should* have handled things.
Face it, girl! Your life seems to be an endless stream of missed opportunities.
You really do need to make some serious changes.
You also need to safeguard Nancy, but first...
A quick side trip!
MIDTOWN MEDICAL CEN

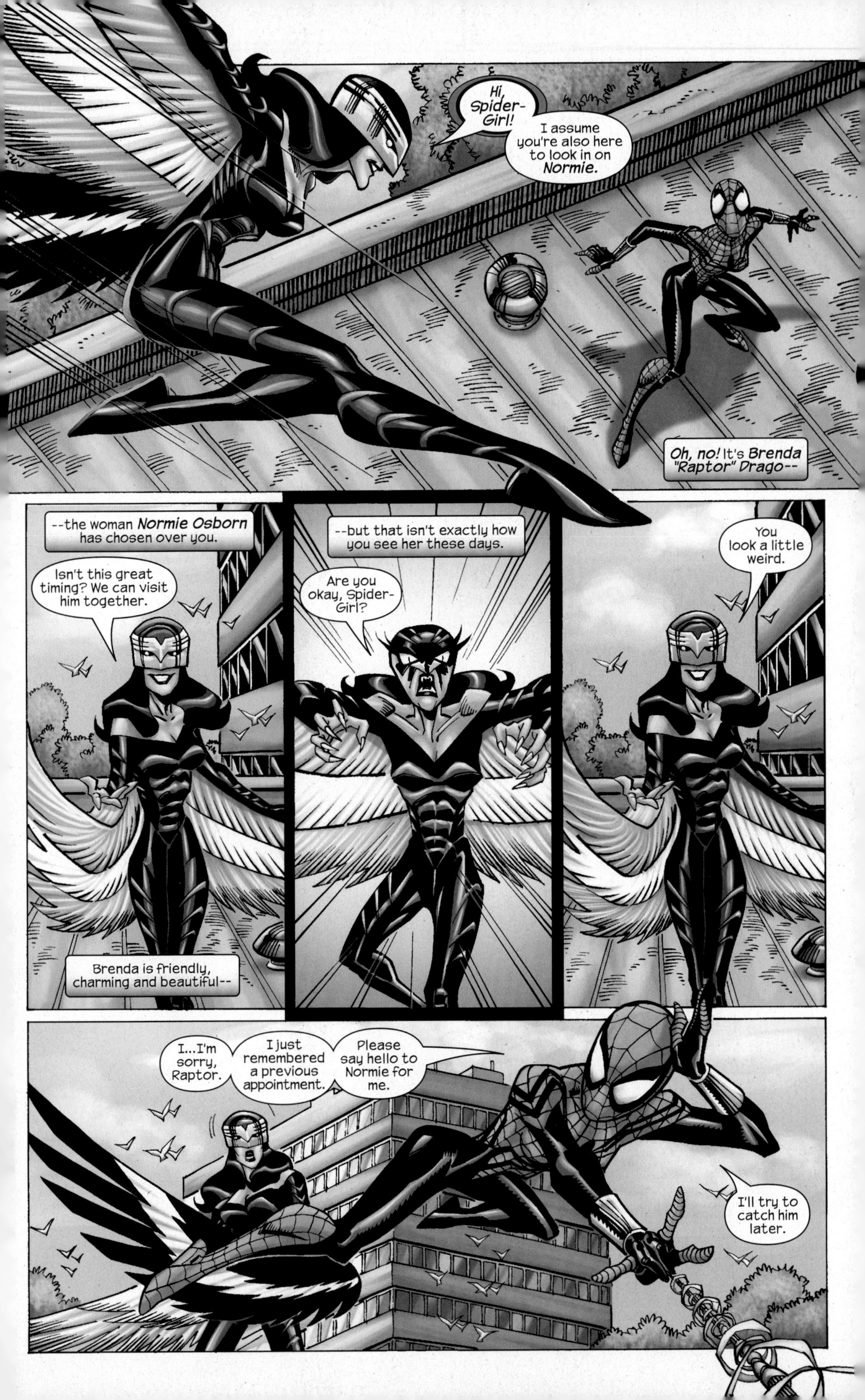
Hi, Spider-Girl!
I assume you're also here to look in on Normie.
Oh, no! It's Brenda "Raptor" Drago--
--the woman Normie Osborn has chosen over you.
Isn't this great timing? We can visit him together.
Brenda is friendly, charming and beautiful--
--but that isn't exactly how you see her these days.
Are you okay, Spider-Girl?
You look a little weird.
I...I'm sorry, Raptor.
I just remembered a previous appointment.
Please say hello to Normie for me.
I'll try to catch him later.

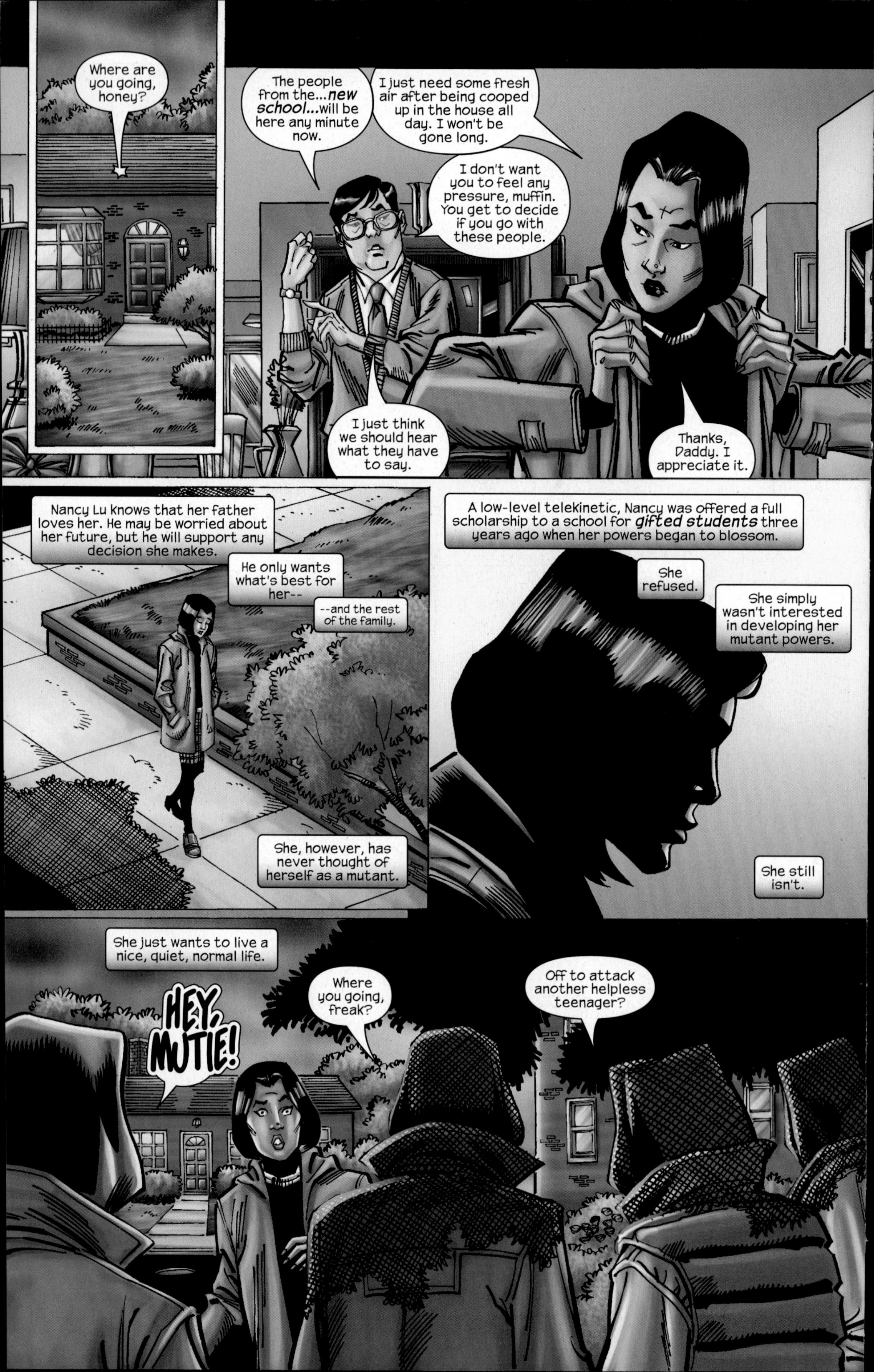

Where are you going, honey?
The people from the...new school...will be here any minute now.
I just need some fresh air after being cooped up in the house all day. I won't be gone long.
I don't want you to feel any pressure, muffin. You get to decide if you go with these people.
I just think we should hear what they have to say.
Thanks, Daddy. I appreciate it.
Nancy Lu knows that her father loves her. He may be worried about her future, but he will support any decision she makes.
He only wants what's best for her--
--and the rest of the family.
She, however, has never thought of herself as a mutant.
A low-level telekinetic, Nancy was offered a full scholarship to a school for gifted students three years ago when her powers began to blossom.
She refused.
She simply wasn't interested in developing her mutant powers.
She still isn't.
She just wants to live a nice, quiet, normal life.
HEY, MUTIE!
Where you going, freak?
Off to attack another helpless teenager?

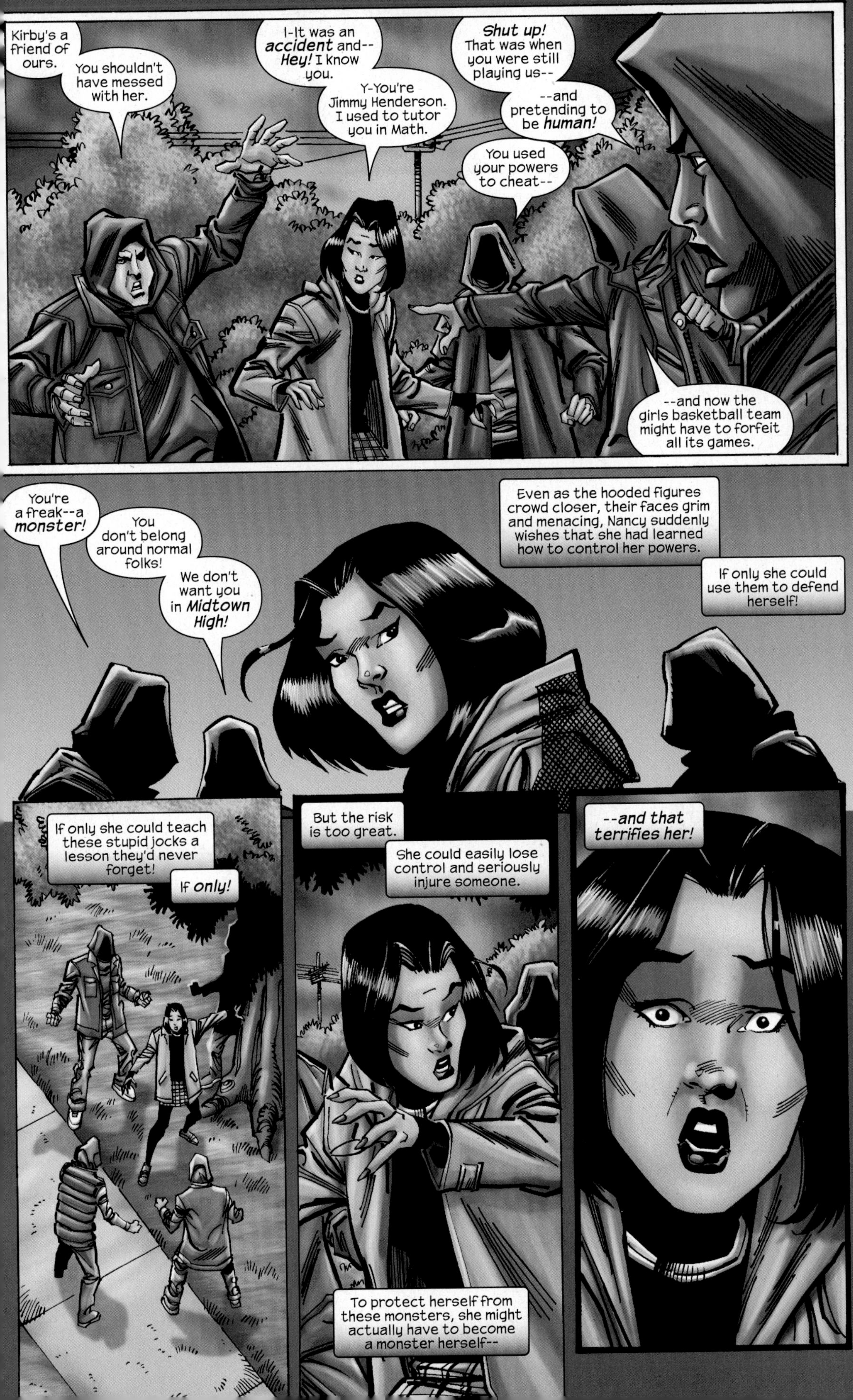
Kirby's a friend of ours.
You shouldn't have messed with her.
I-It was an *accident* and-- *Hey!* I know you.
Y-You're Jimmy Henderson. I used to tutor you in Math.
Shut up! That was when you were still playing us--
--and pretending to be *human!*
You used your powers to cheat--
--and now the girls basketball team might have to forfeit all its games.
You're a freak--a *monster!*
You don't belong around normal folks!
We don't want you in *Midtown High!*
Even as the hooded figures crowd closer, their faces grim and menacing, Nancy suddenly wishes that she had learned how to control her powers.
If only she could use them to defend herself!
If only she could teach these stupid jocks a lesson they'd never forget!
If *only!*
But the risk is too great.
She could easily lose control and seriously injure someone.
To protect herself from these monsters, she might actually have to become a monster herself--
--and that terrifies her!

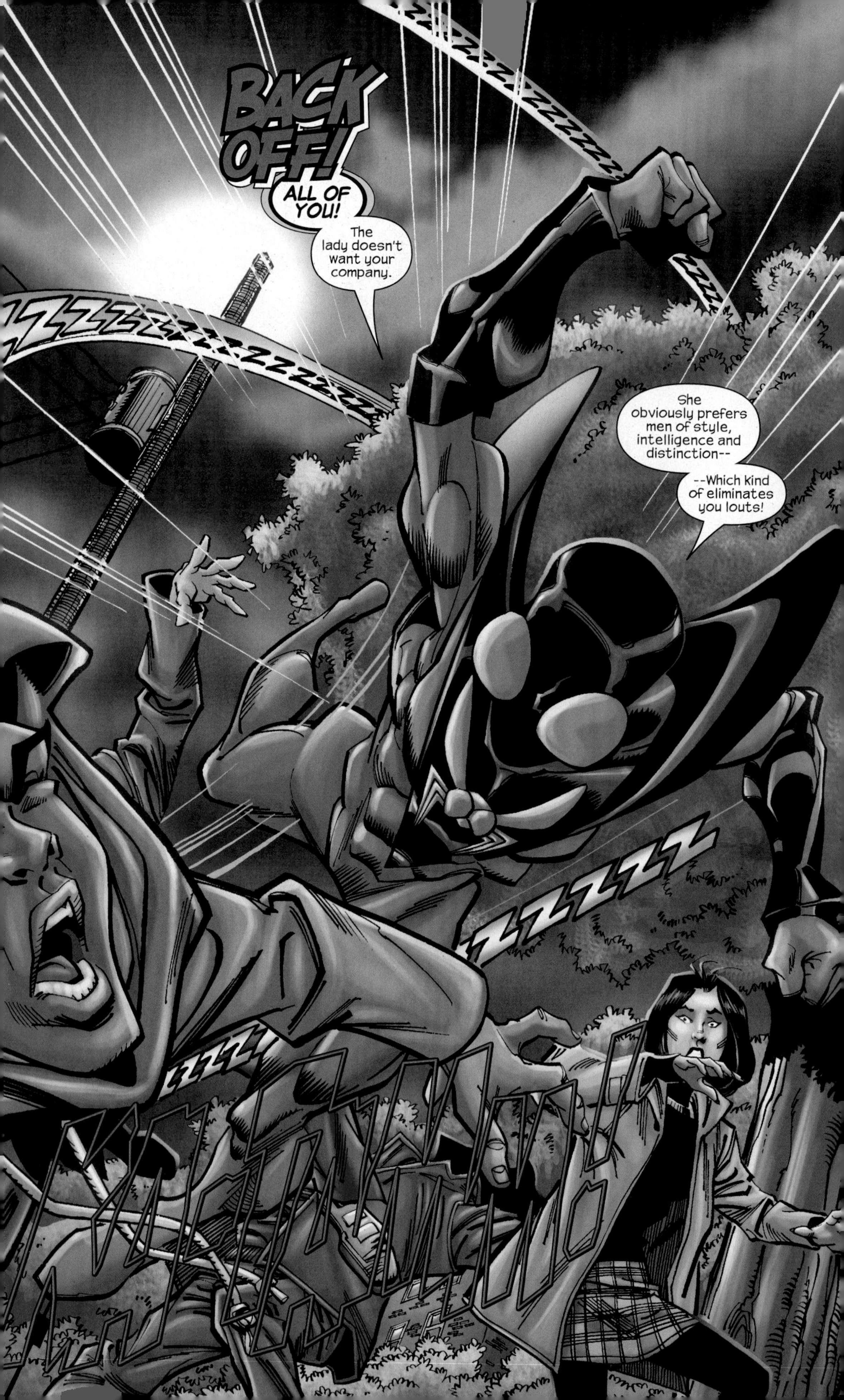
BACK OFF!
ALL OF YOU!
The lady doesn't want your company.
She obviously prefers men of style, intelligence and distinction--
--Which kind of eliminates you louts!

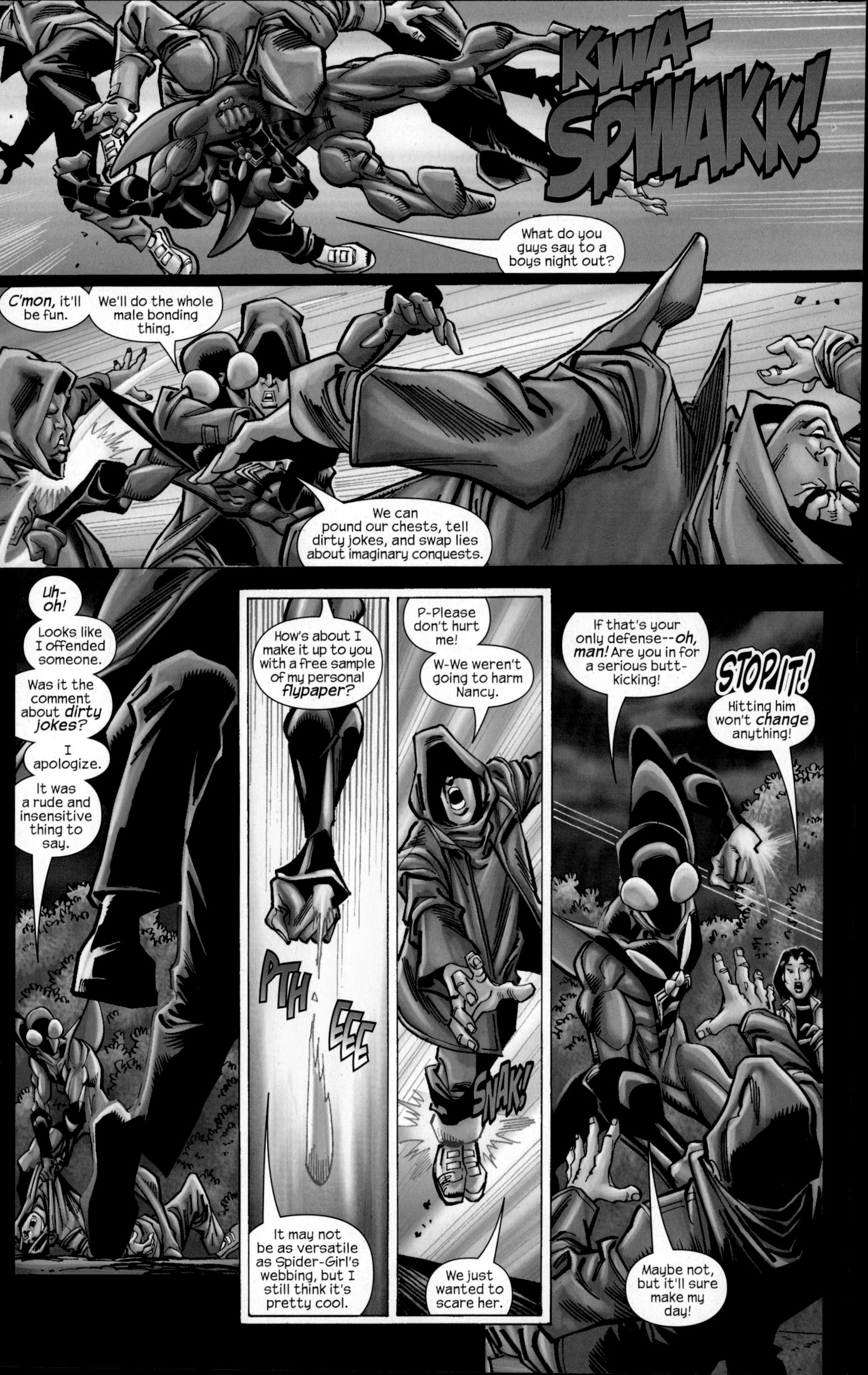
KWA-SPWAKK!
What do you guys say to a boys night out?
C'mon, it'll be fun.
We'll do the whole male bonding thing.
We can pound our chests, tell dirty jokes, and swap lies about imaginary conquests.
Uh-oh!
Looks like I offended someone.
Was it the comment about dirty jokes?
I apologize.
It was a rude and insensitive thing to say.
How's about I make it up to you with a free sample of my personal flypaper?
PTH
EEE
It may not be as versatile as Spider-Girl's webbing, but I still think it's pretty cool.
P-Please don't hurt me!
W-We weren't going to harm Nancy.
SNAK!
We just wanted to scare her.
If that's your only defense--oh, man! Are you in for a serious butt-kicking!
STOP IT!
Hitting him won't change anything!
Maybe not, but it'll sure make my day!

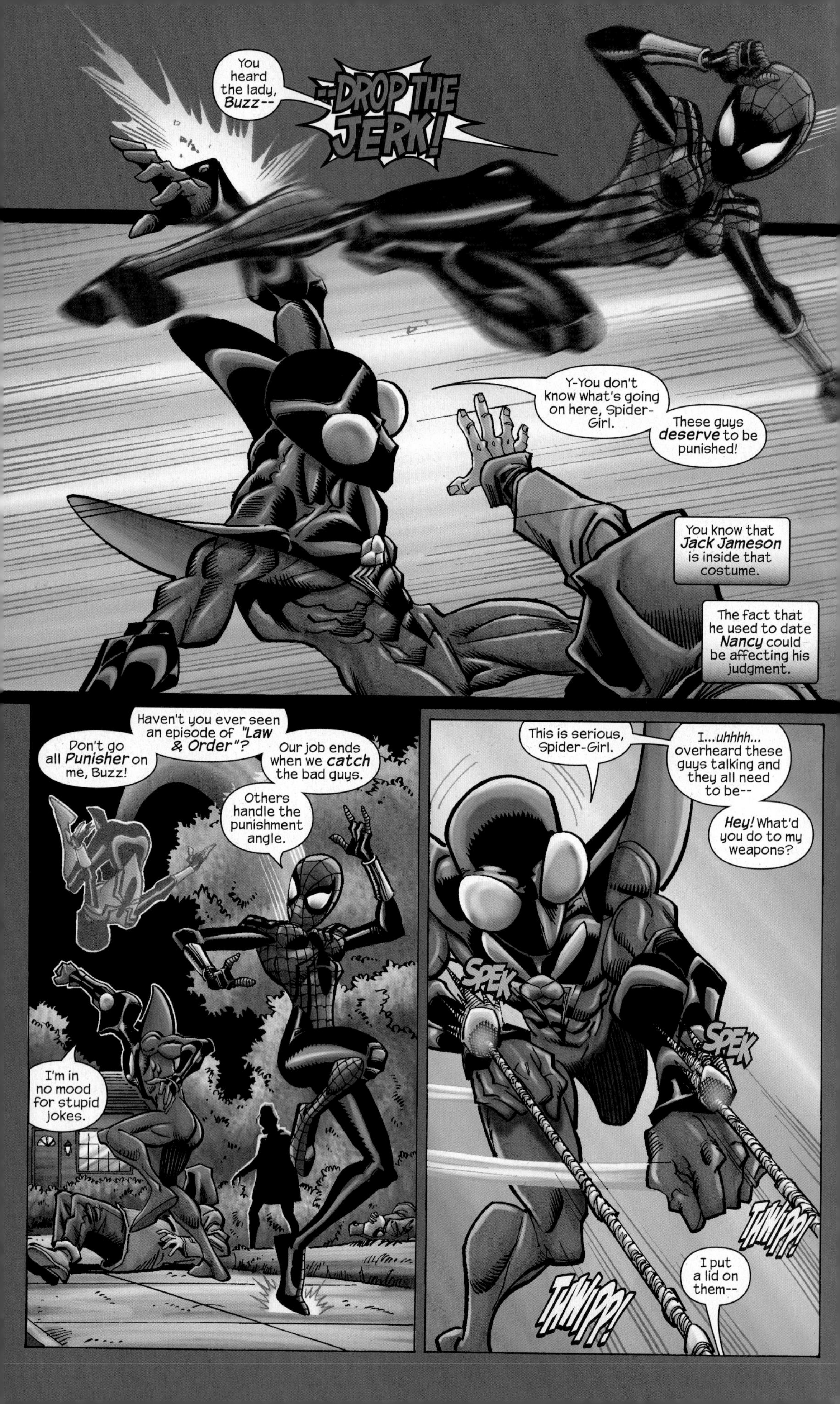
You heard the lady, Buzz--
--DROP THE JERK!
Y-You don't know what's going on here, Spider-Girl.
These guys *deserve* to be punished!
You know that *Jack Jameson* is inside that costume.
The fact that he used to date *Nancy* could be affecting his judgment.
Don't go all *Punisher* on me, Buzz!
Haven't you ever seen an episode of *"Law & Order"*?
Our job ends when we *catch* the bad guys.
Others handle the punishment angle.
I'm in no mood for stupid jokes.
This is serious, Spider-Girl.
I... *uhhhh*... overheard these guys talking and they all need to be--
SPEK
SPEK
Hey! What'd you do to my weapons?
THWIPP!
THWIPP!
I put a lid on them--

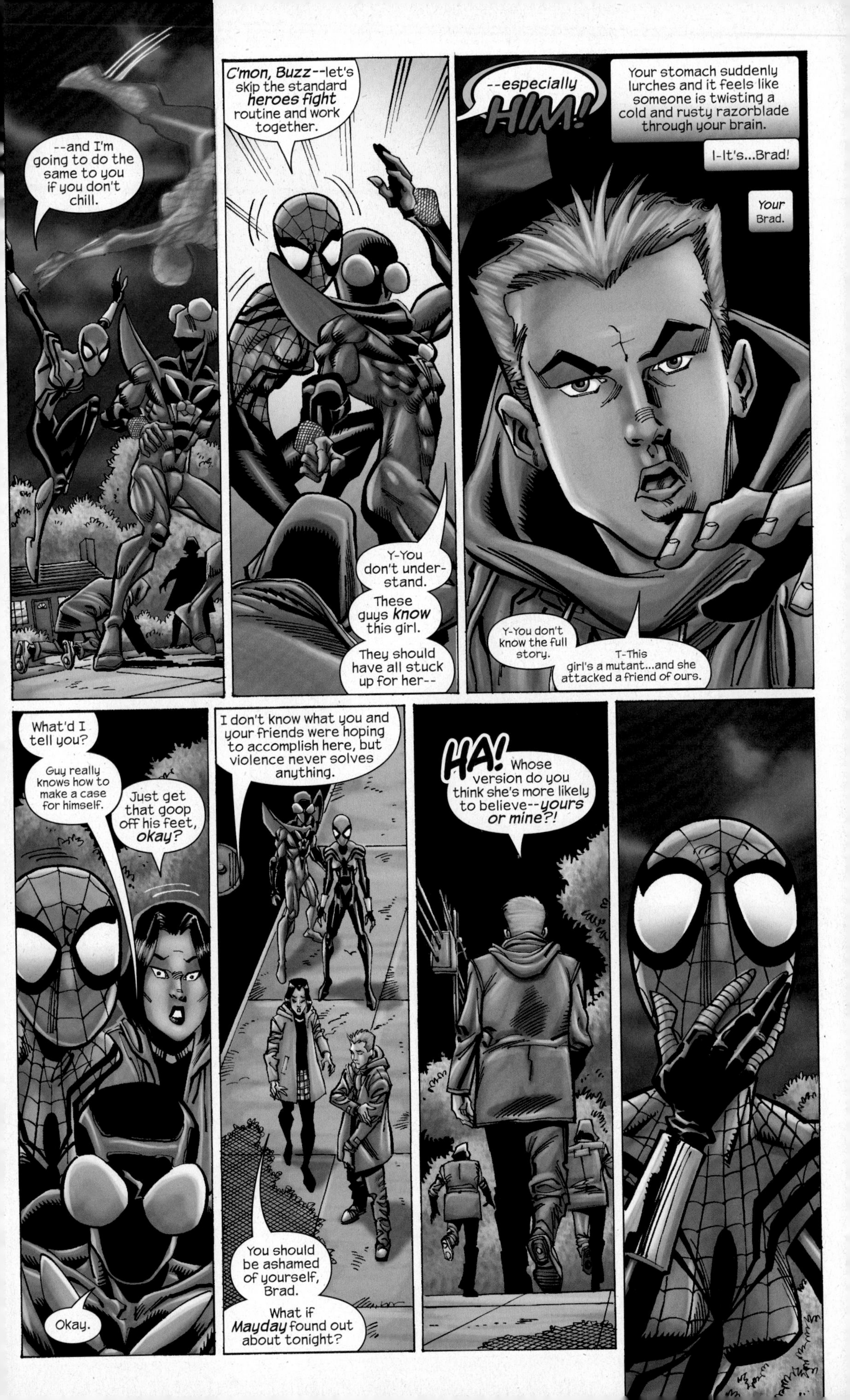
--and I'm going to do the same to you if you don't chill.
C'mon, Buzz--let's skip the standard heroes fight routine and work together.
Y-You don't understand.
These guys know this girl.
They should have all stuck up for her--
--especially HIM!
Your stomach suddenly lurches and it feels like someone is twisting a cold and rusty razorblade through your brain.
I-It's...Brad!
Your Brad.
Y-You don't know the full story.
T-This girl's a mutant...and she attacked a friend of ours.
What'd I tell you?
Guy really knows how to make a case for himself.
Just get that goop off his feet, okay?
Okay.
I don't know what you and your friends were hoping to accomplish here, but violence never solves anything.
You should be ashamed of yourself, Brad.
What if Mayday found out about tonight?
HA! Whose version do you think she's more likely to believe--yours or mine?!

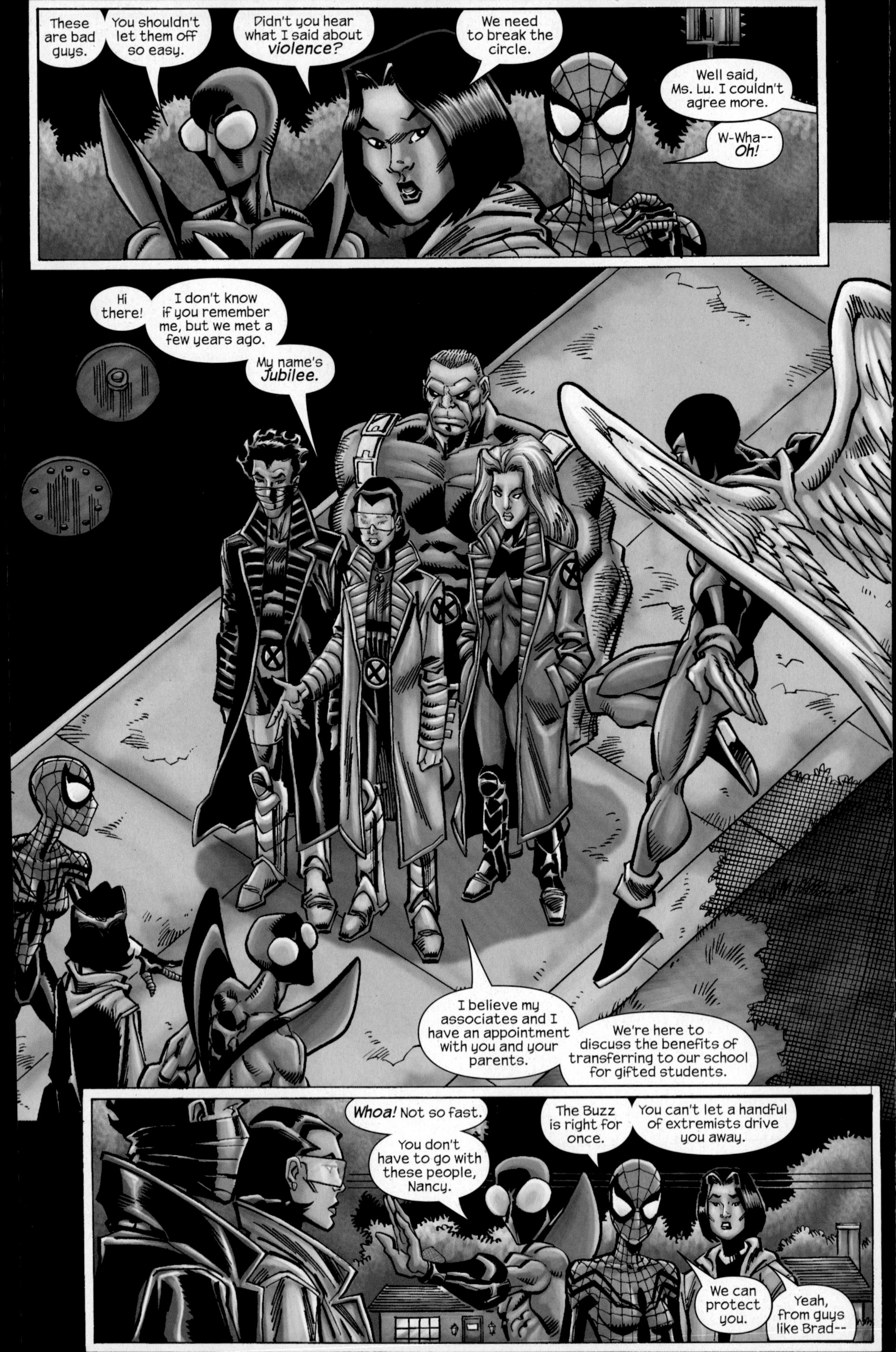
These are bad guys.
You shouldn't let them off so easy.
Didn't you hear what I said about *violence?*
We need to break the circle.
Well said, Ms. Lu. I couldn't agree more.
W-Wha-- *Oh!*
Hi there!
I don't know if you remember me, but we met a few years ago.
My name's *Jubilee.*
I believe my associates and I have an appointment with you and your parents.
We're here to discuss the benefits of transferring to our school for gifted students.
Whoa! Not so fast.
You don't have to go with these people, Nancy.
The Buzz is right for once.
You can't let a handful of extremists drive you away.
We can protect you.
Yeah, from guys like Brad--

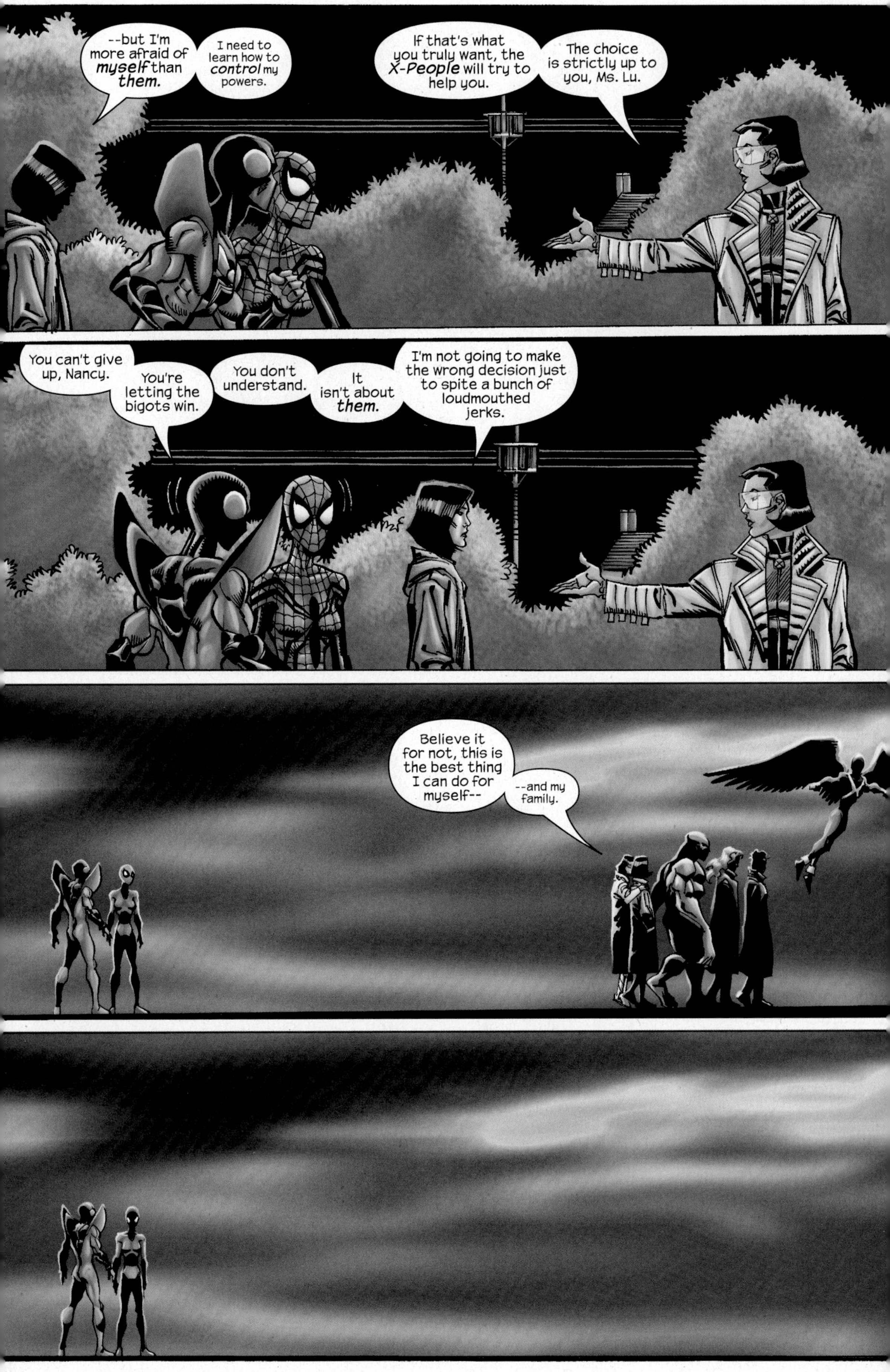
--but I'm more afraid of *myself* than *them.*
I need to learn how to *control* my powers.
If that's what you truly want, the *X-People* will try to help you.
The choice is strictly up to you, Ms. Lu.
You can't give up, Nancy.
You're letting the bigots win.
You don't understand.
It isn't about *them.*
I'm not going to make the wrong decision just to spite a bunch of loudmouthed jerks.
Believe it for not, this is the best thing I can do for myself--
--and my family.

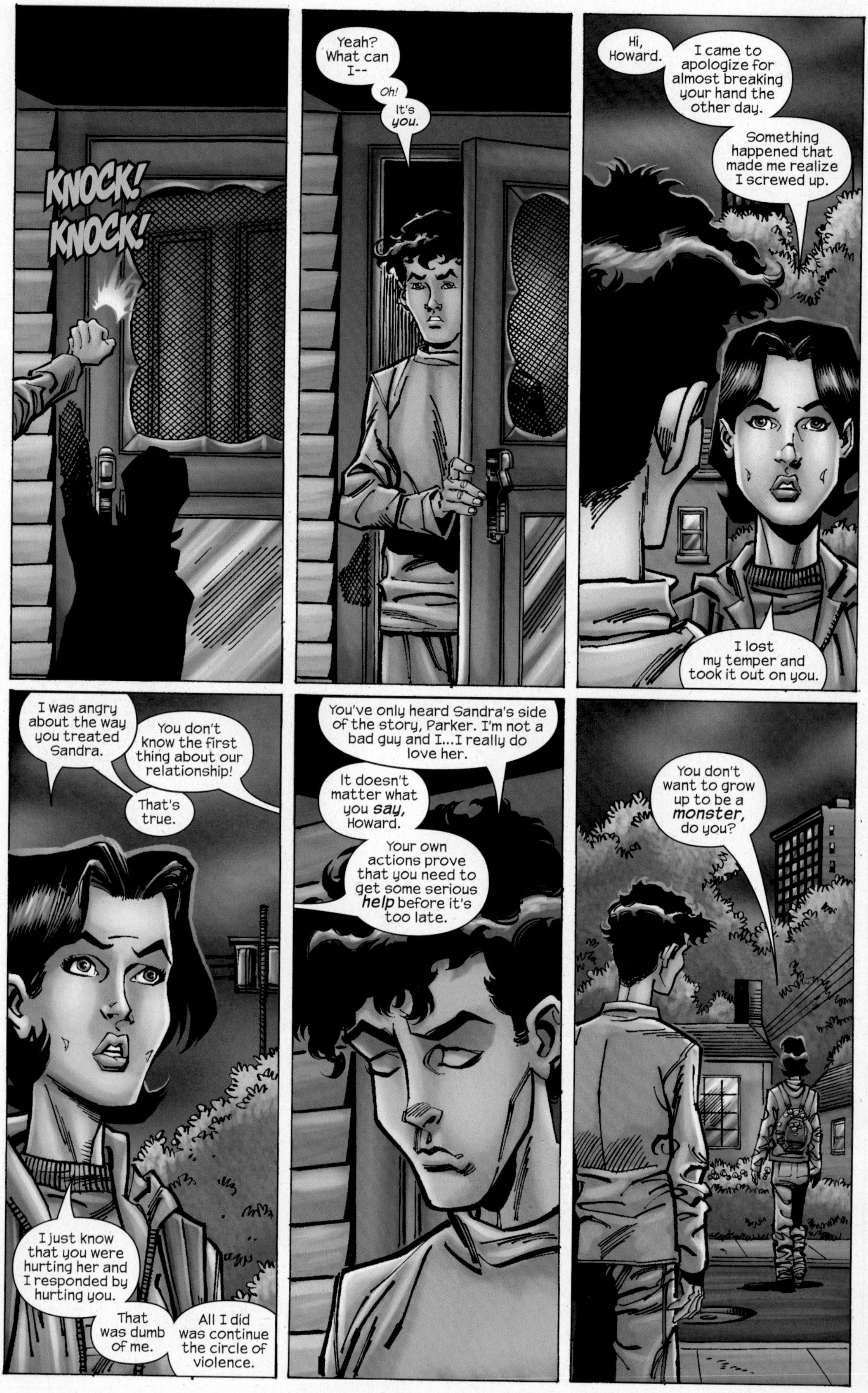
KNOCK! KNOCK!
Yeah? What can I--
Oh!
It's you.
Hi, Howard.
I came to apologize for almost breaking your hand the other day.
Something happened that made me realize I screwed up.
I lost my temper and took it out on you.
I was angry about the way you treated Sandra.
You don't know the first thing about our relationship!
That's true.
I just know that you were hurting her and I responded by hurting you.
That was dumb of me.
All I did was continue the circle of violence.
You've only heard Sandra's side of the story, Parker. I'm not a bad guy and I...I really do love her.
It doesn't matter what you say, Howard.
Your own actions prove that you need to get some serious help before it's too late.
You don't want to grow up to be a monster, do you?

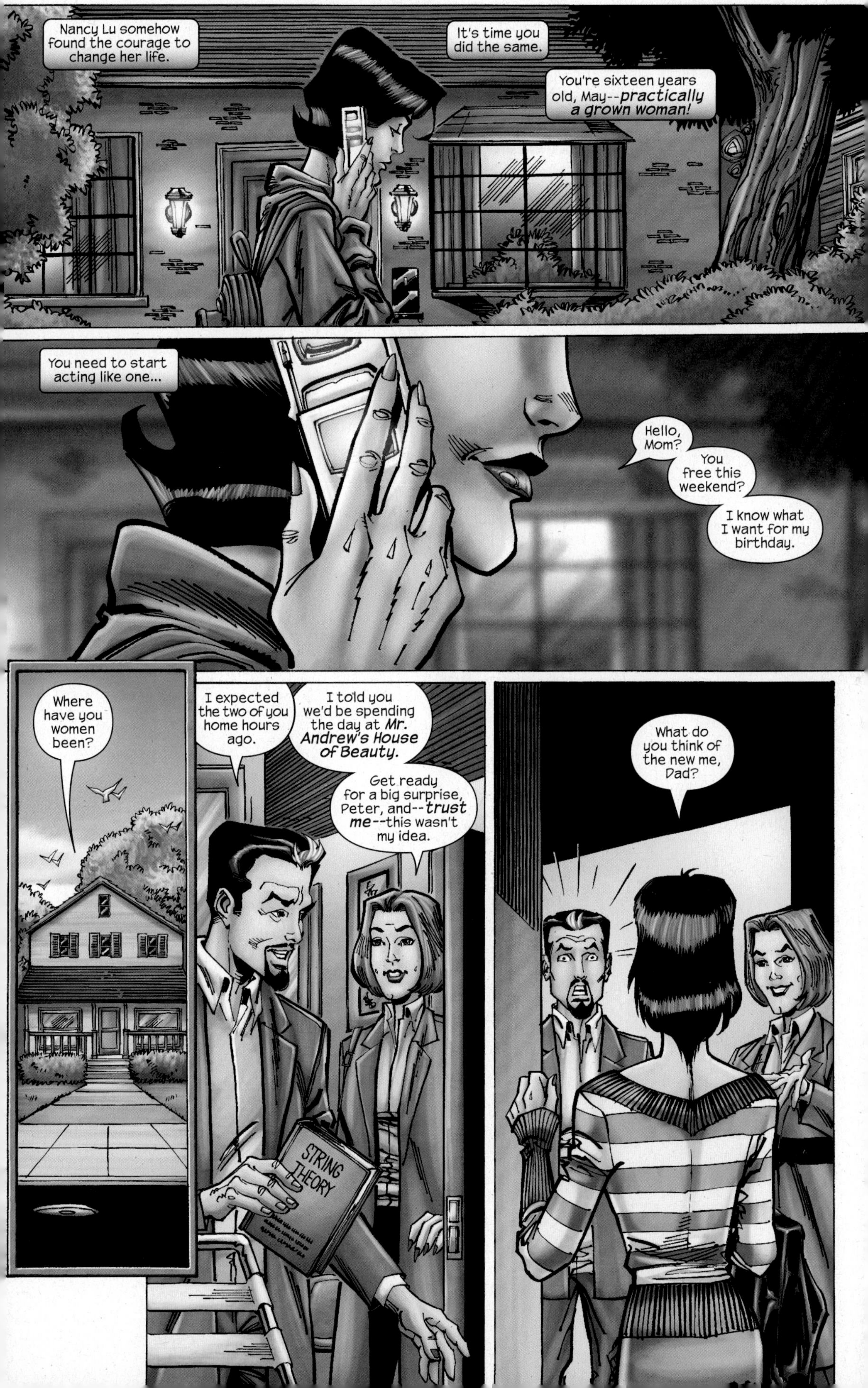
Nancy Lu somehow found the courage to change her life.
It's time you did the same.
You're sixteen years old, May--*practically a grown woman!*
You need to start acting like one...
Hello, Mom?
You free this weekend?
I know what I want for my birthday.
Where have you women been?
I expected the two of you home hours ago.
I told you we'd be spending the day at *Mr. Andrew's House of Beauty.*
Get ready for a big surprise, Peter, and--*trust me*--this wasn't my idea.
STRING THEORY
What do you think of the new me, Dad?

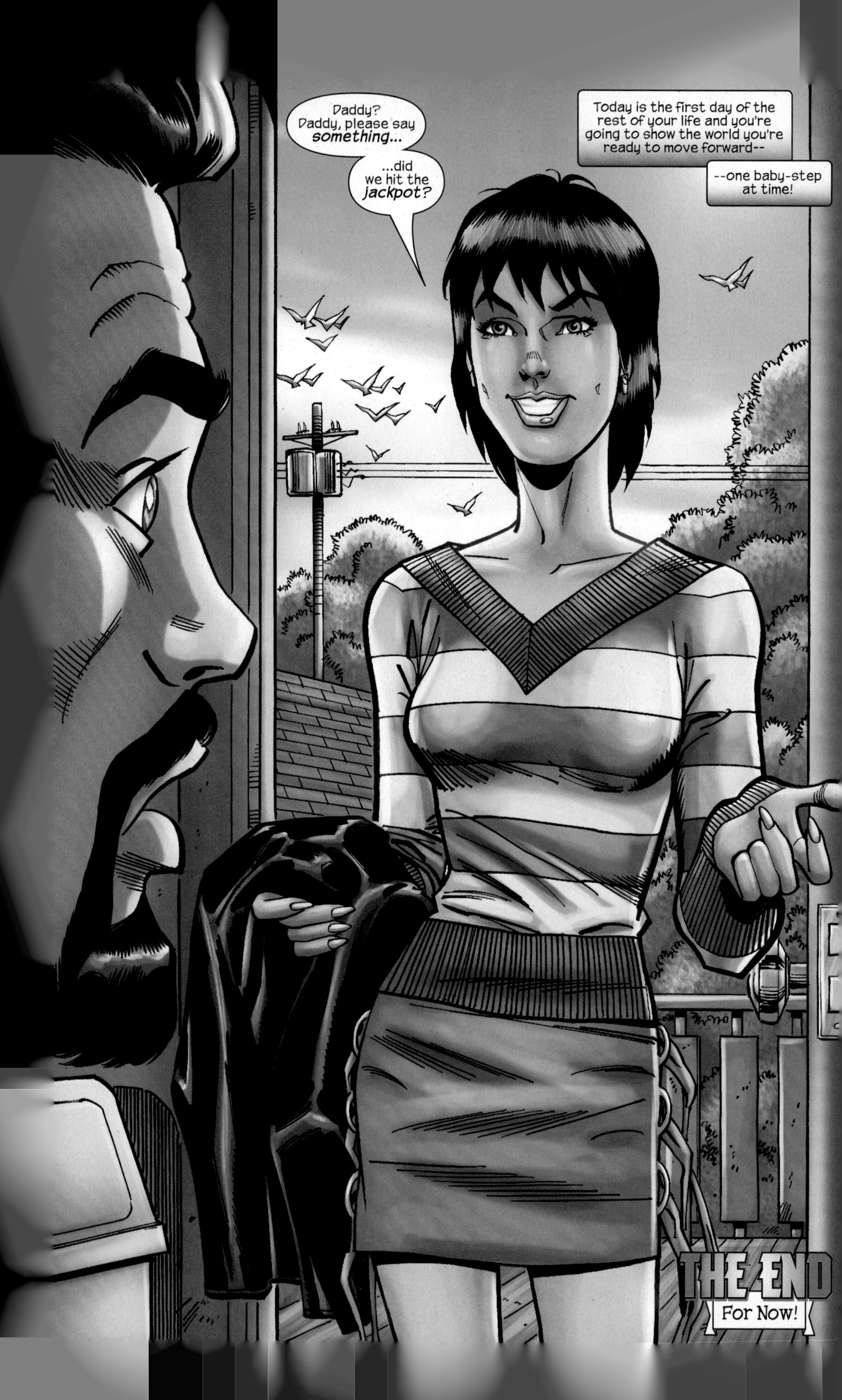

Daddy? Daddy, please say something...
...did we hit the jackpot?
Today is the first day of the rest of your life and you're going to show the world you're ready to move forward--
--one baby-step at time!
THE END
For Now!

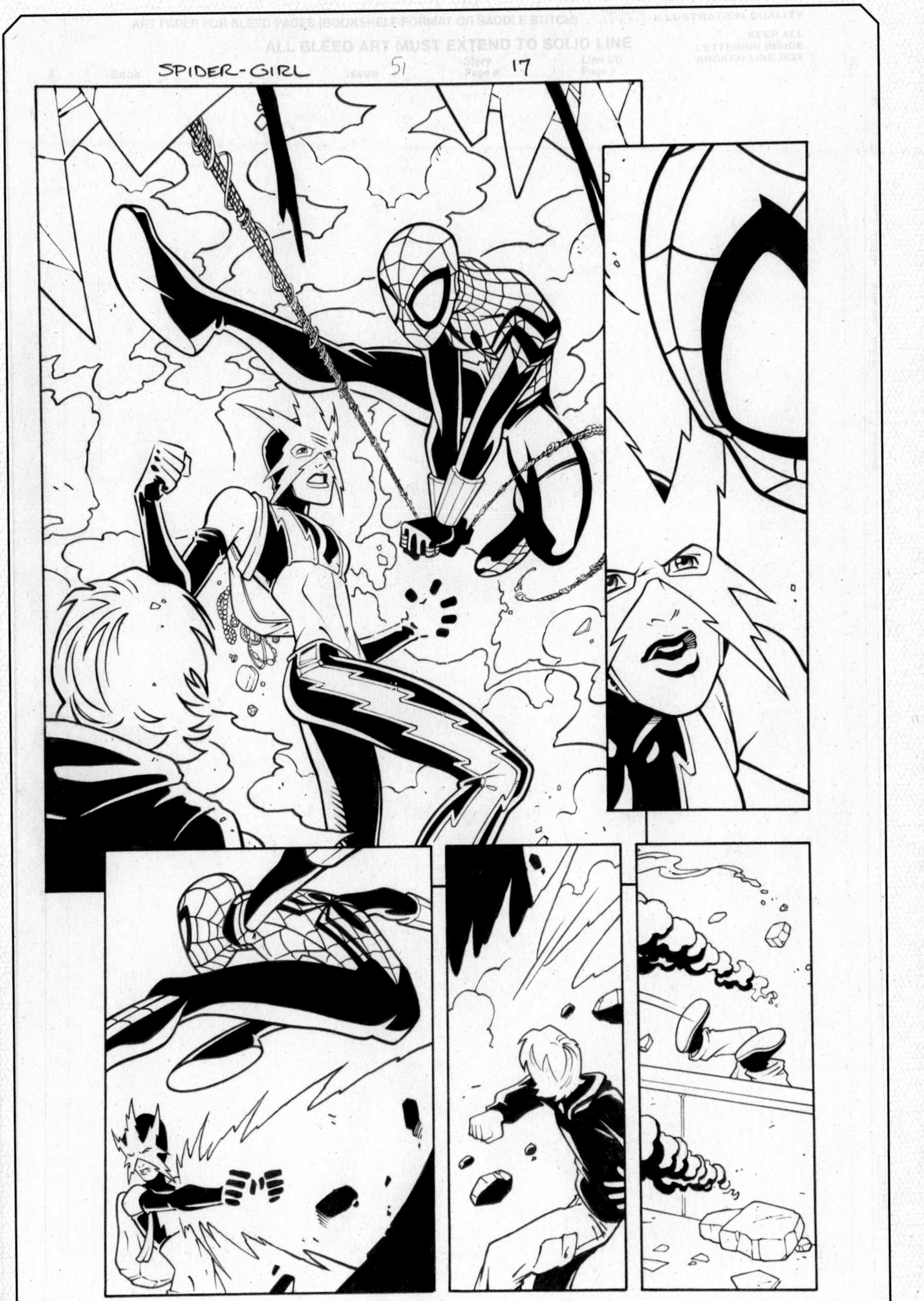
ALL BLEED ART MUST EXTEND TO SOLID LINE
Book SPIDER-GIRL Issue 51 Story Page # 17
CASEY JONES

Spider-Girl #51, page 17 art by **Casey Jones**

Courtesy of HeritageAuctions.com

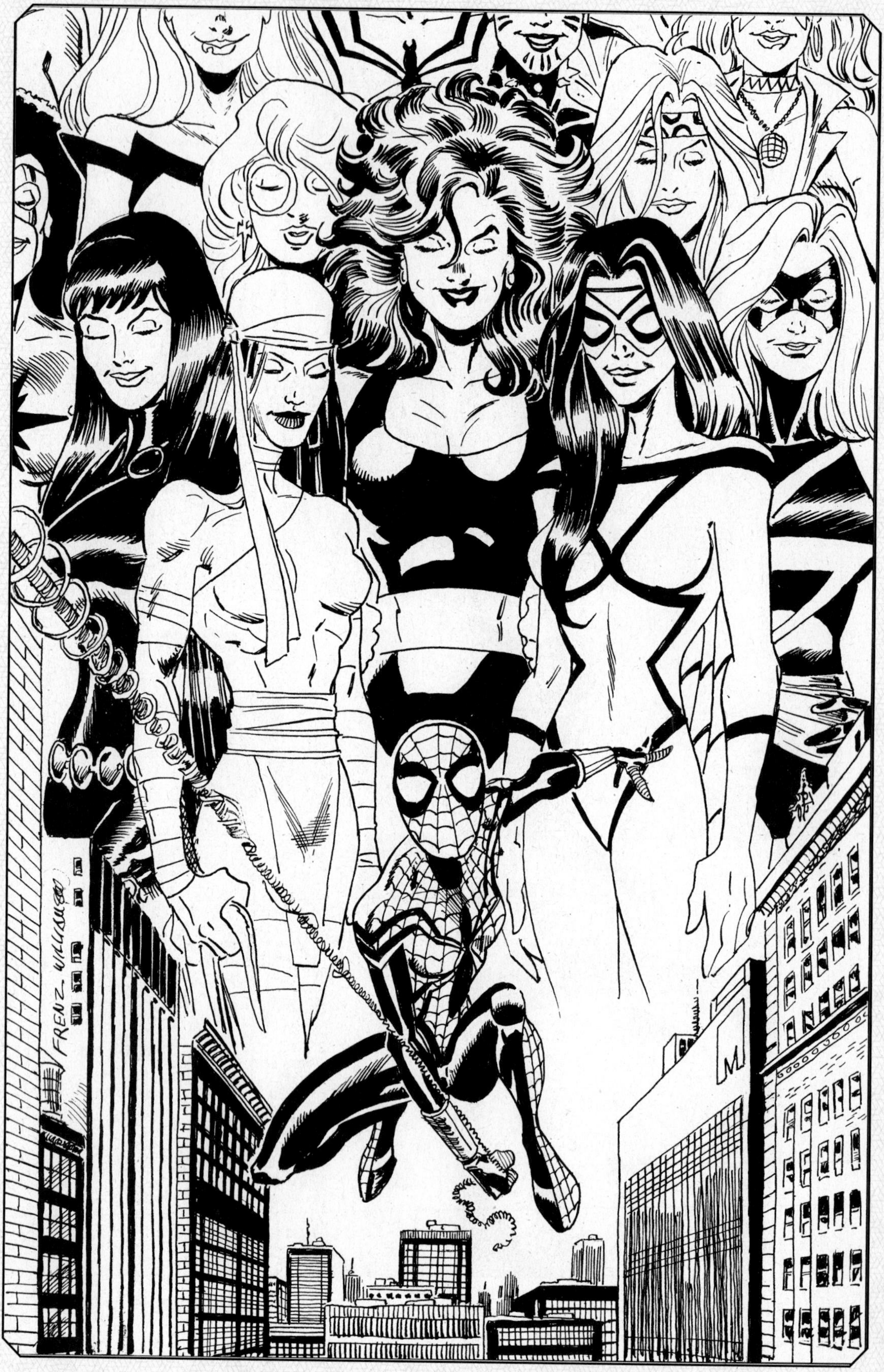

Spider-Girl #60 cover art by **Ron Frenz** & **Al Williamson**

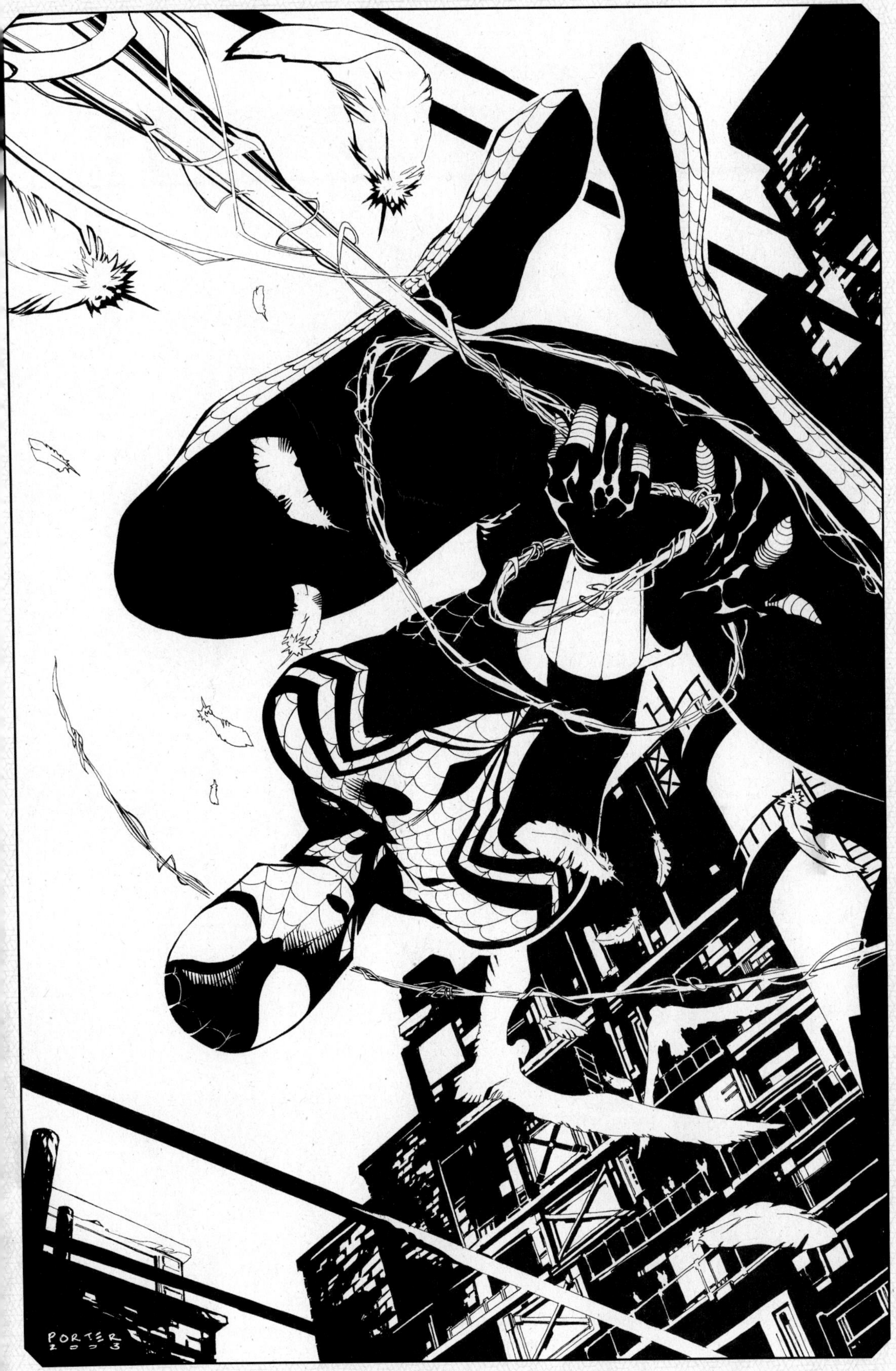
PORTER
2003

Spider-Girl #61 cover art by **Howard Porter**

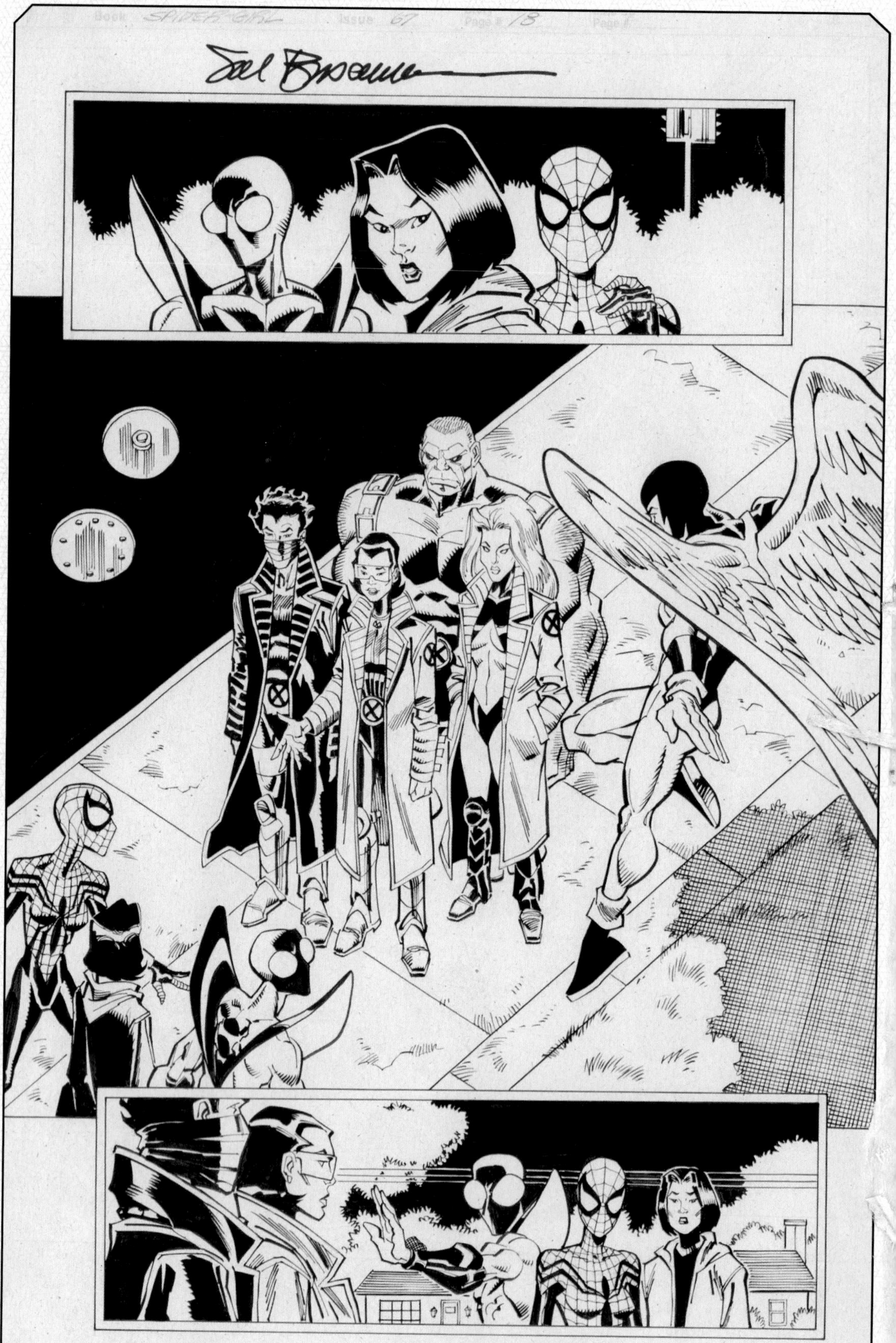
Book SPIDER-GIRL Issue 67 Page # 18

Spider-Girl #67, page 17 art by **Ron Frenz** & **Sal Buscema**

Courtesy of HeritageAuctions.com